# 1001 Great
# Family Pubs

Produced by AA Publishing

Advertisement Sales: advertisingsales@theAA.com
Editorial: lifestyleguides@theAA.com

The Automobile Association would like to thank the following photographers, companies and picture libraries for their assistance in the preparation of this book.
1 The Black Swan, Oldstead; 2 The Pheasant Inn, Keyston ;
3 Hundred House Hotel, Norton; 5 AA/C Sawyer;
Front Cover Photo: A Conway/Alamy
Every effort has been made to trace the copyright holders, and we apologise in advance for any accidental errors. We would be happy to apply any corrections in the following edition of this publication.

Printed in China by Everbest Printing Co Ltd
Directory compiled by the AA Lifestyle Guides Department, managed in the Librios Information Management System and generated from the AA establishment database system.

theAA.com/shop

Published by AA Publishing, a trading name of AA Media Limited whose registered office is Fanum House, Basing View, Basingstoke, Hampshire, RG21 4EA

Registered number 06112600.

A CIP catalogue record for this book is available from the British Library

ISBN 978-0-7495-6457-5
A04298

# Contents

# How to Use the Guide

## 1 LOCATION

**Guide order** Pubs are listed alphabetically by name (ignoring The) under their village or town. Towns and villages are listed alphabetically within their county. The guide has entries for England, Channel Islands, Isle of Man, Scotland and Wales in that order. Some village pubs prefer to be initially located under the nearest town, in which case the village name is included in the address and directions.

## 2 ESTABLISHMENT NAME & SYMBOLS

See Key to symbols in the panel on page 5.

## 3 ADDRESS & CONTACT DETAILS

This gives the street name and the postcode, and if necessary the name of the village is included (see 1 above). This may be up to five miles from the named location.

**☎ Telephone number, ▤ fax number, e-mail and websites:** Wherever possible we have included an e-mail address.

## 4 DIRECTIONS

Directions are given only when they have been supplied by the proprietor.

## 5 DESCRIPTION

Description of the pub and food.

## 6 OPEN

Indicates the hours and dates when the establishment is open and closed.

## 7 BAR MEALS

Indicates the times and days when proprietors tell us bar food can be ordered, and the average price of a main course as supplied by the proprietor. Please be aware that last orders could vary by up to 30 minutes.

## 8 RESTAURANT

Indicates the times and days when proprietors tell us food can be ordered from the restaurant. The average cost of a 3-course à la carte meal and a 3- or 4-course fixed-price menu are shown as supplied by the proprietor. Last orders may be approximately 30 minutes before the times stated.

## 9 BREWERY & COMPANY ⊕

This is the name of the Brewery to which the pub is tied, or the Company which owns it. A free house is where the pub is independently owned and run.

---

**1** ⌐BRANSCOMBE

**2** ⌐**The Masons Arms** ★★ HL ⊕ ♥ ───── **12**

**3** ⌐**EX12 3DJ ☎ 01297 680300** ▤ **01297 680500**
e-mail: reception@masonsarms.co.uk
**4** ⌐dir: *Turn off A3052 towards Branscombe, down hill, hotel at bottom of hill*

The creeper-clad Masons Arms dates back to 1360, when it was just a simple cider house measuring a mere 8ft **5** ⌐x 4ft, squeezed into the middle of a row of cottages. Today that row of cottages is an independent, family-run pub and hotel. Once the haunt of smugglers, the Masons Arms has a bar that can hardly have changed in 200 years, with stone walls, ancient ships' beams, slate floors, and a splendid open fireplace used for spit-roasts, including Sunday lunchtimes. Food is a serious business here and the restaurant maintains a standard of cooking worthy of its AA Rosette. Where possible all ingredients are grown, reared or caught locally, including the lobster and crab landed on nearby Branscombe beach.

**6** ⌐Open all wk Mon-Fri 11-3 6-11 (Sat 11-11 Sun 12-10.30)
**7** ⌐Bar Meals L served Mon-Fri 12-2, Sat-Sun 12-2.15 booking required D served all wk 7-9 booking required Av main course £12 **Restaurant** D served all wk 7-9 **8** booking required Fixed menu price fr £29.95 ⊕ FREE **9** HOUSE ◧ Otter Ale, Masons Ale, Tribute, Branoc, guest **10** ⌐ales. ♥ 14 **Facilities** Children's menu Dogs allowed Garden **11** ⌐Parking **Rooms** 21

## 10 FACILITIES

Indicates if a pub has a children's menu (which might mean children's portions), a garden, allows dogs on the premises, offers parking and has a children's play area. For further information please call the pub.

## 11 ROOMS

Only accommodation that has been inspected is indicated. In the case of AA rated accommodation only, the number of en suite bedrooms is listed. Many pubs have rooms but we only indicate those that are AA rated.

## NOTES

As so many establishments take one or more of the major credit cards we only indicate if a pub does not take cards.

## 12 AA STARS/DESIGNATORS

**AA Stars** are shown at the beginning of an entry.
**AA Designators** are as follows:

**Town House Hotel (TH)** - A small, individual city or town centre property, which provides a high degree of personal service and privacy

**Country House Hotel (CHH)** - Quietly located in a rural area

**Small Hotel (SHL)** - Has fewer than 20 bedrooms and is owner managed

**Metro Hotel (MET)** - A hotel in an urban location that does not offer an evening meal

**Budget Hotel (bud)** - These are usually purpose-built modern properties offering inexpensive accommodation. Often located near motorways and in town or city centres. **They are not awarded stars**

**Bed & Breakfast (B&B)** – Accommodation provided in a private house, run by the owner and with no more than six paying guests

**Guest House (GH)** – Accommodation provided for more than six paying guests and run on a more commercial basis than a B&B. Usually more services, for example dinner, provided by staff as well as the owner

**Farmhouse (FH)** – B&B or guest house rooms provided on a working farm or smallholding

**Restaurant with Rooms (RR)** – Destination restaurant offering overnight accommodation. The restaurant is the main business and is open to non-residents. A high standard of food should be offered, at least five nights a week. A maximum of 12 bedrooms. Most Restaurants with Rooms have been awarded AA Rosettes for their food

**Guest Accommodation (GA)** – Any establishment which meets the entry requirements for the Scheme can choose this designator

**Inn (INN)** – Accommodation provided in a fully licensed establishment. The bar will be open to non-residents and provide food in the evenings

**▲** Refers to hotels rated by another organisation, eg VisitBritain.

For more information on how the AA rates hotels and guest accommodation, please see our website: **theAA.com**

### KEY TO SYMBOLS

| | | |
|---|---|---|
| ◉ | **Rosettes** | – The AA's food award |
| ★★★ | **Stars** | – Accommodation rating |
| ⊞ | **Barrel** | – Name of Brewery, Company or Free House |
| ◧ | **Tankard** | – Principal beers sold |
| ♉ | **Apple** | – Real cider available |
| ♉ | **Wine glass** | – Indicates that at least six wines are available by the glass. For the exact number of wines served this way, see notes at the bottom of each entry |

# BEDFORDSHIRE

## BEDFORD

### The Three Tuns ▼

**57 Main Rd, Biddenham MK40 4BD ☎ 01234 354847**
dir: *On A428 from Bedford towards Northampton 1st left signed Biddenham. Into village, pub on left*

A stone-built, thatched roof pub, The Three Tuns stands in the heart of the beautiful village of Biddenham. It has a large garden with a patio and decking, and a separate children's play area with swings and a climbing frame. The old morgue, situated between the two garden areas, is the oldest building in the village and is said to be haunted. Home-cooked dishes on the regularly-changing menus include pies, steaks, curries, fish, local sausages, burgers and vegetarian specialities.

**Open** all wk 12-3 6-11 (Sun 12-4 7-10.30; 12-11 in summer) **Bar Meals** L served all wk 12-2 D served Mon-Sat 6-9 **Restaurant** L served all wk 12-2 booking required D served Mon-Sat 6-9 booking required ⊕ GREENE KING ◀ Greene King IPA, Abbot Ale, guest ale, Guinness. ▼ 6 **Facilities** Children's menu Play area Family room Dogs allowed Garden Parking

## BROOM

### The Cock

**23 High St SG18 9NA ☎ 01767 314411 📄 01767 314284**
dir: *Off B658 SW of Biggleswade. 1m from A1*

Unspoilt to this day with its intimate quarry-tiled rooms with latched doors and panelled walls, this 17th-century establishment is known as 'The Pub with no Bar'. Real ales are served straight from casks racked by the cellar steps. A straightforward pub grub menu includes jumbo cod, roast chicken, gammon steak, breaded lobster, and breast of Cajun chicken.

**Open** all wk 12-4 6-11 **Bar Meals** L served all wk 12-2.15 D served all wk 7-9 **Restaurant** L served all wk 12-2.15 D served all wk 7-9 ⊕ GREENE KING ◀ Greene King Abbot Ale, IPA, Ruddles County. **Facilities** Children's menu Play area Family room Dogs allowed Garden Parking

## EATON BRAY

### The White Horse ▼

**Market Square LU6 2DG**
**☎ 01525 220231 📄 01525 222485**
e-mail: davidsparrow@onetel.net
web: www.the-whitehorse.co.uk
dir: *A5 N of Dunstable onto A505, left in 1m, follow signs*

For almost 20 years, David and Janet Sparrow have built their reputation on great home cooked food at this traditional 300-year-old village inn with its oak beams and horse brasses. There's a wide ranging menu including comfort food like beef in ale pie, plus daily specials that might include sea bass fillets in lemon butter; Horton's pork with apple sausages and bubble and squeak. It's worth booking for the restaurant, but the same menu is also available in the bar.

**Open** all wk Closed: Sun eve Jan-Mar **Bar Meals** L served all wk 12-2.15 D served all wk 7-9.30 booking required Av main course £9.50 **Restaurant** L served all wk 12-2.15 D served all wk 7-9.30 booking required Av 3 course à la carte fr £21.50 ⊕ PUNCH TAVERNS ◀ Greene King IPA, Shepherd Neame Spitfire. ▼ 8 **Facilities** Children's menu Play area Family room Garden Parking

## LINSLADE

### The Globe Inn ▼

**Globe Ln, Old Linslade LU7 2TA**
**☎ 01525 373338 📄 01525 850551**
e-mail: 6458@greeneking.co.uk

Originally a farmhouse and stables, this friendly waterside inn was converted to serve passing boat crews on the Grand Union Canal. Open fires and candles set the scene for winter evenings, whilst for warmer days there's a large garden and children's play area. Expect an appetising range of light bites and mixed smoked deli board for sharing, as well as hot dishes like pan-seared Barbary duck with dauphinoise potatoes; sweet potato, chick pea and spinach curry; and daily fresh fish specials.

**Open** all day all wk 11-11 **Bar Meals** Av main course £8.95 food served all day **Restaurant** Av 3 course à la carte fr £20 food served all day ⊕ GREENE KING ◀ Greene King Abbot Ale, Old Speckled Hen, IPA & Ruddles County Ale, Hook Norton. ▼ 16 **Facilities** Children's menu Play area Dogs allowed Garden Parking

## NORTHILL

# The Crown ♥

**2 Ickwell Rd SG18 9AA ☎ 01767 627337**
📄 **01767 627279**
e-mail: info@thecrown-northill.com
dir: *Telephone for directions*

A delightful 16th-century pub with chocolate box setting
between Northill church and the village duck pond. Its acre of
garden includes a children's play area, and plenty of tables for
alfresco eating. Inside, the unique copper-covered bar leads to
an informal dining area, where the bar menu of pub favourites
applies. The candlelit split-level restaurant boasts much locally
sourced produce served in home-cooked dishes such as roasted
lamb chump with port and rosemary jus; smoked hake fillets
on tomato sauce; and pork tenderloin medallions wrapped in
bacon.

Open all wk 11.30-3 6-11 (Sun 12-11 Summer Sat 11.30am-
11pm) Closed: 25 Dec eve **Bar Meals** L served Mon-Sat 12-2.30,
Sun 12-8 D served Mon-Sat 6.30-9.30, Sun all day Av main
course £8.95 **Restaurant** L served Mon-Sat 12-2.30, Sun
12-8 booking required D served Mon-Sat 6.30-9.30, Sun all
day booking required Av 3 course à la carte fr £23 ⊕ GREENE
KING ◀ Greene King IPA, Abbot Ale, Old Speckled Hen, Olde
Tripplus, Guest ales. ♥ 9 **Facilities** Children's menu Play area Dogs
allowed Garden Parking

## SALFORD

# The Swan ♥

**2 Warendon Rd MK17 8BD ☎ 01908 281008**
e-mail: swan@peachpubs.com
dir: *M1 junct 13, follow signs to Salford*

Not far from central Milton Keynes is this attractive village and
the tile-hung, Edwardian Swan, which has earned a great local
reputation in recent years. In the kitchen Neil Simons and his
team take pride in using top ingredients from ethical British
producers, not least to cut down on air freight, to produce
starters of pheasant, apricot and smoked bacon terrine with
Cumberland sauce; and Thai crab beignet with pickled ginger
and chilli dressing. From the plentiful main courses come
free-range coq au vin; sea bass with crunchy winter vegetable
slaw; and leek, red onion, broccoli and blue cheese strudel
with Meaux mustard sauce. Deli boards - mixed, charcuterie,
cheese, antipasti, fish and Indian - are a house speciality. The
kitchen will happily prepare children's versions of anything
the grown-ups eat. A short, sensibly priced wine list changes
frequently. On sunny days, check for a barbecue on the terrace.

Open all day all wk 11am-mdnt (Sun 12-10.30) Closed: 25 Dec
**Bar Meals** Av main course £13 food served all day **Restaurant**
food served all day ⊕ Peach Pubs ◀ IPA, Black Sheep,
Guinness. ♥ 8 **Facilities** Children's menu Dogs allowed Garden
Parking

## SHEFFORD

# The Black Horse ♥

**Ireland SG17 5QL ☎ 01462 811398** 📄 **01462 817238**
e-mail: countrytaverns@aol.com
dir: *From S: M1 junct 12, A5120 to Flitwick. Onto A507 by Redbourne
School. Follow signs for A1, Shefford (cross A6). Left onto A600 towards
Bedford*

This traditional pub is set in a lovely garden surrounded by
peaceful countryside. The name of the tiny hamlet is thought
to be derived from the Irish navvies who built the local railway
line in the 1850s. The memorable menu draws a devoted
following, with imaginative meals that might include leg of
lamb roasted with garlic and thyme; locally farmed pork loin
with prune and apple sauce; and fillet of sea bass with warm
fennel and red onion salad.

Open all wk 12-3 6-12 (Sun noon-6pm) Closed: 25-26 Dec, 1 Jan
**Bar Meals** L served Mon-Sat 12-2.30, Sun 12-5 D served Mon-
Sat 6.30-10 **Restaurant** L served Mon-Sat 12-2.30, Sun 12-5
D served Mon-Sat 6.30-10 ◀ Greene King IPA, London Pride,
Village Bike ♻ Westons Stowford Press. ♥ 17 **Facilities** Children's
menu Garden Parking

## SOUTHILL

# The White Horse ♥

**High St SG18 9LD ☎ 01462 813364**
e-mail: paul.e.cluett@virgin.net
dir: *Telephone for directions*

A village pub with traditional values, happily accommodating
the needs of children and those who like to sit outside on
cool days (the patio has heaters). Locally renowned for its
chargrilled steaks from the Duke of Buccleuch's Scottish estate.
Other main courses include Cajun chicken; chargrilled pork loin
steaks; Whitby Bay scampi; and stuffed breaded plaice.

Open all wk **Bar Meals** L served Mon-Fri 12-2.30, Sat-Sun 12-10
booking required D served Mon-Fri 6-10, Sat-Sun 12-10 booking
required Av main course £7.50 **Restaurant** L served Mon-Fri
12-2.30, Sat-Sun 12-10 booking required D served Mon-Fri 6-10,
Sat-Sun 12-10 booking required Fixed menu price fr £5.50 Av 3
course à la carte fr £15 ⊕ ENTERPRISE INNS ◀ Greene King IPA,
London Pride, Speckled Hen, Flowers. ♥ 8 **Facilities** Children's
menu Play area Dogs allowed Garden Parking

## TILSWORTH

# The Anchor Inn ♥

**1 Dunstable Rd LU7 9PU ☎ 01525 210289**
📄 **01525 211578**
e-mail: tonyanchorinn@aol.com
dir: *Exit A5 at Tilsworth. In 1m pub on right at 3rd bend*

The only pub in a Saxon village, the Anchor dates from 1878.
The restaurant is a recent addition to the side of the pub, and
the whole building has been refurbished. The licensees pride

continued

England

themselves on their fresh food and well-kept beers and guest ales. An acre of garden includes patio seating for alfresco dining, an adventure playground and a barbecue. Recent change of hands.

**Open** all day all wk noon-11.30pm **Bar Meals** Av main course £5 food served all day **Restaurant** Fixed menu price fr £10 food served all day ⊕ GREENE KING ◀ Greene King IPA, Abbot Ale, Wadworth 6X, guest ales. ♈ 12 **Facilities** Children's menu Play area Family room Garden Parking

## BERKSHIRE

### ASHMORE GREEN

# The Sun in the Wood ♈

**Stoney Ln RG18 9HF** ☎ **01635 42377** ▤ **01635 528392**
e-mail: info@suninthewood.co.uk
dir: *From A34 at Robin Hood Rdbt left to Shaw, at mini-rdbt right then 7th left into Stoney Ln 1.5m, pub on left*

The name promises woodland beauty and the setting delivers it, yet the centre of Newbury is surprisingly close by. Expect stone floors and plenty of wood panelling within, and a country garden, decking terrace for alfresco dining and crazy golf outside. Enjoy food made using local ingredients at this award-winning country pub: perhaps crisp whitebait with home-made tartare sauce, then chicken breast with wild mushroom sauce.

**Open** Closed: Mon **Bar Meals** L served Tue-Sat 12-2, Sun 12-4 booking required D served Tue-Sat 6-9.30 booking required Av main course £10.95 **Restaurant** L served Tue-Sat 12-2, Sun 12-4 booking required D served Tue-Sat 6-9.30 booking required Av 3 course à la carte fr £19.95 ⊕ WADWORTH ◀ Wadworth 6X, Henrys Original IPA, Badger Tanglefoot ♻ Westons Stowford Press. ♈ 16 **Facilities** Children's menu Play area Garden Parking

### BOXFORD

# The Bell at Boxford ⌂ ★★★ INN ♈

**Lambourn Rd RG20 8DD** ☎ **01488 608721**
▤ **01488 658502**
e-mail: paul@bellatboxford.com
dir: *A338 toward Wantage, right onto B4000, take 3rd left to Boxford*

Mock Tudor country pub at the heart of the glorious Lambourn Valley, noted for its pretty villages and sweeping Downland scenery. Cosy log fires add to the appeal in winter, and the

patio is popular throughout the year with its array of flowers and outdoor heating, hog roasts, barbecues and parties.

**Open** all wk 11-3 6-11 (Sun noon-10.30) **Bar Meals** L served Mon-Sat 12-2, Sun 12-3 D served Mon-Sat 7-9.30, Sun 7-9 Av main course £8.95 **Restaurant** L served Mon-Sat 12-2, Sun 12-3 D served Mon-Sat 7-9.30, Sun 7-9 Av 3 course à la carte fr £28.50 ⊕ FREE HOUSE ◀ Interbrew Bass, Courage Best, Wadworth 6X, Henrys IPA. ♈ 60 **Facilities** Children's menu Dogs allowed Garden Parking **Rooms** 11

### COOKHAM DEAN

# Chequers Brasserie ♈

**Dean Ln SL6 9BQ** ☎ **01628 481232** ▤ **01628 481237**
e-mail: info@chequersbrasserie.co.uk
dir: *From A4094 in Cookham High St towards Marlow, over rail line. On right*

Kenneth Grahame, who wrote The Wind in the Willows, spent his childhood in these parts. He'd surely have enjoyed this historic pub, tucked away between Marlow and Maidenhead in this pretty village. Striking Victorian and Edwardian villas around the green set the tone, whilst the surrounding wooded hills and dales have earned Cookham Dean a reputation as a centre for wonderful walks. Sample the likes of rump of Buckinghamshire lamb with sautéed chorizo, fondant potato and ratatouille, fillet of black bream with marsh samphire, brown shrimp, dill beurre blanc and a bobbin of linguini.

**Open** all day all wk 11-11 **Bar Meals** L served Mon-Sat 12-2.30, Sun 12-9.30 D served Mon-Thu 6.30-9.30, Fri-Sat 6.30-10, Sun 12-9.30 Av main course £12.50 **Restaurant** L served Mon-Sat 12-2.30, Sun 12-9.30 D served Mon-Thu 6.30-9.30, Fri-Sat 6.30-10, Sun 12-9.30 Fixed menu price fr £26.95 Av 3 course à la carte fr £18.95 ⊕ FREE HOUSE ◀ Guinness, Greene King IPA, Rebellion Marlow Brewery ♻ Stowford Press, Thatchers Cox, Aspall. ♈ 14 **Facilities** Children's menu Garden Parking

### EAST GARSTON

# The Queen's Arms Country Inn

**RG17 7ET** ☎ **01488 648757** ▤ **01488 648642**
e-mail: info@queensarmshotel.co.uk
dir: *M4 junct 14, 4m onto A338 to Great Shefford, then East Garston*

This 18th-century inn is located in a small village in the Lambourn Valley, with its racehorse training yards. It is also a good area for walking, being quite close to the Ridgeway. The Queen's Arms offers a warm welcome in stylishly traditional setting. The menu offers a good selection of traditional country food made from fresh local ingredients. On the main menu are dishes such as goats' cheese and black pudding salad; wild boar and leek sausages; lamb cutlets; and roast peppers stuffed with brie, mushrooms and red onion served with tagliatelle. The terrace and large garden are popular in the summer, when barbecues and hog roasts take place.

**Open** all wk **Bar Meals** L served all wk 12-2 D served all wk 7-9 Av main course £16 **Restaurant** L served all wk 12-2 D served all wk 7-9 Av 3 course à la carte fr £32 ⊕ MILLERS

COLLECTION ◄ Guinness, 1664 Ringwood Best, Ringwood 49er, guest ale. **Facilities** Children's menu Dogs allowed Garden Parking

## HERMITAGE

### The White Horse of Hermitage ♥

**Newbury Rd RG18 9TB ☎ 01635 200325**
e-mail: thewh@btconnect.com
web: www.thewhitehorseofhermitage.co.uk
dir: *5m from Newbury on B4009. Follow signs to Chieveley, right into Priors Court Rd, turn left at mini-rdbt, pub approx 1m*

The White Horse has achieved a solid reputation for its pub food, using the freshest and finest local produce to create a daily menu, including signature dishes such as BBQ babyback ribs. The interior bar and restaurant is contemporary in decor, and outside you choose between the Mediterranean-style patio or the large garden which is equipped with swings and a football area.

Open noon-3 5-11 Closed: Sun eve, Mon (ex BH) **Bar Meals** Av main course £10 food served all day **Restaurant** Av 3 course à la carte fr £15 food served all day ● GREENE KING ◄ Abbot Ale, Greene King IPA, Guinness. ♥ 9 **Facilities** Children's menu Play area Dogs allowed Garden Parking

## HUNGERFORD

### The Swan Inn ★★★★ INN

**Craven Rd, Lower Green, Inkpen RG17 9DX**
**☎ 01488 668326 ▤ 01488 668306**
e-mail: enquiries@theswaninn-organics.co.uk
web: www.theswaninn-organics.co.uk
dir: *S down Hungerford High St (A338), under rail bridge, left to Hungerford Common. Right signed Inkpen (3m)*

Organic beef farmers Mary and Bernard Harris preside over this rambling 17th-century free house, which stands in fine walking country just below Combe Gibbet and Walbury Hill. In addition to ramblers, the pub is a magnet for cyclists, hang gliders, shooting parties and organic food enthusiasts. An attractive terraced garden sets the scene for alfresco summer dining, in contrast to the heavily beamed interior with its old photographic prints and open winter fires. Almost everything on the menu is prepared using their own fresh produce; meats are 100% organic and butchered on the premises, earning accreditation by the Soil Association. There's an organic farm shop to visit too.

Open all wk 11-11 (Sun noon-10.30) Closed: 25-26 Dec **Bar Meals** L served all wk 12-2 D served all wk 7-9.30 Av main course £10 **Restaurant** L served Wed-Sun 12-2.30 booking required D served Wed-Sat 7-9.30 booking required Av 3 course à la carte fr £25 ● FREE HOUSE ◄ Butts Traditional & Jester Bitter, Butts Blackguard, guest ales. **Facilities** Children's menu Play area Garden Parking **Rooms** 10

## HURST

### The Green Man ♥

**Hinton Rd RG10 0BP ☎ 0118 934 2599**
**▤ 0118 934 2939**
e-mail: simon@thegreenman.uk.com
dir: *Off A321, adjacent to Hurst Cricket Club*

The pub gained its first licence in 1602, and Brakspear purchased a 1,000 year lease on the building in 1646. The old black beams, low in places, are still to be seen and the building has been developed to include all the old features, while newer areas reflect a similar theme. Inside you'll find open fires, hand drawn beer and good food, from sandwiches to Sunday roasts. The garden, open to fields and woodland, includes a children's play area.

Open all wk 11-3 5.30-11 (Sun noon-10.30) **Bar Meals** food served all day **Restaurant** food served all day ● BRAKSPEAR ◄ Brakspear Bitter, Hobgoblin, seasonal ales. ♥ 8 **Facilities** Children's menu Play area Garden Parking

## KINTBURY

### The Dundas Arms ♥

**53 Station Rd RG17 9UT ☎ 01488 658263**

📠 01488 658568

e-mail: info@dundasarms.co.uk

dir: *M4 junct 13 take A34 to Newbury, then A4 to Hungerford, left to Kintbury. Pub 1m by canal & rail station*

Set in an Area of Outstanding Natural Beauty on the banks of the Kennet and Avon Canal, this free house has been welcoming travellers since the end of the 18th century. Traditional beers are served in the convivial bar, whilst the simply styled restaurant is redolent of a French auberge. On warmer days, outdoor tables offer views of the narrow boats and wildlife on the canal. Meanwhile, a typical restaurant meal might start with crab au gratin or salad of fillet steak with beetroot, grapeseed and horseradish sauce, before moving on to pan-fried venison haunch steak with red wine and pepper sauce, or baked Orkney salmon with fennel and saffron risotto.

**Open** Closed: 25 & 31 Dec, Sun eve **Bar Meals** L served Mon-Sat 12-2 D served Tue-Sat 7-9 Av main course £11.50 **Restaurant** L served Mon-Sat 12-2 D served Tue-Sat 7-9 booking required Av 3 course à la carte fr £23 ⊕ FREE HOUSE ◀ West Berkshire, Mr Chubbs Lunchtime Bitter, Adnams, West Berkshire Good Old Boy, Ramsbury Gold. ♥ 10 **Facilities** Children's menu Family room Parking

## LECKHAMPSTEAD

### The Stag ♥

**Shop Ln RG20 8QG ☎ 01488 638436**

e-mail: enquiries@stagleckhampstead.co.uk

dir: *6m from Newbury on B4494*

The privately owned, white-painted Stag could only be a pub. It lies just off the village green in a sleepy downland village and

close by are the Ridgeway long-distance path and Snelsmore Common, home to nightjar, woodlark and grazing Exmoor ponies. Needless to say, with such beautiful countryside all around, muddy wellies and wet dogs are expected - in fact, the latter are as genuinely welcome as their owners. During the winter months the wood-burning stove is always ready with its dancing flames. The bar and restaurant walls are painted in warm red, or left as bare brick, while old black and white photographs tell of village life many years ago. Surrounding farms and growers supply all produce, including venison, pheasant and fresh river trout. Aberdeen Angus beef from cattle raised next door may also feature as a special, and those lucky enough to find it there agree that its taste and texture are sublime.

**Open** all wk 12-3 6-11 **Bar Meals** L served all wk 12-2.30 booking required D served all wk 6-9.30 booking required Av main course £9 **Restaurant** L served all wk 12-2.30 booking required D served all wk 6-9.30 Av 3 course à la carte fr £15 ⊕ FREE HOUSE ◀ Morlands Original. ♥ 8 **Facilities** Children's menu Dogs allowed Garden Parking

## NEWBURY

### The White Hart ♥

**Moneyrow Green, Holyport SL6 2ND ☎ 01628 621460**

📠 01628 621460

dir: *2m S from Maidenhead. M4 junct 8/9, follow Holyport signs then Moneyrow Green. Pub by petrol station*

A busy 19th-century coaching inn offering quality home-made food, with most vegetables and herbs used freshly picked from its own organic allotment. Typical mains are caramelised breast of duck; calves' liver and bacon; venison sausages; grilled fillet of plaice; and slow-roasted tomato tart with Somerset brie. The wood-panelled lounge bar is furnished with leather chesterfields and warmed by an open fire. There are large gardens to enjoy in summer and a boules pitch. Recent change of hands.

**Open** all day all wk 12-11.30 (Fri-Sat 12-1am, Sun 12-11) **Bar Meals** L served Tue-Sat 12.30-3, Sun 12-4 D served Tue-Sat 6-9 Av main course £7.50 ⊕ GREENE KING ◀ Guinness, IPA, Morland Original ♂ Stowford Press. ♥ 7 **Facilities** Children's menu Dogs allowed Garden Parking

## The Yew Tree Inn ◉◉ ♀

**Hollington Cross, Andover Rd, Highclere RG20 9SE**
☎ **01635 253360** 📠 **01635 255035**
e-mail: info@theyewtree.net
dir: *A34 toward Southampton, 2nd exit bypass Highclere, onto A343 at rdbt, through village, pub on right*

The former 16th-century coaching inn is owned and sympathetically remodelled by the celebrated chef-turned restaurateur, Marco Pierre White, whose famed perfectionism is evident throughout the rambling building, from the immaculate styling that blends original features of old beams, tiled floors, and inglenooks with huge smouldering logs, with the refinement of crisp linen tablecloths, sparkling glassware, and a contemporary finish. He performs a similar trick with the menu, offering both traditional British food and time-honoured classics from the French culinary canon. Kick off a memorable meal with pea and ham soup or Morecambe Bay potted shrimps; then move on to braised oxtail and kidney pudding; Marsh Benham lamb with dauphinoise; or rib-eye steak with béarnaise. Tellingly, the desserts are described as 'puddings' and might include such familiar comforts as rice pudding with red fruit compôte and caramelised apple pie. Good value fixed-price menus are also a feature at lunchtime, early evening and on Sundays.

**Open** all day all wk **Bar Meals** L served Mon-Sat 12-2.30, Sun 12-3 D served all wk 6-9 Av main course £15 **Restaurant** L served Mon-Sat 12-2.30, Sun 12-3 D served all wk 6-9 Fixed menu price fr £15.50 Av 3 course à la carte fr £27 ⊕ FREE HOUSE ◀ Timothy Taylor, Adnams, Butt's Barbus Barbus, Mr Chubbs Ö Westons Old Rosie, Westons Bounds Brand. ♀ 10 **Facilities** Children's menu Dogs allowed Garden Parking

## PALEY STREET

## The Royal Oak ◉◉ ♀

**SL6 3JN** ☎ **01628 620541**
dir: *From Maidenhead take A330 towards Ascot for 2m, turn right onto B3024 signed White Waltham, 2nd pub on left*

Drop by for a drink and relax on one of the comfortable sofas at this traditional English dining pub, owned by Nick Parkinson, son of Sir Michael Parkinson. Fullers provide the reliable ales, but the wine list is undoubtedly the star of the drinks show; around 20 wines are served by the glass, and the main listings begin with a selection of over 20 champagnes. Meanwhile, head chef Dominic Chapman has a solid reputation in the kitchen, using the best seasonal produce to create

outstandingly good British food. Choose from a small selection of bar snacks or sample the lunch and dinner menus. Typical mains include peppered haunch of venison with creamed spinach, Old Spot belly pork with mushy peas and braised onions, or grilled lemon sole with wild mushrooms and watercress. A large beer garden completes the picture for alfresco dining in warmer weather.

**Open** 12-3 6-11 (Sun 12-4) Closed: 25 Dec & 1 Jan, Sun eve **Restaurant** L served Mon-Sat 12-3, Sun 12-4 booking required D served Mon-Thu 6.30-9.30, Fri-Sat 6.30-10 Av 3 course à la carte fr £35 ⊕ FULLERS ◀ Fuller's London Pride. ♀ 20 **Facilities** Children's menu Garden Parking

## READING

## The Flowing Spring ♀

**Henley Rd, Playhatch RG4 9RB** ☎ **0118 969 9878**
e-mail: flowingspring@aol.com
dir: *3m N of Reading*

A lovely country pub on the Henley road, much favoured by walkers and cyclists. It's family friendly too, with a menu for under-12s and a small play area in the large well-kept garden. Representative dishes on the combined bar/restaurant menu include chicken goujons with chips and salad; battered cod and chips; spotted dick; and sticky toffee pudding. Being a Fullers pub, Chiswick, London Pride and ESB are all well kept on tap.

**Open** all wk 11-11 **Bar Meals** L served all wk D served all wk Av main course £6.95 food served all day **Restaurant** L served all wk D served all wk Av 3 course à la carte fr £12 food served all day ⊕ FULLERS ◀ London Pride, ESB, Chiswick, HSB. ♀ 7 **Facilities** Children's menu Play area Family room Dogs allowed Garden Parking

## WINTERBOURNE

## The Winterbourne Arms ♀

**RG20 8BB** ☎ **01635 248200** 📠 **01635 248824**
e-mail: winterbournearms@tiscali.co.uk
dir: *M4 junct 13 into Chieveley Services, follow Donnington signs to Winterbourne sign. Turn right into Arlington Ln, right at T-junct, left into Winterbourne*

This large 300-year-old free house once sheltered a shop and bakery - the remains of the bread oven are in the restaurant. In winter the interior is candle-lit with a log fire, while the extensive gardens offer alfresco dining in summer. Local game and daily fresh fish from Brixham provide the basic ingredients for mainly British-style dishes such as warm goats' cheese and red onion tartlet; beer battered fillet of cod; and pan-fried supreme of salmon with lobster bisque and prawn sauce.

**Open** all wk noon-3 6-11 (Sun noon-10.30) **Bar Meals** L served all wk 12-2.30 D served all wk 6-10 Av main course £10 food served all day **Restaurant** L served all wk 12-2.30 D served all wk 6-10 Fixed menu price fr £10 Av 3 course à la carte fr £15.25 ⊕ FREE HOUSE ◀ Ramsbury Gold, Guinness, Fuller's London Pride. ♀ 20 **Facilities** Children's menu Dogs allowed Garden Parking

# Berkshire-Buckinghamshire

## WORLD'S END

### The Langley Hall Inn ☻

**RG20 8SA ☎ 01635 248332 📄 01635 248571**
dir: *Exit M4 junct 13 north, take 1st slip road signed Beedon & Chieveley. Left & immediately right, inn 1.5m on left*

Friendly, family-run bar/restaurant with a reputation for freshly prepared food, real ales and a good selection of wines. Fresh fish dishes vary according to the daily catch - maybe pan-fried crevettes, grilled Dover sole, salmon fishcakes with spinach and parsley sauce, or roast cod fillet with cheese and herb crust. Other favourites are braised lamb, beef stir-fry, and Thai chicken curry. Outside there is a large patio and garden, plus a petanque court for fine weather use.

**Open** all wk 12-3.30 5.30-11 (Sun 12-6) Closed: 26 Dec-2 Jan **Bar Meals** L served all wk 12-2.30 (Sun 12-4) D served Mon-Sat 6.30-10 booking required **Restaurant** L served all wk 12-2.30 (Sun 12-4) booking required D served Mon-Sat 6.30-10 booking required ⊕ ENTERPRISE INNS ◀ West Berkshire Brewery - Good Old Boy, Mr Chubbs, Lunchtime Bitter, Deuchars IPA, London Pride, Brakspears ♂ Stowford Press. ☻ 12 **Facilities** Children's menu Dogs allowed Garden Parking

## BUCKINGHAMSHIRE

## AMERSHAM

### Hit or Miss Inn ☻

**Penn Street Village HP7 0PX ☎ 01494 713109**
📄 **01494 718010**
e-mail: hit@ourpubs.co.uk
dir: *M25 junct 18, A404 (Amersham to High Wycombe road) to Amersham. Past crematorium on right, 2nd left into Whielden Ln (signed Winchmore Hill). 1.25m, pub on right*

Michael and Mary Macken welcome you to their 18th-century cottage-style dining pub with its fires and old world beams. The Hit or Miss overlooks the cricket ground from which the pub takes its name, and there's a beautiful country garden with lawn, patio and picnic tables for warmer days. Home-cooked dishes range from tempting well-filled sandwiches and baked potatoes to maple syrup and mustard marinated salmon fillet, venison pie with raspberry jus, or a selection of steaks. There are daily specials and Sunday roasts, too.

**Open** all day all wk 11-11 (Sun 12-10.30) **Bar Meals** L served Mon-Sat 12-2.30, Sun 12-8 D served Mon-Sat 6.30-9.30, Sun 12-8 **Restaurant** L served Mon-Sat 12-2.30, Sun 12-8 D served Mon-Sat 6.30-9.30, Sun 12-8 ⊕ HALL & WOODHOUSE ◀ Badger Best, Tanglefoot, Sussex, Hopping Hare ♂ Stowford Press. ☻ 12 **Facilities** Children's menu Dogs allowed Garden Parking

## BEACONSFIELD

### The Royal Standard of England ☻

**Brindle Ln, Forty Green HP9 1XT ☎ 01494 673382**
e-mail: theoldestpub@btinternet.com
dir: *A40 to Beaconsfield, right at church rdbt onto B474 towards Penn, left onto Forty Green Rd, 1m*

Situated in the beautiful Chilterns village of Forty Green, this welcoming country inn traces its roots to Saxon times. During the Civil War the pub was a mustering place for Royalists, and the ancient building is said to be haunted by the ghost of a 12 year-old drummer boy. Today, good hearty food is served amid the striking stained glass windows, beams and flagstone floors, whilst in winter the building is warmed by a large inglenook fireplace. Seasonal wild game is a regular feature on the specials board, supported by an extensive bill of fare. Start, perhaps, with a pork terrine before moving on to main course dishes such as mutton shepherd's pie; seasonal vegetable risotto; or Buckinghamshire bacon badger suet roll. The pub boasts a wide choice of interesting ales and real ciders, with many popular wines served by the glass.

**Open** all day all wk 11-11 **Bar Meals** Av main course £12 food served all day **Restaurant** food served all day ⊕ FREE HOUSE ◀ Marston's Pedigree, Brakspear Bitter, Rebellion IPA, Theakston Old Peculier, Guest Ales ♂ Westons Stowford Press, Old Rosie Scrumpy. ☻ 12 **Facilities** Children's menu Family room Dogs allowed Garden Parking

## BLETCHLEY

### The Crooked Billet ⊛ ☻

**2 Westbrook End, Newton Longville MK17 0DF**
☎ **01908 373936**
e-mail: john@thebillet.co.uk
dir: *M1 junct 13, follow signs to Buckingham. 6m, signed at Buttledump rdbt to Newton Longville*

Built as a farmhouse in about 1665, the Crooked Billet was first licensed in the early 1700s. A brew house was added during the 19th century in response to growing demand. Nevertheless, farming continued into the early 20th century; pigs and hens were kept in a barn, whilst apples were harvested from the orchards. Today, the pub retains much of its traditional charm, with original oak beams, open log fires and a large garden. But the top attraction is the food and wine from husband-and-wife team John and Emma Gilchrist. Emma's regularly-changing menus are based on the finest, freshest ingredients from a multitude of small specialist food producers and suppliers. The emphasis is on taste, combined with modern presentation. Lunchtime in the relaxed bar area brings sandwiches, salads, and pastas, together with traditional pub dishes. Typical choices on the evening menu are cream of white bean soup, followed by pan-fried trout fillet, green beans and buttered Jersey Royals; or chicken Kiev with roasted wild garlic butter and soft herb gnocchi.

**Open** noon-2.30 5-11 (Sun noon-4) Closed: Mon L **Bar Meals** L served Tue-Sat 12-2, Sun 12-4 D served Mon-Sat 7-9.30 Av main course £12.50 **Restaurant** L served Tue-Sat 12-2, Sun 12-4 D served Mon-Sat 7-9.30 booking required Fixed menu price fr £12 Av 3 course à la carte fr £24 ⊕ GREENE KING ◄ Old Speckled Hen, Badger Tanglefoot, Hobgoblin, Ruddles County. ☻ 300 **Facilities** Children's menu Garden Parking

## BOVINGDON GREEN

# The Royal Oak ☻

**Frieth Rd SL7 2JF ☎ 01628 488611** 📄 **01628 478680**
e-mail: info@royaloakmarlow.co.uk
web: www.royaloakmarlow.co.uk
dir: *From Marlow, take A4155. In 300yds right signed Bovingdon Green. In 0.75m pub on left*

This delightful whitewashed village pub is set amid its own spacious surroundings, which include a sunny terrace, pétanque piste and herb garden, while inside you'll find a cosy interior with a wood-burning stove, rich fabrics, a rose-red dining room and lustrous dark floorboards. The imaginative British food on the menu makes good use of fresh local produce. Among the menu's 'small plate' selection you might find devilled lamb's kidneys on eggy bread brioche with crispy pancetta; and bubble and squeak with oak-smoked bacon, poached egg and hollandaise sauce. Main meals include classic fish pie with buttered Chantenay carrots; and crispy herb polenta cake with sautéed wild mushrooms, glazed goats' cheese and balsamic roast beetroot. Sunday roasts are also popular. Among the decent selection of puddings are vanilla bean crème brûlée with lemon thyme shortbread; and spiced apple and blackberry crumble.

**Open** all day all wk 11-11 (Sun 12-10.30) Closed: 26 Dec **Bar Meals** L served Mon-Fri 12-2.30, Sat 12-3, Sun 12-4 D served Sun-Thu 6.30-9.30, Fri-Sat 6.30-10 **Restaurant** L served Mon-Fri 12-2.30, Sat 12-3, Sun 12-4 booking required D served Sun-Thu 6.30-9.30, Fri-Sat 6.30-10 ⊕ SALISBURY PUBS LTD ◄ Brakspears, Marlow Rebellion IPA, Wychwood Hobgoblin. ☻ 19 **Facilities** Children's menu Dogs allowed Garden Parking

## BRILL

# The Pheasant Inn ☻

**Windmill St HP18 9TG ☎ 01844 239370**
e-mail: info@thepheasant.co.uk
dir: *In village centre, by windmill*

Set on the edge of Brill Common, the large garden and veranda at this 17th-century beamed inn make the most of its fine hilltop position, with stunning views over seven counties. The popular menu offers a selection of locally produced steaks; duck breast with blueberry juniper sauce; braised lamb shank with sweet potato and Stilton mash; and red mullet in rich saffron mussel stew. Roald Dahl and JRR Tolkien were both frequent visitors, and the annual Brill Music Festival is on the first Saturday of July.

**Open** all day all wk 11-11 (Fri-Sun 11am-mdnt) **Bar Meals** L served all wk 12-2 D served all wk 6.30-9 **Restaurant** L served all wk 12-2 D served all wk 6.30-9 ◄ Triple B, Courage Best Ỗ Thatchers. ☻ 9 **Facilities** Children's menu Garden Parking

## BUCKINGHAM

# The Wheatsheaf ☻

**Main St, Maids Moreton MK18 1QR**
**☎ 01280 815433** 📄 **01280 814631**
dir: *M1 junct 13, (or M40 junct 9, A34 to Bicester) A421 to Buckingham, then A413 to Maids Moreton*

This thatched inn has been a pub since 1750, and offers an appetising menu in the spacious conservatory overlooking the beer garden. Try baked cod and prawns in cream; roast aubergine stuffed with ratatouille; or home-made Thai chicken curry. Real ales and snacks can also be enjoyed in the bar, with its inglenook fireplaces. Children will love the outdoor play area.

**Open** all wk **Bar Meals** L served all wk 12-2.15 D served Tue-Sat 6.45-9.30 **Restaurant** L served all wk 12-2.15 D served Tue-Sat 6.45-9.30 ⊕ FREE HOUSE ◄ John Smiths, Side Pocket For A Toad, Reverend James, Pitstop. ☻ 10 **Facilities** Children's menu Play area Family room Dogs allowed Garden Parking

# Buckinghamshire

## CHALFONT ST GILES

### The Ivy House ♀

**London Rd HP8 4RS ☎ 01494 872184** 📄 **01494 872870**
e-mail: ivyhouse@fullers.co.uk
dir: *On A413 2m S of Amersham & 1.5m N of Chalfont St Giles*

Set close to John Milton's cottage in Chalfont St Giles, this beautiful 250-year-old brick and flint coaching inn enjoys amazing views of the Chiltern Hills. The pub is handy for local country walks as well as several nearby golf courses, and is well-known for its friendly welcome, great food and extensive wine list. Open fires, comfy armchairs, old beams and brasses all give the place a cosy, warm and welcoming atmosphere. Meals are served in the bar, the former coach house and the restaurant, and in fine weather there's also the option of alfresco dining in the garden. The fresh seasonal menu features daily blackboard specials, with the emphasis on quality local produce, fresh fish, and salads. Lunchtime brings a selection of sandwiches and filled baked potatoes; the Ivy House ploughman's with Stilton, Cheddar and ham; as well as hot dishes like chilli con carne; and hand-carved ham, eggs and French fries. More formal dining might include Shropshire fidget pie with mash and broccoli or Toulouse cassoulet with chunky white bread; or multi award-winning speciality sausages of the day served with bubble and squeak. Desserts include traditional baked apple with cinnamon and raisins.

**Open** all day all wk **Bar Meals** L served Mon-Fri 12-3, Sat-Sun all day D served Mon-Fri 6-10, Sat-Sun all day Av main course £10 **Restaurant** L served Mon-Fri 12-3, Sat-Sun all day booking required D served Mon-Fri 6-10, Sat-Sun all day booking required Fixed menu price fr £9.95 Av 3 course à la carte fr £20 ⊕ FULLERS SMITH & TURNER ◀ Fuller's London Pride, Chiswick, Guest Ale ♻ Scrumpy Jack. ♀ 10 **Facilities** Children's menu Dogs allowed Garden Parking

## CHEDDINGTON

### The Old Swan ♀

**58 High St LU7 0RQ ☎ 01296 668226** 📄 **01296 663811**
e-mail: geoffrsmith@btconnect.com
dir: *From Tring towards Marsworth take B489, 0.5m. Left towards Cooks Wharf onto Cheddington, pub on left*

Formed out of three cottages in the 15th century, this delightful thatched pub is known not only for its real ales and traditional charm but also for its ghosts. A man in 18th-century dress reputedly tries to kiss ladies in the restaurant area! Food ranges from roasted half pheasant with black cherry and port sauce; sea bass fillets with pine nuts and baby spinach; to five bean, vegetable and tomato hotpot. Outside there's a large garden with a children's play area.

**Open** all wk Mon-Fri 12-3, 5-11 (Sat-Sun 11-11) **Bar Meals** L served Mon-Thu 12-2, Fri-Sat 12-2.30, Sun 12-4 D served Mon-Thu 6-9, Fri-Sat 6-9.30 Av main course £10 **Restaurant** L served Mon-Thu 12-2, Fri-Sat 12-2.30, Sun 12-4 D served Mon-Thu 6-9, Fri-Sat 6-9.30 ⊕ PUNCH TAVERNS ◀ Courage Best, St Austell Tribute, Everard's Tiger, Shepherd Neame Spitfire, Adnams Broadside ♻ Stowford Press. ♀ 12 **Facilities** Children's menu Play area Dogs allowed Garden Parking

## CHESHAM

### The Swan ♀

**Ley Hill HP5 1UT ☎ 01494 783075**
e-mail: swanleyhill@btconnect.com
dir: *1.5m E of Chesham by golf course*

Once three cottages, the first built around 1520, qualifying it as one of Buckinghamshire's oldest pubs. Condemned prisoners, heading for nearby gallows, would drink 'a last and final ale' here. During the Second World War, Clark Gable, James Stewart and Glenn Miller frequently drank here after cycling from Bovingdon airbase. Menus change several times monthly, and a blackboard features daily specials. Corn-fed chicken and home honey-roasted ham pie, and venison wrapped in smoked pancetta with confit new potatoes are typical dinner choices.

**Open** all wk 12-3 5.30-11 (Sun 12-10.30) **Bar Meals** L served all wk 12-2.30 D served Tue-Sat 7-9 **Restaurant** L served Tue-Sun 12-2.30 D served Tue-Sat 7-9 booking required ⊕ PUNCH RETAIL ◀ Adnams Bitter, Fuller's London Pride, Timothy Taylor Landlord, Brakspears, guest ales. ♀ 8 **Facilities** Children's menu Garden Parking

## CUDDINGTON

# The Crown ♛

**Spurt St HP18 0BB ☎ 01844 292222**
e-mail: david@anniebaileys.com
web: www.thecrowncuddington.co.uk
dir: *Off A418 between Aylesbury & Thame*

Fans of the popular TV series Midsomer Murders may recognise The Crown, as it has been used several times as a location. This delightful, Grade II listed, thatched and whitewashed enterprise has made a name for itself as a great place to dine. Fullers and Adnams are on tap in the bar, and an extensive wine list suggests the perfect match for every dish on the regularly changing menus. Among the starters to try are marinated sardines with coriander and spring onion pesto and hoi sin duck and bacon salad. Seafood dishes are a major attraction, and usually include seafood pie; smoked haddock with grilled Welsh rarebit, tomato salad and chips; and scallops with pancetta, salad leaves and truffle vinaigrette. Other typical main courses include gnocchi and spinach bake with gorgonzola; medallions of pork with mushroom and paprika sauce, chorizo and boulangère potatoes; and rib-eye steak with pink peppercorn and brandy sauce. A changing selection of desserts is chalked up on a blackboard. Sandwiches and 'small plates' are also available.

**Open** all wk **Bar Meals** L served all wk 12-2.15 D served Mon-Sat 6.30-9.15 Av main course £11 **Restaurant** L served all wk 12-2.15 D served Mon-Sat 6.30-9.15 Fixed menu price fr £12.50 Av 3 course à la carte fr £22 ⊕ FULLERS ◀ Fuller's London Pride, Adnams, Guinness. ♛ 9 **Facilities** Children's menu Garden Parking

## DENHAM

# The Swan Inn ♛

**Village Rd UB9 5BH ☎ 01895 832085   📄 01895 835516**
e-mail: info@swaninndenham.co.uk
web: www.swaninndenham.co.uk
dir: *From A40 take A412. In 200yds follow Denham Village sign on right. Through village, over bridge, last pub on left*

The Swan is the embodiment of the traditional country inn - a double fronted Georgian property swathed in wisteria and set in the beautiful village of Denham. The interior is cosily welcoming with a large log fire and a collection of pictures picked up at local auctions, while outside there is a sunny terrace and large gardens. A private dining room is also available for family occasions or business meetings. Fresh, seasonal produce underpins a menu that re-invigorates some old favourites and makes the most of market availability with a daily-changing specials board. For a starter or light meal look to the 'small plates' section of the menu, with the likes of Marlow rabbit terrine with sauerkraut. Among the main meals you'll find plenty of variety from braised Stockings Farm lamb shoulder shepherd's pie with smoked potato mash to beetroot-cured roast Scottish organic salmon on creamed saffron curly kale with lemon thyme dressing.

**Open** all day all wk 11-11 (Sun 12-10.30) Closed: 26 Dec **Bar Meals** L served Mon-Fri 12-2.30, Sat 12-3, Sun 12-4 D served Sun-Thu 6.30-9.30, Fri-Sat 6.30-10 **Restaurant** L served Mon-Fri 12-2.30, Sat 12-3, Sun 12-4 booking required D served Sun-Thu 6.30-9.30, Fri-Sat 6.30-10 booking required ⊕ SALISBURY PUBS LTD ◀ Wadworth 6X, Courage Best, Marlow Rebellion IPA. ♛ 19 **Facilities** Children's menu Dogs allowed Garden Parking

## FORD

# The Dinton Hermit ★ ★ ★ INN ♛

**Water Ln HP17 8XH ☎ 01296 747473   📄 01296 748819**
e-mail: relax@dintonhermit.co.uk
dir: *Off A418 between Aylesbury & Thame*

Deep in the Vale of Aylesbury, this traditional stone-built inn is a comfortable and friendly place to pop in for a quick drink in front of the open fire. You'll find guest beers and locally brewed ales at the bar, as well as a wide selection of wines. In summer, the large garden is just the place to enjoy the sunshine in the peace and quiet of the Buckinghamshire countryside. Both the restaurant and the bar menus offer

continued

**England**

a range of quality dishes, with locally sourced ingredients wherever possible. Menus change with the seasons, but might include cod cheek and saffron stew; pea and mushroom risotto with a fine leaf salad; or Welsh lamb shank with glazed root vegetables.

**Open** all day all wk 10am-11pm (Sun noon-10.30pm) Closed: 25-26 Dec & 1 Jan **Bar Meals** Av main course £10 food served all day **Restaurant** Fixed menu price fr £15.50 Av 3 course à la carte fr £20 food served all day ⊕ FREE HOUSE ◄ Adnams Bitter, 6X Brakspears, London Pride, Batemans XB. ₹ 13 **Facilities** Children's menu Dogs allowed Garden Parking **Rooms** 13

## FRIETH

## The Prince Albert ₹

**RG9 6PY ☎ 01494 881683**
dir: *4m N of Marlow. Follow Frieth road from Marlow. Straight across at x-rds on Fingest road. Pub 200yds on left*

Set in the Chilterns, close to Hambledon and Marlow, this traditional country pub prides itself on old world values. There are no televisions, juke boxes or games - just good conversation and a welcoming atmosphere. Warm open fires enhance the mood in winter. Expect baguettes, jacket potatoes and ploughman's lunches among the lunchtime light bites, while the evening menu typically offers jumbo battered cod, chilli con carne, lamb shank, and home-made steak and kidney pie.

**Open** all day all wk 11-11 (Sun noon-10.30pm) **Bar Meals** L served Mon-Sat 12.15-2.30, Sun 12.30-3 D served Fri-Sat 7.30-9.30 ⊕ BRAKSPEAR ◄ Brakspear Bitter, Brakspear seasonal ales. ₹ 9 **Facilities** Children's menu Dogs allowed Garden Parking

## GREAT MISSENDEN

## The Rising Sun ₹

**Little Hampden HP16 9PS ☎ 01494 488393 & 488360**
📄 **01494 488788**
e-mail: sunrising@rising-sun.demon.co.uk
web: www.rising-sun.demon.co.uk
dir: *From A413, N of Gt Missenden, take Rignall Rd on left signed Princes Risborough 2.5m. Turn right signed 'Little Hampden only'*

You'll find this 250-year-old inn tucked away in the Chiltern Hills, close to the Ridgeway, down a single track, no-through road, surrounded by beech woods and glorious scenery. An attractive new feature is the landscaped garden area with

comfortable armchair seating and tables for outside wining and dining in beautiful surroundings. There's some good seafood, like fresh mussels with a creamy saffron sauce or pan-fried curried prawns on mango and orange salad. Otherwise look out for roast Deben duck with black cherry and red wine sauce; steak and kidney pie; smoked chicken, sausage and bacon pie; and for something lighter, toasted panini baguette with various fillings; chicken saté with basmati rice and salad; Woodman's lunch - soup, warm roll and butter, four cheeses, mixed pickles and salad; wild mixed mushroom puff pastry basket with a creamy stilton sauce.

**Open** Tue-Sat 11-3, 6.30-10 (Sun 12-3) Closed: Sun eve & Mon **Bar Meals** L served Tue-Sun 12-2 booking required D served Tue-Sat 7-9 booking required Av main course £9.95 **Restaurant** L served Tue-Sun 12-2 booking required D served Tue-Sat 7-9 booking required Fixed menu price fr £20 Av 3 course à la carte fr £21 ⊕ FREE HOUSE ◄ Adnams, Spitfire, Marstons Pedigree, Brakspear Special, Exmoor Gold, Old Speckled Hen. ₹ 10 **Facilities** Children's menu Dogs allowed Garden Parking

## The Nags Head ★★★★ INN ⊛ ₹

**London Rd HP16 0DG ☎ 01494 862200  📄 01494 862685**
e-mail: goodfood@nagsheadbucks.com
web: www.nagsheadbucks.com
dir: *1m from Great Missenden on London Rd. From A413 (Amersham to Aylesbury) turn left signed Chiltern Hospital. After 500mtrs pub on corner of Nags Head Ln & London Rd*

This charming free house was built in the 15th century as three small cottages for the local craftsmen who produced chair spindles and other furniture components. The parts were taken to London for assembly into finished pieces of furniture. Capitalising on their unique position on the London Road, the cottages were later converted into a coaching inn, offering rest and refreshment to weary horses and travellers. Original features including the low oak beams and inglenook fireplace have been carefully retained as a backdrop for the stylish new bar. The dining room is decorated with limited edition prints by local children's author the late Roald Dahl, who was once a regular. The varied menus offer main courses such as slow-cooked lamb shank or steamed salmon and lemon sole with queen scallops, and red pepper and saffron risotto. Leave room for a tempting pudding.

**Open** all day all wk noon-11.30 (closed Sun eve) **Bar Meals** L served Mon-Sat 12-2.30, Sun 12-3.30 booking required D served Mon-Sat 6.30-9.30 booking required Av main course £14.95 **Restaurant** L served Mon-Sat 12-2.30, Sun 12-3.30 booking required D served Mon-Sat 6.30-9.30 booking required Av 3 course à la carte fr £30 ◀ London Pride, Black Sheep, Old Speckled Hen, Jack O'Legs, Rebellion. ☇ 14 **Facilities** Children's menu Dogs allowed Garden Parking **Rooms** 5

## HADDENHAM

### The Green Dragon ⚙⚙ ☇

**8 Churchway HP17 8AA ☎ 01844 291403**
e-mail: enquiries@greendragon.co.uk
web: www.greendragon.co.uk
dir: *SW from Aylesbury on A418 (Oxford road) pass Stone, Upton & Dinton. In 7m left signed Haddenham. Pub approx 1m*

Popular with TV and film crews, Haddenham is a picturesque village with this 18th-century pub at the heart of the old part, close to the green and the 12th-century church. Inside, stone and wooden floors contrast with modern decor and leather sofas in the large bar/dining area. The focus is on good, fresh food and locally sourced produce is used to great effect on monthly-changing menus and the daily chalkboard specials. Fresh fish comes from Cornwall daily. At lunch there's a selection of doorstop sandwiches and baguettes served with twice-cooked, chunky chips and salad; ham, eggs and chips; or a home-made burger with chips and Green Dragon relish. Main courses take in venison and wild mushroom suet pudding with curly kale; pan-roasted skate wing with fennel and cucumber salad and wilted wild garlic; and 28-day aged rib-eye steak with all the trimmings. Great value set lunch and evening menus are available early week. The garden offers two large lawns and an enclosed gravelled area which offers some shade.

**Open** all day all wk noon-11 (Sun noon-10.30) Closed: 26 Dec **Bar Meals** L served all wk 12-2.30 D served all wk 6.30-9.30 Av main course £12.95 **Restaurant** L served all wk 12-2.30 D served all wk 6.30-9.30 ⊞ ENTERPRISE ◀ Sharp's Doom Bar, Timothy Taylor Landlord, Guest ale ♻ Westons Stowford Press. ☇ 6 **Facilities** Children's menu Dogs allowed Garden Parking

## HAMBLEDEN

### The Stag & Huntsman Inn

**RG9 6RP ☎ 01491 571227 📄 01491 413810**
e-mail: andy@stagandhuntsman.com
dir: *5m from Henley-on-Thames on A4155 toward Marlow, left at Mill End towards Hambleden*

Close to the glorious beech-clad Chilterns, this 400-year-old brick and flint village pub has featured in many films and TV series. Ever-changing guest ales are served in the public bar, lounge bar and cosy snug. Food is available in the bars as well as the dining room, from an extensive menu of home-made dishes prepared with local seasonal produce. Hambleden estate game features in season.

**Open** all wk 11-2.30 (Sat-Sun 11-3), 6-11 (Sun 7-10.30), 25 Dec 12-1 Closed: 25-26 Dec & 1 Jan evenings **Bar Meals** L served all wk 12-2 D served Mon-Sat 7-9.30 ⊞ FREE HOUSE ◀ Rebellion IPA, Wadworth 6X, guest ales. **Facilities** Children's menu Garden Parking

## HEDGERLEY

### The White Horse ☇

**SL2 3UY ☎ 01753 643225**
dir: *Telephone for directions*

The original part of the pub is 500 years old, and over 1000 beers take their turn at the pumps each year. At least seven real ales are always available, served by gravity. An annual beer festival is held at the end of May bank holiday. Home-made food ranges from a salad bar with pies, quiches, sandwiches and ploughman's through to curries, chilli, pasta dishes, pies and steaks.

**Open** all wk 11-2.30 5-11 (Sat 11-11, Sun 11-10.30) **Bar Meals** L served Mon-Fri 12-2, Sat-Sun 12-2.30 ⊞ FREE HOUSE ◀ Regularly changing ♻ Regularly changing. ☇ 10 **Facilities** Children's menu Family room Dogs allowed Garden Parking

## LONG CRENDON

## The Angel Inn ⊛ ☐

**47 Bicester Rd HP18 9EE ☎ 01844 208268**
📄 **01844 202497**
e-mail: angelrestaurant@aol.com
dir: *M40 junct 7, A418 to Thame, B4011 to Long Crendon. Inn on B4011*

Wattle-and-daub walls and inglenook fireplaces attest to the age of this former coaching inn, located in the pretty village of Long Crendon. Original materials and classic decorations have been used throughout. There is a warm bar area with leather settees, and a bright conservatory and outside patio area, which come into their own in summer. Real ales are served, along with cocktails, champagne and wine by the glass, but food is the main focus here. At lunch, choose between tempting sandwiches with hot or cold fillings, and the more substantial fare on offer, typically rump of English lamb on chargrilled vegetables, or poached smoked haddock on leek and mustard mash.

**Open** all wk **Bar Meals** L served all wk 12-3 D served all wk 7-10 Av main course £14.95 **Restaurant** L served all wk 12-3 D served all wk 7-10 Fixed menu price fr £19.95 Av 3 course à la carte fr £24.95 ⊕ FREE HOUSE ◀ Oxford Blue, IPA, Brakspear. ☐ 11 **Facilities** Children's menu Garden Parking

## MARLOW

## The Hand and Flowers ⊛⊛⊛ ☐

**126 West St SL7 2BP ☎ 01628 482277**  📄 **01628 401913**
e-mail: theoffice@thehandandflowers.co.uk
web: www.thehandandflowers.co.uk
dir: *M4 junct 9, A404 N into Marlow, A4155 towards Henley-on-Thames. Pub on outskirts on right*

Dedicated chef Tom Kerridge took pub cooking to a new level when he bought the lease to this unassuming pub in 2005. Despite gaining three AA Rosettes in the first year, the pub remains a relaxed and unpretentious place, with beams, timbers, open fires and small bar area serving decent Abbot Ale and a short bar menu – fish and chips, rare roast beef and horseradish sandwich with chips. Tom's cooking is intelligently straightforward and elegant, with simplicity, flavour and skill top of his agenda, and the style is modern Anglo-French built around top-notch produce. From the tiny kitchen comes terrine of Old Spot pork and bacon with hot pickled pineapple; slow-cooked Oxford beef with bone marrow bread pudding; Valrhona chocolate tart with malted milk ice cream, and

rhubarb crumble soufflé with stem ginger anglaise. A class act in a refreshingly informal pub.

**Open** 12-2.30 6.30-9.30 (Sun 12-3.30) Closed: 24-26 Dec, 31 Dec L, 1 Jan D, Sun eve **Bar Meals** L served Mon-Sat 12-2.30 booking required D served Mon-Sat 6.30-9.30 booking required Av main course £9.80 **Restaurant** L served all wk 12-2.30 booking required D served all wk 6.30-9.30 booking required Av 3 course à la carte fr £35 ⊕ Greene King ◀ Abbot Ale, IPA. ☐ 10 **Facilities** Children's menu Garden Parking

## The Kings Head ☐

**Church Rd, Little Marlow SL7 3RZ ☎ 01628 484407**
📄 **01628 484407**
dir: *M40 junct 4 take A4040 S, then A4155 towards Bourne End. Pub 0.5m on right*

Together with the Old Forge, this flower-adorned, 17th-century pub forms part of an attractive group of buildings a few minutes' walk from the Thames Footpath. It has an open-plan but cosy interior with original beams and open fires. In addition to sandwiches and jacket potatoes, the menu offers quite a range of more substantial meals, including salmon fillet hollandaise; mixed fish salad; lamb shank with rich minty gravy; pheasant casserole; and stir-fry duck with plum sauce.

**Open** all day all wk 11-11 **Bar Meals** L served Mon-Sat 12-2.15, Sun 12-7 booking required D served all wk booking required **Restaurant** L served Mon-Sat 12-2.15, Sun 12-7 booking required ⊕ ENTERPRISE INNS ◀ Fuller's London Pride, Timothy Taylor Landlord, Adnam Broadside, St Austell Tribute ⨀ Westons Stowford Press. ☐ 9 **Facilities** Children's menu Garden Parking

## MARLOW BOTTOM

## Pegasus ☐

☎ **01628 484926**
e-mail: pegasusmarlow@hotmail.co.uk
dir: *3m outside Marlow town centre, follow signs to Marlow Bottom*

New chef-landlord Oliver Reichhold snapped up the former TJ O'Reilly's pub late in 2008 and has breathed new life into the building, restoring its old name and offering quality, affordable modern pub food. The short, innovative menu may feature John Dory with cucumber and black pudding to start, followed by local Dexter beef fillet with red wine butter; with Bakewell tart with coffee ice cream to finish. Wash down with a pint of Marlow Rebellion or one of eight wines by the glass.

**Open** 12-3 5.30-11.30 (Sun 12-5) Closed: Mon **Bar Meals** L served Tue-Sun 12-2.30 D served Tue-Sun 6-9 Av main course £8 **Restaurant** L served Tue-Sun 12-2.30 booking required D served Tue-Sun 6.30-10 booking required Fixed menu price fr £15 Av 3 course à la carte fr £25 ⊕ FREE HOUSE ◀ Rebellion IPA, London Pride, Greene King. ☐ 8 **Facilities** Children's menu Garden Parking

## MENTMORE

# Il Maschio@ The Stag ▼

**The Green LU7 0QF ☎ 01296 668423** 📄 **01296 660264**
e-mail: info@ilmaschio.com
dir: *Telephone for directions*

The imposing Stag stands in a picture-postcard village with a lovely summer garden, overlooking Mentmore Towers, a huge Elizabethan-style stately home built in 1855 for Baron Amschel de Rothschild. In this idyllic setting there is a wealth of fresh resources, and head chef and co-owner Mani Rebelo has tapped into the local Chiltern farming community and suppliers for his raw materials. The cooking is a distinctive fusion of British and Mediterranean cuisine. From the seasonally-changing lunch menu you can enjoy freshly made pizzas, pasta gamberetti (prawns, garlic, white wine and cream), and decent salads, perhaps mixed seafood marinated in oil, lemon, garlic and parsley. Evening additions may include venison steak, tuna cooked in lemon juice, olive oil and fresh thyme, seafood mixed grill, and free-range chicken breast with mushroom, brandy and cream sauce. Check out the cocktail bar for some exotic flavoured infusions in the form of martinis, daiquiris and margaritas.

Open all wk Bar Meals  food served all day ⊕ CHARLES WELLS ◀ Youngs Bitter, Guinness, Bombardier. ▼ 8
Facilities Children's menu Dogs allowed Garden Parking

## MILTON KEYNES

# The Swan Inn ▼

**Broughton Rd, Milton Keynes Village MK10 9AH**
**☎ 01908 665240** 📄 **01908 395091**
e-mail: info@theswan-mkvillage.co.uk
dir: *M1 junct 14 towards Milton Keynes. Pub off V11 or H7*

Lots of pubs claim to source their menu ingredients locally, but not many take home-grown vegetables as currency. This one does. Its 13th-century thatch shelters a cosy yet stylish interior, with log fires, flagstone floors, a snug, and a spacious garden at the back. From his open plan kitchen, Toni the Italian chef dispenses a simple yet creative menu that changes monthly with the seasons. Crusty ciabatta sandwiches, daily pies and pasta dishes; and pub classics like hand-made lamb and coriander burgers, and salmon and spring onion fishcakes, are fine examples of the fare.

Open all day all wk 11-11 (Fri-Sat 11-mdnt, Sun noon-10.30) Closed: 25-26 Dec, 1 Jan (morning) Bar Meals L served Mon-Sat 12-9.30, Sun 12-6 D served Mon-Sat 12-9.30, Sun 12-6 Av main course £9.50 food served all day Restaurant L served Mon-Sat 12-3, Sun 12-6 booking required D served Mon-Sat 6-9.30 booking required Av 3 course à la carte fr £22 ◀ Adnams, Old Speckled Hen. ▼ 6 Facilities Children's menu Dogs allowed Garden Parking

## PENN

# The Old Queens Head ▼

**Hammersley Ln, Tylers Green HP10 8EY ☎ 01494 813371**
📄 **01494 816145**
e-mail: info@oldqueensheadpenn.co.uk
web: www.oldqueensheadpenn.co.uk
dir: *B474 (Penn road) through Beaconsfield New Town towards Penn, approx 3m left into School Rd, left in 500yds into Hammersley Ln. Pub opp church*

In 1666, local builders made good use of the plentiful supplies of local timber to build the barn that, with several additions, today houses the dining room of this charming pub. The owners have spent many hours at local auctions finding lovely old furniture and pictures in keeping with the age of the pub. A sunny terrace overlooks the church of St Margaret's and there's a large garden in which to eat and drink. The versatile kitchen is responsible for a modern British menu offering a good choice, with starters such as crispy smoked haddock fishcake with saffron mayonnaise and slow-roast tomato relish. You might then find yourself torn between pan-fried duck breast on confit duck hash with purple sprouting broccoli and Madeira jus; and roast leek, spring onion and thyme gnocchi with creamy Barkham blue cheese sauce. Puddings include steamed apple and sherried raisin roly-poly with cinnamon ice cream.

Open all day all wk 11-11 (Sun 12-10.30) Closed: 26 Dec Bar Meals L served all wk 12-2.30, Sat 12-3, Sun 12-4 D served all wk 6.30-9.30, Fri & Sat 6.30-10 Restaurant L served all wk 12-2.30, Sat 12-3, Sun 12-4 booking required D served all wk 6.30-9.30, Fri & Sat 6.30-10 booking required ⊕ SALISBURY PUBS LTD ◀ Ruddles County, Greene King IPA, Guinness. ▼ 19
Facilities Children's menu Dogs allowed Garden Parking

## PRESTON BISSETT

# The White Hart ▼

**Pound Ln MK18 4LX ☎ 01280 847969**
dir: *2.5m from A421*

Seek out this pretty thatched free house in the winter months for traditional game dishes from the local shoots. The Grade II listed building dates from 1545 and lies amid the rolling hills of rural Buckinghamshire. There's a good selection of wines and local real ales, and a small select menu that changes with the seasons; expect classic dishes like steak and ale pie, and slow-cooked belly of pork. There's a nice, secluded garden, too.

continued

England

Open 12-2.30 6-11 (Sat-Sun noon-11pm) Closed: Mon Bar Meals L served Tue-Sun 12-2.30 D served Tue-Sun 6-11 Av main course £9.50 Restaurant L served Tue-Sun 12-2.30 booking required D served Tue-Sun 6-10 booking required Av 3 course à la carte fr £20 ◗ Hooky Best Bitter, Old Hooky, Timothy Taylor Landlord, Rev James, Tribute. 🍷 6 Facilities Children's menu Dogs allowed Garden Parking

## RADNAGE

## The Three Horseshoes Inn 🍷

**Horseshoe Rd, Bennett End HP14 4EB ☎ 01494 483273**
e-mail: threehorseshoes@btconnect.com
dir: M40 junct 5 Stokenchurch to High Wycombe, turn left Radnage 1.8m, left & follow road

Dating from 1748, this delightful little inn is tucked away down a leafy lane. Stone floors, original beams, bread oven and open fire are among the features. The modern English and European menu changes daily, and award-winning chef/owner Simon Cranshaw uses as much local produce as possible. Enjoy a Rebellion Ale at the bar, or wander outside in the gardens.

Open 12-3 6-11 (Sun 12-4) Closed: Mon Bar Meals L served Wed-Sun 12-2.30 D served Tue-Sat 6-9.30 Av main course £9.50 Restaurant L served Wed-Sun 12-2.30 D served Tue-Sat 6-9.30 Fixed menu price fr £25 Av 3 course à la carte fr £28.50 ⊕ FREE HOUSE ◗ Rebellion beers. 🍷 10 Facilities Children's menu Dogs allowed Garden Parking

## TURVILLE

## The Bull & Butcher 🍷

**RG9 6QU ☎ 01491 638283 📠 01491 638836**
e-mail: info@thebullandbutcher.com
dir: M40 junct 5 follow Ibstone signs. Right at T-junct. Pub 0.25m on left

You'll probably recognise the Bull & Butcher, even if you've never been there before. For Turville, with its 16th-century pub and 10th-century church, has taken part in many film and TV productions: Midsomer Murders, The Vicar of Dibley, Goodbye Mr Tom, and Chitty Chitty Bang Bang. After an exhilarating walk amid the glorious Chilterns scenery, drop down from the windmill on Turville Hill and unwind with a pint in the Well Bar or Windmill Lounge with their natural oak beams and open fires. There's also a large garden and patio area. Menu choices begin with starters that include a platter of cured meats with olives and bread, whilst main course dishes range from cod, chips and mushy peas or pan-fried duck with rice and stir-fried vegetables to roasted vegetable cannelloni with spinach.

Open all day all wk 11-11 (Sun noon-10.30pm) Bar Meals L served Mon-Fri 12-2.30, Sat-Sun 12-4 booking required D served Mon-Fri 6.30-9.30, Sat 6-9.30, Sun 7-9 booking required Av main course £12 Restaurant L served Mon-Fri 12-2.30, Sat-Sun 12-4 booking required D served Mon-Fri 6.30-9.30, Sat 6-9.30, Sun 7-9 booking required Av 3 course à la carte fr £22.50 ⊕ BRAKSPEAR ◗ Brakspear Bitter, Hooky Dark, Oxford Gold, Brewers selections. 🍷 36 Facilities Children's menu Dogs allowed Garden Parking

## WHITELEAF

## Red Lion

**Upper Icknield Way HP27 0LL ☎ 01844 344476**
📠 **01844 344476**
e-mail: tim_hibbert@hotmail.co.uk
dir: A4010 through Princes Risborough, turn right into The Holloway, at T-junct turn right, pub on left

Family-owned 17th-century traditional country inn in the heart of the Chilterns, surrounded by National Trust land and situated close to the Ridgeway national trail. There are plenty of good local walks with wonderful views. A cosy fire in winter and a secluded summer beer garden add to the appeal. Hearty pub fare is served in the bar area and includes rib-eye steak, sausage and mash, vegetarian lasagne, haddock and chips, warm baguettes and jacket potatoes. You can also dine in the recently built restaurant.

Open all wk Bar Meals L served all wk 12-2 D served Mon-Sat 7-9 booking required Av main course £8.50 Restaurant L served all wk 12-2 booking required D served Mon-Sat 7-9 booking required Fixed menu price fr £9.50 ⊕ FREE HOUSE ◗ Brakspear Bitter, Hook Norton, Tribute, Guinness. Facilities Children's menu Family room Dogs allowed Garden Parking

## WOOBURN COMMON

## Chequers Inn ★★★ HL ◉ 🍷

**Kiln Ln HP10 0JQ ☎ 01628 529575 📠 01628 850124**
e-mail: info@chequers-inn.com
dir: M40 junct 2, A40 through Beaconsfield Old Town towards High Wycombe. 2m from town left into Broad Ln. Inn 2.5m

Oak posts and beams, flagstone floors and a wonderful open fireplace blackened by a million blazing logs: this 17th-century inn is an absolute charmer. It has been owned and run by the same family for 35 years, ensuring a friendly, relaxed and welcoming atmosphere. Overlooking open Chiltern Hills countryside, its interior includes an attractively decorated restaurant, but an alternative dining option is the extensive lunch and dinner bar menu backed by a large selection of beers, guest ales and wines; the same menu is served in the contemporary lounge. The restaurant is as ideal for a quick business lunch as for a long romantic dinner. Fresh, predominantly local ingredients are used in dishes such as slow-cooked Oxfordshire pork belly with cauliflower purée, black pudding and caramelised apple sauce; pan-fried fillet of brill with samphire, boulangère potatoes and a light chicken and tomato jus; and chocolate torte with orange sorbet. Outside is a garden area where barbecues are held in summer.

Open all day all wk noon-mdnt Bar Meals L served Mon-Fri 12-2.30, Sat 12-10, Sun 12-9.30 D served Mon-Thu 6-9.30, Fri 6-10, Sat 12-10, Sun 12-9.30 Av main course £10.95 Restaurant L served all wk 12-2.30 booking required D served all wk 7-9.30 booking required Fixed menu price fr £13.95 Av 3 course à la carte fr £29.95 ⊕ FREE HOUSE ◗ IPA, Rebellion Smuggler, Old Speckled Hen. 🍷 12 Facilities Children's menu Garden Parking Rooms 17

## CAMBRIDGESHIRE

### BABRAHAM

## The George Inn at Babraham ◉

**High St CB2 4AG ☎ 01223 833800** 📄 **01223 833800**
e-mail: stevelythall@btinternet.com
dir: *In High St, just off A11/A505 & A1307*

An 18th-century coaching inn once renowned for the Whitsun and May Day revels hosted here. Set in the heart of rural Cambridgeshire, it was devastated by fire in 2004 but new kitchens and three restaurant areas have restored this village dining pub to its former glory. At the bar, Greene King's reliable beers include Old Speckled Hen, while the food operation continues to maintain 'a passion for detail'. For lunch you could snack on roasted cashews, marinated olives, toasted herb and garlic croutons, and sun-blushed tomatoes; alternatively a freshly baked ciabatta with poached salmon and baby prawns might suffice. Favourites from the bar menu include beer-battered fresh cod fillet, and home-made lasagne with garlic bread. A full à la carte choice could include seared queen scallops to start, Suffolk rack of lamb with herb and Stilton crust, and brandy snap basket filled with exotic fruit salad. Roasts on Sunday include Norfolk turkey, and all are served with fresh market vegetables.

**Open** all wk noon-3 6-11 **Bar Meals** L served all wk 12-3 D served all wk 6-9.30 Av main course £9 **Restaurant** L served all wk 12-3 D served all wk 6-9.30 Fixed menu price fr £7.95 Av 3 course à la carte fr £25 ⊕ GREENE KING ◀ Old Speckled Hen, Greene King IPA, Abbot Ale. **Facilities** Children's menu Dogs allowed Garden Parking

### BARRINGTON

## The Royal Oak ♸

**31 West Green CB22 7RZ ☎ 01223 870791**
📄 **01223 870791**
e-mail: info@royaloak.uk.net
dir: *From Barton off M11, S of Cambridge*

One of the oldest thatched pubs in England, this rambling, timbered 13th-century building overlooks one of the largest village greens in England. It's is only six miles from Cambridge, three miles from the M11 and a mile from Shepreth Station. A wide range of fish dishes includes scallops, trout, scampi, tuna, swordfish, tiger prawns, squid and other seasonal offerings. There is also a carvery on Sunday which could be accompanied by a pint of IPA Potton Brewery or Young's Bitter.

**Open** all wk noon-2.30 6-11 (Sun 12-3 6.30-10.30) **Restaurant** L served noon-2, Sun noon-2.30 booking required D served 6.30-9.30, Sun 7-9 booking required ⊕ FREE HOUSE ◀ IPA Potton Brewery, Adnams, Young's Bitter, Morland Original. ♸ 6 **Facilities** Children's menu Garden Parking

### BROUGHTON

## The Crown ♸

**Bridge Rd PE28 3AY ☎ 01487 824428**
e-mail: info@thecrowninnrestaurant.co.uk
dir: *Just off A141 between Huntingdon & Warboys, by church in village centre*

Quality, flavour and the freshest seasonal food are the hallmarks of this picturesque 18th-century free house, just across the road from the church. The Crown lies at the heart of a thriving local community; it's popular with walkers and visitors alike, and the extensive rear garden is perfect for leisurely summer afternoons. The restaurant combines a traditional pub interior with touches of contemporary design, and this is the place to sample good, honest British food with a French and Italian twist. Begin with roast parsnip soup with aged balsamic vinegar; Bottisham smoked duck salad; or carrot and coriander roulade. Moving on to the main course, the choices might include four-hour roast pork belly; fish pie with mashed potato; or braised fennel and goats' cheese tart. Round off with apple and sultana crumble, pear and almond frangipane tart, or decadent chocolate Nemesis.

**Open** 11.30-3 6.30-11 (Sun 11.30-6) Closed: 1-11 Jan, Mon-Tue **Bar Meals** L served Wed-Sun 12-2.30 D served Wed-Sun 7-10 Av main course £13 **Restaurant** L served Wed-Sun 12-2.30 booking required D served Wed-Sun 7-10 booking required Fixed menu price fr £11.50 ⊕ FREE HOUSE ◀ Adnams Broadside, Elgoods Black Dog, Greene King IPA, City of Cambridge Hobson Choice, Potton Brewery Shambles ♂ Aspalls. ♸ 10 **Facilities** Children's menu Dogs allowed Garden Parking

### CAMBRIDGE

## Cambridge Blue ♸

**85 Gwydir St CB1 2LG ☎ 01223 471680**
dir: *City centre*

A friendly 1860s backstreet pub with an unexpected garden. Inside are two real fires and lots of memorabilia. The tap room has seven handpumps, but there are always at least 12 real ales to choose from, such as Bishop's Farewell and Nethergate Dewdrop (the pub used to be called the Dew Drop Inn, a Victorian pun). Good value pub grub made on the premises ranges from ciabattas and jackets to curries, pies, chilli con carne and sticky toffee pudding.

**Open** all wk noon-2.30 5-11 (Thu-Sat noon-11 Sun noon-10.30)

continued

Bar Meals L served Mon-Fri 12-2, Sat-Sun 12-4 D served all wk 6-9 Av main course £7 ⊕ FREE HOUSE ◀ Woodforde's Wherry, Oakham Bishops Farewell, guest ales. ♟ 8 **Facilities** Children's menu Family room Dogs allowed Garden

## Free Press ♟

**Prospect Row CB1 1DU ☎ 01223 368337**
e-mail: craig.bickley@ntlworld.com
dir: *Telephone for directions*

Students, academics, locals and visitors rub shoulders in this atmospheric and picturesque back-street pub near the city centre. It has open fires and a beautiful walled garden - but no music, mobile phones or gaming machines. Punters are attracted by first-rate real ales and nourishing home-made food such as chilli with garlic bread; goat's cheese salad; filled toasted ciabattas; venison sausages; salmon filled with couscous and vegetables.

Open all wk noon-2.30 6-11 (Fri noon-2.30 4.30-11, Sat noon-11, Sun noon-3 7-10.30) Closed: 25-26 Dec, 1 Jan ⊕ GREENE KING ◀ Greene King IPA, Abbot Ale, Dark Mild, guest ales. ♟ 10 **Facilities** Children's menu Dogs allowed Garden

## ELSWORTH

## The George & Dragon ♟

**41 Boxworth Rd CB3 8JQ ☎ 01954 267236**
📄 01954 267080
e-mail: www.georgeanddragon-elsworth.co.uk
dir: *SE of A14 between Cambridge & Huntingdon*

Set in a pretty village just outside Cambridge, this pub offers a wide range of satisfying food to locals and visitors alike. Look out for halibut mornay, steak and kidney pie, and fresh cod, haddock or plaice from Lowestoft. For a lighter meal, ploughman's lunches and sandwiches are available. There are special menus for occasions such as Valentine candlelit dinner and Mother's Day. Friday night is Aberdeen Angus steak night.

Open all wk 11-2.30 6-11 Bar Meals L served all wk 11-2.30 D served all wk 6-11 Av main course £11.50 **Restaurant** L served all wk 11-2.30 D served all wk 6-11 Fixed menu price fr £10.50 Av 3 course à la carte fr £16 ⊕ FREE HOUSE ◀ Greene King IPA, Ruddles County, Greene King Old Speckled Hen. ♟ 8 **Facilities** Children's menu Garden Parking

## ELTON

## The Crown Inn ★★★★★ INN ♟

**8 Duck St PE8 6RQ ☎ 01832 280232**
e-mail: inncrown@googlemail.com
dir: *A1(M) junct 17, W on A605 signed Oundle/Northampton. In 3.5m right to Elton, 0.9m left signed Nassington. Inn 0.3m on right*

Almost hidden by a towering chestnut tree, The Crown is a beautiful, 17th-century thatched building opposite the village green. Chef/owner Marcus Lamb places great emphasis on the food, using local supplies for everything from sandwiches to salmon and prawn ravioli in a Thai broth followed by pork

loin layered with mushroom, leek and Stilton, and served with mashed potato and a mustard sauce. Annual treats include a May Day hog roast and a summer beer festival.

Open all wk noon-11 (Mon 5-11 (BH noon-11)) Closed: 1-7 Jan (Restaurant ) Bar Meals L served Tue-Sun 12-2 D served Tue-Sat 6.30-8.45 Av main course £13.95 **Restaurant** L served Tue-Sun 12-2 booking required D served Tue-Sat 6.30-8.45 booking required Fixed menu price fr £12 Av 3 course à la carte fr £32 ⊕ FREE HOUSE ◀ Golden Crown Bitter, Greene King IPA, Adnams, Jeffrey Hudson Bitter, Black Sheep. ♟ 10 **Facilities** Children's menu Dogs allowed Garden Parking **Rooms** 5

## ELY

## The Anchor Inn ★★★★ RR 🏵 ♟

**Sutton Gault CB6 2BD ☎ 01353 778537**
📄 01353 776180
e-mail: anchorinn@popmail.bta.com
web: www.anchorsuttongault.co.uk
dir: *From A14, B1050 to Earith, take B1381 to Sutton. Sutton Gault on left*

Gault, as in the hamlet's name, is the type of thick clay used for the banks of the rivers and dykes that criss-cross the billiard-table-flat fen country. The Anchor was built to provide shelter for the Scottish prisoners of war who built the Old and New Bedford Rivers to drain the fens. It's been an inn, today a family-run free house, ever since. Scrubbed pine tables on gently undulating floors, old prints, evening candle glow and winter log fires help to engender its timeless charm and character. The core of its monthly menus, for which it continues to win wide recognition, is traditional British in the best sense, using local produce wherever possible, including daily deliveries of fresh seafood, such as hand-dressed Cromer crab and Brancaster oysters and mussels, and game from the market. The house speciality is grilled dates wrapped in bacon in a mild grain mustard cream sauce. The Sunday lunch menu always includes roast beef, along with another roast, fresh fish and vegetarian dishes. Some of the suites and rooms overlook the river.

Open all wk 12-2.30 7-10.30 (Sat 12-3 6.30-11) Bar Meals Av main course £13 **Restaurant** L served Mon-Sat 12-2, Sun 12-2.30 booking required D served Mon-Fri 7-9, Sat 6.30-9.30, Sun 6.30-8.30 booking required Fixed menu price fr £11.95 Av 3 course à la carte fr £25 ⊕ FREE HOUSE ◀ Pegasus. ♟ 12 **Facilities** Children's menu Garden Parking **Rooms** 4

## FEN DITTON

### Ancient Shepherds ☻

**High St CB5 8ST ☎ 01223 293280** 📠 **01223 293280**
e-mail: ancientshepherds@hotmail.co.uk
dir: *From A14 take B1047 signed Cambridge/Airport*

Named after the ancient order of Shepherders who used to meet here, this heavily-beamed pub and restaurant was built originally as three cottages in 1540. The two bars, a lounge and a dining room all boast inglenook fireplaces. Located three miles from Cambridge in a riverside setting, it provides a welcome escape for those who like to enjoy their refreshments without the addition of music, darts or pool. Among the fish dishes on the menu are fillet of sea bass on a bed of creamed leeks and home-made fishcakes. Meat eaters are equally well catered for with perhaps half a casseroled guinea fowl in Burgundy with roast vegetables, Barnsley lamb chops, and pork loin steaks in cream and mustard sauce to choose from.

Open noon-2.30 6-11 Closed: 25-26 Dec, Mon eve & Sun eve **Bar Meals** L served all wk 12-2.30 Av main course £7.95 **Restaurant** L served all wk 12-2.30 D served Tue-Sat 6.30-9 booking required Av 3 course à la carte fr £22 🟁 PUNCH TAVERNS ◀ Adnams Bitter, Greene King IPA. ☻ 8 **Facilities** Children's menu Dogs allowed Garden Parking

## FORDHAM

### White Pheasant ☻

**CB7 5LQ ☎ 01638 720414**
e-mail: chef@whitepheasant.com
web: www.whitepheasant.com
dir: *From Newmarket A142 to Ely, approx 5m to Fordham. Pub on left*

This 18th-century building stands in a fenland village between Ely and Newmarket. In recent years its considerable appeal has been subtly enhanced by improvements that preserve its period charm. You can enjoy the locally brewed ale, a glass of wine or home-made lemonade or strawberryade while perusing the menus. Food is taken seriously here: the kitchen offers globally-influenced, traditional British dishes ranging from light bites to full à la carte meals. Prime produce is used from local suppliers and all the meat is free range. Lighter meals might include the lunchtime deli board; or a choice of 'old favourites' such as Suffolk ham with fried free-range eggs and chips, while an evening meal could start with home-made local game pâté with cranberry and caper relish, followed by slow-roasted belly of free-range Suffolk pork with black pudding. Fish and game

are often found on the specials board. The pub also offers hog and spit roast catering.

Open all wk noon-3 6-11 (Sun 7-9.30) Closed: 26-29 Dec, 1 Jan **Bar Meals** L served Mon-Sat 12-2.30 booking required Av main course £14 **Restaurant** L served Mon-Sun 12-2.30 booking required D served Mon-Sat 6-9.30, Sun 7-9 booking required Av 3 course à la carte fr £27 🟁 FREE HOUSE ◀ Rusty Bucket, Woodforde's Wherry, Nethergate 🍎 Aspalls. ☻ 14 **Facilities** Children's menu Garden Parking

## GRANTCHESTER

### The Rupert Brooke ☻

**2 Broadway CB3 9NQ ☎ 01223 840295** 📠 **01223 841251**
e-mail: info@therupertbrooke.com
dir: *M11 junct 12, follow Grantchester signs*

Only five minutes from the centre of Cambridge, yet set in an idyllic location overlooking the meadows close to the River Cam, sits the Rupert Brooke, named after the WWI poet. Inside, you'll find timber beams and winter log fires, with relaxing sofas and tub chairs. Using local, seasonal produce and with regularly changing menus, watch the chefs at work in the theatre-style kitchen, creating their range of modern British dishes - winter squash and sage risotto; Grasmere Farm sausages with creamy mash are typical choices.

Open all wk 11.30-11 (Fri-Sat 11.30-mdnt) **Bar Meals** L served Mon-Sat 12-3 D served Mon-Fri 6-9.30 Av main course £11 **Restaurant** L served Mon-Sat 12-3 (Sun 12-6 (8 May-Sep)) booking required D served Mon-Sat 6-9.30 booking required Av 3 course à la carte fr £25 🟁 ENTERPRISE INNS ◀ Harveys Sussex Best, Woodforde's Wherry, London Pride, Timothy Taylor Landlord 🍎 Westons Stowford Press. ☻ 12 **Facilities** Children's menu Family room Garden Parking

## HEMINGFORD GREY

### The Cock Pub and Restaurant ☻

**47 High St PE28 9BJ ☎ 01480 463609** 📠 **01480 461747**
e-mail: cock@cambscuisine.com
dir: *2m S of Huntingdon and 1m E of A14*

There's been a spring in the step of this village pub since Oliver Thain and Richard Bradley arrived a few years ago; it has had a recent refurbishment too. Transforming it into an dining pub, they've retained traditional values, with well kept real ales,

continued

log fires blazing when the weather demands and a delightful garden in summer, and a welcome for walkers, children and dogs. In the wooden-floored restaurant fresh fish, including seared sea bream and mushroom sauce, and chef's various home-made sausages, may prove irresistible. Gluten-free dishes offered.

**Open** all wk 11.30-3 6-11 **Restaurant** L served all wk 12-2.30 D served all wk 6.15-9.30 Fixed menu price fr £11 Av 3 course à la carte fr £20 ⊕ FREE HOUSE ◀ Golden Jackal, Wolf Brewery, Victoria Bitter, Buntingford Highwayman IPA, seasonal ale from Nethergate. ♀ 13 **Facilities** Children's menu Dogs allowed Garden Parking

## HINXTON

### The Red Lion ★★★★ INN ⊛ ♀

**32 High St CB10 1QY ☎ 01799 530601** 📄 **01799 531201**
e-mail: info@redlionhinxton.co.uk
dir: *1m from M11 junct 9*

The Red Lion has been in Hinxton, a conservation village, since the 16th century. The bar is in the oldest part, while the spacious oak-built extension is the dining room. Pub policy is always to use fresh local produce where possible to create imaginative dishes such as Poché-grillé pheasant breast wrapped in streaky bacon; or pork belly confit with sage dauphinoise potato, fine beans and apple jus. Enjoy your visit with a pint of Rusty Bucket, Village Bike or Aspall cider, or stay over and explore the area.

**Open** all wk 11-3 6-11 **Bar Meals** L served Mon-Thu 12-2, Fri-Sun 12-2.30 D served Sun-Thu 7-9, Fri-Sat 7-9.30 Av main course £11 **Restaurant** L served Mon-Thu 12-2, Fri-Sun 12-2.30 D served Sun-Thu 7-9, Fri-Sat 7-9.30 Av 3 course à la carte fr £22 ⊕ FREE HOUSE ◀ Adnams, Greene King IPA, Woodforde's Wherry, Rusty Bucket, Village Bike, guest ales ♂ Aspall. ♀ 12 **Facilities** Children's menu Dogs allowed Garden Parking **Rooms** 8

## HOLYWELL

### The Old Ferryboat Inn ⏢ ★★ HL ♀

**Back Ln PE27 4TG ☎ 01480 463227** 📄 **01480 463245**
e-mail: 8638@greeneking.co.uk
dir: *From Cambridge on A14 right onto A1096, then right onto A1123, right to Holywell*

Renowned as England's oldest inn, built some time in the 11th century, but with a history that goes back to the 6th. In a tranquil setting beside the Great Ouse river, The Old Ferryboat has immaculately maintained thatch, white stone walls, cosy interior and bags of charm and character. A pleasant atmosphere - despite the resident ghost of a lovelorn teenager - in which to enjoy grilled bacon and warm poached egg salad; British beef and Ruddles ale pie, mash, seasonal vegetables and onion gravy; or sweet potato, chick pea and spinach curry.

**Open** all wk 11-11 (Sun noon-10.30) **Bar Meals** food served all day **Restaurant** food served all day ⊕ OLD ENGLISH INNS & HOTELS ◀ Greene King Abbot Ale/IPA, guest ales. ♀ 18 **Facilities** Children's menu Garden Parking **Rooms** 7

## HORNINGSEA

### The Crown & Punchbowl

**CB5 9JG ☎ 01223 860643** 📄 **01223 441814**
e-mail: info@thecrownandpunchbowl.co.uk
dir: *Please telephone for directions*

Soft colours and wooden floors create a warm and cosy atmosphere beneath the tiled roof of this whitewashed free house, not far from Cambridge city centre. The large restaurant caters equally for business lunches and those with more time to relax; expect roast guinea fowl with braised lentils; stuffed field mushroom with goats' cheese, spinach and beans; and home-made pie with seasonal vegetables. Fresh fish and home-made sausages also feature on the chalkboard menus.

**Open** noon-2.30 6.30-9 Closed: Sun eve & BH eve **Bar Meals** Av main course £12.95 **Restaurant** L served all wk 12-2.30 booking required D served Mon-Sat 6.30-9 booking required Fixed menu price fr £11.95 Av 3 course à la carte fr £19.95 ⊕ FREE HOUSE ◀ Hobson's Choice. **Facilities** Children's menu Garden Parking

## KEYSTON

### Pheasant Inn ⊛ ♀

**Village Loop Rd PE28 0RE**
**☎ 01832 710241** 📄 **01832 710340**
e-mail: info@thepheasant-keyston.co.uk
dir: *0.5m off A14, clearly signed, 10m W of Huntingdon, 14m E of Kettering*

A 15th-century, thatched inn, set in a sleepy village. Its unspoilt bar is full of oak beams and simple wooden furniture, and is warmed by large open fires. Three distinct dining areas are all comfortable, intimate and relaxed. In fine weather enjoy the garden at the rear of the pub, or sit on one of the benches out front. Expect good things of the restaurant, where the cooking owes much to the South of France, as well as to the best seasonal produce from mostly local suppliers. Menus may offer starters of potato, spring onion and chive soup with poached egg; or lamb pie with piccalilli and watercress. Among typical mains are coq au vin with confit garlic mashed potato and cavolo nero; steak and ale suet pudding with green peppercorn sauce, new potatoes and Italian chicory; and crisp grey mullet with bourride sauce, tapenade potatoes, brown shrimps and mussels. Puddings include chocolate Pithiviers with thyme ice cream; and banana sticky toffee pudding with butterscotch sauce and Jersey cream.

Open all day Closed: Sun eve, Mon (ex BH) **Bar Meals** L served Mon-Sat 12-2.30 booking required D served Mon-Sat 6.30-9.30 booking required Av main course £14 **Restaurant** L served all wk 12-2.30 booking required D served all wk 6.30-9.30 booking required Fixed menu price fr £15 ⊕ THE PHEASANT KEYSTON LTD ◄ Adnams, Village Bike Potton Brewery, Augustinian Nethergate Brewery. ☻ 16 **Facilities** Children's menu Dogs allowed Garden Parking

## MADINGLEY

# The Three Horseshoes ◉ ♀

**High St CB3 8AB ☎ 01954 210221  📄 01954 212043**
e-mail: thethreehorseshoes@huntsbridge.co.uk
dir: *M11 junct 13, 1.5m from A14*

This picturesque thatched inn enjoys a charming location; its large garden extends towards meadowland and the local cricket pitch. Inside is a small, bustling bar and a conservatory restaurant. Chef-Patron Richard Stokes is a local who's style is a modern take on Italian cuisine, characterised by imaginative dishes and intense flavours. After antipasti, you could try risotto di pesce or aqua cotta (a 'boiled water' classic Italian soup), followed by line-caught grey mullet with Casteluccio lentils, Italian sea kale, slow cooked fennel and salsa verde; or pot-roasted free-range organic chicken stuffed with garlic, thyme, butter and lemon, potato purée, cavolo nero and chicken liver crostino. Desserts might include lemon tart with Seville orange and Campari sorbet. Prior booking advisable.

Open all wk 11.30-3 6-11 (Sun 6-9.30) **Bar Meals** L served Mon-Fri 12-2, Sat-Sun 12-2.30 D served all wk 6.30-9.30 Av main course £15 **Restaurant** L served all wk 12-2.30 D served Mon-Sat 6.30-9.30 Fixed menu price fr £20 Av 3 course à la carte fr £30 ⊕ FREE HOUSE ◄ Adnams Bitter, Hook Norton Old Hooky, Smile's Best, Cambridge Hobsons Choice, guest ales. ☻ 20 **Facilities** Children's menu Garden Parking

## MILTON

# Waggon & Horses

**39 High St CB24 6DF ☎ 01223 860313**
e-mail: winningtons.waggon@ntlworld.com
dir: *A14/A10 junct. Past Tesco, through village, approx 1m set back on left*

Elgood Brewery's most southerly house, the pub is an imposing mock-Tudor building famed for its large collection of hats. Real cider is also served, from local producer Cassels. Wednesday night is quiz night and baltis are the speciality on Thursdays. Meals are good value and the chilli is recommended. Bar billiards is popular, and outside there's a large child-safe garden with slide and swings, and a pétanque terrain.

Open all wk noon-2.30 5-11 (Fri 5-mdnt, Sat noon-3 6-11.30, Sun noon-3 7.30-10.30) **Bar Meals** L served all wk 12-2 D served all wk 7-9 Av main course £5 ⊕ ELGOOD & SONS LTD ◄ Elgoods Cambridge Bitter, Black Dog Mild, Golden Newt, seasonal and guest ales ♻ Cassells. **Facilities** Children's menu Dogs allowed Garden Parking

## SPALDWICK

# The George Inn ♀

**High St PE28 0TD ☎ 01480 890293  📄 01480 896847**
e-mail: info@georgeofspaldwick.co.uk
dir: *6m W of Huntingdon on A14, junct 18 towards Spaldwick/Stow Longa*

Refurbished to create a pleasing blend of traditional and modern, this fine old building retains historic features such as original beams and fireplaces. It started life as a large private residence belonging to the Dartington family, and became a coaching inn in 1679. Today it remains a serene presence beside the manor house, overlooking the village green. The bar is relaxing with its comfortable leather sofas, while the restaurant, set in a beautifully converted barn, offers a pleasing selection of traditional British and Mediterranean-influenced dishes. Typical choices include a starter of crispy duck salad with spicy chorizo, bacon lardons, croutons and plum dressing, followed by wood pigeon breasts with herb dumplings, mash, red cabbage and a chocolate red wine sauce. Finish with apple crumble tart or a delightful selection of cheeses.

Open all day all wk noon-11.30pm Closed: 1 Jan **Bar Meals** L served all wk 12-2.30 D served all wk 6-9.30 **Restaurant** L served all wk 12-2.30 D served all wk 6-9.30 ⊕ PUNCH TAVERNS ◄ Adnams Broadside, Greene King IPA, Youngs Special. ☻ 25 **Facilities** Children's menu Garden Parking

## STAPLEFORD

# The Rose at Stapleford ♀

**81 London Rd CB22 5DE ☎ 01223 843349**
e-mail: paulnbeer@aol.com

Having made a success of the George and Dragon at Elsworth (see entry), Paul and Karen Beer are weaving their magic at the Rose, a traditional village pub close to Cambridge and Duxford Imperial War Museum. Expect a comfortably refurbished interior, replete with low beams and inglenook fireplaces, and extensive menus that draw on local Suffolk produce, particularly meat with fish from Lowestoft. Typical dishes take in calves' liver and bacon with onion gravy, fish pie, and local farm-reared steaks with pepper sauce.

Open 12-2.30 6-11 Closed: Sun eve **Bar Meals** L served all wk 12-2.30 D served all wk 6-9.30 Av main course £12 food served all day **Restaurant** L served all wk 12-2.30 D served all wk 6-9.30 Fixed menu price fr £11 Av 3 course à la carte fr £20 food served all day ⊕ Enterprise ◄ IPA, Tribute, Guest Ale. ☻ 9 **Facilities** Children's menu Dogs allowed Garden Parking

**England**

## STRETHAM

### The Lazy Otter

**Cambridge Rd CB6 3LU ☎ 01353 649780**
📄 01353 649314
e-mail: restaurant@lazy-otter.com
dir: *Telephone for directions*

Just off the A10 between Ely and Cambridge, the Lazy Otter stands overlooking the marina beside the River Great Ouse. There's been a pub on this site since the 18th century, but the old building was redeveloped in 1986. Today, the large beer garden and riverside restaurant are popular summer attractions. Lunchtime brings baguettes, sandwiches and jacket potatoes, whilst main course choices include ham and eggs; baked cod au gratin; and home-made spinach lasagne. Enjoy your meal with a pint of Lazy Otter best bitter or Pickled Pig cider.

**Open** all day all wk 11-11 (Sun noon-10.30pm) **Bar Meals** L served Mon-Sat 12-2, Sun 12-7 booking required D served Mon-Sat 6.30-9, Sun 12-7 booking required Av main course £8.50 **Restaurant** L served Mon-Sat 12-2, Sun 12-7 booking required D served Mon-Sat 6.30-9, Sun 12-7 booking required ⊕ FREE HOUSE ◀ Greene King, IPA, Guest ales Ŏ Pickled Pig. **Facilities** Children's menu Play area Garden Parking

## CHESHIRE

## BURLEYDAM

### The Combermere Arms ▾

**SY13 4AT ☎ 01948 871223** 📄 01948 661371
e-mail: combermere.arms@brunningandprice.co.uk
dir: *From Whitchurch take A525 towards Nantwich, at Newcastle/Audlem/Woore sign, turn right at junct. Pub 100yds on right*

Popular with local shoots, walkers and town folk alike, this busy 17th-century inn retains great character and warmth. Three roaring fires complement the wealth of oak, pictures and old furniture. Dishes range from light bites and sandwiches to shin of beef and Weetwood ale pie or pot-roasted Combermere Abbey pheasant; and puddings like steamed blackcurrant roly poly with custard. There is a very impressive cheese list.

**Open** all wk 11.30-11 **Bar Meals** Av main course £10 food served all day **Restaurant** food served all day ⊕ FREE HOUSE ◀ Woodlands Oak Beauty, Weetwood Cheshire Cat, Thornbridge Jaipur Monsoon, St Austells Tribute, Storm Hurricane Hubert Ŏ Weston Stowford Press, Thatchers Gold, Inch's Stonehouse. ▾ 15 **Facilities** Children's menu Dogs allowed Garden Parking

## BURWARDSLEY

### The Pheasant Inn ★★★★★ INN ▾

**CH3 9PF ☎ 01829 770434** 📄 01829 771097
e-mail: info@thepheasantinn.co.uk
dir: *A41 (Chester to Whitchurch), after 4m left to Burwardsley. Follow 'Cheshire Workshops' signs*

Tucked away in a peaceful corner of rural Cheshire, this 300-year-old half-timbered former farmhouse is just quarter of an hour's drive from historic Chester. Standing way up in the Peckforton Hills, the views from the terrace are magnificent. The wholesome food is good, the service friendly and relaxed; please note children are welcome during the day but not in the evenings. The menu breaks down into light-bites, deli-boards and sandwiches for those who want to make a quick pit-stop; a selection for those who fancy eating gastro-pub style; and principally British and European main courses for those who want something more substantial. Puddings follow traditional lines with warm chocolate fudge cake and vanilla ice cream; and homemade apple and blackberry crumble with custard. There's also a selection of ice creams made by Gog's Cheshire Farm just down the road.

**Open** all wk **Bar Meals** L served all wk (no food Mon 3-6) D served all wk (no food Mon 3-6) Av main course £11.50 food served all day **Restaurant** L served all wk (no food Mon 3-6) D served all wk (no food Mon 3-6) Av 3 course à la carte fr £21.50 food served all day ⊕ FREE HOUSE ◀ Weetwood Old Dog, Eastgate, Best, guest Bitter Ŏ Stowford Press. ▾ 8 **Facilities** Children's menu Dogs allowed Garden Parking **Rooms** 12

## CHOLMONDELEY

### The Cholmondeley Arms ▾

**SY14 8HN ☎ 01829 720300** 📄 01829 720123
e-mail: guy@cholmondeleyarms.co.uk
dir: *On A49, between Whitchurch & Tarporley*

Formerly the village school, this elegant pub had been closed for six years when in 1988 the current owners embarked on its conversion. Set in quiet countryside adjoining the grounds of historic Cholmondeley Castle, home to Lord and Lady Cholmondeley, it is close to the Sandstone Trail, Shropshire Union Canal, and Beeston Castle. All food is freshly prepared, using local produce wherever possible, and is offered from a daily changing menu. Main courses range from beer battered haddock or hot Madras beef curry to pan-fried gurnard fillet with sautéed samphire grass and steamed mussels. There is also an extensive choice of home-made puddings.

**Open** all wk 10-3.30 6-11 (Sat-Sun 10-11) Closed: 25 Dec **Bar Meals** L served Mon-Fri 12-2.30, Sat-Sun 12-10 D served Mon-Fri 6-10, Sat-Sun 12-10 Av main course £10 ⊕ FREE HOUSE ◀ Weetwood Eastgate Ale, Salopian Gold, Woodlands Light Oak, Cumberland Ale. ♚ 11 **Facilities** Children's menu Dogs allowed Garden Parking

## HAUGHTON MOSS

### The Nags Head ♚

**Long Ln CW6 9RN ☎ 01829 260265** 🖹 **01829 261364**
e-mail: roryk1@btinternet.com
dir: *Turn off A49 S of Tarporley at Beeston/Haughton sign into Long Ln, continue for 1.75m*

Set amid beautiful Cheshire countryside, this 16th-century black and white building, once a smithy, is every inch the friendly, traditional pub. Inside are low ceilings, crooked beams, exposed brickwork and real fires. Outside, there are spacious gardens and a bowling green. The extensive menu might offer moules marinière or stilton and Guinness pâté to start, followed by steak and chips or fajitas. An impressive choice of home-made desserts could include syrup and pear sponge or triple chocolate roulade.

**Open** all day all wk 11-mdnt **Bar Meals** L served all wk 12-10 D served all wk 12-10 Av main course £10 food served all day **Restaurant** L served all wk 12-10 D served all wk 12-10 Fixed menu price fr £8.85 Av 3 course à la carte fr £20 food served all day ⊕ FREE HOUSE ◀ Flowers IPA, Sharps Doom Bar, guest ales. ♚ 14 **Facilities** Children's menu Play area Dogs allowed Garden Parking

## HUXLEY

### Stuart's Table at the Farmer's Arms ♚

**Huxley Ln CH3 9BG ☎ 01829 781342** 🖹 **01829 781794**
e-mail: stuart@stuartstable.com
dir: *Telephone for directions*

Reputedly a hospital during the civil war, the Farmers Arms was first recorded as a pub in 1802. It has grown into an inviting country pub and restaurant specialising in quality British steaks, served with an appealing range of sauces and accompaniments. Other choices include lunchtime tapas and sandwiches, and meals such as game terrine with parsley and shallot sauce and crab apple jelly followed by slow-roasted belly pork with chorizo and white bean cassoulet.

**Open** all wk noon-3 5-11 (Fri-Sat noon-mdnt, Sun noon-10.30, Mon 5-11) **Bar Meals** L served Tue-Sat 12-2 **Restaurant** L served Tue-Sat 12-2, Sun 12-4 D served Tue-Thu 6.30-9, Fri-Sat 6.30-9.30 Fixed menu price fr £16.95 Av 3 course à la carte fr £20 ⊕ ADMIRAL TAVERNS ◀ Black Sheep, Adnams, guest ale. ♚ 30 **Facilities** Children's menu Garden Parking

## LACH DENNIS

### The Duke of Portland ♚

**Penny's Ln CW9 7SY ☎ 01606 46264**
e-mail: info@dukeofportland.com
web: www.dukeofportland.com
dir: *M6 junct 19, A556 towards Northwich. Left onto B5082 to Lach Dennis*

Eat well at this independent family-run pub set in the heart of the glorious Cheshire plain. The sunny, landscaped garden complements the attractively refurbished building, and the owners are strongly committed to local producers, many of whom have never supplied other commercial customers. Share some antipasti while enjoying a drink. Other dishes include seared chicken breast and fresh tomato purée with crushed new potatoes or The Dukes legendary fish and chips.

**Open** all wk **Restaurant** Fixed menu price fr £9.95 Av 3 course à la carte fr £10.95 food served all day ◀ Thwaites Bomber, Marstons Pedigree, Banks Original, Sneck Lifter. ♚ 7 **Facilities** Children's menu Garden Parking

## MACCLESFIELD

### The Windmill Inn ♚

**Holehouse Ln, Whitely Green, Adlington SK10 5SJ ☎ 01625 574222**
e-mail: mail@thewindmill.info
dir: *Between Macclesfield & Poynton. Follow brown tourist signs on main road. Pub in 1.5m*

Close to the Macclesfield Canal and the Middlewood Way, this former farmhouse is ideal for country strollers. It has an extensive landscaped garden, complete with children's maze, while the interior has a real fire and sofas. The menu runs from light lunches - potted Goosnargh duck with spiced plum relish and toasted sourdough, - to meals such as smoked haddock and leek tart with hollandaise sauce followed by braised steak and onions with horseradish mash and roast parsnips.

**Open** all wk noon-3 5-11 (Fri-Sat noon-11, Sun noon-10.30) **Bar Meals** L served Mon-Fri 12-2.30, Sat-Sun 12-4 booking required D served Mon-Fri 5.30-9.30, Sat 12-9.30, Sun 12-8 booking required Av main course £10.95 **Restaurant** L served Mon-Fri 12-2.30, Sat 12-9, Sun 12-8 booking required D served Mon-Fri 5.30-9.30, Sat 12-9.30, Sun 12-8 booking required ⊕ Mitchels & Butler - Moyo Ltd ◀ Black Sheep, Old Speckled Hen, Wadworth 6X, guest ale. ♚ 14 **Facilities** Children's menu Dogs allowed Garden Parking

## MARTON

### The Davenport Arms ♟

**Congleton Rd SK11 9HF ☎ 01260 224269**
📄 **01260 224565**
e-mail: enquiries@thedavenportarms.co.uk
web: www.thedavenportarms.co.uk
dir: *3m from Congleton off A34*

Trials took place upstairs in this 18th-century pub, then a farmhouse, the miscreants being hanged from a gibbet that is thought to have been attached to a farm building opposite. Cushioned settles and leather armchairs by a log fire characterise the traditional bar, while in the middle of the restaurant is a well, now purely decorative. With Theakston Yorkshire Bitter and Courage Directors being regulars, there are always two guest ales on the pumps. All food - and this includes chutneys, sauces and desserts - is freshly made on the premises from local suppliers. In addition to speciality baguettes, lunchtime temptations include starters of Bury black pudding on sweet potato rösti with shallot purée and green peppercorn sauce; then for a main course you might try Cajun salmon fillets with mango and plum, red onion and sweet chilli salsa. The lovely beer garden contains a discreet children's play area.

Open noon-3 6-mdnt (Fri-Sun noon-mdnt) Closed: Mon L (ex BH) Bar Meals L served Tue-Sat 12-2.30, Sun 12-3 D served Tue-Sat 6-9, Sun 6-8.30 Av main course £8.95 Restaurant L served Tue-Sat 12-2.30, Sun 12-3 booking required D served Tue-Sat 6-9, Sun 6-8.30 booking required Av 3 course à la carte fr £22 ⊕ FREE HOUSE ◖ Copper Dragon, Storm Brewing, Directors, Weetwood, Theakstons. ♟ 9 Facilities Children's menu Play area Garden Parking

## MOULDSWORTH

### The Goshawk ♟

**Station Rd CH3 8AJ ☎ 01928 740900  📄 01928 740965**
dir: *A51 from Chester onto A54. Left onto B5393 towards Frodsham. Enter Mouldsworth, pub on left opposite rail station*

A welcoming pub with log fires and stripped pine floors, The Goshawk is conveniently located opposite the railway station in Mouldsworth, one stop from Chester on the Manchester to Stockport line. Close by are the Delamere Forest and Country Park, and the Mouldsworth Motor Museum. The menu has something for everyone, with light snacks of Bury black pudding with chicken and beetroot, or eggs Benedict, and

shellfish starters like potted shrimps or seared scallops. There is a good choice of salads, and more substantial fare, with up to 12 fish dishes, steaks from the chargrill, and vegetarian options such as stuffed roasted red peppers. House favourites are lobster thermidor and steak and kidney pudding made with Timothy Taylor's Ale.

Open all wk noon-11 (Sun noon-10.30) Closed: 25 Dec & 1 Jan Bar Meals  food served all day Restaurant  food served all day ◖ Timothy Taylor Landlord, Greene King IPA, Deuchars, Old Speckled Hen. ♟ 14 Facilities Children's menu Play area Family room Garden Parking

## PLUMLEY

### The Golden Pheasant Hotel ♟

**Plumley Moor Rd WA16 9RX ☎ 01565 722261**
📄 **01565 723804**
dir: *M6 junct 19, A556 signed Chester. 2m, left at Plumley/Peover signs. Through Plumley, pub 1m opp rail station*

Set in the beautiful Cheshire countryside, The Golden Pheasant is convenient for Chester and Manchester, with trains from the station opposite hourly. This 200-year-old, traditional wayside inn is privately owned and proud of its locally sourced food served in the dining room and lounge bar areas. Expect roaring log fires, comfy sitting areas, alfresco dining, a children's play area and a locals' bar with a darts board.

Open all day all wk 11-11 (Sun noon-10.30) Bar Meals Av main course £10.95 food served all day Restaurant  Fixed menu price fr £15.95 Av 3 course à la carte fr £21.95 food served all day ⊕ J W LEES ◖ J W Lees Bitter, John Willies Bitter, Guinness. ♟ 12 Facilities Children's menu Play area Garden Parking

### The Smoker ♟

**WA16 0TY ☎ 01565 722338  📄 01565 722093**
e-mail: smoker@plumley.fsword.co.uk
dir: *From M6 junct 19 take A556 W. Pub 1.75m on left*

This 400-year-old thatched coaching inn is actually named after a white racehorse bred by the Prince Regent, although recent legislation has prompted the addition of a covered smokers' courtyard complete with heating and seating. The pub's striking wood-panelled interior of three connecting rooms provides a traditional welcoming atmosphere, with log fires, beams and copper kettles. The menu has an appealing and lengthy array of starters; main courses include Barnsley chop; deep-fried haddock; and lamb Henry.

Open all wk 10-3 6-11 (Sun 10am-10.30pm) Bar Meals L served Mon-Fri 10-2.30, Sun 10-9 D served Mon-Fri 6-9.30, Sun 10-9 Av main course £10 Restaurant L served Mon-Fri 10-2.30, Sun 10-9 booking required D served Mon-Fri 6-9.30, Sun 10-9 booking required Av 3 course à la carte fr £18.50 ⊕ FREDERIC ROBINSON ◖ Robinson's Best, Double Hop, Robinsons Smooth. ♟ 10 Facilities Children's menu Play area Garden Parking

## SHOCKLACH

### The Bull ☤

**Worthenbury Rd SY14 7BL ☎ 01829 250239**
e-mail: info@thebullshocklach.com
dir: *12m S of Chester, 3m W of Malpas*

Recently completely refurbished, this village pub retains its old beams, cosy rooms and log fire but has a new bar, distinctive furniture and attractive stone and wood flooring. The menu is locally sourced and dishes, such as belly pork, steak pie and fish and chips, are freshly made. Look out for daily specials and Fish Friday options. Five local ales are served along with a 60-bin wine list and a malt whisky collection approaching 35.

**Open** all wk noon-3 6-11 (Sun 10-8) **Bar Meals** L served Mon-Sat 12-2.30, Sun 10-8 booking required D served Mon-Thu 6-9.30, Fri-Sat 6-10, Sun 10-8 booking required Av main course £10 **Restaurant** L served Mon-Sat 12-2.30, Sun 10-8 booking required D served Mon-Thu 6-9.30, Fri-Sat 6-10, Sun 10-8 booking required Av 3 course à la carte fr £22 ⊕ Admiral Taverns ◄ Stonehouse Station Bitter, Guinness, guest ales. ☤ 10 **Facilities** Children's menu Garden Parking

## SWETTENHAM

### The Swettenham Arms ☤

**Swettenham Ln CW12 2LF ☎ 01477 571284**
🖹 01477 571284
e-mail: info@swettenhamarms.co.uk
dir: *M6 junct 18 to Holmes Chapel, then A535 towards Jodrell Bank. 3m right (Forty Acre Lane) to Swettenham*

Winter in this delightful 600-year-old pub means log fires and mulled wine; summer means abundant lavender and sunflowers in the meadow; in autumn there are the arboretum and nature reserve. And spring? Well, everywhere's lovely in spring, so just enjoy the high standards of food and service, which of course are year-round. The pub was once a nunnery, linked to the village church by an underground passage where corpses 'rested' before burial. So, expect ghost stories: indeed, in 2005, after seeing an apparition in the fireplace, a lady customer sought urgent counselling from the vicar. Begin your meal with smoked halibut salad and quenelles of mascarpone; then 21-day roast Cheshire beef and Yorkshire pudding, or one of Chef's signature dishes; supreme of chicken, brie and spring onion in filo pastry, and white wine and basil cream sauce, perhaps. Vegetarians have a good choice.

**Open** all wk noon-3.30 6-11 (Sat-Sun noon-11) **Bar Meals** L served Mon-Sat 12-2.30, Sun 12-9.30 booking required D served Mon-Sat 6.30-9.30, Sun 12-9.30 booking required Av main course £10 **Restaurant** L served Mon-Sat 12-2.30, Sun 12-9.30 booking required D served Mon-Sat 6.30-9.30, Sun 12-9.30 booking required Av 3 course à la carte fr £20 ⊕ FREE HOUSE ◄ Landlord, Hydes, Beartown, Pride of Pendle, guest ales Ŏ Addlestones. ☤ 8 **Facilities** Children's menu Garden Parking

## CORNWALL & ISLES OF SCILLY

## BODINNICK

### Old Ferry Inn ☤

**PL23 1LX ☎ 01726 870237 🖹 01726 870116**
e-mail: royce972@aol.com
dir: *A38 towards Dobwalls, left onto A390. After 3m left onto B3359 then right to Bodinnick/Polruan for 5m*

This friendly, family-run free house stands just 50 yards from the scenic River Fowey, where the car ferry still makes regular crossings to Fowey itself. Inside the 400-year-old building, old photographs and nautical bric-a-brac set the scene for sampling Sharp's Bitter and an extensive bar menu. Choices range from snacks to home-cooked food like steak and ale pie, curries, vegetarian and fish dishes.

**Open** all day all wk 11-11 (summer), noon-10 (winter) Closed: 25 Dec **Bar Meals** L served all wk 12-3 (summer), 12-2.30 (winter) D served all wk 6-9 (summer), 6.30-8.30 (winter) Av main course £8.50 **Restaurant** D served all wk 7-8.30 booking required Av 3 course à la carte fr £20 ⊕ FREE HOUSE ◄ Sharp's Bitter, Guinness Ŏ Stowford Press. ☤ 6 **Facilities** Children's menu Family room Dogs allowed Garden Parking

## BOLVENTOR

### Jamaica Inn ☤

**PL15 7TS ☎ 01566 86250 🖹 01566 86177**
e-mail: enquiry@jamaicainn.co.uk
dir: *Follow A30 from Exeter. 10m after Launceston take Bolventor road, follow signs*

The setting for Daphne du Maurier's famous novel, this 18th-century inn stands high on Bodmin Moor. Its Smugglers Museum houses fascinating artefacts, while the Daphne du Maurier room honours the great writer. The place is big on atmosphere, with a cobbled courtyard, beamed ceilings and roaring fires. Lunches range from hot ciabattas to grills; the evening menu served from 3pm could start with warm melted goats' cheese bruschetta, and follow with barbecued pork ribs or poached fillet of Port Isaac salmon.

**Open** all day all wk 9am-11pm **Bar Meals** L served all wk Av main course £9 food served all day ⊕ FREE HOUSE ◄ Doom Bar, Tribute, Jamaica Inn Ale. ☤ 8 **Facilities** Children's menu Play area Dogs allowed Garden Parking

## CALLINGTON

### The Coachmakers Arms ☤

**6 Newport Square PL17 7AS ☎ 01579 382567**
🖹 01579 384679
dir: *Between Plymouth & Launceston on A388*

Traditional stone-built pub on the A388 between Plymouth and Launceston. Clocks, plates, pictures of local scenes,

continued

England

old cars and antique trade advertisements contribute to the atmosphere, as do the fish tank and aviary. There's plenty of choice on the menu, from chargrilled steaks, steak and kidney pie or hot-pot, to oven-baked plaice, vegetable balti or salads. Regulars range from the local football team to the pensioners dining club. On Wednesday there's a charity quiz night, and Thursday is steak night.

Open all day all wk all wk **Bar Meals** L served all wk 12-2 D served all wk 7-9.30 Av main course £5 **Restaurant** L served all wk 12-2 D served all wk 7-9.30 Av 3 course à la carte fr £15 ⊕ ENTERPRISE INNS ◀ Sharp's Doom Bar, Worthing Best Bitter, Bass. ♥ 7 **Facilities** Children's menu Dogs allowed Parking

### Manor House Inn ♥

**Rilla Mill PL17 7NT ☎ 01579 362354**
dir: *5m from Callington, just off B3257*

Set by the River Lynher, once a granary for the mill next door, Manor House is a traditional pub that offers a reasonably-priced selection of home-made food. Careful attention is paid to use of local ingredients, including fresh fish. Typical choices include steak and ale pie, battered haddock and chips, chicken chasseur, and curry of the week. Lighter options include club sandwich, tuna melt, toasted sandwiches and salads.

Open Closed: Mon **Bar Meals** L served Tue-Sun 11.30-2 D served Tue-Sun 6-9 Av main course £5 **Restaurant** L served Tue-Sun 11.30-2 D served Tue-Sun 6-9 Av 3 course à la carte fr £18 ⊕ FREE HOUSE ◀ Sharp's Own & Special, Doom Bar, Betty Stogs ♂ Thatchers Gold, Westons Scrumpy, Cornish Rattler. ♥ 8 **Facilities** Children's menu Dogs allowed Garden Parking

## CONSTANTINE

### Trengilly Wartha Inn ★★★ INN ⊛ ♥

**Nancenoy TR11 5RP ☎ 01326 340332    ⌨ 01326 340332**
e-mail: reception@trengilly.co.uk
dir: *Follow signs to Nancenoy, left towards Gweek until 1st sign for inn, left & left again at next sign, continue to inn*

The name is Cornish and means 'a settlement above the trees', in this case the wooded valley of Polpenwith Creek, an offshoot of the lovely Helford River. The six acres of gardens and meadows that surround the inn include a vine-shaded pergola just perfect for summer dining. There's a small bistro on one side of the inn, and plenty more space for eating in the informal bar area, where a conservatory extension houses the family room. Talented chefs prepare everything from scratch using the best locally produced meats, game, fish and shellfish

from local waters. The bar menu offers pub favourites as well as less traditional choices and the bistro always has a good seafood selection, but watch out, because in summer the day's boatload of fresh fish can sell out fast. Fresh home-made steak and kidney puddings are sold through the winter on Wednesday nights.

Open all wk 11-3 6-12 **Bar Meals** L served all wk 12-2.15 D served all wk 6.30-9.30 Av main course £10 **Restaurant** L served all wk 12-2.15 booking required D served all wk 6.30-12 booking required Av 3 course à la carte fr £20 ⊕ FREE HOUSE ◀ Skinners Cornish Knocker, Betty Stogs, Sharp's Doom Bar, Sharp's Edenale, Guest Ales ♂ Cornish Rattler, Thatchers Gold. ♥ 15 **Facilities** Children's menu Play area Family room Dogs allowed Garden Parking **Rooms** 8

## CUBERT

### The Smugglers' Den Inn ♥

**Trebellan TR8 5PY ☎ 01637 830209    ⌨ 01637 830580**
e-mail: info@thesmugglersden.co.uk
web: www.thesmugglersden.co.uk
dir: *From Newquay take B3075 to Cubert x-rds, then right, then left signed Trebellan, 0.5m*

Set in a valley leading to the coast, this thatched 16th-century pub comprises a long bar, family room, children's play area, courtyards and huge beer garden. The no-nonsense, modern menu might offer houmous and flatbread with rocket and sun-blushed tomatoes at lunch, or tempura king prawns followed by Falmouth Bay moules marinière in the evening.

Open all day all wk 11-3 6-11 (Sat-Sun 11-3 6-mdnt, summer open all day) Closed: Jan-Mar closed Mon-Tue L **Bar Meals** L served all wk 12-2.30 (winter 12-2) D served all wk 6-9.30 (winter Sun-Thu 6-9, Fri-Sat 6-9.30) **Restaurant** L served all wk 12-2.30 (winter 12-2) booking required D served all wk 6-9.30 (winter Sun-Thu 6-9, Fri-Sat 6-9.30) booking required ⊕ FREE HOUSE ◀ Skinner's Smugglers Ale, Sharp's Doom Bar, St Austell Tribute, Rotating Guest ales ♂ Healey's Cornish Rattler. ♥ 12 **Facilities** Children's menu Play area Family room Dogs allowed Garden Parking

## FEOCK

### The Punch Bowl & Ladle ♥

**Penelewey TR3 6QY ☎ 01872 862237** 📄 **01872 870401**
dir: *Off Truro to Falmouth road, after Shell garage at 'Playing Place' rdbt
follow signs for King Harry Ferry to right. 0.5m, pub on right*

This ancient and fascinating thatched building comprises three
cob-built 17th-century farm workers' cottages and a former
customhouse. There are delightful rural views from the inn's
patio, and in warmer weather you can enjoy a drink in the
walled garden. The menu uses 99 per cent Cornish goods,
and choices include fish pie; local mussels in Cornish cider;
Malaysian chicken; and venison steak in chocolate sauce. There
is live music monthly, and regular food theme nights.

**Open** all day all wk 11.30am-11pm (Fri 11.30am-mdnt, Sun
noon-10.30) **Bar Meals** L served all wk 12-5 Av main course
£9 food served all day **Restaurant** L served all wk 12-2.30 D
served all wk 6-8.30 booking required Av 3 course à la carte fr
£17 ⊕ St Austell Brewery ◀ Tribute, Tinners, Proper Job, Cornish
Cream. ♥ 8 **Facilities** Children's menu Dogs allowed Garden
Parking

## FOWEY

### The Ship Inn

**Trafalgar Square PL23 1AZ ☎ 01726 832230**
e-mail: shipinnfowey@hotmail.com
dir: *From A30 take B3269 & A390*

One of Fowey's oldest buildings, The Ship was built in 1570
by John Rashleigh, who sailed to the Americas with Walter
Raleigh. Given Fowey's riverside position, assume a good
choice of fish, including River Fowey mussels, pan-fried
scallops with mushrooms and bacon, and Ship Inn fish pie.
Other options include beef and Guinness pie or local butcher's
sausages and mash. St Austell ales, real fires and a long
tradition of genial hospitality add the final touches.

**Open** all day all wk 11am-mdnt (Fri-Sat 11am-1am) **Bar Meals** L
served Mon-Sat 12-2.30, Sun 12-4 D served Mon-Sat 6-9 Av
main course £10 **Restaurant** L served Mon-Sat 12-2.30 (summer
only), Sun 12-4 D served Mon-Sat 6-9, (Sun 6-9 summer only)
Fixed menu price fr £12.50 ⊕ ST AUSTELL BREWERY ◀ St
Austell Tinners Ale, Tribute, Proper Job ☼ Cornish Rattler.
**Facilities** Children's menu Family room Dogs allowed

## GUNWALLOE

### The Halzephron Inn ♥

**TR12 7QB ☎ 01326 240406** 📄 **01326 241442**
e-mail: halzephroninn@gunwalloe1.fsnet.co.uk
dir: *3m S of Helston on A3083, right to Gunwalloe, through village. Inn
on left*

The name of this ancient inn derives from Als Yfferin, old
Cornish for 'cliffs of hell', an appropriate description of its
situation on this hazardous stretch of coastline. Once a
haunt of smugglers, the pub stands just 300 yards from the
famous South Cornwall footpath and is the only pub on the
stretch between Mullion and Porthleven. Today it offers a
warm welcome, a wide selection of ales including Organic
Halzephron Gold and whiskies, and meals prepared from fresh
local produce. Lunch brings a choice of platters, plus specials
such as seafood chowder. The evening menu shifts comfortably
from the classic (beef bourguignon) to the modern: perhaps
whole roast partridge en croûte; or roast saddle of rabbit
wrapped in prosciutto filled with mushroom and herb duxelle.
There is an excellent Junior Menu available.

**Open** all wk all wk Closed: 25 Dec **Bar Meals** L served all wk
12-2 D served all wk 7-9 **Restaurant** L served all wk 12-2 D
served all wk 7-9 ⊕ FREE HOUSE ◀ Sharp's Own, Doom Bar &
Special, St Austell Tribute, Organic Halzephron Gold ☼ Cornish
Rattler. ♥ 8 **Facilities** Children's menu Family room Garden
Parking

continued

England

England

## LANLIVERY

### The Crown Inn ★★★ INN ♛

**PL30 5BT ☎ 01208 872707**
e-mail: thecrown@wagtailinns.com
dir: *Signed from A390. Follow brown sign about 1.5m W of Lostwithiel*

This pub was built in the 12th century to house the stonemasons constructing the church. Fowey is just a few miles away, so expect the menu to offer fresh crab, scallops, mackerel and much more. Other local produce also features strongly, including meats from a butcher's in Par, fruit and vegetables from Bodmin and dairy products from Lostwithiel. Main courses include slow roasted belly pork; fresh Cornish crab gratin; and wild mushroom risotto. Have a fresh Fowey crab sandwich at lunchtime, or a Cornish brie, bacon and watercress ciabatta; or just a proper Cornish pasty. The pretty front garden is a lovely spot to enjoy a summer evening, perhaps with a glass of Pimms.

**Open** all day all wk **Bar Meals** L served all wk 12-2.30 booking required D served all wk 6.30-9 booking required Av main course £10 **Restaurant** L served all wk 12-2.30 booking required D served all wk 6.30-9 booking required Fixed menu price fr £10 ⊕ FREE HOUSE ◀ Sharp's Doom Bar, Skinners Betty Stogs, Skinners Cornish Knocker, Edenale. ♛ 7 **Facilities** Children's menu Dogs allowed Garden Parking **Rooms** 9

## LUDGVAN

### White Hart ♛

**Churchtown TR20 8EY ☎ 01736 740574**
dir: *From A30 take B3309 at Crowlas*

Built somewhere between 1280 and 1320, the White Hart retains the peaceful atmosphere of a bygone era and offers splendid views across St Michael's Mount and Bay. Although there has been a recent change of hands, things haven't changed that much. Real ales are still sold from the back of the bar, and the food is still as popular as ever. Mr and Mrs Gibbard, the new owners, also run the Turk's Head in Penzance.

**Open** all wk all wk **Bar Meals** L served all wk 12-2.30 booking required D served all wk 6-9.30 booking required Av main course £7 **Restaurant** L served all wk 12-2.30 booking required D served all wk 6-9.30 ⊕ PUNCH TAVERNS ◀ Sharp's Doom Bar, Flowers IPA, Betty Stogs, Abbots. ♛ 12 **Facilities** Children's menu Dogs allowed Garden Parking

## MALPAS

### The Heron Inn

**Trenhaile Ter TR1 1SL ☎ 01872 272773**
📄 01872 272773
e-mail: theheron@hotmail.co.uk
dir: *From Trafalgar rdbt in Truro exit towards BBC Radio Cornwall, & pub sign. Follow Malpas Rd for 2m into village. Pub on left*

Two miles from Truro's city centre, the pub enjoys panoramic River Fal views from its large terrace. The building may be old but its interior is light and airy, echoing the colours of the river. Local produce is used in traditional home-made dishes such as local roast ham, fried egg and chips; beef lasagne with garlic bread; and a pan-fried trio of Cornish fish.

**Open** all wk 11-3 6-11 (all day Fri-Sat (Sun till 10.30) summer all day every day) **Bar Meals** Av main course £9 **Restaurant** L served all wk 12-2 booking required D served Mon-Sat 6.30-9, Sun 7-9 booking required ⊕ ST AUSTELL BREWERY ◀ Tribute, IPA, Black Prince ⚫ Cornish Rattler. **Facilities** Children's menu Garden Parking

## MEVAGISSEY

### The Ship Inn ★★★ INN ♛

**Fore St PL26 6UQ ☎ 01726 843324** 📄 01726 844368
e-mail: shipinnian@hotmail.co.uk
dir: *7m S of St Austell*

The inn stands just a few yards from Mevagissey's picturesque fishing harbour, so the choice of fish and seafood dishes comes as no surprise: moules marinière, beer-battered cod, and oven-baked fillet of haddock topped with prawns and Cornish Tiskey cheese and served with a lemon and dill sauce. Other options take in baguettes, burgers, jacket potatoes, steaks, and trio of Cornish sausages served with mash and rich red onion gravy.

**Open** all wk all wk **Bar Meals** L served all wk 12-6 D served all wk 6-9 food served all day ⊕ ST AUSTELL BREWERY ◀ St Austell Ales. ♛ 8 **Facilities** Children's menu Family room Dogs allowed **Rooms** 5

## MITCHELL

### The Plume of Feathers ★★★★ INN ♛

**TR8 5AX ☎ 01872 510387** 📄 01637 839401
e-mail: enquiries@theplume.info
dir: *Exit A30 to Mitchell/Newquay*

Over the years, this 16th century building has welcomed various historical figures - John Wesley preached Methodism from the pillared entrance, and Sir Walter Raleigh used to live locally. The present owners have established it as a successful destination pub restaurant; the imaginative kitchen has an excellent reputation for its food, based on a fusion of modern European and classical British dishes, with an emphasis on fresh fish and the best Cornish ingredients. Lunch brings starters such as home-made fishcake with sweet chilli and mixed leaves followed by a home-made beef burger with home-made relish and fries, while dinner could start with smoked mackerel fillet with houmous and toasted crostini followed by confit of Cornish duck leg with Toulouse sausage, tomato and mixed bean cassoulet.

**Open** all day all wk 9am-11/mdnt (25 Dec 11-5) **Bar Meals** Av main course £10 food served all day **Restaurant** Av 3 course à la carte fr £22 food served all day ⊕ FREE HOUSE ◀ Doom Bar, John Smiths Smooth, Betty Stogs. ♥ 7 **Facilities** Children's menu Play area Dogs allowed Garden Parking **Rooms** 7

## NEWQUAY

# The Lewinnick Lodge Bar & Restaurant ♥

**Pentire Headland TR7 1NX** ☎ **01637 878117**
📄 **01637 870130**
e-mail: ask@lewinnick-lodge.info
dir: *From Newquay take Pentire Rd 0.5m, pub on right*

Originally built as a small stone cottage in the late 18th century, the Lodge enjoys stunning views of Cornwall's Atlantic coast. One of only two properties on this rugged headland, the pub has established a great reputation, built up by the current owners over the last 20 years, with locals and visitors alike. Menu choices include fishcakes with sweet chilli, mixed leaves and fries; steak with braised shallots and slow-roasted vine tomatoes; and roasted red pepper, ricotta and spinach linguine.

**Open** all day all wk **Bar Meals** Av main course £5 food served all day **Restaurant** Fixed menu price fr £12 Av 3 course à la carte fr £18 food served all day ⊕ FREE HOUSE ◀ Sharp's Doom Bar, Skinner's Betty Stogs. ♥ 10 **Facilities** Children's menu Dogs allowed Garden Parking

## PERRANUTHNOE

# The Victoria Inn ★★★ INN ⊛ ♥

**TR20 9NP** ☎ **01736 710309**
e-mail: enquiries@victoriainn-penzance.co.uk
dir: *Off A394 (Penzance to Helston road), signed Perranuthnoe*

Reputedly Cornwall's oldest inn, the Victoria dates from the 12th century. Set within sight of the sea, it's popular with walkers and has a restful, Mediterranean-style garden. Food is taken seriously here, not least local fish and seafood offered on a daily board of specials. Using the best of local ingredients, typical dishes are goats' cheese and sweet pepper fondue; roasted pork belly with champ, black pudding and apple and bay sauce; and poached pear with caramel sauce, shortbread and ginger ice cream.

**Open** 12-2 6.30-11 **Closed:** 25-26 Dec, 1 Jan, 1st wk Jan, Sun eve & Mon (off season) **Bar Meals** L served all wk 12-2 booking required D served all wk 6.30-11 booking required Av main course £14 **Restaurant** L served all wk 12-2 booking required D served all wk 6.30-11 booking required Av 3 course à la carte fr £19.85 ◀ Doom Bar, Tribute. ♥ 6 **Facilities** Children's menu Dogs allowed Garden Parking **Rooms** 2

## PORT GAVERNE

# Port Gaverne Hotel ★★ HL ♥

**PL29 3SQ** ☎ **01208 880244** 📄 **01208 880151**
web: www.chycor.co.uk/hotels/port-gaverne
dir: *Signed from B3314, S of Delabole via B3267 on E of Port Isaac*

Close to a secluded cove, is this delightful 17th-century inn. A meandering building with lots of period detail, the hotel has long association with fishing and smuggling. Locally supplied produce includes plenty of fresh fish. For example, along with a ploughman's, try a half pint of prawns at lunchtime, or a seafood pie. At dinner expect starters like crab soup; or lobster and monkfish Thermidor; and mains of sautéed pan-fried John Dory with olive oil mash; or chargrilled sirloin steak au poivre.

**Open** all day all wk **Bar Meals** L served all wk 12-2.30 D served all wk 6-9 Av main course £9 **Restaurant** D served all wk 7-9 Av 3 course à la carte fr £27 ⊕ FREE HOUSE ◀ Sharp's Doom Bar, Bass, St Austell Tribute. ♥ 9 **Facilities** Children's menu Dogs allowed Garden Parking **Rooms** 14

## PORTHLEVEN

# The Ship Inn

**TR13 9JS** ☎ **01326 564204** 📄 **01326 564204**
e-mail: cjoakden@yahoo.co.uk
dir: *From Helston follow signs to Porthleven, 2.5m. On entering village continue to harbour. Take W road by side of harbour to inn*

Dating from the 17th century, this smugglers' inn is actually built into the cliffs, and is approached by a flight of stone steps. In winter two log fires warm the interior, while the flames of a third flicker in the separate Smithy children's room. Expect a good selection of locally caught fish and seafood, such as crab and prawn mornay, or the smoked fish platter, all smoked in Cornwall. The pub has declared itself a 'chip-free zone'.

**Open** all day all wk 11.30am-11.30pm (Sun noon-10.30) **Bar Meals** L served all wk 12-2 D served all wk 6.30-9 ⊕ FREE HOUSE ◀ Courage Best, Sharp's Doom Bar & Special, guest ales. **Facilities** Children's menu Family room Dogs allowed Garden

## PORTREATH

# Basset Arms

**Tregea Ter TR16 4NG** ☎ **01209 842077**
e-mail: bassettarms@btconnect.com
dir: *From Redruth take B3300 to Portreath. Pub on left near seafront*

Tin-mining and shipwreck paraphernalia adorn the low-beamed interior of this early 19th-century Cornish stone cottage, built as a pub to serve harbour workers. At one time it served as a mortuary for ill-fated seafarers, so there are plenty of ghost stories! The menu makes the most of local seafood, such as mussels and fries, and home-made fish pie, but also provides a wide selection of alternatives, including half chicken in barbecue sauce; 12oz gammon steak; curry of the day; and salads including crab, when available.

continued

Open all day all wk 11am-11pm (Fri-Sat 11am-mdnt, Sun 11-10.30) **Bar Meals** L served all wk 12-2 D served all wk 6-9 Av main course £9.50 **Restaurant** L served all wk 12-2 D served all wk 6-9 Av 3 course à la carte fr £18 ⊕ FREE HOUSE ◀ Sharp's Doom Bar, Courage, John Smith's Smooth. **Facilities** Children's menu Play area Dogs allowed Garden Parking

## ST AGNES

### Driftwood Spars ★★★★ GA ♈

**Trevaunance Cove TR5 0RT ☎ 01872 552428**
🖨 01872 553701
e-mail: driftwoodspars@hotmail.com
dir: *A30 onto B3285, through St Agnes, down steep hill, left at Peterville Inn, onto road signed Trevaunance Cove*

Just off the South West Coastal Path, and a short walk from the beach, this family-run pub with rooms, restaurant, beer gardens and micro-brewery, is housed in a 300-year-old tin miners' store, chandlery and sail loft, complete with its own smugglers' tunnel. The name comes from the huge beams that were originally spars from a shipwrecked boat. Daily changing specials supplement the seasonal menu and seafood figures strongly. There is live music at weekends.

Open all day all wk 11-11 (Fri-Sat 11-1am, 25 Dec 11am-2pm) **Bar Meals** L served all wk 12-2.30 Av main course £9.50 **Restaurant** L served Sun 12-2.30 booking required D served all wk 7-9, (winter Thu-Sat 7-9) booking required Av 3 course à la carte fr £25 ⊕ FREE HOUSE ◀ Tinners, Blue Hills Bitter, Tribute, Betty Stogs, Doom Bar ♊ Cornish Rattler, Addlestones. ♈ 10 **Facilities** Children's menu Dogs allowed Garden Parking Rooms 15

## ST BREWARD

### The Old Inn & Restaurant ♈

**Churchtown, Bodmin Moor PL30 4PP ☎ 01208 850711**
🖨 01208 851671
e-mail: theoldinn@macace.net
dir: *A30 to Bodmin. 16m, right just after Temple, follow signs to St Breward. B3266 (Bodmin to Camelford road) turn to St Breward, follow brown signs*

Located high up on Bodmin Moor, one of Cornwall's oldest inns is now owned and run by local man Darren Wills, the latest licensee in its 1,000-year history. The solid granite pub has slate flagstone floors and two huge granite fireplaces with real fires in winter. It is well-known throughout the area for its

wholesome home-cooked food, frequented by many who are drawn by its Moorland Grills and Sunday roasts. Check out the local Cornish wines as well. There is also a large beer garden with children's pet corner.

Open all day all wk 11-11 **Bar Meals** L served Sun-Fri 11-2, Sat 11-9 D served Sun-Fri 6-9, Sat 11-9 Av main course £8.95 **Restaurant** L served Mon-Fri 11-2, Sat-Sun 11-9 booking required D served Mon-Fri 6-9, Sat-Sun 11-9 booking required Av 3 course à la carte fr £19 ⊕ FREE HOUSE ◀ Sharp's Doom Bar & Special, guest ales. ♈ 20 **Facilities** Children's menu Family room Dogs allowed Garden Parking

## ST JUST (NEAR LAND'S END)

### The Wellington ★★ INN

**Market Square TR19 7HD ☎ 01736 787319**
🖨 01736 787906
e-mail: wellingtonhotel@msn.com
dir: *Take A30 to Penzance, then A3071 W of Penzance to St Just*

Standing in the market square of an historic mining town, this family-run inn makes an ideal base for exploring the spectacular beaches and countryside of West Penwith. Low ceilings, Cornish stonework and a secluded walled garden help to evoke the atmosphere of old Cornwall. The blackboard menu features fresh crab, local fish and daily home-cooked specials: smoked mackerel salad; country ham, eggs and chips; and a prize-winning ploughman's are typical selections.

Open all day all wk **Bar Meals** L served all wk 12-2 D served all wk 6-9 (winter 6-8.30) Av main course £8 **Restaurant** D served all wk 6-9 (summer) ⊕ ST AUSTELL BREWERY ◀ St Austell Tinners, St Austell Tribute, HSD ♊ Cornish Rattler. **Facilities** Children's menu Play area Dogs allowed Garden Rooms 11

## ST MAWES

### The Victory Inn ♈

**Victory Hill TR2 5PQ ☎ 01326 270324   🖨 01326 270238**
e-mail: contact@victory-inn.co.uk
dir: *Take A3078 to St Mawes. Pub up Victory Steps adjacent to harbour*

A friendly fishermen's local, close to St Mawes Harbour on the Roseland Peninsula, and named after Nelson's flagship. It is a traditional pub with a modern approach to food, which is served at lunch and dinner seven days a week. The warm welcome from Phil and Debbie Heslip embraces one and all, including children who are provided with paper, crayons and their own menu. The first-floor restaurant connects to an outside terrace, which looks across the rooftops to the harbour. Not surprisingly, the freshest local seafood is high on the list of ingredients - all Cornish - and the choice of fish and shellfish changes almost daily.

Open all day all wk 11am-mdnt **Bar Meals** L served all wk 12-3 D served all wk 6-9.30 booking required Av main course £8.95 **Restaurant** L served all wk 12-3 D served all wk 6-9.15 booking required Fixed menu price fr £10.95 Av 3 course à la carte fr £16.95 ⌖ PUNCH TAVERNS ◀ Sharp's, Bass, Wadworth 6X, Adnams Broadside, Brains Reverend James, Otter Ale Ò Addlestones. ⏶ 8 **Facilities** Children's menu Dogs allowed Garden

## ST MAWGAN

## The Falcon Inn ★★★★ INN ⏶

**TR8 4EP** ☎ 01637 860225 📄 01637 860884
e-mail: info@thefalcon-stmawgan.co.uk
dir: *From A30 (8m W of Bodmin) follow signs to Newquay/St Mawgan Airport. After 2m right into village, pub at bottom of hill*

Nestling in the sheltered Vale of Lanherne conservation area is the wisteria-covered Falcon, with large attractive garden, a lovely magnolia tree and cobbled courtyard. The interior is cosy and relaxed, with flagstone floors and log fires in winter; two en suite letting rooms make the inn a handy overnight stop before catching a plane from Newquay. Beers from St Austell Brewery are augmented by Scrumpy and Rattler ciders; half a dozen wines available by the glass complete the range of refreshments. At lunchtime you'll find home-made soup, sandwiches, jacket potatoes, and main courses such as chicken and mushroom pie. Weather permitting, summer barbecues are planned for the garden. Dishes in the more formal restaurant may feature starters of antipasto misto or roast vegetable bruschetta. Main courses always include fresh fish options such as red mullet, hake or trout, and vegetarians are well catered for.

Open all wk 11-3 6-11 (Jul-Aug open all day) Closed: 25 Dec (open 12-2) **Bar Meals** L served all wk 12-2 D served all wk 6-9 **Restaurant** L served all wk 12-2 D served all wk 6-9 ⌖ ST AUSTELL BREWERY ◀ St Austell HSD, Tinners Ale, Tribute Ò Cornish Rattler. ⏶ 7 **Facilities** Children's menu Dogs allowed Garden Parking **Rooms** 2

## TREBARWITH

## The Mill House Inn ⏶

**PL34 0HD** ☎ 01840 770200 📄 01840 770647
e-mail: management@themillhouseinn.co.uk
web: www.themillhouseinn.co.uk
dir: *From Tintagel take B3263 S, right after Trewarmett to Trebarwith Strand. Pub 0.5m on right*

Originally known as Treknow Mill, the building dates from 1760 and was still working in the late 1930s, becoming a pub in 1960. Set in seven acres of wooded gardens on the north Cornish coast, this beautifully atmospheric stone building has log fires in the residents' lounge and Delabole slate-floored bar, where wooden tables and chapel chairs give off a relaxed, family-friendly feel. Lunches, evening drinks and barbecues can be enjoyed outside on the attractive split-level terraces, while dinner in the restaurant over the millstream is a particular treat. Sharp's Doom Bar and other local ales and an unusual and creative wine list complement the regularly changing lunch menus, all featuring the best local fresh fish, meat and other produce. At lunchtime, traditional pub favourites, such as sausages and mash, or battered haddock and chips, appear alongside Tuscan bean cassoulet with dressed leaves, Parmesan and ciabatta. In the restaurant, a typical meal might be lobster and sea trout terrine with light herb salad and asparagus cream; then honey-glazed Tintagel duck breast with fondant potatoes and roasted carrot and maple purée; and to finish chocolate and orange cheesecake with mint ice cream. Live music is popular on either Friday or Saturday nights every week.

Open all wk 11-11 (Fri-Sat 11am-mdnt) (Sun noon-10.30) Closed: 25 Dec **Bar Meals** L served Mon-Sat 12-2.30, Sun 12-3 D served all wk 6.30-8.30 **Restaurant** D served all wk 6.30-9 ⌖ FREE HOUSE ◀ Sharp's Doom Bar, Red Stripe, Skinners Cornish Knocker Ò Inch's Stonehouse, Stowford Press. ⏶ 7 **Facilities** Children's menu Play area Family room Dogs allowed Garden Parking

## TREBURLEY

### The Springer Spaniel ♏

**PL15 9NS ☎ 01579 370424**

e-mail: enquiries@thespringerspaniel.org.uk
web: www.thespringerspaniel.org.uk
dir: *On A388 halfway between Launceston & Callington*

This country dining pub aims to provide the best that a traditional Cornish hostelry can offer - delectable ales, delicious food, fine wines and friendly service. The old creeper-clad walls conceal a cosy bar with high-backed wooden settles, farmhouse-style chairs and a wood-burning stove. You can bring your dog, join in with the chat, read the papers or cast an eye over the many books in the snug. Children are always welcome, and will have fun with the 'Little Jack Russell' menu which serves up organic sausages, burgers and chips, and seasonal vegetable pasta bake. The restaurant is full of plants and flowers, with flickering candles in the evenings adding to the romantic atmosphere. In summer the newly landscaped, sheltered garden is a great place to relax and enjoy the sunshine with a pint of Skinners. Food is a big draw here, with beef from the owners' own nearby organic farm as a speciality, from home-made burgers and sausages to fine steaks. Daily specials are strong on fish and game, such as chargrilled tuna steak with tomato, roast red pepper relish and chilli lime dressing; and braised rabbit with bacon, sun-dried tomatoes and rosemary.

Open all wk noon-2.30 6-10.30 Bar Meals L served all wk 12-1.45 D served all wk 6.15-8.45 Av main course £8.95 Restaurant L served all wk 12-1.45 D served all wk 6.15-8.45 Av 3 course à la carte fr £22 ⊕ FREE HOUSE ◀ Sharp's Doom Bar, Skinner's Betty Stogs, St Austell Tribute, guest ale ♻ Rattler, Cornish Orchard's Black & Gold. ♏ 7 Facilities Children's menu Family room Dogs allowed Garden Parking

## TREGADILLETT

### Eliot Arms (Square & Compass) ♏

**PL15 7EU ☎ 01566 772051**

dir: *From Launceston take A30 towards Bodmin. Then follow brown signs to Tregadillett*

The extraordinary décor in this charming creeper-clad coaching inn includes Masonic regalia, horse brasses and 54 clocks. It was believed to have been a Masonic lodge for Napoleonic prisoners, and even has its own friendly ghost! Customers can enjoy real fires in winter and lovely hanging baskets in summer. Food is served in the bar or bright and airy restaurant and includes home-made soup, pie and curry of the day; steak and chips; chargrills; and home-made vegetarian dishes such as spinach and mushroom lasagne or spicy vegetable curry.

Open all day all wk 11.30-11 (Fri-Sat 11.30am-mdnt, Sun noon-10.30) Bar Meals L served all wk 12-2 booking required D served all wk 6-9 booking required Av main course £8.95 Restaurant L served all wk 12-2 booking required D served all wk 6-9 booking required ⊕ FREE HOUSE ◀ Sharp's Doom Bar, Courage Best. ♏ 9 Facilities Children's menu Family room Dogs allowed Parking

## TYWARDREATH

### The Royal Inn ★★★★ INN ♏

**66 Eastcliffe Rd PL24 2AJ ☎ 01726 815601**
📄 **01726 816415**

e-mail: info@royal-inn.co.uk
dir: *A3082 Par, follow brown tourist signs for 'Newquay Branch line' or railway station. Pub opp rail station*

Travellers and employees of the Great Western Railway once frequented this 19th-century inn, which was named after a visit by King Edward VII to a local copper mine. These days it's much extended and smartly refurbished, with food and drink offerings that support Cornwall's micro-breweries and food producers. The open-plan bar with large log fire is a great place for, say, simple trio of local pork sausages and mash, while the restaurant and conservatory might offer creamy mushroom and tarragon chicken.

Open all day all wk 11.30am-11pm (Sun 12-10.30) Bar Meals L served all wk 12-2 D served Mon-Sat 6.30-9, Sun 7-9 Restaurant L served all wk 12-2 D served Mon-Sat 6.30-9, Sun 7-9 booking required ⊕ FREE HOUSE ◀ Sharp's Doom Bar & Special Ale, Wells Bombardier, Shepherd Neame Spitfire, Cotleigh Barn Owl ♻ Cornish Rattler. ♏ 11 Facilities Children's menu Dogs allowed Garden Parking Rooms 15

## ZENNOR

### The Tinners Arms ♏

**TR26 3BY ☎ 01736 796927**

e-mail: tinners@tinnersarms.com
dir: *Take B3306 from St Ives towards St Just. Zennor approx 5m*

The only pub in the village, this 13th-century, granite-built free house is close to the South West coastal path and is particularly popular with walkers. It has changed very little over the years, with its stone floors and low ceilings. The main bar has open fires at both ends and outside there is a large terrace with sea views. A sample menu features sirloin steak, chicken pie, slow-cooked duck leg, and butternut squash risotto. For a lighter bite enjoy a fresh Newlyn crab sandwich.

Open all wk Bar Meals L served all wk 12-2 D served all wk 6.30-9 ⊕ FREE HOUSE ◀ Zennor Mermaid, Tinners Ale, Sharps Own ♻ Burrow Hill. ♏ 12 Facilities Children's menu Family room Dogs allowed Garden Parking

## CUMBRIA

### AMBLESIDE

## Drunken Duck Inn ★★★★★ INN 🏵🏵 ☘

**Barngates LA22 0NG ☎ 015394 36347** 📄 **015394 36781**
e-mail: info@drunkenduckinn.co.uk
web: www.drunkenduckinn.co.uk
dir: *From Kendal on A591 to Ambleside, then follow Hawkshead sign. In 2.5m inn sign on right, 1m up hill*

This 17th-century inn which stands in some glorious Lakeland countryside, just a short drive from Tarn Hows. In the same ownership for over three decades and constantly evolving, the traditional whitewashed inn continues to offer good service, excellent food and drink and a friendly, relaxed atmosphere. Real ales are served in the oak-floored and beamed bar, with open fire, numerous pictures, leather club chairs and beautiful Brathay Black slate bar top from the local quarry. Excellent locally sourced food is served in three informal restaurant areas, from lunchtime dishes like braised beef and dumplings; lamb hotpot with pickled red cabbage; and rare roast beef and horseradish sandwiches (walkers can take these away), to more imaginative evening meals like duck breast with confit garlic risotto and duck jus, and roast halibut with red wine reduction. Desserts are equally tempting: steamed marmalade sponge pudding with clotted cream and vanilla sauce. After a walk there's nothing better than relaxing on the front verandah with a pint and soaking up the view to Lake Windermere.

Open all wk Closed: 25 Dec **Bar Meals** L served all wk 12-4 Av main course £20 **Restaurant** D served all wk 6-9.30 booking required Av 3 course à la carte fr £40 ⊕ FREE HOUSE ◀ Barngates Cracker Ale, Chesters Strong & Ugly, Tag Lag, Catnap, Mothbag, 1 guest ale. ☘ 20 **Facilities** Children's menu Garden Parking **Rooms** 17

### APPLEBY-IN-WESTMORLAND

## Tufton Arms Hotel ☘

**Market Square CA16 6XA ☎ 017683 51593**
📄 **017683 52761**
e-mail: info@tuftonarmshotel.co.uk
dir: *In town centre*

Appleby-in-Westmorland is a medieval market town nestling in the heart of a valley so magically unspoilt that the only possible name for it is Eden. The Milsom family have lovingly restored the Tufton Arms to its former Victorian splendour with rich drapes, period paintings and antique furniture. The elegant conservatory restaurant overlooks a cobbled mews courtyard; light and airy in the daytime, this room takes on an attractive glow in the evening when the curtains are closed and the lighting is low. Chef David Milsom and his kitchen team have won many accolades for their superb food, a selection of dishes made from the finest and freshest local ingredients.

Open all day all wk 7am-11pm Closed: 25-26 Dec **Bar Meals** L served all wk 12-2 D served all wk 6.30-9 **Restaurant** L served all wk 12-2 D served all wk 6.30-9 ⊕ FREE HOUSE ◀ Tufton Arms Ale, Flowers IPA, Tennants. ☘ 15 **Facilities** Children's menu Dogs allowed Parking

### ARMATHWAITE

## The Dukes Head Inn ★★★ INN ☘

**Front St CA4 9PB ☎ 016974 72226**
e-mail: info@dukeshead-hotel.co.uk
dir: *9m from Penrith, 10m from Carlisle between junct 41 & 42 of M6*

Originally a farm, this pub was licensed during the construction of the Settle to Carlisle railway. Set in the pretty red sandstone village of Armathwaite, it has been proudly run by the Lynch family for over 21 years. The River Eden runs through the village and provides wonderful walks along its banks and up into the woods beyond. Re-fuel with hot steak sandwich or a starter of home-made salmon and haddock fishcake followed by venison, pheasant and rabbit hotpot with home-pickled cabbage. Look out for the many special events and offers.

Open all wk 11.30-11.30 Closed: 25 Dec **Bar Meals** L served Mon-Sat 12-2, Sun 12-2.30 D served all wk 6.30-9 **Restaurant** L served Mon-Sat 12-2, Sun 12-2.30 D served all wk 6.30-9 ⊕ PUNCH TAVERNS ◀ Jennings Cumberland Ale, Black Sheep Bitter, Deuchars IPA, Black Cat Mild Ô Aspall's Premier Cru, Westons, Thatchers. ☘ 6 **Facilities** Children's menu Dogs allowed Garden Parking **Rooms** 5

### BLENCOGO

## The New Inn ☘

**CA7 0BZ ☎ 016973 61091** 📄 **016973 61091**
dir: *From Carlisle take A596 towards Wigton, then B5302 towards Silloth. After 4m Blencogo signed on left*

This late Victorian sandstone pub has superb views of the north Cumbrian fells and Solway Plain. It is located in a farming hamlet, and the impressive menu makes good use of produce from the region - perhaps chargrilled tenderloin of pork topped with apricot and herb crust; fresh salmon served with hollandaise sauce and asparagus; or yellow-fin tuna with mild curried mango and Armagnac sauce.

Open Closed: 1st 2wks Jan, Mon-Wed **Bar Meals** Av main course £15 **Restaurant** L served Sun 12-2 booking required D served Thu-Sun 6.30-9 booking required Fixed menu price fr £18.50 Av 3 course à la carte fr £26 ⊕ FREE HOUSE ◀ Yates, Carlisle State Bitter, Hesket Newmarket, Black Sheep. ☘ 10 **Facilities** Children's menu Garden Parking

## BOOT

# The Boot Inn

**CA19 1TG** ☎ **019467 23224** 📄 **019467 23337**
e-mail: enquiries@bootinn.co.uk
web: www.bootinn.co.uk
dir: *From A595 follow signs for Eskdale then Boot*

The Boot takes its name from the pretty pink granite village in which it sits, which also boasts England's oldest working watermill. This is some of England's finest walking country, and the award-winning, traditional Boot Inn sits slap bang in the middle of it. A beck wends its way through the valley, crossed by a 17th-century packhorse bridge. Scafell Pike and Wastwater are within rambling distance and, naturally enough, the pub attracts many cold and hungry climbers. Fortunately there's a roaring fire on cooler days, and plenty of hearty home-made dishes to restore them. The beer garden has two children's play areas. Tempting sandwiches, jacket potatoes and ploughman's platters (ham or cheese) on the lunch menu are supported by hearty options such as Cumberland sausage with home-made chips or great home-made pies. Local produce is taken seriously here, with lamb, beef, eggs, cheese and sausages all coming from nearby suppliers. In the evening the range broadens with starters of mozzarella and tomatoes or prawn cocktail; main courses such as home-made curry or gammon, chips and peas; and traditional puddings like fruit crumble or sticky toffee pudding. Children can opt for small versions of several dishes from the main menu, or for the likes of local sausages and chips. Dogs under control are welcome.

**Open** all wk Closed: 25 Dec **Bar Meals** Av main course £7.95 food served all day **Restaurant** D served all wk 6-8.30 booking required ⊕ ROBINSONS ◀ Double Hop, Unicorn, Dizzy Blonde, Dark Hatters Ö Westons Stowford Press Organic. **Facilities** Children's menu Play area Family room Dogs allowed Garden Parking

---

## BORROWDALE

# The Langstrath Country Inn 🍷

**CA12 5XG** ☎ **017687 77239**
e-mail: info@thelangstrath.com
dir: *B5289 past Grange, through Rosthwaite, left to Stonethwaite. Inn on left after 1m*

Refurbishments over the years at this 16th-century, family-run inn, include the addition of a restaurant with spectacular views up the Langstrath valley. A meal here could start with

Cumbrian cheese soufflé or smoked Borrowdale trout and avocado salad; continue with Goosnargh chicken breast on olive oil mash or Cumbrian sirloin steak; and wind up with some delicious sticky toffee pudding. The bar offers decent ales and an extensive wine list. Set on the coast-to-coast and Cumbrian Way walks, this is an ideal spot for hikers.

**Open** noon-10.30 Closed: Dec-Jan, Mon **Bar Meals** L served Tue-Sun 12-2.30 D served Tue-Sun 6-9 Av main course £12 **Restaurant** L served Tue-Sun 12-2.30 D served Tue-Sun 6-9 Av 3 course à la carte fr £21 ⊕ FREE HOUSE ◀ Jennings Bitter, Black Sheep, Hawkshead Bitter, Cocker Hoop Ö Thatchers Gold. 🍷 8 **Facilities** Children's menu Garden Parking

---

## BOUTH

# The White Hart Inn 🍷

**LA12 8JB** ☎ **01229 861229** 📄 **01229 861836**
e-mail: nigelwhitehart@aol.com
dir: *1.5m from A590. 10m from M6 junct 36*

Bouth today reposes quietly in the Lake District National Park, although once it housed an occasionally noisy gunpowder factory. When this closed in 1928 villagers turned to woodland industries and farm labouring instead, and some of their tools now adorn this 17th-century coaching inn. Ever-changing specials are served in the upstairs restaurant that looks out over woods, fields and fells, or the horseshoe-shaped bar.

**Open** all day all wk noon-11 (Sun noon-10.30) **Bar Meals** L served Mon-Fri 12-2 booking required D served all wk 6-8.45 booking required **Restaurant** L served Mon-Fri 12-2 booking required D served all wk 6-8.45 booking required ⊕ FREE HOUSE ◀ Black Sheep Best, Jennings Cumberland Ale, Coniston Bluebird, Ulverston. 🍷 7 **Facilities** Children's menu Dogs allowed Garden Parking

---

## BRAITHWAITE

# Coledale Inn

**CA12 5TN** ☎ **017687 78272** 📄 **017687 78272**
e-mail: info@coledale-inn.co.uk
dir: *M6 junct 50, A66 towards Cockermouth for 18m. Turn to Braithwaite then towards Whinlatter Pass. Follow sign on left, over bridge to Inn*

Set in a peaceful spot above Braithwaite village, this inn is ideal for exploring the footpaths that begin nearby. The building started life as a woollen mill in the 1820s, and is full of attractive Victorian prints, furnishings and antiques. Home-made meals, such as steak and kidney pie, are backed by an impressive wine list. Don't expect an explanation of the strange-shaped tree in the garden, because no-one knows.

**Open** all day all wk 11-11 **Bar Meals** L served all wk 12-2 D served all wk 6-9 Av main course £8.95 ⊕ FREE HOUSE ◀ Yates, Theakstons, Jennings Best, John Smiths. **Facilities** Children's menu Play area Dogs allowed Garden Parking

## The Royal Oak ★★★★ INN ♛

**CA12 5SY ☎ 017687 78533** 📄 **017687 78533**
e-mail: tpfranks@hotmail.com
dir: *Exit M6 junct 40, A66 to Keswick, 20m. Bypass Keswick & Portinscale juncts, take next left, pub in village centre*

The Royal Oak is set in the centre of Braithwaite village in a walkers' paradise surrounded by high fells and beautiful scenery. The interior is all oak beams and log fires, and the menu offers hearty pub food in the bar area or restaurant, served alongside local ales.

**Open** all wk **Bar Meals** L served all wk 12-2 D served all wk 6-9 Av main course £9 **Restaurant** L served all wk 12-2 D served all wk 6-9 ⊕ MARSTONS ◄ Jennings Lakeland Ale, Cumberland Ale, Cocker Hoop, Sneck Lifter. ♛ 8 **Facilities** Children's menu Dogs allowed Garden Parking **Rooms** 10

## BRAMPTON

## Blacksmiths Arms ★★★★ INN ♛

**Talkin Village CA8 1LE ☎ 016977 3452** 📄 **016977 3396**
e-mail: blacksmithsarmstalkin@yahoo.co.uk
dir: *From M6 take A69 E, after 7m straight over rdbt, follow signs to Talkin Tarn then Talkin Village*

This attractive family-run village inn stands in some lovely countryside; the Borders, Hadrian's Wall and the Lakes are all close by. The original smithy, dating from 1700, remains part of inn along with the bar, restaurant and accommodation. Enjoy the warm hospitality and a pint of ale from Brampton Brewery, while choosing from the menus that range from bar snacks to full à la carte offerings. Dishes typically include lasagne, assorted pies, Cumberland sausages, and fresh local trout.

**Open** all wk noon-3 6-mdnt **Bar Meals** L served all wk 12-2 D served all wk 6-9 Av main course £9.95 **Restaurant** L served all wk 12-2 D served all wk 6-9 Av 3 course à la carte fr £15.95 ⊕ FREE HOUSE ◄ Yates, Brampton, Black Sheep. ♛ 20 **Facilities** Children's menu Garden Parking **Rooms** 8

## BROUGHTON-IN-FURNESS

## The Old Kings Head ★★★★ INN

**Church St LA20 6HJ ☎ 01229 716293**
e-mail: russell@clar7jw.freeserve.co.uk
dir: *Telephone for directions*

With a history spanning 400 years, the spick-and-span former coaching inn is one of the oldest buildings in the town.

Perfectly located for exploring the southern Lakes, the pub offers freshly prepared food using local ingredients. Look to the chalkboard for daily fish specials, perhaps hot potted prawns, and whole bass with lemon and lime cream, or tuck into winter lamb casserole, rack of lamb, or a classic steak and ale pie.

**Open** all wk noon-3 5-mdnt **Bar Meals** L served all wk 12-2 booking required D served all wk 5-9 booking required **Restaurant** L served all wk 12-2 booking required D served all wk 5-9 booking required ⊕ ENTERPRISE INNS ◄ Beckstones, Black Sheep, IPA, Black Dog. **Facilities** Children's menu Play area Garden Parking **Rooms** 6

## BUTTERMERE

## Bridge Hotel ★★★ CHH ♛

**CA13 9UZ ☎ 017687 70252** 📄 **017687 70215**
e-mail: enquiries@bridge-hotel.com
web: www.bridge-hotel.com
dir: *Take B5289 from Keswick*

An 18th-century former coaching inn set between Buttermere and Crummock Water in an outstandingly beautiful area, surrounded by the Buttermere Fells. There are wonderful walks right from the front door. Good food and real ales are served in the character bars (Cumberland sausage, rainbow trout or Scottish salmon), and a four-course dinner in the dining room - including, perhaps, roast Lakeland lamb with Cumberland sauce and crispy leeks, or venison braised with mushrooms and Old Peculier jus.

**Open** all day all wk all wk 10.30am-11.30pm **Bar Meals** food served all day **Restaurant** D served all wk 6-8.30 Av 3 course à la carte fr £31.50 ⊕ FREE HOUSE ◄ Theakston's Old Peculier, Black Sheep Best, Buttermere Bitter, Boddingtons, Hawkshead Gold. ♛ 12 **Facilities** Children's menu Garden Parking **Rooms** 21

## CALDBECK

## Oddfellows Arms

**CA7 8EA ☎ 016974 78227** 📄 **016974 78056**
dir: *Telephone for directions*

This 17th-century former coaching inn is set in a scenic conservation village in the northern fells. Popular with coast-to-coast cyclists and walkers on the Cumbrian Way, the Oddfellows serves Jennings Bitter and Cumberland Ale. Lunchtime snacks include jacket potatoes, sandwiches, or hot beef in a roll, whilst specials and vegetarian blackboards

continued

supplement the regular menu. Expect bacon chops with stilton; sirloin steaks; and local trout fillets. There's a daily curry, too.

**Open** all day all wk **Bar Meals** L served all wk 12-2 D served all wk 6.15-8.30 Av main course £8.50 **Restaurant** L served all wk 12-1.30 booking required D served all wk 6.15-8.30 booking required Av 3 course à la carte fr £15 ⊕ MARSTONS ◂ Jennings Bitter, Cumberland Ale. **Facilities** Children's menu Dogs allowed Garden Parking

## CONISTON

## The Black Bull Inn & Hotel ⏝

1 Yewdale Rd LA21 8DU ☎ 015394 41335 & 41668 ▤ 015394 41168
e-mail: i.s.bradley@btinternet.com
dir: *M6 junct 36, A590. 23m from Kendal via Windermere & Ambleside*

A cosy refuge in the heart of the Lake District, this 400-year-old coaching inn has been run by the same family for nearly 30 years. Set at the foot of the Old Man of Coniston mountain and adjacent to Coniston Water, it has welcomed some famous faces over the years, from Coleridge and Turner to Anthony Hopkins. Back in the 1990s the owners' son started a micro-brewery behind the inn, which has gone from strength to strength; the award-winning real ales are not only sold behind the bar, but shipped out to 30 neighbouring hostelries. For hungry ramblers calling in at lunchtime, there is an excellent and unfussy range of snacks including toasted sandwiches, soups and jacket potatoes. Alternatively, the restaurant menu runs from hearty winter warmers such as a bowl of home-made chilli through to a salad of local Esthwaite trout fillets - perfect on a summer's day.

**Open** all wk Closed: 25 Dec **Bar Meals** food served all day **Restaurant** D served all wk 6-9 booking required ⊕ FREE HOUSE ◂ Coniston Bluebird, Old Man Ale, Opium, Blacksmith, XB, Oatmeal Stout. ⏝ 10 **Facilities** Children's menu Family room Dogs allowed Garden Parking

## CROOK

## The Sun Inn ⏝

LA8 8LA ☎ 01539 821351 ▤ 01539 821351
dir: *Off B5284*

A welcoming inn which has grown from a row of cottages built in 1711, when beer was served to travellers from a front room. The same pleasure is dispensed today by the winter fires or on the summer terrace. The bar and regular menus feature steak and mushroom pie, beer battered cod and chips, curries, steaks, salads and vegetarian dishes. The seasonal menus use locally sourced produce.

**Open** all wk **Bar Meals** L served Mon-Fri 12-2.30, Sat-Sun 12-10.30 D served Mon-Fri 6-9, Sat-Sun 12-10.30 **Restaurant** L served Mon-Fri 12-2.30, Sat-Sun 12-10.30 D served Mon-Fri 6-9, Sat-Sun 12-10.30 booking required ◂ Scottish & Newcastle ◂ Theakston, John Smiths's, Courage Directors, Coniston Bluebird, Hawkeshead. ⏝ 14 **Facilities** Children's menu Dogs allowed Garden Parking

## CROSTHWAITE

## The Punch Bowl Inn ★★★★★ INN ◉ ⏝

LA8 8HR ☎ 015395 68237 ▤ 015395 68875
e-mail: info@the-punchbowl.co.uk
dir: *M6 junct 36, A590 towards Barrow, A5074 & follow signs for Crosthwaite. Pub by church on left*

Located in the Lyth Valley beside a parish church, this classy inn operates as a bar; an elegant restaurant; accommodation witn swish, boutique-style rooms; and the village post office. Although remodelled with a contemporary feel, it still has bags of character. Oak beams, roaring log fires, gleaming wooden floors, and elegant dining rooms with white linen and local artwork. The menu is served throughout bar and restaurant and champions local suppliers. Lunchtime snacks take in roast beef and horseradish sandwiches.

**Open** all wk noon-mdnt **Bar Meals** Av main course £12 food served all day **Restaurant** Av 3 course à la carte fr £25.30 food served all day ⊕ FREE HOUSE ◂ Tag Lag, Cat Nap, Erdinger, Westmorland Gold, Coniston Bluebird, Hawkshead Gold ♨ Thatchers Gold. ⏝ 16 **Facilities** Children's menu Dogs allowed Garden Parking **Rooms** 9

## ENNERDALE BRIDGE

## The Shepherd's Arms Hotel

CA23 3AR ☎ 01946 861249 ▤ 01946 861249
e-mail: shepherdsarms@btconnect.com
web: www.shepherdsarmshotel.co.uk
dir: *A66 to Cockermouth (25m), A5086 to Egremont (5m) then follow sign to Ennerdale*

Located on a beautiful stretch of Wainwright's Coast to Coast footpath, this informal free house is a favourite with walkers. The bar has a long serving counter, a long case clock and wood-burning stove below a large beam hung with copper and brass pieces. The carpeted main area has an open log fire and comfortable seating, and is a venue for local musicians; it opens into a small conservatory with pub tables and an additional outdoor sitting area. Shepherd's Arms own brew heads the beers, and a nicely varied menu is served throughout. There's plenty of choice for vegetarians, as well as daily specials and à la carte options in the dining room.

**Open** all wk **Bar Meals** L served all wk 12-2 D served all wk 6-9 Av main course £8 ⊕ FREE HOUSE ◂ Jennings Bitter, Cumberland, Guest ales. **Facilities** Children's menu Dogs allowed Garden Parking

## ESKDALE GREEN

### Bower House Inn ★★ HL

**CA19 1TD** ☎ **019467 23244** 📄 **019467 23308**
e-mail: info@bowerhouseinn.co.uk
dir: *4m off A595, 0.5m W of Eskdale Green*

Despite its out-of-the-way location, in unspoilt Eskdale overlooking Muncaster Fell, the traditional appeal of this 17th-century inn finds favour with an eclectic clientele, from walkers and tourists to business folk and wedding parties. Headquarters of the village cricket team (the pitch is next door), the bar has a distinctly clubby feel, with oak beams, ticking clocks, crackling log fires and local ales on tap, and opens out on to an enchanting, enclosed garden. The rambling restaurant is a charming room with candlelit tables, exposed stone, log fires and equestrian pictures creating a welcoming, traditional setting for some hearty, imaginative food. Try Morecambe Bay potted shrimps or smoked Herdwick lamb with minted apple chutney for starters, followed by beef fillet cooked in red wine; roast venison with juniper berry sauce; local wild duck and trout; or poached salmon with white wine and cucumber sauce.

Open all day all wk 11-11 **Bar Meals** L served all wk D served all wk Av main course £10.50 food served all day **Restaurant** D served 7-9 Av 3 course à la carte fr £22 ⊕ FREE HOUSE ◀ Theakston Bitter, Jennings Bitter, Coniston Bluebird, Hawkshead Bitter, Dent Ales. **Facilities** Children's menu Dogs allowed Garden Parking **Rooms** 29

## GRASMERE

### The Travellers Rest Inn 🍷

**Keswick Rd LA22 9RR** ☎ **015394 35604** 📄 **017687 72309**
e-mail: stay@lakedistrictinns.co.uk
dir: *From M6 take A591 to Grasmere, pub 0.5m N of Grasmere*

Located on the edge of picturesque Grasmere and handy for touring and exploring the ever-beautiful Lake District, the Travellers Rest has been a pub for more than 500 years. Inside, a roaring log fire complements the welcoming atmosphere of the beamed and inglenooked bar area. An extensive menu of traditional home-cooked fare is offered, ranging from Westmorland terrine and eggs Benedict, to wild mushroom gratin and rump of Lakeland lamb.

Open all day all wk **Bar Meals** food served all day ⊕ FREE HOUSE ◀ Jennings Bitter & Cocker Hoop, Cumberland Ale, Sneck

Lifter, guest ales. 🍷 10 **Facilities** Children's menu Family room Dogs allowed Garden Parking

## GREAT SALKELD

### The Highland Drove Inn and Kyloes Restaurant 🍷

**CA11 9NA** ☎ **01768 898349** 📄 **01768 898708**
e-mail: highlanddroveinn@btinternet.com
dir: *Exit M6 junct 40, take A66 E'bound then A686 to Alston. After 4m, left onto B6412 for Great Salkeld & Lazonby*

A 300-year-old country inn, nestling by the church in a picturesque village deep in the lovely Eden Valley. Looking more like an old farmhouse, the pub is a great all-round inn, the area's social hub with a well-deserved reputation for high quality food and conviviality. Inside, there's an attractive brick and timber bar, old tables and settles in the main bar area, and a lounge with log fire, dark wood furniture and tartan fabrics. Menus list traditional local dishes, alongside daily specials reflecting the availability of local game and fish, and meat from herds reared and matured in Cumbria. Typical meals might be rabbit and bacon pie baked in a double crust with cider and cream; honeyed duck breast with black pudding; pan-fried plaice fillet with spiced melon and lime butter; then pannacotta and stewed rhubarb. Despite the excellence of the food, the Highland Drove is still a pub where locals come to enjoy the wide range of cask-conditioned real ales, plenty of other beers and ciders, and a good selection of wines.

Open all wk noon-2 6-late (Closed Mon L) **Bar Meals** L served Tue-Sun 12-2 D served all wk 6-9 **Restaurant** L served Tue-Sun 12-2 D served all wk 6-9 ⊕ FREE HOUSE ◀ Theakston Black Bull, John Smiths Cask, John Smiths Smooth, Theakstons Best, Theakstons Mild, guest ale. 🍷 25 **Facilities** Children's menu Dogs allowed Garden Parking

## HAWKSHEAD

### Kings Arms ★★★ INN

**The Square LA22 0NZ** ☎ **015394 36372** 📄 **015394 36006**
e-mail: info@kingsarmshawkshead.co.uk
dir: *M6 junct 36, A590 to Newby Bridge, right at 1st junct past rdbt, over bridge, 8m to Hawkshead*

Overlooking the picturesque square at the heart of this virtually unchanged Elizabethan Lakeland village, made famous by Beatrix Potter who lived nearby, this 16th-century inn throngs

continued

in summer. In colder weather, bag a table by the fire in the traditional carpeted bar, quaff a pint of Hawkshead bitter and tuck into lunchtime rolls (bacon and brie with cranberry sauce), or for dinner try lamb Henry (slow braised shoulder with red wine and rosemary gravy, or chargrilled rib-eye steak with peppercorn sauce. Look out for the carved figure of a king in the bar.

**Open** all day all wk 11am-mdnt **Bar Meals** L served all wk 12-2.30 D served all wk 6-9.30 Av main course £8.50 **Restaurant** L served all wk 12-2.30 booking required D served all wk 6-9.30 booking required Fixed menu price fr £11.50 ⊕ FREE HOUSE ◀ Tetley Bitter, Black Sheep Best, Hawkshead Gold, Hawkshead Bitter, Coniston Bluebird, guest ales. **Facilities** Children's menu Dogs allowed Garden **Rooms** 8

## Queens Head Hotel ★★ HL ⊚ ♀

**Main St LA22 0NS** ☎ 015394 36271 📠 015394 36722
e-mail: enquiries@queensheadhotel.co.uk
web: www.queensheadhotel.co.uk
dir: *M6 junct 36, A590 to Newby Bridge, 1st right, 8m to Hawkshead*

Behind the Queen's Head's flower-bedecked exterior you'll find low oak-beamed ceilings, wood-panelled walls, an original slate floor and a welcoming fire. An extensive wine list and a selection of real ales is offered, plus a full menu and an ever-changing specials board. Dishes draw from the wealth of quality produce on the doorstep: trout from Esthwaite Water, pheasant from Graythwaite, traditionally cured hams and Cumberland sausage from Waberthwaite, and slow-maturing Herdwick lamb. For lunch try sandwiches, salads or light bites such as a steamed, naturally-smoked haddock fillet with mixed leaves or chicken liver pâté with orange and tequila served with toasted brioche. Heartier lunch options include a 'pot of fish' in a lemon and parsley cream sauce; or Thai curry with saffron rice. An evening meal might open with game and wild mushroom terrine with juniper berry oil, brioche toast with pear and date chutney, followed by venison casserole; Fellside lamb cutlets; or pan-fried West Coast sea bass fillet. The area is a haven for walkers, and Esthwaite Water is close by.

**Open** all wk 11am-11.45pm Sun 12-11.45 **Bar Meals** L served 12-2.30 Sun 12-5 D served all wk 6.15-9.30 Av main course £12.95 **Restaurant** L served 12-2.30 Sun 12-5 booking required D served all wk 6.15-9.30 booking required ⊕ FREDERIC ROBINSON ◀ Hartleys Cumbria Way, Double Hop, Guest Ale. ♀ 11 **Facilities** Children's menu Family room Garden **Rooms** 13

## KESWICK

## The Farmers ♀

**Portinscale CA12 5RN** ☎ 01768 773442
e-mail: grew2157@tiscali.co.uk
dir: *Exit M6 junct 40 (Penrith) onto A66, pass Keswick B5289 junct, turn left to Portinscale*

Set in a small village a mile from bustling Keswick, this historic village pub has traditional decor and long-standing ties with the local hunt. Expect well-kept ales, a friendly welcome and traditional home-cooked food. Typical offerings include home-made lasagne; fish and chips; home-made steak and ale pie; and sweet and sour chicken in batter. Leave room for dessert, perhaps a chocolate brownie or home-made strawberry pie.

**Open** all wk noon-11pm (winter Mon-Fri 3-11 Sat-Sun noon-11) **Bar Meals** L served all wk 12-3 (winter Sat-Sun 12-3) D served Mon-Sat 5-9, Sun 6-9 Av main course £7.95 **Restaurant** Fixed menu price fr £12.95 ◀ Jennings Bitter, Jennings Cumberland, guest ale. ♀ 6 **Facilities** Children's menu Dogs allowed Garden

## The Horse & Farrier Inn ♀

**Threlkeld Village CA12 4SQ**
☎ 017687 79688 📠 017687 79823
e-mail: info@horseandfarrier.com web: www.horseandfarrier.com
dir: *M6 junct 40 follow Keswick (A66) signs, after 12m turn right signed Threlkeld. Pub in village centre*

The Horse & Farrier stands at the foot of Blencathra, with views of Skiddaw and Helvellyn. Within its thick stone walls you'll find slate-flagged floors, beamed ceilings and all the essential features of an inn built over 300 years ago. The inn has an excellent local reputation for food, from hearty Lakeland breakfasts to home-cooked meals served in either the bar, or the charming restaurant. Lunchtime brings a range of open sandwiches and baguettes, as well as hot favourites like deep fried breaded Whitby scampi. A more formal dinner might begin with duck liver and brandy pâté with fresh beetroot chutney. Then, turn to steamed sea bass on tagliatelle verdi; or pan-fried fillet steak with shallot and port wine sauce. The dessert menu includes a range Swiss ice creams, pink grapefruit and orange sorbet and chocolate mint parfait.

**Open** all day all wk 7.30am-mdnt **Bar Meals** food served all day **Restaurant** food served all day ⊕ JENNINGS BROTHERS PLC ◀ Jennings Bitter, Cocker Hoop, Sneck Lifter, Cumberland Ale, guest ale. ♀ 9 **Facilities** Children's menu Family room Dogs allowed Garden Parking

## KIRKBY LONSDALE

### The Sun Inn ★★★★★ INN

**Market St LA6 2AU ☎ 015242 71965 015242 72485**
e-mail: email@sun-inn.info
dir: *From M6 junct 36 take A65 for Kirkby Lonsdale. In 5m left signed Kirkby Lonsdale. At next T-junct turn left. Right at bottom of hill*

Natural stone and oak floors, log fires and window seats create a relaxed atmosphere at this welcoming 17th century inn, just a few minutes' walk from Ruskin's View, famously painted by Turner. Lunchtime choices include sandwiches and light bites, as well as main course dishes like rare breed beef cheeseburger with watercress salad; fish goujons with herb mayonnaise; and a locally-made charcuterie platter. The restaurant menu changes regularly to include options such as mushroom suet pudding with baby root vegetables; and Gloucester Old Spot pork belly with bubble and squeak. The Sun an ideal base from which to explore the Lake District and Yorkshire Dales.

**Open** all day all wk 10am-11pm **Bar Meals** L served Tue-Sun 12-2.30 D served all wk 7-9 Av main course £7.95 **Restaurant** L served Tue-Sun 12-2.30 D served all wk 7-9 Av 3 course à la carte fr £20 FREE HOUSE Jennings Cumberland Ale, Timothy Taylor Landlord, guest ales. 7 **Facilities** Children's menu Dogs allowed **Rooms** 11

## LITTLE LANGDALE

### Three Shires Inn ★★★★ INN

**LA22 9NZ ☎ 015394 37215 015394 37127**
e-mail: enquiry@threeshiresinn.co.uk
web: www.threeshiresinn.co.uk
dir: *Turn off A593, 2.3m from Ambleside at 2nd junct signed 'The Langdales'. 1st left 0.5m. Inn in 1m*

The traditional Cumbrian slate and stone inn was built in 1872 and enjoys a stunning location in the beautiful Little Langdale valley. Named after the nearby meeting point of three county shires - Westmorland, Cumberland and Lancashire – it has been personally run by the Stephenson family since 1983. The bars boasting bare beams and slate walls are warmed in winter by cosy log fires, while on fine summer days, locals, walkers and tourists head for the picnic tables by a lakeland stream in the landscaped garden – the fell views are magnificent. Refreshments include tip-top Cumbrian ales from Jennings, Hawkshead and Coniston breweries. Food is locally sourced and very popular, with evening booking advisable. Light lunches start with tempting sandwiches, baguettes, soups and the perfect walkers' lunch, a ham and cheese ploughman's, or hot food such as Angus steak burger and beef and ale pie. Hearty evening choices take in marinated rump of Lakeland lamb with garlic and herb mash and port and redcurrant sauce, and rib-eye steak with all the trimmings.

**Open** all wk 11-3 6-10.30 Dec-Jan, 11-10.30 Feb-Nov (Fri-Sat 11-11 ) Closed: 25 Dec **Bar Meals** L served all wk 12-2 (ex 24 Dec) D served all wk 6-8.45 (ex mid wk Dec-Jan) booking required Av main course £12.95 **Restaurant** D served all wk 6-8.45 (ex mid wk Dec-Jan) booking required Fixed menu price fr £18.95 Av 3 course à la carte fr £18 FREE HOUSE Jennings Best & Cumberland, Coniston Old Man, Hawkshead Bitter, Blacksheep Bitters. **Facilities** Children's menu Garden Parking **Rooms** 10

## LOWESWATER

### Kirkstile Inn ★★★★ INN

**CA13 0RU ☎ 01900 85219 01900 85239**
e-mail: info@kirkstile.com
dir: *From Cockermouth B5289 to Lorton, past Low Lorton, 3m to Loweswater. At red phone box left, 200yds*

Standing in the shadow of Melbreak, the Kirkstile Inn has offered shelter and hospitality amidst the stunning Cumbrian fells for some 400 years. Located between Loweswater and Crummock Water, the inn is an ideal base for walking, climbing, boating and fishing. Of course, you may simply prefer relaxing over a beer from one of the local breweries. Here the food matches the quality of the views, with plenty of choice from the regular menus and daily changing blackboard specials. Expect a choice of baguettes, sandwiches and jacket potatoes at lunchtime, as well as a range of hot dishes like pan-fried chicken with salad and wild rice; the evening menu may begin with black pudding in beer batter with a red wine sauce; or smoked chicken salad with olive dressing. Move on to roasted hake fillet with sweet potato; goats' cheese, spinach and roasted vegetable lasagne; or slow-cooked Lakeland lamb shoulder with rosemary mash. Dessert options include Cumberland rum Nicky, pecan pie and chocolate marquise.

**Open** all wk Closed: 25 Dec **Bar Meals** L served all wk 12-3 booking required D served all wk 6-9 booking required Av main course £10.25 **Restaurant** D served all wk 6-9 booking required Av 3 course à la carte fr £21 FREE HOUSE Kirkstile Gold, Yates Bitter, Melbreak, Grasmoor Ale Stowford Press. 10 **Facilities** Children's menu Family room Dogs allowed Garden Parking **Rooms** 8

## NEAR SAWREY

### Tower Bank Arms ♥

**LA22 0LF ☎ 015394 36334**

e-mail: enquiries@towerbankarms.com
dir: *On B5285 SW of Windermere.1.5m from Hawkshead.*

This 17th-century Lakeland inn was immortalised in Beatrix Potter's Tales of Jemima Puddleduck. The author's former home, Hilltop, now a National Trust property, is just behind the pub. Food based on local produce is served in the bar or restaurant, and children are made welcome. Typical menu starts with plate of smoked salmon and crayfish tails or flat field mushroom topped with local blue cheese, continues with breast of Barbary duck with sweet plum and ginger sauce or Cumbrian beef and ale stew, and winds up with bread and butter pudding. There is also an excellent cheese slate.

Open all wk open all day Etr-Oct Bar Meals L served all wk 12-2 D served Mon-Sat 6-9, Sun & BH 6-8 (Mon-Thu in winter) Av main course £9.50 Restaurant D served Mon-Sat 6-9, Sun & BH 6-8 (Mon-Thu in winter) Av 3 course à la carte fr £18.45 ⊕ FREE HOUSE ◀ Barngates Tag Lag, Hawkshead Bitter, Brodies Prime, Keswick, Ulverston. ♥ 7 Facilities Children's menu Dogs allowed Garden Parking

## NETHER WASDALE

### The Screes Inn

**CA20 1ET ☎ 019467 26262   📄 019467 26262**

e-mail: info@thescreesinnwasdale.com
dir: *A595 to Gosforth, in 3m turn right signed Nether Wasdale. In village on left*

This friendly family-run pub is situated in the picturesque village of Nether Wasdale and makes an excellent base for walking, mountain biking or diving in this lovely area, particularly Scawfell. It dates back 300 years and offers a log fire, real ales and large selection of malt whiskies. There is a good choice of sandwiches at lunchtime, and other dishes include lasagne, roast leg of lamb off the bone, vegetarian chilli, chick pea and sweet potato curry, or goats' cheese strudel.

Open all day all wk 11-11 (Sun 11-10.30) Closed: 25 Dec, 1 Jan Bar Meals L served all wk 12-3 D served all wk 6-9 Av main course £9 Restaurant L served all wk 12-3 D served all wk 6-9 ⊕ FREE HOUSE ◀ Yates Bitter, Derwent, Black Sheep. Facilities Children's menu Dogs allowed Garden Parking

## OUTGATE

### Outgate Inn ♥

**LA22 0NQ ☎ 015394 36413**

e-mail: outgate@outgate.wanadoo.co.uk
dir: *Exit M6 junct 36, by-pass Kendal, A591 towards Ambleside. At Clappersgate take B5285 to Hawkshead then Outgate 3m*

Once a mineral water manufacturer, and now part of Robinson's and Hartley's Brewery, whose ales are served in the bar. During the winter there's a real fire, while summer warmth should be available in the secluded beer garden. Daily specials supplement grilled local gammon with free range egg and pineapple, pan-fried rib-eye steak, Cumberland sausage and mash, and lightly grilled fillet of lemon sole. Live jazz on Fridays from March to October.

Open all wk all day Mar-Nov Bar Meals L served all wk 12-2 D served all wk 6-9 Restaurant L served all wk 12-2 D served all wk 6-9 ⊕ FREDERIC ROBINSON ◀ Hartleys XB, Old Stockport Bitter, Robinsons Smooth. ♥ 10 Facilities Children's menu Dogs allowed Garden Parking

## RAVENSTONEDALE

### The Black Swan ★★★★ INN ♥

**CA17 4NG ☎ 015396 23204**

e-mail: enquiries@blackswanhotel.com
dir: *M6 junct 38 take A685 E towards Brough*

A grand, family-run Victorian inn in a peaceful conservation village in the upper Eden Valley. Its lovely riverside garden is home to red squirrels, which will let you share their space to relax after you've walked the Howgill Fells, explored the Lakes or toured the Yorkshire Dales. Local ales are served in the bar, while in the beautifully decorated dining rooms main meals include award-winning local sausage casseroled with red wine, mushrooms and shallots or fresh cod or haddock in Black Sheep beer batter with mushy or garden peas and chips. Menus feature sourcing information about all their suppliers.

Open all wk 8.30am-11.30pm Bar Meals L served all wk 12-2 D served all wk 6-9 Av main course £8.95 Restaurant L served all wk 12-2 booking required D served all wk 6-9 ⊕ FREE HOUSE ◀ Black Sheep, John Smith's, Dent, Tirril Brewery, Hawkshead Brewery ♂ Thatchers. ♥ 7 Facilities Children's menu Dogs allowed Garden Parking Rooms 10

### The Fat Lamb Country Inn ★★ HL

**Crossbank CA17 4LL ☎ 015396 23242   📄 015396 23285**

e-mail: enquiries@fatlamb.co.uk
dir: *On A683 between Sedbergh & Kirkby Stephen*

Modern amenities blend with old fashioned hospitality at this 350 year-old free house, a former coaching inn solidly built of local stone, and standing in open countryside between the Lake District and the Yorkshire Dales National Parks. An open fire warms the bar in winter; this is the oldest part of the building, and was converted from the former kitchen and living area. Snacks and meals are served here and in the relaxed restaurant, and the table d'hôte menu might feature local lamb cutlets in mint jus; pan-fried tuna steak with black olive and red onion dressing; or roast guinea fowl with caramelised onion and apple sauce. Whatever you choose, it will have been prepared on site using the best available local ingredients.

Open all wk **Bar Meals** L served all wk 12-2 booking required D served all wk 6-9 booking required Av main course £9.60 **Restaurant** L served all wk 12-2 booking required D served all wk 6-9 booking required Fixed menu price fr £22 Av 3 course à la carte fr £12.50 ⊕ FREE HOUSE ◗ Black Sheep Bitter. **Facilities** Children's menu Play area Dogs allowed Garden Parking **Rooms** 12

## TIRRIL

## Queen's Head Inn ♏

**CA10 2JF ☎ 01768 863219**
e-mail: bookings@queensheadinn.co.uk
dir: *A66 towards Penrith then A6 S towards Shap. In Eamont Bridge turn right just after Crown Hotel. Tirril in 1m on B5320*

Situated on the edge of the Lake District National Park, this 18th-century English country inn is chock-full of beams, flagstones and memorabilia, as you would expect from an old inn. While in the bar, look for the Wordsworth Indenture, signed by the great poet himself, his brother, Christopher, and local wheelwright John Bewsher, to whom the Wordsworths sold the pub in 1836. You can eat in the bar or restaurant, and a meal might include bacon and black pudding salad; oven-baked chicken stuffed with Blengdale Blue and spinach; and chocolate and orange tart. In August the a beer and sausage festival is held here. The village shop is at the back of the inn.

Open all day all wk noon-11pm Sun-Thu, noon-mdnt Fri-Sat **Bar Meals** L served all wk 12-8.30 Mar-Oct, 12-2.30 Nov-Feb D served all wk 12-8.30 Mar-Oct, 5.30-8.30 Nov-Feb Av main course £9.95 **Restaurant** L served all wk 12-8.30 Mar-Oct,

12-2.30 Nov-Feb D served all wk 12-8.30 Mar-Oct, 5.30-8.30 Nov-Feb Fixed menu price fr £8.95 Av 3 course à la carte fr £17.95 ⊕ ROBINSONS ◗ Unicorn, Cumbria Way, Dizzy Blonde. ♏ 10 **Facilities** Children's menu Dogs allowed Parking

## TROUTBECK

## Queens Head ★★★★ INN ♏

**Townhead LA23 1PW ☎ 015394 32174 ▤ 015394 31938**
e-mail: feast@queensheadhotel.com
dir: *M6 junct 36, A590/591, W towards Windermere, right at mini-rdbt onto A592 signed Penrith/Ullswater. Pub 2m on left*

The lovely undulating valley of Troutbeck, with its maze of footpaths and felltop views, is a magnet for ramblers. True to its roots, this smart 17th-century coaching inn offers sustenance and comfortable accommodation to the weary and footsore. The bar is perhaps its most remarkable feature, carved from a four-poster bed that once resided in Appleby Castle. Nooks and crannies, low beams stuffed with old pennies by farmers on their way home from market, and a log fire throughout the year complete the heart-warming picture. The menu proffers hearty fare – from tempting baguettes filled with warm Cumberland sausage, caramelised onion and English mustard mayonnaise, to pan-roasted chicken supreme with bubble and squeak. In addition a three-course set menu, with meat, fish and vegetarian options at each course, is always available.

Open all day all wk **Bar Meals** food served all day **Restaurant** booking required food served all day ⊕ FREDERIC ROBINSON ◗ Hartleys XB, Cumbria Way, Double Hop, Old Tom, Dizzy Blonde. ♏ 8 **Facilities** Children's menu Dogs allowed Parking **Rooms** 15

## ULVERSTON

## Farmers Arms ♏

**Market Place LA12 7BA ☎ 01229 584469**
**▤ 01229 582188**
dir: *In town centre*

A warm welcome is extended at this lively 16th-century inn located at the centre of the attractive, historic market town. The visitor will find a comfortable and relaxing beamed front bar with an open fire in winter. The Sunday lunches are famous locally, and at other times there's a varied and tempting specials menu, and lunchtime choice of hot and cold sandwiches, baguettes or ciabatta, and various salads.

Open all wk ⊕ FREE HOUSE ◗ Hawkshead Best Bitter, John Smiths. ♏ 12 **Facilities** Children's menu Garden

WASDALE HEAD

## Wasdale Head Inn

**CA20 1EX ☎ 019467 26229 & 26333 019467 26334**
e-mail: wasdaleheadinn@msn.com
dir: *From A595 follow Wasdale signs. Inn at head of valley*

Famous historic mountain inn dramatically situated at the foot of England's highest mountains and beside her deepest lake. The oak-panelled walls are hung with photographs reflecting a passion for climbing. Exclusive real ales are brewed in the pub's own micro brewery and celebrated by annual beer festivals. Abraham's Restaurant offers dishes like seared venison steak on maris piper mash and juniper berry sauce.

**Open** all day all wk 11-11 (Sun noon-10.30) **Bar Meals** L served all wk 12-9 D served all wk 12-9 Av main course £9.50 food served all day **Restaurant** D served all wk 7-8 booking required Fixed menu price fr £28 FREE HOUSE Great Gable, Wasd Ale, Burnmoor, Yewbarrow, Illgill, Liar. 15 **Facilities** Children's menu Dogs allowed Garden Parking

WINDERMERE

## The Angel Inn

**Helm Rd LA23 3BU ☎ 015394 44080 015394 46003**
e-mail: rooms@the-angelinn.com
dir: *From Rayrigg Rd (parallel to lake) into Crag Brow, then right into Helm Rd*

City chic style is offered at this sophisticated gastro-pub in a great location five minutes' from Lake Windermere in the centre of Bowness-on-Windermere. Good food based on local produce is available throughout the day from a choice of menus: breakfast/brunch; sandwiches and light lunches; starters, nibbles and salads; main courses - braised Cumbrian farmed pork belly with parmentier potatoes, carrot purée and black pudding - desserts and a children's menu. In warmer weather head for the garden terrace where there are great views.

**Open** all day all wk 9am-11pm Closed: 25 Dec **Bar Meals** L served all wk 11.30-4 D served all wk 5-9 **Restaurant** L served all wk 11.30-4 D served all wk 5-9 FREE HOUSE Coniston Bluebird Bitter, Hawkshead Bitter. 12 **Facilities** Children's menu Garden Parking

## Eagle & Child Inn ★★★ INN

**Kendal Rd, Staveley LA8 9LP ☎ 01539 821320**
e-mail: info@eaglechildinn.co.uk
web: www.eaglechildinn.co.uk
dir: *M6 junct 36, A590 towards Kendal then A591 towards Windermere. Staveley approx 2m*

The rivers Kent and Gowan meet at the gardens of this friendly inn, and it's surrounded by miles of excellent walking, cycling and fishing country. Several pubs in Britain share the same name, which refers to a legend of a baby found in an eagle's nest. Dishes include Fleetwood mussels in tomato, garlic and white wine sauce, local rump steak braised with onions; and roast cod loin in anchovy and parsley butter.

**Open** all wk all wk 11am-11pm **Bar Meals** L served Mon-Fri 12-2.30, Sat-Sun 12-3 D served Mon-Fri 6-8.45, Black Sheep Best Bitter, Coniston, Hawkshead Bitter, Dent Ales, Yates Bitter, Tirril Brewery Westons. 10 **Facilities** Children's menu Dogs allowed Garden Parking **Rooms** 5

WORKINGTON

## The Old Ginn House

**Great Clifton CA14 1TS ☎ 01900 64616**
**01900 873384**
e-mail: enquiries@oldginnhouse.co.uk
dir: *Just off A66, 3m from Workington & 4m from Cockermouth*

The inn was converted from a 17th-century farmstead. The Ginn Room was where farm horses were harnessed to a grindstone to crush crops. Today the unique rounded room is the main bar offering warm hospitality and a well stocked bar; there is also a cosy lounge. The butter yellows, bright check curtains and terracotta tiles of the dining areas exude a warm Mediterranean glow. A menu of the usual bar food is supplemented by larger dishes such as a Ginn House steak, which is stuffed with ham and onion and topped with stilton or cheddar.

**Open** all day all wk 11am-mdnt Closed: 24-26 Dec, 1 Jan **Bar Meals** L served all wk 12-2 D served all wk 6-9.30 Av main course £8 **Restaurant** L served all wk 12-2 D served all wk 6-9.30 Av 3 course à la carte fr £16 FREE HOUSE Jennings Bitter, John Smiths Bitter. **Facilities** Children's menu Garden Parking

England

## YANWATH

## The Yanwath Gate Inn ♟

**CA10 2LF ☎ 01768 862386**
e-mail: enquiries@yanwathgate.com
dir: *Telephone for directions*

The Yanwath Gate Inn has been offering hospitality in the North Lakes since 1683. Today the ethos of owner Matt Edwards is to offer good quality informal dining based on produce which is usually local and organic if possible. Fish is delivered fresh every morning so there are always half a dozen fish and seafood specials on the carte menu. A typical dinner choice could be white bean and garlic soup; followed by smoked venison loin; or gilthead bream; then sticky date pudding to finish. A cosy reading area in the bar ensures a relaxed mood for diners who can choose to eat here by the log fire or at a table in one of the dining rooms.

**Open** all day all wk noon-11pm **Bar Meals** L served all wk 12-2.30 booking required D served all wk 6-9 booking required Av main course £10 **Restaurant** L served all wk 12-2.30 booking required D served all wk 6-9 booking required Av 3 course à la carte fr £30 ⊕ FREE HOUSE ◀ Hesket Newmarket Doris's 90th Birthday Ale, Tirril, Keswick, Paulaner Hefeweizen, De Koninck. ♟ 12 **Facilities** Children's menu Dogs allowed Garden Parking

---

## DERBYSHIRE

## BAKEWELL

## The Bull's Head

**Church St, Ashford-in-the-Water DE45 1QB**
**☎ 01629 812931**
e-mail: bullshead.ashford@virgin.net
dir: *Off A6, 2m N of Bakewell, 5m from Chatsworth Estate*

A family affair for several generations, the Bull's Head has seen the London and Manchester coaches come and go, though the village's famous well dressing is still a sight to see. Everything about this pub is smartly turned out, from the roses round the door to the brassware in the bar. The interior is unpretentious, with dark wooden beams, open brick fires and comfy banquettes. There is no restaurant as such; dishes from a frequently changing menu are cooked to order and served in the small lounge bar. Lunchtime sees a range of sandwiches on offer, or delicious home-made soups such as tomato and lovage; or yellow split pea. Steak and Old Stockport ale pie served with braised red cabbage and dripping-roasted potatoes is a popular main course choice, with blueberry crumble pie and vanilla ice cream to finish.

**Open** all wk 11-3 (summer) noon-3 (winter) 6-11 (Sun noon-3 7-10.30) **Bar Meals** L served all wk 12-2 D served Mon-Sat (ex Thu in winter) 6.30-9, Sun 7-9 ⊕ ROBINSONS ◀ Old Stockport, Unicorn, Double Hop. **Facilities** Children's menu Family room Dogs allowed Garden Parking

## The Monsal Head Hotel ★★ HL ◉ ♟

**Monsal Head DE45 1NL ☎ 01629 640250**
📄 **01629 640815**
e-mail: enquiries@monsalhead.com
dir: *A6 from Bakewell towards Buxton. 1.5m to Ashford. Follow Monsal Head signs, B6465 for 1m*

Set in the heart of the Peak District National Park just three miles from Bakewell, this hotel enjoys lovely views over Monsal Dale. The hotel's real ale pub, the Stables, reflects its earlier role as the home of railway horses which collected passengers from Monsal Dale station. Today, this delightful venue features original flagstone floors and seating in the former horse stalls, with horse tack on the walls and a hay rack at the back of the bar. You'll find welcoming winter fires, and a range of cask ales that includes Theakstones and Lloyds Monsal. Food is served all day in the bar and Longstone restaurant, or in fine weather you may prefer to eat in the large enclosed garden. There's a full range of snacks, sandwiches and jacket potatoes, as well as a children's menu. Typical choices from the main menu might start with chestnut and sweet potato risotto cakes, main course options include seared venison medallions with red cabbage and mashed potato, or crusted roast salmon tournedos. There are daily choices of brûlée or fruit crumble to round things off, or you might prefer a sorbet or sticky toffee pudding.

**Open** all day all wk 8am-11pm **Bar Meals** L served Mon-Sat 12-9.30, Sun 12-9 D served Mon-Sat 12-9.30, Sun 12-9 Av main course £12 food served all day **Restaurant** L served Mon-Sat 12-9.30, Sun 12-9 D served Mon-Sat 12-9.30, Sun 12-9 Av 3 course à la carte fr £25 food served all day ⊕ FREE HOUSE ◀ Theakstons, Bradfield ales, Lloyds Monsal, Thornbridge ales, Abbeydale. ♟ 17 **Facilities** Children's menu Dogs allowed Garden Parking **Rooms** 7

# Derbyshire

## BAMFORD

### Yorkshire Bridge Inn ★★★★ INN ♥

**Ashopton Rd S33 0AZ ☎ 01433 651361**
📄 01433 651361
e-mail: info@yorkshire-bridge.co.uk
web: www.yorkshire-bridge.co.uk
dir: *A57 from M1, left onto A6013, pub 1m on right*

The old packhorse bridge that crosses the River Derwent here on Derbyshire's border with Yorkshire gives this early 19th-century inn its name. The inn's beamed and chintz-curtained bars are cosy and welcoming in winter, although in warmer weather you might want to be in the stone-built conservatory, outside in the courtyard, or in the spacious beer garden. Good quality, freshly made pub food is prepared to order using local produce; the standard menu, complemented by daily specials, lists submarines, toasted sandwiches and filled jacket potatoes (lunchtime only), plus grills and other hot dishes which are available throughout the day. Among the main courses are rosemary and garlic lamb steaks; home-made steak and kidney pie; fish of the day; and sweet potato and leek crumble. There's also a good choice of salads and grilled steaks. For dessert, try a home-made crumble.

Open all wk all wk 11am-11pm Bar Meals L served Mon-Sat 12-2, Sun 12-8.30 D served Mon-Thu 6-9, Fri-Sat 6-9.30, Sun 12-8.30 ⊕ FREE HOUSE ◖ Bakewell Best, Pale Rider, Golden Pippen, Scotts 1816. ♥ 13 Facilities Children's menu Garden Parking Rooms 14

## BARLOW

### The Trout at Barlow

**33 Valley Rd S18 7SL ☎ 0114 289 0893**
📄 0114 289 0893
e-mail: mikenorie@btconnect.com
dir: *From Chesterfield follow the Newbold Rd B619 for 4.5m*

This country pub, a few miles outside Chesterfield at the start of the Peak District, has recently changed hands. It is strong on food and jazz, with Jazz Club every Saturday night and Jazz Dining the first Monday of the month. There is also a quiz on a Wednesday night. A weekly-changing choice of two real ales is offered and freshly prepared, home-cooked food. All special occasions are catered for, such as weddings and parties.

Open all wk 12-3 6-11 (Sun noon-9.30) Bar Meals booking required Av main course £10.95 Restaurant L served Mon-Sat 12-2, Sun 12-4 booking required D served Mon-Sat 6-9 booking required ⊕ MARSTON'S ◖ Marston's Pedigree, Mansfield Smooth, Marston's Finest Creamy, Guest. Facilities Children's menu Garden Parking

## BARROW UPON TRENT

### Ragley Boat Stop ♥

**Deepdale Ln, Off Sinfin Ln DE73 1HH ☎ 01332 703919**
e-mail: ragley@king-henry-taverns.co.uk
dir: *Please telephone for directions*

When King Henry's Taverns bought this canalside pub, its outbuildings were in a dangerous condition, there was no sewerage, and three acres of overgrown garden sloped down to the waterside. But now it offers pub grub to satisfy the appetites of boaters hungry after hours sitting motionless at the tiller. Traditional favourites include bangers and mash; fisherman's pie; and for the truly ravenous a Mighty Man mixed grill. Pan-fried swordfish and steaks in different guises, such as fillet steak fajitas, are other tempting choices.

Open all day all wk noon-11 Bar Meals Av main course £3 food served all day Restaurant food served all day ⊕ KING HENRY TAVERNS ◖ Greene King IPA, Marstons Pedigree, Guinness. ♥ 15 Facilities Children's menu Play area Family room Garden Parking

## BIRCHOVER

### The Druid Inn ♥

**Main St DE4 2BL ☎ 01629 650302**
e-mail: thedruidinn@hotmail.co.uk
dir: *From A6 between Matlock & Bakewell take B5056 signed Ashbourne. Approx 2m left to Birchover*

This family-run free house was built in 1607, and retains its original tiled floor and real log fires. Choose between a leisurely lunch and a pint of Druid Ale in the bar and snug, or go for a more formal experience in the upper or lower restaurant. On bright, sunny days, the outside terrace presents a further option, with views over the surrounding Derbyshire countryside. The same menu is served throughout, offering a selection of light bites; classic or hot sandwiches; and full meals. Starters such as honey-roasted belly pork with hoi sin sauce, spring onion and cucumber salad herald main course dishes like penne pasta with peas, pesto and Parmesan; Druid game pie with garlic mash; and grilled pollack with tomato and grain mustard herb crust. The pub is especially popular on summer weekends, when many visitors walk up to the moors behind the inn.

Open 11-3 6-11 (Sat 11am-mdnt) Closed: Sun eve Bar Meals L served Mon-Sat 12-2.30, Sun 12-3 booking required D served Mon-Thu 6-9, Fri-Sat 6-9.30 booking required Restaurant L served Mon-Sat 12-2.30, Sun 12-3 booking required D served Mon-Thu 6-9, Fri-Sat 6-9.30 booking required ⊕ FREE HOUSE ◖ Druid Bitter, Guest ale. ♥ 12 Facilities Children's menu Garden Parking

England

## The Red Lion

**Main St DE4 2BN ☎ 01629 650363**
e-mail: matteo@frau36.fsnet.co.uk
dir: *5.5m from Matlock, off A6 onto B5056*

Druids practised their magic amidst Rowter Rocks, a 70-yard-long pile of gritstone with fine views of the wooded hillside and valley below. Originally a farmhouse, the Red Lion was built in 1680, and gained its first licence in 1722. Its old well, now glass-covered, still remains in the Tap Room. The exposed stone walls, scrubbed oak tables and quarry tiled floor add to the cosy and welcoming atmosphere. Expect reasonably priced home-cooked food made with local ingredients, with dishes ranging from a simple sandwich to a rustic Sardinian dish from co-owner Matteo's homeland.

**Open** 12-2.30 7-11.30 (Sat & BH Mons noon-mdnt) Closed: Mon in winter **Bar Meals** L served Tue-Sun 12-2 D served Tue-Sun 7-9 Av main course £8 **Restaurant** L served Tue-Sun 12-2 D served Tue-Sun 7-9 Fixed menu price fr £11.95 Av 3 course à la carte fr £8 ⊕ FREE HOUSE ◖ Boddingtons, Nine Ladies, Black Sheep, Ichinusa (Sardinian), Peakstone's Rock Brewery Bitters. **Facilities** Children's menu Dogs allowed Garden Parking

## BRADWELL

## The Old Bowling Green Inn ♟

**Smalldale S33 9JQ ☎ 01433 620450**
e-mail: dalesinns@aol.com
dir: *Off A625 onto B6049 towards Bradwell. Turn right onto Gore Lane up side of park. Through bottleneck into Smalldale. Pub 150 yds on the right*

A 16th-century coaching inn with impressive views over glorious countryside. Traditional country cooking and good value daily specials supplemented by weekly changing ales produce grilled goats' cheese with sun-dried tomatoes and caramelised onions; chicken breast in mushroom, white wine and mustard grain cream sauce; sea bass fillets on celeriac mash; and meat and potato pie. Bakewell tart and apple crumble feature among a range of tempting home-made puddings.

**Open** all day all wk **Bar Meals** L served Mon-Sat 12-2.30, Sun 12.30-4 D served Mon-Sat 6-9 Av main course £7.50 **Restaurant** L served Mon-Sat 12-2.30, Sun 12.30-4 D served Mon-Sat 6-9 ⊕ ENTERPRISE INNS ◖ Stones, Tetleys, Copper Dragon, Black Sheep, John Smiths. ♟ 6 **Facilities** Children's menu Garden Parking

## BRASSINGTON

## Ye Olde Gate Inne

**Well St DE4 4HJ ☎ 01629 540448 ▤ 01629 540448**
e-mail: theoldgateinn@supanet.com
dir: *2m from Carsington Water off A5023 between Wirksworth & Ashbourne*

Built in 1616 out of local stone and timbers allegedly salvaged from the wrecked Armada fleet, this venerable inn stands beside an old London to Manchester turnpike in the heart of Brassington, a hill village on the southern edge of the Peak District. Oak beams, black cast iron log burner, an antique clock, charmingly worn quarry-tiled floors and a delightful mishmash of polished furniture give the inn plenty of character. Hand-pumped Marston's Pedigree Bitter takes pride of place behind the bar, alongside guest ales such as Jennings Cumberland. The menu offers firm lunchtime favourites, such as home-roasted ham, egg and home-made chips; and Cumberland sausages with creamed mash and onion gravy. In the evening, start with crevettes cooked in garlic butter and choose from the likes of roast pheasant breast wrapped in bacon with a port sauce, or pan-fried fillet of beef served with an oxtail broth.

**Open** Closed: Mon (ex BH), Tue L **Bar Meals** L served Wed-Sat 12-2, Sun 12-2.30 D served Tue-Sat 6.30-8.45 Av main course £9 ⊕ MARSTON'S ◖ Marston's Pedigree, Jennings Cumberland, guest ales. **Facilities** Children's menu Family room Dogs allowed Garden Parking

## CASTLETON

## Ye Olde Nag's Head

**Cross St S33 8WH ☎ 01433 620248 & 620443**
**▤ 01433 621501**
e-mail: info@yeoldenagshead.co.uk
web: www.yeoldenagshead.co.uk
dir: *A625 from Sheffield, W through Hope Valley, through Hathersage & Hope. Pub on main road*

A grey-stone, traditional 17th-century inn situated in the heart of the Peak District National Park, close to Chatsworth House, Haddon Hall and miles of wonderful walks. Walkers are welcome to seek refreshment in the cosy bars, warmed by open fires and kitted out with antiques, and where you'll find three ales on handpump and a good choice of pub food, including the all-day giant Derbyshire breakfast, sausages and mash, liver and onions and steak and ale pie.

**Open** all day all wk **Bar Meals** food served all day **Restaurant** food served all day ⊕ FREE HOUSE ◖ Black Sheep, Guinness. **Facilities** Children's menu Dogs allowed Parking

## CHESTERFIELD

### Red Lion Pub & Bistro ⚑

**Darley Rd, Stone Edge S45 0LW ☎ 01246 566142**
🖳 **01246 591040**
e-mail: ewen@redlionpubandbistro.com
dir: *Telephone for directions*

Located on the edge of the Peak District, the Red Lion is rumoured to stand at the very centre of Great Britain. Despite its wooden beams and stone walls, this stylish free house is an effortless blend of old and new, with discreet lighting and comfy leather armchairs. Ian Daisley's striking black and white photographs decorate the walls, whilst local jazz bands liven up the bar on Thursdays evenings. Home-grown salads and fresh, seasonal produce feature on the menus, and the chefs make everything from chutneys to black pudding. Meals are served in the bar and bistro, or beneath white umbrellas in the large garden.

Open all day all wk **Bar Meals** Av main course £16 food served all day **Restaurant** Av 3 course à la carte fr £35 food served all day ⊕ FREE HOUSE ◖ Timothy Taylor Landlord. ⚑ 8 **Facilities** Children's menu Garden Parking

## FENNY BENTLEY

### Bentley Brook Inn ★★★ INN ⚑

**DE6 1LF ☎ 01335 350278 🖳 01335 350422**
e-mail: all@bentleybrookinn.co.uk
web: www.bentleybrookinn.co.uk

Completely refurbished but still full of traditional charm and atmosphere, this lovely building began life as a medieval farmhouse made from wattle and daub. The house became a restaurant in 1954, and a full drinks licence was granted in the 1970s. Both the bar and the restaurant, which overlooks the terrace and garden, serve everything from sandwiches to substantial home-cooked dishes. Lunch might include black pudding and bacon tartlet with mustard sauce, followed by chicken breast in a pesto sauce served on a bed of tagliatelle. The menus are changed with the seasons and in response to the usually plentiful supply of local game. Home-made desserts include sticky toffee pudding with butterscotch sauce and ice cream. Traditional English Sunday lunch is served as a three-course, three-roast carvery, and during the summer the barbecue in the garden is fired up. In the winter, snuggle up by the central open log fire and play dominoes, cards or chess.

Open all day all wk **Bar Meals** L served all wk 12-9 (Oct-Mar 12-3) booking required D served all wk 12-9 (Oct-Mar 6-9) booking required **Restaurant** L served all wk 12-9 (Oct-Mar 12-3) booking required D served all wk 12-9 (Oct-Mar 6-9) booking required ◖ Leatherbritches Bespoke, Leatherbritches Hairy Helmet, Goldings, Marstons Pedigree. ⚑ 7 **Facilities** Children's menu Play area Dogs allowed Garden Parking **Rooms** 11

## FROGGATT

### The Chequers Inn ★★★★ INN ◎ ⚑

**Froggatt Edge S32 3ZJ ☎ 01433 630231**
🖳 **01433 631072**
e-mail: info@chequers-froggatt.com
dir: *On A625, 0.5m N of Calver*

Originally four stone-built 18th-century cottages, the Chequers stands above Calver on the steep banks of Froggatt Edge; its westward panorama of the Peak District National Park reached by a steep, wild woodland footpath from the elevated secret garden. The civilised interior of wooden floors, Windsor chairs, antique furnishings, blazing log fires is perfect for a contemplative pint of Kelham Island Easy Rider or your choice from an innovative modern European menu (with some British favourites). The food is prepared from locally sourced produce, ranging from sandwiches and salads through to starters as varied as grilled sardines with caper oil, and pork belly with saffron and red pepper potatoes. Mains take in smoked haddock and parsley fishcake; roast duck breast with pumpkin mash; and pan-fried calves' liver with mash, pancetta and fruit chutney. Finish with Bakewell pudding and custard.

Open all wk 12-2 6-9.30 (Sat 12-9.30, Sun 12-9) Closed: 25 Dec **Bar Meals** L served Mon-Fri 12-2, Sat-Sun 12-6 D served Mon-Sat 6-9.30, Sun 6-9 Av main course £15 ⊕ FREE HOUSE ◖ Greene King IPA, Black Sheep, Kelham Island Easy Rider. ⚑ 9 **Facilities** Children's menu Garden Parking **Rooms** 5

## HARTSHORNE

### The Mill Wheel ★★★★ INN ⚑

**Ticknall Rd DE11 7AS ☎ 01283 550335 🖳 01283 552833**
e-mail: info@themillwheel.co.uk
dir: *A511 from Burton-on-Trent towards Leicester. Left at island signed A514/Derby. Pub a short distance*

This old building's huge mill wheel has survived for some 250 years. In 1945 a dispute over water rights cut off the supply and the site became derelict. Since being restored in 1987, the wheel has been slowly turning once again, and is very much the focus of attention in the bar and restaurant. Here dishes such as pan-fried Cornish mackerel with tapenade bruschetta are served, followed perhaps by roast loin of lamb with dauphinoise potatoes.

Open all wk **Bar Meals** food served all day **Restaurant** L served 12-2.30 (Sun 12-8.30) D served 6-9.15 Mon-Thu (6-9.30 Fri-Sat, 12-8.30 Sun) ⊕ FREE HOUSE ◖ Abbot Ale, Oakham Ale, Summer Lightning, Bass, Pedigree. ⚑ 8 **Facilities** Children's menu Garden Parking **Rooms** 4

## HATHERSAGE

### Millstone Inn ★★★★ INN ♟

**Sheffield Rd S32 1DA** ☎ **01433 650258** 🖨 **01433 650276**
e-mail: jerry@millstone.co.uk
dir: *Telephone for directions*

Striking views over the picturesque Hope Valley are afforded from this former coaching inn, set amid the beauty of the Peak District yet convenient for the city of Sheffield. The atmospheric bar serves six traditional cask ales all year round and the menu offers a good choice of dishes prepared from local produce, including a popular Sunday carvery of freshly roasted joints.

**Open** all day all wk 11.30am-11pm **Bar Meals** L served all wk 12-9 booking required Av main course £9 food served all day ⊕ FREE HOUSE ◀ Timothy Taylor Landlord, Black Sheep, guest ales. ♟ 16 **Facilities** Children's menu Dogs allowed Garden Parking **Rooms** 8

### The Scotsmans Pack Country Inn ★★★★ INN ♟

**School Ln S32 1BZ** ☎ **01433 650253** 🖨 **01433 650712**
web: www.scotsmanspack.com
dir: *Hathersage is on A625 8m from Sheffield*

This historic inn in the beautiful Hope Valley is located on one of the old packhorse trails used by Scottish 'packmen' or travelling drapers. Just a short walk away from Hathersage church and Little John's Grave, the inn is ideally placed for walking and touring the Peak District. Hearty pub dishes include braised steak in red wine sauce, home-made lasagne and salad, and lamb's liver and bacon with onion gravy.

**Open** all day all wk 11-3 6-mdnt (all day Fri-Sun) **Bar Meals** L served Mon-Fri 12-2 booking required D served Mon-Fri 6-9, Sat-Sun 12-9 booking required ⊕ MARSTONS PLC ◀ Jennings Cumberland, Pedigree, Mansfield Bitter. ♟ 7 **Facilities** Children's menu Family room Garden Parking **Rooms** 5

## MELBOURNE

### The Melbourne Arms ★★★ INN ♟

**92 Ashby Rd DE73 8ES**
☎ **01332 864949** & **863990** 🖨 **01332 865525**
e-mail: info@melbournearms.co.uk

This restaurant on the village outskirts was tastefully converted from an 18th-century pub over 10 years ago. There are two bars, a coffee lounge and the restaurant itself, where an extensive menu of authentic Indian dishes is offered. With a range of English dishes and a children's menu too, there's no reason why the whole family can't find plenty to enjoy.

**Open** all day all wk 11.30am-11.30pm **Bar Meals** Av main course £6.99 food served all day **Restaurant** Fixed menu price fr £12.99 Av 3 course à la carte fr £19 food served all day ⊕ FREE HOUSE ◀ Pedigree, Tetley's Smooth, Guinness. ♟ 12 **Facilities** Children's menu Play area Family room Garden Parking **Rooms** 7

## MILLTOWN

### The Nettle Inn ♟

**S45 0ES** ☎ **01246 590462**

A 16th-century hostelry on the edge of the Peak District, this inn has all the traditional charm you could wish for, from flower-filled hanging baskets to log fires and a stone-flagged taproom floor. Expect well-kept ales and impressive home-made food (including breads, pickles and sauces), using the best of seasonal, local produce. Typical dishes are locally made chorizo with pancetta, quail egg and salad; and pollack with broad bean and mint risotto and breaded deep-fried tripe.

**Open** all wk Sat-Sun all day **Bar Meals** Av main course £6.75 food served all day **Restaurant** Av 3 course à la carte fr £25 food served all day ⊕ FREE HOUSE ◀ Bradfield Farmers Best Bitter, Bradfield Farmers Blonde, Hardy & Hansons, Olde Trip, Bradfield Belgian Blue, Bradfield Farmers Brown Cow. ♟ 9 **Facilities** Children's menu Dogs allowed Garden Parking

## RIPLEY

### The Moss Cottage Hotel

**Nottingham Rd DE5 3JT** ☎ **01773 742555**
e-mail: doug-ashley@hotmail.co.uk
dir: *Telephone for directions*

This red-brick free house specialises in carvery dishes, with four roast joints each day. Expect popular menu choices like prawn cocktail or mushroom dippers; ham, egg and chips; liver and onions; or battered haddock. Hot puddings include rhubarb crumble and chocolate fudge cake.

**Open** 12-3 5-11 (Sun 5-8) Closed: Sun eve Mon L **Bar Meals** L served Tue-Sun 12-2 D served Mon-Sat 6-8 Av main course £8 **Restaurant** L served Tue-Sun 12-2 D served Mon-Sat 6-8 ⊕ FREE HOUSE ◀ Old Tripp, Guinness, Guest ale ♻ Old Rosie Scrumpy. **Facilities** Children's menu Parking

## SHARDLOW

# The Old Crown Inn

**Cavendish Bridge DE72 2HL ☎ 01332 792392**
e-mail: the.oldcrowninn@btconnect.com
dir: *M1 junct 24 take A6 towards Derby. Left before river, bridge into Shardlow*

A family-friendly pub on the south side of the River Trent, where up to seven guest ales are served. It was built as a coaching inn during the 17th century, and retains its warm and atmospheric interior. Several hundred water jugs hang from the ceilings, while the walls display an abundance of brewery and railway memorabilia. Traditional food is lovingly prepared by the landlady, including sandwiches, jackets, omelettes, ham and eggs, and Cumberland sausages.

Open all day all wk 11am-mdnt (Fri-Sat 11am-1am) **Bar Meals** L served Mon-Fri 12-2, Sat 12-8, Sun 12-3 D served Mon-Fri 5-8, Sat 12-8 Av main course £6.50 **Restaurant** L served Mon-Fri 12-2, Sat 12-8, Sun 12-3 D served Mon-Fri 5-8, Sat 12-8 Fixed menu price fr £9.25 (Sun L only) ⊕ MARSTONS ◖ Marston's Pedigree, Jennings Cocker Hoop, Guest ales. **Facilities** Children's menu Play area Dogs allowed Garden Parking

# DEVON

## ASHBURTON

# The Rising Sun ★★★★ INN ♐

**Woodland TQ13 7JT ☎ 01364 652544**
e-mail: admin@therisingsunwoodland.co.uk
dir: *From A38 E of Ashburton take lane signed Woodland/Denbury. Pub on left, approx 1.5m*

A former drovers' inn, largely rebuilt following a fire in 1989, The Rising Sun is set in beautiful Devon countryside, convenient for Exeter, Plymouth and Torbay. Owner Paul is the chef and is dedicated to using local and seasonal produce on his menus. There's a good choice of fish from Brixham – baked Brixham sea bass - and excellent West Country cheeses; children's menu too. As well as dishes like roasted rack of Woodland lamb or belly of Tamworth pork, the pub is also well known for its home-made pies (available to take home).

Open all wk noon-3 6-11 (Sun noon-3 6.30-11, all day mid Jul-mid Sep) Closed: 25 Dec **Bar Meals** Av main course £8.50 food served all day **Restaurant** Av 3 course à la carte fr £17 food served all day ⊕ FREE HOUSE ◖ Princetown Jail Ale, IPA, Teignworthy Reel Ale, guest ales Ò Thatchers. ♐ 10 **Facilities** Children's menu Play area Family room Dogs allowed Garden Parking **Rooms** 5

## AVONWICK

# The Avon Inn ♐

**TQ10 9NB ☎ 01364 73475**
e-mail: dfreresmith@yahoo.co.uk
dir: *Telephone for directions*

There's a change of ownership at this handsome whitewashed free house, just off the busy Exeter to Plymouth trunk road. The focus is on great home-cooked food using fresh local produce, with fruit and vegetables from the owners own allotment. Warm and cosy in winter, the large beer garden is perfect for the warmer weather with its three areas – lawn and flowers, new family area and a secluded section that goes down to the river Avon. Look out for barbecues at weekends.

Open all day all wk 10.30am-11.30pm (Sun 10.30am-11pm) **Bar Meals** Av main course £7 food served all day **Restaurant** Av 3 course à la carte fr £20 food served all day ⊕ FREE HOUSE ◖ Otter Bitter, Otter Bright, Blackawton 44 Special, Guinness Ò Thatchers Gold. ♐ 6 **Facilities** Children's menu Play area Dogs allowed Garden Parking

## AXMOUTH

# The Harbour Inn

**Church St EX12 4AF ☎ 01297 20371**
e-mail: theharbourinn@live.co.uk
dir: *Main street opposite church, 1m from Seaton*

The River Axe meanders through its valley into Lyme Bay, but just before they meet is Axmouth harbour, which accounted for one sixth of Devon's trade during the 16th century. This cosy, oak-beamed, harbourside inn was built four centuries earlier, however. Gary and Graciela Tubb have maintained three principles - local ingredients bought from small family businesses, nothing frozen, and everything home made. A bar and bistro menu offers scampi and chips, lasagne, sausages or faggots with mash and gravy, jacket potatoes, baguettes and sandwiches. From a daily updated blackboard menu, you might want to consider pork tenderloin with prunes and bacon; swordfish steak with niçoise salad; or tagliatelle, wild mushrooms and spicy tomato sauce. The Harbour makes a great stop if you are walking the South West Coast Path between Lyme Regis and Seaton.

Open all wk **Bar Meals** L served 12-2 D served 6.30-9 (Sun 7-9) **Restaurant** L served 12-2 D served 6.30-9 (Sun 7-9) ⊕ HALL & WOODHOUSE ◖ Badger 1st Gold, Tanglefoot, Sussex Ò Stowford Press, Applewood. **Facilities** Children's menu Play area Dogs allowed Garden Parking

## The Ship Inn ♥

**EX12 4AF ☎ 01297 21838**

dir: *1m S of A3052 between Lyme & Sidmouth. Signed to Seaton at Boshill Cross*

There are long views over the Axe estuary from the beer garden of this creeper-clad family-run inn. It was built soon after the original Ship burnt down on Christmas Day 1879, and is able to trace its landlords back to 1769; the current ones have been there for over 40 years. Well kept real ales complement an extensive menu including daily blackboard specials where local fish and game feature, cooked with home-grown herbs.

**Open** all day all wk 11am-11pm **Bar Meals** L served all wk 12-2.30 booking required D served all wk 6-9 booking required **Restaurant** L served all wk 12-2.30 booking required D served all wk 6-9 booking required ⊕ PUNCH TAVERNS ◼ Otter Bitter, Guinness, 6X ♻ Stowford Press. ♥ 10 **Facilities** Children's menu Play area Family room Dogs allowed Garden Parking

## BARBROOK

## The Beggars Roost

**EX35 6LD ☎ 01598 752404**

e-mail: info@beggarsroost.co.uk
dir: *A39, 1m from Lynton*

Originally a manor farmhouse with attached cow barn, the buildings were converted into a hotel in the 1970s with the barn becoming the Beggars Roost. The long, low bar has tables around a warm log-burner; the restaurant on the floor above extends up into the beamed apex and is popular for parties. The pub menu offers a great range of reasonably priced favourites such as casseroles, terrines and ploughman's, while the restaurant focuses on more sophisticated fare.

**Open** noon-2.30 6-close Closed: Mon (Nov-Feb) **Bar Meals** L served all wk 12-2.30 D served all wk 6-9 **Restaurant** L served all wk 12-2.30 D served all wk 6-9 ⊕ FREE HOUSE ◼ Exmoor Ale, Cotleigh Barn Owl, Exmoor Silver Stallion, Cotleigh Tawny ♻ Thatchers. **Facilities** Children's menu Dogs allowed Garden Parking

## BEER

## Anchor Inn ♥

**Fore St EX12 3ET ☎ 01297 20386 ▤ 01297 24474**

e-mail: 6403@greeneking.co.uk
dir: *A3052 towards Lyme Regis. At Hangmans Stone take B3174 into Beer. Pub on seafront*

Fish caught by local boats feature strongly on the menu at this pretty colour-washed hotel, which overlooks the sea in the picture-perfect Devon village of Beer. Dine on beer-battered cod and chips; local crab with salad; smoked haddock on Cheddar cheese mash with a mustard cream sauce; or chicken breast stuffed with brie, wrapped in bacon and served with a cranberry and red wine sauce.

**Open** all day all wk 8am-11pm **Bar Meals** L served Mon-Fri 11-2.30, Sat-Sun 11-4 D served Sun-Thu 6-9, Fri-Sat 6-9.30 **Restaurant** L served Mon-Fri 12-2.30, Sat-Sun 12-3 D served Sun-Thu 6-9, Fri-Sat 6-9.30 ⊕ GREENE KING ◼ Otter Ale, Greene King IPA, Abbot Ale. ♥ 14 **Facilities** Children's menu Garden

## BICKLEIGH

## Fisherman's Cot ♥

**EX16 8RW ☎ 01884 855237 ▤ 01884 855241**

e-mail: fishermanscot.bickleigh@marstons.co.uk
dir: *Telephone for directions*

Well-appointed thatched inn by Bickleigh Bridge over the River Exe with food all day and large beer garden, just a short drive from Tiverton and Exmoor. The Waterside Bar is the place for snacks and afternoon tea, while the restaurant incorporates a carvery and à la carte menus. Sunday lunch is served, and champagne and smoked salmon breakfast is optional.

**Open** all day all wk 11am-11pm (Sun noon-10.30pm) **Bar Meals** L served all wk 12-9 booking required D served all wk 12-9 booking required food served all day **Restaurant** L served all wk 12-9 booking required D served all wk 12-9 booking required food served all day ⊕ ELDRIDGE POPE ♥ 8 **Facilities** Children's menu Garden Parking

## BRAMPFORD SPEKE

## The Lazy Toad Inn ♥

**EX5 5DP ☎ 01392 841591 ▤ 01392 841591**

e-mail: thelazytoadinn@btinternet.com
dir: *From Exeter take A377 towards Crediton 1.5m, right signed Brampford Speke*

Substantial renovation at this Grade II listed 19th-century free house has created a series of cosy, beamed rooms in which to enjoy good food, real ales and traditional ciders. Winter fires and a new walled beer garden mark the passage of the seasons, whilst home-grown herbs complement meat and fish cured in the pub's own smokery. Menu choices might include steamed port and pigeon pudding; or Gloucester Old Spot sausages with bubble and squeak.

**Open** 11.30-2.30 6-11 (Sun 12-3) Closed: 2 wks Jan, Sun eve & Mon **Bar Meals** L served Tue-Sun 12-2 booking required D served Tue-Sat 6-9 booking required Av main course £11.50 **Restaurant** Av 3 course à la carte fr £24 ⊕ FREE HOUSE ◼ St Austell Tribute, Exmoor Fox, Otter Ale & Bitter, Exe Valley Exeter Old ♻ Sandford Devon Red, Traditional Farmhouse, Old Kirton. ♥ 12 **Facilities** Children's menu Family room Dogs allowed Garden Parking

## BRANSCOMBE

### The Masons Arms ★★ HL 🏵 🍷

**EX12 3DJ** ☎ **01297 680300** 📠 **01297 680500**

e-mail: reception@masonsarms.co.uk

dir: *Turn off A3052 towards Branscombe, down hill, hotel at bottom of hill*

The creeper-clad Masons Arms dates back to 1360, when it was just a simple cider house measuring a mere 8ft x 4ft, squeezed into the middle of a row of cottages. Today that row of cottages is an independent, family-run pub and hotel. Once the haunt of smugglers, the Masons Arms has a bar that can hardly have changed in 200 years, with stone walls, ancient ships' beams, slate floors, and a splendid open fireplace used for spit-roasts, including Sunday lunchtimes. Food is a serious business here and the restaurant maintains a standard of cooking worthy of its AA Rosette. Where possible all ingredients are grown, reared or caught locally, including the lobster and crab landed on nearby Branscombe beach.

**Open** all wk Mon-Fri 11-3 6-11 (Sat 11-11 Sun 12-10.30) **Bar Meals** L served Mon-Fri 12-2, Sat-Sun 12-2.15 booking required D served all wk 7-9 booking required Av main course £12 **Restaurant** D served all wk 7-9 booking required Fixed menu price fr £29.95 🍺 FREE HOUSE ◀ Otter Ale, Masons Ale, Tribute, Branoc, guest ales. 🍷 14 **Facilities** Children's menu Dogs allowed Garden Parking **Rooms** 21

## BRENDON

### Rockford Inn

**EX35 6PT** ☎ **01598 741214**

e-mail: enquiries@therockfordinn.com

dir: *A39 through Minehead follow signs to Lynmouth. Turn left off A39 to Brendon approx 5m before Lynmouth*

Standing on the water's edge overlooking the River Lyn, this 17th-century free house is popular with fisherman (permits available in the pub) and handy for several walking routes. There's a choice of good home-made pub meals with an international twist. Eat in the garden in fine weather, or come indoors to the open fire and wood burning stoves when the nights draw in.

**Open** noon-11 (Mon 6-11) Closed: Mon L **Bar Meals** L served Tue-Sun 12-4 D served all wk 6-9 **Restaurant** L served Tue-Sun 12-4 D served all wk 6-9 booking required 🍺 FREE HOUSE ◀ Barn Owl, Tribute, Cotleigh 25, Exmoor, Cavalier ♂ Thatchers. **Facilities** Children's menu Dogs allowed Garden Parking

## CHARDSTOCK

### The George Inn

**EX13 7BX** ☎ **01460 220241**

e-mail: info@george-inn.co.uk

dir: *A358 from Taunton through Chard towards Axminster, left at Tytherleigh. Signed from A358*

Graffiti from 1648 can be seen in the snug of this 700-year-old pub, which was once a parish house. A friendly parson named Copeland haunts the cellar, while cheerful locals who've been drinking in the George for the past 40 years preside over 'Compost Corner'. Hearty dishes include feta, spinach and mozzarella pie; pan-fried lambs' liver or beer battered cod.

**Open** all wk **Bar Meals** L served all wk 12-2 D served all wk 6.30-9.30 Av main course £9 **Restaurant** L served all wk 12-2 D served all wk 6.30-9.30 Av 3 course à la carte fr £15 🍺 FREE HOUSE ◀ Ruddles County Bitter, Branoc, guest ale ♂ Stowford Press. **Facilities** Children's menu Dogs allowed Garden Parking

## CHERITON BISHOP

### The Old Thatch Inn 🍷

**EX6 6HJ** ☎ **01647 24204**

e-mail: mail@theoldthatchinn.f9.co.uk

dir: *0.5m off A30, 7m SW of Exeter*

This charming 16th-century free house sits within the Dartmoor National Park, just half a mile off the main A30. It's a popular halfway house for travellers, and once welcomed stagecoaches on the London to Penzance road. For a time during the inn passed into private hands and became a tea room, before its licence was renewed in the early 1970s. All food is prepared using fresh ingredients from the southwest, with seafood featuring strongly. Dishes change every day depending on supplies; examples include grilled whole sardines with garlic herb butter. Look out for the speciality pumpkin and sunflower seed mini loaf sandwich filled with a variety of choices such as Somerset brie, smoked chicken and redcurrant sauce.

**Open** all wk 11.30-3 6-11 Closed: 25-26 Dec, Sun eve **Bar Meals** L served all wk 12-2.30 D served Mon-Sat 6.30-9 Av main course £12 **Restaurant** L served all wk 12-2.30 D served Mon-Sat 6.30-9 Av 3 course à la carte fr £22.50 🍺 FREE HOUSE ◀ Otter Ale, Port Stout, O'Hanlon's Royal Oak, Skinners Betty Stogs, Yellowhammer ♂ Thatchers Scrumpy Jack. 🍷 9 **Facilities** Children's menu Family room Dogs allowed Garden Parking

## CLAYHIDON

# The Merry Harriers ♥

**Forches Corner EX15 3TR ☎ 01823 421270**
📄 01823 421270
e-mail: peter.gatling@btinternet.com
dir: *Wellington A38, turn onto Ford Street (marked by brown tourist sign). At top of hill turn left, 1.5m on right*

The Merry Harriers is a 15th-century inn that stands high on the Blackdown Hills, with plenty of space for a large beer garden and a five-lane skittle alley, one of the longest in the county. Inside the characterful bar are beamed ceilings, a cosy inglenook and attractive dining areas. More than 90 per cent of kitchen ingredients are from the surrounding hills, or further afield in the West Country. The regularly changing menus offer a wide choice, including Somerset pork chop with apple sauce; pan-fried Somerset lamb's liver and bacon; grilled fillets of Combe St Nicholas rainbow trout; smoked North Petherton duck breast served on a mixed leaf and pomegranate salad; or West Country chicken korma. Children can select from a menu that contains kiddie curry, mad cow (steak and kidney) pie, and whizzers (organic pork and apple sausages) and chips.

**Open** noon-3 6.30-11 Closed: Sun eve & Mon **Bar Meals** L served Tue-Sat 12-2, Sun 12-2.15 booking required D served Tue-Sat 6.30-9 booking required Av main course £9 food served all day **Restaurant** L served Tue-Sat 12-2, Sun 12-2.15 booking required D served Tue-Sat 6.30-9 booking required food served all day ⊕ FREE HOUSE ◀ Otter Head, Cotleigh Harrier, Exmoor Gold, St Austell Tinners Ö Thatchers Gold. ♥ 14 **Facilities** Children's menu Play area Family room Dogs allowed Garden Parking

## COLEFORD

# The New Inn ★★★★ INN ♥

**EX17 5BZ ☎ 01363 84242** 📄 01363 85044
e-mail: enquiries@thenewinncoleford.co.uk
dir: *From Exeter take A377, 1.5m after Crediton turn left for Coleford, continue for 1.5m*

A pretty, 13th-century cob and thatch inn set in a sleepy conservation village, deep in the heart of unspoilt countryside. 'Captain', the chatty resident parrot, welcomes folk into the rambling interior - the ancient, slate-floored bar features old carved chests, polished brass and roaring log fires, and blends effortlessly with the dining room extension: warm red carpets, fresh white walls, original oak beams, simple wooden furniture and cushioned settles, antique prints and assorted

bric-a-brac. Bar food is reliable and home cooked, relying on fresh local ingredients: Brixham fish, Devon cheeses and produce sourced from surrounding farms and villages. The menu takes in lunchtime sandwiches and ploughman's platters to posh bangers and mash. For something more substantial, tuck into venison and red wine pie, fruity lamb tagine,or whole plaice with herb butter. Leave room for an indulgent pudding, perhaps a selection of local farm-made ice creams, or a plate of West Country cheeses. Make the most of the idyllic, willow-fringed riverside garden, perfect for summer alfresco dining and the summer hog roasts.

**Open** all wk 12-3 6-11 (Sun 7-10.30 winter) Closed: 25-26 Dec **Bar Meals** L served all wk 12-2 D served all wk 7-9.30 Av main course £7.50 **Restaurant** L served all wk 12-2 D served all wk 7-9.30 Av 3 course à la carte fr £20 ⊕ FREE HOUSE ◀ Doom Bar, Otter Ale, Exmoor Ale, Spitfire, Rev James Ö Thatchers, Winkleigh Sam's. ♥ 10 **Facilities** Children's menu Dogs allowed Garden Parking **Rooms** 6

## COLYFORD

# The Wheelwright Inn ♥

**Swanhill Rd EX24 6QQ ☎ 01297 552585**
dir: *Please telephone for directions*

This pretty thatched inn has earned a reputation for outstanding food and service since Gary and Toni Valentine took over in 2007. The 17th-century pub has undergone substantial refurbishment, but the low beams, wooden floors and log fire ensure that it retains its authentic country feel. Expect a varied contemporary menu, including well-filled sandwiches on locally baked bread; local pork cutlet with creamy potato and swede mash; and moules marinière with crusty bread.

**Open** all day all wk **Bar Meals** food served all day **Restaurant** food served all day ⊕ HALL & WOODHOUSE ◀ Badger First Gold, Tanglefoot, Hopping Hare, Guinness Ö Stowford Press. ♥ 8 **Facilities** Children's menu Family room Dogs allowed Garden Parking

## CORNWORTHY

### Hunters Lodge Inn ♊

**TQ9 7ES ☎ 01803 732204**
dir: *Off A381, S of Totnes*

Built in 1740, this country local is at the hub of village life, sponsoring a football team, charity events and a dog show (it's a dog friendly pub). There's even a Christmas party for children. Other notable features are the real log fire and resident ghost. An extensive menu offers dishes from the sea (sesame battered Brixham cod fillet), and from the land (gammon steak, Cornworthy hens' eggs) as well as a selection of pasta dishes (spaghetti carbonara).

**Open** all wk 11.30am-2.30 6.30-close (Closed Mon L) **Bar Meals** L served Tue-Sun 11.30-2 booking required D served all wk 6.30-9 booking required **Restaurant** L served Tue-Sun 11.30-2 booking required D served all wk 6.30-9 booking required ⊕ FREE HOUSE ◀ Teignworthy Reel Ale, Sharp's Doom bar, Guest ales. ♊ 14 **Facilities** Children's menu Play area Dogs allowed Garden Parking

## CULMSTOCK

### Culm Valley Inn ♊

**EX15 3JJ ☎ 01884 840354 ▤ 01884 841659**
e-mail: culmvalleyinn@btinternet.com
dir: *2m from A38, 3m from Wellington*

A former station hotel in which the owners exposed a long-hidden bar during renovations. The ever-changing blackboard menu displays a lengthy list of home-made dishes, mostly using locally-grown or raised ingredients, including chicken breast with a cider brandy sauce. Fish and shellfish mostly from South Devon or Cornwall, including shellfish platters and Portuguese fish stew.

**Open** all wk noon-3 7-11pm (Fri-Sat noon-11pm Sun noon-10.30pm Open all day in summer) Closed: 25 Dec eve **Bar Meals** L served all wk 12-2 D served Mon-Sat 7-9 **Restaurant** L served all wk 12-2 D served Mon-Sat 7-9 ⊕ FREE HOUSE ◀ O'Hanlons Firefly, Branscombe Branoc. ♊ 50 **Facilities** Children's menu Dogs allowed Garden Parking

## DARTMOUTH

### Royal Castle Hotel ★★★ HL ♊

**11 The Quay TQ6 9PS ☎ 01803 833033 ▤ 01803 835445**
e-mail: becca@royalcastle.co.uk
dir: *In town centre, overlooking inner harbour*

Dating in part from the 1630s, and originally two neighbouring quayside houses, one of which became The New Inn; by 1782 it had been combined with its neighbour to become The Castle Inn. Further rebuilds incorporated the battlemented turrets and cornice that gave it an appearance worthy of its name. The Nu restaurant occupies a large first floor room with and river views, and bar food is served in both the Galleon and Harbour Bars. In the former you can have your meat roasted

on the Lydstone Range, forged in Dartmouth over 300 years ago. Dishes range from trio of local pork sausages, to catch of the day on the specials board and river Exe mussels steamed in creamy white wine and garlic. Spiral staircases and priest holes are other intriguing features, along with many fine antiques.

**Open** all day all wk 8am-11.30pm **Bar Meals** Av main course £9.95 food served all day **Restaurant** L served all wk 12-2 D served all wk 6-9 Fixed menu price fr £12.50 Av 3 course à la carte fr £25 ⊕ FREE HOUSE ◀ Jail Ale, Bays Gold, Doom Bar ⚬ Thatchers Gold. ♊ 24 **Facilities** Children's menu Family room Dogs allowed Parking **Rooms** 25

## DENBURY

### The Union Inn ♊

**Denbury Green TQ12 6DQ ☎ 01803 812595 ▤ 01803 814206**
e-mail: unioninn@hotmail.co.uk
dir: *2m form Newton Abbot, signed Denbury*

The Union Inn is at least 400 years old and counting. Inside are the original stone walls that once rang to the hammers of the blacksmiths and cartwrights who worked here many moons ago. Choose freshly prepared, mouth-watering starters such as moules marinière or smoked chicken in mango vinaigrette, and follow with slow-roasted shoulder of lamb with mint garlic and redcurrant jelly, or a rib-eye steak on a bed of haggis with stilton and whisky sauce.

**Open** all wk noon-3 6-11.30 (Fri-Sat noon-mdnt) **Bar Meals** L served all wk 12-2 D served all wk 6-9 **Restaurant** L served all wk 12-2 D served all wk 6-9 ⊕ ENTERPRISE INNS ◀ Otter, London Pride, guest ale. ♊ 9 **Facilities** Children's menu Dogs allowed Garden Parking

## EXETER

### The Twisted Oak ♊

**Little John's Cross Hill EX2 9RG ☎ 01392 273666**
e-mail: info@twistedoakpub.com
dir: *A30 to Okehampton, follow signs for pub*

Set in a beautiful part of Ide just outside Exeter, this large pub has been turned into a quality, food-driven venue in the last few years. There is a choice of dining areas - an informal place where you can relax on the leather sofas and eat; a separate lounge bar restaurant; and a more formal conservatory area, which is adult only in the evenings. During the summer months the huge garden provides seating and a children's play area.

Open all wk 11am-3 5-11pm (Fri-Sun 11am-mdnt) **Bar Meals** L served Mon-Thu 12-2.30, Fri-Sun all day D served Mon-Thu 6-9, Fri-Sun all day **Restaurant** L served Mon-Thu 12-2.30, Fri-Sun all day D served Mon-Thu 6-9, Fri-Sun all day ◀ Sharp's Doom Bar, Exmoor Ale. ♀ 7 **Facilities** Children's menu Play area Family room Dogs allowed Garden Parking

---

## EXTON

### The Puffing Billy ♀

**Station Rd EX3 0PR** ☎ **01392 877888** 📄 **01392 876232**
dir: *A376 signed Exmouth, through Ebford. Follow signs for Puffing Billy, turn right into Exton*

Named for its proximity to the Exeter-Exmouth branch line, the 16th-century Puffing Billy enjoys views of the Exe estuary. Enjoy mackerel rillette with marinated aubergine, pink fir potato and tapenade salad; caramelised scallops with truffled baby leek terrine; confit duck leg and fennel risotto; twice-baked Cornish Blue soufflé with walnuts and French bean salad; slow honey-roasted pork belly with creamed potato and pine nut salad; and Crediton duckling with fondant potato, turnip, apples and fig jus. Rhubarb crumble soufflé with ginger ice cream is a typical dessert.

Open all wk noon-3 6-11 Closed: selected days over Xmas **Bar Meals** L served Mon-Sat 12-2 Av main course £11.50 **Restaurant** L served Mon-Sat 12-2 (Sun 12-2.30) booking required D served Mon-Sat 6.30-9.30 (Sun 6-9) booking required Av 3 course à la carte fr £22 ⊕ FREE HOUSE ◀ Otter, Bays. ♀ 12 **Facilities** Children's menu Garden Parking

---

## HARBERTON

### The Church House Inn ♀

**TQ9 7SF** ☎ **01803 863707**
dir: *From Totnes take A381 S. Turn right for Harberton, pub by church in village centre*

Built to house masons working on the church next door (around 1100), the inn has some fascinating historic features, including a Tudor window frame and latticed window with 13th-century glass; there's even a resident ghost. The extensive menu is supplemented by daily specials and a traditional roast on Sundays. There's plenty of seafood/fish, and a family room is provided.

Open all wk noon-3 6-11pm **Bar Meals** L served all wk 12-2 D served all wk 6.30-9 **Restaurant** L served all wk 12-2 D served all wk 6.30-9 ⊕ FREE HOUSE ◀ Skinners, Dartmoor IPA, Dartmoor Jail Ale, Guest ales. ♀ 8 **Facilities** Children's menu Family room Dogs allowed

---

## HORNS CROSS

### The Hoops Inn & Country Hotel
★★★ HL ◉ ♀

**Clovelly EX39 5DL** ☎ **01237 451222** 📄 **01237 451247**
e-mail: sales@hoopsinn.co.uk web: www.hoopsinn.co.uk
dir: *On A39 between Bideford & Clovelly*

Having evaded the revenue men, smugglers would share out their spoils in this thatched, cob-walled, 13th-century inn. Set in 16 acres of gardens and meadows on the Atlantic coast, it now offers the freshest produce Devon can offer, including vegetables from the garden. Guests can eat in the bar, morning room or restaurant, where oak-panelled walls, period furniture and tables set with crisp white napkins create the right level of formality. Seasonal menus focus on local produce, and house specialities include terrine of Devon game with home-made piccalilli, and Exmoor venison with griottine cherry sauce.

Open all day all wk 7am-11pm (Sun 8.30am-10.30pm) **Bar Meals** L served all wk 12-6 D served all wk 6-9 Av main course £13.50 food served all day **Restaurant** D served all wk 7-9 booking required Fixed menu price fr £20 Av 3 course à la carte fr £27.50 ⊕ FREE HOUSE ◀ Hoops Old Ale & Best, Golden Pig, Doom Bar ♻ Thatchers Gold, Winkleigh. ♀ 20 **Facilities** Children's menu Play area Family room Dogs allowed Garden Parking **Rooms** 13

---

## HORSEBRIDGE

### The Royal Inn ♀
**PL19 8PJ** ☎ **01822 870214**
e-mail: paul@royalinn.co.uk
dir: *S of B3362 (Launceston-Tavistock road)*

The pub, with a façade enlivened by superb pointed arched windows, was once a nunnery. Standing near a bridge built over the Tamar in 1437 by Benedictine monks, it was the Packhorse Inn until Charles I pitched up one day - his seal is in the doorstep. Beef for the steaks, casseroles and stews, and the pheasant and venison on the specials board are all locally supplied. Chilli cheese tortillas are much appreciated.

Open all wk noon-3 6.30-11pm **Bar Meals** L served all wk 12-2 booking required D served all wk 6.30-9 booking required **Restaurant** L served all wk 12-2 booking required D served all wk 6.30-9 booking required ⊕ FREE HOUSE ◀ Eastreet, Bass, Skinners, St Austell Proper Job. ♀ 6 **Facilities** Children's menu Dogs allowed Garden Parking

### KINGSKERSWELL

## Barn Owl Inn ☻

**Aller Mills TQ12 5AN ☎ 01803 872130**
e-mail: barnowl.allermills@hall-woodhouse.co.uk
dir: *Telephone for directions*

Handy for Dartmoor and the English Riviera towns, this recently renovated and beautifully restored, 16th-century former farmhouse has many charming features, including flagged floors, a black-leaded range, and oak beams in a high-vaulted converted barn with a minstrels' gallery. Lunchtime snacks include toasties, wraps and baguettes, while the main menu features lots of traditional pub favourites all washed down with a pint of Tanglefoot or Badgers First Gold.

**Open** all wk noon-11 (Sun noon-10.30) **Bar Meals** Av main course £5 food served all day **Restaurant** food served all day ⊕ WOODHOUSE INNS ◀ Tanglefoot, Badger First Gold. ☻ 24 **Facilities** Children's menu Dogs allowed Garden Parking

### KING'S NYMPTON

## The Grove Inn ☻

**EX37 9ST ☎ 01769 580406**
e-mail: info@thegroveinn.co.uk
dir: *2.5m from A377 (Exeter to Barnstaple road)*

A true taste of Devon is offered at this 17th-century thatched inn, set in a beautiful conservation village. Working closely with local farmers and producers, the food is sourced as close to home as possible. Look out for dishes such as roast rib of Lakeland Farm beef with Exmoor Ale Yorkshire pudding, breast of Devon chicken stuffed with mozzarella, sage and Parma ham, or Devon fish pie.

**Open** noon-3 6-11 (BH noon-3) Closed: Mon L ex BH **Bar Meals** L served Tue-Sat 12-2 **Restaurant** L served Tue-Sun 12-2 booking required D served Tue-Sat 7-9 booking required food served all day ⊕ FREE HOUSE ◀ Exmoor Ale, Otter Ale, Bath Gem Ale, Sharps Doom Bar, Teignworthy Springtide Ö Winkleigh. ☻ 7 **Facilities** Children's menu Dogs allowed Garden

### KINGSTON

## The Dolphin Inn

**TQ7 4QE ☎ 01548 810314 ▤ 01548 810314**
e-mail: info@dolphininn.eclipse.co.uk
web: www.dolphin-inn.co.uk
dir: *From A379 (Plymouth to Kingsbridge road) take B3233 for Bigbury-on-Sea. Follow brown inn signs*

The Dolphin is just a mile from the beaches of the South Hams and the beautiful Erme Estuary, ideal for walkers, golfers and surfers. The inn dates from the 16th century and was originally built as cottages for stone masons working on the village church next door. All the food is home made and the menu includes pies, crab bake, lobster bisque, lamb stew, and stuffed chicken breast. Specials provide daily fish and game dishes.

**Open** noon-3 6-11 (Sun 7-10.30) Closed: Sun eve Winter **Bar Meals** L served Mon-Fri 12-2 (Sat-Sun 12-2.30) D served all wk 6-9 (closed Sun & Mon eve winter) Av main course £8.95 **Restaurant** L served Mon-Fri 12-2 (Sat-Sun 12-2.30) D served all wk 6-9 (closed Sun & Mon eve winter) ⊕ PUNCH TAVERNS ◀ Teignworthy Spring Tide, Courage Best, Sharp's Doom Bar, Otter. **Facilities** Children's menu Play area Family room Dogs allowed Garden Parking

### LEWDOWN

## The Harris Arms ☻

**Portgate EX20 4PZ ☎ 01566 783331 ▤ 01566 783359**
e-mail: whiteman@powernet.co.uk
dir: *From A30 take Lifton turn, halfway between Lifton & Lewdown in hamlet of Portgate*

A 16th-century inn with wonderful views to Brent Tor, this establishment lives up to its promotional strapline: 'Eat Real Food and Drink Real Wine'. Located on the old A30 close to the boundary between Devon and Cornwall, it's an accessible spot for honest food with substance and style, plus real ales and excellent wines. The pub's excellent reputation, which reaches far beyond the local area, is built on exact cooking and locally-sourced ingredients. Example starters are fillets of warm home-smoked Cornish mackerel with horseradish cream; and grilled local goats' cheese on toasted baguette with mixed leaves, walnuts and pesto. Main courses might include slow-roasted confit of Devon pork belly with braised cabbage, potato and black pudding croquette, and sage and apple jus; and pub classics such as home-cooked ham with eggs and chips.

**Open** Closed: Mon & Sun eve **Bar Meals** L served Tue-Sun 12-2 booking required D served Tue-Sat 6.30-9 booking required Av main course £8.95 **Restaurant** L served Tue-Sun 12-2 booking required D served Tue-Sat 6.30-9 booking required Fixed menu price fr £13.95 Av 3 course à la carte fr £22.50 ⊕ FREE HOUSE ◀ Sharp's Doom Bar, Guinness Extra Cold, guest ales. ☻ 18 **Facilities** Children's menu Dogs allowed Garden Parking

## LIFTON

## The Arundell Arms ★★★ HL ⊛⊛ ♀

**PL16 0AA ☎ 01566 784666** 🖹 **01566 784494**
e-mail: reservations@arundellarms.com
web: www.arundellarms.com
dir: *1m off A30 dual carriageway, 3m E of Launceston*

Set in a valley of five rivers, close to the uplands of Dartmoor, Anne Voss-Bark's upmarket, creeper-clad old Devon inn is a favourite destination for those who enjoy country pursuits - in particular fishing - the River Tamar flows past the bottom of the garden and guests have 20 miles of fishing rights along its length. Today, it exudes warmth and a truly civilised air pervades the smart interior - not only in the 'locals' bar, with its babble of conversation and simple food at lunchtime, but also in the smarter dining bar which has two AA Rosettes for its food. You can choose to eat sandwiches (roast Devon beef with horseradish), or select from the starters and light snacks menu. Here you're likely to find tomato and red pepper soup, or a smooth chicken liver pâté with red onion marmalade for starters; and main courses like braised oxtail with roast vegetables; and spiced venison burgers with dressed leaves and chips. Three-course table d'hôte and à la carte menus are served in the elegant restaurant; typical dishes include asparagus with chervil hollandaise, casserole of John Dory, sea trout, scallops and sole, and hot chocolate pudding with whipped rum cream.

**Open** all wk 12-3 6-11 **Bar Meals** L served all wk 12-2.30 D served all wk 6-9.30 Av main course £12 **Restaurant** L served all wk 12-2.30 booking required D served all wk 6-9.30 booking required Fixed menu price fr £30 ⊕ FREE HOUSE ◀ Tribute, Guest Ales Ŏ Thatchers, Cornish Rattler. ♀ 9 **Facilities** Children's menu Dogs allowed Garden Parking **Rooms** 21

## LYMPSTONE

## The Globe Inn ♀

**The Strand EX8 5EY ☎ 01395 263166**
dir: *Telephone for directions*

Set in the estuary village of Lympstone, this traditional beamed inn has a good local reputation for seafood. The separate restaurant area serves as a coffee bar during the day. Look out for bass fillets with plum sauce; monkfish kebabs; seafood platter; and seafood grill. Weekend music and quiz nights are a feature.

**Open** all wk 10am-3 5.30-mdnt (Sun all day) **Bar Meals** L served all wk 10-2 booking required D served all wk 6.30-9.30 booking required **Restaurant** L served all wk 10-2 booking required D served all wk 6.30-9.30 booking required ⊕ HEAVITREE ◀ London Pride, Otter, Bass Ŏ Aspall. ♀ 10 **Facilities** Children's menu Dogs allowed

## MARLDON

## The Church House Inn ♀

**Village Rd TQ3 1SL ☎ 01803 558279** 🖹 **01803 664865**
dir: *Take Torquay ring road, follow signs to Marldon & Totnes, follow brown signs to pub*

An ancient inn with a contemporary feel located between Torbay and the market town of Newton Abbott. The building dates from around 1400, when it was a hostel for the builders of the adjoining village church, but it was rebuilt in 1750 incorporating beautiful Georgian windows. Typical evening menus include honey roast duck breast with a mixed berry sauce, slow-cooked shoulder of lamb in Moroccan spiced sultana and almond sauce, or fillet of salmon with a spring onion, mussel and white wine sauce.

**Open** all wk 11.30-2.30 5-11 (Fri-Sat 5-11.30 Sun 12-3 5.30-10.30) **Bar Meals** L served all wk 12-2 D served all wk 6.30-9.30 Av main course £13.50 **Restaurant** L served all wk 12-2 D served all wk 6.30-9.30 Av 3 course à la carte fr £26.30 ⊕ FREE HOUSE ◀ Dartmoor Best, Bass, Old Speckled Hen, Greene King IPA, London Pride. ♀ 10 **Facilities** Children's menu Dogs allowed Garden Parking

## MEAVY

## The Royal Oak Inn ♀

**PL20 6PJ ☎ 01822 852944**
e-mail: sjearp@aol.com
dir: *B3212 from Yelverton to Princetown. Right at Dousland to Meavy, past school. Pub opposite village green*

Flagstone floors, oak beams and a welcoming open fire set the scene at this traditional 15th-century free house. Standing by the village green and close to the shores of Burrator reservoir on the edge of Dartmoor, the inn is popular with cyclists and walkers – 'muddy boots and muddy paws are always welcome'. Local cask ales and ciders accompany the carefully sourced ingredients in a menu ranging from lunchtime baguettes and jackets to steak and Jail Ale pie; and monkfish and salmon kebabs.

**Open** all wk 11-3 6-11 (Sat-Sun & May-Oct all day) **Bar Meals** L served Mon-Fri 12-2.30, Sat-Sun 12-3 D served all wk 6-9 Av main course £5 **Restaurant** L served Mon-Fri 12-2.30, Sat-Sun 12-3 D served all wk 6-9 Fixed menu price fr £8 ⊕ FREE HOUSE ◀ Dartmoor Jail Ale, Dartmoor IPA, St Austell Tribute, Royal Oak, Guest Ŏ Westons Scrumpy, Old Rosie, Thatchers Gold. ♀ 12 **Facilities** Children's menu Dogs allowed Garden

## MODBURY

## California Country Inn

**California Cross PL21 0SG ☎ 01548 821449**
📄 **01548 821566**
e-mail: california@bellinns.entadsl.com
web: www.californiacountryinn.co.uk
dir: *Telephone for details*

Oak beams and exposed stonework are features of this whitewashed 14th-century free house. Brass, copper and old photographs decorate the interior, and there's a landscaped garden for summer use. Menus are created from only locally supplied produce, with prime meats from the chargrill, and dishes ranging from lasagne and beer-battered cod in the bar to roast monk fish with Yealm mussels, or loin of Plympton venison in the restaurant.

Open all day all wk 11-11 **Bar Meals** L served Mon-Sat 12-2, Sun 12-8 D served Mon-Sat 6-9, Sun 12-8 Av main course £9 **Restaurant** L served Sun 12-2 D served Wed-Sun 6-9 booking required Av 3 course à la carte fr £20 ⊕ FREE HOUSE ◄ Guinness, Abbot Ale, London Pride, Doom Bar. **Facilities** Children's menu Family room Dogs allowed Garden Parking

## MOLLAND

## The London Inn

**EX36 3NG ☎ 01769 550269**
dir: *Telephone for directions*

New owners at this 15th-century inn passionately believe that Exmoor needs to retain at least one of its traditional pubs. The London has many historic features and remains a centre for the shooting and hunting crowd. Home-made locally sourced food and ale straight from the cask are served, and the latest venture is a micro-brewery. Typical dishes include wood pigeon salad, venison sausages with bubble and squeak and gravy, and jam roly poly.

Open 12-3 6.30-11.30 (Sun 12-5) Closed: Sun eve **Bar Meals** L served Mon-Sat 12-2, Sun 12-3 D served Mon-Sat 7-9 Av main course £7 **Restaurant** L served Mon-Sat 12-2, Sun 12-3 booking required D served Mon-Sat 7-9 booking required ⊕ FREE HOUSE ◄ Exmoor Ale, Cotleigh Tawny Bitter ♂ Winkleigh Cider. **Facilities** Children's menu Family room Dogs allowed Garden Parking

## MORETONHAMPSTEAD

## The White Hart Hotel ★★★ HL ◉ ♟

**The Square TQ13 8NF ☎ 01647 441340** 📄 **01647 441341**
e-mail: enquiries@Whitehartdartmoor.co.uk
dir: *From A30 at Whiddon Down take A382 for Chagford & Moretonhampstead. Pub in village centre. Parking in 20yds*

Set in the heart of Dartmoor, this Grade II listed building dates from 1639 and has a recently refurbished bar, lounge and brasserie restaurant area for informal dining and drinking. Locally brewed ales are served alongside locally sourced food and dishes include rump of Dartmoor lamb with mini moussaka and feta cheese, and steamed stone bass with scallop and mushroom fricassee. Customers can also call in for morning coffee or afternoon tea.

Open all day all wk 11-11 **Bar Meals** L served all wk 12-2.30 D served all wk 6-9.30 Av main course £7.95 **Restaurant** L served all wk 12-2.30 booking required D served all wk 6-9.30 booking required Fixed menu price fr £15.95 Av 3 course à la carte fr £25 ⊕ HART INNS LTD ◄ St Austell Tribute, Otter, Doom Bar ♂ Thatchers. ♟ 18 **Facilities** Children's menu Dogs allowed Garden **Rooms** 28

## NEWTON ST CYRES

## The Beer Engine ♟

**EX5 5AX ☎ 01392 851282** 📄 **01392 851876**
e-mail: info@thebeerengine.co.uk
dir: *From Exeter take A377 towards Crediton. Signed from A377 towards Sweetham. Pub opp rail station in village*

Originally a railway hotel opened in 1852, this whitewashed free house is now acknowledged as one of Devon's leading micro-breweries. Engine ales with names like Piston bitter and Sleeper Heavy evoke the pub's antecedents, whilst cider drinkers can wash down their ploughman's with Dragon Tears. With local suppliers listed, expect a wide choice of fish dishes, as well as braised lamb shank, breaded veal escalope, and pan-fried venison sausages on bubble and squeak.

Open all day all wk 11am-11pm (Sun noon-10.30) **Bar Meals** L served all wk 12-2 D served Tue-Sat 6.30-9.15, Sun-Mon 6.30-8.30 Av main course £9 **Restaurant** L served all wk 12-2 booking required D served Tue-Sat 6.30-9.15, Sun-Mon 6.30-8.30 booking required ⊕ FREE HOUSE ◄ Engine Ales: Piston Bitter, Rail Ale, Sleeper Heavy ♂ Stowford Press. ♟ 7 **Facilities** Children's menu Dogs allowed Garden Parking

## NORTH BOVEY

# The Ring of Bells Inn ♥

**TQ13 8RB ☎ 01647 440375** 📠 **01647 440746**
e-mail: info@ringofbellsinn.com
dir: *1.5m from Moretonhampstead off B3212. 7m S of Whiddon Down junct on A30*

The Ring of Bells is one of Dartmoor's most historic inns, an attractive thatched property located just off the village green. It was built in the 13th century as lodgings for the stonemasons who were working on the church, and remains very much at the heart of the village's social life. Visitors too are attracted by the good Devon pub food and West Country ales. The short daily menus are full of interesting options – to start perhaps, a warm salad of goats' cheese, parmesan and olive oil, followed by loin of venison with celeriac and braised lentils; leave a little room for crème brûlée with figs or a home-made crumble.

Open all day all wk Closed: 25 Dec Bar Meals L served all wk all day Etr-Oct, all wk 12-2.30 Nov-Etr D served all wk all day Etr-Oct, all wk 6.30-9.30 Nov-Etr Av main course £10 Restaurant D served all wk 6.30-9.30 booking required ⊕ FREE HOUSE ◼ Otter Ale, St Austell Tribute, Sharps Doom Bar. ♀ 12 Facilities Children's menu Family room Dogs allowed Garden

## NOSS MAYO

# The Ship Inn ♥

**PL8 1FW ☎ 01752 872387** 📠 **01752 873294**
e-mail: ship@nossmayo.com web: www.nossmayo.com
dir: *5m S of Yealmpton on River Yealm estuary*

Reclaimed English oak and local stone characterise this beautifully renovated 16th-century free house. Huddled on Noss Mayo's tidal waterfront on the south bank of the Yealm estuary, the style is simple and properly pub-like. The deceptively spacious building has wooden floors, old bookcases, log fires and dozens of local pictures. The inn's superb location makes it a popular port of call for sailing enthusiasts; walkers, too, throng the bar, and dogs are allowed downstairs. The ever-changing menu is served from midday until 9:30pm, and majors on local produce, notably fish. For the hearty three-course appetite, classic starters like grilled goats' cheese on mixed salad, and traditional crayfish cocktail with Marie rose sauce, could be followed by pan-fried duck breast on potato rosti; or seared sea bass fillet on stir-fried vegetables with noodles and hoi sin sauce. Round off with crème brûlée; bread and butter pudding with custard; or sticky toffee pudding with butterscotch sauce and vanilla ice cream.

Open all day all wk Bar Meals Av main course £12 food served all day Restaurant Av 3 course à la carte fr £23 food served all day ⊕ FREE HOUSE ◼ Tamar, Jail Ale & Butcombe Blonde, Dartmoor IPA. ♀ 10 Facilities Children's menu Dogs allowed Garden Parking

## PARRACOMBE

# The Fox & Goose ♥

**EX31 4PE ☎ 01598 763239** 📠 **01598 763621**
web: www.foxandgoose-parracombe.co.uk
dir: *1m from A39 between Blackmoor Gate (2m) & Lynton (6m). Signed to Parracombe. Fox & Goose sign on approach*

It's hard to believe that this striking building in this sleepy Exmoor village was once a couple of tiny thatched cottages serving the local farming community. It was changed beyond recognition when it was enlarged to compete with nearby hotels after the narrow gauge Lynton and Barnstaple Railway linked Parracombe with the outside world in 1898. The village has remained unspoilt and the pub continues to thrive, drawing locals and visitors for good home-made food listed on changing blackboard menus, which can be enjoyed in the homely bar and restaurant, or in the paved courtyard garden overlooking the river. Menus may champion meat and seasonal game from surrounding farms and estates, but fish dominates proceedings, all landed locally along the North Devon coast. Meat lovers will not be disappointed with slow-braised shoulder of lamb with roasted root vegetables and creamy mash, while starters take in smoked mackerel and horseradish pâté, and indulgent puddings may include hot chocolate brownie and a traditional rice pudding served with home-made jam. Don't miss the Sunday roast lunches.

Open all wk Bar Meals L served 12-2 D served 6-9 (Sun 7-9) Av main course £12.95 Restaurant L served 12-2 D served 6-9 (Sun 7-9) ⊕ FREE HOUSE ◼ Cotleigh Barn Owl, Dartmoor Best, Exmoor Fox, Guinness Ô Winkleigh. ♀ 10 Facilities Children's menu Dogs allowed Garden Parking

## RATTERY

### Church House Inn ♟

**TQ10 9LD** ☎ **01364 642220** 📄 **01364 642220**
e-mail: ray12@onetel.com
dir: *1m from A38 Exeter to Plymouth Rd*

This venerable 11th-century inn is filled with brasses, bare beams, large fireplaces and other historic features. Some customers encounter the wandering spirit of a monk; fortunately he seems to be friendly. In the dining room, the menu offers fresh fish of all kinds (snowcrab cocktail; lemon sole), as well as home-made moussaka, game pie and chilli, and lighter options such as salads or toasted sandwiches, plus vegetarian balti and stroganoff.

**Open** all wk 11-2.30 6-11 (Sun noon-3 6-10.30) **Bar Meals** L served Mon-Sat 11.30-2, Sun 12-2 booking required D served all wk 6.30-9 booking required **Restaurant** L served Mon-Sat 11.30-2, Sun 12-2 booking required D served all wk 6.30-9 booking required ⊕ FREE HOUSE ◼ Princetown IPA, Princetown Jail Ale, Butcombe Best Bitter, Otter Ale. ♟ 8 **Facilities** Children's menu Dogs allowed Garden Parking

---

## SIDMOUTH

### The Blue Ball ★★★★ INN ♟

**Stevens Cross, Sidford EX10 9QL**
☎ **01395 514062** 📄 **01395 519584**
e-mail: rogernewton@blueballinn.net web: www.blueballinn.net
dir: *M5 junct 30 exit to A3052. Through Sidford towards Lyme Regis, on left after village, approx 13m*

The Newton family has run this 14th-century thatched, cob-and-flint pub since 1912. The inn is a hugely attractive, lovingly maintained building, festooned with colourful hanging baskets in summer, and cosy in winter within the rambling carpeted bars. Arrive early to bag one of the fireside seats (there are

three log fires) and peruse the extensive menus. Classic pub favourites feature on the main menu, from fishcakes with tartare sauce and deep-fried whitebait for starters, to steak and kidney pudding; battered cod and chips; rib-eye steak with peppercorn sauce and all the trimmings, and various jacket potatoes with fillings; salads; and a good choice of sandwiches. Typical puddings include chocolate and walnut sponge pudding and range of Salcombe ice creams.

**Open** all day all wk Closed: 25 Dec eve **Bar Meals** L served all wk 12-3 D served all wk 6-9 Av main course £9.50 **Restaurant** L served all wk 12-3 D served all wk 6-9 ⊕ PUNCH TAVERNS ◼ Otter Bitter, Tribute, John Smiths, Guest Ale ♂ Stowford Press. ♟ 10 **Facilities** Children's menu Play area Family room Dogs allowed Garden Parking **Rooms** 9

### Dukes ★★★★ INN ♟

**The Esplanade EX10 8AR**
☎ **01395 513320** 📄 **01395 519318**
e-mail: dukes@hotels-sidmouth.co.uk
dir: *M5 junct 30 onto A3052, take 1st exit to Sidmouth on right then left onto Esplanade*

Situated at the heart of Sidmouth town centre on the Regency Esplanade, Dukes is a contemporary inn, with traditional values. The interior is stylish and lively, with a relaxed Continental feel in the bar and public areas. In fine weather the patio garden overlooking the sea is the perfect place to sit with a mid-morning Italian freshly ground coffee and home-baked pastry. Varied menu choices include traditional English-style favourites and a specials board that offers a variety of fresh fish from Brixham and Lyme Bay, and prime meats from West Country farms. If you just want a snack, possibilities range from a wide choice of stone baked pizzas and thick cut sandwiches made with local bread, to loaded nachos and home-made jacket wedges. Sundays mean traditional roasts – topside of West Country beef, leg of lamb, loin of pork. In the afternoon some might feel like a Devon cream tea.

**Open** all day all wk **Bar Meals** L served Sun-Thu 12-9. Fri-Sat 12-9.30 D served Sun-Thu 12-9, Fri-Sat 12-9.30 Av main course £12 food served all day **Restaurant** L served Sun-Thu 12-9. Fri-Sat 12-9.30 booking required D served Sun-Thu 12-9. Fri-Sat 12-9.30 booking required Fixed menu price fr £15 Av 3 course à la carte fr £18 food served all day ⊕ FREE HOUSE ◼ Branscombe Vale Branoc & Summa That, O'Hanlon's Firefly, Princetown Jail Ale, Otter Ale. ♟ 16 **Facilities** Children's menu Play area Dogs allowed Garden Parking **Rooms** 13

England

## SOUTH ZEAL

## Oxenham Arms ★★ HL ♏

**EX20 2JT ☎ 01837 840244** 🖹 **01837 840791**
e-mail: relax@theoxenhamarms.co.uk
dir: *Just off A30 4m E of Okehampton, in village centre*

Probably built by monks in the 12th century, this inn on the edge of Dartmoor is one of the oldest in England. First licensed in 1477, the pub retains a historical feel with beams, flagstone floors, blazing fires and a prehistoric monolith – archaeologists believe the monks just built around it. Burgoynes restaurant serves an eclectic seasonal menu based on fine local produce. Expect the likes of a choice of home-made pâtés, followed by coq au vin, Cornish crab salad, and The Oxenham chicken curry.

**Open** all wk 10.30-3.30 5-11 **Bar Meals** L served all wk 11.30-3 D served all wk 6-9.30 Av main course £11 **Restaurant** L served all wk 11.30-3 D served all wk 6-9.30 Av 3 course à la carte fr £17 ⊕ FREE HOUSE ◀ Sharp's Doom Bar, Otter, guest. ♏ 8 **Facilities** Children's menu Dogs allowed Garden Parking **Rooms** 7

## SPREYTON

## The Tom Cobley Tavern ♏

**EX17 5AL ☎ 01647 231314**
dir: *From A30 at Whiddon Down take A3124 N. Take 1st right after services then 1st right over bridge.*

From this pub, one day in 1802, a certain Thomas Cobley and his companions set forth for Widecombe Fair, an event immortalised in song. Today, this traditional village local offers a selection of bar snacks, lighter fare and home-made main meals, including pies, salads, duck and fish dishes, as well as a good vegetarian selection. Finish off with one of the great ice creams or sorbets. There is a pretty garden to enjoy in the warmer months.

**Open** 12-3 6-11 (Sun 12-4 7-11 Mon 6.30-11 Fri-Sat 6-1am) Closed: Mon L **Bar Meals** L served Tue-Sat 12-3 D served Sun-Thu 7-10 Av main course £6 food served all day **Restaurant** L served all wk 12-3 booking required D served all wk 7-10 Fixed menu price fr £10 food served all day ⊕ FREE HOUSE ◀ Cotleigh Tawny Ale, Doom Bar, Tribute, Otter Ale, Proper Job, Ŏ Winkleigh Cider, Stowford Press. ♏ 7 **Facilities** Children's menu Dogs allowed Garden Parking

## STOCKLAND

## The Kings Arms Inn ♏

**EX14 9BS ☎ 01404 881361** 🖹 **01404 881387**
e-mail: info@thekingsarmsinn.org.uk
dir: *Off A30 to Chard, 6m NE of Honiton*

A traditional 16th-century thatched, whitewashed former coaching inn tucked away in the Blackdown Hills. After passing through the impressive flagstone entrance, you'll encounter two interesting features - a medieval oak screen and an original bread oven. Locals and visitors in the bar will, as likely

as not, share a fondness for Otter and Exmoor real ales. Pub food here uses local suppliers and might include ham, egg and chips; filled jacket potatoes with salad; local pork sausages and mash; and chef's own recipe beefburgers. The restaurant offers other choices: pigeon breasts, ostrich fillets and gravadlax from the blackboards, and from the carte menu rare fillet steak with Roquefort cheese; poached salmon with Cajun seasoning; king prawn Thermidor; and vegetarian options. At lunchtime filled ciabattas are served with chips and salad; soups are home made, and there's usually a curry. Look out for the lively annual Stockland Fair.

**Open** all wk 11.30-3 6-11 (Sun 12-3 6.30-10.30) **Bar Meals** L served Mon-Sat 12-2 **Restaurant** L served all wk 12-2 booking required D served all wk 6.30-9 booking required ⊕ FREE HOUSE ◀ Otter Ale, Exmoor Ale Ŏ Thatchers. ♏ 15 **Facilities** Children's menu Dogs allowed Garden Parking

## STRETE

## Kings Arms ◉ ♏

**Dartmouth Rd TQ6 0RW ☎ 01803 770377** 🖹 **01803 771008**
e-mail: kingsarms_devon_fish@hotmail.com
dir: *On A379 (Dartmouth-Kingsbridge road), 5m from Dartmouth*

You can't miss this striking, 18th-century pub, with its unique cast-iron balcony, as it stands smack beside the coast road and the South West coast path passes the front door. Pop in for a pint of Otter Ale, bag a seat by the fire in the traditional, terracotta-walled bar, or head up the few steps into the light and airy contemporary-styled restaurant, replete with modern artwork and stunning views across Start Bay. Chef Rob Dawson's motto is 'keep it fresh, keep it simple' and on his daily lunch and dinner menus you'll find wonderfully fresh seafood, simply prepared with some modern twists, including crab, lobster and fish from a local boat (the boat trawls exclusively for the pub once a week).

**Open** 11.30-3 6-11 (Sat-Sun 11.30-11) **Bar Meals** L served Mon-Fri 12-2, Sat-Sun 11.30-11 booking required D served Mon-Fri 6.30-9, Sat-Sun 11.30-11 booking required Av main course £12 **Restaurant** L served Tue-Fri 12-2, Sat-Sun 11.30-11 booking required D served Tue-Fri 6.30-9, Sat-Sun 11.30-11 booking required Av 3 course à la carte fr £24 ⊕ HEAVITREE ◀ Otter Ale, Adnams Bitter, Guinness Ŏ Aspalls. ♏ 15 **Facilities** Children's menu Dogs allowed Garden Parking

## TOTNES

## The Durant Arms ★★★★ INN ♏

**Ashprington TQ9 7UP ☎ 01803 732240**
dir: *Exit A38 at Totnes junct, to Dartington & Totnes, at 1st lights right for Kingsbridge on A381, in 1m left for Ashprington*

Locally renowned as a dining pub, the delightful Durant Arms is situated in the picturesque village of Ashprington, just outside Totnes in the heart of the South Hams. Proprietors Graham and Eileen Ellis are proud to uphold British values of

continued

England

hospitality at the award-winning 18th-century hostelry. The small bar is fitted out in a traditional style, with work by local artists on display alongside horse-brasses, ferns and cheerful red velvet curtains. All dishes are cooked to order, with a wide variety of meat, fish and fresh steamed vegetables, all sourced locally wherever possible. Local fish and seafood figure strongly in dishes such as Dartmouth smoked salmon with black pepper; or shell-on whole prawns with garlic dip, to start, and main courses of sea bass fillet on roasted vegetables with pepper sauce; or fillets of lemon sole roulade. Desserts range from chocolate fondant with clotted cream to treacle sponge pudding with vanilla ice cream. Award-winning, hand-made English cheeses from nearby Sharpham's organic dairy are another speciality of the house, and wines from the Sharpham vineyard are offered on the wine list. The little courtyard to the rear provides a cosy spot to linger over a summer meal.

Open all wk **Bar Meals** L served all wk 12-2 D served all wk 7-9.15 **Restaurant** L served all wk 12-2 D served all wk 7-9.15 ⊕ FREE HOUSE ◀ Dartmoor Bitter, Tetley, Tribute. ♀ 8 **Facilities** Children's menu Family room Dogs allowed Garden Parking **Rooms** 8

## Royal Seven Stars Hotel ♀

**The Plains TQ9 5DD ☎ 01803 862125**
e-mail: enquiry@royalsevenstars.co.uk
dir: *From A382 signed Totnes, left at 'Dartington' rdbt. Through lights towards town centre, through next rdbt, pass Morrisons car park on left. 200yds on right*

A Grade II listed pub dating from 1640 in the heart of Totnes. The traditional saloon bar with open fire serves Jail Ale and Doom Bar among others, with home-cooked bar meals available all day. Bar 7's more contemporary atmosphere, with slate floors and black leather sofas, is the setting for Mediterranean-inspired snacks, fruit smoothies, speciality coffees and a selection of cakes. The restaurant, called TQ9 after its town centre location, serves good local produce– including a Sunday carvery – in a relaxed, stylish environment.

Open all day all wk **Bar Meals** Av main course £8 food served all day **Restaurant** L served Sun 12-2.30 booking required D served all wk 6.30-9.30 booking required Av 3 course à la carte fr £20 ⊕ FREE HOUSE ◀ Jail Ale, Doom Bar, Bays Gold, Courage Best. ♀ 20 **Facilities** Children's menu Family room Dogs allowed Parking

## Steam Packet Inn ★★★★ INN ♀

**St Peter's Quay TQ9 5EW ☎ 01803 863880**
📄 **01803 862754**
e-mail: steampacket@buccaneer.co.uk
dir: *Exit A38 towards Plymouth, 18m. A384 to Totnes 6m. Left at mini-rdbt, pass Morrisons on left, over mini-rdbt, 400yds on left*

The inn's sign depicts the Amelia, a steam packet ship that regularly called here with passengers, parcels and mail before the days of modern road and rail transport. These days the building is a welcoming riverside pub with great views, particularly from the conservatory restaurant, and plenty of waterside seating for sunny days. Typical dishes from the menu include fresh Brixham sea bass fillet; haddock in 'jail ale' batter; roasted pork cutlet with carrot and swede purée; and creamy pumpkin and goats' cheese gnocchi. Good local cheese selection.

Open all day all wk **Bar Meals** L served Mon-Fri 12-2.30, Sat 12-3, Sun 12-4 D served Mon-Sat 6-9.30, Sun 6-9 **Restaurant** L served Mon-Fri 12-2.30, Sat 12-3, Sun 12-4 D served Mon-Sat 6-9.30, Sun 6-9 ⊕ BUCCANEER HOLDINGS LTD ◀ Courage Best, Otter Bright, Jail Ale, Guest ale Ŏ Stowford Press. ♀ 8 **Facilities** Children's menu Dogs allowed Garden Parking **Rooms** 4

## TRUSHAM

## Cridford Inn ♀

**TQ13 0NR ☎ 01626 853694**
e-mail: reservations@vanillapod-cridfordinn.com
web: www.cridfordinn.co.uk
dir: *A38 take junct for Teign Valley, turn right follow signs Trusham for 4m*

A thatched former longhouse with origins in the mid-9th century, but rebuilt in the late 11th, which means that the rough stone walls, the fireplaces in the bar and mosaic floor in the Vanilla Pod restaurant, plus the stained glass window in the bar, have all been here for a long, long time. The window, in fact, is probably the earliest surviving domestic example in Britain. In the bar (Doom Bar and Otter real ales) the menu changes seasonally, although there are daily specials. Here you can try smoked Dartmouth salmon; game pie, containing braised wild boar, venison, pheasant and rabbit; baked field mushrooms with smoked applewood and herb crust; steak and kidney pie; honey-baked West Country ham and eggs; seafood mornay; or one of a selection of chargrills. A three-course dinner from the monthly-changing restaurant menu might feature pan-fried red mullet with red wine, beetroot, creamed leeks and crispy bacon; followed by roasted guinea fowl; and hand-made Belgian chocolate pudding. Most of the vegetarian options are on a separate board. Outside is a terrace from which the rose-covered longhouse looks wonderful.

**Open** all wk 11-3 6-11 (Sat 11-11 Sun noon-10.30) **Bar Meals** L served all wk 12-2 D served all wk 7-9.30 Av main course £8.95 **Restaurant** L served Sun 12-1.30 booking required D served Mon-Sat 7-9.30 booking required Fixed menu price fr £21.95 Av 3 course à la carte fr £23.45 ⊕ FREE HOUSE ◀ Doom Bar, Otter Ale Ö Thatchers. ♥ 8 **Facilities** Children's menu Family room Garden Parking

## TUCKENHAY

# The Maltsters Arms ♥

TQ9 7EQ ☎ 01803 732350 📄 01803 732823
e-mail: pub@tuckenhay.demon.co.uk
dir: *A381 from Totnes towards Kingsbridge. 1m, at hill top turn left, follow signs to Tuckenhay, 3m*

Accessible only along high-banked lanes, or by boat either side of high tide, this old stone country inn on Bow Creek off the River Dart was once owned by TV chef, Keith Floyd. The daily changing menu may feature pan-fried skate wing, beef and bell pepper balti, mushroom tortelloni, stone bass fillet and salmon in white wine sauce, or T-bone steak with mushroom and tarragon sauce. Famous for summer barbecues and occasional music events.

**Open** all day all wk 11-11 (25 Dec 12-2) **Bar Meals** L served all wk 12-3 D served all wk 7-9.30 Av main course £11 food served all day **Restaurant** L served all wk 12-3 booking required D served all wk 7-9.30 booking required Av 3 course à la carte fr £20 ⊕ FREE HOUSE ◀ Princetown Dartmoor IPA, Young's Special, Teignworthy Maltsters Ale, Sharps Doom Bar, Skinners Betty Stoggs Ö Westons Perry. ♥ 18 **Facilities** Children's menu Family room Dogs allowed Garden Parking

## TYTHERLEIGH

# Tytherleigh Arms Hotel

EX13 7BE ☎ 01460 220400 & 220214 📄 01460 220814
e-mail: tytherleigharms@aol.com
dir: *Equidistant from Chard & Axminster on A358*

Beamed ceilings and huge roaring fires are notable features of this family-run, 16th-century former coaching inn. It is a food-led establishment, situated on the Devon, Somerset and Dorset borders. Great pride is taken in sourcing local ingredients, and fish dishes are a speciality with fish landed locally – perhaps Lyme Bay scallops, crème fraîche and sweet chilli sauce. Other fresh home-cooked dishes might include liver and bacon, mash with onion gravy; and pork tenderloin with black pudding and wholegrain mustard sauce. To finish perhaps try Barbara's lemon posset or Tom's banoffee pie and delicious cheesecakes.

**Open** all wk 11-2.30 6.30-11 (Sun eve in winter) **Bar Meals** L served all wk 11-2.30 booking required D served all wk 6.30-9 booking required Av main course £9.95 **Restaurant** L served all wk 11-2.30 booking required D served all wk 6.30-9 booking required ⊕ FREE HOUSE ◀ Butcombe Bitter, Otter, Murphy's, Boddingtons Ö Ashton Press. **Facilities** Children's menu Garden Parking

## WINKLEIGH

# The Kings Arms ♥

Fore St EX19 8HQ ☎ 01837 83384 📄 01834 83055
e-mail: kingsarmswinkleigh@googlemail.com
dir: *Village signed from B3220 (Crediton to Torrington road)*

Scrubbed pine tables and traditional wooden settles set the scene at this ancient thatched country inn in Winkleigh's central square. Wood-burning stoves keep the beamed bar and dining rooms warm in chilly weather, and traditional pub games are encouraged. Generous servings of freshly-made food include sandwiches and hot snacks, as well as steak and kidney parcel, loin of lamb with rosemary and redcurrant sauce, and Lucy's fish pie. Booking is recommended at weekends.

**Open** all day all wk 11-11 (Sun noon-10.30) **Bar Meals** food served all day **Restaurant** food served all day ⊕ ENTERPRISE INNS ◀ Butcombe Bitter, Sharp's Doom Bar, Cornish Coaster Ö Winkleigh Cider. ♥ 9 **Facilities** Children's menu Dogs allowed Garden

## YEALMPTON

# Rose & Crown ♥

Market St PL8 2EB ☎ 01752 880223 📄 01752 881058
e-mail: info@theroseandcrown.co.uk

From the classic brown and cream décor to the comfy leather sofas and open fire, the interior of this stylish bar restaurant reflects a perfect balance between contemporary and traditional features. The head chef regularly changes his tempting à la carte and set menus, and sources his ingredients

continued

locally wherever possible. Many dishes are traditional classics with an extra touch of class, whilst others feature a Pacific Rim twist with exotic Indonesian and Malaysian flavours. 'Lite bites' are served in the sunken lounge, whilst the restaurant menu might include options like pan-seared pork with mustard potatoes and roasted carrots; wild sea bass on mussel chowder with chargrilled new potatoes; or courgette cannelloni with Parmesan and rocket. Look out for the newly landscaped terraced garden - the perfect place to enjoy a hot summer's afternoon.

Open all wk **Bar Meals** L served all wk 12-2.30 D served all wk 6.30-9.30 Av main course £11 **Restaurant** L served all wk 12-2.30 booking required D served all wk 6.30-9.30 booking required Fixed menu price fr £9.95 Av 3 course à la carte fr £24 ⊕ INNTRA WEST LTD ◀ Doom Bar, London Pride, Courage Best, IPA Greene King, Otter, Tribute. ♀ 8 **Facilities** Children's menu Family room Dogs allowed Garden Parking

# DORSET

## BOURTON

# The White Lion Inn

**High St SP8 5AT ☎ 01747 840866**
e-mail: office@whitelionbourton.co.uk
dir: *Off A303, opposite B3092 to Gillingham*

Dating from 1723, the White Lion is a beautiful, stone-built, creeper clad Dorset inn. The bar is cosy, with beams, flagstones and an open fire, and serves a range of real beers and ciders. Imaginative menus draw on the wealth of quality local produce. Dishes range from home-made burger with Montgomery Cheddar, chutney, salad and chips in the bar, to pork belly slowly braised in Calvados, Cheddar Valley cider and thyme in the restaurant.

Open all wk noon-3 5-11 **Bar Meals** L served Mon-Sat 12-2.30, Sun 12-3.30 D served all wk 6-9 Av main course £9 **Restaurant** L served Mon-Sat 12-2.30, Sun 12-3.30 D served all wk 6-9 ⊕ ADMIRAL TAVERNS ◀ Fuller's London Pride, Greene King IPA, guest ale Ö Thatchers. **Facilities** Children's menu Dogs allowed Garden Parking

## BRIDPORT

# The West Bay ♀

**Station Rd, West Bay DT6 4EW**
**☎ 01308 422157  🖹 01308 459717**
e-mail: info@thewestbay.co.uk
dir: *From A35 (Bridport by-pass) take B3157 (2nd exit) towards West Bay. After mini-rdbt 1st left (Station Road). Pub on left*

Built in 1739, this traditional bar/restaurant lies at the foot of East Cliff, part of the World Heritage Jurassic Coast. Specialities are fish and seafood: West Bay velvet crab soup; and Lyme Bay hot crab pâté on toasted sourdough are starter examples, which could be followed by lemon sole with brown shrimps and caper butter; or roast huss with surf clams and sea beet.

Open noon-3 6-11 Closed: Sun eve & winter Mon L **Bar Meals** L served all wk 12-2 (Tue-Sun 12-2 winter) D served Mon-Sat 6.30-9 (Tue-Sat 6.30-9 winter) Av main course £14.50 **Restaurant** L served all wk 12-2 (Tue-Sun 12-2 winter) booking required D served Mon-Sat 6.30-9 (Tue-Sat 6.30-9 winter) booking required Fixed menu price fr £15 Av 3 course à la carte fr £26.50 ⊕ PALMERS ◀ Palmers IPA, Palmers Copper, Palmers 200, Guinness, Tally Ho! Ö Thatcher's Gold. ♀ 9 **Facilities** Children's menu Dogs allowed Garden Parking

## BUCKHORN WESTON

# Stapleton Arms ♀

**Church Hill SP8 5HS ☎ 01963 370396**
e-mail: relax@thestapletonarms.com
dir: *3.5m from Wincanton in village centre*

A stylish but unstuffy pub in a pretty village, with a spacious bar, elegant dining room and secluded garden. Hand-pumped ales, draught farm ciders, organic fruit juices and wines from new, old and emerging wine regions accompany simple, innovative food based on quality produce from small local suppliers. For starters try winter vegetable and thyme soup with a hunk of freshly delivered bread; or pan-fried scallops with celeriac purée, crispy Parma ham and toasted fennel seeds. Main courses include slow-roasted belly pork with apple mash and a cider sauce; and ruby red beetroot and fresh horseradish risotto. Fish caught off Dorset's south coast is delivered daily, and the award-winning menus continue to broaden – most recently with products from a smokery near Bath. You can even decide on your Sunday joint and the pub will prepare and cook it for you.

Open all wk 11-3 6-11 (Sun noon-10.30) **Bar Meals** L served all wk 12-3 D served all wk 6-10 Av main course £12 **Restaurant** L served all wk 12-3 booking required D served all wk 6-10 booking required Av 3 course à la carte fr £23 ⊕ FREE HOUSE ◀ Butcombe, Hidden Brewery, Moor's Revival Ö Thatchers Cheddar Valley, Butcombe's Ashton Press, Orchard Pig. ♀ 12 **Facilities** Children's menu Dogs allowed Garden Parking

## BUCKLAND NEWTON

# Gaggle of Geese ♟

**DT2 7BS ☎ 01300 345249**
e-mail: gaggle@gaggleofgeese.co.uk
dir: *On B3143 N of Dorchester*

Mark and Emily Hammick have breathed new life into this now thriving community local since taking over in 2008. Fresh flowers and candles top scrubbed tables in the spruced-up bar, where you can sup West Country ales and local ciders, and tuck into some cracking pub food. Prepared from local seasonal produce, including meat from Mark's family farm, dishes include pork terrine with apple chutney, roasted butternut squash risotto, and rib-eye steak and peppercorn sauce. Well worth the diversion off the A352 south of Sherborne.

Open all wk 11.30-3 6 11.30 (Sun 11.30-11.30, Sat 11.30-11.30 in summer) Closed: 1 wk Jan, 25 Dec Bar Meals L served Mon-Sat 12-2, Sun 12-3 booking required D served Sun-Thu 7-9, Fri-Sat 7-9.30 booking required Av main course £10 Restaurant L served Mon-Sat 12-2, Sun 12-3 booking required D served Sun-Thu 7-9, Fri-Sat 7-9.30 booking required Av 3 course à la carte fr £25 ⊕ FREE HOUSE ◀ Ringwood, Proper Job, Tribute, Butcombe Bitter, Hop Back Summer Lightning ♂ Thatchers Gold, Lulworth Skipper, Bridge Farm Traditional. ♟ 10 Facilities Children's menu Play area Dogs allowed Garden Parking

## BURTON BRADSTOCK

# The Anchor Inn ♟

**High St DT6 4QF ☎ 01308 897228**
e-mail: info@dorset-seafood-restaurant.co.uk
dir: *2m SE of Bridport on B3157 in centre of Burton Bradstock*

A 300-year-old coaching inn, the Anchor is located just inland from the Jurassic Coast World Heritage Site, near Chesil Beach. As you might expect from its name, the pub is full of marine memorabilia: fishing nets hang from ceilings, and old fishing tools and arty things made by the chef-proprietor from shellfish adorn the walls. Seafood is a speciality, and there is an extensive selection of main fish courses on the menu, plus 'catch of the day' specials. The bouillabaisse is a substantial version of the celebrated French dish, including a wide variety of local fish and shellfish in a creamy lobster, white wine and brandy jus, served with a hot baguette. Dorset scallops, dived for around West Bay, are seared in butter and served in their shells with a creamy bacon and mushroom sauce, on a bed of savoury rice garnished with salad and prawns.

Open all wk Closed: 1 Jan Bar Meals L served all wk 12-2 booking required D served all wk 6-9.30 booking required food served all day Restaurant L served all wk 12-2 booking required D served all wk 6-9.30 booking required food served all day ⊕ PUNCH TAVERNS ◀ Otter Bitter, Tribute, Theakston Best Bitter, John Smith's ♂ Thatchers. ♟ 10 Facilities Children's menu Dogs allowed Parking

## CATTISTOCK

# Fox & Hounds Inn ♟

**Duck St DT2 0JH ☎ 01300 320444    ▤ 01300 320444**
e-mail: lizflight@yahoo.co.uk
web: www.foxandhoundsinn.com
dir: *On A37, between Dorchester & Yeovil, follow signs to Cattistock*

This attractive 16th-century inn is set in the beautiful village of Cattistock. Original features include beams, open fires in winter and huge inglenooks, one with an original bread oven. It is a fascinating building, full of curiosities, such as the hidden cupboard reached by a staircase that winds around the chimney in one of the loft areas. Traditional home-made meals include locally made faggots; mushroom stroganoff; steak and kidney pudding; and Dorset apple cake. A superb garden is available in the summer. Recent change of ownership.

Open noon-2.30 7-11 (Thu-Sat 12-2.30 6-11) Closed: Mon L Bar Meals L served Tue-Sun 12-2 D served Tue-Sat 7-11 booking required Av main course £8.95 Restaurant L served Tue-Sun 12-2 D served Tue-Sat 7-11 booking required ⊕ PALMERS ◀ Palmers IPA, Copper Ale, Palmers 200, Dorset Gold ♂ Thatchers Traditional. Facilities Children's menu Play area Dogs allowed Garden Parking

## CHEDINGTON

# Winyards Gap Inn ♟

**Chedington Ln DT8 3HY ☎ 01935 891244**
e-mail: enquiries@winyardsgap.com
web: www.winyardsgap.com
dir: *5m S of Crewkerne on A356*

An ancient inn tucked under an ancient earthwork on the edge of the Dorset Down, with a stunning view towards the Quantock Hills that inspired Thomas Hardy's poem 'At Winyard's Gap'. Savour the view from the beamed bar or the terraced garden with a pint of Exmoor Ale and a decent meal – scallops with lemon butter sauce, lamb steak with redcurrant

continued

England

England

jus, Eton mess, or a traditional bar meal, perhaps, ham, egg and chips or a smoked salmon sandwich.

Open all wk 11.30-3 6-11 (Sat-Sun 11.30-11) Closed: 25 Dec **Bar Meals** L served Mon-Sat 12-2 D served all wk 6-9 Av main course £12 **Restaurant** L served all wk 12-2 booking required D served all wk 6-9 booking required Av 3 course à la carte fr £22 ⊕ FREE HOUSE ◀ Doom Bar, Exmoor Ale, Otter Ale ♂ Thatchers Gold. ♀ 8 **Facilities** Children's menu Dogs allowed Garden Parking

## CORFE CASTLE

### The Greyhound Inn ♀

**The Square BH20 5EZ** ☎ **01929 480205** ▤ **01929 480205**
e-mail: eat@greyhoundcorfe.co.uk
dir: *W from Bournemouth, take A35 to Dorchester, after 5m left onto A351, 10m to Corfe Castle*

A classic coaching inn, set beneath the ruins of Corfe Castle, the Greyhound has a large beer garden with views of Swanage Steam Railway. A full diary of events features two annual beer festivals in May and August and a West Country sausage and cider festival in October half term. The convivial atmosphere embraces families, cyclists and walkers enjoying local food and ale, including winter game and summer shellfish.

Open all wk 11-11 **Bar Meals** L served all wk 11-3 D served all wk 6-9 Av main course £10.75 ⊕ ENTERPRISE INNS ◀ Fuller's London Pride, Timothy Taylor Landlord, Black Sheep, Ringwood Best, Purbeck Brewery Fossil Fuel, Marston's Pedigree ♂ Westons Organic, Stowford Press. ♀ 6 **Facilities** Children's menu Play area Family room Dogs allowed Garden

## EAST MORDEN

### The Cock & Bottle ♀

**BH20 7DL** ☎ **01929 459238**
dir: *From A35 W of Poole turn right B3075, pub 0.5m on left*

Originally a cob-walled Dorset longhouse, dating back some 400 years, the pub acquired a brick skin around 1800, and remained thatched until 1966. The original interiors are comfortably rustic with low-beamed ceilings and lots of nooks and crannies around the log fires. Lovely pastoral views over farmland include the pub's paddock, where vintage car and motorcycle meetings are occasionally hosted during the summer. The experienced chef serves up an appealing mix of traditional and inventive cooking, with wholesome bar and light lunch menus supporting a varied daily carte. Dishes might include fresh dressed local crab to start, followed by loin of

venison with wild mushroom ragout, and rum and raisin white chocolate tart to finish. A children's choice is also available.

Open all wk 11.30-2.30 6-11 (Sun noon-3 7-10.30) **Bar Meals** L served all wk 12-2 D served Mon-Sat 6-9 (Sun 7-9) **Restaurant** L served all wk 12-2 booking required D served Mon-Sat 6-9 (Sun 7-9) booking required ⊕ HALL & WOODHOUSE ◀ Badger Dorset Best, Tanglefoot & Sussex. ♀ 6 **Facilities** Children's menu Dogs allowed Garden Parking

## EVERSHOT

### The Acorn Inn ★★★★ INN ◉ ♀

**DT2 0JW** ☎ **01935 83228** ▤ **01935 83707**
e-mail: stay@acorn-inn.co.uk
web: www.acorn-inn.co.uk
dir: *A303 to Yeovil, Dorchester Rd, on A37 right to Evershot*

Immortalised in Thomas Hardy's Tess of the D'Urbervilles, this 16th-century free house stands in an Area of Outstanding Natural Beauty, with walking, fishing, shooting and riding all nearby. The two oak-panelled bars are warmed by log fires, blazing in carved hamstone fireplaces. It's rumoured that the residents' sitting room was once used as Judge Jeffreys' court room. Most food is locally sourced, and menus include starters such as chicken, wild mushroom and herb terrine. Typical main course choices include roasted butternut squash, Parmesan, cherry tomato and pine nut tagliatelle; sea bass on herb crushed new potatoes with basil pesto; and West Country sausages with grain mustard mash and rosemary jus. Finish with raspberry and Amaretto crème brulée; or creamed mango fool with sesame tuile biscuit and blackberries.

Open all day all wk 11-11 **Bar Meals** L served all wk 12-2 D served all wk 7-9 **Restaurant** L served all wk 12-2 booking required D served all wk 7-9 booking required ⊕ FREE HOUSE ◀ Draymens, guest ale ♂ Thatchers Gold, Thatchers Scrumpy. ♀ 7 **Facilities** Children's menu Family room Dogs allowed Garden Parking **Rooms** 10

## FARNHAM

# The Museum Inn ◉ ♈

**DT11 8DE** ☎ **01825 516261** 📄 **01825 516988**

e-mail: enquiries@museuminn.co.uk

dir: *From Salisbury take A354 to Blandford Forum, 12m. Farnham signed on right. Pub in village centre*

The part-thatched 17th-century Museum owes its name and present existence to the archaeologist General Pitt-Rivers, who took over the Gypsy School nearby to house one of his museums. Beautifully refurbished, the inn retains many original features throughout its civilised beamed rooms, from the stone flagged floors and inglenook fireplace to a traditional bread oven. The same attention to detail is evident in the accomplished kitchen, where a commitment to sourcing local produce reared in traditional ways results in well prepared and presented modern British dishes. Try smoked haddock leek fishcake with lightly curried beurre blanc, followed by confit duck leg with spring onion mash. For dessert, perhaps iced nougat parfait with star anise roasted plum, or treacle tart with blackcurrant coulis.

Open all wk noon-3 6-11 **Bar Meals** L served 12-2 D served 7-9 Av main course £17 **Restaurant** L served Sun 12-2.30 booking required D served Fri-Sat 7-9 booking required Av 3 course à la carte fr £32 ⊕ FREE HOUSE ◀ Ringwood Old Thumper, Timothy Taylor, Jimmy Riddle, Sunchaser Ō Stowford Press, Westons Organic. ♈ 13 **Facilities** Children's menu Dogs allowed Garden Parking

## GILLINGHAM

# The Kings Arms Inn ♈

**East Stour Common SP8 5NB** ☎ **01747 838325**

e-mail: nrosscampbell@aol.com

dir: *4m W of Shaftesbury on A30*

A family-run, 200-year-old free house, this village inn makes a great base for exploring Dorset's countryside and coast. There is a public bar with a log fire, the Mallard and Garden Room and an enclosed acre of attractive beer garden. The menus offer an extensive choice of restaurant fare and traditional pub grub. Popular choices include chicken breast stuffed with haggis on black pudding mash in a Drambuie sauce, or steak and kidney pudding with red onion marmalade. A separate menu is available for children.

Open all wk **Bar Meals** L served Mon-Sat 12-2.30, Sun 12-9.15 booking required D served Mon-Sat 5.30-9.15, Sun 12-9.15 booking required **Restaurant** L served Mon-Sat 12-2.30, Sun 12-9.15 booking required D served Mon-Sat 5.30-9.15, Sun 12-9.15 booking required ⊕ FREE HOUSE ◀ London Pride, Copper Ale, Tribute, Wadworth 6X. ♈ 8 **Facilities** Children's menu Family room Dogs allowed Garden Parking

## LOWER ANSTY

# The Fox Inn ★★★★ INN ♈

**DT2 7PN** ☎ **01258 880328** 📄 **01258 881440**

e-mail: fox@anstyfoxinn.co.uk

dir: *A35 from Dorchester towards Poole for 4m, exit signed Piddlehinton/ Athelhampton House, left to Cheselbourne, then right. Pub in village opposite post office*

Looking more like a grand rectory than a pub, the 250-year-old Fox was built for brewer Charles Hall, later to co-found Blandford's Hall & Woodhouse brewery, whose Badger beers are served in the bar. Typical main courses are pot-roasted half duck with cherry compote and red wine jus; sautéed tiger prawn in sweet pepper and tomato sauce; and grilled fillet steak glazed with Dorset Blue Vinny cheese and herb mash.

Open all wk 11-11 **Bar Meals** L served all wk 12-2.30 D served all wk 6.30-9 Av main course £7.25 **Restaurant** L served all wk 12-2.30 D served all wk 6.30-9 Av 3 course à la carte fr £21 ⊕ HALL & WOODHOUSE ◀ Badger Tanglefoot, Badger Best, Badger Smooth, seasonal guest ale. ♈ 11 **Facilities** Children's menu Dogs allowed Garden Parking **Rooms** 11

## MARSHWOOD

# The Bottle Inn ♈

**DT6 5QJ** ☎ **01297 678254** 📄 **01297 678739**

e-mail: thebottleinn@msn.com

dir: *On B3165 (Crewkerne to Lyme Regis road) 5m from the Hunters Lodge*

The thatched Bottle Inn was first mentioned as an ale house back in the 17th century, and was the first pub in the area during the 18th century to serve bottled beer rather than beer from the jug - hence the name. Its rustic interior has simple wooden settles, scrubbed tables and a blazing fire. The lunch menu keeps it simple with jacket potatoes, grilled paninis, burgers like wild boar and apple, ploughman's, baguettes, lite bites (perhaps crab cakes; pâté; or deep fried brie) plus haddock and chips; chilli; and gammon steak. At dinner choices could be smoked duck with raspberry coulis, followed by traditional suet steak and kidney pudding or supreme of chicken stuffed with smoked salmon with whisky and mustard cream sauce. The pub is home to the annual World Stinging-Nettle Eating Championships. Look out for live music, and remember Tuesday is steak night and Thursday is curry night.

Open all wk noon-3 6-11 **Bar Meals** L served all wk 12-2 booking required Av main course £8 **Restaurant** L served all wk 12-2 booking required D served all wk 6-9 booking required Fixed menu price fr £9.50 ⊕ FREE HOUSE ◀ Otter Ale, Otter Bitter, Stargazer, guest ale Ō Stowford Press, Thatchers Gold. ♈ 7 **Facilities** Children's menu Play area Family room Garden Parking

## MILTON ABBAS

### The Hambro Arms ♀

**DT11 0BP ☎ 01258 880233**
e-mail: info@hambroarms.co.uk
dir: *A354 (Dorchester to Blandford road), turn off at Royal Oak*

This 18th-century thatched pub, now owned by a partnership of villagers, is set in the midst of a picturesque village of thatched, whitewashed cottages, believed to be the first planned settlement in England. The owners' aim is to provide a traditional country pub atmosphere with exceptional food, most of it locally sourced, whether you're looking for a lunchtime snack or fine dining experience. Regular gourmet and oriental evenings are featured.

**Open** all wk 11-3 6-11 (Sat-Sun 11-11) **Bar Meals** L served all wk 12-2.30 D served Sun-Thu 6.30-9, Fri-Sat 6.30-9.30 Av main course £8.95 **Restaurant** L served all wk 12-2.30 D served Sun-Thu 6.30-9, Fri-Sat 6.30-9.30 Fixed menu price fr £11.95 ⊕ FREE HOUSE ◀ Ringwood, Piddle Ales, Durdle Door ♂ Stowford Press. ♀ 8 **Facilities** Children's menu Garden Parking

## MOTCOMBE

### The Coppleridge Inn ⚏ ★★★ INN ♀

**SP7 9HW ☎ 01747 851980 ▤ 01747 851858**
e-mail: thecoppleridgeinn@btinternet.com
web: www.coppleridge.com
dir: *Take A350 to Warminster for 1.5m, left at brown tourist sign.*

Previously a dairy farm, this 18th-century building retains plenty of traditional features, including flagstone floors and log fires. Run by the Goodinge family for nearly 20 years, it offers a good range of real ales and a daily-changing menu of sophisticated pub food, ranging from roasted lamb rump on sweet potato mash with sage jus to grilled lemon sole with dill velouté. For sunny days there is a large garden and terrace with Blackmore Vale views and a secure children's playground.

**Open** all wk 11-3 5-11 (Sat 11am-mdnt Sun noon-11) **Bar Meals** L served all wk 12-2.30 D served all wk 6-9 Av main course £11.50 **Restaurant** L served all wk 12-2.30 D served all wk 6-9 Av 3 course à la carte fr £22 ⊕ FREE HOUSE ◀ Butcombe Bitter, Greene King IPA, Wadworth 6X, Fuller's London Pride, Sharp's Doom Bar. ♀ 10 **Facilities** Children's menu Play area Family room Dogs allowed Garden Parking **Rooms** 10

## NORTH WOOTTON

### The Three Elms ♀

**DT9 5JW ☎ 01935 812881**
e-mail: mark@threeelms.co.uk
dir: *From Sherborne take A352 towards Dorchester then A3030. Pub 1m*

Recently re-opened under new management, The Three Elms has been refurbished but retains its original features, including beams and a log fire. Just outside Sherborne on the edge of the beautiful Blackmore Vale, the inn has a large beer garden with fabulous views. Freshly cooked British classics are served at candlelit tables, including Sunday roasts and regularly-changing blackboard specials. Typical dishes are roast leg of free-range lamb, beer-battered pollock with hand-cut chips, and local pork sausages with mash and caramelised onion jus.

**Open** all wk 11-2.30 6.30-11 (Sun noon-3 7-10.30) Closed: 25-26 Dec **Bar Meals** L served Mon-Sat 12-2, Sun 12-2.30 booking required D served Mon-Sat 6.30-9.30, Sun 7-9 booking required **Restaurant** L served Mon-Sat 12-2, Sun 12-2.30 booking required D served Mon-Sat 6.30-9.30, Sun 7-9 booking required ⊕ FREE HOUSE ◀ Butcombe Bitter ♂ Thatchers Burrow Hill. ♀ 10 **Facilities** Children's menu Dogs allowed Garden Parking

## OSMINGTON MILLS

### The Smugglers Inn ♀

**DT3 6HF ☎ 01305 833125**
e-mail: smugglers.weymouth@hall-woodhouse.co.uk
dir: *7m E of Weymouth towards Wareham, pub signed*

Set on the cliffs at Osmington Mills with the South Coast Footpath running through the garden, the inn has beautiful views across Weymouth Bay. In the late 18th century (the inn dates back to the 13th century) it was the base of infamous smuggler Pierre La Tour who fell in love with the publican's daughter, Arabella Carless, who was shot dead while helping him to escape during a raid. These days you can enjoy a tasty menu with typical dishes like chicken and bacon salad, chargrilled rump steak, and Sussex smokey (fish pie).

**Open** all wk 11-11 (Sun noon-10.30) **Bar Meals** L served all wk 12-9.30 D served all wk 12-9.30 Av main course £9 food served all day **Restaurant** L served all wk 12-9.30 D served all wk 12-9.30 food served all day ⊕ HALL & WOODHOUSE ◀ Badger, Tanglefoot, guest ale. ♀ 12 **Facilities** Children's menu Play area Dogs allowed Garden Parking

## PIDDLEHINTON

### The Thimble Inn

**DT2 7TD ☎ 01300 348270**
e-mail: thimbleinn@googlemail.com
dir: *A35 W'bound, right onto B3143, Piddlehinton in 4m*

Friendly village local with open fires, traditional pub games and good food cooked to order. The pub stands in a pretty valley on the banks of the River Piddle, and the riverside patio is popular in summer. The extensive menu ranges from sandwiches and jacket potatoes to fish choices like poached halibut on leek and white sauce; and grilled trout with almonds.

**Open** all wk 11.30-2.30 6-11 Closed: 25 Dec **Bar Meals** L served all wk 11.30-2 booking required D served all wk 6.30-9 booking required **Restaurant** L served all wk 11.30-2 booking required D served all wk 6.30-9 booking required ⊕ FREE HOUSE ◀ Ringwood Best, Palmer Copper Ale & Palmer IPA, Ringwood Old Thumper, Summer Lightning Ŏ Thatchers Gold, Thatchers Dry. **Facilities** Children's menu Dogs allowed Garden Parking

## PIDDLETRENTHIDE

## The European Inn ♀

DT2 7QT ☎ 01300 348308
e-mail: info@european-inn.co.uk **web:** www.european-inn.co.uk
dir: *5m N of Dorchester on B3143*

Mark and Emily Hammick bought and renovated this inn a few years ago. Whether you want a pint and a snack at the bar, or a three-course dinner with fine wine, the aim is to please you. From the menu, starters of salt cod fritters with watercress and garlic mayo; or game terrine with toast and 'gaggle' chutney. To follow might come Sydling Brook organic pork three ways; or pumpkin risotto with sage butter, rocket, Parmesan and balsamic vinegar. Puddings include rice pudding with home-made damson jam; Piddlehinton apple crumble and custard; and Craig's Farm ice creams.

Closed: 25 Dec, 1 Jan, last 2 wks Jan, Sun eve & Mon
**Bar Meals** L served all wk 12-2 booking required D served Mon-Sat 7-9 booking req Av main course £12 **Restaurant** L served all wk 12-2 booking req D served Mon-Sat 7-9 booking required Av 3 course à la carte fr £23 ⊕ FREE HOUSE ◀ Palmers Copper, St Austell Tribute, Yeovil Stargazer, Sharps Doom Bar, Otter Bright. ♀ 9 **Facilities** Children's menu Dogs allowed Garden Parking

## The Poachers Inn ★★★★ INN ♀

DT2 7QX ☎ 01300 348358 ⌨ 01300 348153
e-mail: info@ thepoachersinn.co.uk
dir: *6m N from Dorchester on B3143. At church end of village*

This family-run inn beside the River Piddle continues to provide real ales, good food, fires and traditional pub games right in the heart of Thomas Hardy country. There's an extensive menu, supported by daily specials that may include home-made spaghetti Bolognese, seafood salad with lemon and dill, or pork and leek sausages with mustard mash. Leave room for traditional red and blackcurrant crumble!

**Open** all day all wk 8am-mdnt **Bar Meals** food served all day **Restaurant** food served all day ⊕ FREE HOUSE ◀ Wadworth 6X, Palmers Copper Ale, Guinness, Hopback, John Smiths Ŏ Thatchers Gold. ♀ 6 **Facilities** Children's menu Dogs allowed Garden Parking **Rooms** 21

## POOLE

## The Guildhall Tavern ♀

15 Market St BH15 1NB ☎ 01202 671717
⌨ 01202 242346
e-mail: sewerynsevfred@aol.com
dir: *2 mins from Quay*

Originally a cider house, this pub stands in the heart of Poole's Old Town, just two minutes from the historic quay. Beautifully fresh fish and seafood dominate the bilingual menus, which reflect the owners' Gallic roots. Moules marinière followed by pan-fried skate wing with butter jus and fresh caper berries are typical offerings, but meat eaters should be satisfied with the likes of pan-fried Scotch beef with Roquefort blue cheese sauce. French themed evenings are held every month.

**Open** Closed: 1st 2wks Nov, Mon **Bar Meals** L served Tue-Sun 12-2.30 Av main course £17 **Restaurant** L served Tue-Sun 12-2.30 D served Tue-Sun 6-10 Fixed menu price fr £14.25 Av 3 course à la carte fr £30 ⊕ PUNCH TAVERNS ◀ Ringwood Best. ♀ 7 **Facilities** Children's menu Dogs allowed Parking

## PUNCKNOWLE

## The Crown Inn ♀

Church St DT2 9BN ☎ 01308 897711
e-mail: crownpuncknowle@btinternet.com
dir: *From A35, into Bridevally, through Litton Cheney. From B3157, inland at Swyre*

There's a traditional atmosphere within the rambling, low-beamed bars at this picturesque 16th-century thatched inn, which was once the haunt of smugglers on their way from nearby Chesil Beach to visit prosperous customers in Bath. Food ranges from light snacks and sandwiches to home-made dishes like lamb chops with mint sauce; mushroom and nut pasta with French bread; and tuna steak with basil and tomato sauce. Recent change of hands.

**Open** 12-3 6-11 Closed: Sun eve **Bar Meals** L served all wk 12-2 D served Mon-Sat 6-9 Av main course £8 **Restaurant** L served all wk 12-2 D served Mon-Sat 6-9 Av 3 course à la carte fr £18 ⊕ PALMERS ◀ Palmers IPA, 200 Premium Ale, Copper, Tally Ho! Ŏ Thatchers Gold. ♀ 10 **Facilities** Children's menu Family room Dogs allowed Garden Parking

**Puncknowle continued**

## Queen's Head

**High St, Milborne Port DT9 5DQ ☎ 01963 250314**
**e-mail:** info@queenshead.co.uk
**dir:** *On A30, 2.5m W of Sherborne towards Sailsbury*

Milborne Port has no facilities for shipping, the suffix being Old English for 'borough', a status it acquired in 1249. The building came much later, in Elizabethan times, although no mention is made of it as a hostelry until 1738. Charming and friendly bars, restaurant, beer garden and skittle alley combine to make it a popular free house in these parts.

**Open** all wk 11-2.30 5.30-11.30 (Fri-Sat 11am-mdnt) **Bar Meals** L served all wk 12-2.30 booking required D served all wk 5.30-9.30 booking required Av main course £7.50 **Restaurant** L served all wk 12-2.30 booking required D served all wk 5.30-9.30 booking required ⊕ ENTERPRISE INNS ◀ Butcombe Bitters, Fuller's London Pride, Hopback Summer Lightning. **Facilities** Children's menu Dogs allowed Garden Parking

## SHROTON OR IWERNE COURTNEY

## The Cricketers

**DT11 8QD ☎ 01258 860421** 🖹 01258 861800
**e-mail:** cricketers@heartstoneinns.co.uk
**dir:** *7m S of Shaftesbury on A350, turn right after Iwerne Minster. 5m N of Blandford Forum on A360, past Stourpaine, in 2m left into Shroton. Pub in village centre*

The Cricketers is a classically English pub, built at the turn of the 20th century, which guarantees a warm welcome. The open plan interior comprises a main bar, comfy bars and pleasant eating areas - all light and airy rooms leading to the restaurant at the rear. This in turn overlooks a lovely garden, well stocked with trees and flowers. Inside, the cricket theme is taken up in the collection of sports memorabilia on display, and during the summer months the local cricket team really does frequent the establishment. The pub is also popular with hikers, lured from the Wessex Way, which runs conveniently through the garden. Expect a menu which contains freshly prepared local favourites and a fine selection of specials, with perhaps locally shot venison and pheasant, and fish direct from the Cornish coast. Themed nights and regular events put the Cricketers firmly at the heart of the community.

**Open** all wk 11-3 6-11 (Sat-Sun 11-11 summer only) **Bar Meals** L served all wk 12-2.30 booking required D served Mon-Sat 6-9.30 booking required Av main course £9.95 **Restaurant** L served all

wk 12-2.30 booking required D served Mon-Sat 6-9.30 booking required ⊕ FREE HOUSE ◀ Tribute Cornish Ale, Ringwood Best, Butcombe, Piddle Ale ♂ Stowford Press. **Facilities** Children's menu Garden Parking

## STRATTON

## Saxon Arms ♥

**DT2 9WG ☎ 01305 260020**
**e-mail:** rodsaxonlamont1@yahoo.co.uk
**dir:** *3m NW of Dorchester on A37, pub at back of village green between church & new village hall*

With its solid oak beams, log-burning stove and flagstone floors, this pretty thatched free house stands overlooking the village green. Popular with fishermen and cycling clubs, the pub is also handy for riverside walks. Menu choices include Dorset ham, egg and chips; smoked haddock and spring onion fishcake; and warm spinach and feta cheese pie.

**Open** all wk 11-3 5.30-late (Sat-Sun 11am-late) **Bar Meals** L served Mon-Sat 11-2.15, Sun 12-9 booking required D served Mon-Sat 6-9.15, Sun 12-9 booking required Av main course £8.95 **Restaurant** L served Mon-Sat 11-2.15, Sun 12-9 booking required D served Mon-Sat 6-9.15, Sun 12-9 booking required Av 3 course à la carte fr £15 ⊕ FREE HOUSE ◀ Fuller's London Pride, Palmers IPA, Ringwood, Timothy Taylor, Butcombe, Abbot, Ruddles ♂ Stowford Press. ♥ 15 **Facilities** Children's menu Dogs allowed Garden Parking

## SYDLING ST NICHOLAS

## The Greyhound Inn ★★★★ INN ◉ ♥

**DT2 9PD ☎ 01300 341303**
**e-mail:** info@thegreyhounddorset.co.uk
**dir:** *Off A37 (Yeovil to Dorchester road), turn off at Cerne Abbas/Sydling St Nicholas*

A 17th-century inn with a walled garden, The Greyhound is set in a picturesque village complete with stream. Food is served in the bar or cosy restaurant, ranging from snacks to the full dining experience. Local seafood is a speciality, with dishes such as pan-fried monkfish with chorizo, fresh basil, cherry tomatoes and sherry, and there is a good choice of meat and game.

**Open** all wk 11-2.30 6-11 Closed: Sun eve **Bar Meals** L served all wk 12-2 booking required D served Mon-Sat 6-9 booking required **Restaurant** L served all wk 12-2 booking required D served Mon-Sat 6-9 booking required ⊕ FREE HOUSE ◀ Palmer IPA, Wadworth 6X, St Austell Tinners, Old Speckled Hen, Spitfire ♂ Thatchers Gold. ♥ 7 **Facilities** Children's menu Play area Dogs allowed Garden Parking **Rooms** 6

## TARRANT MONKTON

### The Langton Arms ★★★★ INN ⛾

**DT11 8RX** ☎ **01258 830225** 🖹 **01258 830053**
e-mail: info@thelangtonarms.co.uk
dir: *A31 from Ringwood, or A357 from Shaftesbury, or A35 from Bournemouth*

Occupying a peaceful spot close to the village church, this attractive 17th-century thatched inn offers the sort of fulfilling meal that on a weekday might comprise marinated crispy beef from the Tarrant Valley, followed by real ale battered haddock, and then home-made mango, pineapple and passion fruit parfait. Or at lunchtime on Sunday, the same degree of satisfaction could well be derived from home-cured gravadlax; roast loin of pork and caramelised onion gravy; and a selection of West Country cheeses with biscuits, celery, grapes and chutney. A comprehensive menu is also available in both bars.

Open all day all wk **Bar Meals** L served Mon-Fri 12-2.30, Sat-Sun all day D served Mon-Thu 6-9.30, Fri 6-10, Sat-Sun all day **Restaurant** L served Mon-Fri 12-2.30, Sat-Sun all day D served Mon-Thu 6-9.30, Fri 6-10, Sat-Sun all day ⊕ FREE HOUSE 🍺 Guest ales (all local). ⛾ 7 **Facilities** Children's menu Play area Family room Dogs allowed Garden Parking **Rooms** 6

## TRENT

### Rose & Crown Trent ⛾

**DT9 4SL** ☎ **01935 850776** 🖹 **01935 850776**
e-mail: hkirkie@hotmail.com **web:** www.roseandcrowntrent.com
dir: *Just off A30 between Sherborne & Yeovil*

You'll find this thatched, ivy-clad inn tucked away in the conservation village of Trent, opposite St Andrew's church. The original building was created in the 14th century for workers erecting the church spire. The present structure was completed in the 18th century, and has been a farmhouse and an inn. Although recently refurbished, the pub's interior speaks eloquently of its past; the Trent Barrow Room, with an open fire, plenty of seating, old bottles and books, is the perfect place to retire with a drink. Owners Heather Kirk and Stuart Malcom have established a menu of impressive home-cooked food using an array of regional ingredients, from village eggs to local cheeses. The light bites and lunch menu brings ploughman's lunches with home-made bread, and platters of tapas to share, as well as more substantial offerings such as a salmon, crab and coriander fishcake with sweet chilli dressing, followed by roast corn-fed chicken breast with black pudding

and a tarragon cream sauce with sautéed potatoes and seasonal vegetables. In the evening, dinner might comprise grilled goats' cheese bruschetta with a beetroot and pear dressing followed by rump of lamb with a herb crust, crushed new potatoes and a redcurrant and port sauce. Traditional puddings include Bramley apple and sultana crumble with vanilla custard; and warm sticky toffee pudding with clotted cream ice cream and butterscotch sauce.

Open 12-3 6-11 (Sat-Sun 12-11) Closed: Mon **Bar Meals** L served Tue-Sun 12-3 booking required D served Tue-Sat 6-9 booking required Av main course £8.95 **Restaurant** L served Tue-Sun 12-3 D served Tue-Sat 6-9 booking required Fixed menu price fr £12.95 Av 3 course à la carte fr £26.95 ⊕ WADWORTH 🍺 6X, Henry's IPA, Horizon, Bishops Tipple, guest ale Ŏ Stowford Press, Thatchers Gold. ⛾ 8 **Facilities** Children's menu Family room Dogs allowed Garden Parking

## WEST LULWORTH

### The Castle Inn ⛾

**Main Rd BH20 5RN** ☎ **01929 400311** 🖹 **01929 400415**
e-mail: office@lulworthinn.com
dir: *Follow village signs from A352 (Dorchester to Wareham road). Inn on right on B3070 through West Lulworth. Car park opposite*

In a delightful setting near Lulworth Cove, this family-run thatched village inn is great for walkers. The bars offer a traditional atmosphere, and outside, you'll find large tiered gardens packed with plants. The wide-ranging menu includes chicken stroganoff, seafood stew, sirloin steak grill, and tuna steak. There's also a good vegetarian choice.

Open all wk Closed: 25 Dec **Bar Meals** L served all wk 12-2 D served all wk 7-10 Av main course £8.50 ⊕ FREE HOUSE 🍺 John Smiths, Sharps, Isle of Purbeck, Piddle Ales, Palmers. ⛾ 8 **Facilities** Children's menu Dogs allowed Garden Parking

## CO DURHAM

## AYCLIFFE

### The County ⛾

**13 The Green, Aycliffe Village DL5 6LX** ☎ **01325 312273**
🖹 **01325 312273**
e-mail: colettefarrell@btinternet.com
dir: *Off A167 into Aycliffe Village. Off Junct 59 A1(M)*

Quietly positioned overlooking the village green, the award-winning County can be found in Aycliffe village some four miles north of Darlington. Using the best of local ingredients, especially top quality fish and game, the bistro-type daily specials board adds variety to the menu.

Open all wk 12-3 6-11 Closed: 25 Dec, 1 Jan **Bar Meals** L served Mon-Sat 12-2, Sun 12-2.30 D served all wk 6-9 Av main course £8.95 **Restaurant** L served Mon-Sat 12-2, Sun 12-2.30 D served all wk 6-9 Av 3 course à la carte fr £22 ⊕ FREE HOUSE 🍺 Jennings Cumberland Ale, Castle Eden. ⛾ 7 **Facilities** Children's menu Parking

# Co Durham

## BARNARD CASTLE

### The Bridge Inn & Restaurant
**Whorlton Village DL12 8XD ☎ 01833 627341**
📠 01833 627995
e-mail: info@thebridgeinnrestaurant.co.uk
web: www.thebridgeinnrestaurant.co.uk

It was a bold move that brought chef/patron Paul O'Hara to this quaint village near Barnard Castle, after six years in charge of the kitchen at Durham's renowned Bistro 21. No longer, then, do the good people of Teesdale have to travel miles to experience the taste and sophistication of city dining. In either the restaurant or outside, start with roast wood-pigeon breasts, and then try to decide between champagne risotto with wild mushrooms and Parmesan crisp; salmon and cod fishcakes; fillet and slow-cooked beef with shallots and two celeries; pot-roast pheasant with bacon, chestnuts and Brussels sprouts, or something from the vegetarian menu. Blackboards display specials such as poached fillet of wild sea bass, monkfish tails and scallops with spring onion risotto. To finish, perhaps profiteroles; apple and cinnamon crumble; creamed rice pudding; dark chocolate soufflé with boozy cherries and pistachio ice cream; or sticky toffee pudding with butterscotch sauce.

**Open** noon-2 6.30-11 (Sun 5.30-10) **Closed:** 24 Dec eve, 25-26 Dec, Mon-Tue **Bar Meals** L served Wed-Sun 12-2 booking required D served Wed-Sat 6.30-11 booking required Av main course £15.50 **Restaurant** Fixed menu price fr £14 Av 3 course à la carte fr £26 🍺 Timothy Taylor Landlord, Theakstons Black Bull. **Facilities** Children's menu Dogs allowed Garden Parking

### The Morritt Arms Hotel ★★★ HL 🍷
**Greta Bridge DL12 9SE ☎ 01833 627232**
📠 01833 627392
e-mail: relax@themorritt.co.uk
dir: *At Scotch Corner take A66 towards Penrith, after 9m turn at Greta Bridge. Hotel over bridge on left*

Situated in rural Teesdale, The Morritt Arms has been an inn for two centuries. Full of character, the bar is very much focused on food. Here the carte offers starters of pressed ham, black pudding, Wensleydale cheese and home-made chutney; chilli and garlic tiger prawns with soft egg noodles, spring onions and coriander; British beef carpaccio with garlic dressing; wild mushrooms on toast with poached Neasham egg, truffle and tarragon dressing. Main courses include slow roasted belly pork with bubble and squeak, roasted roots and

mustard jus; pan-fried trout, saffron and pea risotto, parsley oil; Teesdale lamb rack, leek and mustard mash, parsnips and redcurrant jus; and Mediterranean vegetables, sun blushed tomatoes, goats' cheese and tomato sauce. You can also dine in the oak-panelled hotel restaurant, Pallatt's bistro, or the landscaped gardens.

**Open** all day all wk 7am-11pm **Bar Meals** food served all day **Restaurant** L served all wk 12-3 D served all wk 7-9.30 ⊕ FREE HOUSE 🍺 John Smith's, Timothy Taylor Landlord, Black Sheep Best. 🍷 20 **Facilities** Children's menu Play area Family room Dogs allowed Garden Parking **Rooms** 27

## COTHERSTONE

### The Fox and Hounds 🍷
**DL12 9PF ☎ 01833 650241**
e-mail: foxenquiries@tiscali.co.uk
dir: *4m W of Barnard Castle. From A66 onto B6277, signed*

This delightful 18th-century coaching inn in the heart of Teesdale is a perfect holiday base. Both the restaurant and the heavily beamed bar boast welcoming winter fires in original fireplaces. Fresh local ingredients are the foundation of home-made food such as a warm salad of Wensleydale cheese, bacon, cranberries and apple; steak, black pudding and Black Sheep ale pie; or pan-fried crown of Holwick pheasant on bubble and squeak mash with rich gravy.

**Open** all wk 12-2.30 6.30-11 (Sun 6.30-10.30) **Closed:** 25-26 Dec **Bar Meals** L served all wk 12-2 D served all wk 6.30-9 **Restaurant** D served all wk 6.30-9 ⊕ FREE HOUSE 🍺 Black Sheep Best, Village Brewer Bull Bitter, Black Sheep Ale, Daleside Special, Yorkshire Terrier. 🍷 10 **Facilities** Children's menu Garden Parking

## MIDDLESTONE

### Ship Inn 🍷
**Low Rd DL14 8AB ☎ 01388 810904**
e-mail: tony.theshipinn@googlemail.com
dir: *On B6287 (Kirk Merrington to Coundon road)*

Beer drinkers will appreciate the string of real ale-related accolades received by this family-run pub on the village green. In the last five years regulars could have sampled well over 800 different beers. Home-cooked food is served in the bar and restaurant, using beef, pork and lamb reared locally. The Ship has three unique attributes – it is 23 miles from the sea, 550 feet above sea level and the cellar is 9 feet above the bar! The rooftop patio has spectacular views over the Tees Valley and Cleveland Hills.

**Open** all wk 4-11 (Fri-Sun noon-11) **Bar Meals** L served Fri-Sun 12-2 D served all wk 6-9 Av main course £4.95 ⊕ FREE HOUSE 🍺 6 guest ales. 🍷 13 **Facilities** Children's menu Play area Family room Dogs allowed Parking

England

## MIDDLETON-IN-TEESDALE

# The Teesdale Hotel ★★ HL

**Market Square DL12 0QG ☎ 01833 640264**
🖹 01833 640651
e-mail: enquiries@teesdalehotel.com
dir: *Telephone for directions*

Just off the Pennine Way, this tastefully modernised, family-run former coaching inn enjoys some of Britain's loveliest scenery. It has a striking 18th-century stone exterior and archway, while the interior is warm and friendly, with an open fire in the bar. All food is home-made using local produce. A typical meal might include black pudding with a spicy plum sauce followed by steak and ale pie with chips and mushy peas.

Open all day all wk **Bar Meals** L served all wk 12.30-2.30 D served all wk 7-9 Av main course £6.50 **Restaurant** D served all wk 7-9 Fixed menu price fr £8.50 Av 3 course à la carte fr £16.50 ⊕ FREE HOUSE ◀ Guinness, Tetley Smooth, Black Sheep Best Bitter. **Facilities** Children's menu Dogs allowed Parking Rooms 14

## NEWTON AYCLIFFE

# Blacksmiths Arms ♀

**Preston le Skerne, (off Ricknall Lane) DL5 6JH**
☎ 01325 314873
dir: *Telephone for directions*

A former smithy dating from the 1700s, and still relatively isolated in its farmland setting. Enjoying an excellent reputation locally as a good dining pub, it offers starters of hot smoked mackerel and potato salad; cod and prawn brandade; chicken fillet goujons; and potted mushrooms. Requiring their own page on the menu are fish dishes such as grilled halibut steak with risotto, and gingered salmon. Chef's specialities include Gressingham duck breast, and pork au poivre.

Open Closed: 1 Jan, Mon ⊕ FREE HOUSE ◀ Ever changing selection of real ales. ♀ 10 **Facilities** Children's menu Play area Garden Parking

## SEDGEFIELD

# Dun Cow Inn ♀

**43 Front St TS21 3AT ☎ 01740 620894 🖹 01740 622163**
e-mail: dunn_cow@btconnect.com
dir: *At junct of A177 & A689. Inn in village centre*

An interesting array of bric-a-brac can be viewed inside this splendid old village inn, which has many flower baskets bedecking its exterior in summer. Typical offerings include Angus sirloin steaks, locally-made sausages, spring lamb cutlets, fresh Shetland mussels, and mushroom stroganoff. Pudding choices often include gooseberry crumble and chocolate fudge cake with butterscotch sauce.

Open all wk all wk 11am-3pm, 6pm-mdnt **Bar Meals** L served Mon-Sat 12-2, Sun 12-8 D served Mon-Sat 6.30-9.30, Sun 12-8 **Restaurant** L served Mon-Sat 12-2, Sun 12-8 booking required D served Mon-Sat 6.30-9.30, Sun 12-8 booking required ⊕ FREE HOUSE ◀ Theakston Best Bitter, John Smiths Smooth, Black Sheeps Bitter, Guest ales. ♀ 8 **Facilities** Children's menu Parking

## ESSEX

## BRAINTREE

# The Green Dragon at Young's End ♀

**Upper London Rd, Young's End CM77 8QN**
☎ 01245 361030 🖹 01245 362575
e-mail: info@thegreendragonyoungsend.co.uk
dir: *At Braintree bypass take A131 S towards Chelmsford, exit at Young's End on Great Leighs bypass*

The Green Dragon provides a comfortable venue for good drinking and dining, with winter fires creating a cosy atmosphere in the friendly bars, which are smartly decked in contemporary designs and lots of original exposed beams and stylish furnishings. The spacious restaurant maintains the rustic theme with bare brick walls and wonderful old beams. Outside there's a large garden and heated patio area. The bar menu offers the likes of beer-battered cod and chips, Essex bangers and mash, omelettes, jackets and sandwiches, while the restaurant goes in for dishes like chicken breast stuffed with brie and bacon, steak and ale pie, or halibut with mussels and tagliatelle of leek. There is also the option of private dining in the Hayloft Restaurant.

Open all wk **Bar Meals** L served Mon-Sat 12-3, Sun all day D served Mon-Sat 6-9, Sun all day Av main course £7.50 **Restaurant** L served Mon-Sat 12-3, Sun all day booking required D served Mon-Sat 6-9, Sun all day booking required Av 3 course à la carte fr £9.95 ⊕ GREENE KING ◀ Greene King IPA , Abbot Ale. ♀ 10 **Facilities** Children's menu Garden Parking

England

## CASTLE HEDINGHAM

# The Bell Inn 🍷

**Saint James St CO9 3EJ ☎ 01787 460350**
e-mail: bell-castle@hotmail.co.uk
web: www.hedinghambell.co.uk
dir: *On A1124 N of Halstead, right to Castle Hedingham*

Run by the same family for over 40 years, this unspoilt pub began life in the 15th century as a coaching inn. Today it oozes traditional charm, from log fires in winter to a huge orchard garden and vine-covered patio for summer lounging. Food from quality local suppliers is home cooked and largely traditional, although the Turkish chef offers interesting specials such as grilled lamb meatballs. Fish is hand-picked from Billingsgate or delivered fresh from Colchester. Summer and winter beer festivals are a feature.

Open all wk 11.45-3 6-11 (Fri-Sat noon-mdnt Sun noon-11) Closed: 25 Dec eve **Bar Meals** L served Mon-Fri 12-2, Sat-Sun 12-2.30 D served Sun-Mon 7-9, Tue-Sat 7-9.30 Av main course £8.50 ⊕ GRAYS ◀ Maldon Gold Mighty Oak, Adnams Bitter, Mighty Oak IPA, guest ale Ŏ Stowford Press. 🍷 8 **Facilities** Children's menu Play area Family room Dogs allowed Garden Parking

## CLAVERING

# The Cricketers 🍷

**CB11 4QT ☎ 01799 550442 📄 01799 550882**
e-mail: info@thecricketers.co.uk
dir: *From M11 junct 10, A505 E. Then A1301, B1383. At Newport take B1038*

With landlords called Sally and Trevor Oliver, it might come as no surprise to learn that this newly refurbished, 16th-century village pub is where celebrity chef Jamie first learnt to devil a kidney. Its proximity to the cricket pitch long ago suggested that appropriate memorabilia should decorate the beamed, log fire-warmed bar and restaurant, both of which offer seasonally changing menus and daily specials. Head chef, Justin Greig, is passionate about using excellent produce. Typical are meat and vegetarian antipasti; braised rabbit with home-made gnocchi

and mixed wild mushrooms; pavé of Scottish salmon on crab spaghetti; sautéed calf's liver and bacon with Szechuan spiced potatoes; and spinach and feta filo pastry pie, while there's always plenty of fish, and a roast every Sunday. The celebrity chef himself supplies the vegetables, herbs and leaves from his certified organic garden nearby. The children's menu steers clear of the 'dreaded nuggets'.

Open all day all wk Closed: 25-26 Dec **Bar Meals** L served all wk 12-2 booking required D served all wk 6.30-9.30 booking required Av main course £13 **Restaurant** L served all wk 12-2 booking required D served all wk 6.30-9.30 booking required Av 3 course à la carte fr £29.50 ⊕ FREE HOUSE ◀ Adnams Bitter, Tetley Bitter, Greene King IPA, Adnams Broadside, Woodforde's Wherry, Nog Ŏ Aspall. 🍷 10 **Facilities** Children's menu Play area Family room Garden Parking

## COLCHESTER

# The Rose & Crown Hotel ★★★ HL 🍷

**East St CO1 2TZ ☎ 01206 866677 📄 01206 866616**
e-mail: info@rose-and-crown.com
dir: *From M25 junct 28 take A12 N. Follow Colchester signs*

The Rose & Crown is a beautiful timber-framed building dating from the 14th century, believed to be the oldest hotel in the oldest town in England, just a few minutes' from Colchester Castle. The Tudor bar with its roaring fire is a great place to relax with a drink. Food is served in the Oak Room, the main restaurant awarded two AA rosettes, or the Tudor Room brasserie, an informal alternative serving classic bar food.

Open all wk **Bar Meals** L served all wk 12-2.30 D served all wk 6.30-9.30 Av main course £10 ⊕ FREE HOUSE ◀ Tetley's Bitter, Rose & Crown Bitter, Adnams Broadside. 🍷 7 **Facilities** Children's menu Family room Parking **Rooms** 38

## DEDHAM

# Marlborough Head Inn 🍷

**Mill Ln CO7 6DH ☎ 01206 323250**
e-mail: jen.pearmain@tiscali.co.uk
dir: *E of A12, N of Colchester*

Tucked away in glorious Constable Country, a 16th-century building that was once a clearing-house for local wool merchants. In 1660, after a slump in trade, it became an inn. Today it is as perfect for a pint, sofa and newspaper as it is for a good home-cooked family meal. Traditional favourites such as steak, Guinness and mushroom pie; and lamb shank with red wine and rosemary appear on the menu, plus fish is given centre stage on Fridays.

Open all wk 11.30-11 **Bar Meals** Av main course £8.95 food served all day **Restaurant** food served all day ⊕ PUNCH ◀ Adnams Southwold, Greene King IPA Ŏ Aspall. 🍷 8 **Facilities** Children's menu Family room Dogs allowed Garden Parking

## AIRSTEAD

# The Square and Compasses ♟

**Fuller St CM3 2BB** ☎ **01245 361477** 📄 **01245 361548**
**e-mail:** info@thesquareandcompasses.co.uk
**web:** www.thesquareandcompasses.co.uk
**dir:** *A131 Chelmsford to Braintree. Take Great Leighs exit, enter village
turn right into Boreham rd. Turn left signed Fuller St & Terling. Pub on
left as you enter hamlet*

Brought back to life following a two-year closure, this lovingly
restored 17th-century pub stands in a sleepy hamlet and is
worth seeking out for local micro-brewery ales and hearty pub
food cooked from local seasonal produce. Eat in the main bar,
adorned with old farming tools, or at old oak tables by the fire
in the dining room. Choose a classic chicken and leek pie or
follow chilli and lime squid with pheasant and rabbit casserole,
and chocolate cheesecake.

**Open** all wk 11.30-3 6-11 (Sat-Sun noon-11) **Bar Meals** L served
Mon-Fri 12-2, Sat 12-2.30, Sun 12-4 D served Tue-Sat 6.30-9.30
booking required Av main course £10 **Restaurant** L served Tue-Fri
12-2, Sat 12-2.30, Sun 12-4 D served Tue-Sat 6.30-9.30 booking
required Av 3 course à la carte fr £22 ⊕ FREE HOUSE ◀ Stokers
Ales, Oscar Wilde, Mighty Oak, Suffolk County, Nethergate,
Hophead Dark Star ♂ Stowford Press, Thatchers. ♟ 14
**Facilities** Children's menu Dogs allowed Garden Parking

## FEERING

# The Sun Inn ♟

**Feering Hill CO5 9NH** ☎ **01376 570442** 📄 **01376 570442**
**e-mail:** andy.howard@virgin.net
**dir:** *On A12 between Colchester & Witham. Village 1m*

Real ale and real food are at the heart of this pretty, timbered
pub that dates from 1525. There's a large garden for the
summer months, while winter warmth comes from two
inglenook fireplaces. There are no TVs or games machines; the
customers create the atmosphere. Food-wise, expect simple,
seasonal dishes; perhaps tempura-battered prawns followed
by fresh fish in a Spitfire ale batter with chips, peas and home-
made tartare sauce, with plum crumble for pudding.

**Open** all wk **Bar Meals** L served Mon-Sat 12-2.30, Sun
12-9 D served Mon-Sat 6-9.30, Sun 12-9 Av main course £8
**Restaurant** L served Mon-Sat 12-2.30, Sun 12-9 D served Mon-
Sat 6-9.30, Sun 12-9 ⊕ SHEPHERD NEAME ◀ Master Brew,
Spitfire, Bishops Finger, seasonal ale. ♟ 8 **Facilities** Children's
menu Dogs allowed Garden Parking

## FELSTED

# The Swan at Felsted ♟

**Station Rd CM6 3DG** ☎ **01371 820245** 📄 **01371 821393**
**e-mail:** info@theswanatfelsted.co.uk
**web:** www.theswanatfelsted.co.uk
**dir:** *Exit M11 junct 8 onto A120 signed Felsted. Pub in village centre*

Venture through the door of this red brick-and-timber building
and be pleasantly surprised. Rebuilt after a disastrous fire in
the early 1900s and formerly the village bank, then a run-
down boozer, it was rescued and stylishly refurbished by Jono
and Jane Clarke in 2002. Today it's very much a gastro-pub,
with polished wood floors, leather sofas, chunky furnishings
and colourful modern art, and successfully balances being a
traditional pub and a quality restaurant. The atmosphere is
friendly and informal and locals beat a path to the door for
imaginative menus that champion locally sourced produce.
Menus are sensibly short, the pubby lunch choice taking in
honey roast ham, egg and hand-cut chips, macaroni cheese
with tomato and herb crust, and beer-battered fish and chips.
Cooking moves up a gear in the evening, with pan-seared
scallops with cauliflower purée and lamb rump with Puy lentils
and winter vegetables to choose from.

**Open** all wk noon-3 5-11 (Sun noon-6) **Bar Meals** L served
Mon-Sat 12-2.30, Sun 12-4 D served Mon-Sat 6-9.30
**Restaurant** L served Mon-Sat 12-2.30, Sun 12-4 booking
required D served Mon-Sat 6-9.30 booking required ⊕ GREENE
KING ◀ IPA, Prospect, Guinness, guest ale ♂ Stowford Press. ♟ 9
**Facilities** Children's menu Dogs allowed Garden Parking

## HORNDON ON THE HILL

# Bell Inn & Hill House ♟

**High Rd SS17 8LD** ☎ **01375 642463** 📄 **01375 361611**
**e-mail:** info@bell-inn.co.uk
**dir:** *M25 junct 30/31 signed Thurrock*

The Bell is a 15th-century coaching inn, as the archway
through to the courtyard testifies. Once you are inside, look
for the original king post that supports the inn's ancient roof
timbers. The bar menu offers lunchtime sandwiches and light
meals such as pan-fried fishcakes with poached egg and
hollandaise; and braised lamb's liver with mustard mash and
red wine sauce. From the daily-changing restaurant menu,
built around the freshest produce, you might start with Loch
Fyne smoked salmon with scrambled egg and cheddar rarebit;

continued

pan-fried snails with Café de Paris butter in puff pastry; or cream of parsnip soup with croutons. For your main course, options might include roast duck with balsamic roast fig and cranberry compote; pan-fried scallops with mushy peas and oyster dressing; or wild mushroom ravioli with sauté of wild mushroom and Parmesan. Stylish desserts could prove somewhat tempting: try caramelised pannacotta with rhubarb compote, ginger ice cream and lemon shortbread.

Open all wk Closed: 25-26 Dec **Bar Meals** L served all wk 12-1.45 D served all wk 6.30-9.45 Av main course £15.95 **Restaurant** L served Mon-Sat 12-1.45, Sun 12-2.30 booking required D served all wk 6.30-9.45 booking required Av 3 course à la carte fr £23 ⊕ FREE HOUSE ◀ Greene King IPA, Interbrew Bass, Crouchvale Brewers Gold, Ruddles County, Spitfire. ♀ 16 **Facilities** Children's menu Dogs allowed Garden Parking

## LITTLE CANFIELD

## The Lion & Lamb ♀

**CM6 1SR** ☎ **01279 870257** 📄 **01279 870423**
e-mail: info@lionandlamb.co.uk
dir: *M11 junct 8, B1256 towards Takeley & Little Canfield*

A favourite for business or leisure, this traditional country pub restaurant is handy for Stansted airport and the M11. Inside you'll find oak beams, winter log fires, and an extensive food selection. From the bar menu choose sandwiches, steak and ale pie, Lion & Lamb beef burger, lasagne or sausage and mash. In the restaurant sample vegetable moussaka of red lentils and aubergine, Thai red beef curry, or a kangaroo fillet from the grill!

Open all wk 11-11 **Bar Meals** Av main course £9 food served all day **Restaurant** Av 3 course à la carte fr £25 food served all day ⊕ GREENE KING ◀ Old Speckled Hen, Greene King IPA, Old Bob, guest ales. ♀ 10 **Facilities** Children's menu Play area Garden Parking

## MANNINGTREE

## The Mistley Thorn ⊛⊛ ♀

**High St, Mistley CO11 1HE** ☎ **01206 392821**
📄 **01206 390122**
e-mail: info@mistleythorn.com
dir: *From Ipswich A12 junct 31 onto B1070, follow signs to East Bergholt, Manningtree & Mistley. From Colchester A120 towards Harwich. Left at Horsley Cross. Mistley in 3m*

Built as a coaching inn around 1723, this historic free house overlooking the two-mile wide River Stour estuary, offers award-winning dining and accommodation in tastefully designed surroundings. Stylewise, the interior is a touch New England, with terracotta-tiled floors, exposed beams and high-quality furnishings. American-born executive chef Sherri Singleton, who also runs the Mistley Kitchen cookery school, develops accomplished menus using abundant quantities of the best local produce – world-famous rock oysters from Mersea Island; lobsters from Harwich; Suffolk beef and lamb; and salad leaves and herbs grown by a certified-organic smallholder. Among the line-up worthy of the pub's two AA Rosettes are crayfish ceviche; smoked haddock chowder; chicken liver and smoked bacon rosemary skewer with balsamic onions and toast; roasted duck breast with spring onion potato cake, braised red cabbage and cherry jus; chargrilled rib-eye with tempura onion rings, grilled cherry tomatoes and garlic field mushrooms; and aubergine rollatini with ricotta, Parmesan and pesto.

Open all wk 12-2.30 6.30-9 (Sat-Sun all day) **Bar Meals** L served Mon-Fri 12-2.30, Sat-Sun all day D served Mon-Fri 6.30-9, Sat 6.30-9.30 Av main course £12 **Restaurant** L served Mon-Fri 12-2.30, Sat-Sun all day D served Mon-Fri 6.30-9, Sat 6.30-9.30 Fixed menu price fr £10.95 Av 3 course à la carte fr £21 ⊕ FREE HOUSE ◀ Adnams. ♀ 17 **Facilities** Children's menu Dogs allowed Parking

## NORTH FAMBRIDGE

## The Ferry Boat Inn

**Ferry Ln CM3 6LR** ☎ **01621 740208**
e-mail: sylviaferryboat@aol.com
dir: *From Chelmsford take A130 S then A132 to South Woodham Ferrers, then B1012. right to village*

Owned by the same family for 26 years, this 500-year-old traditional weatherboard inn has beams, log fires and a resident ghost. It is tucked away at the end of a lovely village on the River Crouch, next to the marina, and was once a centre for smugglers. These days it is understandably popular with the sailing fraternity. In addition to the extensive menu and chef's specials, dishes might include minted lamb chop, grilled sea bass, chicken korma or beef chilli.

**Open** all wk 11.30-3 6.30-11 (Sun 12-4 6.30-10.30 & all day in summer) **Bar Meals** food served all day **Restaurant** food served all day ⊕ FREE HOUSE ◀ Greene King IPA, Abbot Ale, Morland. **Facilities** Children's menu Family room Dogs allowed Garden Parking

## PATTISWICK

# The Compasses at Pattiswick ⚑

**Compasses Rd CM77 8BG** ☎ **01376 561322**
📄 **01376 564343**
**e-mail:** info@thecompassesatpattiswick.co.uk
**web:** www.thecompassesatpattiswick.co.uk
**dir:** *From Braintree take A120 E towards Colchester. After Bradwell 1st left to Pattiswick*

Once two estate workers' cottages, The Compasses is now an award-winning dining pub, whose owners' passion for good food translates into straightforward but superbly cooked dishes, jam-packed with local produce. At lunchtime try potted shrimps; local pork pie with home-made piccalilli; grilled plaice fillets with scallop butter and cavolo nero; or a daily special. The dinner menu is studded with dishes like sweet potato and parsnip curry with braised rice and raita, rib-eye steak with sautéed mushrooms and peppercorn butter; roasted sea bass fillets with anchovy mash and chive clotted cream; and blackboard specials, such as Cajun-crusted sea trout with ginger and garlic-roasted peppers. The desserts list favours the classics – apple and rhubarb crumble with vanilla ice cream; and spotted dick with home-made custard. A roaring log fire make a welcoming sight in winter after a local walk, while in summer the large garden is inviting.

**Open** all wk 11-3 5.30-11 (Sat 5.30-mdnt, Sun noon-4.30, Sun eve in Summer) **Bar Meals** L served all wk 12-3 D served Mon-Thu 6-9.30, Fri-Sat 6-9.45 **Restaurant** L served Mon-Sat 12-3, Sun 12-4.30 booking required D served Mon-Thu 6-9.30, Fri-Sat 6-9.45 booking required ⊕ FREE HOUSE ◀ Woodforde's Wherry, Adnams, Adnams Broadside, St Austell Tribute ♂ Aspalls. ⚑ 12 **Facilities** Children's menu Play area Dogs allowed Garden Parking

## STOCK

# The Hoop ⚑

**21 High St CM4 9BD** ☎ **01277 841137**
**e-mail:** thehoopstock@yahoo.co.uk
**dir:** *On B1007 between Chelmsford & Billericay*

This 15th-century free house on Stock's village green is every inch the traditional pub. Expect a warm welcome, real ales and a pleasing lack of music or fruit machines. The annual beer festival enjoys growing popularity, but the food is also a major draw. In keeping with the gorgeously traditional interior, a meal might include potted shrimps with brown bread; calves' liver with bacon, mash and onion rings; and bread and butter pudding for dessert.

**Open** all wk 11-11 (Sun 12-10.30) **Bar Meals** L served Mon-Sat 12-2.30, Sun 12-5 D served Mon-Sat 6-9 Av main course f9 **Restaurant** L served Tue-Fri 12-2.30, Sun 12-5 booking required D served Tue-Sat 6-9 booking required Av 3 course à la carte fr £25 ⊕ FREE HOUSE ◀ Adnams Bitter, 4 guest ales ♂ Westons, Thatchers. ⚑ 10 **Facilities** Children's menu Dogs allowed Garden

## WOODHAM MORTIMER

# Hurdle Makers Arms ⚑

**Post Office Rd CM9 6ST** ☎ **01245 225169**
📄 **01245 225169**
**e-mail:** gary@hurdlemakersarms.co.uk
**dir:** *From Chelmsford A414 to Maldon/Danbury. 4.5m, through Danbury into Woodham Mortimer. Over 1st rdbt, 1st left, pub on left. Behind golf driving range*

A Grade II listed building dating back 400 years, the Hurdle Makers Arms has been a pub since 1837. Right at the heart of village life, it has live music, quiz nights and regular themed food evenings. Real ale lovers will be delighted by the wide range of micro-brewery products, and there are even guest ciders. Home-made pub food is served seven days a week, and in summer there are weekend barbecues in the large garden.

**Open** all wk all day summer (winter Mon-Thu noon-3 5.30-11 Fri-Sat all day Sun 12-9) **Bar Meals** L served Mon-Fri 12-3, Sat 12-9.30, Sun 12-8 D served Mon-Fri 6-9.30, Sat 12-9.30, Sun 12-8 **Restaurant** L served Mon-Fri 12-3, Sat 12-9.30, Sun 12-8 D served Mon-Fri 6-9.30, Sat 12-9.30, Sun 12-8 ⊕ GRAY & SONS ◀ Abbot, Mighty Oak, Crouch Vale, Farmers ales, Guest ales ♂ Old Rosie. ⚑ 8 **Facilities** Children's menu Play area Garden Parking

## GLOUCESTERSHIRE

### ALDERTON

## The Gardeners Arms ♀

**Beckford Rd GL20 8NL ☎ 01242 620257**
e-mail: gardeners1@btconnect.com
web: www.gardenersarms.biz
dir: *Please telephone for directions*

This family-run, 16th-century thatched free house is in a quiet Cotswolds village. You can play boules in the large beer garden, and shove ha'penny or other traditional bar games in the stone-walled bar. Seasonal local produce and daily fresh fish underpin simple dishes such as home-made beef lasagne; tiger prawn Thai green curry; liver, bacon and onions; broccoli and cauliflower cheese gratin; and Mediterranean vegetable Wellington. Monthly-changing specials include slow-braised Cotswold lamb shoulder; and pan-fried halibut steak. Two beer festivals are held, one in May and the other at Christmas.

Open all wk 10-2 5-10 (Sun all day, Fri till mdnt) **Bar Meals** L served all wk 12-2 D served all wk 5.30-9 Av main course £4.50 **Restaurant** L served Mon-Sat 12-2, Sun all day booking required D served all wk 5.30-9.30 booking required Fixed menu price fr £10 Av 3 course à la carte fr £15 ⊕ FREE HOUSE ◀ Doom Bar, Butcombe Best, Courage Best, Local Guest Ales Ŏ Westons GWR. ♀ 8 **Facilities** Children's menu Dogs allowed Garden Parking

### ALMONDSBURY

## The Bowl ♀

**16 Church Rd BS32 4DT ☎ 01454 612757**
🖹 01454 619910
e-mail: bowlinn@sabrain.com
dir: *M5 junct 16 towards Thornbury. 3rd left onto Over Ln, 1st right onto Sundays Hill, next right onto Church Rd*

Originally built to house monks building the village church, The Bowl became an inn in 1550. Its name derives from the shape of the valley around the nearby Severn Estuary, which can be seen from the inn. Brains ales are on offer, and food can be eaten in the bar or the restaurant, which may offer roasted free range chicken breast, Vichycoisse and crisp pancetta; hand-made cheddar, garlic and mushroom ravioli; or pan-fried sea bass with courgette spaghetti.

Open all wk 12-3 5-11 (Sat noon-11 Sun noon-10.30) **Bar Meals** L served Mon-Fri 12-2.30, Sat 12-10, Sun 12-8 D served Mon-Fri 6-10 Av main course £9 **Restaurant** L served Sun 12-2 booking required D served Mon-Sat 6-9 booking required Av 3 course à la carte fr £28 ⊕ BRAINS BREWERY S.A.BRAIN & CO LTD ◀ Butcombe, Tribute Ŏ Stowford Press. ♀ 9 **Facilities** Children's menu Parking

### ARLINGHAM

## The Old Passage Inn ★★★★ RR 🏵🏵 ♀

**Passage Rd GL2 7JR ☎ 01452 740547  🖹 01452 741871**
e-mail: oldpassage@ukonline.co.uk
dir: *5m from A38 adjacent M5 junct 13*

In a tranquil location on the banks of the tidal River Severn, surrounded by fields and wonderful views, this ancient inn was once a ferry station for services crossing the river. Although it's more restaurant-with-rooms than a pub, expect an informal atmosphere in the open and airy dining room, and a relaxed approach in summer when the riverside terrace throngs at lunchtimes. First-class seafood cookery is the real draw, the almost exclusively fish and shellfish menu attracting lovers of seafood. Start, perhaps, potted shrimps, fish soup with saffron mayonnaise, or simple smoked salmon with capers and lemon dressing. Fruits de mer are served hot or cold, with other fish dishes including wild sea bass with saffron and vanilla sauce, and fish stew. Non-fish alternatives may include chargrilled sirloin steak and roast partridge.

Open 11-3 6-finish (all day Etr-Sep) Closed: 25 Dec, Sun eve & Mon **Bar Meals** Av main course £17.50 **Restaurant** L served Tue-Sat 12-2.30, Sun 12-3 booking required D served Tue-Sat 6-9 booking required Fixed menu price fr £15 Av 3 course à la carte fr £80 ⊕ FREE HOUSE ◀ Wickwar Ŏ Westons Organic. ♀ 14 **Facilities** Children's menu Dogs allowed Garden Parking **Rooms** 3

### BERKELEY

## The Malt House ★★★ INN ♀

**Marybrook St GL13 9BA ☎ 01453 511177**
🖹 01453 810257
e-mail: the-malthouse@btconnect.com
web: www.themalthouse.uk.com
dir: *M5 junct 13/14, A38 towards Bristol. Pub on main road towards Sharpness*

Within walking distance of Berkeley Castle and its deer park, this family-run free house is also handy for the Edward Jenner

museum, dedicated to the life of the founding father of immunology. Inside the heavily beamed pub you'll find a varied selection of lunchtime bar food, as well as weekly home-made specials. Pub favourites like steak and ale pie rub shoulders with vegetarian stuffed peppers; and grilled halibut, butter and lime.

**Open** all wk 4-11 (Fri-Sat noon-mdnt Sun noon-4) **Bar Meals** L served Fri-Sun 12-2 D served Mon-Sat 6-9 **Restaurant** L served Fri-Sun 12-2 D served Mon-Sat 6-9 ⊕ FREE HOUSE ◄ Old Speckled Hen, Theakstons Best Ö Stowford Press, Thatchers Gold. ♀ 6 **Facilities** Children's menu Garden Parking **Rooms** 10

---

## BIBURY

# Catherine Wheel

**Arlington GL7 5ND ☎ 01285 740250**
dir: *Telephone for directions*

This low-beamed 15th-century pub is situated in a Cotswold village described by William Morris as 'the most beautiful in England'. Inside is an original ship's timber beam, as well as various prints and photographs of Old Bibury, and blazing log fires in winter. Traditional pub food includes fresh Bibury trout, salmon and prawns, and tuna steak.

**Open** all day all wk 10am-11pm (Mon-Fri 3-6 closed during winter) **Bar Meals** L served all wk 12-2.30 D served all wk 6-9.30 **Restaurant** L served all wk 12-2.30 D served all wk 6-9.30 Av 3 course à la carte fr £20 ⊕ BARNSLEY HOUSE LTD ◄ Hook Norton, Sharps Doom Bar Ö Westons Stowford Press. **Facilities** Children's menu Dogs allowed Garden Parking

---

## BIRDLIP

# The Golden Heart ♀

**Nettleton Bottom GL4 8LA ☎ 01242 870261**
🗎 **01242 870599**
e-mail: cathstevensgh@aol.com
dir: *On A417 Gloucester to Cirencester. 8m from Cheltenham. Pub at base of dip in Nettleton Bottom*

This centuries-old Cotswold stone inn has glorious views from its terraced gardens. It probably started life as a drovers' inn, and retains plenty of original features. Excellent local ales and traditional ciders are the focus of the bar, while the extensive menus show an equal commitment to local produce, particularly prize-winning meat from livestock markets and shows. On the other hand, it also makes room for exotic meats including a low fat ostrich casserole or a crocodile, zebra and rattlesnake mixed grill.

**Open** all wk 11-3 5.30-11 (Fri-Sun open all day) Closed: 25 Dec **Bar Meals** L served Mon-Sat 12-3, Sun all day D served Mon-Sat 6-10, Sun all day Av main course £11.25 **Restaurant** L served Mon-Sat 12-3, Sun all day D served Mon-Sat 12-3, Sun all day ⊕ FREE HOUSE ◄ Otter Bitter, Wickwar, Cotswolds Way, Wye Valley, Otter, Gold Festival Ö Westons, Henney, Thatchers. ♀ 10 **Facilities** Children's menu Family room Dogs allowed Garden Parking

---

## BOURTON-ON-THE-HILL

# Horse and Groom ♀

**GL56 9AQ ☎ 01386 700413** 🗎 **01386 700413**
e-mail: greenstocks@horseandgroom.info
dir: *2m W of Moreton-in-Marsh on A44*

Owned and run by the Greenstock brothers, this is a honey-coloured Grade II listed Georgian building with a contemporary feel combined with original period features. This is a serious dining pub, as well as a friendly place for the locals to drink. The bar offers a selection of local favourites and guest ales, whilst the blackboard menu of regularly changing dishes provides plenty of appeal for even the most regular diners. With committed local suppliers backed up by the pub's own vegetable patch, the Horse and Groom's kitchen has plenty of good produce to work with. A typical menu might feature fragrant Thai broth of diver-caught scallops, prawns and steamed mussels; pan-roast stuffed duck breast with braised red cabbage and Madeira jus; or grilled organic salmon fillet with braised herb lentils and bacon. Leave room for puddings like apple and blueberry flapjack crumble or pear and almond tart. In summer, the mature garden offers panoramic hilltop views.

**Open** 11-3 6-11 Closed: 25 Dec, Sun eve **Bar Meals** L served all wk 12-2 booking required D served Mon-Sat 7-9 booking required **Restaurant** L served all wk 12-2 booking required D served Mon-Sat 7-9 booking required ⊕ FREE HOUSE ◄ Hook Norton Hooky, Dorothy Goodbody-Wye Valley, Pure UBU, Goffs Jouster, Cotswold Wheat Ö Westons Stowford Press. ♀ 14 **Facilities** Children's menu Garden Parking

---

## CHARLTON KINGS

# The Reservoir ♀

**London Rd GL54 4HG ☎ 01242 529671**
e-mail: susan@thereservoirinn.co.uk
dir: *On A40, 5m E of Cheltenham*

Andy and Susan Proctor took over this friendly pub a few miles out of Cheltenham in March 2008, following three years at The Hinds Head, Heston Blumenthal's pub in Bray. The surroundings here are beautiful, while the atmosphere inside is by any measure relaxing. The daily-changing menus are subtitled 'A Celebration of British Food' and use fresh, seasonal and locally sourced ingredients in a range broad enough to satisfy everyone from Cotswold Way walkers looking for a

continued

ploughman's and a pint, to weekend diners with hearts set on locally shot game, washed down with a jolly decent wine. Behind all these classic dishes is business partner Martin Blunos, a regular guest TV chef. Using fresh, seasonal and locally sourced ingredients, he produces Cotswold ham, eggs and triple-cooked chips; Old Spot sausages, mash and onion gravy; chunky fish stew with garlic mayonnaise; Angus rump steak with shallot and peppercorn butter; and creamed pearl barley with roasted butternut squash. Desserts continue the British classics theme with spotted dick and custard pudding; warm fig and almond tart; and winter fruit mess. And if it's just a bar snack you want, the choice runs from a mug of soup to beer-battered fish with mushy peas and triple-cooked chips. A covered patio and large beer garden are ideal for those alfresco drinks and meals.

**Open** 11-3 5-11 (Fri-Sun open all day) Closed: 26 Dec, Mon **Bar Meals** Av main course £8 food served all day **Restaurant** L served Tue-Sat 12-2.30, Sun 12-8 D served Tue-Sat 5.30-9.30 Fixed menu price fr £10 Av 3 course à la carte fr £22 ⊕ Greene King ◀ IPA, Abbot, Morland Original ♉ Stowford Press. ♟ 9 **Facilities** Children's menu Dogs allowed Garden Parking

---

## CHEDWORTH

## Hare & Hounds ♟

**Foss Cross GL54 4NN ☎ 01285 720288**
e-mail: stay@hareandhoundsinn.com
dir: *On A429 (Fosse Way), 6m from Cirencester*

A 14th-century inn with various interconnecting dining areas often described as a rabbit warren. Open fires, beams and stone and polished wood floors add to the charm. It's ideally placed for touring the Cotswolds or attending Cheltenham race meetings. There's a daily changing blackboard, along with a menu typically listing breast of Gressingham duck; baked fillet of cod; and Burmese vegetable tofu curry.

**Open** all wk 11-3 (Sat 6-close Sun 7- close) **Bar Meals** L served all wk 12-2.30 booking required D served Mon-Sat 6.30-9.30, Sun 7-9 booking required **Restaurant** L served all wk 12-2.30 booking required D served Mon-Sat 6.30-9.30, Sun 7-9 booking required ⊕ ARKELLS ◀ Arkells 2B, 3B, Moonlight ♉ Stowford Press. ♟ 10 **Facilities** Children's menu Family room Dogs allowed Garden Parking

## CHIPPING CAMPDEN

## The Bakers Arms ♟

**Broad Campden GL55 6UR ☎ 01386 840515**
dir: *1m from Chipping Campden*

There is a friendly family atmosphere at this country Cotswold inn, where you can expect to find exposed stone walls, beams and an inglenook fireplace. A choice of four to five real ales is offered alongside reasonably priced meals. Choose from sandwiches, warm baguettes and filled giant Yorkshire puddings, or dishes such as mariner's pie, Thai red vegetable curry, and liver, bacon and onions with rich gravy.

**Open** all wk 11.30-2.30 4.45-11 (Fri-Sun 11.30-11 Apr-Oct all wk 11.30-11) Closed: 25 Dec **Bar Meals** L served Mon-Fri 12-2, Sat 12-2.30, Sun 12-6 D served Mon-Sat 6-9 Av main course £7.50 **Restaurant** L served Mon-Fri 12-2, Sat 12-2.30, Sun 12-6 D served Mon-Sat 6-9 ⊕ FREE HOUSE ◀ Stanway Bitter, Bombardier, Donnington BB. ♟ 6 **Facilities** Children's menu Play area Garden Parking **Notes** ☺

## Eight Bells ♟

**Church St GL55 6JG ☎ 01386 840371** ▤ 01386 841669
e-mail: neilhargreaves@bellinn.fsnet.co.uk
dir: *8m from Stratford-upon-Avon, M40 Junct 15*

A lovely old inn, located just off the High Street of this popular Cotswold destination, the Eight Bells was built in the 14th century to house stonemasons working on the nearby church and to store the eight church bells. A cobbled entranceway leads into two atmospheric bars, which retain original oak beams, open fireplaces and a priest's hole. In summer, the exterior is hung with flower baskets, and guests spill out into the enclosed courtyard or the terraced garden. Freshly prepared local food is offered in the bar or the modern dining room. Lunchtime sandwiches on fresh ciabatta bread are available Monday to Saturday, and dishes range through home-made soup, bruschetta, traditional fish and chips, monkfish tail wrapped in Parma ham, and Mr Lashford's sausage of the day. There is a tempting children's menu available.

**Open** all day all wk noon-11 (Sun noon-10.30) Closed: 25 Dec **Bar Meals** L served Mon-Thu 12-2, Fri-Sun 12-2.30 D served Mon-Thu 6.30-9, Fri-Sat 6.30-9.30, Sun 6.30-8.45 **Restaurant** L served Mon-Thu 12-2, Fri-Sun 12-2.30 D served Mon-Thu 6.30-9, Fri-Sat 6.30-9.30, Sun 6.30-8.45 ⊕ FREE HOUSE ◀ Hook Norton Best & guest ales, Goff's Jouster, Marston Pedigree, Purity UBU ♉ Old Rosie. ♟ 8 **Facilities** Children's menu Family room Dogs allowed Garden

## CIRENCESTER

# The Crown of Crucis ★★★ HL ☗

**Ampney Crucis GL7 5RS ☎ 01285 851806**
📄 **01285 851735**
e-mail: reception@thecrownofcrucis.co.uk
dir: *On A417 to Lechlade, 2m E of Cirencester*

This 16th-century inn stands beside the Ampney brook in picturesque Ampney Crucis at the gateway to the Cotswolds. The name 'Crucis' refers to the Latin cross in the nearby churchyard. The inn itself retains its historical charm while feeling comfortably up-to-date. It overlooks the village cricket green, and on summer days the evocative sound of willow on leather and the quiet stream meandering past the lawns conspire to create a perfect picture of quintessential England. With its traditional beams, log fires and warm, friendly atmosphere, the bar has been recently restored. Bar food is served all day, along with a range of daily specials.

**Open** all day all wk **Closed:** 25 Dec **Bar Meals** Av main course £9 food served all day **Restaurant** L served all wk 12-2.30 booking required D served all wk 7-9.30 booking required Av 3 course à la carte fr £25 ⊕ FREE HOUSE ◀ Doom Bar, Archers Village, John Smiths. ☗ 10 **Facilities** Children's menu Dogs allowed Garden Parking **Rooms** 25

## CLIFFORD'S MESNE

# The Yew Tree ☗

**Clifford's Mesne GL18 1JS ☎ 01531 820719**
📄 **01531 820912**
e-mail: cass@yewtreeinn.com
dir: *From Newent High Street follow signs to Clifford's Mesne. Pub at far end of village on road to Glasshouse*

Although it might stretch your map-reader's skills, it is well worth the effort finding The Yew Tree, a welcoming halt on the slopes of the National Trust's May Hill, Gloucestershire's highest point. From its 971ft summit you can, weather conditions permitting, see the bluish outlines of the Welsh Mountains and the Malvern Hills, as well as the River Severn - across seven counties, in fact. The interior features quarry-tiled floors, pleasant furnishings, winter log fires and a good choice of real ales (Wye Valley) and varieties of local artisan cider and perry are offered, while all the wines are imported by the inn and sold in its own wine shop. Free-range chickens provide eggs for the kitchen and many of the herbs, salad leaves, vegetables and fruit are home grown. Dishes are

freshly prepared, and starters could include gravadlax with dill dressing; and chargrilled courgette and sun-dried tomato risotto. Daily specials complement old favourites such as slow-roasted belly of Old Spot pork with caramelised celeriac, and the pub's trademark rabbit and bacon pudding. Other main courses include seared duck breast with blackberry and shallot compote; line-caught fish with chunky tartare dressing; and mushroom, spinach and mascarpone roulade. There's a selection of local farmhouse cheeses too. Special events are a regular feature with monthly quiz and supper nights through the winter and occasional performances by guest musicians. In May, the Yew Tree holds a beer, cider and local produce festival.

**Open** Closed: Mon, Tue L, Sun eve **Bar Meals** L served Wed-Sat 12-2 booking required D served Tue-Sat 6-9 booking required Av main course £12 **Restaurant** L served Sun 12-4 booking required Av 3 course à la carte fr £20 ⊕ FREE HOUSE ◀ Wye Valley HPA, Cotswold Spring Brewery Glory, Local Ales Ⓒ Stowford Press, Old Rosie. ☗ 16 **Facilities** Children's menu Play area Dogs allowed Garden Parking

## COATES

# The Tunnel House Inn

**GL7 6PW ☎ 01285 770280  📄 01285 700040**
e-mail: bookings@tunnelhouse.com
web: www.tunnelhouse.com
dir: *From Cirencester on A433 towards Tetbury, in 2m turn right towards Coates, follow brown signs to Canal Tunnel & Inn*

Lying between the Cotswold villages of Coates and Tarlton, the Tunnel House enjoys a glorious rural location close to the mouth of the two-mile long Sapperton Tunnel on the Thames and Severn Canal. Once providing accommodation for the 'navvies' building the canal, it is not far from the source of the Thames. In appropriate weather the garden is an ideal place for relaxing with a pint of Uley Bitter or Black Rat cider,

continued

and enjoying the views across the fields, while in the winter months three log fires warm the welcoming bar, where oddities include an upside-down table on the ceiling. You may dine on simple, home-made cooking in the restaurant area or relax in the comfortable seating in the bar. Eat lightly at lunchtime with a bacon and brie sandwich or a ploughman's, or choose from the monthly changing menu, typically featuring good home-prepared dishes such as beer-battered cod and chips with salad; or honey-roasted Wiltshire ham, eggs and chips. Dinner, from a separate menu, could include chicken liver parfait, Melba toast and red onion confit; then blackened fillet of mackerel with roasted winter vegetables and horseradish cream. Children will probably opt for the usual favourites of sausage and mash with gravy; mini beefburger with cheese and bacon; fish and chips; or chicken goujons. A children's play area and spectacular walks in the surrounding countryside add to the pub's popularity.

**Open** all wk Closed: 25 Dec **Bar Meals** L served all wk 12-2.15 D served all wk 6.45-9.15 Av main course £10 **Restaurant** L served all wk 12-2.15 D served all wk 6.45-9.15 Fixed menu price fr £10 Av 3 course à la carte fr £22 ⊕ FREE HOUSE ◀ Uley Old Spot, Uley Bitter, Wye Valley Bitter, Hook Norton, Budding, Butcombe ♻ Cornish Rattler, Black Rat, Westons Organic. **Facilities** Children's menu Play area Family room Dogs allowed Garden Parking

## COWLEY

# The Green Dragon Inn ★★★★ INN ♛

**Cockleford GL53 9NW ☎ 01242 870271**
🖹 **01242 870171**
e-mail: green-dragon@buccaneer.co.uk
web: www.green-dragon-inn.co.uk
dir: *Telephone for directions*

This handsome stone-built inn, dating from the 17th century, is situated in the Cotswold hamlet of Cockleford. The fittings and furniture are the work of Robert Thompson, the 'Mouse Man of Kilburn' (that's Kilburn, North Yorkshire, not London), so-called for his trademark mouse. Here and in the Lower Bar freshly prepared traditional and modern 'pub food with a difference' is served from a weekly menu that includes sandwiches at lunchtime and children's favourites. A good choice of starters/light meals include cullen skink, a rich tasty soup of smoked haddock, potatoes and leeks; and chargrilled gammon steak with free-range fried egg. Typical main meals include game casserole with winter roots and marjoram savoury cobbler;

pan-fried salmon fillet with a saffron risotto flavoured with crayfish tails and crab; and steak and kidney suet pudding with minted mushy peas. The bar here opens out on to a spacious patio area overlooking a lake, making it a lovely place for a meal.

**Open** all wk **Bar Meals** L served Mon-Fri 12-2.15, Sat 12-2.30, Sun 12-3 D served all wk 6-8.30 Av main course £13.50 **Restaurant** L served Mon-Fri 12-2.15, Sat 12-2.30, Sun 12-3 D served all wk 6-8.30 ⊕ BUCCANEER ◀ Hook Norton, Directors, Butcombe, guest ale ♻ Stowford Press. ♛ 9 **Facilities** Children's menu Dogs allowed Garden Parking **Rooms** 9

## FOSSEBRIDGE

# The Inn at Fossebridge ★★★★ INN ♛

**GL54 3JS ☎ 01285 720721  🖹 01285 720793**
e-mail: info@fossebridgeinn.co.uk
dir: *From M4 junct 15, A419 towards Cirencester, then A429 towards Stow. Pub approx 7m on left*

Set in extensive grounds with a lake, this imposing, family-run, 18th-century free house was once a coaching inn on the ancient Fosseway. Exposed beams, stone walls, flagstone floors and open fires provide the setting for the varied bar food and restaurant menus, with snacks ranging from sandwiches, baguettes and jacket potatoes, to light meals and ever-changing specials such as steak and ale pie; and pan-fried sardines with chunky tomato sauce. Turn to the main menu for additional choices: starters of Thai fishcake on pak choi with chilli and lime dressing; duck pancake rolls with cucumber and plum sauce; and smooth game terrine, while main courses could include baked fillet of cod; wild mushroom and butternut squash risotto; and signature dish roasted best end of Cotswold lamb with herb crust.

**Open** all day all wk noon-mdnt (Sun noon-11.30) **Bar Meals** L served all wk 12-3 D served Mon-Sat 6.30-10, Sun 6.30-9.30 Av main course £7.50 **Restaurant** L served all wk 12-3 booking required D served Mon-Sat 6.30-10, Sun 6.30-9.30 booking required ⊕ FREE HOUSE ◀ Tribute, Proper Job ♻ Stowford Press. ♛ 8 **Facilities** Children's menu Dogs allowed Garden Parking **Rooms** 8

## FRAMPTON MANSELL

### The Crown Inn ★★★★ INN 🍷

**GL6 8JG ☎ 01285 760601**
**e-mail:** enquiries@thecrowninn-cotswolds.co.uk
**dir:** *A419 halfway between Cirencester & Stroud*

Overlooking the wooded Golden Valley in the heart of unspoilt Frampton Mansell, stands this 17th-century free house. Once a simple cider house, and now in the fresh hands of Simon Baker, it is the perfect village pub. The interior is full of old world charm, with honey-coloured stone walls, beams and open fireplaces where log fires are lit in winter. There is also plenty of seating in the large garden for the warmer months. Fresh local food with lots of seasonal specials includes chicken, mushroom and leek pie; baby vegetable and lentil stew; slow-cooked lamb shank with chorizo cassoulet; and fish, chips and mushy peas.

**Open** all day all wk noon-11 **Bar Meals** L served Mon-Sat 12-2.30, Sun 12-8.30 booking required D served Mon-Sat 6-9.30, Sun 12-8.30 booking required Av main course £9 FREE HOUSE Butcombe Bitter, Laurie Lee's Bitter. 🍷 12 **Facilities** Children's menu Dogs allowed Garden Parking

**Rooms** 12

## GREAT BARRINGTON

### The Fox 🍷

**OX18 4TB ☎ 01451 844385**
**e-mail:** info@foxinnbarrington.com
**dir:** *3m W on A40 from Burford, turn N signed The Barringtons, pub approx 0.5m on right*

Picturesque 16th-century pub with a delightful patio and large beer garden overlooking the River Windrush - on warm days a perfect summer watering hole and very popular with those attending Cheltenham racecourse. Built of mellow Cotswold stone and characterised by low ceilings and log fires, the inn offers a range of well-kept Donnington beers and a choice of food using the best of local produce. In the Riverview Restaurant expect dishes like beef in ale pie; local pigeon breasts casseroled with button mushrooms; chicken piri-piri; Thai tuna steak; and spinach, leek and chestnut pie.

**Open** all day all wk 11-11 **Bar Meals** L served Mon-Fri 12-2.30, Sat-Sun 12-9.30 D served Mon-Fri 6.30-9.30, Sat-Sun 12-9.30 Av main course £9.95 **Restaurant** L served Mon-Fri 12-2.30, Sat-Sun 12-9.30 D served Mon-Fri 6.30-9.30, Sat-Sun 12-9.30 DONNINGTON Donnington BB, SBA. 🍷 7 **Facilities** Children's menu Dogs allowed Garden Parking

## GREET

### The Harvest Home 🍷

**Evesham Rd GL54 5BH**
**☎ 01242 602430 01242 602094**
**e-mail:** harvesthome07@btinternet.com
**dir:** *M5 junct 9 take A435 towards Evesham, then B4077 & B4078 towards Winchcombe, 200yds from station*

Set in the beautiful Cotswold countryside, this traditional country inn draws steam train enthusiasts aplenty, as a restored stretch of the Great Western Railway runs past the end of the garden. Built around 1903 for railway workers, the pub is handy for Cheltenham Racecourse and Sudeley Castle. Expect a good range of snacks and mains, including locally-reared beef and tempting seafood dishes.

**Open** all wk 12-3 6-11 (Sun 12-10.30) **Bar Meals** L served all wk 12-3 D served all wk 6.30-9 **Restaurant** L served all wk 12-3 D served all wk 6.30-9 ENTERPRISE INNS Goffs Jouster, Timothy Taylor Landlord, Courage Directors Stowford Press. 🍷 11 **Facilities** Children's menu Dogs allowed Garden Parking

## HINTON

### The Bull Inn 🍷

**SN14 8HG ☎ 0117 937 2332**
**e-mail:** diserwhite@aol.com **web:** www.thebullathinton.co.uk
**dir:** *From M4 junct 18, A46 to Bath 1m, turn right 1m, down hill. Pub on right*

Since the 17th century, The Bull has been an inn, a farm and a dairy, and in some of that tradition the owners now rear their own pigs for the table. Inside are two inglenook fireplaces and flagstone flooring, while outside there's a front-facing terrace and a large garden with children's play area. The menu uses locally supplied produce and home-grown fruit and vegetables. Look out for Royal Gloucester steak and ale pie with horseradish pastry; and deep fried cod in soda and lime batter.

**Open** noon-3 6-11.30 (Sat-Sun & BH open all day) Closed: Mon L (ex BH) **Bar Meals** L served Tue-Sat 12-2, Sun 12-3.30 D served Mon-Thu 6-9, Fri-Sat 6-9.30 Av main course £12 **Restaurant** L served Tue-Sat 12-2, Sun 12-3.30 booking required D served Mon-Thu 6-9, Fri-Sat 6-9.30 booking required WADWORTH Wadworth 6X & Henrys IPA, Wadworth Bishops Tipple, Wadworth Summersault, guest ale. 🍷 12 **Facilities** Children's menu Play area Dogs allowed Garden Parking

England

# Gloucestershire

## LOWER APPERLEY

### The Farmers Arms ♈

**Ledbury Rd GL19 4DR ☎ 01452 780307**
e-mail: danieljrpardoe@googlemail.com
dir: *From Tewkesbury take A38 towards Gloucester/Ledbury. 2m, right at lights onto B4213 (signed Ledbury). 1.5m, pub on left*

A popular, 16th-century, timber-framed village pub, close to the River Severn. Low beams, an open fire, regular guest ales and an extensive menu are to be found within. Dishes using locally sourced produce include steak and kidney pie; honey roast ham with free range eggs and chips; and luxury fish pie. Look lout for special themed nights - Italian, French, Irish.

**Open** all wk 11-3 6-12 (Sat-Sun & summer 11-mdnt) **Bar Meals** L served all wk 12-2 D served all wk 6-9.30 Av main course £7.50 **Restaurant** L served all wk 12-2 D served all wk 6-9.30 Av 3 course à la carte fr £22.50 ⊕ WADWORTH ◀ Wadworth 6X, Henry's Original IPA, guest ales ♂ Stowford Press, Thatchers Gold. ♈ 12 **Facilities** Children's menu Play area Dogs allowed Garden Parking

## LOWER ODDINGTON

### The Fox ♈

**GL56 0UR ☎ 01451 870555 & & 870666**
🖹 01451 870666
e-mail: info@foxinn.net
web: www.foxinn.net
dir: *A436 from Stow-on-the-Wold then right to Lower Oddington*

Set in a Cotswold village close to Stow-on-the-Wold, this stone-built and creeper-clad free house dates back to the 17th century. Fresh flowers and antique furniture complete the period feel in the bar, with its polished flagstone floors, beams and log fires. The Fox's reputation for good food and wine at reasonable prices draws people in to enjoy the atmosphere of a traditional English pub. Daily specials take full advantage of seasonal local produce and freshly-caught Cornish fish. Starters like chicken liver pâté with cornichons and French bread, and roasted butternut squash risotto herald main course options that include grilled sirloin steak with mustard and herb butter; and lamb chump with flageolet beans and red wine sauce. Desserts such as orange and apricot brioche bread and butter pudding, and apple and blackberry crumble with custard provide a satisfying conclusion, or you might try the selection of three cheeses with fig chutney. In summer, there's a heated terrace for alfresco dining, as well as a pretty cottage garden.

**Open** all wk Closed: 25 Dec **Bar Meals** L served Mon-Sat 12-2, Sun 12-4 booking required D served Mon-Sat 6.30-10, Sun 7-9.30 booking required Av main course £12.50 **Restaurant** L served Mon-Sat 12-2, Sun 12-4 booking required D served Mon-Sat 6.30-10, Sun 7-9.30 booking required Av 3 course à la carte fr £20 ⊕ FREE HOUSE ◀ Hook Norton Best, Abbot Ale, Ruddles County, Wickwar's Old Bob, Purity UBU. ♈ 12 **Facilities** Children's menu Dogs allowed Garden Parking

## MARSHFIELD

### The Catherine Wheel

**39 High St SN14 8LR ☎ 01225 892220**
e-mail: bookings@thecatherinewheel.co.uk
dir: *Between Bath, Bristol & Chippenham on A420. 5m from M4 junct 18*

Simple, stylish decor complements the clean lines of this impressive, mainly 17th-century inn on the edge of the Cotswolds, with its exposed brickwork and large open fireplaces. Menus are also simple and well presented, with favourites at lunchtime including jacket potatoes and ploughman's. In the evening look forward to smoked mackerel and crab fishcakes, followed by one of the specials such as venison and pheasant stew. A small but sunny patio is a lovely spot for a summertime pint brewed by nearby Cotswold and Bath-based breweries.

**Open** all wk noon-3 6-11 (Sun noon-11) **Bar Meals** L served Mon-Sat 12-2, Sun 12-3 booking required D served Mon-Sat 7-10 booking required **Restaurant** L served Mon-Sat 12-2, Sun 12-3 booking required D served Mon-Sat 7-10 booking required ⊕ FREE HOUSE ◀ Courage Best, guest ales ♂ Stowford Press. **Facilities** Children's menu Dogs allowed Garden Parking

### The Lord Nelson Inn ★★★ INN ♈

**1 & 2 High St SN14 8LP ☎ 01225 891820**
e-mail: thelordnelsoninn.@btinternet.com
dir: *On A420 between Bristol & Chippenham. .*

Located in a village at the edge of the Cotswolds, this 17th-century coaching inn is family run and has a good reputation for its home-made food and quality cask ales. There is a spacious bar, candlelit restaurant, log fires in winter and a patio for summer use. Dishes range from home-made burger with hand cut chips, to collops of monkfish with saffron and red pepper dressing, and timbale of white and wild rice.

**Open** all day all wk noon-11 (Fri-Sun all day) **Bar Meals** L served Mon-Sat 12-2, Sun 12-3 D served Mon-Sat 6.30-9, Sun 6-8 booking required Av main course £10.95 **Restaurant** L served Mon-Sat 12-2, Sun 12-3 D served Mon-Sat 6.30-9, Sun 6-8 booking required Av 3 course à la carte fr £14.95 ⊕ ENTERPRISE INNS ◀ Courage Best, Bath Gem, 6X ♂ Stowford Press. ♈ 12 **Facilities** Children's menu Play area Dogs allowed Garden **Rooms** 3

## MEYSEY HAMPTON

## The Masons Arms ⚲

**28 High St GL7 5JT** ☎ **01285 850164** 🖷 **01285 850164**
dir: *6m E of Cirencester off A417, beside village green*

New landlords have taken over this 17th-century stone pub beside the green in a charming village on the southern edge of the Cotswolds near Cirencester. The hub of the community, expect to find a log fire in the big inglenook, and straightforward pub food.

**Open** all wk **Bar Meals** L served all wk 12-3 D served all wk 3-6 **Restaurant** L served all wk 12-3 D served all wk 3-6 ⊕ FREE HOUSE ◀ Hook Norton Best, Butcombes, Theakstons, guest ales. ⚲ 14 **Facilities** Children's menu Play area Dogs allowed Garden Parking

## MINCHINHAMPTON

## The Old Lodge ★★★★ INN ⚲

**Minchinhampton Common GL6 9AQ** ☎ **01453 832047** 🖷 **01453 834033**
e-mail: old-lodge@food-club.com
dir: *Telephone for details*

A 400-year-old Cotswold inn, high on Minchinhampton Common, where cattle range free. The stylish restaurant, adorned with paintings and sculptures, has floor-to-ceiling windows that look directly onto the common. Typically on the menu are roast monkfish tail with curried parsnip purée and mussel broth; and braised shank of lamb with dauphinoise potato, french beans and paprika sauce.

**Open** all day all wk 11-11 (Sun 11-10.30) Closed: 25 Dec **Bar Meals** L served Mon-Fri 12-3, Sat 12-10, Sun 12-9.30 D served Mon-Fri 6-10, Sat 12-10, Sun 12-9.30 **Restaurant** L served Mon-Fri 12-3, Sat 12-10, Sun 12-9.30 D served Mon-Fri 6-10, Sat 12-10, Sun 12-9.30 ◀ Stroud Budding, Tom Long, Otter Bitter ◑ Stowford Press. ⚲ 10 **Facilities** Children's menu Dogs allowed Garden **Rooms** 6

## The Weighbridge Inn ⚲

**GL6 9AL** ☎ **01453 832520** 🖷 **01453 835903**
e-mail: enquiries@2in1pub.co.uk
dir: *Between Nailsworth & Avening on B4014*

The 17th-century free house stands on the original London to Bristol packhorse trail, now a footpath and bridleway, ideal for exploring the South Cotswolds on foot. At one time the innkeeper also looked after the weighbridge, which served the local woollen mills. Behind the scenes there has been careful renovation, but original features of the bars and the restaurant in the upstairs raftered hayloft, with its massive roof beams reaching almost to the floor, remain untouched. Outside, the patios and sheltered landscaped garden offer good views of the Cotswolds. The inn prides itself on the quality of its food, all cooked from scratch. The famous '2 in 1' pies, served straight from the oven on a wooden board, have been made here for 30 years, comprising the filling of your choice (such as pork, bacon and celery, or salmon in a creamy sauce) topped with home-made cauliflower cheese and a pastry lid. Also popular are the Sunday roasts and the daily specials that supplement the regular menu, which itself changes every five weeks and may list corned beef hash, salmon fishcakes with parsley and chive sauce, and almond and pear tart with Amaretto custard. The future for the inn is really more of the same: great food, great service and great company.

**Open** all day all wk noon-11 (Sun noon-10.30) Closed: 25 Dec & 10 days Jan **Bar Meals** L served all wk 12-9.30 booking required D served all wk 12-9.30 booking required Av main course £10 food served all day **Restaurant** L served all wk 12-9.30 booking required D served all wk 12-9.30 booking required food served all day ⊕ FREE HOUSE ◀ Wadworth 6X, Uley Old Spot, Laurie Lee ◑ Wicked Witch, Westons Bounds Brand. ⚲ 16 **Facilities** Children's menu Family room Dogs allowed Garden Parking

## NORTH CERNEY

## Bathurst Arms ⚲

**GL7 7BZ** ☎ **01285 831281**
e-mail: james@bathurstarms.com
dir: *5m N of Cirencester on A435*

A rambling, creeper-covered building on the Earl of Bathurst's estate, with gardens stretching to the banks of the River Churn, this is a cracking 17th-century inn in an enviably romantic location. The stone-flagged bar exudes character with beams and log fires, and draws walkers and locals in for pints of Hooky and decent pub food prepared from locally sourced ingredients. Bag a settle in the bar or walk through wine room to the restaurant, replete with open kitchen, and tuck into crab ravioli, pork belly and chorizo cassoulet, beer-battered pollack, and vanilla cheesecake.

**Open** all wk noon-3 6-11 (Sun noon-11) **Bar Meals** L served all wk 12-2 D served all wk 6-9 Av main course £12 **Restaurant** L served all wk 12-2 D served all wk 6-9 Fixed menu price fr £12 Av 3 course à la carte fr £25 ⊕ FREE HOUSE ◀ Cotswold Way, Tournament, Festival Gold ◑ Stowford Press. ⚲ 60 **Facilities** Children's menu Dogs allowed Garden Parking

## NORTHLEACH

### The Puesdown Inn ★★★★ INN ◎◎ ♀

**Compton Abdale GL54 4DN ☎ 01451 860262**
📄 01451 861262
e-mail: inn4food@btopenworld.com
dir: *On A40 between Oxford & Cheltenham, 3m W of Northleach*

Said to date from 1236, this refurbished coaching inn is set on the old Salt Way between Burford and Cheltenham. Inside, you'll find cosy sofas, log fires and warm, rich colours on the walls, providing a welcome refuge from the winter weather. For the inn is set 800 feet above sea level, and its unique name - an anagram for 'snowed up' - derives from an old English expression meaning 'windy ridge'. Guests were marooned here in 1947 during the worst blizzard of the century. The restaurant has earned two AA Rosettes for dishes such as roast local partridge with rosti potato and glazed apples; sea bass fillet with parsley potatoes and green beans; and organic pork loin with parsnip purée.

**Open** Closed: Sun eve **Bar Meals** L served Mon-Sat 12-3 D served Tue-Sat 6-10.30 Av main course £7.50 **Restaurant** L served all wk 12-3 booking required D served Tue-Sat 6-10.30 booking required Fixed menu price fr £10 Av 3 course à la carte fr £22.50 ⊕ FREE HOUSE ◀ Hook Norton Best Bitter, Hooky Dark, Old Hooky, Haymaker, Twelve Days. ♀ 15 **Facilities** Children's menu Dogs allowed Garden Parking **Rooms** 3

## POULTON

### The Falcon Inn ♀

**London Rd GL7 5HN ☎ 01285 850844**
e-mail: inn4food@btopenworld.com
dir: *From Cirencester E on A417 towards Fairford*

At the heart of the Cotswold village of Poulton, the Falcon has been transformed from a straightforward village local into a stylish and sophisticated gastro-pub which has become popular with drinkers and diners from far and wide. Especially good value is the fixed-price two-course or three-course lunch menu, which offers choices of two starters and two main courses: pea and tomato risotto or leek and rocket soup followed by chargrilled sardines, new potatoes and salad, or pot roasted shoulder of lamb with winter vegetables. Desserts are along the lines of glazed rice pudding or lemon tart. Loin of Prinknash Abbey organic pork with pommes Anna and parsnip purée, and supreme of Great Farm guinea fowl with blackberry sauce are fine examples dinner main courses.

**Open** Closed: Sun eve & Mon **Bar Meals** L served Tue-Sat 12-3 D served Tue-Sat 6-10 Av main course £7 **Restaurant** L served Tue-Sun 12-3 booking required D served Tue-Sat 6-10 booking required Fixed menu price fr £10 Av 3 course à la carte fr £18.50 ⊕ ENTERPRISE INNS ◀ Hook Norton Best Bitter. ♀ 9 **Facilities** Children's menu Dogs allowed Garden Parking

## SHEEPSCOMBE

### The Butchers Arms ♀

**GL6 7RH ☎ 01452 812113** 📄 01452 814358
e-mail: mark@butchers-arms.co.uk
dir: *1.5m S of A46 (Cheltenham to Stroud road), N of Painswick*

Set on the sunny side of Sheepscombe valley, this award-winning pub has a garden terrace with lovely views of beech-wooded slopes on all sides. The area attracts many walkers, riders and tourists. The menus (a full menu is available at lunchtime and in the evening) include dishes made from produce raised in fields within sight of the pub. Light meals and salads are augmented by traditional favourites such as home-made cottage pie, chef's turkey curry, tomato and mushroom risotto, beer-battered fish and chips, and grilled steaks. Specials may include sea bass, scallops, pork belly, or local shoot pheasant. The 'Young Person's Menu' keeps children happy, or an adult-sized main course can be divided in two. An ever-changing specials board above the fireplace completes the choice and may include Pyll House Farm Barnsley lamb chop with grain mustard mash and redcurrant jus.

**Open** all wk 11.30-2.30 6.30-11 (Sat 11.30-11.30 Sun noon-10.30) **Bar Meals** L served all wk 12-2.30 booking required D served Mon-Sat 6.30-9.30, Sun 6.30-9 booking required Av main course £9.50 **Restaurant** L served all wk 12-2.30 booking required D served Mon-Sat 6.30-9.30, Sun 6.30-9 booking required Av 3 course à la carte fr £17.50 ⊕ FREE HOUSE ◀ Otter Bitter, Goffs Jouster, Butcombe Gold, St Austell Tribute ⓞ Westons Stowford Press, Westons Bottled Ciders. ♀ 10 **Facilities** Children's menu Dogs allowed Garden Parking

## SOMERFORD KEYNES

### The Bakers Arms ♀

**GL7 6DN ☎ 01285 861298**
dir: *Exit A419 signed Cotswold Water Park. Cross B4696, 1m, follow signs for Keynes Park & Somerford Keynes*

A beautiful chocolate box pub built from Cotswold stone, with low-beamed ceilings and inglenook fireplaces. Dating from the 15th century, the building was formerly the village bakery and stands in mature gardens ideal for al fresco dining. Discreet children's play areas and heated terraces add to its broad appeal. Somerford Keynes is in the Cotswold Water Park, and the man-made beach of Keynes Park is within easy walking distance, while the nearby Thames Path and Cotswold Way make the pub popular with walkers.

Open all day all wk 11-11 (Sun 12-10.30) **Bar Meals** L served Mon-Fri 12-2.30, Sat-Sun 12-9 D served Mon-Fri 6-9, Sat-Sun 12-9 **Restaurant** L served Mon-Fri 12-2.30, Sat-Sun 12-9 D served Mon-Fri 6-9, Sat-Sun 12-9 ⊕ ENTERPRISE INNS ◀ Courage Best, Butcombe Bitter, Stroud Budding. ⏺ 8 **Facilities** Children's menu Play area Family room Dogs allowed Garden Parking

## SOUTHROP

### The Swan at Southrop ⊛⊛ ⏺

**GL7 3NU ☎ 01367 850205** 🖹 **01367 850517**
e-mail: info@theswanatsouthrop.co.uk
dir: *Off A361 between Lechlade & Burford*

The Swan is a 17th-century, creeper-clad Cotswold inn on the village green. Sebastian and Lana Snow, both protegés of Antony Worrall-Thompson, relaunched it in September 2008. The interior is surprisingly light and airy for such an historic building, but homely too, especially when the log fire is ablaze. The menu line-up comprises carte, fixed-price, bar and weekend roast, with the former offering starters of salad of figs with Colston Basset Blue cheese, pine-nuts and apples; open ravioli of crab, salt cod, chilli and coconut; and carpaccio of veal with tonnato dressing, capers and basil. Mains include Southrop lamb rump with pea, mint, bacon and wood sorrel fricassée; wild sea bream fillet with pea purée, girolle mushrooms, spinach and pecorino; and chartreuse of Hatherop partridge with Savoy cabbage, cotechino sausage and lentils.

Open all wk **Bar Meals** L served all wk 12-3 D served all wk 6-10.30 Av main course £8 **Restaurant** L served all wk 12-3 booking required D served all wk 6-10.30 booking required Av 3 course à la carte fr £25 ⊕ FREE HOUSE ◀ Hook Norton, Wadworth 6X, Cotswold Way, guest ale. ⏺ 10 **Facilities** Children's menu Dogs allowed

## STONEHOUSE

### The George Inn

**Peter St, Frocester GL10 3TQ ☎ 01453 822302**
🖹 **01453 791612**
e-mail: info@georgeinn.co.uk
dir: *M5 junct 13, onto A419 at 1st rdbt 3rd exit signed Eastington, left at next rdbt signed Frocester. Approx 2m on right in village*

An award-winning 18th-century coaching inn, unspoiled by juke box or fruit machine. Instead, crackling log fires and a sunny courtyard garden give the place all-year-round appeal. The Cotswold Way and a network of leafy paths and lanes are on the doorstep. Expect a warm welcome, a selection of real ales including three local brews, and good home-cooked food from nearby suppliers. Tuck in to half a roast chicken, or Frocester Fayre faggots with mash, peas and gravy.

Open all day all wk 7.30am-mdnt **Bar Meals** food served all day **Restaurant** food served all day ⊕ FROCESTER BEER CO LTD ◀ Deuchars IPA, Blacksheep, 3 guest ales. **Facilities** Children's menu Play area Family room Dogs allowed Garden Parking

## STROUD

### The Ram Inn

**South Woodchester GL5 5EL ☎ 01453 873329**
🖹 **01453 873329**
e-mail: raminnwoodchester@hotmail.co.uk
dir: *A46 from Stroud to Nailsworth, right after 2m into South Woodchester, follow brown tourist signs*

From the plentiful seating on terrace of the 17th-century Cotswold stone Ram Inn, there are splendid views over five valleys, although proximity to the huge fireplace may prove more appealing in winter. Rib-eye steak, at least two fish dishes, home-made lasagne and Sunday roasts can be expected. The Stroud Morris Men regularly perform.

Open all day all wk 11-11 **Bar Meals** L served all wk 12-2 D served all wk 6-9 Av main course £7.50 **Restaurant** L served all wk 12-2 D served all wk 6-9 ⊕ FREE HOUSE ◀ Uley Old Spot, Stroud Budding, Butcombe Bitter, Guests. **Facilities** Children's menu Family room Dogs allowed Garden Parking

### The Woolpack Inn ⏺

**Slad Rd, Slad GL6 7QA ☎ 01452 813429**
🖹 **01452 813429**
e-mail: info@thewoolpackinn-slad.com
dir: *2m from Stroud, 8m from Gloucester*

The Woolpack is a friendly local, situated in the beautiful Slad Valley close to the Cotswold Way, an area immortalised by Laurie Lee in his book Cider with Rosie. Indeed, the author was a regular at the pub. Not surprisingly, the place is popular with walkers. Walking boots and wellies aren't frowned upon here, and children and dogs are made welcome. Honest, straightforward food is freshly prepared from the best local produce, all washed down with a pint of Uley bitter.

Open all day all wk noon-mdnt (Sun noon-11pm) **Bar Meals** L served Mon-Sat 12-2, Sun 12-3.30 booking required D served Tue-Sat 6.30-9 booking required Av main course £11.50 **Restaurant** L served Mon-Sat 12-2, Sun 12-3.30 booking required D served Tue-Sat 6.30-9 booking required Av 3 course à la carte fr £18 ⊕ FREE HOUSE ◀ Uley Pig's Ear, Old Spot, Uley Bitter, guest ale ◔ Old Rosie, Stowfords Press. ⏺ 8 **Facilities** Children's menu Family room Dogs allowed Garden Parking

## TETBURY

### Gumstool Inn ⏺

**Calcot Manor GL8 8YJ ☎ 01666 890391**
🖹 **01666 890394**
e-mail: reception@calcotmanor.co.uk
dir: *3m W of Tetbury*

The traditional country inn, Gumstool, is part of Calcot Manor Hotel, set in 220 acres of Cotswold countryside. The hotel is a successful conversion of a 14th-century stone farmhouse built by Cistercian monks, set around a flower-filled courtyard. The food at the inn is top notch gastro-pub quality. Monthly menus offer a good choice, with typical starters of crisp goats' cheese

continued

parcel, roasted beetroot salad; or Cajun spiced calamari salad with chilli jam. Starters or a larger portion for a light main course include warm Cornish crab and leek tart with rocket and frisée salad; crispy Asian duck noodle salad with Thai dressing; and grilled haloumi cheese, polenta and wood-roasted Mediterranean vegetables. Among the mains might be roasted pheasant with bacon, bread sauce and potato gratin; Moroccan spiced lamb tagine with lemon, rose harissa and coriander; or roasted halibut, curried mussels and leeks.

Open all wk 11.30-2.30 5.30-11 **Bar Meals** L served all wk 11.30-2 booking required D served all wk 7-9.30 booking required Av main course £8 **Restaurant** L served all wk 12-2 booking required D served all wk 7-9.30 booking required Av 3 course à la carte fr £35 ⊕ FREE HOUSE ◼ Atlantics Sharp's IPA, Matthews Bob Wool, Wickwar Cotswold Way, Butcombe Blonde. ♟ 12 **Facilities** Children's menu Play area Family room Garden Parking

## The Trouble House ◉◉ ♟

### Cirencester Rd GL8 8SG ☎ 01666 502206
e-mail: info@thetroublehouse.co.uk
dir: *On A433 between Tetbury & Cirencester*

There's a warm welcome from husband and wife team Martin and Neringa Caws – and original features like ancient beams, fireplaces and a charmingly crooked ceiling all add to this pub's very English allure. The Trouble House has an enviable reputation for food; bread is baked daily with organic flour from nearby Shipton Mill, whilst many other local ingredients appear on the menu. Begin, perhaps, with grilled sea scallops and apple purée; or warm beetroot tart, caramelised onion and goats' cheese. Main course dishes include slow-cooked Gloucestershire Old Spot pork belly with fondant potato; and Cornish lobster risotto with peas, tomato and tarragon. Praline parfait with raspberries; and coffee crème brûlée are typical desserts.

Open 11.30-3 7-11 Closed: 25-26 Dec, Sun eve, Mon **Bar Meals** L served Tue-Fri 12-2 booking required Av main course £10.50 **Restaurant** L served Tue-Sun 12-2 booking required D served Tue-Sat 7-9.30 booking required Av 3 course à la carte fr £25.50 ⊕ WADWORTH ◼ Wadworth 6X, Henrys IPA Ở Stowford Press. ♟ 12 **Facilities** Children's menu Dogs allowed Garden Parking

## TORMARTON

# Best Western Compass Inn ★★ HL ♟
### GL9 1JB ☎ 01454 218242 ▤ 01454 218741
e-mail: info@compass-inn.co.uk
web: www.compass-inn.co.uk
dir: *From M4 junct 18 take A46 N towards Stroud. After 200mtrs 1st right towards Tormarton. Inn in 300mtrs*

A charming 18th-century inn, set in six acres of grounds in the heart of the Gloucestershire countryside, right on the Cotswold Way. Light bites and more filling meals can be taken in the bar, while the restaurant offers the likes of chicken liver pâté with brioche, followed by roasted pork fillet with sage mash, caramelised apple and grain mustard sauce.

Open all day all wk 7am-11pm (Sat-Sun 8am-11pm) Closed: 25-26 Dec **Bar Meals** Av main course £9 food served all day **Restaurant** Av 3 course à la carte fr £20 food served all day ⊕ FREE HOUSE ◼ Interbrew Bass, Butcombe Gold, Butcombe Ở Ashton Press. ♟ 9 **Facilities** Children's menu Dogs allowed Garden Parking **Rooms** 26

## UPPER ODDINGTON

# The Horse and Groom Inn ♟
### GL56 0XH ☎ 01451 830584
e-mail: info@horseandgroom.uk.com
dir: *1.5m S of Stow-on-the-Wold, just off A436*

A 16th-century stone-built inn, the Horse & Groom is located in a Cotswold conservation village just a mile and a half from Stow-on-the-Wold. It is immaculately kept, with pale polished flagstone floors, beams, stripped stone walls and log fires in the inglenook. In fine weather you can enjoy the terrace and gardens, with grape vines bounded by dry stone walls. Menus comprise regional food sourced from as close to the kitchen door as possible. Bread, for example, is made daily from Cotswold Flour Millers flour. Dishes might include pan-fried breast of Adlestrop pheasant with thyme and garlic roasted sweet potatoes and orange glazed chicory, or hand-cut, finest 21-day aged Hereford beef steaks served with a choice of sauces. Fish is featured on the daily blackboard menu.

Open all wk noon-3 5.30-11 (Sun 6.30-10.30) **Bar Meals** L served all wk 12-2 D served Mon-Sat 6.30-9, Sun 7-9 **Restaurant** L served all wk 12-2 D served Mon-Sat 6.30-9, Sun 7-9 ⊕ FREE HOUSE ◼ Wye Valley Butty Bach, Wye Valley Best, Hereford Pale Ale, Wickwar Bob Cotswold Premium Lager. ♟ 25 **Facilities** Children's menu Play area Garden Parking

## WOODCHESTER

# The Old Fleece ♥

**Bath Rd, Rooksmoor GL5 5NB ☎ 01453 872582**
e-mail: pheasantpluckers2003@yahoo.co.uk
dir: *2m S of Stroud on A46*

Set amid beautiful countryside, this delightful 18th-century coaching inn was built from Cotswold stone and has a traditional stone roof. From the Old Fleece, you can walk to Rodborough, Minchinhampton and Selsley Commons, or connect with the scenic Cotswold Way. The beautifully refurbished interior includes wooden floors, wood panelling and exposed stone. There's a comprehensive menu of British and continental dishes, ranging from classics such as Old Spot sausage and mash with onion gravy to the likes of confit duck leg with hoi sin noodles, whole sea bream with braised fennel, or pork loin steak with apple and Calvados purée.

Open all day all wk 11-11 Closed: 25 Dec **Bar Meals** L served all wk 11-2.45 D served all wk 5.30-10 **Restaurant** L served all wk 11-2.45 D served all wk 5.30-10 ⊕ PHEASANT PLUCKERS LTD ◾ Bass, Greene King Abbot Ale, Otter Bitter. ♥ 12 **Facilities** Children's menu Dogs allowed Garden Parking

# GREATER MANCHESTER

## DENSHAW

# The Rams Head Inn ♥

**OL3 5UN ☎ 01457 874802   📄 01457 820978**
e-mail: ramsheaddenshaw@aol.com
dir: *From M62 junct 22, 2m towards Oldham*

From its position 1212 feet above sea level, this 400-year-old country inn offers panoramic views over Saddleworth. Log fires and collections of memorabilia are features of the interior, where blackboard menus list everything available and food is cooked to order. Seafood figures strongly, with dishes such as crayfish tails with ginger crème fraîche, and monkfish wrapped in Parma ham. Another attraction is The Pantry at The Rams Head, a farm shop, deli, bakery, tearooms and patisserie.

Open noon-2.30 6-11 Closed: 25 Dec, Mon (ex BH) **Bar Meals** Av main course £10.95 **Restaurant** Fixed menu price fr £12.95 Av 3 course à la carte fr £20 food served all day ⊕ FREE HOUSE ◾ Carlsberg-Tetley Bitter, Timothy Taylor Landlord, Black Sheep Bitter, Copper Dragon. ♥ 8 **Facilities** Children's menu Parking

# The Oddfellows Arms ♥

**73 Moor End Rd SK6 5PT ☎ 0161 449 7826**
dir: *Telephone for details*

A friendly welcome can be expected in this c1650 building, which has had a liquor licence since 1805. It changed its name from 'The Angel Inn' in 1860 to accommodate the Oddfellows Society, a forerunner of the Trades Unions.

Open all wk 4-late (Thu-Fri 12-late Sat 11-late Sun 11-6) Closed: 25-26 Dec, 31 Dec-1 Jan **Bar Meals** L served Thu-Fri 12-6, Sat-Sun 11-6 D served Thu-Fri 12-6, Sat-Sun 11-6 **Restaurant** L served Thu-Fri 12-2.30, Sun 12-5 booking required D served Wed-Sat 5.30-9 booking required ⊕ ENTERPRISE INNS PLC ◾ Adnams Southwold, Marston's Pedigree, Bitter, Fennicks Arizona, guest. ♥ 8 **Facilities** Children's menu Dogs allowed Garden Parking

## OLDHAM

# The White Hart Inn ◉◉ ♥

**Stockport Rd, Lydgate OL4 4JJ ☎ 01457 872566**
📄 01457 875190
e-mail: bookings@thewhitehart.co.uk
dir: *From Manchester A62 to Oldham. Right onto bypass, A669 through Lees. In 500yds past Grotton, at brow of hill turn right onto A6050*

An attractive 18th-century coaching inn, the White Hart is renowned for its award-winning restaurant, and the fact that the characters Compo, Clegg and Cyril from Last of the Summer Wine were based on former regulars here. A variety of eating areas includes the brasserie, a contemporary restaurant, the intimate library and the newer Oak Room. The pub menu offers plenty of choice, including six options for children and some classic local dishes. In the restaurant expect the likes of roast dorade fillet with cockle linguini, dill and fennel purée and vanilla nage, or Goosnargh duck breast with confit leg and Puy lentils, blackcurrants and carrot fondant.

Open all day all wk **Bar Meals** L served Mon-Sat 12-2.30, Sun 1-7 booking required D served all wk 6-9.30 booking required Av main course £12 **Restaurant** L served Sun 12-3 booking required D served Mon-Sat 6-9.30 booking required Fixed menu price fr £19.95 Av 3 course à la carte fr £19.95 ⊕ FREE HOUSE ◾ Timothy Taylor Landlord, J W Lees Bitter, Carlsberg-Tetley Bitter, Copper Dragon, Golden Best. ♥ 16 **Facilities** Children's menu Dogs allowed Garden Parking

## STALYBRIDGE

# The Royal Oak

**364 Huddersfield Rd, Millbrook SK15 3EP**
☎ 0161 338 7118
dir: *From Stalybridge turn onto Huddersfield rd, pub located on the right next to Country Park*

This family-run pub, once a coroner's evidence room, was later owned by the late Jackie Blanchflower of Manchester United, who took it on in the 1960s, and rumour has it that the players used to drink here. It stands next to a country park, which is great for walks before or after eating. The food is Italian influenced, and everything is freshly prepared and cooked to order. The wine list is short but well chosen.

Open Wed-Fri 5.30-11 (Tue 6-9 only by prior reservation, Sat 4.30-11, Sun noon-10.30) Closed: 1 Jan, Mon **Bar Meals** D served Tue 6-9, Wed-Fri 5.30-9, Sat 4.30-9, Sun 12-7 Av main course £7 **Restaurant** D served Tue 6-9, Wed-Fri 5.30-9, Sat 4.30-9, Sun 12-7 Fixed menu price fr £10.50 ⊕ ENTERPRISE INNS ◾ Boddingtons, John Smiths. **Facilities** Children's menu Garden Parking

**England**

## STOCKPORT

## The Arden Arms ▼

**23 Millgate SK1 2LX ☎ 0161 480 2185**
e-mail: steve@ardenarms.com
dir: *M60 junct 27 to town centre. Across mini-rdbt, at lights turn left. Pub on right of next rdbt behind Asda*

Last modernised in 1908, this Victorian coaching inn close to Stockport's historic market place ranks high among the country's timeless gems. Come to see the classic unspoilt layout, the original tiled floors and panelling, and order pint of Robinson's from the traditional curved bar, quaffing it by the coal fire in the tiny snug bar. Quality lunches include hot sandwiches, tempting ciabattas, gammon, egg and chips or grilled halloumi and vegetable kebabs, and banana and toffee pudding. There's a sheltered courtyard for summer drinking.

Open all wk noon-11.45 Closed: 25-26 Dec, 1 Jan **Bar Meals** L served Mon-Fri 12-2.30, Sat-Sun 12-4 Av main course £8.95 ⊕ ROBINSONS ◀ Unicorn Bitter, Hatters Mild, Robin Bitter, Double Hop, seasonal ales. ▼ 8 **Facilities** Children's menu Dogs allowed Garden **Notes** ◙

## The Nursery Inn ▼

**Green Ln, Heaton Norris SK4 2NA ☎ 0161 432 2044**
▤ 0161 442 1857
e-mail: nurseryinn@hydesbrewery.com
dir: *Green Ln off Heaton Moor Rd. Pass rugby club on Green Ln, at end on right. Little cobbled road, pub 100yds on right*

Set in a conservation area complete with bowling green, the Nursery was originally the main headquarters of Stockport County Football Club, with players changing in what is now the pub's interior, and the pitch at the rear. Dating back to 1939, the pub's wood panelling in the lounge/dining room and other original features reflect that period. With Hydes beers on offer, food is available at lunchtime only - jacket potatoes, sandwiches and baguettes in the bar, and smoked haddock and tuna steak in the restaurant.

Open all wk **Bar Meals** L served Tue-Sun 12-2.30 Av main course £6.50 **Restaurant** L served Tue-Sun 12-2.30 ⊕ HYDES BREWERY ◀ Hydes Bitter, Hydes Jekylls Gold, Hydes Seasonal Ales, Hydes Smooth. ▼ 7 **Facilities** Children's menu Dogs allowed Garden Parking **Notes** ◙

## HAMPSHIRE

## ALTON

## The Anchor Inn ◉◉ ▼

**Lower Froyle GU34 4NA ☎ 01420 23261**
▤ 01420 520467
e-mail: info@anchorinnatlowerfroyle.co.uk
dir: *A31 signed Bentley, follow brown tourist signs to Anchor Inn*

The boarded and tile-hung Anchor Inn has been sympathetically remodelled to create a classic gastro-pub with bags of atmosphere and appeal. The cosy snug and saloon

bar are decked out with open fires, wooden floors and lots of original features, whilst period furnishings and old prints hint at a bygone era. In the informal dining room, candlesticks and polished wooden tables combine with the painted wall panelling to create a dark, romantic interior. The accomplished seasonal menu is driven by fresh local produce, blending modern presentation with simplicity and clear flavours. Typical menu choices might start with chicken liver and foie gras parfait with red onion marmalade, before moving on to halibut and Jerusalem artichoke risotto, or Donald Russell rib-eye steak with béarnaise sauce and hand-cut chips. The dessert selection includes buttermilk pannacotta with poached Yorkshire rhubarb, and treacle tart with clotted cream.

Open all day all wk **Bar Meals** L served all wk 12-2 D served all wk 7-9 Av main course £9 **Restaurant** L served all wk 12-2 booking required D served Mon-Sat 7-9 booking required Av 3 course à la carte fr £35 ⊕ THE MILLERS COLLECTION ◀ Ringwood Best, Ringwood 49er, guest ales ♉ Thatchers. ▼ 9 **Facilities** Children's menu Dogs allowed Garden Parking

## ANDOVER

## Wyke Down Country Pub & Restaurant ▼

**Wyke Down, Picket Piece SP11 6LX ☎ 01264 352048**
▤ 01264 324661
e-mail: info@wykedown.co.uk
dir: *3m from Andover town centre/A303. Follow signs for Wyke Down Caravan Park*

Combining a pub/restaurant with a caravan park and golf driving range, this establishment is a diversified farm on the outskirts of Andover. It still raises beef cattle, but the pub started in a barn 25 years ago and the restaurant was built 11 years ago. Dishes range from lasagne, curry and Cajun chicken supreme on the bar menu to restaurant fare such as maple roasted pork chop, nut loaf, or steaks from the griddle.

Open all wk noon-3 6-11 Closed: 25 Dec-2 Jan **Bar Meals** L served all wk 12-2 booking required D served all wk 6-9 booking required **Restaurant** L served all wk 12-2 booking required D served all wk 6-9 booking required ⊕ FREE HOUSE ◀ Guinness, Timothy Taylor, real ale. ▼ 6 **Facilities** Children's menu Play area Garden Parking

## BAUGHURST

## The Wellington Arms ◉◉ ▼

**Baughurst Rd RG26 5LP ☎ 0118 982 0110**
e-mail: info@thewellingtonarms.com
web: www.thewellingtonarms.com
dir: *M4 junct 12 follow Newbury signs on A4. At rdbt left signed Aldermaston. Through Aldermaston. Up hill, at next rdbt 2nd exit, left at T-junct, pub 1m on left*

Blackboard menus and Edwardian furniture set the scene at this tiny whitewashed pub. Fields and woodland surround the large lawned garden, an ideal setting for the free-range chickens whose eggs are used in the kitchen. There are beehives too; herbs are grown just outside the kitchen door, the bread is baked by a craft baker, and nearby Henwood Farm delivers fresh organic vegetables and salads every day. The impressive menus show attention to detail – and so must you; check the food service times and book in advance to sample the mouth-watering fare. Starters might include local rabbit and free-range pork terrine with apple chutney and hot toast, followed by main course options such as roast rack of English lamb with fennel gratin and oven-dried tomatoes, or seared Brixham turbot on sautéed marsh samphire. Leave space for dessert; steamed apple and syrup sponge with custard is a typical choice.

**Open** Closed: Mon, Sun eve, Tue L **Bar Meals** Av main course £15 **Restaurant** L served Wed-Sun 12-2.30 booking required D served Tue-Sat 6.30-9.30 booking required Fixed menu price fr £15 Av 3 course à la carte fr £28 Wadworth 6X. 12 **Facilities** Children's menu Dogs allowed Garden Parking

## BEAUWORTH

### The Milburys

**SO24 0PB ☎ 01962 771248 01962 7771910**
e-mail: info@themilburys.co.uk
dir: *A272 towards Petersfield, after 6m turn right for Beauworth*

A rustic hill-top pub dating from the 17th century and named after the Bronze Age barrow nearby. It is noted for its massive, 250-year-old treadmill that used to draw water from the 300ft well in the bar, and for the far-reaching views across Hampshire that can be savoured from the lofty garden. The African Oasis restaurant has a distinctly South African flavour.

**Open** all wk FREE HOUSE Theakstons Old Peculier, Triple FFF Altons Pride, Deuchars, guest ale. 8 **Facilities** Dogs allowed Garden Parking

## BENTLEY

### The Bull Inn

**GU10 5JH ☎ 01420 22156 01420 520772**
dir: *2m from Farnham on A31 towards Winchester*

15th-century beamed coaching inn in a Hampshire village made famous by a reality TV show called 'The Village'. Inside are open log fires, two separate bars and a restaurant. Extensive selection of pub food complemented by braised shank of lamb with sweet potato mash and rosemary sauce; pan-fried fillet of salmon with a lemon and chive butter; and roasted hock of ham with swede and potato purée.

**Open** all day all wk 10.30am-mdnt (Sun 12.30-10.30) **Bar Meals** L served Mon-Sat 12-2.30, Sun 12-8.30 D served Mon-Sat 6.30-9.30, Sun 12-8.30 Courage Best, Ringwood Best, Young's Bitter, Timothy Taylor Landlord Thatchers Pear. 8 **Facilities** Dogs allowed Garden Parking

## BENTWORTH

### The Sun Inn

**Sun Hill GU34 5JT ☎ 01420 562338**
dir: *Telephone for directions*

This delightful flower-decked pub is either the first building you pass as you enter Bentworth from the Basingstoke-Alton road, or the last one out, depending on which way you are travelling, and it always seems to come as a surprise. Originally two cottages, it now has three interconnecting rooms, each with its own log fire and brick and wood floors. The bar is the middle room, right in front of the door. Pews, settles, scrubbed pine tables with lit candles in the evening add to the homely atmosphere. Food is hearty and traditional, with beef Stroganoff; minted lamb; a range of meat and vegetarian curries; liver and bacon; cheesy haddock bake; filled Yorkshire puddings; braised steak in red wine and mushroom sauce; and Mediterranean lamb. Game in season includes venison, cooked in Guinness with pickled walnuts, and pheasant. Everything, from the soup to the dessert, is home made.

**Open** all wk FREE HOUSE Cheriton Pots Ale, Ringwood Best & Old Thumper, Brakspear Bitter, Fuller's London Pride. 6 **Facilities** Family room Dogs allowed Garden Parking

# Hampshire

## BOLDRE

## The Red Lion ♟

**Rope Hill SO41 8NE** ☎ **01590 673177** 🖹 **01590 674036**
dir: *1m from Lymington off A337. From M27 junct 1 through Lyndhurst &
Brockenhurst towards Lymington, follow signs for Boldre*

The Red Lion has a mention in the Domesday Book, although
today's inn dates from the 15th century, when it was created
from a stable and two cottages. Inside you'll find a rambling
series of beamed rooms packed with rural memorabilia. Menus
offer traditional, home-made dishes featuring local venison
and fish from local catches; the inn is proud to hold the New
Forest Marque for use and promotion of food produced in the
New Forest area. Pie and Pudding evenings are very popular
– a choice of six or seven home-made pies and a home-made
pudding for £10. Another innovation is to eat at a patio hot
table, where you cook your choice of meat, fish or game on a
central hotplate. Typical dishes are trio of Sway Butcher's Red
Lion sausages; foresters chicken; Ringwood ale battered fish,
and crab and spring onion fishcakes.

Open all wk 11-3 5.30-11 (Sun noon-4 6-10.30) **Bar Meals** L
served Mon-Sat 12-2.30, Sun 12-3.30 D served Mon-Sat 6-9.30,
Sun 6-9 Av main course £6 **Restaurant** L served Mon-Sat
12-2.30, Sun 12-3.30 D served Mon-Sat 6-9.30, Sun 6-9 Av
3 course à la carte fr £18 ⊕ FREE HOUSE ◀ Ringwood Best,
Ringwood Fortyniner, Marstons Pedigree, Guinness, guest
ales. ♟ 18 **Facilities** Children's menu Dogs allowed Garden
Parking

## BRANSGORE

## The Three Tuns Country Inn 🏵🏵 ♟

**Ringwood Rd BH23 8JH** ☎ **01425 672232**
e-mail: threetunsinn@btconnect.com
dir: *1.5m from A35 Walkford junct. 3m from Christchurch & 1m from
Hinton Admiral railway station*

This award-winning, 17th-century inn is one of the few in the
New Forest still under thatch. It offers five distinct public areas:
a comfortable Lounge Bar, with no music, TV screens or games,
and in winter a log fire; an oak-beamed Snug Bar, again with
a log fire, and biscuits and water for dogs; a large terrace
with its water feature; a south-facing garden, surrounded by
fields, trees and ponies, and not a bouncy castle in sight, but
space galore (on sunny days, out comes the barbecue); and
finally, the restaurant. Here you'll find how fresh produce and
seasonings from around the world are fused into classic dishes

and seasonal specials, recognised for their quality by two AA
rosettes. Expect venison bourguignonne, bacon and glazed
onions; roasted halibut, polenta and artichoke, salsify, olives
and squid fricassée; and wild mushroom risotto with truffle oil,
Parmesan, rocket and tomato.

Open all day all wk 11.30-11 (Sun 12-10.30) **Bar Meals** L
served Mon-Fri 12-2.15, Sat-Sun 12-9.15 booking required D
served Mon-Fri 6.30-9.15, Sat-Sun 12-9.15 booking required
Av main course £12 **Restaurant** L served Mon-Fri 12-2.15,
Sat-Sun 12-9.15 booking required D served Mon-Fri 6.30-9.15,
Sat-Sun 12-9.15 booking required Av 3 course à la carte fr
£20 ⊕ ENTERPRISE INNS ◀ Hop Back Summer Lightning,
Ringwood Best Bitter, Fortyniner, Marstons Porter, Timothy
Taylor Ô Thatchers Gold, New Forest Traditional Farmhouse. ♟ 11
**Facilities** Children's menu Dogs allowed Garden Parking

## BUCKLERS HARD

## The Master Builders House
## Hotel ★★★ HL 🏵 ♟

**SO42 7XB** ☎ **01590 616253** 🖹 **01590 616297**
e-mail: enquiries@themasterbuilders.co.uk
dir: *From M27 junct 2 follow signs to Beaulieu. Left onto B3056. Left to
Bucklers Hard. Hotel 2m on left*

Once home to master shipbuilder Henry Adams, this idyllic
18th-century inn is situated on the banks of the River Beaulieu,
in the historic ship-building village of Bucklers Hard. Ducks,
boats and river walks are all on the doorstep. Bar food includes
grilled Lymington mackerel, tomato and red onion salad; Old
Spot sausages, creamed potato and roast onions; and linguine
with New Forest mushrooms, garlic and parsley.

Open all day all wk 11-11 (Sun 11-10.30) **Bar Meals** Av main
course £9.50 food served all day **Restaurant** L served Mon-Sat
12-2.30, Sun 12-3 booking required D served all wk 7-9.30
booking required Fixed menu price fr £15 Av 3 course à la carte
fr £25 ⊕ HILLBROOKE HOTELS ◀ Ringwood Best, Ringwood
Thumper Ô Stowford Press. ♟ 8 **Facilities** Children's menu Dogs
allowed Garden Parking **Rooms** 25

## BURGHCLERE

## Carnarvon Arms ♟

**Winchester Rd RG20 9LE** ☎ **01635 278222**
🖹 **01635 278444**
e-mail: info@carnarvonarms.com
web: www.carnarvonarms.com
dir: *M4 junct 13, A34 S to Winchester. Exit A34 at Tothill Services, follow
Highclere Castle signs. Pub on right*

The Carnarvon Arms is a modern country inn offering good
food, good beer and sensible prices. The word 'modern' needs
putting into context, however, because it was actually built
in the mid-1800s as a coaching inn providing a stop-off for
travellers to nearby Highclere Castle, the family seat of the
Earls of Carnarvon. The warm and friendly bar, decorated in
fresh natural colours and furnished with rich leather upholstery,
offers a menu of sandwiches, salads, pan-fried liver and

England

bacon with mash and shallot sauce; and tomato and basil shepherd's pie topped with butternut squash and Parmesan. Modern British food, with a strong emphasis on fresh seasonal ingredients at sensible prices, is head chef Justin Brown's objective. From the carte come starters of pan-fried scallops with buttered samphire and herb fish cream; and risotto of leeks, Oxford Blue cheese and toasted walnuts. Among the main courses are fillet of John Dory with sautéed potato, bacon and spinach and dill fish cream; and pan-roasted rump of pork with Jersey Royals, baby leeks and herb red wine sauce. Puddings include traditional tarts and crumbles, in addition to contemporary favourites such as trio of chocolate desserts - mousse, brûlée and fondant. An excellent cheeseboard is served with pressed fruits. Vegetarian and set-price lunch menus are also available.

**Open** all day all wk **Bar Meals** L served all wk 12-2.30 D served all wk 6.30-9.30 **Restaurant** L served all wk 12-2.30 D served all wk 6.30-9.30 🍺 Guinness, guest ales. 🍷 15 **Facilities** Children's menu Dogs allowed Garden Parking

## CHALTON

## The Red Lion 🍷

**PO8 0BG** ☎ 023 9259 2246   📄 023 9259 6915
e-mail: redlionchalton@fullers.co.uk
*dir: Just off A3 between Horndean & Petersfield. Follow signs for Chalton*

Believed to be Hampshire's oldest pub, The Red Lion was built in 1147 as a workshop and residence for the craftsmen working on St Michael's church across the road. By 1460 it had become a hostel for church dignitaries, and was later extended to accommodate coachmen on their journey from London to Portsmouth. Constructed from wood, white daub and thatch, the ancient building blends effortlessly into the hills and trees of the South Downs, and original features inside include an inglenook fireplace. There are spectacular views from the large garden and modern dining room. The pub has a good reputation locally for the quality of its food. You can choose from the daily changing menu of freshly cooked dishes, which relies heavily on locally sourced produce, or the popular snack menu of traditional pub fare.

**Open** all day all wk 11.30-11 (Sun 11.45-10.30) **Bar Meals** food served all day **Restaurant** food served all day 🌐 FULLER, SMITH & TURNER PLC 🍺 Fuller's, HSB, London Pride, Discovery, ESB, seasonal ales 🍏 Heart of Hampshire, Boxing Dog, Sweet Russett. 🍷 20 **Facilities** Children's menu Family room Dogs allowed Garden Parking

## CHARTER ALLEY

## The White Hart Inn 🍷

**White Hart Ln RG26 5QA** ☎ 01256 850048
📄 01256 850524
e-mail: enquiries@whitehartcharteralley.com
*dir: From M3 junct 6 take A339 towards Newbury. Turn right to Ramsdell. Right at church, then 1st left into White Hart Lane*

On the outskirts of the village overlooking open farmland and woods, this pub draws everyone from cyclists and walkers to real ale enthusiasts. Dating from 1818, it originally refreshed local woodsmen and coach drivers visiting the farrier next door. Today's more modern menu is likely to include confit of duck leg with orange and tarragon sauce; venison steak with red wine and redcurrant sauce; or vegetarian stir-fry. Look to the blackboard for specials and fish dishes.

**Open** all wk noon-2.30 7-11 (Sun 7-10.30) Closed: 25-26 Dec, 1 Jan **Bar Meals** L served all wk 12-2 D served Tue-Sat 7-9 Av main course £10 **Restaurant** L served Tue-Sun 12-2 booking required D served Tue-Sat 7-9 booking required 🌐 FREE HOUSE 🍺 West Berkshire Mild, Palmers IPA, Triple FFF Alton Pride, Stonehenge Great Bustard, Loddon Ferryman's Gold. 🍷 7 **Facilities** Children's menu Family room Dogs allowed Garden Parking

## CRAWLEY

## The Fox and Hounds 🍷

**SO21 2PR** ☎ 01962 776006   📄 01962 776006
e-mail: liamlewisairey@aol.com
*dir: A34 onto A272 then 1st right into Crawley*

Just north west of Winchester, at the heart of a peaceful Hampshire village, this mock Tudor traditional inn enjoys a burgeoning reputation for simple well-cooked food. Restored to former glories, it features beamed rooms warmed by log fires that create a welcoming, lived-in atmosphere. Typical dishes are roast beetroot salad with goats' cheese; smokey chicken with bacon leek and cream sauce; home-made beef lasagne; and sticky toffee pudding.

**Open** all wk 11-3 6-mdnt **Bar Meals** L served all wk 12-2 booking required **Restaurant** L served all wk 12-2 booking required D served all wk 6.30-9.30 booking required 🌐 ENTERPRISE INN 🍺 Wadworth 6X, Ringwood Best, Ringwood 49, Bombardier. 🍷 36 **Facilities** Children's menu Play area Garden Parking

## DAMERHAM

### The Compasses Inn ♀

**SP6 3HQ ☎ 01725 518231** 📄 **01725 518880**
e-mail: linda@compassesinn.co.uk
web: www.compassesinn.uk.com
dir: *From Fordingbridge (A338) follow signs for Sandleheath/Damerham. Signed from B3078*

The Compasses is a perfect example of the traditional family-run country free house. Set next to the village green, it is an ideal spot for a tranquil summer pint or a winter warmer round the welcoming open fires. Freshly prepared food is served in the bar, dining room or garden: it ranges from a simple home-baked bread ploughman's to pan-fried sea bass with prawns.

**Open** all wk 11-3 6-11 (Sat-Sun all day) **Bar Meals** L served all wk 12-3 D served all wk 6.30-9.30 ⊕ ENTERPRISE INNS ◀ Ringwood Best, Hop Back Summer Lightning, Courage Best, Ringwood 49er, Guest Ale. ♀ 8 **Facilities** Children's menu Dogs allowed Garden Parking

## DOWNTON

### The Royal Oak ♀

**Christchurch Rd SO41 0LA ☎ 01590 642297**
e-mail: royaloak@alcatraz.co.uk
dir: *On A337 between Lymington & Christchurch*

Two miles south of the New Forest and just one mile from the beach at Lymington, this renovated pub is renowned for its food. Snack on a traditional ploughman's platter or daytime sandwiches such as warm chicken, chorizo and rocket or brie and bacon. Main meals include salmon fish cakes with tomato and chilli jam; sirloin steak with peppercorn sauce; and gourmet burgers.

**Open** all wk 11-11.30 **Bar Meals** food served all day **Restaurant** Fixed menu price fr £9.95 Av 3 course à la carte fr £19 food served all day ⊕ ENTERPRISE INNS ◀ Ringwood Best Bitter, Fuller's London Pride, HSB. ♀ 15 **Facilities** Children's menu Garden Parking

## DROXFORD

### The Bakers Arms ◉ ♀

**High St SO32 3PA ☎ 01489 877533**
e-mail: enquiries@thebakersarmsdroxford.com
dir: *10m E of Winchester on A32 between Fareham & Alton.*

This unpretentious, white-painted pub and restaurant oozes country charm and character, the staff are smiley, and the locals clearly love it. Over the big log fire a blackboard menu lists the simple, well cooked and locally sourced food, while in the bar customers make short work of its barrels of Wallops Wood from the village's own Bowman Brewery. Mostly classic British cuisine includes pea and ham soup; potted mackerel with toast and piccalilli; gratinated Hampshire pike quenelles; grilled chicken breast with rösti potato and wild mushroom sauce; crispy duck leg with chorizo, sautéed potatoes and thyme gravy; roasted polenta with blue cheese and field mushrooms; and orechiette pasta with lamb ragout. Every village should have a local like this.

**Open** 11.45-3 6-11 (Sun 12-3) Closed: Sun eve & Mon **Bar Meals** L served Tue-Sun 12-2 booking required D served Tue-Sun 7-9 booking required Av main course £12.95 **Restaurant** L served Tue-Sun 12-2 booking required D served Tue-Sun 7-9 booking required ◀ Bowman Swift one, Bowman Wallops Wood Ö Stowford Press. ♀ 7 **Facilities** Children's menu Dogs allowed Garden Parking

## EASTON

### The Chestnut Horse ♀

**SO21 1EG ☎ 01962 779257** 📄 **01962 779037**
dir: *From M3 junct 9 take A33 towards Basingstoke, then B3047. Take 2nd right, then 1st left*

This 16th-century pub is located in the pretty Itchen Valley village of Easton and there are some good walks directly from the door. Old tankards and teapots hang from the low-beamed ceilings in the two bar areas, where a large open fire is the central focus through the winter months. The restaurants are equally inviting: plates adorn the light, panelled Green Room, and there's a wood-burning stove in the darker low-beamed Red Room. A good-value set price menu is offered Monday to Saturday lunchtime (12-2pm) or Monday to Thursday early evening (6-7.30pm). This might include fish and chips, local pheasant casserole or chilli con carne. Typical main menu dishes are baked trout fillet with chestnut and herb crust, or slow braised shoulder of lamb with butternut mash. A vegetarian alternative could be tagliatelle with Alresford watercress and gruyère cheese sauce.

**Open** all wk noon-3.30 5.30-11 (Sun eve closed winter) **Bar Meals** L served all wk 12-2.30 booking required D served Mon-Sat 6-9.30 booking required Av main course £12 **Restaurant** L served all wk 12-2 booking required D served Mon-Sat 6-9.30 booking required Fixed menu price fr £12 Av 3 course à la carte fr £24 ⊕ HALL & WOODHOUSE ◀ Chestnut Horse Special, Badger First Gold, Tanglefoot Ö Stowford Press. ♀ 9 **Facilities** Children's menu Dogs allowed Garden Parking

## EAST TYTHERLEY

### The Star Inn Tytherley ★★★★ INN ◉ ☖

**SO51 0LW ☎ 01794 340225**

e-mail: info@starinn.co.uk

dir: *5m N of Romsey off A3057, left for Dunbridge on B3084. Left for Awbridge & Kents Oak. Through Lockerley then 1m*

The 16th-century Star Inn stands overlooking the village cricket green in the smallest village in the Test Valley. You'll find Hidden Brewery beers and other guest ales behind the bar, plus an extensive international wine list. Dine where you like, in the bar, at dark-wood tables in the main dining room, or outside on the patio in summer, where you can also play king-sized chess. Lunchtime brings a variety of platters (fish, Barkham Blue, or Winchester farmhouse cheese), sandwiches (perhaps smoked salmon, crème fraîche and dill, or Cumberland sausage with caramelised onion), and a good value two-course menu (stir-fried tiger prawns with chorizo and gremolata, and roast chicken supreme). The evening menu might offer crab soufflé with watercress and saffron cream, and braised belly pork with sage polenta and celeriac purée. There's a good choice at Sunday lunch, too, including traditional roasts. Children of well behaved parents are welcome.

**Open** 11-2.30 6-10 Closed: Sun eve & Mon (ex BH) **Bar Meals** L served Tue-Sun 12-2 booking required D served Tue-Fri 7-9 booking required Av main course £8.50 **Restaurant** L served Tue-Sun 12-2 booking required D served Tue-Sat 7-9 booking required Av 3 course à la carte fr £20 ⊕ FREE HOUSE ◖ Hidden Quest, Hidden Pint, guest ales ♂ Thatchers Gold. ☖ 8 **Facilities** Children's menu Dogs allowed Garden Parking **Rooms** 3

## EMSWORTH

### The Sussex Brewery ☖

**36 Main Rd PO10 8AU ☎ 01243 371533**

🖨 01243 379684

e-mail: info@sussexbrewery.com

dir: *On A259 (coast road), between Havant & Chichester*

The Sussex Brewery is set in the picturesque village of Emsworth, renowned for its annual food festival in September. This 17th-century pub upholds traditional values with its sawdust covered floors, real ales and open fires, and the two dining rooms that have recently been refurbished. The menu includes a large variety of sausages, from beef and Guinness to tomato and garlic (there's a good choice for vegetarians too). Breakfast and light lunch menus are also available.

**Open** all wk 7am-mdnt **Bar Meals** L served all wk 12-2.30 D served all wk 6.30-9.30 **Restaurant** L served all wk 12-2.30 booking required D served all wk 6.30-9.30 booking required ⊕ YOUNG & CO BREWERY PLC ◖ Youngs Special, Youngs Ordinary, Waggle Dance, Bombardier Tribute. ☖ 12 **Facilities** Children's menu Dogs allowed Garden Parking

## EVERSLEY

### The Golden Pot ☖

**Reading Rd RG27 0NB ☎ 0118 973 2104**

e-mail: jcalder@goldenpot.co.uk

web: www.golden-pot.co.uk

dir: *Between Reading & Camberley on B3272*

Dating back to the 1700s, this well-established hostelry has recently converted to a free house. A warming fire connects the bar and restaurant, while the Snug and Vineyard are comfortable outside areas surrounded by colourful tubs and hanging baskets for summer relaxation. All food is home-made, offering traditional and modern choices, and prepared on the premises; children are not only welcome but also specially catered for.

**Open** all wk 11.30-3 5.30-10.30 Closed: 25-26 & 31 Dec, 1 Jan, (Sun eve) **Bar Meals** L served all wk 12-2.45 booking required D served Mon-Sat 6-9 booking required **Restaurant** L served all wk 12-2.45 booking required D served Mon-Sat 6-9 booking required ⊕ FREE HOUSE ◖ Andwell Brewery, Loddon Brewery, West Berkshire, Hogs Back Brewery, Shepherd Neame. ☖ 8 **Facilities** Children's menu Dogs allowed Garden Parking

## EXTON

### The Shoe Inn ☖

**Shoe Ln SO32 3NT ☎ 01489 877526**

dir: *Exton is on A32 between Fareham & Alton*

In the heart of the Meon Valley, this popular village pub owes much of its success to the food on offer. And that in turn is due to extensive use by the kitchen of local ingredients, including from an ever-expanding herb garden that produces organic vegetables, salad leaves and fruit nourished by compost and manure from the local stud farm. You can enjoy a light meal from the Cobbler's menu, or from a seasonal menu, home-made faggots; slow-cooked leg of Hampshire pork; fillet of organic sea trout; Mediterranean cassoulet; or rigatone with roasted vegetables. Eat inside or in the garden overlooking Old Winchester Hill, while watching the river drift by.

**Open** 11-3 6-11 Closed: 25 Dec, Mon eve **Bar Meals** L served all wk 12-2 **Restaurant** L served all wk 12-2 D served Tue-Sun 6-9 ⊕ WADWORTH ◖ Wadworth 6X, IPA ♂ Stowford Press. ☖ 18 **Facilities** Children's menu Dogs allowed Garden Parking

## FORDINGBRIDGE

### The Augustus John ♀

**116 Station Rd SP6 1DG ☎ 01425 652098**
e-mail: enquiries@augustusjohn.com
dir: *12m S of Salisbury on A338 towards Ringwood*

In keeping with its name, this pub and restaurant has a collection of paintings by Augustus John, who lived in the village. Set on the edge of the New Forest, it's a friendly, welcoming refuge offering a good selection of drinks including Ringwood Best Bitter and Wychwood cider. The extensive menu includes Thai food, fresh fish and hearty meals such as creamy garlic mushrooms followed by roast lamb with a red wine sauce.

**Open** all wk 10.30-3 5-11.30 (wknds open until 1.30am) **Bar Meals** Av main course £5 food served all day **Restaurant** Fixed menu price fr £8.95 Av 3 course à la carte fr £22 food served all day ⊕ MARSTONS ◀ Ringwood Best, Pedigree, Porter, Fortyniner ○ Wychwood. ♀ 8 **Facilities** Children's menu Dogs allowed Garden Parking

## GOSPORT

### The Seahorse ♀

**Broadsands Dr PO12 2TJ ☎ 023 9251 2910**
e-mail: simonl29@aol.com
dir: *A32 onto Military Rd, 2nd exit rdbt onto Gomer Ln, 0.5m on left*

Much more than just a local pub, the refurbished Seahorse includes Leonard's restaurant, as well as a large bar with terrace. This is a family-run business, where head chef Simon Leonard uses locally sourced ingredients to create a wide range of traditional and speciality dishes. Typical choices include boiled ham, duck egg and hand-cut chips; mutton suet pudding; and chargrilled steak with wild mushrooms.

**Open** all day all wk 11-11 Closed: 25 Dec **Bar Meals** L served all wk 12-2.30 D served Sun-Thu 6-8.45, Fri-Sat 6-9.45 (no food Mon eve) ⊕ ENTERPRISE INNS ◀ London Pride, Worthington. ♀ 8 **Facilities** Children's menu Dogs allowed Garden Parking

## HANNINGTON

### The Vine at Hannington ♀

**RG26 5TX ☎ 01635 298525    ▤ 01635 298027**
e-mail: info@thevineathannington.co.uk
web: www.thevineathannington.co.uk
dir: *Hannington signed from A339 between Basingstoke & Newbury*

A traditional village pub high up on the beautiful Hampshire Downs, with views across the countryside from its sheltered garden and attractive conservatory. Visitors can be assured of friendly service and good home-made pub food, many of the herbs, salad leaves and vegetables used coming from the pub garden. Seasonal menus of home-cooked, affordable dishes, including daily specials, might suggest starting with local watercress and spinach soup with focaccia bread; or maybe a share of a generous plate of antipasti. Then follows a selection of mains, among which you'll find home-baked ham with egg and chips; free-range Hampshire pork loin with cider and apple sauce and stuffing; and spinach and Parmesan risotto. Turn your attention to the specials board for local venison pie with juniper, orange and honey; or grilled skate wing with black butter and capers. Should you just want a bar snack, there are ploughman's and sandwiches, or you could again consider the antipasti. The compact wine list should satisfy most tastes. The garden behind the Vine is large, but a cosy wood-burner might make staying inside preferable when the sun isn't shining.

**Open** 12-3 6-11 (Sat-Sun all day) Closed: 25 Dec, Sun eve & Mon in Winter **Bar Meals** L served Mon-Fri 12-2, Sat-Sun 12-2.30 D served all wk 6-9 Av main course £9 **Restaurant** L served Mon-Fri 12-2, Sat-Sun 12-2.30 D served all wk 6-9 Av 3 course à la carte fr £20 ◀ Black Sheep, Bombardier. ♀ 10 **Facilities** Children's menu Play area Family room Dogs allowed Garden Parking

England

## HIGHCLERE

### The Furze Bush Inn ★★★ INN ♟

**Hatt Common, East Woodhay RG20 0NQ**
☎ 01635 253228   ▤ 01635 254883
**e-mail:** info@furzebushinn.co.uk **web:** www.furzebushinn.co.uk
**dir:** *Please telephone for directions*

Handy for Highclere Castle, the M4, Newbury Races and hiking the Berkshire Downs, the Furze Bush lies tucked down lanes in a glorious rural location. Expect a good range of pub food. In the bar, order favourites like chicken pie and ham, egg and chips, or book a restaurant table for game casserole, neck of lamb and rosemary sauce, and treacle tart and custard. There is a large front beer garden.

**Open** all day all wk **Bar Meals** L served Mon-Fri 12-2.30, Sat-Sun & BH all day D served Mon-Sat 6-10, Sun 6-9 Av main course £10 **Restaurant** L served Mon-Fri 12-2.30, Sat-Sun & BH 12-6 booking required D served Mon-Sat 6-10, Sun 6-9 booking required Fixed menu price fr £15 Av 3 course à la carte fr £22 ⊕ FREE HOUSE ◀ Flowers IPA, guest ale. ♟ 8 **Facilities** Children's menu Play area Dogs allowed Garden Parking **Rooms** 10

## HOOK

### The Hogget ♟

**London Rd, Hook Common RG27 9JJ** ☎ 01256 763009
**e-mail:** home@hogget.co.uk
**dir:** *M3 junct 5 0.5m. Located on the A30 between Hook and Basingstoke*

Following a major refurbishment in 2008, The Hogget has quickly established a local reputation for good food and wine in a relaxed setting. Local ingredients from named suppliers are the foundation of freshly-cooked dishes like sausages with colcannon and onion gravy; poached smoked haddock on mustard mash; and roast butternut squash with wild mushrooms and sautéed leeks.

**Open** all wk noon-3 6-11 (Fri 5-11 Sun 7-11) Closed: 25 Dec **Bar Meals** L served all wk 12-2 booking required D served all wk 6.30-9 booking required Av main course £8.50 **Restaurant** L served all wk 12-2 booking required D served all wk 6.30-9 booking required Av 3 course à la carte fr £25 ⊕ MARSTONS PUB COMPANY ◀ Ringwood Best, Ringwood 49er, Jennings Sneck Lifter, Marstons Oyster Stout Ŏ Thatchers Gold. ♟ 14 **Facilities** Children's menu Dogs allowed Garden Parking

## HURSLEY

### The Dolphin Inn ♟

**SO21 2JY** ☎ 01962 775209
**e-mail:** mandy@dolphininn.demon.co.uk
**web:** www.dolphinhursley.co.uk
**dir:** *Please telephone for directions*

Reputedly built from the timbers of an early HMS Dolphin, hence the pub name, the roadside village inn dates from the 16th century and was once a thriving coaching inn. Follow a stroll through nearby Farley Mount Country Park with a traditional pub lunch in the mature garden or in the beamed bars – ham, egg and chips, steak and Guinness pie, sausage and onion baguette, or a healthy tuna Niçoise. Look out for the local butcher's meat draw in Fridays nights.

**Open** all wk Mon-Thu 11-3 6-11 (Fri-Sat 11-11 Sun 12-10.30) **Bar Meals** L served Mon-Thu 12-2, Fri-Sat 12-2.30, Sun 12-8.30 booking required D served Mon-Thu 6-9, Fri-Sat 6.30-9.30, Sun 12-8.30 booking required Av main course £8 **Restaurant** Fixed menu price fr £15 ⊕ ENTERPRISE ◀ Ringwood, Summer Lightning, HBB, HSB Ŏ Thatchers dry, Thatchers Premium. ♟ 23 **Facilities** Children's menu Play area Family room Dogs allowed Garden Parking

## IBSLEY

### Old Beams Inn ♟

**Salisbury Rd BH24 3PP** ☎ 01425 473387
▤ 01202 743080
**e-mail:** hedi@alcatraz.co.uk
**dir:** *On A338 between Ringwood & Salisbury*

Old Beams is a beautiful 14th-century thatched and timber-framed village inn located at the heart of the New Forest with views of countryside and ponies. It has a beer garden with a decked area and patio, and a cosy old world interior revitalised by a recent refurbishment. Pub food favourites based on local and New Forest produce dominate the menu, and on Friday night (fish night) there's a large selection.

**Open** all wk 11-11.30 **Bar Meals** Av main course £10 food served all day **Restaurant** Fixed menu price fr £11.95 food served all day ◀ IPA, Speckled Hen. ♟ 10 **Facilities** Children's menu Garden Parking

## LINWOOD

### The High Corner Inn ♀

**BH24 3QY ☎ 01425 473973**
e-mail: highcorner@wadworth.co.uk
dir: *From A338 (Ringwood to Salisbury road) follow brown tourist signs into forest. Pass Red Shoot Inn, after 1m turn down gravel track at Green High Corner Inn*

This early 18th-century inn is set in seven beautiful acres of woodland in the heart of the New Forest. The cluster of buildings began life as a farm in the early 1700s. A quiet hideaway in winter, mobbed in summer, it is a popular retreat for families with its numerous bar-free rooms, an outdoor adventure playground and miles of wildlife-rich forest and heathland walks and cycle trails. The beamy bars, replete with roaring winter log fires and the full range of Wadworth ales on tap, and the lovely forest garden are very agreeable settings for sampling an extensive range of home-cooked meals and bar snacks; daily specials are shown on chalkboards and a carvery is available on Sunday. Rest and refuel during or following a forest ramble with a refreshing pint of 6X and a bowl of home-made soup and a plate of sandwiches or a ploughman's lunch, best enjoyed on the flower-filled terrace or in the garden with its forest views, or tuck into something more substantial from the traditional pub menu. Dogs and horses are welcome.

Open all wk 11-3 6-11 (3-6 winter) **Bar Meals** L served all wk 12-2.30 D served all wk 6-9 **Restaurant** L served all wk 12-2.30 D served all wk 6-9 ⊕ WADWORTH ◀ Wadworth 6X, Horizon, IPA, Red Shoot New Forest Gold, Toms Tipple ♂ Westons, Thatchers Gold. ♀ 14 **Facilities** Children's menu Play area Dogs allowed Garden Parking

## LITTLETON

### The Running Horse ★★★★ INN ⊛ ♀

**88 Main Rd SO22 6QS ☎ 01962 880218**
▤ 01962 886596
e-mail: runninghorseinn@btconnect.com
web: www.runninghorseinn.co.uk
dir: *3m from Winchester, signed from Stockbridge Rd*

Situated on the western outskirts of Winchester, this pretty rural gastro-pub offers a special blend of atmosphere, food and luxurious accommodation. The bar is a successful marriage of the traditional and the modern, with stripped wooden floor, leather tub chairs around an original fireplace, and white walls. But the focus here is undoubtedly on good eating, and the

chefs' sourcing of seasonal produce of impeccable freshness helped the Running Horse to gain its AA Rosette for the quality of its modern international cuisine. Choose between dining outside on the front or rear terrace, casually in the bar, or more formally in the stylish restaurant. Dinner might begin with tomato and grilled cheese millefeuilles, or oriental crab and salmon fishcakes. Main courses include pan-fried fillet of sea bass with creamed leeks; steak and Winchester ale shortcrust pie; and crispy shoulder of lamb with dauphinoise potatoes. The garden behind the Running Horse and the patio to the front are large and peaceful. The rear garden is particularly good for children as it is a safe distance from the road and there's a huge expanse of grass for them to run on while you enjoy a quiet drink on the verandah.

Open all wk **Bar Meals** L served all wk 12-2 D served all wk 6-9.30 **Restaurant** L served all wk 12-2 D served all wk 6-9.30 ⊕ FREE HOUSE ◀ Ringwood Best, Flower Pots. ♀ 10 **Facilities** Children's menu Dogs allowed Garden Parking **Rooms** 9

## LYMINGTON

### Mayflower Inn ♀

**Kings Saltern Rd SO41 3QD ☎ 01590 672160**
▤ 01590 679180
e-mail: info@themayflower.uk.com
dir: *A337 towards New Milton, left at rdbt by White Hart, left to Rookes Ln, right at mini-rdbt, pub 0.75m*

A favourite with yachtsmen and dog walkers, this solidly built mock-Tudor inn overlooks the Lymington River, with glorious views to the Isle of Wight. There's a magnificent garden with glorious sun terraces, a purpose-built play area for children and an on-going summer barbecue in fine weather. Light bites and big bowl salads are backed up with heartier choices like traditional lamb and rosemary hotpot, pan-fried liver and bacon, and beer battered fish of the day.

Open all day all wk **Bar Meals** Av main course £8.50 food served all day **Restaurant** food served all day ⊕ ENTERPRISE INNS ◀ Ringwood Best, Fuller's London Pride, 6X, Goddards Fuggle Dee Dum. ♀ 8 **Facilities** Children's menu Play area Dogs allowed Garden Parking

## LYNDHURST

## New Forest Inn ☉

**Emery Down SO43 7DY ☎ 023 8028 4690**
e-mail: info@thenewforestinn.co.uk
dir: *M21 junct 1 follow signs for A35/Lyndhurst. In Lyndhurst follow signs for Christchurch, turn right at Swan Inn towards Emery Down*

The inn, which prides itself on its friendliness, is located in the heart of the New Forest, with ponies constantly trying to get in the front door. The pub has its own local walk and dogs are made welcome. Inside you'll find oak beams and floors and two open fires in feature fireplaces. Outside there's a lovely garden for summer use. Home-cooked food includes local game, locally sourced meat and vegetarian options.

**Open** all day all wk **Bar Meals** Av main course £8 food served all day **Restaurant** food served all day ⊕ ENTERPRISE INNS ☖ Ringwood Best, Ringwood 49, guest ales ♂ Stowford Press. ☉ 8 **Facilities** Children's menu Dogs allowed Garden Parking

## The Oak Inn ☉

**Pinkney Ln, Bank SO43 7FE ☎ 023 8028 2350**
📄 023 8028 4601
e-mail: oakinn@fullers.co.uk
dir: *From Lyndhurst signed A35 to Christchurch, follow A35 1m, turn left at Bank sign*

Ponies, pigs and deer graze outside this former ciderhouse. Behind the bay windows are a traditional woodburner, antique pine and an extensive collection of bric-a-brac. There is also a large beer garden for those fine summer days. A wide selection of fresh seafood, including Selsey crab gratin, and seared tuna steak, features among an interesting choice of dishes, including the local wild boar sausages and daily pies.

**Open** all wk **Bar Meals** L served all wk 12-2.30 booking required D served Mon-Sat 6-9.30, Sun 5-9 booking required **Restaurant** L served all wk 12-2.30 booking required D served Mon-Sat 6-9.30, Sun 5-9 booking required ⊕ FULLERS BREWERY ☖ Ringwood Best, Hop Back Summer Lightening, London Pride, Fuller's HSB. ☉ 9 **Facilities** Children's menu Dogs allowed Garden Parking

## MAPLEDURWELL

## The Gamekeepers ☉

**Tunworth Rd RG25 2LU ☎ 01256 322038**
📄 01256 322038
e-mail: costellophil@hotmail.co.uk
dir: *M3 junct 6, take A30 towards Hook. Turn right after The Hatch pub. The Gamekeepers signed*

A 19th-century pub/restaurant with an indoor well, the Gamekeepers has a very rural location with a large secluded garden. Relax on a leather settee with a pint of Fursty Ferret or Stinger and enjoy the cosy atmosphere of low beams and flagstone floors. An impressive range of game and seafood (Dover sole, John Dory, monkfish) is offered, with dishes like oven-baked salmon topped with fontina cheese and wrapped in Parma ham, or chargrilled beef fillet on dauphinoise potatoes with blue cheese and pink peppercorn butter.

**Open** all day all wk **Bar Meals** Av main course £9 food served all day **Restaurant** Av 3 course à la carte fr £30 food served all day ⊕ HALL & WOODHOUSE ☖ Badgers First Gold, Tanglefoot, Sussex Best, Fursty Ferret, Stinger. ☉ 12 **Facilities** Children's menu Dogs allowed Garden Parking

## NEW ALRESFORD

## The Woolpack Inn ☉

**Totford, Nr Northington SO24 9TJ ☎ 0845 293 8066**
📄 0845 293 8055
e-mail: info@thewoolpackinn.co.uk
dir: *M3 south towards A27, take A339 to Alton and first right to B3046 Candovers & Alresford*

Approach this old drovers' inn at night and just as you prepare to descend a steep hill you'll see its welcoming lights down below. The inn changed hands in 2008 and the new owners have really smartened it up, creating a sense of calm modernity while still retaining a traditional feel. Its new seasonal menus offers, in the traditional bar area, bacon butty on farmhouse bread, and Heineken-battered fish and chips; and in the dining room, warm smoked trout and crispy bacon salad; pot-roast Candover Park partridge; and pan-roasted salmon with bacon, pea and potato broth.

**Open** 11.30am-3 6-close (Sat open all day) Closed: Sun eve in winter **Bar Meals** L served all wk 11.30-3 D served Mon-Sat 6-close Av main course £9.50 **Restaurant** L served all wk 11.30-3 D served Mon-Sat 6-close Av 3 course à la carte fr £20 ⊕ FREE HOUSE ☖ Palmers IPA, Palmers Copper, Moondance Triple FFF ♂ Thatchers Gold. ☉ 9 **Facilities** Children's menu Play area Dogs allowed Garden Parking

## NORTH WALTHAM

### The Fox ☙

**RG25 2BE ☎ 01256 397288**
e-mail: info@thefox.org
dir: *From M3 junct 7 take A30 towards Winchester. Village signed on right. Take 2nd signed road*

A peaceful village pub down a quiet country lane enjoying splendid views across fields and farmland - an ideal stop off the M3 just south of Basingstoke. Built as three farm cottages in 1624, the Fox can offer families three large level gardens, one of which is a dedicated children's play area, and superb flower borders and hanging baskets in summer. A dedicated bar menu proffers the likes of ham, double egg and chips; and cottage pie. The monthly-changing restaurant choice may include Hampshire venison; trio of seafood (crevette, marlin and tuna); Barbary duck breast; and slow roasted pork belly with grain mustard mash.

**Open** all day all wk 11-11 **Bar Meals** L served all wk 12-2.30 D served all wk 6-9.30 **Restaurant** L served all wk 12-2.30 booking required D served all wk 6-9.30 booking required ⊕ PUNCH TAVERNS ◖ Ringwood Best Bitter, Adnams Broadside, Brakspear, guest ale ♻ Aspall. ☙ 17 **Facilities** Children's menu Play area Dogs allowed Garden Parking

## ROCKBOURNE

### The Rose & Thistle ☙

**SP6 3NL ☎ 01725 518236**
e-mail: enquiries@roseandthistle.co.uk
web: www.roseandthistle.co.uk
dir: *Follow Rockbourne signs from A354 (Salisbury to Blandford Forum road), or from A338 at Fordingbridge follow signs to Rockbourne*

This is a picture postcard pub if ever there was one, with a stunning rose arch, flowers around the door and a delightful village setting. The low-beamed bar and dining area are furnished with country house fabrics, polished oak tables and chairs, cushioned settles and carved benches, and homely touches include floral arrangements and a scatter of magazines. Open fires make this a cosy retreat in cold weather, whilst the summer sun encourages visitors to sit in the neat cottage garden. Lunchtime favourites are listed as steak and kidney pudding; scrambled egg with smoked salmon; or mixed mushroom stroganoff. In the evening look out for rack of lamb with champ; pesto cous cous with roasted vegetables; or a variety of fish specials on the blackboard.

**Open** all wk **Bar Meals** L served all wk 12-2.30 booking required D served Mon-Sat 7-9.30 booking required Av main course £10 **Restaurant** L served all wk 12-2.30 booking required D served Mon-Sat 7-9.30 booking required ⊕ FREE HOUSE ◖ Fuller's London Pride, Palmers Copper Ale, Timothy Taylor Landlord. ☙ 12 **Facilities** Children's menu Dogs allowed Garden Parking

## ROMSEY

### The Three Tuns ☙

**58 Middlebridge St SO51 8HL ☎ 01794 512639**
e-mail: guru.palmer@yahoo.co.uk
dir: *Romsey bypass, 0.5m from main entrance of Broadlands Estate*

Centrally located in the abbey town, the 400-year-old Three Tuns is just a short walk from the front gates of Broadlands, country seat of Earl Mountbatten. In the last couple of years new owners Hannah and David have sought out local suppliers, aiming at a gastro-pub style operation. Typical dishes are braised shoulder of Romsey lamb, and Swish and Chips (plaice, haddock, king prawn and scallop in beer batter with real tartare and pea purée).

**Open** all day Closed: Mon L **Bar Meals** L served Tue-Sat 12-3, Sun 12-9 D served all wk 6.30-10.30 Av main course £7 **Restaurant** L served Tue-Sat 12-3, Sun 12-9 booking required D served all wk 6.30-10 booking required Av 3 course à la carte fr £25 ⊕ SWISH CATERING LTD ◖ Ringwood Best, Ringwood 49er, Sharp's Doom Bar, Hobgoblin ♻ Old Rosie. ☙ 8 **Facilities** Children's menu Dogs allowed Garden Parking

## SILCHESTER

### Calleva Arms ☙

**Little London Rd, The Common RG7 2PH
☎ 0118 970 0305**
dir: *A340 from Basingstoke, signed Silchester. M4 junct 11, 20 mins signed Mortimer then Silchester*

Standing opposite the village green, the pub is popular with walkers, cyclists, and visitors to the nearby Roman town of Calleva Atrebatum with the remains of its town walls and amphitheatre. A pleasant, airy conservatory added to the 19th-century building overlooks a large garden. Lunchtime favourites include steaks, bangers and mash and salads. Typical dinner selection starts with Thai spiced crab cakes with mango salsa or Indian, nacho or antipasti sharing platters;

followed by aromatic half duck with hoi sin sauce; and chef's fruit crumble with custard.

**Open** all wk 11-3 5.30-11.30 (Sat 11-11.30 Sun noon-11) **Bar Meals** L served all week 12-2 D served all wk 6.30-9 **Restaurant** L served all wk 12-2 booking required D served all wk 6.30-9 booking required ⊕ FULLER, SMITH & TURNER ◗ London Pride, HSB, Guinness, Butser Bitter. ♀ 8 **Facilities** Children's menu Dogs allowed Garden Parking

## STOCKBRIDGE

### The Peat Spade ◉ ♀

**Longstock SO20 6DR ☎ 01264 810612**
e-mail: info@peatspadeinn.co.uk
dir: *Telephone for directions*

Unusual paned windows overlook the peaceful village lane and idyllic thatched cottages at this striking, redbrick and gabled Victorian pub, which stands tucked away in the heart of the Test Valley, only 100 yards from the famous trout stream. Former Hotel du Vin chefs Lucy Townsend and Andrew Clark have created a classy country inn, one where you will find a relaxed atmosphere in the cosy fishing and shooting themed bar and dining room, and a simple, daily-changing menu listing classic English food. Using locally-sourced produce, including allotment fruit and vegetables and game from the Leckford Estate, the choice may take in devilled whitebait with tartare sauce for starters, with main dishes ranging from rump steak with garlic butter to roast halibut with squid ink risotto and sweet fennel. For pudding, try the Cambridge burnt cream or the lemon meringue pie.

**Open** all day all wk Closed: 25-26 Dec **Bar Meals** L served all wk 12-2 booking required D served all wk 7-9 booking required Av main course £15.50 **Restaurant** L served all wk 12-2 booking required D served all wk 7-9 booking required Av 3 course à la carte fr £35 ⊕ FREE HOUSE ◗ Ringwood Best, Ringwood 49er, guest ales. ♀ 10 **Facilities** Children's menu Dogs allowed Garden Parking

### The Three Cups Inn ★★★ INN ♀

**High St SO20 6HB ☎ 01264 810527**
e-mail: manager@the3cups.co.uk
web: www.the3cups.co.uk
dir: *M3 junct 8, A303 towards Andover. Left onto A3057 to Stockbridge*

There are many reasons to visit Stockbridge, and this 15th-century, timber-framed building at the western end of its wide main street is one. The pub's name derives from an Old English phrase for a meeting of three rivers, although the only river here is the Test, which splits into several streams through the village. The interior is low-beamed, with some floors of stone, some of wood, with high-backed chairs and hand-crafted tables arranged through a series of snugs. Modern European and traditional selections on the four menus, including a daily changing blackboard, blend Hampshire's freshest local ingredients to create an excellent choice. Typically, you might well find warm goats' cheese on toast and salad; and seafood cassoulet as starters, with main courses of caramelised shoulder of pork and mangetout; poached chunky sea bass with mousseline of celeriac and citrus shallot sauce; and vegetarian moussaka. Desserts include chocolate and cardamom brownie with home-made blueberry ripple ice cream; and vanilla macaroon with raspberry mousse. A lovely riverside terrace overlooks a rose-filled garden, where you can dine alfresco while trying to spot a wild brown trout in the river.

**Open** all day all wk 10am-10.30pm **Bar Meals** L served all wk 12-2.30 D served all wk 6-9.30 Av main course £10 **Restaurant** L served all wk 12-2.30 D served all wk 6-9.30 Fixed menu price fr £12.95 Av 3 course à la carte fr £20 ⊕ FREE HOUSE ◗ Fagin's Itchen Valley, Ringwood, Flower Pots, guest ales Ō Stowford Press. ♀ 10 **Facilities** Children's menu Dogs allowed Garden Parking **Rooms** 8

## TICHBORNE

### The Tichborne Arms ♀

**SO24 0NA ☎ 01962 733760   🖹 01962 733760**
e-mail: tichbornearms@xln.co.uk
dir: *Off A31 towards Alresford, after 200yds right at Tichborne sign*

A picturesque thatched free house in the heart of the Itchen valley. Three pubs have been built on this site, the first in 1429, but each has been destroyed by fire; the present red-brick building was erected in 1939. An interesting history is attached to this idyllic rural hamlet, which was dramatised in a feature film The Tichborne Claimant; it told the story of a butcher's boy from Australia who impersonated the son of Lady Tichborne (with her support) to claim the family title and estates. The pub interior displays an eclectic mix of artefacts, from stuffed animals and antiques to a chiming grandfather clock. A glowing wood-burning stove matches the warmth of the welcome from Patrick and Nicky Roper, who serve a range of real ales at the bar including Hopback, Palmers and Bowman;

continued

England

Mr Whitehead's Cirrus Minor cider is pulled straight from the barrel. A large, well-stocked garden is ideal for summer eating and drinking.

**Open** 11.30-3 6-11.30 Closed: Sun eve **Bar Meals** L served all wk 11.30-2 D served all wk 6.30-9 ⊕ FREE HOUSE ◀ Hopback Brewery, Palmers, Bowman, Sharps Downton. ♀ 9 **Facilities** Children's menu Dogs allowed Garden Parking

## UPPER FROYLE

### The Hen & Chicken Inn ♀

**GU34 4JH ☎ 01420 22115**
e-mail: bookings@henandchicken.co.uk
dir: *2m from Alton, on A31 next to petrol station*

Highwayman Dick Turpin is said to have hidden upstairs in this 18th-century coaching inn. It still has a traditional atmosphere thanks to large open fires, wood panelling and beams - but the post boxes above the inglenook remain empty. Food ranges from snacks to meals such as home-made linguine niçoise with a poached quail egg, followed by pan-fried calves' liver with bubble and squeak and red wine sauce; and then spotted dick with custard.

**Open** all wk 11.45-3 5.30-close (Sat-Sun all day) **Bar Meals** L served Mon-Sat 12-2.30, Sun 12-7 booking required D served Mon-Thu 6-9, Fri-Sat 6-9.30, Sun 12-7 booking required **Restaurant** L served Mon-Sat 12-2.30, Sun 12-7 booking required D served Mon-Thu 6-9, Fri-Sat 6-9.30, Sun 12-7 booking required ⊕ HALL & WOODHOUSE ◀ Badger Best, Tanglefoot, King, Barnes Sussex Ale Ŏ Stowford Press. ♀ 8 **Facilities** Children's menu Play area Dogs allowed Garden Parking

## WICKHAM

### Greens Restaurant & Pub ♀

**The Square PO17 5JQ ☎ 01329 833197**
e-mail: DuckworthGreens@aol.com
dir: *2m from M27, on corner of historic Wickham Square. 3m from Fareham*

The enduring popularity of Greens, on a corner of Wickham's picturesque square, is entirely down to the standards set by Frank and Carol Duckworth, who have run it for 25 years. Front-of-house staff are trained in guest care ensure a warm and welcoming reception for diners. Modern European cooking may offer Rosary goats' cheese salad with walnut and raspberry dressing; braised beef with red wine and chorizo with basil mash; and spiced apricot bread and butter pudding.

**Open** 10-3 6-11 (Sun & BH noon-4) Closed: Sun eve & Mon **Bar Meals** L served Tue-Sat 12-2.30, Sun 12-3 booking required D served Tue-Sat 6.30-9.30 booking required **Restaurant** L served Tue-Sat 12-2.30, Sun 12-3 booking required D served Tue-Sat 6.30-9.30 booking required Fixed menu price fr £9.95 Av 3 course à la carte fr £20 ⊕ FREE HOUSE ◀ Hopback Summer Lightning, Youngs Special, Guinness, Timothy Taylor, Local ales. ♀ 10 **Facilities** Children's menu Garden Parking

## WINCHESTER

### The Bell Inn ♀

**83 St Cross Rd SO23 9RE ☎ 01962 865284**
e-mail: the_bellinn@btconnect.com
dir: *M3 junct 11, follow B rd into Winchester for approx 1m. Pub on right*

Edge of town local that's worth noting as it stands close to the 12th-century St Cross Hospital, with its fine Norman church, and glorious walks through the River Itchen water meadows to Winchester College and the city centre. Very much a community local, with Greene King ales and good-value food served in the main bar and the pine-furnished lounge, plus a warm welcome to families and dogs. Head for the sunny walled garden on warm summer days.

**Open** all day all wk 11-11 (Fri-Sat 11am-mdnt Sun noon-10.30) **Bar Meals** L served all wk 12-2 booking required D served all wk 6.30-9 booking required Av main course £8 ⊕ GREENE KING ◀ IPA, 2 guest ales Ŏ Stowford Press. ♀ 8 **Facilities** Children's menu Play area Dogs allowed Garden Parking

## HEREFORDSHIRE

## ASTON CREWS

### The Penny Farthing Inn ♀

**HR9 7LW ☎ 01989 750366 🖹 01989 750366**
e-mail: info@pennyfarthinginn.co.uk
dir: *5m E of Ross-on-Wye*

This whitewashed 17th-century blacksmith's shop and coaching inn is located high above the River Wye valley. From its large, sloping garden you can take in views of the Malvern Hills, the Black Hills and the Forest of Dean. Inside are lots of nooks and crannies with oak beams, antiques, saddlery and cheerful log fires. At least two real ales and local cider are guaranteed to be on tap, and the wine list focuses on lesser known wineries to bring quality at a reasonable price. The same objective applies to the menu, which capitalises on the wealth of local vegetable and fruit growers' produce, and some of the best meat in the country. The lunchtime bar menu ranges from sandwiches, baguettes and jacket potatoes, to the pub's pie of the week, and chef's home-made curry. Main courses in the restaurant are likely to feature local lamb and renowned Hereford beef.

**Open** 12-3 6-11 Closed: Mon in winter **Bar Meals** food served all day **Restaurant** food served all day ◀ John Smith's, Black Sheep, Spitfire Ŏ Westons Stowford Press. ♀ 7 **Facilities** Children's menu Dogs allowed Garden Parking

## AYMESTREY

### The Riverside Inn ♉

**HR6 9ST ☎ 01568 708440** 📠 **01568 709058**
e-mail: theriverside@btconnect.com
dir: *On A4110, 18m N of Hereford*

A handsome half-timbered 16th-century inn on the banks of the River Lugg, overlooking an old stone bridge, peaceful woodland and lush meadows. It's a popular pit-stop for walkers hiking the Mortimer Way as the pub stands at the halfway point. Anglers are also drawn to inn as it offers a mile of private fishing for brown trout and grayling. The interior, with its wood panelling, low beams and log fires, engenders a relaxed atmosphere reflecting 300 years of hospitality. Locally grown and reared produce is used as much as possible in the kitchen, and visitors are welcome to take a stroll round the pub's extensive vegetable, herb and fruit gardens. Typical starters may include Lugg trout gravadlax with beetroot and horseradish relish, and Hereford Hop and smoked haddock soufflé with a creamy mustard sauce. Main dishes range from traditional favourites like lambs' liver and bacon with shallot gravy, and beer-battered cod with home-made chips, to more adventurous specials like organic belly pork cooked in local cider served with garden rhubarb and apple sauce; rack of Welsh lamb with pea purée and mint jus, and wild sea bass with creamy mushroom sauce. As befits a Herefordshire location, locally bred fillet and sirloin of beef always feature. Gluten and dairy free diets catered for.

**Open** 11-3 6-11 (Sun 12-3 6-10.30) Closed: 26 Dec & 1 Jan, Mon lunch, Sun eve in winter **Bar Meals** L served Tue-Sun 12-2 D served Mon-Sat 7-9 Av main course £9.95 **Restaurant** L served Tue-Sun 12-2 D served Mon-Sat 7-9 Av 3 course à la carte fr £21 ⊕ FREE HOUSE ◖ Wye Valley Bitter & Butty Bach, Hobsons Best Bitter, Spinning Dog, Owd Bull ♉ Brooke Farm Medium Dry, Westons Stowford Press. ♉ 7 **Facilities** Children's menu Dogs allowed Garden Parking

## CANON PYON

### The Nags Head Inn

**HR4 8NY ☎ 01432 830252**
dir: *Telephone for directions*

More than four hundred years old, with flagstone floors, open fires and exposed beams to prove it. A comprehensive menu might entice you into starting with slices of smoked salmon drizzled with brandy, lemon and cracked pepper, then to

follow with medallions of lamb in a sticky Cumberland sauce, breast of Gressingham duck in a rich morello cherry sauce, or butterflied sea bass on sautéed strips of carrot and chopped coriander. Vegetarian options include stuffed peppers and tagliatelle. Curry nights and Sunday carvery. The large garden features a children's adventure playground.

**Open** all wk Mon-Thu 3-12.30 (Fri-Sun 3-mdnt) **Bar Meals** L served Mon-Fri 4-7, Sat-Sun 12-7 D served Mon- Fri 4-7, Sat-Sun 12-7 **Restaurant** L served Mon-Fri 4-7, Sat-Sun 12-7 D served Mon-Fri 4-7, Sat-Sun 12-7 ⊕ FREE HOUSE ◖ Fuller's London Pride, Boddingtons, Flowers, Nags Ale ♉ Stowford Press. **Facilities** Children's menu Play area Dogs allowed Garden Parking

## HAMPTON BISHOP

### The Bunch of Carrots ♉

**HR1 4JR ☎ 01432 870237** 📠 **01432 870237**
e-mail: bunchofcarrots@buccaneer.co.uk
dir: *From Hereford take A4103, A438, then B4224*

The name has nothing to do with crunchy orange vegetables - it comes from a rock formation in the River Wye, which runs alongside this friendly pub. Inside, expect real fires, old beams and flagstones. There is an extensive menu plus a daily specials board, a carvery, salad buffet, and simple bar snacks. Real ale aficionados should certainly sample the local organic beer, or enjoy a pint of Wye Valley Bitter or Black Bull, plus Westons real cider is available.

**Open** all wk **Bar Meals** L served Mon-Fri 12-2.30, Sat-Sun all day D served Mon-Fri 5.30-9, Sat-Sun all day **Restaurant** L served Mon-Fri 12-2.30, Sat-Sun all day booking required D served Mon-Fri 5.30-9, Sat-Sun all day booking required ⊕ FREE HOUSE ◖ Directors, Wye Valley Bitter, Black Bull Bitter, Organic Bitter ♉ Westons Stowford Press. ♉ 11 **Facilities** Children's menu Play area Dogs allowed Garden Parking

## KIMBOLTON

### Stockton Cross Inn ♉

**HR6 0HD ☎ 01568 612509**
e-mail: info@stocktoncrossinn.co.uk
dir: *On A4112, 0.5m off A49, between Leominster & Ludlow*

A drovers' inn dating from the 16th century, the Stockton Cross Inn stands beside a crossroads where witches, rounded up from the surrounding villages such as Ludlow, were allegedly hanged. This grisly past is at odds with the peace and beauty

continued

of the setting, which includes a pretty country garden with umbrellas and trees for shade. The building itself is regularly photographed by tourists and featured on calendars and chocolate boxes. Children are welcome and enjoy their own menu. A popular traditional Sunday roast and a list of pub favourites (gammon steak with egg, plum tomato, field mushroom and home-made chips, for example) keep hungry customers coming.

**Open** Closed: Sun & Mon eve **Bar Meals** L served Tue-Sun 12-2 D served Tue-Sun 7-9 Av main course £10 **Restaurant** L served Tue-Sun 12-2 D served Tue-Sun 7-9 ⊕ FREE HOUSE ◖ Wye Valley Butty Bach & HPA, Hobson's Town Crier, Flowers Best Bitter, Murphys, Tetley's Smooth Flow, guest ales. ♍ 6 **Facilities** Children's menu Garden Parking

## MADLEY

### The Comet Inn ♍

**Stoney St HR2 9NJ ☎ 01981 250600**
e-mail: thecometinn-madley@hotmail.co.uk
dir: *6m from Hereford on B4352*

Originally three cottages, this black and white 19th-century inn occupies a prominent corner position and is set in two and a half acres. Inside it retains many original features and a roaring open fire. Expect simple, hearty pub food ranging from baguettes and jacket potatoes to comforting options such as steak and ale pie, shank of lamb, grilled gammon, chicken curry, cod in crispy batter, mushroom stroganoff, and a variety of steaks.

**Open** all wk 12-3 6-11 (Fri-Sun all day) **Bar Meals** Av main course £4.95 food served all day **Restaurant** Fixed menu price fr £9.95 food served all day ⊕ FREE HOUSE ◖ Wye Valley Bitter ♂ Stowford Press. ♍ 6 **Facilities** Children's menu Play area Garden Parking

## ORLETON

### The Boot Inn

**SY8 4HN ☎ 01568 780228  ▤ 01568 780228**
e-mail: traceytheboot65@live.co.uk
web: www.thebootinnorleton.co.uk
dir: *Follow A49 S from Ludlow (approx 7m) to B4362 (Woofferton), 1.5m off B4362 turn left. Inn in village centre*

A black and white half timbered village inn, The Boot dates from the 16th century, and in winter a blazing fire in the

inglenook warms the bar. You will be welcomed with excellent service, a good quality English menu with locally sourced produce and a fine range of cask ales. The wine list has been chosen to compliment the menu and to suit all pockets.

**Open** all wk 12-3 5-11 (Sat-Sun noon-11) **Bar Meals** L served all wk 12-3 D served all wk 6-9 Av main course £10 **Restaurant** L served all wk 12-3 D served all wk 6-9 ⊕ VILLAGE GREEN INNS LTD ◖ Hobsons Best, Local Real Ales, Woods, Wye Valley ♂ Stowford Press. **Facilities** Children's menu Play area Dogs allowed Garden Parking

## ROSS-ON-WYE

### The Moody Cow

**Upton Bishop HR9 7TT ☎ 01989 780470**
e-mail: info@themoodycow.biz
dir: *M50 take Newent exit then left at the junction. After 1.5m the pub is straight ahead.*

The pub's name causes endless speculation – it was once called the Wellington - but chef/proprietor Jonathan Rix certainly knows his onions, having previously worked in several establishments recognised for their culinary prowess. He serves local ales as well as Weston's ciders, and sources much of his produce from within 20 miles. Menus cover light lunches, pub classics and dinner options such as carpaccio of swordfish with avocado salsa; and roast breast and confit leg of Madgetts farm duck with apricot and thyme jus. Separate vegetarian menu.

**Open** 11-3.30 6-11 (Sun 6-10.30) Closed: Mon **Bar Meals** L served Tue-Sun 11.30-2.30 D served Tue-Sat 6.30-10 Av main course £13 **Restaurant** L served Tue-Sun 11.30-2.30 D served Tue-Sat 6.30-10 booking required Fixed menu price fr £14 Av 3 course à la carte fr £24.50 ⊕ ENTERPRISE ◖ Wye Valley Bitter, Butty Bach, Spitfire ♂ Stowford Press, Westons Organic. **Facilities** Children's menu Garden Parking

## ST OWENS CROSS

### The New Inn ♍

**HR2 8LQ ☎ 01989 730274  ▤ 01989 730557**
e-mail: info@newinn.biz
web: www.newinn.biz
dir: *Off A4137 W of Ross-on-Wye*

This delightful, multi-award-winning 16th-century inn has been under the caring eye of Nigel and Tee Maud since

February 2006. The spacious beer garden overlooks rolling Herefordshire countryside, with views stretching to the Black Mountains in the distance. Family-friendly outdoor games include giant versions of Jenga and Connect Four. The interior refurbishments have preserved characterful features such as exposed beams and woodwork, creating a cosy and traditional backdrop for a drink, a quick snack or a leisurely meal. At the helm in the kitchen is award-winning chef Tee, whose cooking is recognised with a plaque from the Hairy Bikers. Her ever-changing menus reveal a keen sense of the seasons and a commitment to sourcing excellent local ingredients. Typical starters such as deep-fried brie with cranberry sauce or creamy garlic mushrooms on toasted baguette might be followed by steak, ale and mushroom pie made with Herefordshire beef; oven-baked chicken breast with Hereford Hop and leek sauce; or shank of local lamb with red wine sauce and champ. An irresistible list of traditional puddings takes in Bakewell tart; and local perry jelly with home-made elderflower ice cream.

**Open** all day all wk 11-11 **Bar Meals** L served all wk from 12 D served all wk from 12 Av main course £8.75 food served all day **Restaurant** L served all wk from 12 D served all wk from 12 Av 3 course à la carte fr £20 food served all day ⊕ MARSTONS ♈ 8 **Facilities** Children's menu Play area Dogs allowed Garden Parking

## SHOBDON

# The Bateman Arms ★★★★ INN

**HR6 9LX ☎ 01568 708374**
e-mail: diana@batemanarms.co.uk
dir: *On B4362 off A4110 NW of Leominster*

An 18th-century three-storey coaching inn of striking appearance, with old cobbled paving lining its street frontage. The only pub in the village of Shobdon, there's character inside too; in the bar you can sit beneath ancient oak beams on 300-year-old wooden settles and enjoy a light meal, or head for the restaurant and its menu based on locally-sourced produce. Enjoy gammon steak, chips and peas or seafood fishcakes with green salad and new potatoes; desserts are all home made. There is also a games room and a large beer garden.

**Open** all day all wk noon-11 (Sat 11am-mdnt) **Bar Meals** food served all day **Restaurant** L served all wk 12-2 D served Mon-Sat 7-9 ⊕ FREE HOUSE ◀ Butty Bach, Hobgoblin, Mansfield Bitter. **Facilities** Children's menu Garden Parking **Rooms** 9

# Herefordshire

## SYMONDS YAT (EAST)

# The Saracens Head Inn ★★★★ INN ♈

**HR9 6JL ☎ 01600 890435 📄 01600 890034**
e-mail: contact@saracensheadinn.co.uk
web: www.saracensheadinn.co.uk
dir: *From Ross-on-Wye take A40 to Monmouth. In 4m take Symonds Yat East turn. 1st right before bridge. Right in 0.5m. Right in 1m*

Once a cider mill, the Saracens Head lies on the east bank of the River Wye where it flows into a steep wooded gorge. This is the yat, the local name for a gate or pass, while Robert Symonds was a Sheriff of Herefordshire in the 17th century. The inn's own ferry across the river to Symonds Yat West is hand operated, just as it has been for the past 200 years. You can eat in the lounge, dining room, flag-floored bar, or on one of the two sunny riverside terraces. Regularly changing menus and daily specials boards offer both traditional – moules marinière, for example - and modern, such as gnocchi in sun-dried tomato and pesto cream. Main courses might be rump of rump of Welsh Mountain lamb with dauphinoise potatoes; roasted butternut squash, goats' cheese and pine nut risotto cake; breast of local pheasant with game sausage black pudding and smoked bacon potato cake.

**Open** all wk 11-11 Closed: 25 Dec **Bar Meals** L served all wk 12-2.30 D served all wk 6.30-9 Av main course £11 **Restaurant** L served all wk 12-2.30 D served all wk 6.30-9 Fixed menu price fr £28 Av 3 course à la carte fr £25 ⊕ FREE HOUSE ◀ Theakstons Old Peculier, Old Speckled Hen, Wye Valley Hereford Pale Ale, Wye Valley Butty Bach, Buttcombe Bitter ♂ Westons Organic, Stowford Press, Lyne Down's Roaring Meg. ♈ 7 **Facilities** Children's menu Dogs allowed Garden Parking **Rooms** 10

## WALFORD

### The Mill Race ♟

**HR9 5QS ☎ 01989 562891**
e-mail: enquiries@millrace.info
dir: *From Ross-on-Wye take B4234 to Walford. Pub 3m on right after village hall*

There's a great mix of old and new in this comfortable, contemporary village pub. In winter there's a roaring fire, while in summer the patio doors are flung open into the external dining area, from where Goodrich Castle is visible across the fields. The pub has its own 1000-acre farm, rearing free-range cattle, rare-breed pigs, poultry and game. Dishes on the menu change weekly, often to feature cottage pie; beer-battered coley and chips; Madgetts Farm chicken breast with potato rösti, chestnut mushrooms and sage sauce; oxtail faggots with crushed root vegetables and red wine sauce; and mushroom Stroganoff. Afterwards, should, inexplicably, neither apple and cinnamon crumble nor sticky toffee pudding appeal, there's a good farmhouse cheese selection. The wine list includes a Welsh Seyval Blanc.

**Open** all wk 11-3 5-11 (Sat-Sun all day) **Bar Meals** L served Mon-Fri 12-2, Sat-Sun 12-2.30 booking required D served Mon-Sat 6-9.30, Sun 6-9 booking required Av main course £8 **Restaurant** L served Mon-Fri 12-2, Sat-Sun 12-2.30 booking required D served Mon-Sat 6-9.30, Sun 6-9 booking required Fixed menu price fr £8 Av 3 course à la carte fr £23 ⊕ FREE HOUSE ◀ Wye Valley Bitter, Guest Ales, Guinness ♂ Westons, Stowfords Press, Roaring Meg. ♟ 9 **Facilities** Children's menu Garden Parking

## WELLINGTON

### The Wellington ♟

**HR4 8AT ☎ 01432 830367**
e-mail: thewellington@hotmail.com
dir: *Off A49 into village centre. Pub 0.25m on left*

Owners Ross and Philippa Williams came from London to create one of Herefordshire's finest gastro-pubs. They've done well, with Ross quickly becoming an award-winning champion of food prepared from local, seasonal produce. Start with Parma ham and porcini mushroom lasagne, followed by slow-roasted belly and pan-fried tenderloin of Welsh white pork with cider sauce and mustard mash, and then lemon semifreddo with home-made orange shortbread. Sunday lunch could include roast leg of local venison.

**Open** 12-3 6-11 Closed: Mon L, Sun eve in winter **Bar Meals** L served Tue-Sun 12-2 D served all wk 7-9 Av main course £8.50 **Restaurant** L served Tue-Sun 12-2 D served all wk 7-9 Av 3 course à la carte fr £25 ⊕ FREE HOUSE ◀ Hobsons, Wye Valley Butty Bach, Wye Valley HPA, Guest ales ♂ Westons Scrumpy. ♟ 8 **Facilities** Children's menu Play area Dogs allowed Garden Parking

## WHITNEY-ON-WYE

### Rhydspence Inn ★★★★ INN

**HR3 6EU ☎ 01497 831262 📄 01497 831751**
e-mail: info@rhydspence-inn.co.uk
dir: *N side of A438, 1m W of Whitney-on-Wye*

This charming inn dates from 1380 and was extended in the 17th and 20th centuries. It was most likely built to provide comfort for travellers and pilgrims from Abbey Cwmhir to Hereford Cathedral, but it later became a watering hole for drovers taking cattle, sheep and geese to market in London. These days the pub is rather more elegant, with a cosy bar and spacious dining room giving way to stunning views over the Wye Valley. Food options range from deep-fried cod in lemon batter and French fries or braised shank of lamb from the bar bites and brasserie selection, to main menu dishes such as peppered venison with fricassee of mushrooms and port and redcurrant reduction or pan-fried sea bass with tempura courgettes and lemon aïoli. There is also a good choice of steaks from the grill. The friendly ghost of a former landlady is said to frequent the inn, though only when young children are staying.

**Open** all wk 11-2.30 7-11 **Bar Meals** L served all wk 11-2 D served all wk 7-9 Av main course £9 **Restaurant** L served all wk 11-2 booking required D served all wk 7-9 booking required Av 3 course à la carte fr £25 ⊕ FREE HOUSE ◀ Robinsons Best, Interbrew Bass. **Facilities** Children's menu Family room Garden Parking **Rooms** 7

## WOOLHOPE

### The Crown Inn ♀

**HR1 4QP ☎ 01432 860468  ▤ 01432 860770**
e-mail: menu@crowninnwoolhope.co.uk
dir: *B4224 to Mordiford, left after Moon Inn. Pub in village centre*

Every cider and perry producer in Herefordshire is represented at this real, old fashioned free house, and over 100 types of real ale are served in a year. Good quality local ingredients – wet and dry – are to the fore, with lunchtime baguettes and pub favourites such as chilli, Hereford beef burger, or cider braised ham with chunky chips. There is also an outdoor bar with a heated smoking area and beautiful views.

**Open** all wk 12-2.30 6.30-11 (Sat-Sun all day) **Bar Meals** L served all wk 12-2 D served all wk 6.30-9 Av main course £10 **Restaurant** L served all wk 12-2 D served all wk 6.30-9 Fixed menu price fr £18 Av 3 course à la carte fr £18 ⊕ FREE HOUSE ◖ Wye Valley Best, Black Sheep, guest ales ○ Westons Stowford Press. ♀ 6 **Facilities** Children's menu Garden Parking

## HERTFORDSHIRE

## ALDBURY

### The Valiant Trooper ♀

**Trooper Rd HP23 5RW ☎ 01442 851203**
**▤ 01442 851071**
e-mail: info@thevalianttrooper.co.uk
dir: *A41 at Tring junct, follow rail station signs 0.5m, at village green turn right, 200yds on left*

This country pub and restaurant is set in a pretty village at the foot of the Chiltern Hills. The large beer garden now has a wooden adventure trail, and children are handsomely catered for with their own healthy home-cooked menu. Dogs are also welcome in the bar or garden. The emphasis is on quality local produce in a menu of British classics. Snacks take in tempting sandwiches, cured meat or seafood platters, and savouries such as Welsh rarebit on toast. Typical main courses are pie of the day or five-bean chilli.

**Open** all day all wk 11.30am-11pm (Sun noon-10.30) **Bar Meals** Av main course £9.50 food served all day **Restaurant** Fixed menu price fr £13.50 Av 3 course à la carte fr £19 food served all day ⊕ FREE HOUSE ◖ Fuller's London Pride, Tring Jack O'Legs, 2 Guest ales. ♀ 8 **Facilities** Children's menu Play area Family room Dogs allowed Garden Parking

## ARDELEY

### The Rabbit's Foot

**SG2 7AH ☎ 01438 861350  ▤ 01438 861350**
e-mail: info@therabbitsfoot.co.uk
dir: *Follow B1037 6m from Stevenage, 2m from Walkern*

Formerly known as The Jolly Waggoner, this 500-year-old village pub has recently changed hands. Fresh local ingredients

are used in the seasonal menus – venison stew with caramelised shallots. Families are welcome and the children's menu has a simple, freshly prepared theme. The pub is also dog friendly. There's a large garden to enjoy in summer and open fires in winter.

**Open** 12-3 6-11 Closed: Mon, Tue **Bar Meals** L served Wed-Sun 12-3 D served Wed-Sat 6-9 **Restaurant** L served Wed-Sun 12-3 booking required D served Wed-Sat 6-9 booking required ⊕ ADMIRAL ◖ Greene King IPA, 2 Guest ales. **Facilities** Children's menu Dogs allowed Garden Parking

## ASHWELL

### The Three Tuns ♀

**High St SG7 5NL ☎ 01462 742107  ▤ 01462 743662**
e-mail: claire@tuns.co.uk
dir: *Telephone for directions*

The building, dating from 1806, replaces an earlier one first recorded as a public house in 1700. Original features survive in the two bars and large dining room, probably once a smokehouse, judging by the rows of old hanging hooks. Traditional pub food and an à la carte menu are on offer. The menu might offer steak and kidney pie; Spanish pork casserole and a selection of steaks with interesting sauces.

**Open** all day all wk 11am-11.30pm (Fri-Sat 11am-12.30am) **Bar Meals** L served Mon-Fri 12-2.30, Sat-Sun all day booking required D served Mon-Fri 6.30-9.30, Sat-Sun all day booking required Av main course £18 **Restaurant** L served Mon-Fri 12-2.30, Sat-Sun all day booking required D served Mon-Fri 6.30-9.30, Sat-Sun all day booking required Av 3 course à la carte fr £20 ⊕ GREENE KING ◖ Greene King IPA, Abbot, Guest. ♀ 12 **Facilities** Children's menu Play area Family room Dogs allowed Garden Parking

## BARLEY

### The Fox & Hounds ♀

**High St SG8 8HU ☎ 01763 848459  ▤ 01763 849080**
e-mail: info@foxandhoundsbarley.co.uk
dir: *A505 onto B1368 at Flint Cross, pub 4m*

Set in a pretty village, this former 17th-century hunting lodge is notable for its pub sign which extends across the lane. It has real fires, a warm welcome and an attractive garden. A typical menu includes wild mushroom risotto, beef burger with chunky-cut chips, Irish stew, and beer-battered fish and chips.

**Open** 10-3 6-late (Sat 10am-late, Sun 10-6) Closed: Mon **Bar Meals** L served Tue-Fri 12-3, Sat 12-late, Sun 12-5.30 booking required D served Tue-Sun 6-10 booking required Av main course £8.95 food served all day **Restaurant** L served Tue-Fri 12-3, Sat 12-4, Sun 12-5 booking required D served Tue-Sun 6-10 booking required Av 3 course à la carte fr £20 food served all day ⊕ SAFFRON LEISURE ◖ Adnams Best, Flowers IPA, Woodforde's Wherry. ♀ 12 **Facilities** Children's menu Play area Garden Parking

**England**

## BUNTINGFORD

### The Sword Inn Hand ★★★★ INN ▼

**Westmill SG9 9LQ ☎ 01763 271356**
e-mail: welcome@theswordinnhand.co.uk
dir: *Off A10 1.5m S of Buntingford*

Midway between London and Cambridge in the lovely village of Westmill, and welcoming travellers since the 14th century - you can't miss the oak beams, flag floor and open fireplace. It styles itself a 'real English', family-run pub offering a large selection of snacks, specials, beers and wines. Fresh produce is delivered daily to create herb-crushed rack of lamb, sea bass fillet with stir-fry vegetables, escalope of veal with melted brie or cod and chips.

**Open** all wk 12-3 5-11 (Sun Sep-Apr 12-7, May-Aug 12-10) **Bar Meals** L served Mon-Sat 12-2.30, Sun 12-4 D served Mon-Sat 6.30-9.30 **Restaurant** L served Mon-Sat 12-2.30, Sun 12-4 D served Mon-Sat 6.30-9.30 ⊕ FREE HOUSE ◀ Greene King IPA, Young's Bitter, Timothy Taylor Landlord, Guest ales ♂ Aspalls. ▼ 8 **Facilities** Children's menu Play area Dogs allowed Garden Parking Rooms 4

## FLAUNDEN

### The Bricklayers Arms ▼

**Hogpits Bottom HP3 0PH**
**☎ 01442 833322   ▤ 01442 834841**
e-mail: goodfood@bricklayersarms.com
web: www.bricklayersarms.com
dir: *M25 junct 18 onto A404 (Amersham road). Right at Chenies for Flaunden*

Dating back to 1722, this award-winning pub and restaurant was once an ordinary pair of cottages, one belonging to a butcher, the other to a blacksmith. Tucked away in deepest Hertfordshire, it has featured in many films and TV shows, and is a favourite with locals, walkers, and horse-riders. The ivy-covered façade gives way to an immaculate interior, with low beams, exposed brickwork, candlelight and open fires. Another is a happy marriage between traditional English and French fusion cooking. The Gallic influence comes from Michelin-trained head chef, Claude Paillet, and his team who use fresh organic produce from local suppliers to create seasonal lunch and dinner menus, plus daily specials. Main courses might include fillet of Scotch beef with a choice of freshly prepared sauces; or pan-fried sea bass with smoked paprika and scallop cream sauce. Don't stop there, as the Bricklayers has an

excellent pudding menu, on which you're likely to find crêpe filled with Cointreau-flavoured mascarpone and citrus fruits; and lemon tart with pannacotta and raspberry ice cream.

**Open** all wk 12-11.30 (25 Dec 12-3) **Bar Meals** L served Mon-Sat 12-2.30, Sun 12-3.30 booking required D served Mon-Sat 6.30-9.30, Sun 6.30-8.30 Av main course £13 **Restaurant** L served Mon-Sat 12-2.30, Sun 12-3.30 booking required D served Mon-Sat 6.30-9.30, Sun 6.30-8.30 Av 3 course à la carte fr £28 ⊕ FREE HOUSE ◀ Old Speckled Hen, Greene King IPA, London Pride, Jack O'Legs (Tring Brewery), Rebellion. ▼ 12 **Facilities** Children's menu Dogs allowed Garden Parking

## HEMEL HEMPSTEAD

### Alford Arms ▼

**Frithsden HP1 3DD ☎ 01442 864480   ▤ 01422 876893**
e-mail: info@alfordarmsfrithsden.co.uk
web: www.alfordarmsfrithsden.co.uk
dir: *From Hemel Hempstead on A4146 take 2nd left at Water End. In 1m left at T-junct, right after 0.75m. Pub 100yds on right*

An attractive Victorian pub, the Alford Arms is set in the hamlet of Frithsden surrounded by National Trust woodland. The garden overlooks the village green, and Ashridge Forest is close by. You'll immediately pick up on the warm and lively atmosphere, derived in part from the buzz of conversation and the background jazz music, and partly from the rich colours and eclectic mixture of furniture and pictures. The staff are renowned for their good humour and they do their utmost to ensure an enjoyable experience for customers. The seasonal menu balances innovative dishes with more traditional fare, and everything is prepared from fresh local produce when possible. There's a great choice of light dishes or 'small plates', from rustic breads with roast garlic, balsamic and olive oil, to roast local wood pigeon breast on baked apple tarte Tatin; or potted organic Scottish salmon with sour dough toast. Main meals include baked Chiltern lamb and rabbit shepherd's pie; Ashridge Estate venison steak and kidney pudding; and beer battered haddock with hand-cut chips. Puddings include warm fig chocolate brownie with crème fraîche ice cream; or vanilla and ginger cheesecake. The British cheese plate is a tempting finish, with Alford oatcakes, sticky malt loaf and fig jam.

**Open** all day all wk 11-11 (Sun 12-10.30) Closed: 26 Dec **Bar Meals** L served Mon-Fri 12-2.30, Sat 12-3, Sun 12-4 D served Mon-Thu 6.30-9.30, Fri-Sat 6.30-10, Sun 7-9.30 **Restaurant** L served Mon-Fri 12-2.30, Sat 12-3, Sun 12-4 booking required D served Mon-Thu 6.30-9.30, Fri-Sat 6.30-10, Sun 7-9.30

booking required ⊕ SALISBURY PUBS LTD ◖ Marstons Pedigree, Brakspear, Flowers Original, Marlow Rebellion IPA. ♇ 19
**Facilities** Children's menu Dogs allowed Garden Parking

## HEXTON

### The Raven ♇

**SG5 3JB ☎ 01582 881209** 📄 **01582 881610**
e-mail: jack@ravenathexton.f9.co.uk
dir: *5m W of Hitchin. 5m N of Luton, just outside Barton-le-Clay*

This neat 1920s pub is named after Ravensburgh Castle in the neighbouring hills. It has comfortable bars and a large garden with a terrace and play area. Snacks include ploughman's and salad platters, plus tortilla wraps, filled baguettes and jacket potatoes. The main menu offers lots of steak options, and dishes like smoky American chicken, whole rack of barbecue ribs, Thai red vegetable curry and an all-day breakfast.

**Open** all wk **Bar Meals** L served 12-2.15 (Fri-Sun all day) D served 6-9 (Fri-Sun all day) Av main course £9 **Restaurant** L served 12-2.15 (Fri-Sun all day) D served 6-9 (Fri-Sun all day) Av 3 course à la carte fr £15 ⊕ ENTERPRISE INNS ◖ Greene King, Old Speckled Hen, Fuller's London Pride, Greene King IPA. ♇ 24
**Facilities** Children's menu Play area Garden Parking

## HITCHIN

### The Greyhound ★★★ INN ♇

**London Rd, St Ippolyts SG4 7NL ☎ 01462 440989**
e-mail: greyhound@freenet.co.uk
web: www.thegreyhoundpubhotel.co.uk
dir: *1.5m S of Hitchin on B656*

There has been a pub on the site for 300 years although the current building dates from 1900. The Greyhound was rescued from dereliction by the present owner who used to work for the London Fire Brigade. It is now a popular, family-run hostelry surrounded by pleasant countryside and open farmland. The shotguns over the bars are said to have been owned by notorious poacher twins who used each other as an alibi. The food is unpretentious, generous and competitively priced.

**Open** all wk 7am-2.30 5-11 (Sun 7am-8pm) **Bar Meals** L served Mon-Sat 7-2, Sun 7am-8pm D served Mon-Sat 5-9, Sun 7am-8pm Av main course £9 **Restaurant** L served Mon-Sat 7-2, Sun 7am-8pm D served Mon-Sat 5-9, Sun 7am-8pm Av 3 course à la carte fr £18.75 ⊕ FREE HOUSE ◖ Adnams, guest. ♇ 8
**Facilities** Children's menu Dogs allowed Parking **Rooms** 5

## HUNSDON

### The Fox and Hounds ♇

**2 High St SG12 8NH ☎ 01279 843999** 📄 **01279 841092**
e-mail: info@foxandhounds-hunsdon.co.uk
web: www.foxandhounds-hunsdon.co.uk
dir: *From A414 between Ware & Harlow take B180 in Stanstead Abbotts N to Hunsdon*

Nestled in a sleepy village in the heart of the Hertfordshire countryside, this pub has a warm, welcoming atmosphere and a large pretty garden, with a heated covered terrace. Meals can be taken in the bar and the lounge, or in the more formal dining room with its chandelier and period furniture on Friday evenings and weekends. Expect serious, inspired cooking that combines classics with modern touches. Lunch could begin with mussels, cider, leeks and cream; or sautéed squid, chorizo and butter beans, followed by roast skate wing, lentils and salsa verde; or perhaps calves' liver persillade and duck fat potato cake. For dinner, perhaps try smoked eel, crispy Parma ham and potato pancake; or rabbit rillettes, pickles and toast, followed by Black Angus côte de boeuf, fat chips and sauce bearnaise; or fillet of wild line caught sea bass with purple sprouting broccoli and anchovy and chilli dressing. Roast black figs, honey and mascarpone is an elegant way to round matters off.

**Open** noon-4 6-11 Closed: Sun, Mon eve **Bar Meals** L served Tue-Sun 12-3 D served Tue-Sat 6.30-9.30 Av main course £15 **Restaurant** L served Sun 12-3 booking required D served Fri-Sat 7-9.30 booking required Fixed menu price fr £12.50 Av 3 course à la carte fr £26 ⊕ FREE HOUSE ◖ Adnams Bitter, Adnams Broadside, Guinness ♥ Aspall. ♇ 10 **Facilities** Children's menu Play area Dogs allowed Garden Parking

## LITTLE HADHAM

### The Nags Head ♇

**The Ford SG11 2AX ☎ 01279 771555** 📄 **01279 771555**
e-mail: paul.arkell@virgin.net
dir: *M11 junct 8 take A120 towards Puckeridge & A10. Left at lights in Little Hadham. Pub 1m on right*

Formerly a coaching inn, this 16th-century pub has also been a brewery, a bakery and Home Guard arsenal in its time. Open brickwork and an old bakery oven are among the features at this village inn. An extensive menu offers everything from braised lamb joint and roast spiced duck breast to pasta

continued

**England**

carbonara and mixed grill. Plenty of starters available and more than 20 fish choices.

**Open** all wk **Bar Meals** L served Mon-Sat 12-2, Sun 12-3 D served Mon-Sat 6-9, Sun 7-9 Av main course £10 **Restaurant** L served Mon-Sat 12-2, Sun 12-3 booking required D served Mon-Sat 6-9, Sun 7-9 booking required ⊕ GREENE KING ◀ Greene King Abbot Ale, IPA, Old Speckled Hen & Ruddles County Ale, Marstons Pedigree. ♀ 6 **Facilities** Children's menu Garden

## ROYSTON

## The Cabinet Free House and Restaurant ♀

**High St, Reed SG8 8AH ☎ 01763 848366**
**e-mail:** thecabinet@btconnect.com
**dir:** *2m S of Royston, just off A10*

The Cabinet is a 16th-century country inn and restaurant located in the little village of Reed just off the A10. Now in the capable hands of Tracey Hale and Angus Martin, the refurbished inn has a cosy and comfortable interior with low beamed ceilings and an open fire. The surroundings lend themselves to special occasions, particularly weddings, and the premises are licensed for civil ceremonies. As well as a great selection of real ales, the menu is an eclectic mix, based on personal taste and sound cooking techniques rather than a particular type of cuisine. Food is prepared from the best local produce, but draws inspiration from around the world. The restaurant and snug lunchtime offerings range from soup of the day or macaroni cheese, to toad-in-the-hole with scallion mash, or pea and gorgonzola risotto. Comfort desserts include rice pudding with home-made jam, and Eton mess. Evening suppers are equally appealing while moving up a gear or two in complexity: a typical choice could start with "Crayfish Bloody Mary" or bouillabaisse of red mullet; continue with daube of venison with dumplings, roasted beetroot and mustard mash or lobster and chicken casserole; and round off with chocolate torte with walnut meringue. Mind the resident ghost - an old gentleman in a dark coat.

**Open** 12-3 6-11 (Sat-Sun 12-11) Closed: 1 Jan, Mon L **Bar Meals** L served Tue-Sun 12-3 D served Tue-Sat 6-9 Av main course £10 **Restaurant** L served Tue-Sun 12-3 booking required D served Tue-Sat 6-9 booking required Fixed menu price fr £10-25 Av 3 course à la carte fr £25 ⊕ FREE HOUSE ◀ Woodforde's Wherry, Adnams, Old Speckled Hen, Nelson's Revenge, Timothy Taylor, Augustinian Ö Aspall. ♀ 12 **Facilities** Children's menu Family room Dogs allowed Garden Parking

## ST ALBANS

## Rose & Crown ♀

**10 Saint Michael St AL3 4SG**
**☎ 01727 851903 ▤ 01727 761775**
**e-mail:** ruth.courtney@ntlworld.com
**dir:** *Telephone for details*

Traditional 16th-century pub situated in a beautiful part of Saint Michael's 'village', opposite the entrance to Verulanium Park and the Roman Museum. It has a classic beamed bar with a huge inglenook, open fire in winter and a lovely walled garden. The pub offers a distinctive range of American deli-style sandwiches, which are served with potato salad, kettle crisps and pickled cucumber. There is traditional folk music on Thursday nights, live music on Monday nights.

**Open** all day all wk 11.30-3 5.30-11 (Sat 11.30-11.30) **Bar Meals** L served Mon-Sat 12-2.30, Sun 12-5 D served Mon-Sat 6-9 ⊕ PUNCH TAVERNS ◀ Adnams Bitter, Tetley Bitter, Fuller's London Pride, Courage Directors, guest ales. ♀ 20 **Facilities** Children's menu Dogs allowed Garden Parking

## KENT

## BIDDENDEN

## The Three Chimneys ♀

**Biddenden Rd TN27 8LW ☎ 01580 291472**
**dir:** *From A262 midway between Biddenden & Sissinghurst, follow Frittenden signs. (Pub seen from main road). Pub immediately on left in hamlet of Three Chimneys*

A 15th-century Wealden treasure of a classic country pub, the original, small-roomed layout and old-fashioned furnishings remain delightfully intact. There are old settles, low beams, wood-panelled walls, worn brick floors, crackling log fires, soft evening candlelight, and no music or electronic games. Modern-day demand for dining space has seen the addition of the rear Garden Room and a tasteful new conservatory, and drinkers and diners spill out onto the secluded heated side patio and vast shrub-filled garden, perfect for summer eating. Food is bang up-to-date and listed on daily-changing chalkboards. Tuck into a hearty ploughman's lunch, red lentil and tomato soup or potted shrimps, or something more substantial, perhaps roast cod on wilted spinach with chive velouté or local pork sausages with mash and port and red wine gravy. If you have room for a pudding, try the rhubarb and apple crumble. Adnams and Shepherd Neame ales and the heady Biddenden cider are tapped direct from cask.

**Open** all wk 11.30-3 5.30-11 (Sat-Sun 11.30-4, 5.30-11) Closed: 25 Dec **Bar Meals** L served all wk 12-2.30 booking required D served all wk 6.30-9.30 booking required **Restaurant** L served all wk 12-2.30 booking required D served all wk 6.30-9.30 booking required ⊕ FREE HOUSE ◀ Adnams, Harveys Old, Special Ö Biddenden. ♀ 10 **Facilities** Children's menu Dogs allowed Garden Parking

England

## BOSSINGHAM

## The Hop Pocket

**The Street CT4 6DY** ☎ 01227 709866 📠 01227 709866
dir: *Telephone for directions*

Birds of prey and an animal corner for children are among the more unusual attractions at this family pub in the heart of Kent. Canterbury is five miles away and the county's delightfully scenic coast and countryside are in easy reach. Menu may include fish pie, supreme of chicken, spicy salmon, Cajun beef, chilli nachos and fish platter. There's also an extensive range of sandwiches and omelettes.

**Open** all wk 11-3 6-mdnt (Sun noon-3 7-11) **Bar Meals** L served all wk 12-2.30 D served Mon-Sat 7-9.30 **Restaurant** L served all wk 12-2.30 D served Mon-Sat 7-9.30 ⊞ FREE HOUSE ◀ London Pride, Master Brew, Wadworth 6X, Spitfire. **Facilities** Children's menu Dogs allowed Garden Parking

## BOUGHTON MONCHELSEA

## The Mulberry Tree ◉◉

**Hermitage Ln ME17 4DA** ☎ 01622 749082 & 714058
e-mail: info@themulberrytreekent.co.uk
dir: *M20 to junct 8. B2163 towards Coxheath, left after Ralphs Garden Centre into Wierton Rd, over x-rds, 1st left down East Hall Hill.*

In beautiful Kent countryside, this contemporary country bar and restaurant attracts people from a wide area, simply because it is eminently capable of providing very good food. Seasonal, free-range and organic produce is used in modern British and European cuisine. From the skilled hands of head chef Alan Irwin and his team come dishes such as raviolo of scallop with roasted native lobster; slow-roast belly of Kentish pork, boulangère potato and hispi cabbage; and gratin of spiced tangerines and Cox's apples with white chocolate cheesecake.

**Open** noon-3 6.30-11 (Sun noon-4) Closed: Sun eve, Mon **Bar Meals** L served Tue-Sat 12-2 (Sun 12-2.30) booking required D served Tue-Thu 6.30-9, Fri-Sat 6.30-9.30 booking required Av main course £12.95 **Restaurant** L served Tue-Sat 12-2 (Sun 12-2.30) booking required D served Tue- Thu 6.30-9, Fri-Sat 6.30-9.30 Fixed menu price fr £12.95 Av 3 course à la carte fr £25 ⊞ FREE HOUSE ◀ Harveys, Goacher's. **Facilities** Children's menu Garden Parking

## CANTERBURY

## The Chapter Arms ☿

**New Town St, Chartham Hatch CT4 7LT** ☎ 01227 738340
e-mail: david.durell@vmicombox.co.uk
dir: *3m from Canterbury. Off A28 in Chartham Hatch or A2 at Upper Harbledown*

Situated on the North Downs Way, this charming free house is set in over an acre of gardens overlooking apple orchards and oast houses. It was once three cottages owned by Canterbury Cathedral's Dean and Chapter - hence the name. Any day's menu might offer Kentish lamb crusted with garlic and thyme, Thai salmon fishcakes, or steak and kidney pie. Live Sixties music and jazz evenings are popular.

**Open** all wk Closed: 25 Dec eve **Bar Meals** L served all wk 12-2.30 D served Mon-Sat 6.30-9 booking required Av main course £8.95 **Restaurant** L served all wk 12-2.30 D served Mon-Sat 6.30-9 booking required Av 3 course à la carte fr £25 ⊞ FREE HOUSE ◀ Shepherd Neame Master Brew, Adnams, Harveys, Youngs, Wells Bombardier, guest ales. ☿ 10 **Facilities** Children's menu Play area Dogs allowed Garden Parking

## The Dove Inn ◉ ☿

**Plum Pudding Ln, Dargate ME13 9HB**
☎ 01227 751360 📠 01227 751360
e-mail: pipmacgrew@hotmail.com
dir: *5m NW of Canterbury, A299 Thanet Way, turn off at Lychgate service station*

The Dove is a splendid vine-covered Victorian country pub, tucked away in a sleepy hamlet, surrounded by orchards and farmland. It has established a reputation for good food based on locally sourced ingredients. The interior is simple and relaxed with stripped wooden floors and scrubbed tables. Outside is a large formal garden where a dovecote and doves present a scenic backdrop for a meal or quiet pint. The menu offers something for everyone, including light lunches, snacks and restaurant quality food. The chef has a talent for producing country cooking with a strong French influence. Local gamekeepers provide much of the meat and game, and fresh fish features. Both children and dogs are made welcome.

**Open** noon-3 6-mdnt (Fri noon-mdnt Sun noon-9 (Apr-Oct) noon-4 (Nov-Mar)) Closed: Mon **Bar Meals** L served Tue-Sat 12-2.30 D served Tue-Thu 6.30-9 Av main course £10 **Restaurant** L served Tue-Sun 12-2.30 booking required D served Tue-Sat 7-9 booking required Av 3 course à la carte fr £25 ⊞ SHEPHERD NEAME ◀ Shepherd Neame Master Brew, Spitfire, seasonal ale. ☿ 8 **Facilities** Children's menu Dogs allowed Garden Parking

## FAVERSHAM

## Shipwright's Arms ☿

**Hollowshore ME13 7TU** ☎ 01795 590088
dir: *A2 through Ospringe then right at rdbt. Right at T-junct then left opposite Davington School, follow signs*

Step back in time to this remote pub on the Swale marshes which is well over 300 years old, and once a favourite with sailors and fishermen waiting to dock in Faversham. The pub still draws its water from a well. Examine the maritime artefacts in the many nooks and crannies, while downing a Kent-brewed cask ale. Home cooked food includes locally caught fish in season, and English pies and puddings during the winter, where four open fires keep things cosy.

**Open** Closed: Mon (Oct-Mar) **Bar Meals** L served Tue-Sat 11-2.30, Sun 12-2.30 D served Tue-Sat 7-9 **Restaurant** L served Tue-Sat 11-2.30, Sun 12-2.30 D served Tue-Sat 7-9 ⊞ FREE HOUSE ◀ Local ales. ☿ 6 **Facilities** Children's menu Family room Dogs allowed Garden Parking

## FOLKESTONE

### The Lighthouse Inn ♀

**Old Dover Rd, Capel le Ferne CT18 7HT ☎ 01303 223300**
🖹 01303 842270
e-mail: james@thelighthouseinn.net
dir: *M20 junct 13 follow signs for Capel le Ferne*

There are sweeping Channel views from this pub on the edge of Dover's famous White Cliffs. The Lighthouse began as an ale house in 1840, later becoming, successively, a billiard hall, convalescent home, psychiatric hospital and country club while, more recently still, Channel Tunnel builders headquartered here. Expect decent home-made food along the lines of traditional prawn cocktail followed by local sausages with mash and onion jus, Channel fisherman's pie or classic ham, egg and chips.

**Open** all day all wk 11-11 **Bar Meals** Av main course £12.50 food served all day **Restaurant** Fixed menu price fr £14 Av 3 course à la carte fr £25 food served all day ⊕ FREE HOUSE ◀ IPA, 6X, Adnams. ♀ 14 **Facilities** Children's menu Play area Family room Dogs allowed Garden Parking

## FORDCOMBE

### Chafford Arms ♀

**TN3 0SA ☎ 01892 740267 🖹 01892 740703**
e-mail: chaffordarms@btconnect.com
dir: *On B2188 (off A264) between Tunbridge Wells, East Grinstead & Penshurst*

A lovely mid-19th-century tile-hung village pub, with a working red telephone kiosk in the car park and a large garden with great views across the weald. The menu offers a great range of traditional pub food. While mum and dad choose between chicken, ham and leek pie or a crock of chilli con carne, the children can pick their favourites from the likes of golden whale with chips, or crispy chicken teddies and salad.

**Open** all day all wk 11am-mdnt **Bar Meals** L served 12-9 (Sun 12-4) D served 12-9 (Sun 12-4) Av main course £9 food served all day **Restaurant** L served 12-9 (Sun 12-4) D served 12-9 (Sun 12-4) food served all day ⊕ ENTERPRISE INNS ◀ Larkins Bitter, Harvey's Best. ♀ 9 **Facilities** Children's menu Dogs allowed Garden Parking

## GOODNESTONE

### The Fitzwalter Arms ♀

**The Street CT3 1PJ ☎ 01304 840303**
e-mail: thefitzwalter arms@gmail.com
dir: *Signed from B2046 & A2*

The 'Fitz', hostelry to the Fitzwalter Estate, has been a pub since 1702. Quintessentially English, it is a place of conviviality and conversation. Jane Austen was a frequent visitor to nearby Goodnestone Park after her brother, Edward, married into the family. On the menu, home cured ham with figs and parmesan; roast partridge with bread sauce and bacon; baked line-caught cod fillet, fishcake and old-fashioned egg sauce; treacle tart and custard.

**Open** all wk noon-3 6-11 (Fri-Sun noon-11) Closed: 25 Dec, 1 Jan **Restaurant** L served Mon & Wed-Sun 12-2 booking required D served Mon & Wed-Sat 7-9 booking required Fixed menu price fr £12.50 Av 3 course à la carte fr £20 ⊕ SHEPHERD NEAME ◀ Master Brew, Spitfire. ♀ 12 **Facilities** Children's menu Dogs allowed Garden

## GOUDHURST

### Green Cross Inn

**TN17 1HA ☎ 01580 211200 🖹 01580 212905**
dir: *A21 from Tonbridge towards Hastings turn left onto A262 towards Ashford. 2m, Goudhurst on right*

A food orientated pub in an unspoiled corner of Kent, originally built to serve the Paddock Wood-Goudhurst railway line, which closed in 1968. The dining room is prettily decorated with fresh flowers. The pub specialises in fresh seafood including oysters, crab, mussels, smoked eel – the list goes on. Main courses in the bar range from home-made steak, kidney and mushroom pie with shortcrust pastry, to calves' liver and bacon Lyonnaise.

**Open** all wk noon-3 6-11 Closed: Sun eve **Bar Meals** L served all wk 12-2.30 booking required D served Mon-Sat 7-9.45 booking required Av main course £13.50 **Restaurant** L served all wk 12-2.30 booking required D served Mon-Sat 7-9.45 booking required Av 3 course à la carte fr £30 ⊕ FREE HOUSE ◀ Harvey's Sussex Best Bitter, Guinness ◔ Biddenden. **Facilities** Children's menu Garden Parking

### The Star & Eagle ★★★★ INN ♀

**High St TN17 1AL ☎ 01580 211512 🖹 01580 212444**
e-mail: starandeagle@btconnect.com
dir: *Just off A21 towards Hastings. Take A262 into Goudhurst. Pub at top of hill next to church*

A commanding position at 400 feet above sea level gives the 14th-century Star & Eagle outstanding views of the orchards and hop fields of Kent. The vaulted stonework suggests that this rambling, big-beamed building may once have been a monastery, and the tunnel from the cellars probably surfaces underneath the neighbouring parish church. These days, it's a place to unwind and enjoy fine food, prepared under the guidance of Spanish chef/proprietor Enrique Martinez. A typical bar meal might be field mushrooms stuffed with bacon and stilton; and cod, salmon and smoked haddock fish pie. From the restaurant menu might come soupe de poisson laced with brandy and cream; and Scottish rope mussels with chilli. Follow with pot-roast shoulder of lamb baked Spanish style; or sautéed calves' livers.

**Open** all wk 11-11 (Sun 12-3 6.30-10.30) **Bar Meals** L served all wk 12-2.30 D served all wk 7-9.30 Av main course £15 **Restaurant** L served all wk 12-2.30 D served all wk 7-9.30 Fixed menu price fr £24 Av 3 course à la carte fr £30 ⊕ FREE HOUSE ◀ Adnams Bitter, Harvey's, Grasshopper. ♀ 24 **Facilities** Children's menu Family room Garden Parking **Rooms** 10

## HAWKHURST

# The Great House ♟

**Gills Green TN18 5EJ ☎ 01580 753119** 🖹 **01622 851881**
e-mail: enquiries@thegreathouse.net
dir: *Just off A229 between Cranbrook & Hawkhurst*

The Great House is a wonderfully atmospheric 16th-century free house with a warm and comfortable ambience. There are three dining areas to choose from, and the Orangery which opens onto a Mediterranean-style terrace overlooking a pretty garden. The food is fresh and seasonal, and all meat comes from a local organic farm. Favourites from the bar menu might include Park Farm Cumberland sausages and mash, liver and bacon, or one of various ploughman's. Alongside the deli board selection (cheese, fish, antipasti, charcuterie), there are starters of grilled goats' cheese with sesame crust and sweet chilli dressing, or Nicoise-style fish soup with potato aioli, which may be followed by slow-cooked lamb shank with olive mash; sweet and sour pumpkin risotto; or roast breast of Norfolk chicken with haricot beans and bacon ragout. Imaginative desserts might take in Bailey's chocolate parfait with cherry sauce, or Kentish apple and cinnamon crumble. Part of the pub has been transformed into a deli/farmers' market.

Open all wk noon-11 Bar Meals L served Mon-Fri 12-3, Sat 12-10, Sun 12-8 D served Mon-Fri 6.30-9.30, Sat 12-10, Sun 12-8 Av main course £11 Restaurant L served Mon-Fri 12-3, Sat 12-10, Sun 12-8 D served Mon-Fri 6.30-9.30, Sat 12-10, Sun 12-8 Fixed menu price fr £11 Av 3 course à la carte fr £22 ⊕ FREE HOUSE ◀ Harvey's, Guinness, Youngs. ♟ 13 Facilities Children's menu Garden Parking

## HODSOLL STREET

# The Green Man

**TN15 7LE ☎ 01732 823575**
e-mail: the.greenman@btinternet.com
dir: *On North Downs between Brands Hatch & Gravesend on A227*

Set in the picturesque village of Hodsoll Street on the North Downs, this 300-year-old, family-run pub is loved for its decent food and real ales. Food is prepared to order using fresh local produce, and includes a wide variety of fish (especially on Wednesday, which is fish night). Curry takes centre stage on Thursday nights, while Tuesday night is steak and rib night. Live music features every second Thursday of each month.

Open all wk Bar Meals L served Mon-Fri 12-2, Sat-Sun 12-3 D served Mon-Sat 6.30-9.30, Sun 6.30-9 Restaurant L served Mon-Fri 12-2, Sat-Sun 12-3 D served Mon-Sat 6.30-9.30, Sun 6.30-9 ⊕ HAYWOOD PUB COMPANY LTD ◀ Timothy Taylor Landlord, Harvey's, Old Speckled Hen, guest ale. Facilities Children's menu Play area Dogs allowed Garden Parking

## IDEN GREEN

# The Peacock ♟

**Goudhurst Rd TN17 2PB ☎ 01580 211233**
dir: *A21 from Tunbridge Wells to Hastings, onto A262, pub 1.5m past Goudhurst*

A Grade II listed building dating from the 17th century with low beams, an inglenook fireplace, old oak doors, real ales on tap, and a wide range of traditional pub food. A large enclosed garden with fruit trees and picnic tables on one side of the building is popular in summer, and there's also a patio.

Open all wk 12-11 (Sun 12-6) Bar Meals L served Mon-Fri & Sun 12-2.30, Sat all day D served Mon-Fri 6-8.45, Sat all day Restaurant L served Mon-Fri & Sun 12-2.30, Sat all day D served Mon-Fri 6-8.45, Sat all day ⊕ SHEPHERD NEAME ◀ Shepherd Neame Master Brew, Spitfire, seasonal ales. ♟ 12 Facilities Children's menu Family room Dogs allowed Garden Parking

## IVY HATCH

# The Plough at Ivy Hatch ♟

**High Cross Rd TN15 0NL ☎ 01732 810100**
e-mail: theploughpubco@tiscali.co.uk
dir: *Off A25 between Borough Green & Sevenoaks, follow signs to Ightham Mote*

Set deep in Kent countryside, and just a quarter of a mile from the National Trust's Ightham Mote, the 17th-century Plough is the perfect spot for a lingering lunch or supper. Now the last bastion of a once-thriving community, it is an integral part of village life, even more so since a refurbishment provided smart oak flooring and a new seating area around the fireplace. Plans to establish a kitchen garden within the grounds will complement the locally sourced produce that's already used, including a wide selection of seafood from the south coast and seasonal game from local shoots. Starters might include lentil and lovage soup; and fruits de mer, consisting of langoustines, crevettes, North Atlantic prawns and Colchester rock oysters. To follow, stay with the fish, perhaps, with Isle of Shuna mussels in white wine and cream sauce with hand-cut chips; or tackle a Sussex rib-eye steak with caramelised banana shallots and peppercorn sauce; or, for vegetarians, wild mushroom pie with new potatoes, green beans and cep sauce. Desserts include a range of ice creams; lemon tart with mascarpone; and crème brûlée. Lunch on Sunday need not be limited to

continued

roasts, but roasts there are, namely rump of beef, leg of lamb, loin of pork and haunch of venison. There's a terrace and garden ideal for alfresco dining. If you go on one of the many good walks in the area, don't worry about how muddy your boots are when you squelch to the pub.

**Open** all wk noon-3 6-11 (Sat noon-11 Sun 10-6) **Bar Meals** L served Mon-Sat 12-2.45, Sun 12-6 D served Mon-Sat 6-9.30 Av main course £10 **Restaurant** L served Mon-Sat 12-2.45, Sun 12-6 D served Mon-Sat 6-9.30 Fixed menu price fr £15 Av 3 course à la carte fr £19.50 ⊕ FREE HOUSE ◀ Harveys Best, Seasonal ales, Westerham Finchcocks ♻ Stowford Press. ♈ 8 **Facilities** Children's menu Garden Parking

## MAIDSTONE

### The Black Horse Inn ★★★★ INN ♈

**Pilgrims Way, Thurnham ME14 3LD**
☎ **01622 737185** 🖷 **01622 739170**
e-mail: info@wellieboot.net
dir: *M20 junct 7, A249, right into Detling. Opposite Cock Horse Pub turn onto Pilgrims Way*

Tucked beneath the steep face of the North Downs on the Pilgrims Way, this welcoming free house has oak beams, exposed brickwork and an open log fire in winter. The building is thought to have been a forge before its conversion to an inn during the middle of the 18th century. The bar and restaurant menus range from traditional favourites like honey and mustard roasted ham on bubble and squeak to grilled fillet of sea bass with Mediterranean vegetables.

**Open** all day all wk 11-11 **Bar Meals** Av main course £8.95 food served all day **Restaurant** Fixed menu price fr £8.95 Av 3 course à la carte fr £11.95 food served all day ⊕ FREE HOUSE ◀ Kents Best, London Pride, Greene King IPA, Black Sheep, Late Red ♻ Biddendens. ♈ 30 **Facilities** Children's menu Dogs allowed Garden Parking **Rooms** 30

## NEWNHAM

### The George Inn ♈

**44 The Street ME9 0LL** ☎ **01795 890237**
🖷 **01795 890726**
dir: *4m from Faversham*

The George is an attractive country inn with a large beer garden. Despite the passing of the centuries, the inn retains much of its historic character with beams, polished wooden

floors, inglenook fireplaces and candlelit tables. Food is served in the bar and 50-seater restaurant. Bar snacks range from sandwiches to sausage and mash, while main meals could include pan-fried fillet of red snapper with crushed potatoes, baby fennel, fresh scampi and rosemary butter; or peppered duck breast with celeriac mash and cherry and port sauce. Regular events include live jazz, quizzes and murder mystery evenings.

**Open** all wk 11-3 6.30-11 (Sun noon-4 7-10.30) **Bar Meals** L served all wk 12-2.30 booking required D served all wk 7-9.30 booking required Av main course £10 **Restaurant** L served all wk 12-2.30 booking required D served all wk 7-9.30 booking required Av 3 course à la carte fr £20 ⊕ SHEPHERD NEAME ◀ Shepherd Neame Master Brew, Spitfire, Bishops Finger, Kent Best, seasonal ale. ♈ 8 **Facilities** Children's menu Garden Parking

## PENSHURST

### The Bottle House Inn ♈

**Coldharbour Rd TN11 8ET** ☎ **01892 870306**
🖷 **01892 871094**
e-mail: info@thebottlehouseinnpenshurst.co.uk
web: www.thebottlehouseinnpenshurst.co.uk
dir: *From Tunbridge Wells take A264 W, then B2188 N. After Fordcombe left towards Edenbridge & Hever. Pub 500yds after staggered x-rds*

A well-regarded dining pub, The Bottle House was built as a farmhouse in 1492. The pub was said to be the originator of the ploughman's lunch, made with bread from the old bakery next door and cheese donated by Canadian soldiers billeted nearby. Today, low beams and a copper-topped counter give the bar a warm, welcoming atmosphere. The menu has something for everyone, starting with grilled green lip mussels stuffed with Welsh rarebit, duck liver and orange parfait with toasted brioche, or deep-fried sesame-coated brie and breaded mozzarella with plum and apple chutney. Lighter meals are also available and may include smoked fish platter or linguini in creamy basil pesto sauce. Moving on to main courses, diners may enjoy trio of Kentish sausages with mustard mash; oven-roasted skate wing with cracked black pepper crust; braised lamb shank with mint and rosemary gravy; or red snapper fillet with soy, ginger, chilli and spring onion dressing.

**Open** all day all wk 11-11 (Sun 11-10.30) Closed: 25 Dec **Bar Meals** food served all day **Restaurant** food served all day ⊕ FREE HOUSE ◀ Larkins Ale, Harveys Sussex Best Bitter. ♈ 8 **Facilities** Children's menu Dogs allowed Garden Parking

## The Leicester Arms

**High St TN11 8BT ☎ 01892 870551**
dir: *From Tunbridge Wells take A26 towards Tonbridge. Left onto B21765 towards Penshurst*

A large and picturesque country inn at the centre of a picturesque village, the Leicester Arms stands in its own pretty gardens looking out over the River Medway. It was once part of the Penshurst Place estate. The wood-panelled dining room is worth a visit for the views over the weald and river alone. Dishes range from traditional pub food in the bar to the likes of pressed pork belly with crackling, chicken curry, or Moroccan vegetable tagine from the carte menu.

Open all wk 11am-mdnt **Bar Meals** Av main course £10 food served all day **Restaurant** Av 3 course à la carte fr £19 ⊕ ENTERPRISE INNS ◀ Harvey's Sussex Bitter, Shepherd Neame Master Brew, Sharp's Doom Bar. **Facilities** Children's menu Dogs allowed Garden Parking

## The Spotted Dog ♥

**Smarts Hill TN11 8EE ☎ 01892 870253  📄 01892 870107**
e-mail: info@spotteddogpub.co.uk
dir: *Off B2188 between Penshurst & Fordcombe*

Deep in the Kent countryside, this 16th-century white weather-boarded free house enjoys fine views over the Weald from the rear terrace. The rambling interior with its tiled and oak floors, low beams and three open fireplaces creates a welcoming atmosphere for both locals and visitors alike. But don't expect fast food or a huge menu, because everything here is freshly prepared to order, using traceable local produce wherever possible. Starters like rare roasted venison salad with red wine vinaigrette set the stage for main course choices that might include mushroom stroganoff with rice; calves' liver and bacon with creamy mash, vegetables and rich gravy; or grilled whole sea bass, lemon hollandaise sauce, new potatoes and vegetables. If you fancy re-creating some of those dishes at home, then help is at hand; just pop into the adjacent Spotted Dog Farm Shop for a comprehensive range of produce from local suppliers.

Open all wk noon-3 6-11 (Sun noon-10.30) **Bar Meals** L served Mon-Sat 12-2.30 D served Mon-Sat 6-9 **Restaurant** L served Mon-Sat 12-2.30, Sun 12-5 D served Mon-Fri 6-9, Sat 6-9.30 ⊕ FREE HOUSE ◀ Sharp's Doom Bar, Larkins Traditional, guest ale Ŏ Chiddingstone. ♥ 20 **Facilities** Children's menu Dogs allowed Garden Parking

**PLUCKLEY**

## The Dering Arms ♥

**Station Rd TN27 0RR ☎ 01233 840371  📄 01233 840498**
e-mail: jim@deringarms.com
web: www.deringarms.com
dir: *M20 junct 8, A20 to Ashford. Right onto B2077 at Charing to Pluckley*

Pluckley's residents cherish its claim to fame as the most haunted village in England; they're also proud of its starring role in the 1990s TV series, The Darling Buds of May. It has two simply furnished traditional bars with mounted stags' heads and fishing rods, roaring fires in winter, an intimate restaurant, and a family room with a baby grand piano (there to be played). Chef/patron James Buss has managed this distinctive inn with passion and flair since 1984. He does the main cooking himself, preparing every meal to order using only the finest, freshest produce. The extensive daily menus reflect his love of fresh fish and seafood, such as starters of Sussex mackerel smokies and grilled Irish oysters with chorizo. Appearing as main course options might be confit of duck with bubble and squeak potato cake and wild mushroom sauce; pan-fried tuna steak with garlic and lemon butter; and grilled skate wing with capers and beurre noisettes. Do check the blackboards for specials, as well. Jim's Seafood Special, a traditional fruits de mer for a minimum of two people, requires 24 hours' notice. Desserts range from oranges in caramel with Grand Marnier, to prunes marinated in Cointreau. Black tie gourmet evenings, featuring seven courses of unusual and intriguing dishes, are held throughout the winter, and classic car meetings are held every second Sunday of the month.

Open 11.30-3.30 6-11 Closed: 26-29 Dec, Sun eve & Mon **Bar Meals** L served Tue-Sun 12-2 booking required D served Tue-Sat 7-9.30 booking required Av main course £17 **Restaurant** L served Tue-Sun 12-2 booking required D served Tue-Sat 7-9.30 booking required Av 3 course à la carte fr £32 ⊕ FREE HOUSE ◀ Goacher's Dering Ale, Maidstone Dark, Gold Star, Old Ale. ♥ 7 **Facilities** Children's menu Family room Dogs allowed Garden Parking

England

**Pluckley continued**

## The Mundy Bois ♟

**Mundy Bois TN27 0ST ☎ 01233 840048**
📠 01233 840193
e-mail: helen@mundybois.com
dir: *From A20 at Charing exit towards Pluckley. Right into Pinnock at bottom of Pluckley Hill. Next right into Mundy Bois Rd. 1m left*

An ale house since 1780 and formerly named the Rose and Crown, this creeper-clad pub is on the outskirts of Pluckley. A blackboard menu features frequently changing dishes created from local produce where possible, and a nearby farm specializing in rare breeds — rare breed Welsh pork chops on mustard mash with caramelised apples and cider sauce. A patio dining area allows alfresco eating, and the garden has an adventure playground.

Open all wk **Bar Meals** L served all wk 12-2 D served all wk 6.30-9 **Restaurant** L served all wk 12-2 D served all wk 6.30-9 ⊕ FREE HOUSE ◀ Master Brew, Youngs. ♟ 8 **Facilities** Children's menu Play area Dogs allowed Garden Parking

## ST MARGARET'S AT CLIFFE

## The Coastguard

**St Margaret's Bay CT15 6DY ☎ 01304 853176**
e-mail: thecoastguard@talk21.com
dir: *2m off A258 between Dover & Deal, follow St Margaret's at Cliffe signs. Through village towards sea*

The Coastguard is set in one of the most delightful spots on the Kentish coast, St Margaret's Bay, with its breathtaking white cliffs and beach walks. The pub stands only a stone's throw from the water's edge and has spectacular views out to sea. It is renowned for its food and hospitality, and everything is freshly made on the premises, including the breads and sauces, using local produce whenever possible. The menu changes daily, even during service, depending on the weather and what is available, and features award-winning fish dishes, beef from a local farm and 'garden of Kent' fresh salad. The cheeseboard is highly regarded and has attracted many accolades. The regular selection of traditional British beers and cask ales is supplemented by guest ales, and there are some rare single malts including some from defunct distilleries.

Open all day all wk 11-11 (Sun 11-10.30) **Bar Meals** L served all wk 12.30-2.45 D served all wk 6.30-8.45 food served all day **Restaurant** L served all wk 12.30-2.45 D served all wk 6.30-8.45 ⊕ FREE HOUSE ◀ Gadds of Ramsgate, Hop Daemon, Adnams, Caledonian, Isle of Arran. **Facilities** Children's menu Play area Dogs allowed Garden Parking

## SELLING

## The Rose and Crown

**Perry Wood ME13 9RY ☎ 01227 752214**
e-mail: perrywoodrose@btinternet.co.uk
dir: *From A28 right at Badgers Hill, left at end. 1st left signed Perry Wood. Pub at top*

Set amidst 150 acres of woodland in the middle of an Area of Outstanding Natural Beauty, this 16th-century pub's beamed interior is decorated with hop garlands, corn dollies, horse brasses and brass cask taps. The perfumed summer garden includes a children's play area and bat and trap pitch. The ploughman's is served with huffkin, a bread made with eggs, milk and ground paragon wheat - a little like brioche but less sweet. A game menu is available in season.

Open all wk noon-3 6.30-11 Closed: 25-26 Dec eve, 1 Jan eve, Mon eve **Bar Meals** L served all wk 12-2 D served Tue-Sun 7-9 **Restaurant** L served all wk 12-2 D served Tue-Sun 7-9 ⊕ FREE HOUSE ◀ Adnams Southwold, Harvey's Sussex Best Bitter, guest ale. **Facilities** Children's menu Play area Dogs allowed Garden Parking

## SMARDEN

## The Chequers Inn

**The Street TN27 8QA ☎ 01233 770217   📠 01233 770623**
e-mail: spaldings@thechequerssmarden.com
dir: *Through Leeds village, left to Sutton Valence/Headcorn then left for Smarden. Pub in village centre*

A ghost is said to haunt the Chequers, an atmospheric 14th-century inn with clapboard façade in the centre of one of Kent's prettiest villages. The inn has its own beautiful landscaped garden with large duck pond and attractive south-facing courtyard. Real ales by Harveys and Adnams are served in the low beamed bars. Food ranges from traditional to modern, with something for every taste and appetite including further options on the specials board. The bar menu tempts with sausages and mash or home-made spaghetti bolognaise, while main courses may include steak and ale pie; chicken chasseur; or roasted cod rarebit. Fish specials change daily according to the season, and Sundays offer a popular choice of two roasts and a reduced à la carte menu. The pub host lots of community events throughout the year.

Open all wk **Bar Meals** L served all wk 12-3 D served all wk 6-9 **Restaurant** L served all wk 12-3 D served all wk 6-9 ⊕ FREE HOUSE ◀ Harvey's, IPA, Adnams. **Facilities** Children's menu Dogs allowed Garden Parking

## SPELDHURST

# George & Dragon ♈

**Speldhurst Hill TN3 0NN ☎ 01892 863125**
📠 01892 863216
e-mail: julian@speldhurst.com
dir: *Telephone for directions*

Built around 1500, the George and Dragon is a venerable timber-clad village hostelry. Some say its origins are earlier, when Speldhurst would have seen archers departing for the Battle of Agincourt. At the beginning of the 17th century the curative powers of the village's iron-rich waters were discovered, which put nearby Tunbridge Wells on the map. Today's customers enjoy a modern gastro-pub, where the menu offers half a dozen eclectic choices at each stage: you could start with parsnip and coriander soup with parsnip crisps and follow with Ashdown Forest venison stew, sautéed potatoes and wilted greens; roast guinea fowl with chilli and tarragon butter; or fillet of wild sea bass with brown shrimp and caper butter. Food can be served in the two gardens - one with a 200-year-old olive tree.

**Open** all wk **Bar Meals** L served all wk 12-2.45 D served Mon-Sat 7-9.45 Av main course £9 **Restaurant** L served Sat-Sun 12-3 booking required D served Fri-Sun 7-10 booking required Av 3 course à la carte fr £25 ⊕ FREE HOUSE ◀ Harvey's Best, Sussex Pale, Larkins, Porter. ♈ 10 **Facilities** Children's menu Family room Dogs allowed Garden Parking

## TENTERDEN

# White Lion Inn ♈

**57 High St TN30 6BD ☎ 01580 765077** 📠 01580 764157
e-mail: whitelion.tenterden@marstons.co.uk
dir: *On A28 (Ashford to Hastings road)*

A 16th-century coaching inn on a tree-lined street of this old Cinque Port, with many original features retained. The area is known for its cricket connections, and the first recorded county match between Kent and London was played here in 1719. The menu offers plenty of choice, from calves' liver and bacon, shoulder of lamb, and Cumberland cottage pie to tuna pasta bake and various ploughman's.

**Open** all wk 10am-11pm (wknds 10am-mdnt) **Bar Meals** food served all day **Restaurant** food served all day ⊕ MARSTONS ◀ Marstons Pedigree, Cumberland. ♈ 10 **Facilities** Children's menu Garden Parking

## TONBRIDGE
**See Penshurst**

## TUNBRIDGE WELLS (ROYAL)

# The Beacon ★★★★ INN ♈

**Tea Garden Ln, Rusthall TN3 9JH ☎ 01892 524252**
📠 01892 534288
e-mail: beaconhotel@btopenworld.com
web: www.the-beacon.co.uk
dir: *From Tunbridge Wells take A264 towards East Grinstead. Pub 1m on left*

Set amid seventeen acres of grounds, the Beacon began life in 1895 as the country home of Sir Walter Harris. The building still oozes with country house charm; the bar, with its moulded plaster ceiling, bookshelves and stained glass windows is a wonderful place to relax with a pint. Today, The Beacon's grounds encompass lakes, woodland walks and a chalybeate spring that was first used some 40 years before its more famous counterpart in Tunbridge Wells. Enjoy a drink on the terrace with amazing views in summer or by the fire in the bar on cooler days; here, you'll find draught and bottled cider, a range of beers and a good wine list offering plenty of choice by the glass. Food is served in both the bar and the elegant restaurant, or in one of three private dining rooms. The menus take full advantage of seasonal local produce to which, as a member of Kentish Fare, the kitchen is strongly committed. You could start with pork and apricot terrine with grape and apple chutney; or Stilton and pine nut salad with Domino quails' eggs and herb croutons. Main course dishes include butter-roasted local cod with pea and smoked halibut ragout with poached egg, and seared rib-eye steak with caramelised onion mash and sauteed green vegetables.

**Open** all day all wk Mon-Sat 11-11 (Sun 12-10.30) **Bar Meals** L served Mon-Thu 12-2.30, Fri-Sun 12-9.30 D served Mon-Thu 6.30-9.30, Fri-Sun 12-9.30 Av main course £9.50 **Restaurant** L served Mon-Thu 12-2.30, Fri-Sun 12-9.30 D served Mon-Thu 6.30-9.30, Fri-Sun 12-9.30 Av 3 course à la carte fr £22 ⊕ FREE HOUSE ◀ Harveys Best, Timothy Taylor Landlord, Larkins Traditional ♻ Stowford Press Draught Cider, Westons Organic Bottled Pear Cider. ♈ 12 **Facilities** Children's menu Play area Garden Parking **Rooms** 3

England

## WESTERHAM

### The Fox & Hounds 🍷

**Toys Hill TN16 1QG ☎ 01732 750328**
e-mail: hickmott1@hotmail.com
dir: *Telephone for directions*

High up on Kent's Greensand Ridge, in an Area of Outstanding Natural Beauty, this late 18th-century ale house adjoins a large National Trust estate incorporating an old water tower now protected as a home for hibernating bats. The pub has a traditionally styled restaurant, where starters include smoked salmon and crab roulade, and deep-fried brie with cranberry sauce, while among the mains are fillet of pork stuffed with dates and apricots on horseradish mash, leg of lamb on bubble and squeak with rosemary jus, and daily specials. A children's menu is available.

**Open** 10-3 6-11 (Sat-Sun 10am-11pm) Closed: 25 Dec, Mon eve **Bar Meals** L served Mon-Sat 12-2, Sun 12-3 D served Tue-Sat 6-9 Av main course £11 **Restaurant** L served Mon-Sat 12-2, Sun 12-3 D served Tue-Sat 6-9 Av 3 course à la carte fr £20 ⊕ GREENE KING ◀ Greene King IPA, Abbot Ale, Ruddles County. 🍷 9 **Facilities** Children's menu Dogs allowed Garden Parking

## WEST MALLING

### The Farmhouse 🍷

**97 The High St ME19 6NA ☎ 01732 843257**
📄 **01622 851881**
e-mail: enquiries@thefarmhouse.biz
dir: *M20 junct 4, S on A228. Right to West Malling. Pub in village centre*

A modern gastro-pub, The Farmhouse occupies a handsome Elizabethan property at the heart of the village of West Malling. It has a relaxing atmosphere with a stylish bar and two dining areas, while outside is a spacious walled garden with an area of decking. There are stone-baked pizzas and toasted paninis alongside the blackboard menu which changes regularly. Starters range from home-made soup with crusty bread to melon and Bayonne ham with blackcurrant dressing. Main courses might include pan-fried sea bass salad with sun-dried tomatoes; steak, Guinness and mushroom pie; or confit duck leg with sweet potato mash. Bar food is available all day. The 15th-century barn at the rear of the pub has been transformed into a deli/farmers' market.

**Open** all day all wk noon-11 **Bar Meals** Av main course £11 food served all day **Restaurant** Fixed menu price fr £11 Av 3 course à la carte fr £22 food served all day ⊕ FREE HOUSE ◀ Harvey's, Guinness, Youngs. 🍷 13 **Facilities** Children's menu Garden Parking

## WHITSTABLE

### The Sportsman ⊛⊛ 🍷

**Faversham Rd CT5 4BP ☎ 01227 273370**
e-mail: contact@thesportsmanseasalter.co.uk
dir: *3.5m W of Whitstable, on the coast road between Whitstable and Faversham*

Reached via a winding lane across open marshland from Whitstable, and tucked beneath the sea wall, the Sportsman may seem an unlikely place to find such good food. The rustic yet comfortable interior, with its wooden floors, stripped pine furniture and interesting collection of prints has a warm and welcoming feel. Remember that food is not served on Sunday evenings or Mondays, or you could be disappointed. The daily menu is based on local produce from farms, boats and game dealers. Fish dishes might include seared Thornback ray with cockles, sherry vinegar and brown butter. Starters also feature lots of seafood, typically rock oysters and hot chorizo. Amongst the mains is Monkshill Farm pork belly and apple sauce. There is also a tasting menu available for a maximum of 6 people.

**Open** all wk noon-3 6-11 Closed: 25 Dec **Bar Meals** Av main course £16 **Restaurant** L served Tue-Sun 12-2 booking required D served Tue-Sat 7-9 booking required Av 3 course à la carte fr £30 ⊕ SHEPHERD NEAME ◀ Shepherd Neame Late Red, Master Brew, Porter, Early Bird, Goldings, Whitstable Bay. 🍷 8 **Facilities** Children's menu Family room Dogs allowed Garden Parking

## LANCASHIRE

## BASHALL EAVES

### The Red Pump Inn 🍷

**Clitheroe Rd BB7 3DA ☎ 01254 826227**
e-mail: info@theredpumpinn.co.uk
dir: *3m from Clitheroe, NW, follow 'Whitewell, Trough of Bowland & Bashall Eaves' signs*

Enjoying panoramic views of Pendle Hill and Longridge Fell, this is one of the oldest inns in the Ribble Valley, its name coming from the old red pump that used to provide horses with water. Public areas divide into a snug with real fire, large and small dining rooms and a bar. If you hear music in the bar it'll probably be an eclectic mix of 60s blues, jazz and whatever else matches the relaxed, slightly quirky atmosphere. The menu changes to reflect the seasons and the whims of the owners and chefs, while the supporting daily specials boards – which is where you'll find the fish - may change during the day. Local produce includes meat, game, cheeses and vegetables, with extra-matured local Pendle beef available every day. Typical dishes include Lancashire game pie in a rich casserole; slow-braised Lancashire lamb shank, served with mashed potato and vegetables in a rich gravy; and open lasagne with garlic-roasted vegetables and tomato and herb sauce. Children are catered for with a fresh and healthy menu that's been known to lead to cases of parental theft of food from their child's plate! The bright and sunny Coach House houses the sumptuous lounge that sells home-made breads, cakes (try the chocolate and beetroot), preserves and patés.

Open noon-3 6-11 (Sat noon-11 Sun noon-9) Closed: Mon (ex BH) **Bar Meals** L served Tue-Sat 12-2, Sun 12-7.30 D served Tue-Sat 6-9, Sun 12-7.30 **Restaurant** L served Tue-Sat 12-2, Sun 12-7.30 D served Tue-Sat 6-9, Sun 12-7.30 ⊕ FREE HOUSE ◖ Timothy Taylor Landlord, Black Sheep, Moorhouses, Tirril Brewery. ♀ 10 **Facilities** Children's menu Garden Parking

---

## BILSBORROW

# Owd Nell's Tavern ♀

**Guy's Thatched Hamlet, Canal Side PR3 0RS**
☎ **01995 640010** ▤ **01995 640141**
e-mail: info@guysthatchedhamlet.com
dir: *M6 junct 32 N on A6. In approx 5m follow brown tourist signs to Guy's Thatched Hamlet*

The Wilkinson family has owned and run Guy's Thatched Hamlet beside the Lancaster Canal for nearly 30 years, of which this country-style tavern forms a part. Flagstone floors, fireplaces and low ceilings create an authentic ambience. All-day fare is typified by home-made steamed chicken, leek and mushroom pudding; famous steak and kidney pudding; spinach and cheese cannelloni; and bacon, brie and cranberry panini. Children's menus are available. There is a cider festival at the end of July.

Open all wk 7am-2am Closed: 25 Dec **Bar Meals** Av main course £7.50 food served all day **Restaurant** L served Mon-Sat 12-2.30, Sun 12-10.30 D served Mon-Sat 5.30-10.30, Sun 12-10.30 Fixed menu price fr £7.95 Av 3 course à la carte fr £17 ⊕ FREE HOUSE ◖ Boddingtons Bitter, Jennings Bitter, Copper Dragon, Black Sheep, Owd Nells Canalside Bitter, Moorhouses Bitter, Pendle Witch ᵟ Thatchers Heritage, Cheddar Valley. ♀ 40 **Facilities** Children's menu Play area Family room Dogs allowed Garden Parking

# Clog and Billycock ♀

**Billinge End Rd, Pleasington BB2 6QB ☎ 01254 201163**
e-mail: enquiries@theclogandbillycock.com
dir: *M6 junct 29 onto M65 junct 3, follow signs for Pleasington*

The Clog and Billycock is named after the favoured attire of a landlord from the 1900s (a billycock is black felt hat, a predecessor of the bowler). The extensively renovated building stands in the quaint village of Pleasington on the quiet edges of Blackburn's western suburbs, where the River Darwen flows out of town. A warm and relaxing environment is provided for the appreciation of Thwaites ales, draught ciders, fine wines and good food prepared from quality Lancashire produce. Elm wood platters are a feature – ploughman's, house cured meats and local seafood – all with home-made bread and pickles. Hot and cold sandwiches, traditional pancakes and home-made organic ice cream and milkshakes are also fixtures. Other options might be Muncaster crab cakes or treacle-baked free range Middlewhite Garstang ribs with devilled black peas to start, followed by Lancashire hot pot, or Sandhams cheese and onion pie with sour cream jackets. A comprehensive young people's menu delivers real food and there is a great range of non-alcoholic drinks.

Open all wk noon-11 (Sun noon-10.30) Closed: 25 Dec **Bar Meals** L served Mon-Sat 12-2, Sun 12-8.30 D served Mon-Fri 6-9, Sat 5.30-9, Sun 12-8.30 Av main course £10.50 **Restaurant** L served Mon-Sat 12-2, Sun 12-8.30 D served Mon-Fri 6-9, Sat 5.30-9, Sun 12-8.30 ⊕ FREE HOUSE ◖ Thwaites Bomber, Wainwright, Original. ♀ 8 **Facilities** Children's menu Dogs allowed Garden Parking

## BURROW

### The Highwayman ♟

**LA6 2RJ** ☎ **01524 273338**

e-mail: enquiries@highwaymaninn.co.uk

dir: *M6 junct 36, A65 to Kirkby Lonsdale. Then A683 S. Burrow approx 2m*

This is a Ribble Valley inn and sister to the Three Fishes at Mitton. The building dates from the 18th century and, as a coaching inn, might well have been frequented by highwaymen as its name suggests. Handsome wooden furniture is set on stone floors by open fires, for this is a proper pub serving real beer by local brewer Daniel Thwaites. Food is very much at the heart of the operation, and the philosophy of head chef Michael Ward focuses on an attractive contemporary interpretation of traditional specialities using regional produce – the menu celebrates local food heroes on every line. The ingredients they supply appear in dishes such as Winnie Swarbrick's corn-fed Goosnargh chicken liver pâté; Muncaster crab cake; Sillfield Farm dry-cured gammon steak; and Andy Roe's tomato and red onion salad. Finish with burnt English custard and stewed rhubarb; or bread and butter pudding with steeped apricots.

**Open** all wk noon-11 (Sun noon-10.30) Closed: 25 Dec **Bar Meals** L served Mon-Sat 12-2, Sun 12-8.30 D served Mon-Fri 6-9, Sat 5.30-9, Sun 12-8.30 Av main course £10.50 ◗ Lancaster Bomber, Double Century. ♟ 8 **Facilities** Children's menu Dogs allowed Garden Parking

## CARNFORTH

### The Longlands Inn and Restaurant ⓐ ★★★★ INN

**Tewitfield LA6 1JH** ☎ **01524 781256** 📄 **01524 781004**

e-mail: info@longlandshotel.co.uk

web: www.longlandshotel.co.uk

dir: *Please telephone for directions*

With its nooks and crannies, old beams and uneven floors, this family-run inn stands next to Tewitfield locks on the Lancaster canal. The bar comes to life for band night on Mondays, with a more relaxed feel during the rest of the week. The appetising menu includes slate platters with deli-style bread; and main course choices ranging from braised Silverdale lamb shank, and tamarind confit duck leg on Chinese noodles to the Longlands fish pie with melted cheese topping.

**Open** all day all wk 11am-1am **Bar Meals** L served Mon-Fri 12-2.30, Sat 12-4, Sun 12-9 D served Mon-Fri 5.30-9.30, Sat 5-9.30, Sun 12-9 Av main course £10 **Restaurant** L served Mon-Fri 12-2.30, Sat 12-4, Sun 12-9 D served Mon-Fri 5.30-9.30, Sat 5-9, Sun 12-9 booking required Av 3 course à la carte fr £18 **Facilities** Children's menu Dogs allowed Garden Parking **Rooms** 11

## CHIPPING

### Dog & Partridge ♟

**Hesketh Ln PR3 2TH** ☎ **01995 61201** 📄 **01995 61446**

dir: *M6 junct 31A, follow Longridge signs. At Longridge left at 1st rdbt, straight on at next 3 rdbts. At Alston Arms turn right. 3m, pub on right*

Dating back to 1515, this pleasantly modernised rural pub in the Ribble Valley enjoys delightful views of the surrounding fells. The barn has been transformed into a welcoming dining area, where home-made food on the comprehensive bar snack menu is backed by a specials board featuring fresh fish and game dishes. A typical menu shows duck and orange pâté; roast Lancashire beef and Yorkshire pudding; home-made steak and kidney pie; and broccoli and Stilton pancakes.

**Open** 11.45-3 6.45-11 (Sat 11.45-3 6-11 Sun 11.45-10.30) Closed: Mon **Bar Meals** L served Tue-Sat 12-1.45 **Restaurant** L served Tue-Sat 12-1.30, Sun 12-3 booking required D served Tue-Sat 7-9 Sun 3.30-8.30 booking required Fixed menu price fr £17.25 ⊕ FREE HOUSE ◗ Carlsberg-Tetley, Black Sheep. ♟ 8 **Facilities** Children's menu Parking

## CLITHEROE

### The Assheton Arms ♟

**Downham BB7 4BJ** ☎ **01200 441227** 📄 **01200 440581**

e-mail: asshetonarms@aol.com

web: www.assheton-arms.co.uk

dir: *A59 to Chatburn, then follow Downham signs*

This stone-built country pub is well placed for a walk up Pendle Hill, which looms over the village. Visitors will find the single bar and sectioned rooms furnished with solid oak tables, wingback settees, a stone fireplace, and a blackboard listing daily specials. Seafood is offered according to availability, and you can expect beer battered haddock and chips, and lemon sole with parsley butter. An interesting selection of small dishes includes black pudding with piccalilli and mustard; and Leagrams organic Lancashire cheese platter with crusty bread and apple cider chutney. Main courses take in a choice of vegetarian dishes (broccoli bake; vegetarian chilli; cauliflower and mushroom provençale), as well as traditional Lancashire hot pot; venison casserole, and a range of steaks.

Open all wk **Bar Meals** L served Mon-Sat 12-2, Sun 12-9 D served all wk 6-9 Av main course £11.50 **Restaurant** Av 3 course à la carte fr £20 ⊕ FREE HOUSE ◀ Lancaster Bomber, Wainwright Thwaites. ♀ 22 **Facilities** Children's menu Dogs allowed Parking

## The Shireburn Arms ★★★ HL ♀

**Whalley Rd, Hurst Green BB7 9QJ**
☎ **01254 826518** 🖹 **01254 826208**
e-mail: sales@shireburnarmshotel.com
dir: *Telephone for directions*

A privately run, 17th-century inn with super views, in the heart of the Ribble Valley. J R R Tolkien used to drink here when visiting his son at Stonyhurst College nearby, and the pub has become home of the 'Tolkien Trail'. Using the finest local produce from around Lancashire, the menu ranges from sandwiches and salads to roasted Goosnargh duck with black cherry jus; wild sea trout on crushed peas; and mushroom, cranberry and brie Wellington. A conservatory links the restaurant with the patio and gardens.

Open all day all wk **Bar Meals** Av main course £8.50 food served all day **Restaurant** L served Mon-Fri 12-2, Sun 12-6 D served all wk 6-9 Fixed menu price fr £10.95 Av 3 course à la carte fr £20 ⊕ FREE HOUSE ◀ Theakstons Best Bitter, guest ales. ♀ 10 **Facilities** Children's menu Play area Family room Dogs allowed Garden Parking **Rooms** 22

## FENCE

## Ye Old Sparrowhawk Inn ♀

**Wheatley Lane Rd BB12 9QG** ☎ **01282 603034**
🖹 **01282 603035**
e-mail: mail@yeoldsparrowhawk.co.uk
web: www.yeoldsparrowhawk.co.uk
dir: *M65 junct 13, A6068, at rdbt take 1st exit 0.25m. Turn right onto Carr Hall Rd, at top turn left 0.25m, pub on right*

Sipping a pint outside the half-timbered Sparrowhawk on a summer's evening is one of life's great pleasures. The pub stands at the gateway to Pendle Forest, famous for its witches, but here you'll find friendly service and stylish surroundings. The classically trained chefs work with locally sourced fresh ingredients to create menus that include stilton-glazed Pendle pork chop with Lyonnaise sauté potatoes and Mr Mellin's traditional sausages with mash and onion gravy.

Open all wk **Bar Meals** L served Mon-Sat 12-2.30, Sun 12-8 booking required D served Mon-Sat 5.30-9.30, Sun 12-8 booking required Av main course £10.50 **Restaurant** L served Mon-Sat 12-2.30, Sun 12-8 booking required D served Mon-Sat 5.30-9.30, Sun 12-8 booking required Fixed menu price fr £9 ◀ Thwaites Cask, Draught Bass, Moorhouse Blonde Witch, Black Sheep Best Õ Addlestones. ♀ 13 **Facilities** Children's menu Dogs allowed Garden Parking

---

## LANCASTER

## The Sun Hotel and Bar ♀

**LA1 1ET** ☎ **01524 66006** 🖹 **01524 66397**
e-mail: info@thesunhotelandbar.co.uk
dir: *6m from M6 junct 33*

By opening at 7.30am (a little later at weekends) and closing only when the last conversation dies, this city centre pub sees a steady and diverse flow of people throughout the day. The original inn was built in the 1600s, on the site of the medieval Stoop Hall, and is now Lancaster's oldest licensed premises. Its popular, award-winning bar serves a wide selection of cask ales, fifty bottled beers, two dozen wines by the glass and an excellent spirits selection. Attractive menus start with luxury breakfasts, and encompass reasonably priced lunches, with their acclaimed cheese and pâté boards, and evening meals. Typical main courses include beef chilli; Lancashire hotpot; steak, mushroom and oyster stout pie; moules marinière; and roasted butternut squash and sage risotto.

Open all day all wk from 7.30am until late **Bar Meals** Av main course £6 food served all day ⊕ FREE HOUSE ◀ Thwaites Lancaster Bomber, Lancaster Amber, Timmermans Strawberry, Lancaster Blonde, Warsteiner. ♀ 24 **Facilities** Children's menu Garden

## PARBOLD

### The Eagle & Child ⚲

**Maltkiln Ln, Bispham Green L40 3SG** ☎ **01257 462297**
🖷 **01257 464718**

dir: *3m from M6 junct 27. Over Parbold Hill, follow signs for Bispham Green on right*

Many years ago, legend has it, the local landowner Lord Derby and his wife were childless, but he fathered a child following an illicit liaison with a girl from the village. The child was placed in an eagle's nest so that when the lord and his wife were out walking they happened to hear the child cry. The lady insisted that the little boy was a gift from God, so they took him home and reared him as their son; hence the pub's name (known locally as the Bird and Bastard). The pub maintains its traditional atmosphere and offers five regularly changing guest ales, real ciders and a beer festival every May. All food is made on the premises with ingredients from local suppliers. The bar menu is extensive with the likes of crayfish and lemon risotto; chargrilled sweet cured gammon; and steak and real ale pie. The carte menu might include pan-fried Gressingham duck strips with orange and brandy sauce. There's a new deli shop in the barn next door.

Open all wk **Bar Meals** L served all wk 12-2 booking required D served Sun-Thu 5.30-8.30, Fri-Sat 5.30-9 booking required Av main course £12 **Restaurant** L served all wk 12-2 booking required D served Sun-Thu 5.30-8.30, Fri-Sat 5.30-9 booking required ⊕ FREE HOUSE ◧ Moorhouse Black Cat Mild, Thwaites Bitter, Southport Golden Sands, guest ales. ⚲ 6 **Facilities** Children's menu Family room Dogs allowed Garden Parking

## RIBCHESTER

### The White Bull ⚲

**Church St PR3 3XP** ☎ **01254 878303**
e-mail: enquiries@whitebullrib.co.uk
dir: *M6 junct 31, A59 towards Clitheroe. B6245 towards Longridge. Pub 100mtrs from Roman Museum in town centre*

Ancient Roman columns welcome patrons to this Grade II listed pub in the centre of Ribchester, with its beer garden overlooking the former Roman bathhouse. Despite its 18th-century origins as a courthouse, you'll find a warm and friendly atmosphere in which to sample the local hand-pumped beers. Lunchtime sandwiches and a variety of specials support a main menu that might include game rillette, cranberry chutney with

toast; bangers, mash and onion gravy; and grilled organic sea bass with spinach and lemon and parsley butter. Large walled garden available.

Open all wk Mon open 6pm **Bar Meals** L served Tue-Sun 12-2.30 D served Tue-Sun 6-9 Av main course £11 **Restaurant** L served Tue-Sun 12-2.30 D served Tue-Sun 6-9 Fixed menu price fr £14 Av 3 course à la carte fr £24 ⊕ ENTERPRISE INNS ◧ John Smiths, Copper Dragon Bitter, Bowland Brewery Bitter, Moorhouses. ⚲ 8 **Facilities** Children's menu Garden Parking

## TUNSTALL

### The Lunesdale Arms ⚲

**LA6 2QN** ☎ **015242 74203** 🖷 **015242 74229**
e-mail: info@thelunesdale.co.uk
dir: *M6 junct 36. A65 Kirkby Lonsdale. A638 Lancaster. Pub 2m on right*

Set in a small village in the beautiful Lune Valley, The Lunesdale Arms has established quite a reputation for its food, wines and fine regional beers. Presided over by an ever-popular landlady, the pub is bright, cheery and welcoming. The food is freshly prepared, with bread baked on the premises. Most of the meat is supplied by local farms, and there is always roast lamb, beef or pork for Sunday lunch. Where possible the salad leaves and vegetables are grown organically. Both lunch and evening menus are likely to change on a daily basis according to the seasonality of ingredients and new ideas. Dishes range from Lancashire cheese rarebit with smoked Cumbrian ham; or free-range boiled egg with asparagus fingers and home-made brown bread, to roasted fillet of salmon on a bed of Puy lentils with roasted tomatoes, peppers and balsamic vinegar, or steak, Guinness and mushroom pie with chips.

Open Closed: 25-26 Dec, Mon (ex BH) **Bar Meals** L served Tue-Fri 12-2, Sat-Sun 12-2.30 booking required D served Tue-Sun 6-9 booking required Av main course £10.75 **Restaurant** L served Tue-Fri 12-2, Sat-Sun 12-2.30 booking required D served Tue-Sun 6-9 booking required Av 3 course à la carte fr £20 ⊕ FREE HOUSE ◧ Black Sheep, Dent Aviator, Guinness. ⚲ 8 **Facilities** Children's menu Family room Dogs allowed Garden Parking

## WHALLEY

### The Three Fishes ⊛ ⚲

**Mitton Rd, Mitton BB7 9PQ** ☎ **01254 826888**
🖷 **01254 826026**
e-mail: enquiries@thethreefishes.com
dir: *M6 junct 31, A59 to Clitheroe. Follow signs for Whalley, take B6246 for 2m*

Mitton lies in a wedge of land between the Rivers Hodder and Ribble, the village name reflecting this position in a corruption of Midtown. The Three Fishes has been a public house for some 400 years, supposedly named after the 'three fishes pendant' in the coat of arms of the last abbot of Whalley Abbey, a carved stone from which is now incorporated over the pub entrance. The 21st-century interior very much respects the past and retains its most attractive features, including the big open fires. The strength of the menu of regional and British classics comes from using best quality produce from 'local food heroes'. A generous selection includes deep-fried Lancaster whitebait; braised shin of Ribble Valley beef; toad in the hole with Forager's Cumberland sausage; and breast of devilled Goosnargh chicken. Salads, lunchtime sandwiches and light meals are also available, while children have their own, quite grown-up, menu. Enjoy the sprawling sun terraces in summer.

Open all day all wk Closed: 25 Dec **Bar Meals** L served Mon-Sat 12-2, Sun 12-10.30 D served Mon-Fri 6-9, Sat 5.30-9, Sun 12-10.30 Av main course £10.95 food served all day ⊕ FREE HOUSE ◀ Thwaites Traditional, Thwaites Bomber, Bowland Brewery Hen Harrier. ♀ 13 **Facilities** Children's menu Dogs allowed Garden Parking

---

## LEICESTERSHIRE

### BELTON

# The Queen's Head ★★★★ RR ◉◉ ♀
**2 Long St LE12 9TP** ☎ 01530 222359 📄 01530 224860
e-mail: enquiries@thequeenshead.org
web: www.thequeenshead.org
dir: *On B5324 between Coalville & Loughborough*

The clean, uncluttered exterior of this white-fronted, village centre pub suggests that its new owners might also have a fair idea of what constitutes good interior design. And so they have. The place has all-round appeal, whether you want to settle into a leather sofa in the contemporary bar, or enjoy the food in the restaurant, garden or terrace. A Lite Bites/Classics

menu incorporates club sandwiches; burger and fries; risotto of the day; and sausage and mash. The modern British set menu offers starters of grilled red mullet with houmous and cucumber spaghetti; and carpaccio of beef, tarragon cream and rocket, with mains including fillet or rump of beef with smoked mash and cauliflower cheese; sweet potato curry with jasmine rice and home-made naan bread; and assiette of rabbit with beetroot purée. The two AA Rosettes the Queen's Head has earned speak volumes.

Open all day all wk Closed: 25-26 Dec **Bar Meals** L served all wk 12-2.30, Sat all day D served Mon-Fri 7-9.30, Sat all day Av main course £11 **Restaurant** L served all wk 12-2.30, Sun 12-4 D served Mon-Sat 7-9 Fixed menu price fr £13 Av 3 course à la carte fr £25 ⊕ FREE HOUSE ◀ Worthington, Pedigree, Queens Special Ŏ Merrydown. ♀ 14 **Facilities** Children's menu Play area Dogs allowed Garden Parking **Rooms** 6

---

### EVINGTON

# The Cedars ♀
**Main St LE5 6DN** ☎ 0116 273 0482
e-mail: cedars@king-henrys-taverns.co.uk
dir: *From London Road out of Leicester turn left at lights, follow road to Evington. Pub located in centre of Evington village*

King Henry's Taverns, the owners, like to say that you get two for the price of one here – and you can. The Bar Restaurant serves the group's usual range of competitively priced, freshly prepared steaks, fish and seafood, rumpburgers, traditional favourites, and international and vegetarian dishes. Take the Titanic Challenge – a 48oz (uncooked) rump steak, too big to be cooked 'well done'. Panoramic windows in the main eating area overlook a fountain and pond, and the gardens are a great place for alfresco dining. Friday nights here are devoted to karaoke – you have been warned!

Open all day all wk noon-11 **Bar Meals** Av main course £3 food served all day **Restaurant** food served all day ⊕ KING HENRY'S TAVERNS ◀ Guinness, IPA, Marstons Pedigree. ♀ 15 **Facilities** Children's menu Play area Family room Garden Parking

---

### GRIMSTON

# The Black Horse
**3 Main St LE14 3BZ** ☎ 01664 812358
e-mail: wymeswold@supanet.com
dir: *Telephone for directions*

A traditional 16th-century coaching inn displaying much cricketing memorabilia in a quiet village with views over the Vale of Belvoir. Overlooking the village green, there are plenty of opportunities for country walks, or perhaps a game of pétanque on the pub's floodlit pitch. Good home-cooked meals with daily specials, including lots of game. Fish choices and specials include monkfish, lemon sole, whole grilled plaice, and Arctic char. There is an alfresco eating area for warmer weather.

continued

**England**

Open all wk 12-3 6-11 (Sun 12-6) **Bar Meals** L served Mon-Sat 12-2, Sun 12-3 booking required D served Mon-Sat 6-9 booking required **Restaurant** L served Mon-Sat 6-9 booking required D served Mon-Sat 6-9 booking required ⊕ FREE HOUSE ◀ Adnams, Marston's Pedigree, St Austell Tribute, Belvoir Mild, guest ales ♂ Thatchers Gold. **Facilities** Children's menu Dogs allowed Garden

## LOUGHBOROUGH

## The Falcon Inn ★★★ INN

**64 Main St, Long Whatton LE12 5DG ☎ 01509 842416**
**▤ 01509 646802**
e-mail: enquiries@thefalconinnlongwhatton.com

Just ten minutes' drive from East Midlands airport and the M1, this traditional country inn offers great food, stylish en suite accommodation, and stunning award-winning flower displays in the outdoor areas in summer. Food choices range from classic pub favourites like filled jacket potatoes; roast rack of lamb; and steak and ale pie to more exotic dishes including a full Lebanese mezzeh that reflects the traditions of Lebanese-born proprietor Jad Otaki. Look out for the special events throughout the year.

Open all day all wk **Bar Meals** L served all wk 12-2 D served all wk 6.30-9 Av main course £9.50 **Restaurant** L served all wk 12-2 D served all wk 6.30-9 booking required Av 3 course à la carte fr £18 ⊕ EVERARDS ◀ Tiger Best Bitter, Everards Original, guest ale. **Facilities** Children's menu Family room Garden Parking Rooms 11

## The Swan in the Rushes ♥

**21 The Rushes LE11 5BE ☎ 01509 217014**
**▤ 01509 217014**
e-mail: swanintherushes@castlerockbrewery.co.uk
dir: *On A6 (Derby road). Pub in front of Sainsbury's, 1m from railway station.*

A 1930s tile-fronted real ale pub, it was acquired by the Castle Rock chain in 1986, making it the oldest in the group. There's a first-floor drinking terrace, a function room and bar that seats 80, and a family/dining area. This real ale pub with a friendly atmosphere always offers ten ales, including seven guests, a selection of real ciders and hosts two annual beer festivals. Expect traditional pub grub. Music nights, folk club and a skittle alley complete the picture.

Open all day all wk 11-11 (Fri-Sat 11-mdnt Sun noon-11) **Bar Meals** L served all wk 12-3 D served Mon-Sat 6-9 Av main course £5.95 ⊕ CASTLE ROCK ◀ Castle Rock Harvest Pale, Castle Rock Sheriff's Tipple, Adnams Bitter, 7 guests ♂ Westons Old Rosie Scrumpy, Broadoak Moonshine. ♥ 11 **Facilities** Children's menu Family room Dogs allowed Parking

## LUTTERWORTH

## Man at Arms ♥

**The Green, Bitteswell LE17 4SB ☎ 01455 552540**
e-mail: man@king-henrys-taverns.co.uk
dir: *Take Ullesthorpe road out of Lutterworth, turn left at small white cottage. Pub on left after college on village green*

This was the first pub bought by the King Henry's Taverns group, named after a bequest left by Henry VIII to the nearby village of Bitteswell to provide a 'man at arms' at times of war. Henry was indeed a big eater and, yes, some pretty sizeable meals are available here, but there are healthy options too. A change of decor and style is promised, modelled on sister pub The Ragley Boat Stop in Barrow-upon-Trent.

Open all day all wk noon-11 **Bar Meals** Av main course £3 served all day **Restaurant** food served all day ⊕ KING HENRY'S TAVERNS ◀ Greene King IPA, Marstons Pedigree, Guinness. ♥ 15 **Facilities** Children's menu Play area Family room Garden Parking

## NETHER BROUGHTON

## The Red House ♥

**23 Main St LE14 3HB ☎ 01664 822429 ▤ 01664 823805**
e-mail: bernie@mulberrypubco.com
dir: *M1 junct 21A take A46. Right onto A606. Or take A606 from Nottingham.*

The Red House is a fine mixture of a 300-year-old village pub with log fires in winter and light contemporary design. The lounge bar opens into an airy restaurant, and a conservatory area overlooks the outdoor bar, terrace and courtyard grill. Immaculate gardens include a small play area and a permanent marquee for weddings, parties and corporate functions. Dishes range from locally sourced pork pie, or sausages of the week in the bar, to diver-caught scallops, or braised lamb shank in the restaurant. An ideal spot for walking, fishing and bird-watching.

Open all day all wk **Bar Meals** Av main course £10 food served all day **Restaurant** Av 3 course à la carte fr £25.30 food served all day ⊕ MULBERRY PUB CO LTD ◀ Guinness, Red House Special, Greene King IPA. ♥ 13 **Facilities** Children's menu Play area Dogs allowed Garden Parking

## OLD DALBY

## The Crown Inn ♥

**Debdale Hill LE14 3LF ☎ 01664 823134**
e-mail: oldcrown@castlerockbrewery.co.uk
dir: *A46 turn for Willoughby/Broughton. Right into Nottingham Ln, left to Old Dalby*

A classic creeper-covered, country pub dating from 1509, set in extensive gardens and orchards, with small rooms, all with open fires. The new owners have returned the pub to its former glory - traditional with a contemporary feel. They place a strong emphasis on fresh seasonal produce: if the food doesn't all come from Leicestershire, the county's suppliers are nonetheless wholeheartedly supported. Expect dishes like pan-fried sea bass with lemon and crayfish risotto, or oven roasted rack and braised shoulder of lamb with minted pea purée. There's a good choice of real ales to help wash down a meal, or to enjoy without food: Castle Rock Hemlock and Harvest Pale are among the selection.

Open all wk noon-close Closed: Mon L Bar Meals L served Tue-Fri 12-2, Sat-Sun 12-3 booking required D served Tue-Sat 6-9 booking required Av main course £8 Restaurant L served Tue-Sun 12-2 booking required D served Tue-Sun 6-9 booking required Av 3 course à la carte fr £25 ⊕ FREE HOUSE ◀ Castle Rock Hemlock, Beaver, Harvest Pale, 3 Guest Ales ⚪ Stowford Press. ♀ 10 Facilities Children's menu Family room Dogs allowed Garden Parking

## REDMILE

## Peacock Inn ★★★★ INN ♀

**Church Corner, Main St NG13 0GA ☎ 01949 842554**
**▤ 01949 843746**
e-mail: reservations@thepeacockinnredmile.co.uk
web: www.thepeacockinnredmile.co.uk
dir: *From A1 take A52 towards Nottingham. Turn left, follow signs for Redmile & Belvoir Castle. In Redmile at x-rds turn right. Pub at end of village*

Set beside the Grantham Canal in the Vale of Belvoir, this 16th-century stone-built pub is only two miles from the picturesque castle. The inn has a local reputation for good quality food and real ales, and offers a relaxed setting for wining and dining. The menus are based on local seasonal produce; try smoked duck salad with orange and basil dressing; pan-fried pork fillet with fennel and apple calvados cream jus; chocolate crème brûlée served with fresh fruit.

Open all day all wk Bar Meals L served all wk 12-2.30 D served all wk 6-9 Av main course £8.95 Restaurant D served all wk 6-9 Fixed menu price fr £8.95 Av 3 course à la carte fr £16.95 ⊕ CHARLES WELLS ◀ Young's Bitter, Bombardier. ♀ 8 Facilities Children's menu Dogs allowed Garden Parking Rooms 10

## SOMERBY

## Stilton Cheese Inn ♀

**High St LE14 2QB ☎ 01664 454394**
dir: *From A606 between Melton Mowbray & Oakham follow signs to Pickwell & Somerby. Enter village, 1st right to centre, pub on left*

This attractive 17th-century inn enjoys a good reputation for its food, beer, wine and malt whiskies. Built from mellow local sandstone, it stands in the centre of the village surrounded by beautiful countryside. An interesting range of food from the regularly-changing specials board includes smoked salmon and mascarpone roulade; Rutland Water trout with prawn and tarragon butter; liver, bacon, onion gravy with bubble and squeak; and ginger and walnut treacle tart.

Open all wk 12-3 6-11 (Sun 7-11) Bar Meals L served all wk 12-2 D served Mon-Sat 6-9, Sun 7-9 Av main course £9 Restaurant L served all wk 12-2 D served Mon-Sat 6-9, Sun 7-9 ⊕ FREE HOUSE ◀ Grainstore Ten Fifty, Brewster's Hophead, Belvoir Star, Tetley's Cask, Marston's Pedigree. ♀ 15 Facilities Children's menu Family room Garden Parking

## STATHERN

## Red Lion Inn ◎ ♀

**Red Lion St LE14 4HS ☎ 01949 860868  ▤ 01949 861579**
e-mail: info@theredlioninn.co.uk
dir: *From A1 (Grantham), A607 towards Melton, turn right in Waltham, right at next x-rds then left to Stathern*

The Red Lion is located in the beautiful Vale of Belvoir and comprises a stone-floored bar, a comfortable lounge with plenty of reading material, an elegant dining room and an informal dining area. Menus change daily in accordance with locally supplied produce and the menus offer a mixture of classic pub food and innovative country cooking. Typical dishes are Red Lion fish and chips with tartare sauce and mushy peas; and roast partridge with chestnut cabbage, caramelised pear, bread sauce and game chips. In collaboration with its sister pub, The Olive Branch at Clipsham, Red Olive Foods sells preserves, wholesale wines, hampers and speciality dishes.

Open 12-3 5.30-11 (Fri-Sat 12-11, Sun 12-6.30) Closed: 1 Jan, Mon Bar Meals L served Tue-Sat 12-2, Sun 12-3 booking required D served Tue-Thu 5.30-9, Fri 5.30-9.30, Sat 7-9.30 booking required Av main course £13.50 Restaurant L served Tue-Sat 12-2, Sun 12-3 booking required D served Tue-Thu 5.30-9, Fri 5.30-9.30, Sat 7-9.30 booking required Fixed menu

England

continued

price fr £10 Av 3 course à la carte fr £21.50 ⊕ RUTLAND INN COMPANY LTD ◧ Grainstore Olive Oil, Brewster's VPA, Exmoor Gold, London Pride. ⚲ 8 **Facilities** Children's menu Dogs allowed Garden Parking

## WELHAM

## The Old Red Lion ⚲

**Main St LE16 7UJ ☎ 01858 565253**
e-mail: redlion@king-henrys-taverns.co.uk

This old country pub was once a coaching inn, and the small area opposite the main bar was originally the archway where the coaches would swing in to offload their weary passengers. In winter the leather chesterfields around the log fires create a cosy feel, while in summer take an evening stroll along one of the many footpaths and bridleways. The menu goes in for traditional pub grub, burgers, curries, and vegetarian dishes.

**Open** all day all wk noon-11 **Bar Meals** Av main course £3 food served all day **Restaurant** food served all day ⊕ KING HENRY'S TAVERNS ◧ Greene King IPA, Marstons Pedigree, Guinness. ⚲ 15 **Facilities** Children's menu Play area Family room Parking

## WOODHOUSE EAVES

## The Wheatsheaf Inn ★★★ INN ⚲

**Brand Hill LE12 8SS ☎ 01509 890320 ▤ 01509 890571**
e-mail: richard@wheatsheafinn.net
dir: *M1 junct 22, follow Quorn signs*

Around the turn of the 19th century, when local quarrymen wanted somewhere to drink, they built themselves the Wheatsheaf. It's what locals call a Dim's Inn, a succession of pubs run by three generations of the Dimblebee family. Bistro-style menus include chargrilled prime steaks and popular Wheatsheaf burgers. Fresh fish is a feature of the daily chalkboard - maybe linguine with prawns and salmon in creamy saffron sauce. An additional dining room is now available called The Mess.

**Open** Closed: Sun eve in winter **Bar Meals** L served Mon-Fri 12-2, Sat 12-2.30, Sun 12-3.30 D served All wk 6.30-9.15 **Restaurant** L served Mon-Fri 12-2, Sat 12-2.30, Sun 12-3.30 D served All wk 6.30-9.15 ⊕ FREE HOUSE ◧ Greene King Abbot Ale, Draught Burton Ale, Timothy Taylor Landlord, Adnams Broadside, Tetley Smooth, guest ale. ⚲ 14 **Facilities** Children's menu Dogs allowed Garden Parking **Rooms** 3

## ALLINGTON

## The Welby Arms ★★★★ INN ⚲

**The Green NG32 2EA ☎ 01400 281361 ▤ 01400 281361**
dir: *From Grantham take either A1 N, or A52 W. Allington 1.5m*

A creeper-covered inn overlooking the green, the Welby Arms has a traditional country pub aspect. An excellent choice of real ales is offered alongside home-cooked food. Bar snacks take in home-made beef burgers, baguettes and chilli, and there is a full restaurant menu. Specials include steak and kidney pudding or monkfish wrapped in Parma ham with king prawns.

**Open** all wk 12-3 6-11 (Sun 12-10.30) **Bar Meals** L served Mon-Sat 12-2 D served Mon-Sun 6-9 Av main course £4.95 **Restaurant** L served Mon-Sun 12-2 booking required D served Mon-Sat 6-9, Sun 6-8.30 booking required Av 3 course à la carte fr £19.95 ⊕ FREE HOUSE ◧ John Smith's, Interbrew Bass, Timothy Taylor Landlord, Jennings Cumberland Ale, Badger Tanglefoot, Adnams Broadside. ⚲ 22 **Facilities** Children's menu Garden Parking **Rooms** 3

## FREISTON

## Kings Head

**Church Rd PE22 0NT ☎ 01205 760368**
dir: *From Boston towards Skegness on A52 follow signs for RSPB Reserve Freiston Shore*

Originally two tied cottages, this pub dates from the 15th century and retains its old world charm. According to the season, you'll be delighted by the award-winning flower displays outside or the large coal fire inside. The landlady, Ann, has been here 27 years and makes all the food, using only local produce, while partner Bill provides a warm welcome in the bar. Hearty dishes, such as steak or rabbit pie, are served with fresh vegetables. R.S.P.B. Freiston Shore is close by.

**Open** all wk 11.30-11 (Sun 11.45-4 Mon 11.30-3.30 7-11) **Bar Meals** L served Tue-Sun 12-2 Av main course £7.70 **Restaurant** L served Tue-Sun 12-2 booking required ⊕ BATEMANS ◧ Batemans XB & Dark Mild, Worthington Cream Flow, John Smiths, Guinness. **Facilities** Children's menu Parking ◉

England

## FROGNALL

# The Goat ♒

**155 Spalding Rd PE6 8SA ☎ 01778 347629**
e-mail: graysdebstokes@btconnect.com
**dir:** *A1 to Peterborough, A15 to Market Deeping, old A16 to Spalding, pub approx 1.5m from A15 & A16 junct*

Families are welcome at this cosy, friendly country free house, which has an open fire, large beer garden and plenty to amuse the children. Main courses include beef stroganoff; pork in sweet and sour sauce; leek and mushroom pie; warm bacon and stilton salad; and home-made prawn curry. Beer is taken seriously, with five different guest ales each week and regular beer festivals throughout the year.

**Open** all wk 11.30-3 6-11.30 (Sun noon-11) Closed: 25 Dec, 1 Jan **Bar Meals** L served Mon-Sat 12-2 booking required D served Mon-Sat 6.30-9.30, Sun 12-9 booking required Av main course £9 **Restaurant** L served Mon-Sat 12-2, Sun 12-9 booking required D served Mon-Sat 6.30-9.30, Sun 12-9 booking required Fixed menu price fr £15.95 Av 3 course à la carte fr £18 ⊕ FREE HOUSE ◀ Guest ales: Elgoods, Batemans, Abbeydale, Nethergate, Hopshackle Ŏ Westons Old Rosie, Broadoak Moonshine, Thatchers Cheddar valley. ♒ 16 **Facilities** Children's menu Play area Family room Garden Parking

---

## KIRTON IN LINDSEY

# The George

**20 High St DN21 4LX ☎ 01652 640600**
e-mail: enquiry@thegeorgekirton.co.uk
**dir:** *From A15 take B1205, turn right onto B1400*

Extensively restored in a modern traditional style by Glen and Neil McCartney, the George is an 18th-century former coaching inn offering locally brewed Bateman's ales and seasonally changing menus. From traditional Lincolnshire sausages with mash and gravy in the bar, the choice extends to beef stroganoff, braised lamb shank with mint pea sauce and rib-eye steak with peppercorn sauce. For pudding, indulge in sticky toffee pudding. Lincoln and The Wolds are within easy reach.

**Open** all wk 12-2 5-11 (Sun 11-3) **Bar Meals** Av main course £6.95 food served all day **Restaurant** Av 3 course à la carte fr £22 food served all day ⊕ FREE HOUSE ◀ Batemans XB. **Facilities** Children's menu Play area Garden

## LINCOLN

# Pyewipe Inn

**Fossebank, Saxilby Rd LN1 2BG ☎ 01522 528708**
📄 01522 525009
e-mail: enquiries@pyewipe.co.uk
**dir:** *From Lincoln on A57 past Lincoln/A46 Bypass, pub signed in 0.5m*

First licensed in 1778, the Pyewipe (local dialect for lapwing) stands in four acres alongside the Roman-built Fossedyke Navigation. From the grounds there's a great view of nearby Lincoln Cathedral. All food is bought locally and prepared by qualified chefs. With up to eight menu boards to choose from, expect shank of lamb in braised in orange and rosemary; slow roasted aubergine gratin with ratatouille and gruyère; and smoked haddock with poached egg and grain mustard sauce.

**Open** all day all wk 11-11 **Bar Meals** Av main course £10.50 food served all day **Restaurant** Av 3 course à la carte fr £18.50 food served all day ⊕ FREE HOUSE ◀ Timothy Taylor Landlord, Greene King Abbot Ale, Interbrew Bass, Bombardier, Wadworth 6X. **Facilities** Children's menu Dogs allowed Garden Parking

# The Victoria ♒

**6 Union Rd LN1 3BJ ☎ 01522 541000**
e-mail: jonathanjpc@aol.com
**dir:** *From city outskirts follow signs for Cathedral Quarter. Pub 2 mins' walk from all major up-hill car parks*

Situated right next to the Westgate entrance of the Castle and within a stone's throw of Lincoln Cathedral. As well as the fantastic views of the castle, the pub also offers splendid meals made from exclusively home-prepared food including hot baguettes and filled bacon rolls, Saturday breakfast and Sunday lunches. House specials include sausage and mash, various pies, chilli con carne and home-made lasagne.

**Open** all day all wk 11-mdnt (Fri-Sat 11-1am) **Bar Meals** L served all wk 12-2.30 Av main course £4.50 ⊕ JPC ◀ Timothy Taylor Landlord, Batemans XB, Castle Rock Harvest Pale, guest ales Ŏ Westons. ♒ 10 **Facilities** Children's menu Play area Dogs allowed Garden Parking

**Lincoln continued**

## Wig & Mitre ♚

**32 Steep Hill LN2 1LU ☎ 01522 535190**

📠 **01522 532402**

e-mail: email@wigandmitre.com

dir: *At top of Steep Hill, adjacent to cathedral & Lincoln Castle car parks*

In the historic heart of Lincoln, the Wig & Mitre has been owned and managed by the same proprietors since 1977. The building is a mix of the 14th and 16th centuries, with some more recent parts too. It's music-free, and food is served in perpetual motion from 8.30am to around midnight every day, all year round. The comprehensive breakfast menu runs until noon. Light meals include hot chicken, parsley and red onion burger with horseradish mayonnaise in a hot ciabatta; and a plate of Scottish smoked salmon. Seasonal main menus offer starters such as creamed white onion soup with parmesan dumplings; main courses like Derbyshire beef with horseradish mash; and puds along the lines of russet apple and pear strudel with home-made custard. Wine recommendations are given on the menus. A specials board which may change as the day progresses completes the food options.

Open all day all wk 8.30am-mdnt **Bar Meals** Av main course £13.48 food served all day **Restaurant** Fixed menu price fr £12.50 Av 3 course à la carte fr £20.85 food served all day ⊕ FREE HOUSE ◧ Black Sheep Special, Batemans XB. ♚ 34 **Facilities** Children's menu Dogs allowed

---

### LITTLE BYTHAM

## The Willoughby Arms

**Station Rd NG33 4RA ☎ 01780 410276**

e-mail: cdhulme@tiscali.co.uk

dir: *B6121 (Stamford to Bourne road), at junct follow signs to Careby/ Little Bytham, inn 5m on right*

This 150 year-old traditional stone, beamed free house was originally built as the booking office and waiting room for Lord Willoughby's private railway line. Now, you'll find a selection of real ales with great, home-cooked food available every lunchtime and evening. Menu options include Lincolnshire sausage and mash; rabbit stew; and steak and kidney pie. There is a large beer garden with stunning views.

Open all day all wk 12-11 **Bar Meals** L served Mon-Sat 12-2, Sun 12-6 D served all wk 6-9 Av main course £7.50 **Facilities** Children's menu Dogs allowed Garden Parking

---

### MARKET RASEN

## The Black Horse Inn

**Magna Mile LN8 6AJ ☎ 01507 313645** 📠 **01507 313645**

e-mail: reedannam@aol.com

dir: *In village on A631, between Louth & Market Rasen*

New owners are breathing new life into this Wolds village inn, which dates back to 1730, having refurbished the bar and dining areas. Expect chunky tables, leather sofas fronting open

fires and a relaxing atmosphere. There is also a display of RAF memorabilia connected with Squadron 101 who were stationed at Ludford airfield. Locals flock in for rustic, home-made food, perhaps game terrine with spiced tomato chutney, lamb hotpot with pickled red cabbage, halibut with caper and parsley butter, and white chocolate rice pudding with rhubarb jam, washed down with local Bateman's XB.

Open 12-2.30 5-11 Closed: 1 wk Jan, Sun eve-Mon **Bar Meals** L served Tue-Sat 12-2.30, Sun 12-6 D served Tue-Sat 5-10 Av main course £10 **Restaurant** L served Tue-Sat 12-2.30, Sun 12-6 D served Tue-Sat 5-10 Av 3 course à la carte fr £15.40 ⊕ FREE HOUSE ◧ Bateman's XB, Marston's Pedigree, Abott Ale, Fulstow Common, Tom Wood's Lincoln Red ♂ Westons Scrumpy, Skidbrooke Cyder. **Facilities** Children's menu Garden Parking

---

### NEWTON

## The Red Lion

**NG34 0EE ☎ 01529 497256**

dir: *10m E of Grantham on A52*

Dating from the 17th century, the Red Lion is particularly popular with walkers and cyclists, perhaps because the flat Lincolnshire countryside makes for easy exercise. Low beams, exposed stone walls and an open fire in the bar help to create a very atmospheric interior. Popular dishes include haddock in beer batter, lemon sole with parsley butter sauce, breadcrumbed scampi, and home-made steak and ale pie. The carvery serves cold buffets on weekdays, hot ones on Friday and Saturday evenings, and Sunday lunchtime.

Open 12-3 6-11 Closed: Sun eve & Mon eve **Bar Meals** Av main course £12 **Restaurant** Av 3 course à la carte fr £20 ⊕ FREE HOUSE **Facilities** Children's menu Dogs allowed Garden Parking

---

### RAITHBY

## Red Lion Inn

**PE23 4DS ☎ 01790 753727**

dir: *A158 from Horncastle, right at Sausthorpe, left to Raithby*

Traditional beamed black-and-white village pub, parts of which date back 300 years. Log fires provide a warm welcome in winter. A varied menu of home-made dishes includes sea bass with lime stir fry vegetables, roast guinea fowl with tomato, garlic and bacon, and medallions of beef with peppercorn sauce. Meals can be taken in the garden in the warmer months.

Open all wk 12-2 6-11 (Mon 6-11) **Bar Meals** L served Tue-Sun 12-2 D served Tue-Sun 7-9 **Restaurant** L served Tue-Sun 12-2 D served Tue-Sun 7-9 ⊕ FREE HOUSE ◧ Raithby, Greene King IPA, Tetley Smooth. **Facilities** Children's menu Garden Parking

## SOUTH WITHAM

### Blue Cow Inn & Brewery

**High St NG33 5QB** ☎ **01572 768432** 📄 **01572 768432**
e-mail: enquiries@bluecowinn.co.uk
dir: *Between Stamford & Grantham on A1*

Just in Lincolnshire, with the Rutland border a few hundred yards away, this once-derelict, 13th-century inn stands close to the source of the River Witham. Part-timbered outside, the interior has a wealth of beamed ceilings and walls, stone floors and open log fires when the easterly winds whip across The Fens from Siberia. Simon Crathorn brews his own beers. The inn has a patio beer garden for warm evenings.

**Open** all day all wk 11-11 **Bar Meals** Av main course £8.50 food served all day **Restaurant** food served all day ⊕ FREE HOUSE **Facilities** Children's menu Family room Dogs allowed Garden Parking

## SUSWORTH

### The Jenny Wren Inn

**East Ferry Rd DN17 3AS** ☎ **01724 784000**
e-mail: info@jennywreninn.co.uk
dir: *Please telephone for directions*

Like many other old inns, the Jenny Wren was once a farmhouse. Beamed ceilings, exposed brickwork, wood panelling and fireplaces make it easy to imagine an 18th-century farmer warming himself in front of some blazing logs. The menu offers typical starters of freshly prepared soup; and prawn cocktail with apple, celery and Marie Rose sauce; main courses include pan-fried salmon with prawn lemon cream; steak and ale pie; and oven-roasted chicken breast with dauphinoise potato. The River Trent flows past the front.

**Open** all wk noon-2.30 5.45-10.30 (Fri-Sun & BH noon-10.30) Closed: 1 Jan **Bar Meals** L served Mon-Thu 12-2, Fri-Sun 12-9 booking required D served Mon-Thu 5.45-9, Fri-Sun 12-9 booking required Av main course £10 **Restaurant** L served Mon-Thu 12-2, Fri-Sun 12-9 booking required D served Mon-Thu 5.45-9, Fri-Sun 12-9 booking required Fixed menu price fr £9.95 Av 3 course à la carte fr £20 ⊕ FREE HOUSE ◧ Old Speckled Hen, IPA Bitter, Theakstons. **Facilities** Children's menu Dogs allowed Garden Parking

## WOODHALL SPA

### Village Limits Country Pub, Restaurant & Motel ♟

**Stixwould Rd LN10 6UJ** ☎ **01526 353312**
📄 **01526 352203**
e-mail: info@villagelimits.co.uk
dir: *At rdbt on main street follow Petwood Hotel signs. Motel 500yds past Petwood Hotel*

The pub and restaurant are situated in the original part of the building, so expect bare beams and old world charm. Typical meals, championing the ingredients of many local Lincolnshire

suppliers, include fillet steak with wild mushrooms; chargrilled rainbow trout; and gammon steak.

**Open** Closed: Mon & Sun eve **Bar Meals** L served Tue-Sat 11.30-2 booking required D served Tue-Sat 6.30-9 booking required Av main course £10 **Restaurant** L served Tue-Sun 11.30-2 booking required D served Tue-Sat 6.30-9 booking required Av 3 course à la carte fr £19 ⊕ FREE HOUSE ◧ Batemans XB, Tetley's Smooth Flow, Highwood Tom Wood's Best, Fulstow IPA, Dixon's Major Bitter. ♟ 8 **Facilities** Children's menu Garden Parking

## LONDON

### EC1

### Coach & Horses ♟

**26-28 Ray St, Clerkenwell EC1 3DJ** ☎ **020 7278 8990**
e-mail: info@thecoachandhorses.com
dir: *From Farringdon tube station right onto Cowcross St. At Farringdon Rd turn right, after 500yds left onto Ray St. Pub at bottom of hill*

On this spot once stood Hockley-in-the-Hole bear garden, a popular entertainment venue in Queen Anne's day. Nearly two centuries later, in about 1855, this now classic Victorian London pub was built to serve the myriad artisans, many of them Italian, who populated this characterful area. What is now the public bar used to be a sweet shop, people lived in the beer cellars, and there was a secret passage to the long-buried River Fleet. Unsurprisingly there are a few ghosts, including an old man and a black cat. Among the reasonably priced dishes, look for herring roes on toast; black pudding hash with fried egg, plus these examples from a dinner menu: braised cuttlefish on toast; venison pie with mash; sea bream with roasted salsify, fennel, chervil and cucumber; cassoulet; and Jerusalem artichoke risotto. Over the road is the original Clerk's Well, from which this district takes its name.

**Open** all wk noon-11 (Sat 5-11 Sun noon-5) Closed: 23 Dec-1st Mon in Jan, BH **Bar Meals** L served Mon-Fri & Sun 12-3 D served Mon-Sat 6-10 Av main course £12.50 **Restaurant** L served Mon-Fri & Sun 12-3 D served Mon-Sat 6-10 Av 3 course à la carte fr £20 ◧ Timothy Taylor Landlord, Adnams Bitter, Guinness, Fuller's London Pride, Staropramen. ♟ 19 **Facilities** Children's menu Dogs allowed Garden

### N1

### The Barnsbury ♟

**209-211 Liverpool Rd, Islington N1 1LX** ☎ **020 7607 5519**
📄 **020 7607 3256**
e-mail: info@thebarnsbury.co.uk
dir: *Please telephone for directions*

The Barnsbury, a 'free house and dining room' in the heart of Islington, is a welcome addition to the London scene. It's a gastro-pub where both the food and the prices are well conceived – and its walled garden makes it a secluded and sought-after summer oasis for alfresco relaxation. At least

continued

**England**

two guest ales are backed by Thatchers Gold cider and an in-depth wine list. The food is cooked from daily supplies of fresh ingredients which have been bought direct from the market, itemised in refreshingly concise terms on the menu. Weekday lunches range from oysters to mushroom tagliatelle or lamb shank shepherd's pie. The à la carte dinner choice is also a no-nonsense selection of the day's produce: grilled sardines, caponata and basil oil could be your starter. Pork fillet with sweet potato purée and caramelised apples gives a flavour of the half dozen main course options. Pear and cranberry crumble with clotted cream rounds things off nicely.

Open all day all wk noon-11 (Sun noon-10.30) Closed: 25-26 Dec, 1 Jan Bar Meals L served Mon-Fri 12-3 Av main course £8 Restaurant L served Sat-Sun 12-4 D served all wk 6.30-10 Av 3 course à la carte fr £26 ⊕ FREE HOUSE ◣ Gravesend Shrimpers, 2 guest ales ♂ Thatchers Gold. ♟ 12 Facilities Children's menu Dogs allowed Garden

## The Duke of Cambridge ♟

**30 Saint Peter's St N1 8JT ☎ 020 7359 3066**
📄 **020 7359 1877**
e-mail: duke@dukeorganic.co.uk
dir: *Telephone for directions*

A pioneer in sustainable eating out, the Duke of Cambridge was the first UK pub certified by the Soil Association. Founder Geetie Singh has combined her passion for food and ethical business to create a leader in green dining. The company recycles and reuses wherever possible, and even the electricity is wind and solar sourced. The Marine Conservation Society has given its stamp of approval to the Duke's fish purchasing policy - and, with 100% organic wines and a daily-changing menu, you can feel really virtuous about tucking into a few courses. Try a delicious starter like langoustine with aioli and grilled bread, followed perhaps by mushroom and cavalo nero lasagne with beetroot and watercress salad; or slow roast mutton with rosemary and garlic roasted potatoes.

Open all day all wk noon-11 Closed: 24-26 & 31 Dec, 1 Jan Bar Meals L served Mon-Fri 12.30-3, Sat-Sun 12.30-3.30 D served Mon-Sat 6.30-10.30, Sun 6.30-10 Av main course £13.50 Restaurant L served Mon-Fri 12.30-3, Sat-Sun 12.30-3.30 booking required D served Mon-Sat 6.30-10.30, Sun 6.30-10 booking required Av 3 course à la carte fr £27 ⊕ FREE HOUSE ◣ Pitfield SB Bitter & Eco Warrior, St Peter's Best Bitter, East Kent Golding, Red Squirrel London Porter ♂ Westons, Dunkertons, Wiscombe. ♟ 12 Facilities Children's menu Dogs allowed

## N19

## The Landseer ♟

**37 Landseer Rd N19 4JU ☎ 020 7263 4658**
e-mail: info@thelandseer.wanadoo.co.uk
dir: *Nearest tube stations: Archway & Tufnell Park*

Sunday roasts are a speciality at this unpretentious gastro-pub. This is an ideal spot to relax with the weekend papers, or while away an evening with one of the pub's extensive library of board games. Weekend lunches and daily evening meals are served from separate bar and restaurant menus.

Open all day all wk noon-mdnt (Mon-Tue & Sun noon-11) Closed: 25 Dec Bar Meals Av main course £11 food served all day Restaurant food served all day ⊕ FREE HOUSE ◣ Timothy Taylor Landlord, Abbot Ale, Adnams ♂ Brothers Pear Cider, Aspall. ♟ 14 Facilities Children's menu Play area Dogs allowed

## NW1

## The Chapel

**48 Chapel Street NW1 5DP**
☎ **020 7402 9220** 📄 **020 7723 2337**
e-mail: thechapel@btconnect.com
dir: *By A40 Marylebone Rd & Old Marylebone Rd junct. Off Edgware Rd by tube station*

There's an informal atmosphere at this bright and airy Marylebone gastro-pub with stripped floors and pine furniture. The open-plan building derives its name from nothing more than its Chapel Street location, but it enjoys one of the largest gardens in central London with seating for over 60 customers. Fresh produce is delivered daily, and served in starters like broccoli and watercress soup, and mains such as pan-roasted chicken breast with sautéed ratte potatoes.

Open all day all wk noon-11 Closed: 25-26 Dec, 1 Jan, Etr Bar Meals Av main course £12 Restaurant L served all wk 12-2.30 D served all wk 7-10 Fixed menu price fr £14 Av 3 course à la carte fr £18 ⊕ PUNCH TAVERNS ◣ Greene King IPA, Adnams. Facilities Children's menu Dogs allowed Garden

## The Engineer ♟

**65 Gloucester Av, Primrose Hill NW1 8JH**
☎ **020 7722 0950** 📄 **020 7483 0592**
e-mail: info@the-engineer.com
dir: *Telephone for directions*

Situated in a residential part of Primrose Hill close to Camden Market, this unassuming corner pub was built by Isambard Kingdom Brunel in 1841. It attracts a discerning crowd for imaginative and well-prepared food and a friendly, laid-back atmosphere. Inside it is fashionably rustic, with a spacious bar area, sturdy wooden tables with candles, simple decor and changing art exhibitions in the restaurant area. The regularly-changing menu features an eclectic mix of inspired home-made dishes and uses organic or free-range meats. Typical examples could be miso-marinated pollock with mash, bok choi and soy sherry sauce; baked Dolcelatte, walnut and beetroot cheesecake; and T bone pork chop with celeriac and red lentil mash. Side dishes include Baker fries or rocket and parmesan salad, while desserts include chocolate sticky toffee pudding.

Open all day all wk 9am-11pm (Sun & BH 9am-10.30pm) Bar Meals Av main course £15.50 food served all day Restaurant L served Mon-Fri 12-3, Sat-Sun 12.30-4 booking required D served Mon-Sat 7-11, Sun & BH 7-10.30 booking required Fixed menu price fr £30 Av 3 course à la carte fr £30 ◣ Erdinger, Bombardier, Amstel. ♟ 10 Facilities Children's menu Family room Dogs allowed Garden

## The Prince Albert ♀

**163 Royal College St NW1 0SG ☎ 020 7485 0270**
**🖹 020 7713 5994**
e-mail: info@princealbertcamden.com
web: www.princealbertcamden.com
dir: *From Camden tube station follow Camden Rd. Right onto Royal College St, 200mtrs on right.*

Standing solidly behind the picnic tables in its small, paved courtyard, the Prince Albert's welcoming interior features polished wooden floors and bentwood furniture. Addlestone's cider teams with Adnam's Broadside and Black Sheep bitters at the bar, whilst menu choices include roast butternut squash penne with goats' cheese and sprout tops; Charolais beef burger with aged Cheddar on ciabatta; and sausages and mash with caramelised onion jus.

Open all day all wk noon-11 (Sun 12.30-10.30) Closed: 25-30 Dec **Bar Meals** L served Mon-Sat 12-3, Sun 12.30-6 D served Mon-Sat 6-10 Av main course £12.50 **Restaurant** L served Mon-Sat 12-3, Sun 12.30-6 D served Mon-Sat 6-10 Av 3 course à la carte fr £22.50 ⊕ FREE HOUSE 🍺 Black Sheep, Adnams Broadside, Hoegaarden, Staropramen, Kirin Ichiban Ö Brothers, Addlestones. ♀ 20 **Facilities** Children's menu Dogs allowed Garden

## North Pole Bar & Restaurant ♀

**131 Greenwich High Rd, Greenwich SE10 8JA**
**☎ 020 8853 3020  🖹 020 8853 3501**
e-mail: natalie@northpolegreenwich.com
dir: *From Greenwich rail station turn right, pass Novotel. Pub on right (2 min walk)*

You can do everything from dining to dancing at this grand old corner pub, which prides itself on offering a complete night out under one roof. Guests like to begin the evening with a signature cocktail in the bar, then climb the spiral staircase to the stylish Piano Restaurant, where the resident pianist tinkles away on the ivories Thursday to Sunday evenings. If at this point you happen to look up and see goldfish swimming around in the chandeliers, don't worry: they're for real and nothing to do with any cocktail consumed earlier. In the basement is the South Pole club, where you can dance until 2am. To complete the picture there's also a terrace, which makes an ideal spot for a glass of Pimms on a summer evening. An extensive bar menu is available all day, every day from 12 until 10pm, with choices including filled baguettes and mezze-style platters. Using the best of local suppliers produce, the cooking style in the Piano Restaurant is modern European, with starters typified by braised baby octopus with chorizo, fennel and salad; oxtail risotto; and smoked duck galette with crispy salad and hoi sin dressing. Any one of these could be followed by lamb chump with potato gratin, roasted parsnips and thyme jus; or perhaps honey-roasted duck breast with spiced red cabbage, raisins, sweet potato fondant and chips, and duck jus. For dessert, maybe choose sticky date pudding with butterscotch sauce and vanilla ice cream; or crème brûlée with almond shortbread. Sundays bring roast dinners in the bar and the restaurant and live jazz, funk and Latin music downstairs.

Open all day all wk noon-2am **Bar Meals** L served all wk 12-10 D served all wk 12-10 Av main course £15 food served all day **Restaurant** L served Sat-Sun 12-5 D served all wk 6-10.30 booking required Fixed menu price fr £17.95 Av 3 course à la carte fr £25 food served all day ⊕ FREE HOUSE 🍺 Guinness, IPA, Staropramen. ♀ 20 **Facilities** Children's menu Garden

## SE22

## Franklins ◉ ♀

**157 Lordship Ln, Dulwich SE22 8HX ☎ 020 8299 9598**
e-mail: info@franklinsrestaurant.com
dir: *0.5m S from East Dulwich station along Dog Kennel Hill & Lordship Lane*

As much a pub as it is a bar/restaurant, Franklins offers real ales and lagers on tap, along with real ciders. The restaurant interior is stripped back, modern and stylish with bare floors, exposed brick walls and smartly clothed tables, while the bar has a more traditional feel. A great selection or real ales and ciders are served. The daily menu is available for both lunch and dinner, and there is a good-value set lunch Monday to Friday (except bank holidays and December), priced for two or three courses. Captivating combinations include pickled pigeon with watercress, pear and walnuts to start, and main courses such as leg of venison with sprouting broccoli and anchovy; or hake with chicory and brown shimp. Finish with chocolate nemesis, lemon meringue tart or a cheeseboard of Ashmore, Stinking Bishop and Norbury Blue. Traditional savouries are a feature: Scotch woodcock, Welsh rarebit, and black pudding on toast.

Open all wk Closed: 25-26 & 31 Dec, 1 Jan **Bar Meals** food served all day **Restaurant** food served all day ⊕ FREE HOUSE 🍺 Whitstable Bay Organic Ale, Guinness, Meantime Pale Ale, Shepherd Neame's Orginal Porter Ö Westons, Aspalls, Biddendens. ♀ 11 **Facilities** Children's menu Dogs allowed

## SW3

### The Admiral Codrington 🍷

**17 Mossop St SW3 2LY ☎ 020 7581 0005**
📄 **020 7589 2452**
e-mail: admiral.codrington@333holdingsltd.com
dir: *See website for directions*

The local nickname for this smart and friendly gastro-pub is, inevitably, The Cod. Although this old Chelsea boozer was given a complete makeover that resulted in a stylish new look when it re-opened, it still retains a relaxed and homely feel. The modern British menu runs to caramelised red onion soup; pumpkin and ricotta ravioli; confit Norfolk port belly; and organic Loch Duart salmon and crab cake. Also look out for the 21-day and 35-day aged steaks. A good proportion of the well-chosen wines are available by the glass.

**Open** all day all wk 11.30am-mdnt (Fri-Sat 11.30am-1am, Sun noon-10.30) **Bar Meals** L served Mon-Fri 12-2.30, Sat 12-3.30, Sun 12-4 D served all wk 6-10.30 Av main course £10 **Restaurant** L served Mon-Fri 12-2.30, Sat 12-3.30, Sun 12-4 booking required D served Mon-Sat 6.30-11, Sun 7-10.30 booking required Av 3 course à la carte fr £27 ⊕ 333 ESTATES LTD ◾ Guinness, Black Sheep, Spitfire. 🍷 20 **Facilities** Children's menu Garden

## SW7

### The Anglesea Arms 🍷

**15 Selwood Ter, South Kensington SW7 3QG**
☎ **020 7373 7960**
e-mail: enquiries@angleseaarms.com
dir: *Telephone for directions*

Feeling like a country pub in the middle of South Kensington, the interior has barely changed since 1827, though the dining area has been tastefully updated with panelled walls and leather-clad chairs, plus there's a heated and covered terrace. The Great Train Robbery was said to have been plotted here. Lunch and dinner menus place an emphasis on quality ingredients, fresh preparation and cosmopolitan flavours. From the daily changing menu expect perhaps a charcuterie plate with celeriac remoulade and capers; chicken and vegetable pie; lightly battered whiting and home-made chips; and apple and blackberry crumble with custard. Sunday lunches are popular, booking is advisable.

**Open** all wk Closed: 25-26 Dec **Bar Meals** L served Mon-Fri 12-3, Sat-Sun 12-5 D served Mon-Fri 6.30-10, Sat 6-10, Sun 6-9.30 Av main course £12 **Restaurant** L served Sat-Sun 12-5 booking required D served Mon-Fri 6.30-10, Sat 6-10, Sun 6-9.30 Av 3 course à la carte fr £19 ⊕ FREE HOUSE ◾ Fuller's London Pride, Adnams Bitter, Broadside, Brakspear, Hogs Back Tea. 🍷 21 **Facilities** Children's menu Dogs allowed Garden

## SW10

### The Sporting Page 🍷

**6 Camera Place SW10 0BH ☎ 020 7349 0455**
📄 **020 7352 8162**
e-mail: sportingpage@foodandfuel.co.uk
dir: *Nearest tube - Sloane Square or South Kensington*

A small whitewashed pub happily tucked away between the King's and Fulham Roads. Its smart interior of varnished pine and rosewood and sporting murals makes it easy to unwind there after a day's work. The popular modern British menu includes traditional comfort food such as Cumberland sausage and mash, cheese and bacon burger, and beer battered haddock and chips. Despite its side street location, there's seating for 60 outside.

**Open** all wk Closed: 25-26 Dec **Bar Meals** L served all wk 12-3 D served all wk 6-10 Av main course £7 **Restaurant** Fixed menu price fr £5 ⊕ FREE HOUSE ◾ Wells Bombardier, Fuller's London Pride. 🍷 12 **Facilities** Children's menu Dogs allowed Garden

## SW13

### The Bull's Head 🍷

**373 Lonsdale Rd, Barnes SW13 9PY ☎ 020 8876 5241**
📄 **020 8876 1546**
e-mail: jazz@thebullshead.com
dir: *Telephone for directions*

Facing the Thames and established in 1684, the Bull's Head has become a major venue for mainstream modern jazz and blues. Traditional home-cooked meals are served in the bar, with dishes ranging from haddock and crab to a variety of roasts and pies. Popular home-made puddings. An important and intrinsic feature of the pub is the Thai menu, available throughout the pub in the evening.

**Open** all day all wk noon-mdnt Closed: 25 Dec **Bar Meals** L served all wk 12-4 Av main course £8 food served all day **Restaurant** D served all wk 6-11 Av 3 course à la carte fr £12 ⊕ YOUNG & CO BREWERY PLC ◾ Young's Special, Bitter, Winter Warmer, St Georges, Ramrod, Guinness. 🍷 32 **Facilities** Children's menu Family room Dogs allowed Garden

## SW15

### The Spencer Arms 🍷

**237 Lower Richmond Rd, Putney SW15 1HJ**
☎ **020 8788 0640** 📄 **020 8788 2216**
e-mail: info@thespencerarms.co.uk
dir: *Corner of Putney Common & Lower Richmond Rd, opposite Old Putney Hospital*

The Spencer Arms was transformed a few years ago from a cosy Victorian tavern overlooking Putney Common's leafy woods into an equally cosy gastro-pub. In the process owner Jamie Sherriff created a large sunlit bar area and dining room, and a relaxed fireside area with leather banquettes, all done out in pastels and dark wood. Parents with children to park quietly while they enjoy a drink should do so near the bookshelves and games chest. On offer are daily-changing lunch and dinner menus which incorporate the best ingredients sourced from outstanding, not necessarily local, suppliers. Lunch includes small plates for sharing – black pudding with apple and horseradish coleslaw, Welsh rarebit, sardines and tomato compote – and dishes like lemon risotto with goats' cheese, watercress soup, or buffalo mozzarella with crayfish and rocket. For dinner expect perhaps British-style tapas such as seared scallops, blue cheese and tomato tart and steak and kidney pie, as well as starters like pea soup, and black pudding on toast with HP sauce. The mains might feature braised turbot ragout; roast poussin; confit of duck with curly kale. 'Staples' such as macaroni cheese and mushroom risotto also feature. Children have their own menu. Parking might be a bit tricky.

**Open** all wk Closed: 25 Dec, 1 Jan **Bar Meals** L served Mon-Thu 12-2.30, Fri-Sun 12-6.30 booking required D served Mon-Sat 6.30-10, Sun 6.30-9.30 booking required Av main course £12.95 **Restaurant** L served Mon-Thu 12-2.30, Fri-Sun 12-6.30 booking required D served Mon-Sat 6.30-10, Sun 6.30-9.30 booking required Av 3 course à la carte fr £25 ⊕ FREE HOUSE ◀ Guinness, London Pride, Adnams Bitter ♂ Aspalls Draught. ☜ 18 **Facilities** Children's menu Dogs allowed Garden

## SW18

## The Alma Tavern ☜

**499 Old York Rd, Wandsworth SW18 1TF**
☎ **020 8870 2537**
e-mail: alma@youngs.co.uk
dir: *Opposite Wandsworth town rail station*

Just a stone's throw from Wandsworth Town Station, The Alma is a classic example of Victorian pub architecture. The carefully restored building boasts shiny green tiles on its outside walls, and a second floor dome that makes it one of the Old York Road's most distinctive landmarks. Once inside, the buzzing central bar gives way to a large and airy dining room, with rustic tables and open French doors that lead into a secluded dining courtyard. The bar menu features some interesting sandwiches, as well as pub favourites such as burgers, or battered cod and chips. Meanwhile, the main menu offers pan-fried halibut on spring onion rosti with curly kale, and spiced pork tenderloin with roast garlic and apple mash. The pub is an established watering hole for rugby internationals at Twickenham, and has long associations with local rugby teams, too.

**Open** all wk **Bar Meals** food served all day **Restaurant** L served Mon-Fri 12-4, Sat 12-10.30, Sun 12-9.30 D served Mon-Fri 6-10.30, Sat 12-10.30, Sun 12-9.30 ⊕ YOUNG & CO BREWERY PLC ◀ Youngs Bitter, Youngs Special, Youngs Winter Warmer, Youngs guest/seasonal ales. ☜ 15 **Facilities** Children's menu Dogs allowed Garden Parking

## W1

## The Argyll Arms ☜

**18 Argyll St, Oxford Circus W1F 7TP ☎ 020 7734 6117**
dir: *Nearest tube - Oxford Circus*

A tavern has stood on this site since 1740, but the present building is mid-Victorian and is notable for its stunning floral displays. The interior is divided into 'snugs' by wood and etched glass partitions dating from the late 1800s. There's a popular range of sandwiches and the hot food menu might offer vegetarian moussaka, beef and Guinness pie, chicken and leek pie, haddock and lasagne.

**Open** all day all wk 10am-11pm (Fri-Sat 10am-11.30pm) Closed: 25 Dec **Bar Meals** Av main course £6.95 food served all day **Restaurant** food served all day ⊕ FREE HOUSE ◀ Fuller's London Pride, Timothy Taylor Landlord, guest ales ♂ Aspalls, Westons Organic. ☜ 15 **Facilities** Children's menu

## W4

## The Devonshire ⊛ ☜

**126 Devonshire Rd, Chiswick W4 2JJ**
☎ **020 7592 7962** 🖨 **020 7592 1603**
e-mail: reservations@gordonramsay.com
dir: *150yds off Chiswick High Rd. 100yds from Hogarth rdbt & A4*

A laid back gastro-pub located in a leafy district of Chiswick, the Devonshire was formerly known as the Manor Tavern, and is a Gordon Ramsay's Holding. Expect high ceilings, large windows, original fireplaces and the restoration of its unique wood panelling and façade as well as an attractive landscaped garden to the rear of the pub. It serves a mix of modern British and Mediterranean dishes, and changes daily depending on produce available. Start with some rabbit terrine with pear chutney, or warm mushroom and cheddar tart from the bar menu. A typical three courses might comprise swede and honey soup with pressed ham hock, or warm salad of quail and cured pork belly; followed by Gloucester pork sausages with champ and red onion gravy, or pan-fried sea bass with clams in a white bean winter broth; and cranberry and Clementine shortcake to finish. Children can play in the garden, and play materials are available.

**Open** all day 12-11 (Wed-Thu 6-12, Sun 12-10.30) Closed: Mon-Tue **Bar Meals** L served Fri-Sun booking required D served Wed-Sun booking required Av main course £12 food served all day **Restaurant** L served Fri 12-3, Sat 12-4, Sun 12-10.30 booking required D served Fri 6-10.30, Sat 5-10.30, Sun 12-10.30 booking required ⊕ GORDON RAMSAY HOLDINGS LTD ◀ London Pride, Guinness, Caledonian Deuchars IPA, San Miguel, Kronenberg. ☜ 12 **Facilities** Children's menu Dogs allowed Garden

England

## The Pilot ☿

**56 Wellesley Rd W4 4BZ ☎ 020 8994 0828**
e-mail: thepilot@london-gastros.co.uk
dir: *Nearest tube station: Gunnersbury*

A friendly pub and eating house, The Pilot has a simple, understated style with local artwork displayed on the walls. The large rear garden comes into its own during the barbecue season, serving unusual cuts of meat such as alligator and bison as well as traditional beef. Throughout the year, dishes from the daily-changing menu take full advantage of seasonal produce.

**Open** all wk Closed: 25-26 Dec **Bar Meals** L served Mon-Fri 12-3, Sat 12-4, Sun 12-9.30 booking required D served Mon-Fri 6-10, Sat-Sun 6-9.30 booking required Av main course £13.50 **Restaurant** L served Mon-Fri 12-3, Sat 12-4, Sun 12-9.30 booking required D served Mon-Fri 6-10, Sat-Sun 6-9.30 booking required Fixed menu price fr £25 Av 3 course à la carte fr £30 ⊕ FULLERS SMITH AND TURNER ◀ Staropramen, Fuller's London Pride, Guinness, Peroni. ☿ 14 **Facilities** Children's menu Dogs allowed Garden

# MERSEYSIDE

## BARNSTON

## Fox and Hounds ☿

**Barnston Rd CH61 1BW**
☎ 0151 648 7685   🖷 0151 648 0872
e-mail: ralphleech@hotmail.com
dir: *M53 junct 4 take A5137 to Heswell. Right to Barnston on B5138. Pub on A551*

The pub, located in a conservation area, was built in 1911 on the site of an alehouse and barn. Its Edwardian character has been preserved in the pitch pine woodwork and leaded windows. Incredible collections of 1920s/1930s memorabilia include ashtrays, horse brasses, police helmets and empty whisky cases. Real ales and 12 wines by the glass are served alongside a range of bar snacks such as toasted ciabattas, jacket potatoes, sandwiches and meat or seafood platters. Daily specials and desserts are posted on the chalkboard.

**Open** all wk 11-11 (Sun noon-10.30) **Bar Meals** L served Mon-Sat 12-2, Sun 12-2.30 booking required Av main course £6.50 ⊕ FREE HOUSE ◀ Websters Yorkshire Bitter, Theakston's Best & Old Peculier, 3 guest ales. ☿ 12 **Facilities** Children's menu Family room Dogs allowed Garden Parking

## HIGHTOWN

## The Pheasant Inn ☿

**20 Moss Ln L38 3RA ☎ 0151 929 2106**
dir: *Off the A565, on the B5193*

An original brick in the restaurant wall is dated 1719, when the pub was known as the 'Ten Billets Inn'; the present name was adopted in 1952. By the 19th century a small on-site brewery was producing just 2½ barrels a week, but today you'll find Timothy Taylor Landlord alongside Aspall's cider. The menu starts with jacket potatoes and sandwiches with interesting fillings, and typical hot dishes include baked salmon fishcakes with capers, smoked salmon and lemon chive crème fraîche; corned beef hash with free-range eggs; and daily fish special.

**Open** all day all wk noon-11pm (Sun noon-10.30pm) **Bar Meals** Av main course £9.50 food served all day **Restaurant** Fixed menu price fr £9.95 Av 3 course à la carte fr £20 food served all day ⊕ MITCHELLS & BUTLERS ◀ Timothy Taylor Landlord ♂ Aspall Draught & Organic. ☿ 6 **Facilities** Children's menu Dogs allowed Garden Parking

# NORFOLK

## BINHAM

## Chequers Inn

**Front St NR21 0AL ☎ 01328 830297**
e-mail: steve@binhamchequers.co.uk
dir: *On B1388 between Wells-next-the-Sea & Walsingham*

The Chequers is home to the Front Street Brewery, but even though they brew their own beer they still have regular Norfolk/East Anglian guest ales, and a large selection of bottled beers. The pub has been owned by a village charity since the early 1640s, and was originally a trade hall. Many stones from the nearby priory were used in its construction. The daily changing menu offers dishes such as Norfolk duck pâté, fresh lobster thermidor and plum crumble.

**Open** all wk 11.30-2.30 6-11 (Fri-Sat 11.30-2.30 6-11.30 Sun noon-2.30 7-11) **Bar Meals** L served all wk 12-2 D served all wk 6-9 ⊕ FREE HOUSE ◀ Binham Cheer 3.9%, Callums Ale 4.3%, Unity Strong 5%, Seasonal specials, micro brewery on site. **Facilities** Children's menu Garden Parking

## BLAKENEY

# The Kings Arms ♀

**Westgate St NR25 7NQ ☎ 01263 740341**
📄 **01263 740391**
e-mail: kingsarmsnorfolk@btconnect.com
dir: *From Holt or Fakenham take A148, then B1156 for 6m to Blakeney*

This Grade II listed free house is located on the beautiful north Norfolk coast, close to the salt marshes. Owners Marjorie and Howard Davies settled here after long and successful showbiz careers and their son Nic, now handles the day-to-day running of the pub. The Kings Arms is an ideal centre for walking, or perhaps a ferry trip to the nearby seal colony and world-famous bird sanctuaries. Locally-caught fish and seasonal seafood feature on the menu – crab in summer and mussels in winter - together with local game, home-made lasagne and steaks.

Open all day all wk 11-11 Closed: 25 Dec eve **Bar Meals** Av main course £6 ⊕ FREE HOUSE ◀ Greene King Old Speckled Hen, Woodforde's Wherry Best Bitter, Marston's Pedigree, Adnams Best Bitter. ♀ 12 **Facilities** Children's menu Play area Family room Dogs allowed Garden Parking

# White Horse Hotel ♀

**4 High St NR25 7AL ☎ 01263 740574** 📄 **01263 741303**
e-mail: info@blakeneywhitehorse.co.uk
dir: *From A148 (Cromer to King's Lynn road) onto A149 signed to Blakeney*

Blakeney is a cluster of narrow streets lined with flint-built fishermen's cottages winding down to a small tidal harbour, with glorious views over creeks, estuary and salt marsh. Close to the quayside stands the 17th-century White Horse, formerly a coaching inn, built of brick-and-flint and set around the old courtyard and stables. Inside, the bar, dining room and airy conservatory are tastefully decorated in creams and darkwood with soft lamplight, and the informal bar is adorned with local artwork. Fish dominates the menu, with lobster, crab and mussels sourced from local fishermen. It also takes advantage of local produce, including meat and game from nearby Holkham Estate, and fruit, salads and vegetables from small farms and suppliers. Both bread and puddings are made on the premises. At lunch, tuck into Cley Smokehouse prawns with chilli mayonnaise, deep-fried soft herring roes, fish pie, smoked haddock and crayfish kedgeree, or a smoked ham and mustard sandwich. From the evening carte, choose seared scallops with butternut squash purée, crab apple aioli and Parma ham, or pork belly with oriental broth and braised bok choi for a starter, then follow with roast red mullet, Morston mussel, bacon and tomato stew, confit duck leg with Lyonnaise potatoes, Savoy cabbage, chestnuts and bacon, or beer-battered haddock with hand-cut chips and tartare sauce. To finish, try the pumpkin tart with clotted cream, or the cinnamon pannacotta with roast plum coulis and cardamom ice cream.

Open all wk 10.30am-11pm Closed: 25 Dec **Bar Meals** L served all wk 12-2.15 D served Thu-Sun 6-9, Fri-Sat 6-9.30 ⊕ FREE HOUSE ◀ Adnams Bitter, Woodforde's Wherry, Adnams Broadside, Yetmans Ö Aspalls. ♀ 12 **Facilities** Children's menu Family room Garden Parking

## BLICKLING

# The Buckinghamshire Arms ♀

**Blickling Rd NR11 6NF ☎ 01263 732133**
e-mail: bucksarms@tiscali.com
dir: *A410 from Cromer exit at Aylsham onto B1354, follow Blickling Hall signs*

Claimed to be Norfolk's most beautiful inn 'The Bucks' stands by the gates of the National Trust's Blickling Hall. A late 17th-century coaching inn, it is said to be haunted by Anne Boleyn's ghost, who wanders in the adjacent courtyard and charming garden. The lounge bar and restaurant, with their solid furniture and wood-burning stoves, have plenty of appeal, and meals can be taken in either. Dishes from the dinner menu include Norfolk rump steak; Gunton Park venison casserole; and Halvergate lamb loin stuffed with apricot, pine nuts and rosemary with braised lentils and smoked bacon. Alternatives might be gnocchi with spinach, roast peppers and goats' cheese, or poached smoked haddock with turmeric crushed new potatoes.

Open all day all wk 11-11 Closed: 25 Dec **Bar Meals** L served Mon-Fri 12-2, Sat-Sun 12-2.30 booking required D served all wk 7-9 booking required Av main course £9.95 **Restaurant** L served Mon-Fri 12-2, Sat-Sun 12-2.30 booking required D served all wk 7-9 booking required Fixed menu price fr £11.95 ⊕ FREE HOUSE ◀ Adnams Bitter & Regatta, Woodforde's Wherry, Nelson's Revenge, Wolf Coyote Bitter Ö Aspalls, Norfolk. ♀ 7 **Facilities** Children's menu Garden Parking

**England**

## BRANCASTER STAITHE

## The White Horse ★★★ HL ◎◎ ♥

PE31 8BY ☎ 01485 210262 ▤ 01485 210930
e-mail: reception@whitehorsebrancaster.co.uk
dir: *A149 (coast road), midway between Hunstanton & Wells-next-the-Sea*

A popular gastro-pub gloriously situated in an Area of Outstanding Natural Beauty, with panoramic views from its conservatory restaurant and sun-deck over tidal creeks and marshes to Scolt Head Island. If you think these views are wonderful in daylight, then catch them at sunrise and sunset. Scrubbed pine tables and high-backed settles help to create a welcoming atmosphere for diners ready for two AA Rosette-quality food based on fresh local produce. The extensive, daily-changing restaurant menus and specials offer cockles, mussels and oysters, when in season, from the beds at the bottom of the garden; slow-roasted belly of Norfolk pork with caramelised root vegetables and apple compote; confit duck leg with mixed beans and chorizo; pan-fried fillet of sea bass with pancetta, broad beans, peas and baby leeks; and wild mushroom and baby spinach risotto.

Open all day all wk 9am-11pm (Sun 9am-10.30pm) **Bar Meals** Av main course £7 food served all day **Restaurant** L served all wk 12-2 booking required D served all wk 6.30-9 booking required Av 3 course à la carte fr £25 ⊕ FREE HOUSE ◖ Adnams Best Bitter, Fuller's London Pride, Woodforde's Wherry, guest ♂ Aspall. ♥ 17 **Facilities** Children's menu Dogs allowed Garden Parking **Rooms** 15

## BRISLEY

## The Brisley Bell Inn & Restaurant ★★★ INN

The Green NR20 5DW ☎ 01362 668686
e-mail: info@brisleybell-inn.co.uk
dir: *On the B1145, between Fakenham and East Dereham*

Enjoying an isolated position close to the village centre, this attractive, 16th-century warm brick-built pub overlooks the largest piece of common land in Norfolk, some 200 acres. Inside, you'll find a small, refurbished bar area with old beams, large brick fireplace and exposed brick walls, a separate, neatly laid-up dining room, and a wide-ranging menu that takes in bar snacks, stir-fries, steaks, daily fish specials, and popular Sunday roast lunches.

Open noon-3 6-11 (Sat 11-11 Sun noon-10.30) Closed: Mon **Bar Meals** L served Tue-Sun 12-2.30 D served Tue-Thu & Sun 6-8, Fri-Sat 6-9 Av main course £5.95 **Restaurant** L served Tue-Sun 12-2.30 D served Tue-Thu & Sun 6-8, Fri-Sat 6-9 booking required Fixed menu price fr £8.25 **Facilities** Children's menu Dogs allowed Garden Parking **Rooms** 3

## EATON

## The Red Lion ♥

50 Eaton St NR4 7LD ☎ 01603 454787 ▤ 01603 456939
e-mail: redlioneaton@hotmail.co.uk
dir: *Off A11, 2m S of Norwich city centre*

This heavily-beamed 17th-century coaching inn has bags of character, thanks to its Dutch gables, panelled walls and inglenook fireplaces. The covered terrace enables customers to enjoy one of the real ales or sample the extensive wine list outside during the summer months. The extensive lunch menu offers everything from steak and kidney suet pudding to grilled red snapper fillets with mango and sweet chilli salsa; or Swannington baked gammon with a Cumberland sauce.

Open all day all wk **Bar Meals** L served all wk 12-2.15 booking required D served all wk 6.30-9 booking required **Restaurant** L served all wk 12-2.15 booking required D served all wk 6.30-9 booking required ⊕ ENTERPRISE INNS ◖ Old Speckled Hen, Courage Directors, Greene King IPA, Adnams Bitter, Woodforde's Wherry, Fuller's London Pride. ♥ 10 **Facilities** Children's menu Garden Parking

## GREAT RYBURGH

## The Blue Boar Inn

NR21 0DX ☎ 01328 829212
dir: *Off A1067 4m S of Fakenham*

Dating back to 1683, this whitewashed free house stands opposite the round towered Saxon church of St Andrew. A large magnolia tree ushers you into the rambling old building with its beams and inglenook fireplace. Local produce features strongly on the extensive chalkboard menu. Typical dishes include breast of Norfolk chicken with prawn thermidor; Ryburgh lamb cutlets with mustard mash; and steamed Brancaster mussels when in season.

Open 11.30-2.30 6.30-11.30 Closed: Tue **Bar Meals** L served Wed-Mon 11.30-2.30 D served Wed-Mon 6.30-10.30 Av main course £10 **Restaurant** L served Wed-Mon 11.30-2.30 D served Wed-Mon 6.30-10.30 ⊕ FREE HOUSE ◖ Adnams Bitter, Bass, Murphy's. **Facilities** Children's menu Play area Family room Garden Parking

## HAPPISBURGH

## The Hill House ♥

NR12 0PW ☎ 01692 650004 ▤ 01692 650004
dir: *5m from Stalham, 8m from North Walsham*

Expect to be corrected if you pronounce Happisburgh the way it's spelt - it's Haze-borough. Once the favourite haunt of the creator of Sherlock Holmes, Sir Arthur Conan Doyle, this Grade II listed, 16th-century coaching inn offers good value bar food including sandwiches, jacket potatoes, a range of ploughman's and local crab and fish dishes in season. The restaurant menu includes a wide selection of fish and seafood, steaks and other meat dishes, as well as a vegetarian selection.

Open all wk noon-11.30 (Mon-Wed noon-3 7-11.30 low season) **Bar Meals** L served all wk 12-2.30 D served Mon-Sat 7-9.30, Sun 7-9 booking required **Restaurant** L served all wk 12-2.30 D served Mon-Sat 7-9.30, Sun 7-9 booking required ⊕ FREE HOUSE ◖ Shepherd Neame Spitfire, Buffy's, Woodforde's Wherry, Adnams Bitter, House Bitter Ŏ Aspall, Westons Stowford Press. ♈10 **Facilities** Children's menu Play area Dogs allowed Garden Parking

## HEVINGHAM

# Marsham Arms
# Freehouse ᴀ ★★★★ INN ♈

**Holt Rd NR10 5NP ☎ 01603 754268**
e-mail: nigelbradley@marshamarms.co.uk
web: www.marshamarms.co.uk
dir: *On B1149 N of Norwich airport, 2m through Horsford towards Holt*

Built as a roadside hostel for poor farm labourers by Victorian philanthropist and landowner Robert Marsham. Some original features remain, including the large open fireplace, and there's a spacious garden with paved patio and a dedicated family room. A good range of fresh fish dishes includes cod, haddock, sea bass, herrings and crab. Specialities such as beef stew with dumplings and beer battered haddock are backed by a daily blackboard. There are vegetarian and gluten-free dishes too. Look out for the monthly jazz nights and wine tasting evenings.

Open all wk **Bar Meals** L served all wk 12-2.30 D served all wk 6-9.30 **Restaurant** L served all wk 12-2.30 D served all wk 6-9.30 ⊕ FREE HOUSE ◖ Adnams Best, Woodforde's Wherry Best Bitter, Mauldens, Worthington, Broadside Ŏ Aspall. ♈6 **Facilities** Children's menu Play area Family room Dogs allowed Garden Parking **Rooms** 11

## HEYDON

# Earle Arms ♈

**The Street NR11 6AD ☎ 01263 587376**
e-mail: haitchy@aol.com
dir: *Signed between Cawston & Corpusty on B1149 (Holt to Norwich road)*

Heydon is one of only 13 privately owned villages in the country and is often used as a film location. It dates from the 16th century, and inside are log fires, attractive wallpapers, prints and a collection of bric-a-brac. One of the two rooms offers service through a hatch, and there are tables outside in the pretty back garden. Locally reared meat goes into dishes

like braised lamb shank or fillet of beef marchand de vin. Fish choices include plaice goujons, crayfish omelette, and sea bass fillet with lemon butter.

Open Closed: Mon **Bar Meals** L served Tue-Sun 12-2 booking required D served Tue-Sun 7-9 booking required **Restaurant** L served Tue-Sun 12-2 booking required D served Tue-Sun 7-9 booking required ⊕ FREE HOUSE ◖ Adnams, Woodforde's Wherry. ♈8 **Facilities** Children's menu Dogs allowed Garden Parking

## HORSEY

# Nelson Head

**The Street NR29 4AD ☎ 01493 393378**
dir: *On B1159 (coast road) between West Somerton & Sea Palling*

Located on a National Trust estate, which embraces nearby Horsey Mere, this 17th-century inn will, to many, epitomise the perfect country pub. It enjoys the tranquillity of a particularly unspoilt part of the Norfolk coast - indeed, the Broads are ½ mile away and glorious beaches only a mile - and the sheltered gardens look out towards the dunes and water meadows. Haddock and chips, cottage pie, and a selection of vegetarian choices are among the dishes available.

Open all day all wk 11-11 **Bar Meals** L served all wk 12-2.30 D served all wk 6-8.30 **Restaurant** L served all wk 12-2.30 D served all wk 6-8.30 ⊕ FREE HOUSE ◖ Woodforde's Wherry, Nelson's Revenge. **Facilities** Children's menu Play area Family room Dogs allowed Garden Parking

## HUNSTANTON

# The King William IV ᴀ ★★★★ INN ♈

**Heacham Rd, Sedgeford PE36 5LU ☎ 01485 571765**
📠 **01485 571743**
e-mail: info@thekingwilliamsedgeford.co.uk
dir: *From A149 turn right at traffic lights in Heacham onto B1454. Pub 2m in village*

Despite being extensively refurbished and extended, The King William retains its traditional appeal. It is tucked away in the village of Sedgeford, conveniently close to the north Norfolk coastline. An ale house since 1836, it has winter log fires and a covered alfresco dining area for warmer months. A choice of light meals includes salads and pasta, while a longer visit might take in smoked salmon with lemon and dill dressing followed by duck breast in red wine and berry sauce.

Open all day 11-11 (Sun 12-10.30) Closed: Mon L (ex BH) **Bar Meals** L served Tue-Sat 12-2, Sun 12-2.30 booking required D served all wk 6.30-9 booking required Av main course £9.95 **Restaurant** L served Tue-Sat 12-2, Sun 12-2.30 booking required D served all wk 6.30-9 booking required Fixed menu price fr £18.95 Av 3 course à la carte fr £20 ⊕ FREE HOUSE ◖ Woodforde's Wherry, Adnams Bitter, Guinness, Greene King Abbot Ale, guest ale. ♈9 **Facilities** Children's menu Dogs allowed Garden Parking **Rooms** 9

## ITTERINGHAM

### Walpole Arms ◉ ♀

**NR11 7AR ☎ 01263 587258** 📄 **01263 587074**
e-mail: goodfood@thewalpolearms.co.uk
web: www.thewalpolearms.co.uk
dir: *From Aylsham towards Blickling. After Blickling Hall take 1st right to Itteringham*

The Walpole Arms has been a pub since 1836, although the oak-beamed bar suggests it building could be older. What is known for certain is that Robert Horace Walpole, a direct descendant of Britain's first prime minister, once owned it. Today, both restaurant and bar offer a daily changing three-course carte; children are welcome and have their own menu to choose from. Bar snacks comprise the likes of pizzetta Margherita, with tomato, mozzarella, olives and basil; and chicken and ham pie with hand-cut chips. For those with a hearty appetite, the carte will not disappoint. Typical starters include escabèche of red mullet with pine nuts, sultanas and butter beans; and chilled soup of yogurt, cucumber, mint, almonds and olive oil with cumin flat bread. Main course choices are equally well considered: Morston mussels steamed in cider, with onions, thyme and served with frites; and home-made Catalonian pork sausage with black-eyed beans and spring cabbage. Desserts are traditional and modern at the same time: a saffron-poached pear with orange flower rice pudding and toasted seeds gives an indication of the kitchen's approach. Extensive gardens to the front and rear of the vine-covered terrace encourage relaxation on summer days.

**Open** all wk noon-3 6-11 (Sun noon-5) Closed: 25 Dec **Bar Meals** L served all wk 12-2 D served all wk 6-9.30 Av main course £11.12 **Restaurant** L served Thu-Sun 12-2 D served Thu-Sun 6-9.30 Av 3 course à la carte fr £25.50 ⊕ NOBLE ROT ASSOCIATES LTD ◀ Adnams Broadside & Bitter, Woodforde's Wherry Best Bitter, Walpole. ♀ 12 **Facilities** Children's menu Play area Dogs allowed Garden Parking

## LARLING

### Angel Inn ♀

**NR16 2QU ☎ 01953 717963** 📄 **01953 718561**
dir: *5m from Attleborough, 8m from Thetford. 1m from station*

Three generations of the Stammers family have been running this 17th-century free house for more than 80 years. The present generation is passionate about real ale, and Adnams Bitter is always supported by at least four guest ales from

both Norfolk and elsewhere. There's a homely, local feel to the heavily-beamed public bar, whilst the lounge bar has wheel-back chairs, an oak settle, cosy log fire and a collection of over 100 water jugs. The cooking is underpinned by local ingredients wherever possible, and the light bites menu supplements sandwiches and jacket potatoes with ham, eggs and chips; and sausages in French bread. Main menu options start with home-made pâté; and deep-fried Camembert; moving on to choices like lamb chops with mint sauce; grilled local trout; and pork in peppered cream sauce. The pub also offers camping in Angel meadow just across the road, and an annual beer festival in August.

**Open** all day all wk 10am-mdnt **Bar Meals** L served Sun-Thu 12-9.30, Fri-Sat 12-10 D served Sun-Thu 12-9.30, Fri-Sat 12-10 Av main course £9.95 food served all day **Restaurant** L served Sun-Thu 12-9.30, Fri-Sat 12-10 D served Sun-Thu 12-9.30, Fri-Sat 12-10 food served all day ⊕ FREE HOUSE ◀ Adnams Bitter, Wolf Bitter, Caledonian Deuchars IPA, Timothy Taylor Landlord, Mauldons ♂ Aspall. ♀ 10 **Facilities** Children's menu Play area Garden Parking

## LITTLE WALSINGHAM

### The Black Lion Hotel ♀

**Friday Market Place NR22 6DB ☎ 01328 820235** 📄 **01328 821407**
e-mail: lionwalsingham@btconnect.com
dir: *From King's Lynn take A148 & B1105. Or from Norwich take A1067 & B1105*

Parts of this former coaching inn date from 1310, when they were built to accommodate Edward III on his numerous pilgrimages to the shrine at Walsingham (the hotel's name comes from his wife's coat of arms). The friendly bar has is warmed by a fire in winter. The menu offers something for every taste: light options include soup and filled baps, while a full meal could feature goats' cheese melt, followed by mixed grill, and hot crumble or pie of the day.

**Open** all wk noon-3 6-mdnt (Sat noon-mdnt) **Bar Meals** L served all wk 12-2 D served all wk 7-9 Av main course £6 **Restaurant** L served all wk 12-2 D served all wk 7-9 booking required Av 3 course à la carte fr £15 ⊕ ENTERPRISE INNS ◀ Woodforde's Wherry, Blacksheep Special, Woodforde's Nelson's Revenge, Tetley's. ♀ 8 **Facilities** Children's menu Dogs allowed Garden

## NORWICH

### The Mad Moose Arms ◉◉ ♀

**2 Warwick St NR2 3LB ☎ 01603 627687** 📄 **01508 494946**
e-mail: madmoose@animalinns.co.uk
web: www.themadmoose.co.uk
dir: *1m from A11*

A warm neighbourhood pub, the result of a stunning refit that created a decidedly stylish ground floor bar, all vibrant red walls, exposed brickwork and gleaming wood. The bar menu offers roast aubergine, coriander crust, spiced fruits and couscous; Caesar salad with chicken; seared salmon, niçoise salad and fresh herb oil; aromatic duck with noodles, ginger star anise, coconut and spring onions; green Thai curry with a choice of chicken, prawn or vegetable; and beefburger and chips. On the first floor is the elegant 1Up restaurant with chandeliers, sea-green drapes, and a feature wall depicting a fairytale forest. Confident and ambitious cooking is typified by starters of gravadlax of salmon, sweet pickled cucumber, baby capers and mustard dressing; balsamic cured beetroot, creamed goats' cheese, black olive and thyme biscotti; and truffled girolles with roast confit garlic, brioche toast, chicory and tarragon emulsion. To follow: pan-fried cod, braised Puy lentils, truffled savoy cabbage, seared scallops, red onion confit and crisp Parma ham; roast breast of Norfolk pheasant, herby gnocchi, braised red cabbage, confit salsify, baby onions and red wine sauce; pan-fried black bream, crushed new potatoes, warm confit fennel, crisp leeks, chorizo sausage and saffron butter sauce; and rump of English lamb, creamed white beans, Jerusalem artichokes, confit garlic wilted baby spinach and truffled herb jus. Among the desserts consider warm lemon polenta cake, fresh orange sorbet, orange syrup and candied zest; or caramelised banana tart Tatin, star anise ice-cream and caraway biscuit. There is a stylish outdoor patio for alfresco dining in warmer weather.

Open all day all wk noon-mdnt Closed: 25 Dec Bar Meals L served Mon-Fri 12-2, Sat-Sun 12-9 D served Mon-Fri 6-10, Sat-Sun 12-9 Av main course £7.50 Restaurant L served Sun 12-3 booking required D served Mon-Sat 7-9.30 booking required Av 3 course à la carte fr £25 ⊕ FREE HOUSE ◾ Woodforde's Wherry, Straw Dog. ♟ 9 Facilities Children's menu Garden

## Ribs of Beef ♟

### 24 Wensum St NR3 1HY ☎ 01603 619517
### ◫ 01603 625446
e-mail: roger@cawdron.co.uk
dir: *From Tombland (in front of cathedral) turn left at Maids Head Hotel. Pub 200yds on right on bridge*

Once used by the Norfolk wherry skippers, this welcoming riverside pub is still popular among boat owners cruising the Broads. Its structure incorporates remnants of the original 14th-century building, which was destroyed in the Great Fire in 1507. The pub is famous for its range of cask ales, excellent wines and traditional English food using locally sourced produce. The menu offers a wide range of sandwiches, burgers and jacket potatoes, while larger appetites should be satisfied with dishes such as Adnams' braised brisket of beef or vegetarian lasagne.

Open all day all wk 11-11 (Fri-Sat 11am-1am) Bar Meals L served Mon-Fri 12-2.30, Sat-Sun 12-5 Av main course £5.95 ⊕ FREE HOUSE ◾ Woodforde's Wherry, Adnams Bitter, Adnams Broadside, Marston's Pedigree, Elgoods Mild. ♟ 8 Facilities Children's menu Family room

---

### RINGSTEAD

## The Gin Trap Inn ★★★★ INN ◉ ♟
### 6 High St PE36 5JU ☎ 01485 525264
e-mail: thegintrap@hotmail.co.uk  web: www.gintrapinn.co.uk
dir: *A149 from King's Lynn towards Hunstanton. In 15m turn right at Heacham for Ringstead*

The 17th-century, white-painted pub stands on the famous Peddars Way, just a few miles from Hunstanton and the North Norfolk coast. From the early 70s until a re-fit just a few years ago, the pub was festooned with old gin traps and farm implements. A few gin traps remain over the front door and incorporated into light fittings in the oak beamed-bar area. The pub has a relaxed and friendly atmosphere with a blazing log burner warming the bar throughout the winter, a cosy dining room and modern conservatory, and a pretty garden for summer drinking and dining. The snacks board includes local mussels in season and a selection of hand-cut sandwiches including some based on speciality breads, such as ciabatta and focaccia. The menu is available throughout and makes good use of local seasonal produce, from organic meats reared at Courtyard Farm in the village, and mussels and oyster delivered from nearby Thornham. Typically, start with six Thornham oysters, served on ice with shallot and red wine vinegar dressing, or chicken, apricot and sage terrine with home-made piccalilli and home-baked bread, then move on to mustard-glazed ham with free-range eggs and bubble-and-squeak; dolcelatte and potato ravioli with fresh sage and white truffle oil; or confit Courtyard Farm organic saddleback pork belly with creamed leeks and wholegrain mustard velouté. Desserts range from crème caramel with poached fruits and mixed berries to warm chocolate pudding with home-made vanilla ice cream. Walkers and dogs are very welcome.

Open all day all wk 11.30am-mdnt (11.30-2.30 6-11 in winter) Bar Meals L served Mon-Fri 12-2, Sat-Sun 12-2.30 D served Sun-Thu 6-9, Fri-Sat 6-9.30 Av main course £10.50 Restaurant L served Mon-Fri 12-2, Sat-Sun 12-2.30 D served Sun-Thu 6-9, Fri-Sat 6-9.30 Av 3 course à la carte fr £20 ⊕ FREE HOUSE ◾ Adnams Best, Woodforde's Wherry, guest ales ♂ Aspall. ♟ 8 Facilities Children's menu Dogs allowed Garden Parking Rooms 3

## STOW BARDOLPH

### The Hare Arms ♈

**PE34 3HT ☎ 01366 382229** 📄 **01366 385522**
e-mail: trishmc@harearms222.wanadoo.co.uk
dir: *From King's Lynn take A10 to Downham Market. After 9m village signed on left*

Trish and David McManus have been licensees at this attractive ivy-clad pub for over 30 years. The pub was built during the Napoleonic wars and takes its name from the surrounding estate, ancestral home of the Hare family since 1553. The Hare has preserved its appeal and become deservedly popular. The L-shaped bar and adjoining conservatory are packed with decades-worth of fascinating bygones; the cat warms itself by the fire and peacocks wander around outside. An extensive menu of regular pub food is supplemented by daily specials, including the award-winning steak and peppercorn pie, and fish dishes like whole sea bream with lemon and lime butter. The silver service restaurant offers an à la carte menu Monday to Saturday evening with a range of steaks, vegetarian options and dishes such as slow-cooked lamb shank; Gressingham duck in caramelised orange sauce, and monkfish medallions with red pepper risotto.

**Open** all wk 11-2.30 6-11 (Sun noon-10.30) Closed: 25-26 Dec **Bar Meals** L served Mon-Sat 12-2, Sun 12-10 D served Mon-Sat 6.30-10, Sun 12-10 Av main course £10 **Restaurant** D served Mon-Sat 7-9 booking required Av 3 course à la carte fr £27 ⊕ GREENE KING ◀ Greene King Abbot Ale, IPA & Old Speckled Hen, guest ale. ♈ 7 **Facilities** Children's menu Play area Family room Garden Parking

## SWANTON MORLEY

### Darbys Freehouse

**1&2 Elsing Rd NR20 4NY ☎ 01362 637647**
📄 **01362 637928**
e-mail: louisedarby@hotmail.co.uk
dir: *From A47 (Norwich to King's Lynn) take B1147 to Dereham*

Built in the 1700s as a large country house, then divided into cottages in the late 19th century. In 1987, after the village's last traditional pub closed, it was converted into the pub you see today, while retaining its old beams and inglenooks. Traditional pub food includes steak and mushroom pudding, braised lamb shank, chargrilled pork loin, scampi, beer-battered haddock, steaks, curries and a vegetarian selection. Children have their own menu and a play area.

**Open** all wk 11.30-3 6-11 (Sat 11.30-11, Sun 12-10.30). Food served all day Sat-Sun ⊕ FREE HOUSE ◀ Woodforde's Wherry, Adnams Broadside & Best, 2 guest ales. **Facilities** Children's menu Play area Family room Dogs allowed Garden Parking

## THORNHAM

### Lifeboat Inn ★★ HL ◉ ♈

**Ship Ln PE36 6LT ☎ 01485 512236** 📄 **01485 512323**
e-mail: reception@lifeboatinn.co.uk
dir: *A149 from Hunstanton for approx 6m. 1st left after Thornham sign*

The Lifeboat is a 16th-century inn overlooking Thornham Harbour and the salt marshes. Despite being extended, its original character has been retained. Inside, the warm glow of paraffin lamps enhances the welcoming atmosphere, while the adjoining conservatory is renowned for its ancient vine and adjacent walled patio garden. The best available fish and game feature on the frequently changing menus, in the form of salmon and dill fishcakes with a sun dried tomato and pesto sauce, or Brancaster mussels steamed in Chardonnay with lemon grass, ginger and cream. For a satisfying main course, try lightly bread-crumbed lamb cutlets with ratatouille and a minted garlic gravy, or local partridge casserole with Guinness and mushrooms.

**Open** all wk **Bar Meals** food served all day ⊕ FREE HOUSE ◀ Adnams, Woodforde's Wherry, Greene King IPA & Abbot Ale, guest ales. ♈ 10 **Facilities** Children's menu Play area Family room Dogs allowed Garden Parking **Rooms** 13

## WARHAM ALL SAINTS

### Three Horseshoes

**NR23 1NL ☎ 01328 710547**
dir: *From Wells A149 to Cromer, then right onto B1105 to Warham*

This gem of a pub first opened its doors in 1725. Inside you'll find a gas-lit main bar, stone floors, scrubbed wooden tables and a grandfather clock in the corner. Ales are served directly from the cask through a hole in the bar wall, and the largely original interior includes a curious green and red dial in the ceiling - Norfolk twister, an ancient pub game. Vintage posters, clay pipes, photographs and memorabilia adorn the walls, while down a step are old one-arm bandits. The pub is well known for its home cooking, with local game and shellfish; steak, kidney and Wherry bitter pie; Norfolk chicken and leek suet pudding; and woodman's pie (mushrooms and nuts in red wine sauce). Home-made puddings, such as spotted dick and syrup sponge, are listed over the fire in the main bar.

**Open** all wk **Bar Meals** L served all wk 12-1.45 D served all wk 6-8.30 Av main course £7.80 ⊕ FREE HOUSE ◀ Greene King IPA, Woodforde's Wherry. **Facilities** Children's menu Family room Dogs allowed Garden Parking ◉

## WELLS-NEXT-THE-SEA

# The Crown ◉ ♦

**The Buttlands NR23 1EX ☎ 01328 710209**
📠 01328 711432
e-mail: reception@thecrownhotelwells.co.uk
dir: *10m from Fakenham on B1105*

Striking contemporary decor and furnishings blend effortlessly with the old-world charm of this 17th-century former coaching inn. The hotel overlooks a tree-lined green near the heart of the town, and has been refurbished to create a traditional atmosphere of uncluttered comfort. Beneath the bar's ancient beams, East Anglian ales and Aspall's Suffolk cyder accompany an informal menu. Lunchtime sandwiches might include smoked salmon, cream cheese and cucumber, or why not try the Crown black slate – a sampler of European and Asian appetizers served on a slate tile, whilst main course dishes such as seared liver and bacon with roast root vegetables, or butternut squash, Parmesan and sage risotto are also available in the evening. Meanwhile, dinner in the restaurant might begin with seared pigeon breast, mushroom and crouton salad, before a main course of baked salmon with tiger prawn, tomato and lemongrass brochette. Meals are also served in the warm and cheerful Orangery or outside with its great views.

Open all wk **Bar Meals** L served all wk 12-2.30 D served all wk 6.30-9.30 **Restaurant** D served all wk 7-9 booking required Av 3 course à la carte fr £34.95 ⊕ FREE HOUSE ◀ Adnams Bitter, Woodforde's Wherry, guest ale ♂ Aspall. ♟ 14 **Facilities** Children's menu Dogs allowed Garden Parking

## WINTERTON-ON-SEA

# Fishermans Return ♦

**The Lane NR29 4BN ☎ 01493 393305**
e-mail: fishermansreturn@yahoo.co.uk
web: www.fishermans-return.com
dir: *8m N of Great Yarmouth on B1159*

Long beaches and National Trust land are within 300 metres of this 350-year-old brick and flint pub – and it's dog-friendly too, making it an ideal spot to finish a walk. Behind the bar are Woodforde's Wherry and Adnams, with seasonal guests from Mauldons and Blackfriars. Menus include popular favourites, from toasted sandwiches to cottage pie. But look to the daily changing blackboard for fish and seafood specials, when freshly caught sea bass and mackerel may be on offer.

Open all wk **Bar Meals** L served all wk 12-2.30 D served all wk 6-9 Av main course £8 **Restaurant** L served all wk 12-2.30 D served all wk 6-9 ⊕ FREE HOUSE ◀ Woodforde's Wherry, Adnams Bitter & Broadside, John Smith's ♂ Westons Stowford Press, Old Rosie Scrumpy. ♟ 10 **Facilities** Children's menu Play area Family room Dogs allowed Garden Parking

## BULWICK

# The Queen's Head ♦

**Main St NN17 3DY ☎ 01780 450272**
e-mail: queenshead-bulwick@tiscali.co.uk
dir: *Just off A43, between Corby & Stamford*

Parts of this quintessential English free house date back to 1400, and the building is thought to have been a pub since the 17th century. The name comes from the Portuguese wife of Charles II, Katherine of Braganza, who was well known for her very elaborate hair-styles. Overlooking the village church, the pub is a warren of small rooms with exposed wooden beams, four open fireplaces and flagstone floors. Local shoots supply seasonal game such as teal, woodcock and partridge, and the other ingredients often include village-grown fruit and vegetables brought in by customers and friends. Lunchtime brings great sandwich choices and interesting snacks such as smoked Scottish salmon with shaved fennel, rocket, lemon and capers; and baked goat's cheese with garlic and roasted peppers. The evening menu opens with the likes of winter bean and vegetable soup with bread and olive oil; and home-cured salt beef with vine tomato and beetroot relish. Main course options might include slow-cooked Cornish lamb with root vegetables, pearl barley and herb suet dumpling; celeriac and porcini mushroom risotto with sage and gorgonzola; or pan-fried Scottish salmon with Portland crab and potato chowder. Typical desserts include dark chocolate terrine with toasted hazelnuts, caramel sauce and crème fraiche; or warm apple and caramel tart with clotted Devonshire cream.

Open Closed: Mon **Bar Meals** L served Tue-Sun 12-2.30 booking required D served Tue-Sat 6-9.30 booking required **Restaurant** L served Tue-Sun 12-2.30 booking required D served Tue-Sat 6-9.30 booking required Fixed menu price fr £12.50 ⊕ FREE HOUSE ◀ Shepherd Neame, Spitfire, Elland, Rockingham Ales, Newby Wyke, Guest Ales. ♟ 9 **Facilities** Children's menu Dogs allowed Garden Parking

**England**

## FARTHINGSTONE

### The Kings Arms

**Main St NN12 8EZ** ☎ **01327 361604** 📠 **01327 361604**

e-mail: paul@kingsarms.fsbusiness.co.uk

dir: *M1 junct 16, A45 towards Daventry. At Weedon take A5 towards Towcester. Right signed Farthingstone*

Tucked away in perfect walking country near Canons Ashby (a National Trust property), this 18th-century Grade II listed inn is every inch the traditional country pub - albeit it a highly distinctive one. On fine days many come for the beautiful garden; in colder weather they warm themselves by the real fires, but there is always a warm welcome. The pub has a retail business specialising in Cornish fish, which is reflected on the short menu, available at weekend lunchtimes. British cheese and Loch Fyne fish platters are also available.

Open 7-11.30 (Sat-Sun 12-3.30 7-11.30) Closed: Mon **Bar Meals** L served Sat-Sun 12-2 Av main course £8.75 ⊕ FREE HOUSE 🍺 Thwaites Original, Adnams, Brakspear Bitter, Young's Bitter, Hoggleys Northamptonshire Bitter ♉ Westons Old Rosie Scrumpy. **Facilities** Children's menu Family room Dogs allowed Garden Parking

## OUNDLE

### The Chequered Skipper

**Ashton PE8 5LD** ☎ **01832 273494**

e-mail: enquiries@chequeredskipper.co.uk

dir: *A605 towards Dundle, at rdbt follow signs to Ashton. 1m turn left into Ashton, pub in village*

At the heart of the Rothschild's glorious model village, all stone and thatch cottages nestling around the village green, the thatched, open-plan pub has a contemporary feel, with stone and oak flooring and an unusual flagstone bar top. Using the best of local produce with suppliers listed on the menu, beer-battered haddock and home-made stone-baked pizzas are available in the bar, while the restaurant menu might include slow braised belly of pork in Aspall's cider with demerara-glazed beetroot.

Open all wk 11.30-3 6-11 (Sat 11.30-11 Sun 11.45-11) **Bar Meals** L served Mon-Fri 12-2, Sat 12-2.30, Sun 12-3 Av main course £8 **Restaurant** L served Mon-Fri 12-2, Sat 12-2.30, Sun 12-3 Av 3 course à la carte fr £25 🍺 Rockingham Ale, Oakham Ale. **Facilities** Children's menu Dogs allowed Garden Parking

## SIBBERTOFT

### The Red Lion 🍷

**43 Welland Rise LE16 9UD** ☎ **01858 880011**

e-mail: andrew@redlionwinepub.co.uk

dir: *From Market Harborough take A4304, through Lubenham, left through Marston Trussell to Sibbertoft*

Wine is the special passion of owner Andrew Banks at this friendly 300-year-old free house. Over 200 bins are included on the ever-growing wine list, with many varieties available by the glass. Near the Naseby battle sites, the pub offers an appealing blend of contemporary and classic decor, with oak beams, leather upholstery and a smartly turned-out dining room. In fine weather, meals are served in the quiet garden, which is a favourite with local walkers and cyclists; there's also an outdoor play area for children. The same monthly-changing menu is served throughout, and features local and seasonal produce wherever possible. Choices might begin with crab and prawn fishcake with lime and sweet chilli dip, whilst typical main course options include pork T-bone with mash and stilton sauce; and roasted vegetables with melting mozzarella. Round off, perhaps, with meringue and mixed berry fool. Regular themed evenings include a weekly curry night.

Open 12-2 6.30-11 Closed: Mon & Tue lunch, Sun eve **Bar Meals** L served Wed-Sun 12-2 booking required D served Mon-Sat 6.30-9.30 booking required Av main course £10 **Restaurant** L served Wed-Sun 12-2 booking required D served Mon-Sat 6.30-9.30 booking required Fixed menu price fr £14.95 Av 3 course à la carte fr £19 ⊕ FREE HOUSE 🍺 Adnams, Timothy Taylor Landlord, Black Sheep. 🍷 20 **Facilities** Children's menu Play area Garden Parking

## STOKE BRUERNE

### The Boat Inn

**NN12 7SB** ☎ **01604 862428** 📠 **01604 864314**

e-mail: info@boatinn.co.uk

web: www.boatinn.co.uk

dir: *In village centre, just off A508 or A5*

Just across the lock from a popular canal museum, this free house has been run by the same family since 1877. Beneath its thatched roof you'll find cosy bars, open fires and flagstone floors, as well as a skittle alley. Trips on the pub's narrowboat can be arranged. Home-made soups, sandwiches, jackets, salads and baguettes support more substantial meals such as pan-fried sea bream, supreme of chicken or Gressingham duck breast with apricot and bacon stuffing.

Open all day all wk 9.30am-11pm (Sun 9.30am-10.30pm) **Bar Meals** L served all wk 9.30-2.30 (all day Mar-Oct) D served all wk 6-9 (all day Mar-Oct) Av main course £8 **Restaurant** L served Tue-Sun 12-2 booking required D served all wk 7-9 booking required Fixed menu price fr £10 Av 3 course à la carte fr £15 ⊕ FREE HOUSE 🍺 Banks Bitter, Marstons Pedigree, Frog Island Best, Marstons Old Empire, Wychwood Hobgoblin ♉ Thatcher's Traditional. **Facilities** Children's menu Dogs allowed Garden Parking

## WADENHOE

### The King's Head ♥

**Church St PE8 5ST ☎ 01832 720024**
e-mail: info@kingsheadwadenhoe.co.uk
dir: *From A605, 3m from Wadenhoe rdbt. 2m from Oundle*

A haven for travellers since the 17th century, The King's Head is a stone-built, partially thatched inn situated at the end of a quiet country lane. Extensive gardens overlook the tranquil River Nene, and customers can sit and watch the boats pass by as they enjoy a pint of King's Head Bitter. The warm, welcoming interior has quarry-tiled and bare-boarded floors, heavy oak-beamed ceilings, pine furniture and open log fires. Indeed, the pub has lost none of its old world charm but with all the modern facilities. Here, you can challenge the locals to a game of Northamptonshire skittles - if you dare. The menu offers lunchtime sandwiches and panini, and hearty hot dishes such as beer-battered haddock with garden peas, home-made tartare sauce and hand-cut chips, or roast partridge wrapped in bacon and stuffed with apricots and sage. Vegetables and herbs come from the inn's own garden, and other local sources supply most of the remaining produce.

**Open** all day 11-11 (Sun 12-10, winter 11-2.30 5.30-11 Sun 12-6) Closed: Sun eve in winter **Bar Meals** Av main course £6.50 food served all day **Restaurant** Fixed menu price fr £10 Av 3 course à la carte fr £25 food served all day ⊕ FREE HOUSE ◀ Kings Head Bitter, Barnwell Bitter, JHB, Black Sheep, Fuller's London Pride ♂ Westons Stowford Press. ♥ 18 **Facilities** Children's menu Dogs allowed Garden Parking

## WOODNEWTON

### The White Swan ♥

**22 Main St PE8 5EB ☎ 01780 470944**
dir: *5m off A605/A47*

The pub, which dates from the 1600s, is a stone-built, Grade II listed building set in the middle of an idyllic English village. It has recently been re-opened following major refurbishment and has wasted no time in establishing a reputation for its good modern British food, beers and wines. Entertainment is provided in the form of traditional pub games, such as dominoes and shove ha'penny, and speciality evenings are held throughout the year, including game suppers and wine dinners.

**Open** 11-2.30 6-11 (Sat 11-3 6-11, Sun 12-5) Closed: Sun eve, Mon **Bar Meals** L served Tue-Sat 12-2, Sun 12-2.30 D served Tue-Thu 6-9, Fri-Sat 6-9.30 Av main course £8.50 **Restaurant** Fixed menu price fr £12 Av 3 course à la carte fr £23 ⊕ FREE HOUSE ◀ Adnams, Timothy Taylor Landlord, Bass, Guinness, Greene King IPA, Woodforde's Wherry ♂ Aspall. ♥ 10 **Facilities** Children's menu Garden Parking

## BELFORD

### Blue Bell Hotel ★★★ HL

**Market Place NE70 7NE ☎ 01668 213543**
🖷 01668 213787
e-mail: enquiries@bluebellhotel.com
dir: *Off A1, 15m N of Alnwick , 15m S of Berwick-upon-Tweed*

A mix of old-world charm and modern comforts at this 17th-century coaching inn, with spectacular views across the gardens to Belford church. The menu takes its cue from the best country kitchens, and choices might include mussels in Lindisfarne mead broth; Eyemouth fish pie; slow roasted lamb Henry with creamed potatoes and vegetables; or tempura vegetables with rice and sweet chilli dip.

**Open** all day all wk 11am-mdnt **Bar Meals** L served all wk 12-3 D served all wk 5-9 Av main course £8.95 **Restaurant** L served Sun 12-3 booking required D served all wk 6-9 booking required Fixed menu price fr £21 Av 3 course à la carte fr £40 ⊕ FREE HOUSE ◀ Calders, Tetleys Smooth, Black Sheep, Timothy Taylor Landlord. **Facilities** Children's menu Play area Family room Garden Parking **Rooms** 28

## BLANCHLAND

### The Lord Crewe Arms

**DH8 9SP ☎ 01434 675251  🖷 01434 675337**
e-mail: lord@crewearms.freeserve.co.uk
dir: *10m S of Hexham via B6306*

Built in the 12th century, once the private chapel of the abbot of Blanchland Abbey, and a significant location in the first Jacobite Rebellion in 1715, this is one of England's oldest inns. Antique furniture, blazing log fires and flagstone floors make for an atmospheric setting. Wide-ranging, good-value bar and restaurant menus with specials offer salads, savoury bean hot pot, and game pie.

**Open** all day all wk 11-11 (Sun 12-10.30) **Bar Meals** L served all wk 12-2 D served all wk 7-9 Av main course £7 **Restaurant** D served all wk 7-9.15 booking required Av 3 course à la carte fr £21 ⊕ FREE HOUSE ◀ Black Sheep, John Smiths, Guinness, Boddingtons ♂ Thatchers. **Facilities** Children's menu Play area Family room Dogs allowed Garden Parking

## CARTERWAY HEADS

### The Manor House Inn ♥

**DH8 9LX ☎ 01207 255268**
dir: *A69 W from Newcastle, left onto A68 then S for 8m. Inn on right*

A traditional free house enjoying spectacular views across open moorland and the Derwent Reservoir from its elevated position. Built circa 1760, the completely refurbished inn is an ideal centre for exploring Northumberland's rolling hills and beaches; for a city visit, Newcastle and Durham

continued

**England**

are a short drive away. The cosy stone-walled bar, with its log fires, low-beamed ceiling and massive timber support, serves five well-kept real ales all year, among which may be found Ruddles County, Theakston's Best and Mordue Workie Ticket. The bar and lounge are ideal for a snack, while the restaurant is divided into two dining areas, the larger of which welcomes families with children. The focus on fresh local produce is typified by dishes such as smoked kippers with crisp side salad; slow-braised oxtail on a bed of black pudding mash; and supreme of chicken breast with sautéed leeks and Northumbrian nettle cheese sauce.

**Open** all day all wk 11-11 (Sun 12-10.30) **Bar Meals** food served all day **Restaurant** food served all day ⊕ FREE HOUSE ◀ Theakstons Best, Mordue Workie Ticket, Greene King Ruddles County, Courage Directors, Wells Bombardier ♂ Westons Old Rosie Scrumpy. ♟ 12 **Facilities** Children's menu Dogs allowed Garden Parking

## FALSTONE

# The Blackcock Inn ★★★ INN

**NE48 1AA ☎ 01434 240200**
e-mail: thebcinn@yahoo.co.uk
dir: *From Hexham take A6079, then B6320 to Bellingham, follow brown signs to Kielder & Falstone*

Stone walls, log fires and original beams reflect the 17th-century origins of this traditional family-run free house. An ideal base for walking, boating and fishing, it sits close to Kielder Water and is handy for the Rievers cycle route. The food draws on excellent local produce, with options ranging from light lunchtime snacks through to full evening meals in the intimate Chatto's restaurant: perhaps Japanese-style king prawns followed by lamb shank in red wine and rosemary.

**Open** Closed: Tue in low season **Bar Meals** L served Wed-Sun 12-2 booking required Av main course £8.80 **Restaurant** L served Wed-Sun 12-2 booking required D served Wed-Mon 7-8.30 booking required Av 3 course à la carte fr £15.85 ⊕ FREE HOUSE ◀ John Smiths, Worthington, guest ale ♂ Westons. **Facilities** Children's menu Play area Family room Dogs allowed Garden Parking **Rooms** 6

# The Pheasant Inn ★★★★ INN

**Stannersburn NE48 1DD ☎ 01434 240382**
📄 **01434 240382**
e-mail: enquiries@thepheasantinn.com
dir: *A69, B6079, B6320, follow signs for Kielder Water*

This sprawling stone-walled building in the north Tyne Valley dates back to 1624. It was originally a large farmstead, but for over 250 years one room was always used as a locals' bar. In 1985 it was taken over by the Kershaws, who have continually improved and upgraded it. However they have succeeded in keeping the rustic atmosphere intact - around the walls old photos record local people engaged in long-abandoned trades and professions. Robin and Irene's cooking is fresh, generous and tasty, producing wholesome traditionally English fare. Meals may be taken alfresco in the pretty grassed courtyard with a stream running through, or in the oak-beamed restaurant with its cottage style furnishings and warm terracotta walls. The bar menu changes daily according to season, but classic dishes like steak and kidney pie, home-made soups, lasagne, ploughman's and sandwiches are always available. Restaurant menu starters could embrace grilled fresh asparagus with a balsamic dressing; sweet marinated herrings; and creamy garlic mushrooms in puff pastry. Main courses from the blackboard might be slow-roasted Northumbrian lamb with rosemary and redcurrant jus; cider baked gammon; home-made game and mushroom pie; and fish from North Shields quay. Sandra's sticky toffee pudding is always an irresistible way to finish.

**Open** 12-3 6.30-11 Closed: 25-26 Dec, Mon-Tue (Nov-Mar) **Bar Meals** L served Mon-Sat 12-2.30 **Restaurant** L served Mon-Sat 12-2.30 booking required D served Mon-Sat 6.30-8.30 booking required ⊕ FREE HOUSE ◀ Timothy Taylor Landlord, Wylam Gold, Wylam Rocket. **Facilities** Children's menu Play area Family room Dogs allowed Garden Parking **Rooms** 8

## HALTWHISTLE

# Milecastle Inn

**Military Rd, Cawfields NE49 9NN ☎ 01434 321372**
e-mail: clarehind@aol.com
web: www.milecastle-inn.co.uk
dir: *From A69 into Haltwhistle. Pub approx 2m at junct with B6318*

There are good views of Hadrian's Wall from the garden of this rural inn, which sits close to some of the most interesting parts of this fascinating landmark. Inside you'll find open fires and, possibly, the resident ghost. Daily specials supplement separate bar and restaurant menus, which offer numerous home-made pies – wild boar and duckling, beef and venison - and grills, as well as please-all dishes such as roasted vegetable and Wensleydale bake; hot and spicy chicken wings; and lasagne with garlic bread.

Open all day noon-11 (noon-3 6-10 Nov-Mar) Closed: Sun eve in Jan-Mar **Bar Meals** L served all wk 12-2.30 D served all wk 6-8.30 **Restaurant** L served all wk 12-2.30 D served all wk 6-8.30 ⊕ FREE HOUSE ◀ Big Lamp, Prince Bishop, Carlsberg-Tetley, Castle Eden. **Facilities** Children's menu Garden Parking

---

## HEDLEY ON THE HILL

## The Feathers Inn ⚑

NE43 7SW ☎ 01661 843607 📄 01661 843607
e-mail: info@thefeathers.net web: www.thefeathers.net
dir: *Telephone for directions*

This small, stone-built free house overlooks the splendid Cheviot Hills. The three-roomed pub is well patronised by the local community, but visitors too are always charmed by its friendly and relaxed atmosphere. Old oak beams, coal fires, rustic settles, and stone walls decorated with local photographs of rural life make an ideal setting for cask ales, and a good selection of traditional pub games, but most people will be here for a meal. Award-winning chef Rhian Cradock puts on daily-changing menus of great British classics and North East regional dishes, for whose ingredients he always knows the full provenance. On lunch menus you'll find beer-battered North Sea fish with chunky chips; jugged hare with tarragon; slow-roast Ravensworth Grange middle white pork; and lentil and chestnut shepherd's pie. In the evening, menus list grilled wild halibut; loin of Bill Fail's Currock Hill lamb stuffed with sweetbreads; and Doddington's cheese, spinach and beetroot pie. Delicious desserts include as gooseberry meringue pie and burnt Northumbrian cream. Groups might like to put together

a feasting menu along the lines of home-made black pudding to begin, whole roast suckling pig as the main course, and a selection of Northumbrian cheeses to follow.

Open all wk noon-11pm (Sun 12-10.30, Mon 6-11) **Bar Meals** L served Tue-Sun 12-2 booking required D served Tue-Sat 6-8.30 booking required Av main course £11 ⊕ FREE HOUSE ◀ Mordue Workie Ticket, Big Lamp Bitter, Fuller's London Pride, Northumberland Pit Pony, Orkney Red McGreggor, Hadrian Gladiator Ŏ Westons 1st Quality, Westons Old Rosie. ⚑ 36 **Facilities** Children's menu Family room Parking

---

## HEXHAM

## Dipton Mill Inn ⚑

Dipton Mill Rd NE46 1YA ☎ 01434 606577
e-mail: ghb@hexhamshire.co.uk
dir: *2m S of Hexham on HGV route to Blanchland, B6306, Dipton Mill Rd*

A former farmhouse, with the millstream running right through the gardens, the pub has recently celebrated its rebuilding 400 years ago. It is surrounded by farms and woodland with footpaths for pleasant country walks, and there is Hadrian's Wall and an assortment of other Roman sites in the area to explore. The Dipton Mill is home to Hexhamshire Brewery ales, including Devil's Water and Old Humbug. Food is served evenings and lunchtimes and all dishes are freshly prepared from local produce where possible. Start with home-made soup, such as carrot and celery served with a warm roll, followed by hearty dishes like mince and dumplings, lamb leg steak in wine and mustard sauce, or tomato, bean and vegetable casserole. Traditional desserts include bread and butter pudding or syrup sponge and custard. Salads, sandwiches and ploughman's are also always available.

Open noon-2.30 6-11 (Sun noon-3) Closed: 25 Dec, Sun eve **Bar Meals** L served all wk 12-2 D served Mon-Sat 6.30-8.30 Av main course £7.50 ⊕ FREE HOUSE ◀ Hexhamshire Shire Bitter, Old Humbug, Devil's Water, Devil's Elbow, Whapweasel Ŏ Westons Old Rosie. ⚑ 17 **Facilities** Children's menu Garden 🐾

## Miners Arms Inn

Main St, Acomb NE46 4PW ☎ 01434 603909
e-mail: info@theminersacomb.com
dir: *17m W of Newcastle on A69. 2m W of Hexham*

Close to Hadrian's Wall in peaceful surroundings, this welcoming village pub with open hearth fire dates from 1746. Pride is taken in the range and quality of the ales and in the good home-cooked food. Sunday lunches are especially popular, when North Acomb beef or lamb roasts are accompanied by home-made Yorkshire puddings, roast potatoes and a selection of vegetables. There is a pleasant beer garden and families are welcome.

Open all wk **Bar Meals** L served Sat 12-2.30 booking required D served Thu-Sat 5-8.30 booking required **Restaurant** L served Sun 12-2.30 booking required D served Thu-Sat 5-8.30 booking required ⊕ FREE HOUSE ◀ Black Sheep, Wylam Bitter, Pilsner Urquell, Mordue, Yates Bitter Ŏ Wylam Perry's Farmhouse Cider. **Facilities** Children's menu Dogs allowed Garden

## LONGFRAMLINGTON

# The Anglers Arms

**Weldon Bridge NE65 8AX ☎ 01665 570271 & 570655**
e-mail: johnyoung@anglersarms.fsnet.co.uk
dir: *From N, 9m S of Alnwick right Weldon Bridge sign. From S, A1 to by-pass Morpeth, left onto A697 for Wooler & Coldstream. 7m, left to Weldon Bridge*

This former coaching inn has commanded the picturesque Weldon Bridge over the River Coquet since the 1760s. The interior is full of nice little touches, and open log fires are a welcoming treat on winter days. Look for a range of bar meals, where main courses include home-made steak and ale pie; grilled salmon fillet with sweet chilli sauce; and vegetable stew with home-made dumplings. Outside, there's plenty of space for alfresco summer dining in the carefully-tended garden, which also includes a children's play park. But for more style and a different set of options, the pub's own Pullman railway carriage provides an unusual restaurant experience. Silver service comes as standard here, and you can choose from starters like shredded duck salad with noodles and hoi sin sauce; twice-cooked belly pork with honey spiced apples; and garlic king prawns with a panache of fresh garden leaves. Moving on to the main course, the alternatives include pan-fried chicken breast on bubble and squeak with mushroom and red wine sauce; rack of Border lamb with roasted chateau potatoes; and vegetable stroganoff with basmati rice. Turn to the blackboard for a daily-changing dessert selection.

**Open** all day all wk 11-11 (Sun 12-11) **Bar Meals** Av main course £8 food served all day **Restaurant** Fixed menu price fr £20 Av 3 course à la carte fr £30 food served all day ⊕ FREE HOUSE ◀ Timothy Taylor Landlord, Old Speckled Hen, Abbot Ale, Theakstons Best Bitter. **Facilities** Children's menu Play area Family room Garden Parking

## NEWTON-ON-THE-MOOR

# The Cook and Barker Inn ★★★★ INN ♟

**NE65 9JY ☎ 01665 575234 📄 01665 575887**
dir: *0.5m from A1 S of Alnwick*

From its elevated position in the village of Newton-on-the-Moor, this traditional country inn commands outstanding views of the Cheviot Hills and the Northumbrian coast. The Cook and Barker is a long-established family business run by Phil Farmer. Kitchen staff strive to prepare quality dishes that are value for money, while the front-of-house team looks after guests with expertise and finesse. The bar lunch menu and à la carte evening menu are backed by daily specials on the blackboard, and a gourmet seven-course fixed-price menu is also available. Appetisers are along the lines of warm toasted muffin with black pudding, king scallop and fresh green pea purée; and pressed ham terrine with apricot and home-made chutney. For a main course, choose from the 'Seafood Selection' for the likes of seared tuna loin with a niçoise salad; or pan-roasted cod supreme with mushy peas. The 'Forest and Fields' listing may include noisettes of pork pan-fried with wild forest mushrooms deglazed with Madeira wine and set on a pillow of roasted vegetables; or roast rack of lamb with seasonal greens and rosemary. With 'Grills and Roasts' the cooking technique comes as no surprise: perhaps a prime sirloin steak with balsamic tomatoes and sautéed button mushrooms; or surf-and-turf T-bone steak with garlic prawns. Finally look to the 'Oriental Dishes' for something a little spicy: beef fillet with ginger and spring onions, for example, or pork and prawn stir fry in a black bean sauce.

**Open** all wk **Bar Meals** Av main course £8.95 food served all day **Restaurant** L served all wk 12-2 booking required D served all wk 7-9 booking required Fixed menu price fr £25 Av 3 course à la carte fr £35 ⊕ FREE HOUSE ◀ Timothy Taylor Landlord, Theakstons Best Bitter, Fuller's London Pride, Batemans XXXB, Black Sheep. ♟ 12 **Facilities** Children's menu Family room Garden Parking **Rooms** 18

## WARDEN

### The Boatside Inn ♟

**NE46 4SQ ☎ 01434 602233**
e-mail: sales@theboatsideinn.com
web: www.theboatsideinn.com
dir: *Off A69 W of Hexham, follow signs to Warden Newborough & Fourstones*

A stone-built country inn, the Boatside is situated where the North and South Tyne rivers meet, beneath Warden Hill Iron Age fort. The name refers to the rowing boat that ferried people across the river before the bridge was built. Children, walkers and cyclists are welcome, and the inn has fishing rights on the river. Dishes include Boatside salads; lime, thyme and asparagus risotto; fresh seafood; and steak and ale pie.

**Open** all day all wk 11-11 (Sun 11-10.30) **Bar Meals** L served Mon-Sat 12-2.30, Sun 12-9 D served Mon-Sat 6-9, Sun 12-9 Av main course f9.95 **Restaurant** L served Mon-Sat 12-2.30, Sun 12-9 D served Mon-Sat 6-9, Sun 12-9 ⊕ FREE HOUSE ◀ Black Sheep, John Smiths, Mordue, Wylam. ♟ 15 **Facilities** Children's menu Dogs allowed Garden Parking

## WHALTON

### Beresford Arms

**NE61 3UZ ☎ 01670 775225  📄 01670 775351**
e-mail: beresford.arms@btconnect.com
dir: *5m from Morpeth town centre on B6524*

Under the management of Wendy Makepeace, this ivy-covered coaching inn has a country pub atmosphere, while at the same time conveying a modern feel. It lies in the picturesque village of Whalton, popular with cyclists and walkers enjoying the delights of nearby Kielder Forest and Northumberland National Park. Set opposite the village hall, it also provides a welcome focus for village life. Your meal could start with home-made soup, or prawn and avocado salad with Marie Rose sauce; follow with grilled Wallington Hall rib-eye steak with tomato, mushrooms, onion rings and chips; and finish with a crumble or something that involves whipped cream or chocolate sauce.

**Open** all wk **Bar Meals** L served Tue-Sat 12-2, Sun 12-3 D served Tue-Sat 12-2 6-9 Av main course £10 **Restaurant** L served Fri-Sat 12-2, Sun 12-3 D served Fri-Sat 6-9 Fixed menu price fr £9 Av 3 course à la carte fr £17.50 ⊕ FREE HOUSE ◀ Black Sheep, Timothy Taylor Landlord, John Smith's. **Facilities** Children's menu Dogs allowed Garden Parking

## BLIDWORTH

### Fox & Hounds ♟

**Blidworth Bottoms NG21 0NW ☎ 01623 792383**
e-mail: info@foxandhounds-pub.com
dir: *Right off B6020 between Ravenshead & Blidworth*

A traditional country pub, extensively refurbished to create attractive surroundings for drinking and dining. It was probably built as a farmhouse in the 19th century, when Blidworth Bottoms was a thriving community. A reputation for good pub food comes from dishes such as steak and ale pie; Mediterranean chicken; blackened salmon in Cajun spices; home-made vegetarian cottage pie; and hot chilli con carne.

**Open** all day all wk 11.30am-11.30pm (Fri-Sat 11.30am-mdnt) **Bar Meals** L served Mon-Wed 11.30-8.30, Thu-Sun 11.30-9 D served Mon-Wed 11.30-8.30, Thu-Sun 11.30-9 food served all day ⊕ GREENE KING ◀ H&H Cask Bitter, Old Speckled Hen, Olde Trip H&H, seasonal guest ales. ♟ 9 **Facilities** Children's menu Play area Dogs allowed Garden Parking

## CAUNTON

### Caunton Beck ♟

**NG23 6AB ☎ 01636 636793  📄 01636 636828**
e-mail: email@cauntonbeck.com
dir: *6m NW of Newark on A616 to Sheffield*

This village pub cum restaurant opens for breakfast and carries on serving food until around midnight. It is built around a beautifully restored 16th-century cottage with herb gardens and a colourful rose arbour. The main menu changes with the seasons and is served throughout. To start you might choose soup of the day or twice-baked Caunton Beck soufflé with portobello mushroom and Roquefort cheese. Mains include locally sourced rib-eye of beef with a choice of sauces, or whole roast sea bass stuffed with piri piri, coriander and lime. Vegetarian and gluten-free options are clearly marked. A sandwich and light meal menu is also available.

**Open** all day all wk 8am-mdnt **Bar Meals** Av main course £16.10 food served all day **Restaurant** Fixed menu price fr £11 Av 3 course à la carte fr £22.20 food served all day ⊕ FREE HOUSE ◀ Batemans Valiant, Marston's Pedigree, Tom Woods Best Bitter. ♟ 34 **Facilities** Children's menu Dogs allowed Garden Parking

**England**

## EDWINSTOWE

### Forest Lodge ★★★★ INN 🍷

**2-4 Church St NG21 9QA** ☎ **01623 824443**
🖷 **01623 824686**
e-mail: audrey@forestlodgehotel.co.uk
web: www.forestlodgehotel.co.uk
dir: *A614 towards Edwinstowe, turn onto B6034. Opp church*

Refurbished by the Thompson family over the past five years, the 18th-century coaching inn stands opposite Edwinstowe church, reputedly where Robin Hood married Maid Marion. Quaff local ales, with a plate of ham, egg and chips in the beamed bars, or linger over garlic king prawns and braised ham hock with smoked bacon and parsley sauce.

**Open** all wk 11.30-3 5.30-11 (Fri 11.30-3 5-11, Sun 12-3 6-10.30) Closed: 1 Jan **Bar Meals** L served all wk 12-2 (booking recommended Thu-Sun) D served all wk 6-9 (booking recommended Thu-Sun) Av main course £8 **Restaurant** L served all wk 12-2 booking required D served all wk 6-9 (booking recommended Thu-Sun) Fixed menu price fr £15.75 Av 3 course à la carte fr £20 ⊕ FREE HOUSE ◀ Bombardier, Kelham Island Pale Rider, Abbeydale Moonshine. 🍷 9 **Facilities** Children's menu Dogs allowed Garden Parking **Rooms** 13

## ELKESLEY

### Robin Hood Inn 🍷

**High St DN22 8AJ** ☎ **01777 838259**
e-mail: a1robinhood@aol.com
dir: *5m SE of Worksop off A1 towards Newark-on-Trent*

Parts of this unassuming village inn date back to the 14th century. Ceilings and floors are deep red, while the green walls are adorned with pictures of food. The comprehensive choice is served in both the bar and restaurant, and includes a fixed price menu, carte and daily specials board. Beef bourguignon; grilled rump or fillet steak; pan-fried Normandy style chicken breast, or sausages, onions and mustard mash will satisfy the heartiest of appetites.

**Open** 11.30-2.30 6-11 Closed: Sun eve & Mon lunch **Bar Meals** L served Tue-Sun 12-2 D served Mon-Sat 6-8 Av main course £9 **Restaurant** L served Tue-Sun 12-2 D served Mon-Sat 6-9 Fixed menu price fr £12.50 Av 3 course à la carte fr £15 ⊕ ENTERPRISE INNS ◀ John Smiths Extra Smooth, Black Sheep Best Bitter, guest ale. 🍷 6 **Facilities** Children's menu Play area Garden Parking

## FARNDON

### The Farndon Boathouse 🍷

**Riverside NG24 3SX** ☎ **01636 676578**    🖷 **01636 673911**
e-mail: info@farndonboathouse.co.uk
dir: *From Newark follow A46 to Farndon x-rds, turn right and follow rd to river. Boathouse on riverside*

A major refurbishment has produced a bar and restaurant in the style of a very fashionable old boathouse. Clad in wood, with chunky exposed roof trusses, stone floors and an abundance of glass, this part-restored, part-new building sits on the banks of the River Trent, which the bar and restaurant overlook through an extensively glazed frontage. Fresh modern cooking uses local produce to provide reasonably priced dishes that include smoked haddock fishcakes with peas, rice and warm curry sauce; beef with Cropwell Bishop Stilton and baby onion pie with mash, garden peas and gravy; spiced bouillabaisse; bell pepper stuffed with mixed bean and vegetable chilli con carne; steaks and a variety of burgers. Add some live music to complete a very appealing picture.

**Open** all day all wk 10am-11pm **Bar Meals** L served Mon- Fri 12-2.30, Sat-Sun 12-3 D served all wk 6-9.30 Av main course £10 **Restaurant** L served Mon-Fri 12-2.30, Sat-Sun 12-3 D served all wk 6-9.30 Fixed menu price fr £12 Av 3 course à la carte fr £20 ⊕ FREE HOUSE ◀ Black Sheep, Caythorpe Dover Beck. 🍷 16 **Facilities** Children's menu Garden Parking

## HARBY

### Bottle & Glass 🍷

**High St NG23 7EB** ☎ **01522 703438**    🖷 **01522 703436**
e-mail: email@bottleandglassharby.com
dir: *S of A57 (Lincoln to Markham Moor road)*

Situated in a charming village a few miles west of Lincoln, the pub's original beams and flagstone floors date back many years. Queen Eleanor reputedly died here in 1290. Proprietor Michael Hope aims to create the reassuringly civilised ambience of a music-free meeting house, reading room, watering hole and restaurant. Seasonal dishes of twice-baked cheese soufflé with roasted red onions may be followed by roast fillet of pollack with Puy lentils.

**Open** all day all wk 12-12 **Bar Meals** Av main course £14.25 food served all day **Restaurant** Fixed menu price fr £12.50 Av 3 course à la carte fr £20.40 food served all day ⊕ FREE HOUSE ◀ Young's Bitter, Farmers Blonde, Black Sheep. 🍷 34 **Facilities** Children's menu Dogs allowed Garden Parking

## KIMBERLEY

### The Nelson & Railway Inn

**12 Station Rd NG16 2NR** ☎ **0115 938 2177**
🖷 **0115 938 2179**
dir: *1m N of M1 junct 26*

The landlord of more than 30 years gives this 17th-century pub its distinctive personality. Next door is the Hardy & Hanson brewery that supplies many of the beers, but the two railway stations that once made it a railway inn are now derelict. A hearty menu of pub favourites includes soup, ploughman's, and hot rolls, as well as grills and hot dishes like home-made steak and kidney pie; gammon steak; and mushroom stroganoff.

**Open** all day all wk 11am-mdnt **Bar Meals** L served all wk 12-2.30 D served all wk 5.30-9 Av main course £5.50 **Restaurant** L served all wk 12-2.30 D served all wk 5.30-9 ⊕ HARDY & HANSONS PLC ◀ Hardys, Hansons Best Bitter, Cool & Dark, Olde Trip, Morlands, Ruddles. **Facilities** Children's menu Family room Dogs allowed Garden Parking

## LAXTON

### The Dovecote Inn ♥

Moorhouse Rd NG22 0SX ☎ 01777 871586
e-mail: dovecote-inn@btconnect.com
dir: *Exit A1 at Tuxford through Egmanton to Laxton*

Like most of the village of Laxton, this family-run, 18th-century pub is Crown Estate property belonging to the Royal Family. Outside is a delightful beer garden with views of the church. The interior includes a bar and three cosy rooms. Here the seasonal, home-cooked dishes could include wild Alaskan salmon, slow-roast belly pork with apple and onion compote, chicken breast and bacon, or 28-day matured steak.

**Open** all wk 11 30-3 6.30-11 (Sun 12-10.30) **Bar Meals** Av main course £9 **Restaurant** L served Mon-Sat 12-2, Sun 12.30-6 D served Mon-Sat 6.30-9.30 booking required Av 3 course à la carte fr £18 ⊕ FREE HOUSE ◀ Mansfield Smooth, John Smith's Smooth, Black Sheep, Greene King Old Speckled Hen, Adnams. ♥ 10 **Facilities** Children's menu Dogs allowed Garden Parking

## MORTON

### The Full Moon Inn ♥

Main St NG25 0UT ☎ 01636 830251 📄 01636 830554
e-mail: info@thefullmoonmorton.co.uk
dir: *Newark A617 to Mansfield. Past Kelham, turn left to Rolleston & follow signs to Morton*

In January 2009 the The Full Moon emerged from a transformation by William and Rebecca White that turned a dark and dated pub, once three cottages from the late 1700s, into one that is light, comfortable and contemporary. They exposed the old beams and brickwork, used reclaimed panels and furniture, and laid new carpets to help create what has fast become a destination pub. There's a charming garden for the summer and two roaring log fires for the winter. Rebecca is in charge of the kitchen, where the emphasis is on mostly local farm-fresh food, with a set menu running alongside the pub menu at lunchtime and in the evenings. There's plenty on offer, from sandwiches, baguettes, pastas, burgers and omelettes to Gonalston Farm Shop bangers with mash, red cabbage and gravy; Moon pie with Nottingham beef and roast vegetables, red cabbage and chips; and fresh haddock in beer batter with minted pea purée and chips. On Friday and Saturday nights

the set menu is replaced with a specials board, featuring fish chosen by a local fishmonger and only chalked up once it's actually delivered. Some of Rebecca's casserole style dishes are available in takeaway foil containers. There's plenty here to keep children occupied too, with a designated indoor play area, an outdoor castle and a sand pit, while dogs are also welcome.

**Open** all wk fr 10.30am **Bar Meals** L served all wk 12-2.30 booking required D served all wk 6-9.30 booking required Av main course £10 **Restaurant** L served all wk 12-2.30 booking required D served all wk 6-9.30 booking required Fixed menu price fr £16 Av 3 course à la carte fr £22 ⊕ FREE HOUSE ◀ Bombardier, Dover Beck, Moonshine, guest ales. ♥ 8 **Facilities** Children's menu Play area Family room Dogs allowed Garden Parking

## TUXFORD

### The Mussel & Crab ♥

NG22 0PJ ☎ 01777 870491 📄 01777 872302
e-mail: musselandcrab1@hotmail.com
dir: *From Ollerton/Tuxford junct of A1& A57. N on B1164 to Sibthorpe Hill. Pub 800yds on right*

Fresh fish and seafood dominate the menu at this quirky pub with a multitude of rooms. The piazza room is styled as an Italian courtyard, with murals by artist Tony Cooke; the beamed restaurant is big on rustic charm; and the gents' toilets is brightened with a tank of fish! Countless blackboards offer ever-changing dishes such as crab chowder; and monkfish in a red wine and mushroom sauce.

**Open** all wk **Bar Meals** L served all wk 11-2.30 booking required D served Mon-Sat 6-10, Sun 6-9 booking required Av main course £10 **Restaurant** L served all wk 11-2.30 booking required D served Mon-Sat 6-10, Sun 6-9 booking required Av 3 course à la carte fr £28 ⊕ FREE HOUSE ◀ Tetley Smooth, Tetley Cask, Guinness. ♥ 16 **Facilities** Children's menu Family room Dogs allowed Garden Parking

**England**

## OXFORDSHIRE

### BAMPTON

## The Romany

**Bridge St OX18 2HA ☎ 01993 850237   📄 01993 852133**
e-mail: romany@barbox.net
dir: *Telephone for details*

A shop until 20 years ago, The Romany is housed in an 18th-century building of Cotswold stone with a beamed bar, log fires and intimate dining room. The choice of food ranges from bar snacks and bar meals to a full carte restaurant menu, with home-made specials like hotpot, Somerset pork, or steak and ale pie. There is a good range of vegetarian choices. Regional singers provide live entertainment a couple of times a month.

**Open** all wk **Bar Meals** L served all wk 12-2.30 D served all wk 6-9.30 Av main course £10 **Restaurant** L served all wk 12-2.30 D served all wk 6-9.30 ⊕ PUNCH ◀ Archers Village, Fuller's London Pride, Brakspears, guest ales ♂ Westons Stowford Press. **Facilities** Children's menu Play area Dogs allowed Garden Parking

### BANBURY

## The Wykham Arms ♀

**Temple Mill Rd, Sibford Gower OX15 5RX**
**☎ 01295 788808**
e-mail: info@wykhamarms.co.uk
dir: *Between Banbury & Shipston-on-Stour off B4035. 20m S of Stratford-upon-Avon*

A charming 18th-century thatched inn built of mellow stone with lovely countryside views, where drinkers and diners congregate in intimate beamed rooms. The bar menu, also available in the terrace and garden, offers great sandwiches like sirloin steak or Wykham club. Restaurant main courses may include Caesar salad with roasted maize-fed chicken or Salcombe crab and mango salad.

**Open** 12-2.30 6-11 Closed: Mon **Bar Meals** L served Tue-Sat 12-2.30 D served Tue-Sat 7-9.30 Av main course £15 **Restaurant** L served Tue-Sun 12-2.30 D served Tue-Sat 7-9.30 Av 3 course à la carte fr £26.50 ⊕ FREE HOUSE ◀ Hook Norton Best, Guinness, St Austell Tribute, Adnams Broadside, London Pride. ♀ 17 **Facilities** Children's menu Family room Dogs allowed Garden Parking

### BLOXHAM

## The Elephant & Castle

**OX15 4LZ ☎ 0845 873 7358**
e-mail: elephant.bloxham@btinternet.com
dir: *M40 junct 11, pub just off A361, in village centre. 11m from Banbury*

The arch of this family-run 15th-century Cotswold-stone coaching inn used to straddle the former Banbury to Chipping Norton turnpike. At night the gates of the pub were closed, and no traffic could get over the toll bridge. Locals play Aunt Sally

or shove-ha'penny in the big wood-floored bar, whilst the two-roomed lounge boasts a bar-billiards table and an inglenook fireplace. The menu offers a range of sandwiches and crusty filled baguettes, plus pub favourites like roast chicken breast with stuffing, crispy battered cod and lasagne verdi.

**Open** all wk 10-3 5-12 (Fri 10-3 5-2am, Sat 10am-2am, Sun 10am-mdnt) **Bar Meals** L served Mon-Sat 12-2 Av main course £5 **Restaurant** L served Mon-Sat 12-2 ⊕ HOOK NORTON BREWERY ◀ Hook Norton Best Bitter, Hook Norton seasonal ales, guest ales ♂ Westons Old Rosie Scrumpy. **Facilities** Children's menu Play area Family room Dogs allowed Garden Parking

### BURCOT

## The Chequers ♀

**OX14 3DP ☎ 01865 407771   📄 01865 407771**
e-mail: enquiries@thechequers-burcot.co.uk
dir: *On A415 (Dorchester to Abingdon road) between Clifton Hampden & Dorchester on Thames*

Once a staging post for barges on the Thames, this 400-year-old thatched and timber framed pub now combines the best of old and new. On winter days the blazing fire surrounded by sofas is the favoured spot, especially for toasting marshmallows; in summer, the enclosed beer garden takes precedence. The food is serious, pubby home cooking: think pan-fried field mushrooms in garlic and herb butter on toast to start; then beer battered haddock with hand cut chips; or slow roasted lamb shank with mint and redcurrant gravy.

**Open** all day all wk 12-11 (Sun 12-4) **Bar Meals** L served all wk 12-3 D served Mon-Sat 6.30-9.30 Av main course £13 **Restaurant** L served all wk 12-3 booking required D served Mon-Sat 6.30-9.30 booking required Av 3 course à la carte fr £23 ⊕ FREE HOUSE ◀ Hook Norton Bitter, Ridgway, Young's, guest ales ♂ Westons Stowford Press. ♀ 21 **Facilities** Children's menu Garden Parking

### CHADLINGTON

## The Tite Inn ♀

**Mill End OX7 3NY ☎ 01608 676475   📄 01608 676475**
dir: *2m S of Chipping Norton & 7m N of Burford*

Seventeenth-century Cotswold-stone free house where, in 1642, Royalist troops sank a few stiffeners before the Battle of Edgehill nearby. Situated in the beautiful countryside of the Cotswolds, the inn has a traditional, warm welcoming feel, with an open fire, flagstone floor and oak topped bar. The restaurant area is separate and the menu offers the finest range of home reared South Devon cross beef from fillet steak to burgers. Expect warm duck salad with redcurrant sauce, or pan fried scallops in lemon butter; followed by grilled ginger and coriander marinated tuna, or pan fried sirloin steak with peppercorn sauce.

**Open** 11-3 6-11 (Sun 12-3 7-10.30) Closed: Mon (ex BH) **Bar Meals** L served Tue-Sun 12-2.30 D served Tue-Sat 7-9 **Restaurant** L served Tue-Sun 12-2.30 booking required D served Tue-Sat 7-9 booking required ⊕ FREE HOUSE ◀ Sharp's, Timothy Taylor Landlord ♻ Westons Stowford Press. ♟ 6 **Facilities** Children's menu Dogs allowed Garden Parking

## CHALGROVE

## The Red Lion Inn ♟

**The High St OX44 7SS ☎ 01865 890625**
e-mail: raymondsexton@btinternet.com
web: www.redlionchalgrove.co.uk
dir: *B480 from Oxford ring road, through Stadhampton, left then right at mini-rdbt. At Chalgrove Airfield right into village*

Rather unusually, the cruck-framed 15th-century Red Lion is one of only two pubs in the country owned by its local parish church. How appropriate, then, that the owners are Suzanne and Raymond Sexton; Raymond, incidentally, was Jamie Oliver's father's chef for 10 years. From the front garden you can see the memorial to Colonel John Hampden, a key political figure fatally wounded in a Civil War skirmish nearby. From a 'menu that tries to please everyone' come starters such as salad of spicy merguez sausage, potatoes and shallots topped with a crispy poached egg; and pan-fried pigeon breasts with wild rice and a port wine jus. Main dishes may include pan-fried kidneys served on a bed of bubble and squeak with bacon lardons and balsamic vinegar; and pork loin chops grilled and served on a rich goats' cheese and sage cream. Sandwiches and side orders are also available at lunchtime.

**Open** all wk 11.30-3 6-mdnt (Sat 11.30-3 6-1am Sat 11.30am-1am Sun 11.30am-mdnt in summer) **Bar Meals** L served Mon-Sat 12-2, Sun 12-3 D served Mon-Sat 6-9 Av main course £11.50 **Restaurant** L served Mon-Sat 12-2, Sun 12-3 D served Mon-Sat 6-9 Fixed menu price fr £6.50 Av 3 course à la carte fr £21 ⊕ FREE HOUSE ◀ Fuller's London Pride, Adnams Best, Timothy Taylor Landlord, Boddingtons, guest ale ♻ Aspalls, Westons Stowford Press. ♟ 8 **Facilities** Children's menu Play area Dogs allowed Garden

## CHINNOR

## The Sir Charles Napier ◎◎ ♟

**Spriggs Alley OX39 4BX ☎ 01494 483011**
📄 01494 485311
dir: *M40 junct 6 to Chinnor. Turn right at rdbt, up hill to Spriggs Alley*

This is a true destination pub, but then it's probably always been one. After all, when the itinerant wood-turners, the bodgers, who once worked up in the hills wanted a beer, this was indeed their destination. Inside and out are stone, marble and wood sculptures by Michael Cooper. Huge log fires, comfortable sofas and an eclectic jumble of old furnishings characterise the interior, while the kitchen is proud of its two AA Rosettes. In summer, lunch is served on the vine- and wisteria-shaded terrace that overlooks extensive lawns and herb gardens. Try Bresse pigeon, wild mushroom ravioli, sausage roll and celeriac purée; or noisettes of venison, red onion tarte Tatin, girolles, nutmeg and orange jus. Skate wing with lemon and caper butter; and Lancashire hotpot are among the blackboard specials. A truly extensive wine list even includes bottles from Oregon and Lebanon.

**Open** noon-4 6-mdnt (Sun noon-6) Closed: 25-26 Dec, Mon, Sun eve **Bar Meals** L served Tue-Fri 12-2.30 D served Tue-Fri 6.30-9 Av main course £11.50 **Restaurant** L served Tue-Sat 12-2.30, Sun 12-3.30 booking required D served Tue-Sat 6.30-10 booking required Fixed menu price fr £14.50 Av 3 course à la carte fr £34 ⊕ FREE HOUSE ◀ Wadworth 6X, Wadworth IPA. ♟ 15 **Facilities** Children's menu Dogs allowed Garden Parking

## CHURCH ENSTONE

## The Crown Inn ♟

**Mill Ln OX7 4NN ☎ 01608 677262**
dir: *Off A44, 15m N of Oxford*

Award-winning chef Tony Warburton runs this stone-built 17th-century free house on the eastern edge of the Cotswolds with his wife Caroline. During summer, eat or drink in the secluded rear garden, which is sheltered from the wind but enjoys the best of the late sunshine. Inside you'll find a traditional rustic bar with an open fire, a spacious slate floored conservatory, and a richly decorated beamed dining room. All meals are prepared on the premises using fresh produce, including pork, beef and game from the local farms and estates. Starters may include cream of spring vegetable soup; or warm salad of woodpigeon, bacon and quails' eggs. Main course choices

continued

range from steak and Hooky pie to fettuccini with wild mushrooms, cream and pesto. A home-made pudding such as cheesecake with blackcurrants will round things off nicely.

**Open** all wk 12-3 6-11 (Sun 12-4) **Closed:** 26 Dec, 1 Jan **Bar Meals** Av main course £9 food served all day **Restaurant** Fixed menu price fr £14.95 Av 3 course à la carte fr £17.95 food served all day ⊕ FREE HOUSE ◗ Hook Norton Best Bitter, Timothy Taylor Landlord, Wychwood Hobgoblin. ♀ 8 **Facilities** Children's menu Dogs allowed Garden Parking

## CUMNOR

### Bear & Ragged Staff ♀

28 Appleton Rd OX2 9QH ☎ 01865 862329
▤ 01865 862048
e-mail: enquiries@bearandraggedstaff.com
dir: *A420 from Oxford, right onto B4017 signposted Cumnor*

After a seemingly lengthy hibernation, the Bear & Ragged Staff reopened early in 2009, its tenancy in the hands of a group led by Mark Greenwood, back in England after 30 years in Asia. As Mark explained, it wasn't difficult to see its enormous possibilities – a recently renovated restaurant with a first class kitchen, attached to a 16th century pub. The pub's name is linked with Warwickshire, particularly with the Earl of Warwick, whose mistress's ghost allegedly haunts the building. New menus reflect the cornucopia of wildlife from the surrounding woods and farmland – pheasant, partridge, deer, muntjac, rabbit, duck and pigeon, for instance. The food is best described as hearty, country-style cooking, and casseroles, stews and pub classics, such as bangers and mash, will always be found on the menus, which change every five to six weeks. Lunch menus might offer a platter of charcuterie, or Greek meze to share; home-made burger with bacon and Cheddar; ale, mushroom and beef pie; and salmon and dill fishcakes. There's a bit more sophistication in the evening, with roast venison loin, cavolo nero and juniper berry jus; confit duck leg with wild mushroom and braised chicory; and sea bass fillet with wilted mache lettuce, Japanese udon noodles and lime leaf and celery white bean broth. As for dessert, Chef says 'Don't forget to try the chocolate fondant'.

**Open** all day all wk 11-11 **Bar Meals** L served all wk 12-3 D served all wk 6.30-10 Av main course £8.50 **Restaurant** L served all wk 12-3 D served all wk 6.30-10 Fixed menu price fr £10.50 Av 3 course à la carte fr £24 ⊕ GREENE KING ◗ IPA, Old Speckled Hen, Abbot Ale, guest ales. ♀ 6 **Facilities** Children's menu Play area Dogs allowed Garden Parking

## CUXHAM

### The Half Moon ♀

OX49 5NF ☎ 01491 614151
e-mail: info@thehalf-moon.com
dir: *M40 junct 6 follow Watlington signs. Right at T-junct, 2nd right to Cuxham. Across rdbt, Pub in 1m on right, just past Cuxham sign*

Eilidh Ferguson grows the vegetables and salad leaves that end up on the dining plates at this 16th-century thatched pub. Her partner and chef Andrew Hill smokes the salmon and prepares the game from surrounding farms. Typically, expect dishes such as duck hearts on toast; fried Harlesford Farm organic mutton with bubble and squeak; roast chicken with Caesar salad; grilled dab with caper butter; mutton pie; and vegetable meze. Enjoy a pint in the large beer garden in summer.

**Open** noon-3 6-11 (Sat noon-11 Sun noon-5) **Closed:** Mon ex BH Sun eve (winter) **Bar Meals** L served Tue-Sat 12-2, Sun 12-3 booking required D served Tue-Sat 6-9 booking required Av main course £14 **Restaurant** L served Tue-Sat 12-2, Sun 12-3 booking required D served Tue Sat 6-9 booking required Av 3 course à la carte fr £25 ⊕ BRAKSPEAR ◗ Brakspear Ordinary ♂ Westons Organic. ♀ 8 **Facilities** Children's menu Dogs allowed Garden Parking

## DEDDINGTON

### The Unicorn Inn ♀

Market Place OX15 0SE ☎ 01869 338838
e-mail: robbie@theunicorninn.net
web: www.theunicorninn.net
dir: *6m S of Banbury on A4260*

Populated by friendly locals and smiling staff, visitors feel welcome too in this Grade II listed 17th-century coaching inn overlooking the market square. Exposed beams and an open fire characterise the bar which serves award-winning cask ales

and a large selection of wines by the glass. For warmer days the tranquillity of the secret walled garden is much enjoyed by couples and families alike. The restaurant offers excellent home-cooked food, using locally sourced fresh produce. The menu includes traditional pub favourites which compliment the more contemporary dishes. Fresh fish deliveries six days per week make seafood a particular strength. Children have their own menu and dietary requirements are catered for.

Open all day all wk 11-11 (Fri-Sat 11am-12.30am, Sun noon-10.30) Bar Meals L served Mon-Sat 12-2.30 D served Mon-Thu 6-9, Fri-Sat 6-9.30 Av main course £9 Restaurant L served Mon-Sat 12-2.30, Sun 12-8 D served Mon-Thu 6-9, Fri-Sat 6-9.30, Sun 12-8 booking required Av 3 course à la carte fr £18 ⊕ Charles Wells Pub Co ◀ Hook Norton, Bombardier, Youngs Special, Guest Ale. ♀ 10 Facilities Children's menu Dogs allowed Garden Parking

## DORCHESTER (ON THAMES)

## Fleur De Lys ♀

**9 High St OX10 7HH ☎ 01865 340502  🖹 01865 340502**
e-mail: info@fleurdorchester.co.uk

Dating from around 1525, this lovely old pub is located on the High Street of the picturesque village. It has retained much of its original character with a pretty garden and cosy bar and dining room. Traditional British fare is served, including steak, stilton and port wine pie; and crab and ginger fishcakes, all made in-house. Vegetarians are well catered for, too, with dishes such as baked aubergines stuffed with ratatouille, or steamed vegetarian pudding.

Open all wk noon-3 6-12.30am (Sat-Sun all day) Closed: Winter 3-6 Bar Meals L served all wk 12-2.30 booking required D served Mon-Sat 6.30-9.30 booking required ⊕ FREE HOUSE ◀ Brakspear, Hooky, Guinness, guest beer Ŏ Stowford Press. ♀ 8 Facilities Children's menu Dogs allowed Garden Parking

## The George ★★ HL ♀

**25 High St OX10 7HH ☎ 01865 340404  🖹 01865 341620**
e-mail: thegeorgehotel@fsmail.net
dir: From M40 junct 7, A329 S to A4074 at Shillingford. Follow Dorchester signs. From M4 junct 13, A34 to Abingdon then A415 E to Dorchester

DH Lawrence was a frequent visitor to this 15th-century coaching inn, believed to be one of the oldest public houses in Britain. The George stands at the centre of the picturesque village of Dorchester. Inside, oak beams and inglenook

fireplaces help to create a welcoming atmosphere, while outside there is an attractive garden. The Potboys bar is a traditional taproom - just the spot to enjoy a pint of Brakspear while tucking into steak and Guinness pie; vegetable curry or goats' cheese and pesto roasted peppers. The Carriages restaurant, with its secret garden, serves a full menu with, for example, chicken and wild mushroom terrine or spiced sausage, black pudding and poached egg salad as starters. Main courses might be sea bass and mushroom risotto; pan-seared tuna steak or tian of roast vegetables with rocket pesto.

Open all day all wk 11am-mdnt Bar Meals L served all wk 12-3 D served all wk 6-9 Restaurant L served all wk 12-3 booking required D served all wk 6-9 booking required ⊕ CHAPMANS GROUP ◀ Butcombe Gold, Wadworth 6X. ♀ 6 Facilities Children's menu Garden Parking Rooms 17

## The White Hart ★★★ HL ◉ ♀

**High St OX10 7HN ☎ 01865 340074  🖹 01865 341082**
e-mail: whitehart@oxfordshire-hotels.co.uk
dir: A4074 (Oxford to Reading), 5m from M40 junct 7/ A329 to Wallingford

If this picture-perfect hotel looks familiar, that could be because it has played a starring role in the TV series Midsomer Murders. Set seven miles from Oxford in heart of historic Dorchester-on-Thames, it has welcomed travellers for around 400 years. Log fires and candlelight create an intimate atmosphere for the enjoyment of innovative dishes prepared from fresh ingredients. A good-value fixed-price lunch is available Monday to Saturday, with a choice of three starters, mains and desserts. The carte menu doubles your choice and includes imaginative dishes such as pumpkin risotto or Thai-style fish cakes, followed by roasted loin of pork with braised red cabbage, caramelised apple and sweet potato crisps; fish and chips in beer batter with crushed minted peas and hand cut chips; or grilled peppered rump steak with fat cut chips grilled tomato and salad.

Open all wk Bar Meals L served all wk 12-2.30 D served all wk 6.30-9.30 Av main course £7.95 Restaurant L served all wk 12-2.30 D served all wk 6.30-9.30 ⊕ FREE HOUSE ◀ Greene King, Marston's Pedigree, St Austell Tribute, Deuchars Caledonian IPA. ♀ 12 Facilities Children's menu Parking Rooms 26

## FARINGDON

## The Trout at Tadpole Bridge ♀

**Buckland Marsh SN7 8RF ☎ 01367 870382**
e-mail: info@troutinn.co.uk
dir: Halfway between Oxford & Swindon on A420 take road signed Bampton, pub approx 2m

Sitting peacefully on the River Thames twenty minutes from Oxford is this historic, multi-award-winning free house with luxurious rooms. A destination in its own right, it offers log fires, cask ales, riverside walks, berthing for six boats and a kitchen that makes expert use of the best local ingredients. Having run several fine-dining restaurants, owners Gareth and

continued

**England**

Helen wanted somewhere to raise their family, so the need for games, toys, space and a decent children's menu is understood. The two of them take food seriously, but not so much as to marginalise the drinker, as the locals coming in every night for the fine range of regional beers would undoubtedly affirm. From a sample menu come smoked eel salad with Noilly Prat jelly and shallot purée; pithivier of ceps, leeks and red onion marmalade with red pepper sauce; steamed beef and ale pudding; and blue brie and sun-blushed tomato strudel.

**Open** 11.30-3 6-11 Closed: 25-26 Dec, Sun eve (1 Nov-30 Apr) **Bar Meals** L served all wk 12-2 booking required D served all wk 7-9 booking required Av main course £14 **Restaurant** L served all wk 12-2 booking required D served all wk 7-9 booking required Av 3 course à la carte fr £30 ⊕ FREE HOUSE ◖ Ramsbury Bitter, Youngs PA Bitter Ô Stowford Press. ⬤ 10 **Facilities** Children's menu Dogs allowed Garden Parking

---

## FYFIELD

# The White Hart ⬤

**Main Rd OX13 5LW ☎ 01865 390585**
e-mail: info@whitehart-fyfield.com
web: www.whitehart-fyfield.com
dir: *6m S of Oxford just off A420 (Oxford to Swindon road)*

Like so many pubs, the White Hart has quite a history. It was built in Henry VI's reign by the executors of the lord of the manor as accommodation for a chantry priest and five almsmen. By 1548, chantries had been abolished and it was sold to St John's College, Oxford, whose tenants converted it into a drinking establishment. The interior is breathtaking, with an arch-braced roof and a tunnel running from the low-ceilinged bar to the manor house. The main restaurant is a grand hall of a place with soaring eaves and beams, huge stone-flanked windows and flagstone floors, overlooked by a minstrels' gallery. Mark and Kay are passionate about serving fresh food, using seasonal produce from mostly local suppliers (including their own kitchen garden) with meats sourced from trusted farms and estates; only fish, delivered from Brixham needs to travel. Mark and his team prepare everything fresh daily, even the bread and pasta, made with flour from the local mill. Menus change frequently to offer fish, antipasti and mezze boards to share; salmon fillet with beetroot risotto and horseradish foam; slow-roasted belly of Kelmscott pork with celeriac purée, crackling and cider jus; and lentil, spinach and paneer cheese tart with spiced cauliflower and coriander yoghurt. Home-made ice creams and sorbets always slip down

well to round things off. Two annual beer festivals are held with hog roasts, live music and at least 14 real ales.

**Open** noon-3 5.30-11 (Sat noon-11 Sun noon-10.30) Closed: Mon ex BH **Bar Meals** L served Tue-Sat 12-2.30, Sun 12-4 booking required D served Tue-Sat 7-9.30 booking required Av main course £15 **Restaurant** L served Tue-Sat 12-2.30, Sun 12-4 booking required D served Tue-Sat 7-9.30 booking required Fixed menu price fr £15 Av 3 course à la carte fr £28 ⊕ FREE HOUSE ◖ Hooky Bitter, Doom Bar, Hullabaloo, guest Ales Ô Thatchers Cheddar Valley. ⬤ 14 **Facilities** Children's menu Play area Garden Parking

---

## GORING

# Miller of Mansfield ★★★★★ RR ⊛ ⬤

**High St RG8 9AW ☎ 01491 872829 ▤ 01491 873100**
e-mail: reservations@millerofmansfield.com
dir: *From Pangbourne take A329 to Streatley. Right on B4009, 0.5m to Goring*

This beautiful old building has been stylishly renovated. There is a full bar menu and a restaurant open for breakfast, lunch and dinner 365 days a year. Modern European menus might offer ham hock terrine; slow roast belly pork; confit duck leg in the restaurant to steamed mussels or steak sandwich in the bar. There is a marble paved area in the garden with plants and statues under a canopy with gas heating. There are thirteen rooms available if you would like to stay over.

**Open** all day all wk 8am-11pm **Bar Meals** L served all wk 12-10 D served all wk 12-10 Av main course £8.95 food served all day **Restaurant** L served all wk 12-4.30 D served all wk 6.30-10 booking required Fixed menu price fr £14.95 Av 3 course à la carte fr £33.95 ⊕ FREE HOUSE ◖ Good Old Boy, Rebellion IPA, Organic Jester. ⬤ 15 **Facilities** Children's menu Dogs allowed Garden Parking **Rooms** 13

---

## HAILEY

# Bird in Hand ★★★★ INN ⬤

**Whiteoak Green OX29 9XP ☎ 01993 868321 ▤ 01993 868702**
e-mail: welcome@birdinhandinn.co.uk
dir: *From Witney N onto B4022 through Hailey to Whiteoak Green for 5m. At Charlbury S onto B4022 for 5m*

Set in the Oxfordshire countryside just outside the village of Hailey, this classic Cotswold stone inn is Grade II listed and dates from the 16th century. The beamed interior has huge inglenook fireplaces, with log fires in winter. Food ranges from traditional rarebit on toast topped with a poached egg, to marinated Cotswold game casserole; or home-made faggots with onion gravy and mashed potato.

Open all wk noon-11.30 Bar Meals L served Mon-Sat 12-2.30, Sun 12-3 D served Mon-Sat 6.30-9.30, Sun 6-9 ⊕ Free House ◧ Ramsbury Ö Stowford Press. ♟ 14 Facilities Children's menu Dogs allowed Garden Parking Rooms 16

## HENLEY-ON-THAMES

## The Five Horseshoes ♟

**Maidensgrove RG9 6EX ☎ 01491 641282**
📄 **01491 641086**
e-mail: admin@thefivehorseshoes.co.uk
dir: *From Henley-on-Thames take A4130, in 1m take B480 to right, signed Stonor. In Stonor left, through woods, over common, pub on left.*

This traditional 16th-century pub enjoys far-reaching views across the surrounding countryside from its two large beer gardens. Once inside, old pub games, log fires, heavy beams and brasses set the scene; there are two snug bars, as well as a large conservatory restaurant. Menus focus on the freshest produce, locally sourced when possible, and begin with classics like shepherd's pie with market vegetables; and Berkshire sausages with bubble and squeak. Other choices include smoked haddock kedgeree with poached duck egg; and butternut risotto with pumpkin seeds and Parmesan. Walkers, cyclists and dogs are all welcome, and a special walkers' snack menu includes soup; cheddar ploughman's; and doorstep sandwiches with chunky chips. Summer weekend barbecues and bank holiday hog roasts are held in one of the gardens.

Open noon-3.30 6-11 (Sat noon-11 Sun noon-6) Closed: Sun eve Bar Meals L served Mon-Fri 12-2.30, Sat 12-3, Sun 12-4 booking required D served Mon-Sat 6.30-9.30 Av main course £10 Restaurant L served Mon-Fri 12-2.30, Sat 12-3, Sun 12-4 booking required D served Mon-Sat 6.30-9.30 booking required Av 3 course à la carte fr £25 ⊕ BRAKSPEAR ◧ Brakspear Ordinary, Oxford Gold. ♟ 11 Facilities Children's menu Dogs allowed Garden Parking

## White Hart Nettlebed ★★★★ GA ❀ ♟

**High St, Nettlebed RG9 5DD ☎ 01491 641245**
📄 **01491 649018**
e-mail: info@whitehartnettlebed.com
dir: *On A4130 between Henley-on-Thames & Wallingford*

This beautifully restored property is favoured by a stylish crowd who appreciate the chic bar and restaurant. A typical three-course meal selection could comprise sweet potato and gruyère tartlet with rocket; spinach, feta and cumin spanakopita with babaganouche; and lemon and thyme pannacotta with red wine poached pear. Continental flavours are equally abundant on the Sunday lunch menu: grilled sardines with romesco sauce; confit of duck leg with butter beans in tomato sauce; and chocolate pot and red wine with Chantilly cream.

Open all day all wk 11am-11pm (Sun 11am-6pm) Bar Meals L served Mon-Sat 12-2.30, Sun 12-3 booking required D served Mon-Sat 6-9.30 booking required Restaurant L served Mon-Sat 12-2.30, Sun 12-3 booking required D served Mon-Sat 6-9.30 booking required ⊕ BRAKSPEAR ◧ Brakspear, Guinness. ♟ 12 Facilities Children's menu Play area Family room Garden Parking Rooms 6

## HOOK NORTON

## Sun Inn ♟

**High St OX15 5NH ☎ 01608 737570** 📄 **01608 737570**
e-mail: thesuninnhooky@hotmail.co.uk
dir: *5m from Chipping Norton, 8m from Banbury, just off A361*

Set in picturesque Hook Norton, this welcoming Cotswold stone inn is just a 10 minute walk from the Hook Norton Brewery – ideal if you're planning a tour! Inside you'll find oak beams, flagstones, an inglenook fireplace and plenty of Hook Norton ales on tap. Food runs from sandwiches and British classics to more poised offerings such as cured haunch of smoked wild boar with parmesan, rocket and truffle oil followed by honey-glazed ham hock with roasted garlic and parsley mash and Meaux mustard sauce.

Open all wk 11-3 6-12 (Sun 12-12) Bar Meals L served all wk 11-3 D served all wk 6.30-9 Restaurant L served all wk 11-3 booking required D served all wk 6.30-9 booking required ⊕ HOOK NORTON BREWERY ◧ Hook Norton Best Bitter, Old Hooky, Hooky Gold, seasonal ales Ö Westons Organic. ♟ 8 Facilities Children's menu Dogs allowed Garden Parking

## LOWER SHIPLAKE

## The Baskerville Arms ★★★★ INN ♟

**Station Rd RG9 3NY ☎ 0118 940 3332** 📄 **0118 940 7235**
e-mail: enquiries@thebaskerville.com
dir: *Just off A4155, 1.5m from Henley*

This welcoming pub stands on the popular Thames Path, close to Shiplake station and just a few minutes from historic Henley-on-Thames. Brick-built on the outside, modern-rustic inside, it boasts an attractive garden where summer barbecues are a common fixture. Light meals are served in the bar, while the restaurant offers the likes of chargrilled tenderloin of marinated pork on a ragout of beans, lentils, tomato and paprika; and 'posh' fish and chips. Booking is essential during Henley Regatta (early July).

continued

Open all wk 11.30-2.30 6-11 (Sun noon-4 7-10.30) Bar Meals L served Mon-Sat 11.30-2.30, Sun 12-3.30 Av main course £9 Restaurant L served Mon-Sat 11.30-2.30, Sun 12-3.30 D served Mon-Thu 7-9.30, Fri-Sun 7-10 booking required Fixed menu price fr £12.50 Av 3 course à la carte fr £28 ◖ London Pride, Loddon Hoppit, Timothy Taylor Landlord. ♥ 8 Facilities Children's menu Play area Dogs allowed Garden Parking Rooms 4

## MILTON

### The Black Boy Inn ♥

OX15 4HH ☎ 01295 722111 📄 01295 722978
e-mail: info@blackboyinn.com
web: www.blackboyinn.com
dir: From Banbury take A4260 to Adderbury. After Adderbury turn right signed Bloxham. Onto Milton Road to Milton. Pub on right

Nestling on the edge of picturesque Milton, this gorgeous 16th-century long building is set well back from the Milton Road. Recent refurbishment has created a charming interior with solid pine furniture that's entirely in keeping with the building. The long room has a wood stove at one end and a dining room at the other; in between is the bar, from which extends a conservatory-style dining room overlooking a gravelled courtyard. Outside, the patio and a lovely half-acre garden offer plenty of seating and space for children to run around. Meanwhile, head chef Kevin Hodgkiss produces modern British food based on fresh, seasonal ingredients. There are plenty of pub classics, including the likes of cottage pie with wholegrain mustard mash, and pan-fried liver and bacon with a rich shallot sauce. On the main menu, starters like pea and ham hock soup, and spiced Thai fishcakes with sweet mustard and herb mayonnaise, herald choices that include goats' cheese and fig tarte Tatin with new potatoes; sea bream fillet on basil tagliatelle with crayfish cream sauce; and Cornish cannon of lamb with gratin potato and roasted butternut squash. Leave space for one of the excellent desserts: Yorkshire rhubarb with vanilla pannacotta is typical. A wide range of fresh salads and interesting sandwiches complete the choice.

Open all wk 12-3 5.30-11.30 (Sat-Sun 12-11.30) Bar Meals L served all wk 12-2.30 D served Mon-Thu 6.30-9, Fri-Sat 6.30-9.30 booking required Restaurant L served all wk 12-2.30 D served Mon-Thu 6.30-9, Fri-Sat 6.30-9.30 booking required ◖ Adnams, Abbot Ale, rotating guest ales. ♥ 8 Facilities Children's menu Play area Dogs allowed Garden Parking

## OXFORD

### The Anchor ♥

2 Hayfield Rd, Walton Manor OX2 6TT ☎ 01865 510282
dir: A34 (Oxford ring road N), exit Peartree rdbt, 1.5m then right at Polstead Rd, follow road to bottom, pub on right

This 1937 Art Deco-styled pub is particularly popular with North Oxford's well-heeled locals, firmly on the map for its good quality seasonal British food. Lunchtime specials include roast monkfish with courgettes, peas, bacon and spinach, while the main menu offers belly pork with black pudding and greens; and smoked haddock fishcakes with ginger lime mayo. Bar snacks and sandwiches are also available.

Open all day all wk noon-11 Closed: Xmas Bar Meals L served all wk 12-2.30 D served all wk 6-9.30 Av main course £11 Restaurant L served all wk 12-2.30 booking required D served all wk 6-9.30 booking required Av 3 course à la carte fr £23 ⊕ WADWORTH ◖ Wadworth 6X, Henrys IPA, Bishops Tipple ♂ Westons Stowford Press. ♥ 11 Facilities Children's menu Dogs allowed Garden Parking

## SOUTH STOKE

### The Perch and Pike ★★★ INN ♥

RG8 0JS ☎ 01491 872415 📄 01491 871001
e-mail: info@perchandpike.co.uk
dir: On Ridgeway Hiking Trail. 1.5m N of Goring & 4m S of Wallingford on B4009

The Perch and Pike, just two minutes' walk from the River Thames, was the village's foremost beer house back in the 1700s. There's plenty of atmosphere in the pub and in the adjoining barn conversion, which houses the restaurant. Food ranges from salads, baguettes and ploughman's to the likes of Barbary duck breast with coriander and lemongrass couscous; braised belly pork with apple mash and onion gravy; and South African dish, bobotie - a spicy minced beef.

Open all wk 11.30-3 5.30-11 (Sat-Sun 11.30-11) Bar Meals L served Mon-Sat 12-2.30 booking required D served Mon-Sat 7-9.30 booking required Av main course £9 Restaurant L served Sun 12-2.30 booking required D served Mon-Sat 7-9.30 booking required Av 3 course à la carte fr £24 ⊕ BRAKSPEAR ◖ Brakspear ales. ♥ 7 Facilities Children's menu Dogs allowed Garden Parking Rooms 4

## STADHAMPTON

### The Crazy Bear ★★★★★ GA ⊛⊛ ♥

Bear Ln OX44 7UR ☎ 01865 890714 📄 01865 400481
e-mail: enquiries@crazybear-stadhampton.co.uk
dir: M40 junct 7, A329. In 4m left after petrol station, left into Bear Lane

It's a fitting name for a fairly quirky place, but the 16th-century Crazy Bear likes to pride itself on being quirky, weaving its ancient features into a modern look with a distinctive interior, which combines contemporary and art deco influences. The bar is quite traditional, except that it serves champagne and oysters as well as more conventional bar snacks. There are two restaurants, one serving Thai food, and the other modern British, as well as a wonderful garden with waterfall and statues. The menus should please everyone: 'all day' breakfasts and brunch dishes are served from 7am to 10am and classic English dishes from noon until 10pm. For breakfast/brunch choose duck eggs Benedict or farm-smoked haddock kedgeree; at lunch order a roast Angus beef and horseradish sandwich; or look to the main menu for seared scallops with a shallot and herb butter, or Old Spot ham hock terrine, followed by seared sea bass with shellfish bisque, or chicken and mushroom pie. Leave room for spiced plum crumble tart with clotted cream.

Open all day all wk 7am-mdnt Bar Meals Av main course £14 food served all day Restaurant Fixed menu price fr £10 food served all day ⊕ FREE HOUSE ◖ Old Speckled Hen, IPA, Timothy Taylor Landlord ♂ Aspall, Stowford Press. ♈ 20 Facilities Children's menu Garden Parking Rooms 17

## SWERFORD

# The Mason's Arms ◉ ♈
**Banbury Rd OX7 4AP ☎ 01608 683212    ▤ 01608 683105**
e-mail: admin@masons-arms.com
dir: *Between Banbury & Chipping Norton on A361*

Originally a Masonic lodge, this award-winning 300-year-old pub is owned by Bill and Charmaine Leadbeater, and business partner, Tom Aldous. 'Bill's Food' and 'Bill's Specials' menus confirm his supremacy in the kitchen, where the modern, personal twist he puts on his creations has earned him an AA Rosette. These range from chicken korma with pilau rice, naan bread and onion bhaji, to 12-hour braised shin of shorthorn beef with cranberry and cinnamon red cabbage, herb roasties and red wine jus. His specials include chargrilled lamb cutlets with fondant potato, asparagus spears, honey and rosemary jus. Treacle tart and custard, and lemon and blueberry Pavlova are typical desserts. There is also a tempting children's menu.

Open Closed: 25-26 Dec, Sun eve Bar Meals L served Mon-Sat 12-2 booking required D served Mon-Sat 7-9 booking required Av main course £10.95 Restaurant L served Mon-Sat 12-2, Sun 12-3.30 booking required D served Mon-Sat 7-9 booking required Fixed menu price fr £14.95 Av 3 course à la carte fr £26 ⊕ FREE HOUSE ◖ Hook Norton Best, Brakspear Special. ♈ 14 Facilities Children's menu Garden Parking

## TOOT BALDON

# The Mole Inn ◉◉ ♈
**OX44 9NG ☎ 01865 340001    ▤ 01865 343011**
e-mail: info@themoleinn.com
dir: *5m SE from Oxford city centre off B480*

This stone-built, Grade II listed pub was the subject of an extensive renovation programme not long ago. The top-notch makeover has earned it a glowing and well-deserved reputation, due in no small measure to the efforts of award-winning chef/host Gary Witchalls. Inside, a great deal of care and attention has been lavished on this classic old local, and

now customers can relax in black leather sofas amid stripped beams and solid white walls. The dining areas are equally striking with their intimate lighting and terracotta floors. Gary's inspired menu draws plenty of foodies from nearby Oxford and further afield, tempted by dishes such as 28-day, dry-aged Aberdeenshire rib steak; braised and roasted shoulder of Cornish lamb with clapshot and curly kale; or twice-cooked belly of Blythburgh pork in an apple jus, with gratin dauphinoise and purple sprouting broccoli.

Open all day all wk 12-12 (Sun 12-11) Closed: 25 Dec, 1 Jan Restaurant L served Mon-Sat 12-2.30, Sun 12-4 booking required D served Mon-Sat 7-9.30, Sun 6-9 booking required ⊕ FREE HOUSE ◖ Hook Norton, London Pride, Spitfire, Guinness. ♈ 11 Facilities Children's menu Garden Parking

## RUTLAND

## EMPINGHAM

# The White Horse Inn ★★★ INN ♈
**Main St LE15 8PS ☎ 01780 460221    ▤ 01780 460521**
e-mail: info@whitehorserutland.co.uk
dir: *From A1 take A606 signed Oakham & Rutland Water. From Oakham take A606 to Stamford*

An ideal place to recharge your batteries following a walk or cycle around Rutland Water, this former 17th-century courthouse has lost none of its period charm. The open fire, beamed bar and friendly staff are a recipe for total relaxation. The home-made food starts with sandwiches, home-made soup and baguettes and runs to hearty meals such as cheese and ale soup followed by Elizabethan pork casserole, or local trout fillets with a herb butter.

Open all day all wk Closed: 25 Dec Bar Meals L served Mon-Thu 12-2.15, Fri-Sun 12-9 D served Mon-Thu 6.30-9, Fri-Sun 12-9 Av main course £9.50 Restaurant L served Mon-Thu 12-2.15, Fri Sun 12-9 D served Mon-Thu 6.30-9, Sun 12-9 Av 3 course à la carte fr £19 ⊕ ENTERPRISE INNS ◖ John Smith's, Adnams Best Bitter, Oakham Ales JHB & Bishops Farewell, Timothy Taylor Landlord. ♈ 9 Facilities Children's menu Dogs allowed Garden Parking Rooms 13

## LYDDINGTON

# Old White Hart ♈
**51 Main St LE15 9LR ☎ 01572 821703    ▤ 01572 821978**
e-mail: mail@oldwhitehart.co.uk
dir: *From A6003 between Uppingham & Corby take B672. Pub on main street opp village green*

Set amongst the sandstone cottages of rural Lyddington, this 17th-century free house close to Rutland Water has retained its original beamed ceilings, stone walls and open fires, and is surrounded by well-stocked gardens. The menu might include home cured gravadlax with horseradish dressing; and roast local pheasant breast with buttered mash. Fish and vegetarian choices plus daily specials and early bird menu also available.

continued

England

Open all wk 12-3 6.30-11 (Sun 12-3 7-10.30) Closed: 25 Dec, 26 Dec eve **Bar Meals** L served Mon-Fri 12-2, Sat-Sun 12-2.30 booking required D served all wk 6.30-9, (Sun in summer 7-9) booking required Av main course £12.95 **Restaurant** L served Mon-Fri 12-2, Sat-Sun 12-2.30 booking required D served all wk 6.30-9 (Sun in summer 7-9) booking required Fixed menu price fr £10.95 Av 3 course à la carte fr £25 ⊕ FREE HOUSE ◀ Greene King IPA & Abbot Ale, Timothy Taylor Landlord, Fuller's London Pride, Timothy Taylor Golden Best. ♀ 8 **Facilities** Children's menu Play area Garden Parking

## STRETTON

## Ram Jam Inn

**The Great North Rd LE15 7QX** ☎ **01780 410776**
📄 **01780 410361**
dir: *On A1 N'bound carriageway past B668, through service station into car park*

The inn was originally a humble ale house called the Winchelsea Arms, and belonged to the Earl of Winchelsea. It is thought that its current name stems from a home-brew invented by a resident publican during the 18th century, when the pub sign advertised 'Fine Ram Jam'. Sadly no recipe survives, so its ingredients are a mystery. Today's informal café-bar and bistro, with a patio overlooking orchard and paddock, welcomes visitors with a daily-changing menu.

Open all day all wk 7.30am-10pm (Sun 8.30am-6pm) Closed: 25 Dec **Bar Meals** Av main course £9 food served all day **Restaurant** Av 3 course à la carte fr £15 food served all day ⊕ FREE HOUSE ◀ John Smith's Smooth, Fuller's London Pride. **Facilities** Children's menu Play area Garden Parking

# SHROPSHIRE

## ADMASTON

## The Pheasant Inn at Admaston

**TF5 0AD** ☎ **01952 251989**
e-mail: info@thepheasantadmaston.co.uk
web: www.thepheasantadmaston.co.uk
dir: *M54 junct 6 follow A5223 towards Whitchurch then follow B5063 towards Shawbirch & Admaston. Pub is on left of main rd*

Once owned by the Great Western Railway, this lovely old country pub dates from the 19th century. Stylish interior décor and a real fire add character to the dining areas, whilst the

large enclosed garden is ideal for families. Using the best of local produce, expect pan-seared lamb's liver with crispy bacon and home-grown sage and red wine gravy; roast sea bass with prawn and cucumber butter; and broccoli, leek and field mushroom pie. There is also a very good 'Little People's' menu.

Open all day all wk **Bar Meals** L served Mon-Sat 12-2, Sun 12-3 D served Mon-Sat 6-9 Av main course £9 ◀ Shropshire Gold, Greene King IPA, Shropshire Lad, Guinness. **Facilities** Children's menu Play area Dogs allowed Garden Parking

## BASCHURCH

## The New Inn ♀

**Church Rd SY4 2EF** ☎ **01939 260335**
e-mail: bean.newinn@btconnect.com
dir: *8m from Shrewsbury, 8m from Oswestry*

Refurbished and revitalised by Marcus and Jenny Bean, this whitewashed village pub overlooks the parish church and draws the crowds for local ales and Marcus's home-cooked food. Sit at oak tables in the spick-and-span bar and dining room, or at teak tables on the landscaped patio, and tuck into lamb noisettes stuffed with rosemary and thyme, or slow roast Moor Farm pork belly with caramelised apples and cider jus, and milk chocolate and honeycomb mousse.

Open all wk 11-3 6-11 (Sun 12-4 7-11) Closed: 26 Dec, 1 Jan **Bar Meals** L served all wk 12-2 D served all wk 6.30-9.30 **Restaurant** L served all wk 12-2 booking required D served all wk 6.30-9.30 booking required ⊕ FREE HOUSE ◀ Greene King Abbot Ale, Banks Bitter, Stonehouse Station, Hobsons Best Bitter Ở Thatchers. ♀ 10 **Facilities** Children's menu Dogs allowed Garden Parking

## BRIDGNORTH

## Halfway House Inn ★★★ INN ♀

**Cleobury Rd, Eardington WV16 5LS** ☎ **01746 762670**
📄 **01746 768063**
e-mail: info@halfwayhouseinn.co.uk
dir: *M5 junct 6, A449 towards Kidderminster. Follow ring road to right. At next rdbt take A442 N towards Bridgnorth. 12m, take A458 towards Shrewsbury. Follow brown tourist signs to pub*

An Elizabethan wall mural is a fascinating feature of this former coaching inn, but the Halfway House owes its current name to a visit in 1823 by Princess Victoria and her entourage. The pub is renowned for its locally sourced, home-cooked food, at least three local real ales, 40 malts, and around 100 wines. Dishes range from bar snacks to braised beef in Guinness, grilled local steaks and Astbury Falls rainbow trout.

Open 5-11.30 (Fri & Sat 11am-11.30pm Sun 11-6) Closed: Sun eve ex BH **Bar Meals** L served Fri-Sun 12-2 D served Mon-Sat 6-9 Av main course £11.50 **Restaurant** D served Mon-Sat 6-9 booking required Fixed menu price fr £22.50 Av 3 course à la carte fr £25 ⊕ FREE HOUSE ◀ Holden's Golden Glow, Wood's Shropshire Lad, Hobson's Town Crier, Draught Guinness Ở Weston's Stowford Export. ♀ 10 **Facilities** Children's menu Play area Garden Parking **Rooms** 10

## CHURCH STRETTON

### The Bucks Head ★★★★ INN ☉

**42 High St SY6 6BX ☎ 01694 722898**
e-mail: lnutting@btinternet.com
dir: *12m from Shrewsbury & Ludlow*

Bring your boots and walk off a hearty lunch with a ramble along the Long Mynd, just minutes from the front door of this recently revamped pub and restaurant. Fuel-up on or return from hills for home-made food using local produce. Expect home-made soups, steaks, lasagne, authentic curries or one of the daily fish specials. There's an attractive summer garden for alfresco drinking.

**Open** all day all wk **Bar Meals** L served all wk 12-2.30 D served all wk 6-9 **Restaurant** L served all wk 12-2.30 D served all wk 6-9 ⊕ Marston's Pub Company ◀ Banks Original, Banks Bitter, Marston's Pedigree, Guinness, Guest Ale. ☉ 6 **Facilities** Children's menu Garden Parking **Rooms** 4

### The Royal Oak

**Cardington SY6 7JZ ☎ 01694 771266 📄 01694 771685**
e-mail: inntoxicated@gmail.com
dir: *Turn right off A49 N of Church Stretton; 2m off B4371 (Church Stretton-Much Wenlock road)*

Reputed to be the oldest continuously licensed pub in the county, this 15th-century free house is set in a conservation village surrounded by lovely countryside close to the South Shropshire hills. It has a low-beamed bar with a vast inglenook, and a comfortable beamed dining room. Four cask ales are served alongside home-cooked food. Fidget pie (gammon, apples and cider) is a house speciality made from a recipe handed down from landlord to landlord.

**Open** 12-2.30 (Sun 12-3.30) 7-mdnt (Fri-Sat 1am) Closed: Mon (ex BH Mon L) **Bar Meals** L served Tue-Sat & BH Mon 12-2, Sun 12-2.30 D served Tue-Sun 7-9 **Restaurant** L served Tue-Sat 12-2, Sun 12-2.30 D served Tue-Sun 7-9 ⊕ FREE HOUSE ◀ Hobsons Best Bitter, Three Tuns XXX, Wye Valley Butty Bach, Bass, Six Bells 1859. **Facilities** Children's menu Garden Parking

## CRAVEN ARMS

### The Sun Inn ☉

**Corfton SY7 9DF ☎ 01584 861239**
e-mail: normanspride@aol.com
dir: *On B4368, 7m N of Ludlow*

First licensed in 1613, this historic pub has a public bar with pool table, jukebox and dartboard, along with a lounge and restaurant. Landlord Norman Pearce brews the Corvedale ales in what was the pub's old chicken and lumber shed, using local borehole water; Mahoral cider, from just down the road, is another drinks option. Teresa Pearce uses local produce in a delicious array of traditional dishes, served with up to six fresh vegetables and a choice of chips or new potatoes. The pub has historic connection with the transportation of criminals to Australia.

**Open** all wk 12-2.30 6-11 (Sun 12-3 7-11) **Bar Meals** L served all wk 12-2 D served all wk 6-9 Av main course £9 **Restaurant** L served 12-2 D served 6-9 ⊕ FREE HOUSE ◀ Corvedale Normans Pride, Dark & Delicious, Julie's Ale, Katie's Pride, Farmer Rays ☉ Mahoral. ☉ 14 **Facilities** Children's menu Play area Dogs allowed Garden Parking

## IRONBRIDGE

### The Malthouse ☉

**The Wharfage TF8 7NH ☎ 01952 433712**
📄 **01952 433298**
e-mail: enquiries@themalthouseironbridge.com
dir: *Telephone for directions*

An inn since the 1800s, the Malthouse is located in the village of Ironbridge next to the river, now a designated UNESCO World Heritage Site famous for its natural beauty and award-winning museums. Party menus are available for both the popular jazz bar and the restaurant, while the main menu ranges from lasagne or faggots to monkfish and pancetta baked and served with sweet chorizo, mussel and tomato cassoulet.

**Open** all wk **Bar Meals** food served all day **Restaurant** food served all day ⊕ PUNCH TAVERNS ◀ Directors, Greene King IPA, Badger. ☉ 10 **Facilities** Children's menu Dogs allowed Garden Parking

## LLANFAIR WATERDINE

### The Waterdine ★★★★★ RR ◉◉ ☉

**LD7 1TU ☎ 01547 528214**
e-mail: info@waterdine.com
dir: *4.5m W of Knighton off B4355, turn right opposite Lloyney Inn, 0.5m into village, last on left opp church*

There's an air of total peace and quiet, and there are fine views down the Teme Valley from this low, stone whitewashed pub-with-rooms, tucked away in a tiny hamlet smack on the border between England and Wales. The old parish church stands opposite, the Teme runs through the bottom of the garden, and chef-landlord Ken Adams proudly continues to provide sustenance and shelter for weary travellers at his 400-year-old former drover's inn. There are two dining rooms, the Garden Room looking out over the river, and the Taproom, tucked away in the oldest part of the building with heavy beams and a stone floor. Menus are based on home-grown and locally supplied organic produce, so dishes like Old Spot pork terrine with fig and raspberry chutney, pan-fried beef fillet with Dijon mustard sauce, and roast turbot on leek confit with girolle mushrooms are appropriately seasonal.

**Open** Closed: 1wk winter, 1wk spring, Sun eve & Mon (ex BH) **Bar Meals** L served Thu-Sun 12.15-1.30 booking required **Restaurant** L served Thu-Sun 12.15-1.30 booking required D served Tue-Sat 7-8.30 booking required ⊕ FREE HOUSE ◀ Wood Shropshire Legends, Parish Bitter, Shropshire Lad. ☉ 8 **Facilities** Children's menu Garden Parking **Rooms** 3

## LUDLOW

### The Clive Bar & Restaurant with Rooms ★★★★★ RR ⊛⊛ ♀

**Bromfield SY8 2JR** ☎ **01584 856565 & 856665**
🖹 **01584 856661**
**e-mail:** info@theclive.co.uk
**web:** www.theclive.co.uk
**dir:** *2m N of Ludlow on A49, between Hereford & Shrewsbury*

This classy bar and eatery was once home to Robert Clive, who laid the foundations of British rule in India. Built as a farm house in the 18th-century, the building became a pub in the 19th for the workers of the Estate. These days it houses a bar with traditional ales, real ciders, a wide range of wines and light snacks. It separates into two sections - an 18th-century lounge area in traditional style with log fire and original coat of arms of Clive of India. A more contemporary upper area leads to an outside courtyard with tables and parasols for warmer weather. There is also a stylish Rosetted restaurant.

**Open** all day all wk Mon-Sat 11-11 (Sun 12-10.30) Closed: 25-26 Dec **Bar Meals** L served Mon-Fri 12-3, Sat-Sun 12-6.30 booking required D served Mon-Sat 6.30-10, Sun 6.30-9.30 booking required Av main course £9.95 **Restaurant** L served all wk 12-3 booking required D served Mon-Sat 6.30-10, Sun 6.30-9.30 booking required Av 3 course à la carte fr £25 ⊕ FREE HOUSE ◀ Hobsons Best Bitter, Ludlow Gold Bitter, Guinness Ŏ Dunkertons Original, Mahoral Farm. ♀ 10 **Facilities** Children's menu Garden Parking **Rooms** 15

### The Roebuck Inn ★★★★ INN ⊛⊛

**Brimfield SY8 4NE** ☎ **01584 711230**
**e-mail:** info@theroebuckludlow.co.uk
**dir:** *Just off A49 between Ludlow & Leominster*

Despite a façade that looks decidedly Victorian, this country inn dates from the 15th century. Its lounge bar retains the inglenook and wood panelling of the period, while the elegantly minimalist dining room is more contemporary. Customers have the choice of eating in either room from the imaginative menus of head chef-patron, Olivier Bossut. Expect his carte to offer starters of butternut squash risotto with aged Parmesan, roast pinenuts, cep oil; gateau of crab in a saffron beurre blanc; and main courses of saddle of lamb Wellington with Jerusalem artichoke and liquorice sauce; and fillet of beef en croûte with truffle sauce. Twice monthly, on Wednesday evenings, the Roebuck has a French night in association with Ludlow's French Pantry.

**Open** all wk 11.30-3 6-mdnt (Sun eve times vary) **Bar Meals** L served Mon-Sat 11.30-2.30 D served Mon-Sat 6.30-9 Av main course £13.50 **Restaurant** L served all wk 11.30-2.30 D served Mon-Sat 6.30-9 ⊕ MARSTONS ◀ Bank's Bitter, Marstons Pedigree plus guests. **Facilities** Children's menu Dogs allowed Garden Parking **Rooms** 3

## MUCH WENLOCK

### The Feathers Inn ♀

**Brockton TF13 6JR** ☎ **01746 785202** 🖹 **01746 712717**
**e-mail:** feathersatbrockton@googlemail.com
**dir:** *From Much Wenlock follow signs to Ludlow on B4378 for 3m*

A vast inglenook, big mirrors, stone busts, reclaimed timbers from old ships and local art are all features of this Grade II listed, 16th-century pub. The Feathers also incorporates a mini shop, a children's cookery school, a ladies' luncheon club, and a takeaway food service. Menus are based on fresh, largely local ingredients, with a regularly updated specials board, traditional Sunday roasts, and good value early suppers.

**Open** 12-2 6.30-11 Closed: 26 Dec, 1-4 Jan, Mon **Bar Meals** L served Tue-Sun 12-2 D served Tue-Sun 6.30-11 Av main course £12 **Restaurant** L served Tue-Sun 12-2 D served Tue-Sun 6.30-11 Fixed menu price fr £10 Av 3 course à la carte fr £16 ⊕ FREE HOUSE ◀ Hobsons Ale, Guinness, Boddingtons, Worfield Brewery Ales. ♀ 6 **Facilities** Children's menu Garden Parking

### The George & Dragon

**2 High St TF13 6AA** ☎ **01952 727312**
**e-mail:** bevmason@btinternet.com
**dir:** *On A458 halfway between Shrewsbury & Bridgnorth*

The George & Dragon is an oak-beamed 17th-century inn at the heart of Much Wenlock. Sited next to the market square, Guildhall and ruined priory, the inn welcomes everyone, from locals to walkers. It oozes history, charm and character, and now and again the spirit of a mistreated 18th-century dog is felt as a cold chill around the legs or heard walking across the quarry tiles. Locals Bev and James pride themselves on serving good quality, home-cooked British food and real cask ales.

**Open** all day all wk 11-11 (Thu 11-mdnt Fri-Sat 11am-1am Sun 11am-11.30pm) **Bar Meals** L served all wk 12-2 D served Mon-Tue, Thu 6-9 Av main course £5.95 **Restaurant** L served all wk 12-2 D served Mon-Tue, Thu-Sat 6-9 Fixed menu price fr £6.95 Av 3 course à la carte fr £10.95 ⊕ PUNCH RETAIL ◀ Greene King Abbot Ale, Wadworth 6X, guest ales. **Facilities** Children's menu Dogs allowed

## Longville Arms

**Longville in the Dale TF13 6DT ☎ 01694 771206**
🗎 01694 771742
e-mail: jill.livingstone@btconnect.com
dir: *From Shrewsbury take A49 to Church Stretton, then B4371 to Longville*

Prettily situated in an Area of Outstanding Natural Beauty in Shropshire, ideally placed for walking and touring, this welcoming country inn has been carefully restored. Solid elm or cast-iron-framed tables, oak panelling and wood-burning stoves are among the features that help to generate a warm, friendly ambience. Favourite main courses on the bar menu and specials board include steak and ale pie, mixed fish platter, and a range of steaks. There are tethering facilities for horses and dogs are welcome.

Open all wk 12-3 6.30-11.30 (Sun 12-3 6.30-10.30) **Bar Meals** L served all wk 12-2.30 D served all wk 6.30-9.30 Av main course £10 **Restaurant** L served Sun & BH 12-2.30 D served Fri-Sat & BH 6.30-9.30 Fixed menu price fr £9.95 Av 3 course à la carte fr £22 ⊕ FREE HOUSE ◀ Local guest ales. **Facilities** Children's menu Play area Dogs allowed Garden Parking

---

## MUNSLOW

## The Crown Country Inn ★★★★ INN ◉◉ ♟

**SY7 9ET ☎ 01584 841205**
e-mail: info@crowncountryinn.co.uk
dir: *On B4368 between Craven Arms & Much Wenlock*

The impressive, three-storey Crown stands in a lovely setting below the rolling hills of Wenlock Edge, in the Vale of the River Corve. A Grade II listed building, it retains in the main bar the sturdy oak beams, flagstone floors and prominent inglenook fireplace that must have been here since it was built in Tudor times. Initially, it was a Hundred House, where courts dished out punishment to local miscreants, including perhaps the black-clothed Charlotte sometimes seen in the pub. Free house status means a good range of local beers. Meals are served in the main bar, the Bay dining area, and the Corvedale Restaurant. He acquires his top quality local produce from trusted sources and is proud to feature it in his dishes, many

of which can be both starter or main course, such as risotto of prawns, basil and crayfish tails topped with home-grown dried cherry tomatoes; hot pavé of organic Clunbury smoked salmon with sweet pickled cucumber and horseradish potato salad; baked flat mushrooms topped with Shropshire Blue cheese and apricot and walnut crust; and roast breast of free-range Breckland duck with dauphinoise potatoes. The cheeseboard lists a dozen English and Welsh cheeses, while for something sweet there's warm spiced banana cake with caramelised banana, butterscotch sauce and The Crown's own home-made ice cream.

Open Closed: Xmas, Sun eve, Mon **Bar Meals** L served Tue-Sun 12-2 booking required D served Tue-Sat 6.45-8.45 booking required Av main course £15 **Restaurant** L served Tue-Sun 12-2 booking required D served Tue-Sat 6.45-8.45 booking required Fixed menu price fr £18 Av 3 course à la carte fr £26 ⊕ FREE HOUSE ◀ Holden's Black Country Bitter, Holden's Golden Glow, Holden's Special Bitter, Three Tuns Brewery XXX ♂ Mahoral. ♟ 7 **Facilities** Children's menu Play area Garden Parking **Rooms** 3 **Notes**

---

## NORTON

## The Hundred House Hotel ★★ HL ◉◉ ♟

**Bridgnorth Rd TF11 9EE ☎ 01952 580240**
🗎 01952 580260
e-mail: reservations@hundredhouse.co.uk
web: www.hundredhouse.co.uk
dir: *On A442, 6m N of Bridgnorth, 5m S of Telford centre*

In medieval England the shires were subdivided into administrative areas called hundreds, and hundred houses were the courthouses. That's what the 14th-century, half-timbered, thatched barn outside the hotel used to be, and opposite are the remains of the old stocks and whipping post where offenders were punished. The hotel, which is mainly Georgian, has been lovingly run by the Phillips family for over two decades. In fact, you enter an amazing interconnecting warren of lavishly decorated bars and dining rooms, with old quarry tiled floors, exposed brickwork, beamed ceilings and oak panelling. Oh, and one more thing to see is a display of twelve plates, each representing the annual award of AA Rosettes. Baskets of pumpkins and marrows lurk in corners at harvest time, while in December huge decorated onions might occupy the same space. Dried herbs hang from beams, and chilli peppers, pots pourris and lavender bunches can all be found. Hearty food in the bar/brasserie includes traditional

continued

steak and kidney pie; spatchcock poussin marinated in rosemary and paprika, grilled and served with couscous, salad and harissa sauce; and tapas for two. And, from the main menu, roast Apley partridge stuffed with mushroom and cotechino (an Italian sausage); prime Bridgnorth sirloin steak; hake fillet baked with caponata (a Sicilian speciality); game pie; breast of Hereford duck with orange sauce, confit duck and black pudding; and sweet red and yellow peppers stuffed with bean casserole and salsa verde. The dessert menu offers raspberry and crème brûlée; pear and almond tart with cinnamon cream; and vanilla pannacotta with mulled red berries.

**Open** all wk 11-11 **Closed:** 25-26 Dec eve **Bar Meals** L served all wk 12-2.30 D served all wk 6-9.30 Av main course £9.95 **Restaurant** L served all wk 12-2.30 D served all wk 6-9.30 Fixed menu price fr £10 Av 3 course à la carte fr £22.50 ⊕ FREE HOUSE ◀ Heritage Bitter, Wells, Bombardier, Apley Ale. ♦ 16 **Facilities** Children's menu Garden Parking **Rooms** 10

---

## OSWESTRY

# The Bradford Arms ★★★★ INN

**Llanymynech SY22 6EJ ☎ 01691 830582**
📄 **01691 839009**
e-mail: robinbarsteward@tesco.net
web: www.bradfordarmshotel.com
dir: *Situated on the A483 5m S of Oswestry*

On the Welsh border, close to Powis and Chirk Castles, this coaching inn offers above-average eating in its quietly elegant bar and dining rooms. Arrive early to ensure a seat and then tuck into, say, a bowl of moules, lamb shank with mint gravy, steak and ale pie, and lemon meringue pie. Good lunchtime sandwiches, traditional Sunday roasts, and Black Sheep Bitter on tap. Once the coaching inn on the Earl of Bradford's estate, it is ideally situated for golfing, fishing and walking.

**Open** 11.30-3 6-mdnt **Closed:** 25 Dec L, Mon **Bar Meals** L served Tue-Sun 11.30-2 **Restaurant** L served Tue-Sun 11.30-2 D served Tue-Sun 6.30-9 ⊕ FREE HOUSE ◀ Black Sheep Best, Tetley Smooth, Guinness, 2 Guest ales. **Facilities** Children's menu Dogs allowed Garden Parking **Rooms** 5

# The Red Lion Inn ★★★ INN

**Bailey Head SY11 1PZ ☎ 01691 656077**
📄 **01691 655932**

A newly refurbished public house on the market square in the town centre with a listed, early 1800s frontage, and a modern, open-plan bar, where cask ales are changed every few days. A menu of inexpensive light meals includes home-made cottage pie; chilli con carne; chicken curry; jumbo cod in crispy batter; a wide range of burgers; jacket potatoes; sandwiches, toasted and au naturel; and salads. A Mediterranean-style courtyard acts as the perfect suntrap.

**Open** all day all wk 11am-11pm (Sun noon-10) **Closed:** 25-26 Dec **Bar Meals** L served Mon-Sat 11-3, Sun 12-3 D served Mon-Thu 5.30-8.30 booking required Av main course £5.50 ⊕ Punch Taverns ◀ John Smiths, Guinness. **Facilities** Children's menu Garden Parking **Rooms** 5

---

## PAVE LANE

# The Fox ♦

**TF10 9LQ ☎ 01952 815940   📄 01952 815941**
e-mail: fox@brunningandprice.co.uk
dir: *1m S of Newport, just off A41*

A big Edwardian-style pub, with a mix of private corners and sunny spacious rooms, all wrapped around a busy central bar. There's a large south-facing terrace with views over wooded hills. In addition to light bites and sandwiches, the comprehensive menu could include mushroom and Shropshire Blue soup; Wenlock Edge air-dried Shropshire ham and fig salad; Shropshire rabbit pie; artichoke heart tortelloni with watercress, caper and parmesan pesto. Desserts to try are chocolate and Shropshire stout cake; and passion fruit cheesecake with raspberry sauce.

**Open** all day all wk noon-11 (Sun noon-10.30) **Bar Meals** food served all day **Restaurant** food served all day ⊕ BRUNNING & PRICE ◀ Timothy Taylor Landlord, Woods Shropshire Lad, Thwaites Original, Titanic Mild, Hobsons Golden Glow. ♦ 6 **Facilities** Children's menu Dogs allowed Garden Parking

---

## SHIFNAL

# Odfellows Wine Bar ♦

**Market Place TF11 9AU ☎ 01952 461517**
📄 **01952 463855**
e-mail: reservations@odley.co.uk
dir: *M54 junct 4, 3rd exit at rdbt, at next rdbt take 3rd exit, past petrol station, round bend under rail bridge. Bar on left*

Quirky, popular wine bar owned by Odley Inns, which explains the 'od' spelling. Drinks include regional real ales and ciders. The carefully prepared food, served in an elevated dining area and attractive conservatory, is ethically sourced from local suppliers. The bar and outdoor areas have now been extended and serve regional real ales and ciders as well as the great wine selection. Seasonal menus might offer devilled kidneys; potato, onion and chorizo soup; creamy, dreamy fish pie; chargilled Ludlow venison; and bacon wrapped pheasant breasts on bubble and squeak. Live music every Sunday.

Open all day all wk noon-mdnt Closed: 25-26 Dec, 1 Jan **Bar Meals** L served all wk 12-2.30 Av main course £6 **Restaurant** L served all wk 12-2.30 D served all wk 6-10 Av 3 course à la carte fr £15 ⊕ FREE HOUSE ◀ Salopian, Wye Valley, Holdens, Ludlow Gold, Three Tuns ○ Thatchers. ♀ 12 **Facilities** Children's menu Garden Parking

## SHREWSBURY

## The Armoury ♀

**Victoria Quay, Victoria Av SY1 1HH ☎ 01743 340525**
📄 **01743 340526**
e-mail: armoury@brunningandprice.co.uk
dir: *Telephone for directions*

The converted Armoury building makes an impressive, large scale pub, just over the bridge on the opposite bank of the river from the new Theatre Severn. Large warehouse windows and huge bookcases dominate the interior of the bar and restaurant area. The comprehensive menu ranges through starters, light bites, main courses, sandwiches, puddings and cheese. Typical dishes are chilli and coriander crab cakes; wild boar and apricot sausages; and pan-fried salmon with crab risotto.

Open all day all wk 11am-mdnt Closed: 25-26 Dec **Bar Meals** Av main course £12 **Restaurant** L served 12-10 D served 12-10 food served all day ⊕ BRUNNING & PRICE ◀ Roosters APA, Salopian Shropshire Gold, Deuchars IPA, Woods Shropshire Lad, Three Tuns Steamer. ♀ 16 **Facilities** Children's menu

## The Mytton & Mermaid Hotel ★★★ HL 🏵🏵 ♀

**Atcham SY5 6QG ☎ 01743 761220** 📄 **01743 761292**
e-mail: admin@myttonandmermaid.co.uk
dir: *From M54 junct 7 signed Shrewsbury, at 2nd rdbt take 1st left signed Ironbridge/Atcham. In 1.5m hotel on right after bridge*

Food is a major attraction at this country house hotel on the banks of the Severn; its chef holds two AA rosettes for the quality of his cooking. The Grade II listed building's tastefully decorated interior recalls the atmosphere of its coaching inn days. Mad Jack's Bar, named after a colourful local squire, offers dishes such as naturally smoked haddock with crushed potatoes and hollandaise, or local venison and Shropshire Lad casserole with blue cheese dauphinoise and parsnip crisps.

Open all day all wk 7am-11pm Closed: 25 Dec **Bar Meals** L

served all wk 12-2.30 D served all wk 6.30-10 Av main course £13.95 **Restaurant** L served all wk 12-2.30 booking required D served all wk 7-10 booking required Fixed menu price fr £29.50 Av 3 course à la carte fr £27.50 ⊕ FREE HOUSE ◀ Shropshire Lad, Shropshire Gold, Hobsons Best. ♀ 12 **Facilities** Children's menu Garden Parking **Rooms** 18

## STOTTESDON

## Fighting Cocks

**1 High St DY14 8TZ ☎ 01746 718270** 📄 **01746 718270**
e-mail: sandrafc-5@hotmail.com
dir: *11m from Bridgnorth off B4376*

The pub, first licensed in 1850, was called the Cock Inn until the 1980s. The village name of Stottesdon means 'stud on the hill' and it used to be the administrative centre for the surrounding area. The unassuming 18th-century coaching inn once reputedly brewed an ale containing chicken for monks at the village church; called cock ale, it was also served to travellers along with chicken jelly. Today's food, home-made with locally-sourced produce, is rather more appealing.

Open all wk 6-mdnt (Fri 5pm-1am Sat-Sun noon-mdnt) **Bar Meals** L served Sat-Sun 12-2.30 booking required Av main course £10 **Restaurant** L served Sat-Sun 12-2.30 booking required D served Mon-Sat 7-9 booking required ⊕ FREE HOUSE ◀ Hobsons Best, Hobsons Town Crier, Hobsons Mild, Wye Valley HPA, Wye Valley Bitter ○ Stowford Press. **Facilities** Children's menu Garden Parking

## WENTNOR

## The Crown Inn

**SY9 5EE ☎ 01588 650613** 📄 **01588 650436**
e-mail: crowninn@wentnor.com
dir: *From Shrewsbury A49 to Church Stretton, follow signs over Long Mynd to Asterton, right to Wentnor*

Outdoor enthusiasts of all persuasions will appreciate the location of this 17th-century coaching inn below the Long Mynd. Its homely atmosphere, which owes much to log fires, beams and horse brasses, makes eating and drinking here a pleasure. Meals are served in the bar or separate restaurant. Typical daily changing, traditional home-made dishes include pork tenderloin filled with marinated fruits; pan-fried breast of duck with a burnt orange sauce; and grilled sea bass with couscous.

Open all wk noon-3 6-11 (Sat noon-mdnt Sun noon-10) Closed: 25 Dec **Bar Meals** L served Mon-Fri 12-2 D served Mon-Fri 6-9 Av main course £7.50 **Restaurant** L served Sat-Sun 12-9 D served Sat-Sun 12-9 ⊕ FREE HOUSE ◀ Hobsons, Old Speckled Hen, Three Tuns, Wye Valley ○ Westons Scrumpy. **Facilities** Children's menu Play area Garden Parking

## WHITCHURCH

### Willeymoor Lock Tavern ♀

**Tarporley Rd SY13 4HF ☎ 01948 663274**
dir: *2m N of Whitchurch on A49 (Warrington to Tarporley road)*

A former lock keeper's cottage idyllically situated beside the Llangollen Canal. Low-beamed rooms are hung with a novel teapot collection; there are open log fires and a range of real ales. Deep-fried fish and a choice of grills rub shoulders with traditional steak pie, chicken curry and vegetable chilli. Other options include salad platters, children's choices and gold rush pie for dessert.

**Open** all wk 12-2.30 6-11 (Sun 12-2.30 6-10.30) Closed: 25 Dec & 1 Jan **Bar Meals** L served all wk 12-2 D served all wk 6-9 **Restaurant** L served all wk 12-2 D served all wk 6-9 ⊕ FREE HOUSE ◀ Abbeydale, Moonshine, Weetwood, Oakham JHB, Best & Eastgate, Timothy Taylor Landlord. ♀ 8 **Facilities** Children's menu Play area Garden Parking  ⊛

## WISTANSTOW

### The Plough ♀

**SY7 8DG ☎ 01588 673251**
e-mail: richardsys@btconnect.com
web: www.ploughwistanstow.co.uk
dir: *1m N of Craven Arms. Turn off A49 to Wistanstow*

Beers don't have to travel far to end up being drawn through century-old hand-pumps in the simply furnished bar of this traditional country pub. Located next to the award-winning Wood Brewery, it is effectively the brewery tap, serving Parish Bitter, Shropshire Lad and Wood's other real ales. An ethically sourced menu includes the ever-popular fish and chips (made with Wood's beer batter, of course); Shropshire sirloin and gammon steaks; and scampi, as well as children's choices. The specials board changes regularly and might feature home-made curries (try the fish cooked in coconut milk and turmeric; or spicy lamb and spinach); and farmhouse pork, bacon and cheese pie. Local faggots, omelettes and baguettes appear on the lunchtime menu. On Sundays, as well as the regular menus, there are traditional beef, pork or free-range chicken roasts.

**Open** all wk noon-2.30 5-mdnt (Sun noon-11) **Bar Meals** L served all wk 12-2 D served all wk 6.30-9 Av main course £7.50 ⊕ WOODS BREWERY ◀ Wood's Shropshire Lad, Parish, Pot O' Gold ♂ Thatchers, Stowford Press. ♀ 9 **Facilities** Children's menu Dogs allowed Garden Parking

---

## SOMERSET

### APPLEY

### The Globe Inn ♀

**TA21 0HJ ☎ 01823 672327**
e-mail: globeinnappley@btconnect.com
dir: *From M5 junct 26 take A38 towards Exeter. Village signed in 5m*

The Globe is known for its large collection of Corgi and Dinky cars, Titanic memorabilia, old advertising posters and enamel signs. The Grade II listed inn dates back 500 years and is hidden in a maze of lanes on the Somerset-Devon border. Produce is sourced locally and uses organic and Fair Trade goods where possible. Food from baguettes to main courses (including plenty for vegetarian options), like twice baked broccoli soufflé; lamb hot pot pie; Moroccan chicken and chickpea tagine; and 3 different varieties of 'multi chilli'.

**Open** Closed: Mon (ex BH) **Bar Meals** L served Tue-Sun 12-2 booking required D served Tue-Sun 7-9.30 booking required Av main course £11.95 **Restaurant** L served Tue-Sun 12-2 booking required D served Tue-Sun 7-9.30 booking required Fixed menu price fr £19.95 Av 3 course à la carte fr £22 ⊕ FREE HOUSE ◀ Palmers 200, Exmoor Ales, Appleys Ale, Doom Bar, Tribute ♂ Thatchers Gold. ♀ 8 **Facilities** Children's menu Play area Garden Parking

### ASHCOTT

### Ring O'Bells ♀

**High St TA7 9PZ ☎ 01458 210232**
e-mail: info@ringobells.com
dir: *M5 junct 23 follow A39 & Glastonbury signs. In Ashcott turn left, at post office follow church & village hall signs*

A free house run by the same family for over 20 years. Parts of the building date from 1750, so the pub interior has beams, split-level bars, an old fireplace and a collection of bells and horse brasses. All food is made on the premises. Look to the good value specials board for ham and lentil soup; roast guinea fowl with apple and local cider sauce, then orange and rhubarb cheesecake to finish. Patio and garden in warmer weather.

**Open** all wk noon-3 7-11 (Sun 7-10.30pm) Closed: 25 Dec **Bar Meals** L served all wk 12-2 D served all wk 7-10 Av main course £8 **Restaurant** L served all wk 12-2 D served all wk 7-10 ⊕ FREE HOUSE ◀ guest ales. ♀ 8 **Facilities** Children's menu Play area Garden Parking

### ASHILL

### Square & Compass ♀

**Windmill Hill TA19 9NX ☎ 01823 480467**
e-mail: squareandcompass@tiscali.co.uk
dir: *Turn off A358 at Stewley Cross service station (Windmill Hill) 1m along Wood Rd, behind service station*

There's a warm, friendly atmosphere at this traditional country pub, beautifully located overlooking the Blackdown Hills in the heart of rural Somerset. Lovely gardens make the most of the views, and the bar area features hand-made settles and tables. There is a good choice of home-cooked food (prepared in the state-of-the-art large kitchen). Dishes might include sweet and sour pork, lambs' kidneys braised with sherry and Dijon mustard, hot garlic king prawns, and mixed grill. The barn next door was built by the owners from reclaimed materials for use as a wedding and village events venue.

**Open** Closed: 25 Dec, Tue-Thu L **Bar Meals** L served Fri-Mon 12-3 D served all wk 6.30-late Av main course £8.50 **Restaurant** L served Fri-Mon 12-3 D served all wk 6.30-late Av 3 course à la carte fr £15 ⊕ FREE HOUSE ◀ Exmoor Ale & Gold Moor Withy Cutter, Wadworth 6X, Branscombe Bitter, WHB, HSD. ⬤ 6 **Facilities** Children's menu Dogs allowed Garden Parking

## BABCARY

## Red Lion ⬤

**TA11 7ED ☎ 01458 223230** ▤ **01458 224510**
e-mail: redlionbabcary@btinternet.com
dir: *Please telephone for directions*

The Red Lion is a beautifully refurbished, stone-built free house, with rich, colour-washed walls, heavy beams and simple wooden furniture setting the tone in the friendly bar, whilst French doors lead out into the garden from the restaurant. Granary sandwiches, ciabattas and hot pub favourites like fish pie and honey-glazed Somerset ham, egg and chips are served in the bar. In the restaurant, expect slow roasted pork belly with celeriac purée; butternut squash and sage risotto; and free range duck breast with wild mushroom cream sauce.

**Open** all wk **Bar Meals** L served all wk 12-2.30 D served Mon-Sat 7-9.30 **Restaurant** L served all wk 12-2.30 D served Mon-Sat 7-9.30 ⊕ FREE HOUSE ◀ Teignworthy Reel Ale, O'Hanlons, Otter, Bath Ales. ⬤ 12 **Facilities** Children's menu Play area Dogs allowed Garden Parking

## BATH

## The Hop Pole

**7 Albion Buildings, Upper Bristol Rd BA1 3AR**
**☎ 01225 446327**
e-mail: hoppole@bathales.co.uk
dir: *20 min walk from City of Bath on A4 towards Bristol. Pub opp Victoria Park*

Opposite the Royal Victoria Park and just off the canal path, this is a great spot for quaffing summer ales. One of just nine pubs belonging to Bath Ales, a fresh young microbrewery, the beers rejoice in names such as Gem, Spa, Wild Hare and Barnstormer. Described as a country pub in the heart of a city, The Hop Pole has a stripped-down, stylish interior, and the lovingly restored, spacious beer garden to the rear is complete with patio heaters and pétanque pitch. The atmospheric old skittle alley has been transformed into a large restaurant, which can accommodate coach parties if pre-booked. Home-cooked food ranges from imaginative bar snacks and sandwiches through to full meals. Children are served smaller

portions from the main menu. You could start with chicken liver parfait before moving on to medallions of monkfish with chargrilled Mediterranean vegetables, sun-dried tomatoes and pesto. Monday night is quiz night.

**Open** all day all wk noon-11 (Fri-Sat noon-mdnt) **Bar Meals** L served Mon-Sat 12-2, Sun 12-3 D served Mon-Sat 6-9 Av main course £8.75 **Restaurant** L served Mon-Sat 12-2, Sun 12-3 D served Mon-Sat 6-9 ⊕ BATH ALES LTD ◀ Bath Ales: Gem, Spa, Barnstormer, Festivity, Wild Hare. **Facilities** Children's menu Garden

## The Marlborough Tavern ⬤

**35 Marlborough Buildings BA1 2LY ☎ 01225 423731**
e-mail: joe@marlborough-tavern.com
dir: *10m from M4 junct 18, 200mtrs from the western end of Royal Crescent on the corner of Marlborough Buildings and a short walk from Bath City Centre*

This 18th-century corner pub stands just a stone's throw from Bath's famous Royal Crescent. Foot-weary from the city's tourist trail, then seek rest and refreshment in the rustic-chic bars or head for the attractive courtyard garden. Expect Butcombe Bitter on tap, a raft of decent wines by the glass, and a classy menu that delivers gutsy, full-flavoured dishes prepared from local seasonal produce, including organic meat from local farms and the Neston Park estate, and fruit and vegetables grown by Eades Greengrocers in fields at nearby Swainswick. This translates to imaginative lunchtime sandwiches (houmous, coriander and rocket), tapas-style dishes like grilled chorizo and chicken skewers, classics like braised beef and onions, and Lackfarm Farm rib-eye steak with chips and mushroom sauce. Evening additions may take in spiced pork and black pudding terrine, whole plaice with caper brown butter and spring onion mash, and lemon and saffron posset with plum Eton mess.

**Open** all day all wk noon-11 (Fri-Sat noon-12 30am) Closed: 25 Dec **Restaurant** L served Mon-Sat 12.30-2.30, Sun 12.30-4 booking required D served Mon-Sat 6-9.30 booking required Av 3 course à la carte fr £20 ⊕ PUNCH TAVERNS ◀ Butcombe Bitter, Sharp's Doom Bar Ö Westons Organic. ⬤ 19 **Facilities** Children's menu Dogs allowed Garden

BAWDRIP

## BAWDRIP

## The Knowle Inn

**TA7 8PN ☎ 01278 683330**
e-mail: peter@matthews3.wanadoo.co.uk
dir: *M5 junct 23 or A39 from Bridgwater towards Glastonbury*

A mile off the M5 (Junct 23), this 16th-century pub nestles beneath the Polden Hills on the edge of the Somerset levels – a great place for walking and cycling. A true community pub, with live music, skittles and darts, it also specialises in fresh seafood, with possibly sea bass and gurnard among the catch delivered from Plymouth. Meat-eaters are not forgotten - try the steak and ale pie or a rib-eye steak with all the trimmings. Head for the Mediterranean-style garden, complete with fish pond, for summer alfresco meals.

continued

**England**

Open all day all wk 11-11 **Bar Meals** L served all wk 11-3 booking required D served all wk 6-9 Av main course £8 **Restaurant** L served all wk 11-3 D served all wk 6-9 Fixed menu price fr £10 Av 3 course à la carte fr £20 ⊕ ENTERPRISE ◀ Otter, Champflower Ale, Revival, Somerland Gold Ŏ Thatchers. **Facilities** Children's menu Dogs allowed Garden Parking

## BECKINGTON

### Woolpack Inn Ⓐ ★★ SHL ♟

**BA11 6SP ☎ 01373 831244** 📄 **01373 831223**
e-mail: 6534@greeneking.co.uk
dir: *Just off A36 near junction with A361*

Standing on a corner in the middle of the village, this charming, stone-built coaching inn dates back to the 1500s. Inside there's an attractive, flagstoned bar and outside at the back, a delightful terraced garden. The lunch menu offers soup and sandwich platters, and larger dishes such as home-made sausages and mash; fresh herb and tomato omelette; steak and ale pie; and beer-battered cod and chips. Some of these are also listed on the evening bar menu.

Open all day all wk 11am-11pm (Sun 11am-10pm) **Bar Meals** L served Mon-Sat 12-2.30, Sun 12-3 booking required D served Mon-Sat 6.30-9.30, Sun 6.30-9 booking required **Restaurant** L served Mon-Sat 12-2.30, Sun 12-3 booking required D served Mon-Sat 6.30-9.30, Sun 6.30-9 booking required ⊕ OLD ENGLISH INNS & HOTELS ◀ Greene King IPA, Abbot Ale, guest ale Ŏ Moles Black Rat. ♟ 8 **Facilities** Children's menu Dogs allowed Garden Parking **Rooms** 12

## BICKNOLLER

### The Bicknoller Inn

**32 Church Ln TA4 4EL ☎ 01984 656234**
e-mail: james_herd@sky.com
dir: *Telephone for directions*

A 16th-century thatched country inn set around a courtyard with a large garden under the Quantock Hills. Inside you'll find traditional inglenook fireplaces, flagstone floors and oak beams, as well as a theatre-style kitchen and restaurant. Meals range from sandwiches and pub favourites like hake in beer batter (priced for an 'adequate' or 'generous' portion), to the full three courses with maybe smoked salmon; chicken supreme cooked in red wine, and warm treacle tart.

Open all wk noon-3 6-11 (Fri-Sun all day) Closed: Mon L ex BH **Bar Meals** L served Tue-Thu 12-3, Fri-Sun all day booking required D served Tue-Thu 6.30-10, Fri-Sun all day booking required **Restaurant** L served Tue-Thu 12-3, Fri-Sun all day booking required D served Tue-Thu 6.30-10, Fri-Sun all day booking required ⊕ PALMERS BREWERY ◀ Palmers Copper, Palmers IPA, Palmers Gold, guest ales Ŏ Thatchers Traditional. **Facilities** Children's menu Play area Dogs allowed Garden Parking

## BLUE ANCHOR

### The Smugglers ♟

**TA24 6JS ☎ 01984 640385**
e-mail: info@take2chefs.co.uk
dir: *Off A3191, midway between Minehead & Watchet*

'Fresh food, cooked well' is the philosophy at this friendly 300-year-old inn, standing just yards from Blue Anchor's sandy bay with a backdrop of the Exmoor Hills. Food, using fresh produce locally sourced, can be enjoyed in the Cellar Bar or the Dining Room. Baguettes, filled baked potatoes, pizzas, pastas, grills, curries, salads, speciality sausages and fish and seafood are available. Honey-roast ham and minted lamb cutlets are in the 'comfort food' selection. In fine weather diners eat in the walled garden, where children can enjoy the animals at the nearby farm and the bouncy castle.

Open noon-3 6-11 Closed: Nov-Etr, Sun eve, Mon-Tue L **Bar Meals** L served all wk 12-2.15 D served all wk 6-9 Av main course £8.95 **Restaurant** L served all wk 12-2.15 D served all wk 6-9 ⊕ FREE HOUSE ◀ Smuggled Otter, Otter Ale. ♟ 6 **Facilities** Children's menu Play area Dogs allowed Garden Parking

## CONGRESBURY

### The White Hart Inn ♟

**Wrington Rd BS49 5AR ☎ 01934 833303**
e-mail: murat@simplywhitehart.co.uk
dir: *From M5 junct 21 take A370 through Congresbury, right towards Wrington. Inn in 2.3m on Wrington Road*

This dining pub has a secluded garden with views of the Mendip Hills, and the beamed bars are country-cosy with log fires in stone inglenooks. Refuel with simple, honest food such as steak and Badger ale pie, venison with blackberry and stilton sauce, or a lunchtime brie and bacon baguette, washed down with a pint of Tanglefoot. The gin list is impressive and don't miss the Turkish night – music and belly dancers.

Open all wk 11.30-3 6-11.30 (Fri-Sun 11.30-11.30) Closed: 25 Dec **Bar Meals** Av main course £8.95 food served all day **Restaurant** Av 3 course à la carte fr £17.50 food served all day ⊕ HALL & WOODHOUSE ◼ Badger, Tanglefoot ♂ Westons Stowford Press. ♛ 8 **Facilities** Children's menu Play area Dogs allowed Garden Parking

---

## CORTON DENHAM

## The Queens Arms ♛
**DT9 4LR ☎ 01963 220317**
e-mail: relax@thequeensarms.com
dir: *From A30 (Sherborne) take B3145 signed Wincanton. Approx 1.5m left at red sign to Corton Denham. 1.5m, left down hill, right at bottom into village. Pub on left*

Enjoy a pint of Abbeydale Riot, Moor Revival or a draft Somerset cider by the open fire of this late 18th-century village free house (AA Pub of the Year 2008-09), situated in beautiful countryside. Food is served throughout, as well as in the rear garden. Menus offer great variety: at lunch, Islay whisky-marinated smokey salmon, with pickled silverskins and gherkins; Old English sausages and mash with red onion marmalade; and pan-fried pollock on winter bean cassoulet, as well as sandwiches. In the evening, try seared scallops with crispy Denhay ham, red pepper and shallot purée; the pub's own pig's liver with caramelised shallots and rich gravy; and slow-roasted shoulder of lamb with fondant parsnip, potato and cauliflower purée. Afterwards, 'proper' Somerset apple pie with cream; or the cheese plate and a Trappist beer, one of many world bottled beers available. The extensive wine and malt whisky lists make for good reading.

Open all wk 11-3 6-11 (Sat-Sun, BH, Xmas wk 11-11) **Bar Meals** L served Mon-Sat 12-3, Sun 12-4 D served Mon-Sat 6-10, Sun 6-9.30 Av main course £7.50 **Restaurant** L served Mon-Sat 12-3, Sun 12-4 D served Mon-Sat 6-10, Sun 6-9.30 Av 3 course à la carte fr £23 ⊕ FREE HOUSE ◼ Moor Revival, Abbeydale Riot, changing guests ♂ Thatchers Cheddar Valley. ♛ 20 Facilities Children's menu Dogs allowed Garden Parking

---

## CREWKERNE

## The George Inn ★★★ INN ♛
**Market Square TA18 7LP ☎ 01460 73650**
🖹 01460 72974
e-mail: georgecrewkerne@btconnect.com
dir: *Please telephone for directions*

The George has been welcoming travellers in the heart of Crewkerne since the 16th century, though the present hamstone coaching inn dates from 1832. Using local produce where possible, the extensive menu includes something for everyone, starting with bar food like all-day breakfast, filled jacket potatoes, and steak and kidney pudding to Courtyard Restaurant dishes such as crispy duck with apple sauce, and poached salmon in white wine, plus grills and skillets.

Open all day all wk **Bar Meals** L served all wk 12-2 D served all wk 7-9 Av main course £8 **Restaurant** L served

all wk 12-2 D served all wk 7-9 Av 3 course à la carte fr £16 ⊕ FREE HOUSE ◼ Old Speckled Hen, Doom Bar, Tribute, Boddington's ♂ Thatchers Dry, Thatchers Gold. ♛ 8 **Facilities** Children's menu Dogs allowed Garden **Rooms** 13

---

## DINNINGTON

## Dinnington Docks
**TA17 8SX ☎ 01460 52397**   🖹 **01460 52397**
e-mail: hilary@dinningtondocks.co.uk
dir: *S of A303 between South Petherton & Ilminster*

Formerly known as the Rose & Crown, this traditional village pub on the old Fosse Way has been licensed for over 250 years. Rail or maritime enthusiasts will enjoy the large collection of memorabilia, and it is an ideal location for cycling and walking. Freshly prepared food includes the likes of crab cakes, Greek salad, faggots, snapper, steak, and lamb shank for two.

Open all wk 11.30-3.30 6-mdnt **Bar Meals** Av main course £6.95 food served all day **Restaurant** food served all day ⊕ FREE HOUSE ◼ Butcombe Bitter, Wadworth 6X, guest ales ♂ Burrow Hill, Stowford Press, Thatchers Gold. **Facilities** Children's menu Play area Family room Dogs allowed Garden Parking

---

## DITCHEAT

## The Manor House Inn ♛
**BA4 6RB ☎ 01/49 860276**   🖹 **0870 286 3379**
e-mail: landlord@manorhouseinn.co.uk
dir: *From Shepton Mallet take A371 towards Castle Cary, in 3m turn right to Ditcheat*

About 150 years ago this delightful 17th-century free house, constructed from Ditcheat red brick, belonged to the lord of the manor and was known as the White Hart. It's tucked away in a charming Mendip village offering easy access to the Royal Bath and West showground and the East Somerset steam railway. Inside you'll find roaring log fires in winter and flagstone floors, with the bar serving Butcombe Bitter and three regular guest ales, local apple brandies and up to eight wines by the glass. Menus are seasonal; in spring, for example, you may find starters such as pan-fried chicken livers with Madeira and wild mushrooms, or traditional prawn and seafood cocktail. Main courses may proffer rack of best British spring lamb with a minted herb crust on bubble and squeak; or roasted Somerset belly pork on leeks, spring greens and lardons with a cider sauce. Choose a home-made dessert from the board in the restaurant.

Open all day all wk 11.30-3 5.30-11 (Fri-Sun noon-mdnt) **Bar Meals** L served all wk 12-2 D served all wk 7-9.30 Av main course £7.50 **Restaurant** L served all wk 12-2 booking required D served all wk 7-9.30 booking required Av 3 course à la carte fr £25 ⊕ FREE HOUSE ◼ Butcombe, John Smiths's, guest ales. ♛ 8 **Facilities** Children's menu Dogs allowed Garden Parking

### DUNSTER

## The Luttrell Arms ★★★ HL

**High St TA24 6SG ☎ 01643 821555** 📄 **01643 821567**
e-mail: info@luttrellarms.fsnet.co.uk
dir: *From A39 (Bridgewater to Minehead), left onto A396 to Dunster (2m from Minehead)*

Built in the 15th-century as a guest house for the Abbots of Cleeve, this atmospheric hotel's open fires and oak beams make the bar a welcoming place in winter. A wild venison casserole with ale and horseradish sauce is just the thing for a chilly day, while in the more formal restaurant you could tuck into smoked haddock fishcakes, followed by wild pigeon and mushroom parcels with cider jus. Desserts include sticky ginger parkin with vanilla-steeped pineapple and ginger ice cream in the restaurant, and clotted cream rice pudding in the bar.

Open all wk 8am-11pm **Bar Meals** L served all wk 11.30-3, all day summer D served all wk 7-10 **Restaurant** L served Sun 12-3 booking required D served all wk 7-10 booking required ⊕ FREE HOUSE ◀ Exmoor Gold Fox, Guest ale ♂ Cheddar Valley Cider. **Facilities** Children's menu Family room Dogs allowed Garden Rooms 28

### EAST COKER

## The Helyar Arms ★★★★ INN ◉

**Moor Ln BA22 9JR ☎ 01935 862332** 📄 **01935 864129**
e-mail: info@helyar-arms.co.uk
dir: *3m from Yeovil. Take A57 or A30, follow East Coker signs*

Reputedly named after Archdeacon Helyar, a chaplain to Queen Elizabeth I, this Grade II listed building dates back in part to 1468. Log fires warm the old world bar in this charming inn. There's a skittle alley, accommodation and a separate restaurant occupying an original apple loft. The kitchen makes full use of local produce, including wood pigeon, rabbit, venison, pheasant and fish from the south Devon coast. Lunchtime bar snacks include salads such as chicken and bacon with toasted pine nuts; and hot beef and blue cheese with cherry tomatoes and red onion. A full meal could start with game keeper's terrine or home-smoked duck breast with beetroot and lentil salad. Main courses include pub classics in addition to the likes of whole roasted local partridge or confit chicken with sautéed thyme potatoes.

Open all wk **Bar Meals** L served all wk 12-2.30 D served all wk 6.30-9.30 Av main course £7 **Restaurant** L served all wk 12-2.30 D served all wk 6.30-9.30 Av 3 course à la

carte fr £25 ⊕ PUNCH TAVERNS ◀ Butcombe Bitter, Black Sheep, Hobgoblin ♂ Stowford Press, Taunton Traditional. **Facilities** Children's menu Family room Dogs allowed Garden Parking Rooms 6

### EXFORD

## The Crown Hotel ★★★ HL ◉ ♀

**TA24 7PP ☎ 01643 831554** 📄 **01643 831665**
e-mail: info@crownhotelexmoor.co.uk
web: www.crownhotelexmoor.co.uk
dir: *From M5 junct 25 follow Taunton signs. Take A358 then B3224 via Wheddon Cross to Exford*

The family-run, 17th-century Crown Hotel was the first purpose-built coaching inn on Exmoor. It is located in a pretty village in three acres of gardens and woodland, through which runs a fast-flowing trout stream. The cosy country bar is very much the social heart of the village. Welcoming log fires are lit in the lounge and bar in winter, and there are lovely water and terrace gardens for summer use. Lunchtime snacks include a range of sandwiches and baguettes, and baked potatoes brimming with cheese and pickle, tuna and red onion, or chicken and bacon. Quality ingredients are sourced locally where possible and cooked to order. In the bar look for Exmoor free-range duck leg and lentil salad; trio of organic sausages with mustard mash; seared Cornish scallops with lemon couscous; and pan-fried sea bass with creamed leek potatoes, black trumpet mushrooms, roasted shallots and orange sauce. Delicious vegetarian options: try warm cep risotto with fresh Parmesan and mascarpone cheese. A fitting finish might be plum tart with frangipane, yoghurt sorbet and praline biscuit.

Open all day all wk noon-11pm **Bar Meals** L served all wk 12-2.30 winter, 12-5.30 summer D served all wk 6-9.30 Av main course £11 **Restaurant** D served all wk 7-9 Av 3 course à la carte fr £37.50 ⊕ FREE HOUSE ◀ Exmoor Ale, Exmoor Gold ♂ Thatchers Gold, Cornish Rattler. ♀ 12 **Facilities** Children's menu Dogs allowed Garden Parking Rooms 17

### HINTON ST GEORGE

## The Lord Poulett Arms ♀

**High St TA17 8SE ☎ 01460 73149**
e-mail: steveandmichelle@lordpoulettarms.com
dir: *2m N of Crewkerne, 1.5m S of A303*

Beautifully restored by owners Michelle Paynton and Steve Hill, this 17th-century thatched pub fronts the street in one of

Somerset's loveliest villages. The bar features bare flagstones and boarded floors and is furnished with a harmonious mixture of old oak and elm tables, and ladderback, spindleback and Windsor chairs. Similarly furnished, the dining room has real fires in open fireplaces, including one with a huge bressemer beam across the top. Most of the food is locally sourced: fish is organic or wild, free-range meat comes from the Somerset/ Dorset border, and herbs are home-grown. The lunch menu offers soups, salads, gourmet sandwiches, bouillabaise and hot dishes like pan-roasted duck magret. In the evening you might expect chicken fillet stuffed with haggis; chowder of monkfish, langoustine and smoked bacon; and braised Somerset pork shoulder with carrot and ginger mash. In summer, enjoy a drink by the boule piste, under the wisteria shaded pergola or dine in the wild flower meadow.

Open all wk noon-3 6.30-11 Closed: 26 Dec, 1 Jan Bar Meals L served all wk 12-2 booking required D served all wk 7-9 booking required Av main course £14 Restaurant L served all wk 12-2 booking required D served all wk 7-9 booking required Av 3 course à la carte fr £22 ⊕ FREE HOUSE ◀ Hopback, Branscombe, Cotleigh, Archers, Otter Ö Thatchers Gold. ♈ 7 Facilities Children's menu Dogs allowed Garden Parking

## HOLCOMBE

## The Holcombe Inn ★★★★ INN ♈

Stratton Rd BA3 5EB ☎ 01761 232478  📄 01761 233737
e mail: bookings@holcombeinn.co.uk
dir: On A367 to Stratton-on-the-Fosse, take concealed left turn opposite Downside Abbey signed Holcombe, take next right, pub 1.5m on left

This country inn boasts comfortable accommodation and a large garden with views of nearby Downside Abbey and the Somerset countryside. The lunch menu runs to various sandwiches and wraps, while the evening choice is supplemented by a specials board: start with crispy squid with sweet chilli dip; or asparagus tips with tomato and basil hollandaise sauce, and move on to grilled Scottish salmon with cucumber and prawn cream; pork stroganoff; or spinach and ricotta ravioli.

Open all wk 11.30-11.30 (Sat 11.30-2.30 6.30-11 Sun noon-3 6.45-10.30) Closed: Sun eve & Mon in winter Bar Meals L served all wk 12-2 D served Mon-Sat 7-9, Sun 7-8.30 Restaurant L served all wk 12-2 D served Mon-Sat 7-9, Sun 7-8.30 ⊕ FREE HOUSE ◀ Otter Ale, Guinness, guest bitter Ö Thatchers Old Rascal. ♈ 7 Facilities Children's menu Dogs allowed Garden Parking Rooms 8

## ILCHESTER

## Ilchester Arms ♈

The Square BA22 8LN ☎ 01935 840220  📄 01935 841353
e-mail: mail@ilchesterarms.com
dir: From A303 take A37 signed Ilchester/Yeovil, left at 2nd Ilchester sign. Hotel 100yds on right

An elegant Georgian fronted house with lots of character, this establishment was first licensed in 1686 and was owned

between 1962 and 1985 by the man who developed Ilchester cheese. Attractive features include open fires and a secluded garden. An extensive bistro menu offers the likes of smoked haddock fishcakes to start, medallions of venison with juniper onion compote, game sauce and pommes Anna, and passion fruit tart, in addition to snacks and salads, battered cod and steaks in the bar.

Open all day all wk 7am-11pm Closed: 26 Dec Bar Meals L served Mon-Sat 12-2.30 D served Mon-Sat 7-9 Av main course £6.50 Restaurant L served all wk 12-2.30 D served Mon-Sat 7-9 Av 3 course à la carte fr £35 ⊕ FREE HOUSE ◀ Butcombe, Flowers IPA, Bass, local ales Ö Thatchers Gold. ♈ 12 Facilities Children's menu Play area Family room Garden Parking

## KILVE

## The Hood Arms ★★★★ INN ♈

TA5 1EA ☎ 01278 741210  📄 01278 741477
e-mail: info@thehoodarms.com
dir: From M5 junct 23/24 follow A39 to Kilve. Village between Bridgwater & Minehead

This traditional, friendly 17th-century coaching inn is set among the Quantocks and provides thirsty walkers with traditional ales in the beamed bar. A good range of fresh fish includes whole sea bass with apple and almond butter, and always on the menu are the inn's famous beef and ale pie, and stilton-topped steaks. Vegetarians get their own menu.

Open all day all wk 12-11 Bar Meals Av main course £9 food served all day Restaurant food served all day ⊕ FREE HOUSE ◀ Guinness, Otter Head, Palmers Copperdale, Fullers London Pride, Guest ales Ö Thatchers Gold. ♈ 13 Facilities Children's menu Play area Family room Dogs allowed Garden Parking Rooms 12

## LANGLEY MARSH

## The Three Horseshoes

TA4 2UL ☎ 01984 623763
e-mail: mark_jules96@hotmail.com
dir: M5 junct 25 take B3227 to Wiveliscombe. Turn right up hill at lights. From square, turn right, follow Langley Marsh signs, pub in 1m

This handsome 17th-century red sandstone pub has had only four landlords during the last century. It remains a free house, with traditional opening hours, child-free bars and a good choice of ales straight from the barrel. The landlord's wife prepares home-cooked meals, incorporating local ingredients and vegetables from the pub garden. Typical specials include halibut steak baked with tomatoes and wine; and pheasant breast with smoked bacon and cranberries. There's an enclosed garden with outdoor seating.

Open noon-2.30 7-11 Closed: Mon, Sun eve Bar Meals L served Tue-Sun 12-1.45 D served Tue-Sat 7-9 ⊕ FREE HOUSE ◀ Palmer IPA, Otter Ale, Exmoor Ale, Cotleigh 25. Facilities Children's menu Garden Parking

## LANGPORT

### The Old Pound Inn ★★★ INN ♟

**Aller TA10 0RA ☎ 01458 250469** 🖷 **01458 250469**
e-mail: oldpoundinn@btconnect.com
dir: *2.5m N of Langport on A372. 8m SE of Bridgwater on A372*

Built as a cider house, the Old Pound Inn dates from 1571 and retains plenty of historic character with oak beams, open fires and a garden that used to be the village pound. It's a friendly pub with a good reputation for its real ale and home-cooked food, but also provides function facilities for 200 with its own bar. There is also a skittle alley.

Open all wk Bar Meals L served all wk 12-2 D served all wk 6-9 Restaurant D served Fri-Sun 6-9 🍺 Tribute, Sharp's, Cotleigh, Branscombe, Glastonbury, Hopback ⚬ Burrow Hill Medium, Burrow Hill Pear. ♟ 8 Facilities Children's menu Dogs allowed Garden Parking Rooms 8

## LONG SUTTON

### The Devonshire Arms ★★★ INN ⊛ ♟

**TA10 9LP ☎ 01458 241271** 🖷 **01458 241037**
e-mail: mail@thedevonshirearms.com
dir: *Exit A303 at Podimore rdbt onto A372. Continue for 4m, left onto B3165.*

A fine-looking, stone-built former hunting lodge on a pretty village green. Step through its imposing portico, decorated with the Devonshire family crest, to discover unexpectedly contemporary styling complementing the large open fire and other original features. The pub is also renowned for its daily changing menu based whenever possible on locally sourced produce. For lunch try a grilled mozzarella open sandwich with fennel, tomato and rocket salad, or a venison burger with local cheddar, home-cut chips and garlic mayonnaise. Desserts may include dark chocolate and pear clafoutis, and apple and frangipane tart. Dinner dishes are equally mouthwatering, with half a dozen choices at each course. You can drink and dine in the courtyard, large walled garden or overlooking the green.

Open all wk noon-3 6-11 Closed: 25-26 Dec Bar Meals L served all wk 12-2.30 booking required D served all wk 7-9.30 booking required Av main course £9.75 Restaurant D served all wk 7-9.30 booking required Av 3 course à la carte fr £25 ⊕ FREE HOUSE 🍺 Teignworthy Real Ale, Bath Spa, Cheddar Potholer, Yeovil Stargazer. ♟ 10 Facilities Children's menu Play area Dogs allowed Garden Parking Rooms 9

## LOVINGTON

### The Pilgrims ★★★★ INN ♟

**BA7 7PT ☎ 01963 240597**
e-mail: jools@thepilgrimsatlovington.co.uk
dir: *A303 onto A37 to Lyford, right at lights, 1.5m to The Pilgrims on B3153*

With disarming honesty, owners Sally and Jools Mitchison admit that The Pilgrims will never be pretty from the outside. Step inside, however, and it's another story. Wicker and leather

seating characterise the bar, and locals' pewter mugs hang ready for the next pint of Cottage ale, brewed just around the corner. 'Local' is a much-used word here; many herbs and vegetables are grown in the pub's own garden, and every effort is made to source nearby produce, particularly cheeses. Starters and light lunches include hot potted haddock in cheese sauce on tomato salsa; pan-fried pigeon breast on bubble and squeak; and baked Capricorn goats' cheese in filo pastry with tomato salsa. The dinner menu continues with stuffed free-range West Country chicken breast with bacon lardons and cider cream sauce; and pan-fried John Dory with pesto mash.

Open noon-3 7-11 Closed: Oct, Sun eve, Mon Bar Meals L served Wed-Sun 12-2.30 D served Tue-Sat 7-9 Av main course £10 Restaurant L served Wed-Sun 12.30-2.30 D served Tue-Sat 7-9 booking required Av 3 course à la carte fr £30 ⊕ FREE HOUSE 🍺 Cottage Brewing Champflower, Erdinger ⚬ Burrow Hill Orchard Pig, Stowford Press. ♟ 12 Facilities Children's menu Dogs allowed Garden Parking Rooms 5

## LOWER VOBSTER

### Vobster Inn ★★★★ INN ⊛ ♟

**BA3 5RJ ☎ 01373 812920** 🖷 **01373 812247**
e-mail: info@vobsterinn.co.uk
dir: *4m W of Frome*

The original part of this long stone building, standing in four acres of grounds, dates back to the 17th century, though there was probably an inn here before that. The simple bar menu makes choosing easy with inexpensive suggestions such as roast chorizo sausages with fried eggs and crusty bread; cheese omelette and fries; and grilled goats' cheese bruschetta with Mediterranean vegetables and home-made crab apple jelly. On the main menu you'll find echoes of the owners' origins on Galicia's wild coast, including a selection of Spanish cured and smoked meats with salad, olives, houmous and crusty bread; and Somerset pork belly stuffed with Asturian black pudding, bubble and squeak and vanilla plum, as well as grilled open cap mushrooms with Welsh rarebit; and prawn, crab and mayonnaise cocktail. Typical among the mains options are mixed bean cottage pie; rack of lamb with black pudding, Savoy cabbage and pine nut sauté and scrumpy syrup; and grilled rib-eye with herb butter, mushrooms, cherry vine tomatoes and fries. Fish comes fresh from Cornwall: brill, perhaps, saffron- and garlic-marinated and served with pak choi risotto. All desserts are home made, with choices like white chocolate and coconut cheesecake; pannacotta with fresh berries; and lemon posset. Children are particularly welcome and have their own menu, although they are also encouraged to try smaller portions from the main menus.

**Open** Closed: Sun eve **Bar Meals** L served all wk 12-2 booking required D served Mon-Sat 6.30-9 booking required Av main course £12.50 **Restaurant** L served all wk 12-2 booking required D served Mon-Sat 6.30-9 booking required Av 3 course à la carte fr £22.50 ⊕ FREE HOUSE ◀ Butcombe Blonde, Butcombe Bitter Ꝺ Ashton Press. ♎ 8 **Facilities** Children's menu Family room Garden Parking **Rooms** 3

## MARTOCK

# The Nag's Head Inn

**East St TA12 6NF ☎ 01935 823432**
dir: *Telephone for directions*

This 200-year-old former cider house is set in a lovely hamstone street in a south Somerset village. The large rear garden is partly walled and has pretty borders and trees. Local real ales, wines and food are served in both the public and lounge bars, where crib, dominoes, darts and pool are available. The pub also has a skittle alley and a smoking area.

**Open** all wk noon-3 6-11 (Fri-Sun noon-mdnt) **Bar Meals** L served all wk 12-2 D served Mon-Thu 6-8, Sat-Sun 6-9 Av main course £5.50 **Restaurant** Av 3 course à la carte fr £14 ⊕ FREE HOUSE ◀ Guinness, Worthington, Toby. **Facilities** Children's menu Family room Dogs allowed Garden Parking

## MONTACUTE

# The Kings Arms Inn ♎

**49 Bishopston TA15 6UU ☎ 01935 822513**
e-mail: info@thekingsarmsinn.co.uk
dir: *From A303 onto A3088 at rdbt signed Montacute. Hotel in village centre*

Mons Acutus (thus Montacute) is the steep hill at whose foot the hamstone-built Kings Arms has stood since 1632. Have a snack in the fire-warmed bar or outside in warmer weather, or something more substantial chosen from the daily-changing restaurant menu; the restaurant was recently refurbished. All food is cooked on the premises using fresh ingredients.

**Open** all wk noon-3 6-11.30 (Sun noon-3 Oct-Feb) **Bar Meals** L served all wk 12-3 D served all wk 6-9 Av main course £4.75 **Restaurant** D served all wk 6-9 booking required Fixed menu price fr £15 ⊕ GREENE KING ◀ Ruddles County, Abbot Ale, Old Speckled Hen. ♎ 10 **Facilities** Children's menu Dogs allowed Garden Parking

# The Phelips Arms ♎

**The Borough TA15 6XB**
☎ 01935 822557 📄 01935 822557
e-mail: phelipsarmsmontacute@talktalk.net
dir: *From Cartgate rdbt on A303 follow signs for Montacute*

A 17th-century listed ham stone building overlooking the village square and close to Montacute House (NT). The

emphasis is on food, and everything is prepared on the premises using the best local and West Country produce. The menu features dishes such as home-made steak and ale pie, stuffed oven-cooked pork belly with pear and apple jus; followed by rhubarb crumble or strawberry Pavlova.

**Open** noon-2.30 6-11 Closed: 25 Dec, Mon (ex BH) **Bar Meals** L served Tue-Sun 12-2 D served Tue-Sun 6.30-9 Av main course £7.95 **Restaurant** L served Tue-Sun 12-2 booking required D served Tue-Sun 6.30-9 booking required ⊕ PALMERS ◀ Palmers IPA & 200 Premium Ale, Copper Ale Ꝺ Thatchers Gold. ♎ 9 **Facilities** Children's menu Dogs allowed Garden Parking

## OVER STRATTON

# The Royal Oak ♎

**TA13 5LQ ☎ 01460 240906**
e-mail: info@the-royal-oak.net
dir: *Exit A303 at Hayes End rdbt (South Petherton). 1st left after Esso garage signed Over Stratton*

Blackened beams, flagstones, log fires, pews and settles set the scene in this welcoming old thatched inn built from warm Hamstone, which has the added attraction of a garden, children's play area and barbecue. Expect dishes ranging from beer battered haddock and chips with home-made tartare sauce to supreme of chicken in an apricot, ginger and white wine sauce.

**Open** Closed: Mon (ex BH) **Bar Meals** L served Tue-Sun 12-2 booking required D served Tue-Sun 6-9 booking required **Restaurant** L served Tue-Sun 12-2 booking required D served Tue-Sun 6-9 booking required ⊕ HALL & WOODHOUSE ◀ Badger Best, Tanglefoot, Sussex Best Bitter. ♎ 6 **Facilities** Children's menu Play area Family room Dogs allowed Garden Parking

## RUDGE

# The Full Moon at Rudge ★★★ INN ♎

**BA11 2QF ☎ 01373 830936 📄 01373 831366**
e-mail: info@thefullmoon.co.uk
dir: *From A36 (Bath to Warminster road) follow Rudge signs*

Strategically placed at the crossing of two old drove roads, this inn enjoys great views of Westbury White Horse. The venerable 16th-century building had been sympathetically updated and retains its small, stone-floored rooms furnished with scrubbed tables. Modern British cooking is the watchword with menus changing to reflect the seasons. Lamb chump chop with bubble and squeak and a rosemary jus or simple steak and kidney pie are examples of the fare.

**Open** all day all wk 11.30-11 (Sun noon-10.30) **Bar Meals** L served Mon-Sat 12-2 D served Mon-Sat 6-9, Sun 7-9 **Restaurant** L served all wk 12-2 D served Mon-Sat 6-9 booking required ⊕ FREE HOUSE ◀ Butcombe Bitter, John Smith's, Potholer Ꝺ Stowford Press, Thatchers Cheddar Valley. ♎ 6 **Facilities** Children's menu Dogs allowed Garden Parking **Rooms** 17

## SHEPTON BEAUCHAMP

# Duke of York ♀

**TA19 0LW ☎ 01460 240314**
e-mail: sheptonduke@tiscali.co.uk
dir: *M5 junct 25 Taunton or A303*

This 17th-century free house is run by husband and wife team Paul and Hayley Rowlands, and Purdy, the 'famous' pub dog. The restaurant's varied menu and blackboard specials offer something for everyone. Local chargrilled steaks and fresh fish from Bridport, as well as a selection of pub classics such as lamb moussaka and trio of lamb chops on minted creamed potato and redcurrant and port sauce, shows the style.

**Open** all day noon-3 6.30-mdnt (Mon 6-mdnt Fri noon-3 6-mdnt Sat noon-mdnt Sun noon-10.30) Closed: Mon L **Bar Meals** L served Tue-Sun 12-2 D served Tue-Sat 6.45-9 booking required **Restaurant** L served Tue-Sun 12-2 D served Tue-Sat 6.45-9 booking required ⊕ FREE HOUSE ◀ Teignworthy Reel Ale, Otter Bright. ♀ 7 **Facilities** Children's menu Family room Dogs allowed Garden Parking

---

## SHEPTON MALLET

# The Waggon and Horses ♀

**Frome Rd, Doulting Beacon BA4 4LA ☎ 01749 880302**
e-mail: dawncorp@yahoo.co.uk
dir: *1.5m N of Shepton Mallet at x-roads with Old Wells-Frome road, 1m off A37*

A pretty, whitewashed building with leaded windows, this rural coaching inn has views over Glastonbury, and is set in a large garden and a flower-filled paddock. Other attractions include the skittle alley, which together with a small bar, is available for hire, and free jazz nights (first Friday of the month) in the relaxed surroundings of the upstairs bar. The menu offers traditional home-made dishes. Expect the likes of fresh battered cod with chips; steak and ale pie; tarragon chicken with a creamy sauce, and home-made faggots. A great range of desserts includes raspberry cheesecake, spotted Dick, pineapple upside down pudding and apple crumble.

**Open** all wk Sat-Sun all day **Bar Meals** L served all wk 12-2.30 D served all wk 6-9 **Restaurant** L served all wk 12-2.30 D served all wk 6-9 ⊕ PUNCH TAVERNS ◀ Wadworth 6X, Butcombe ♂ Addlestones. ♀ 12 **Facilities** Children's menu Dogs allowed Garden Parking

## STANTON WICK

# The Carpenters Arms ♀

**BS39 4BX ☎ 01761 490202 ▤ 01761 490763**
e-mail: carpenters@buccaneer.co.uk
web: www.the-carpenters-arms.co.uk
dir: *A37 to Chelwood rdbt, then A368. Pub 8m S of Bath*

Overlooking the Chew Valley, the hamlet of Stanton Wick is the setting for the Carpenters Arms. Formerly a row of miners' cottages, this delightful, stone-built free house is a quintessential English pub. Outside is a landscaped patio for alfresco drinks or meals, while behind the flower-bedecked façade lies a comfortable bar with low beams and a chatty, music-free atmosphere. Seasonal and local produce is a priority, so menus change regularly to make the best of what's available. There are certainly dishes to suit most tastes: among them you may see West Country barn-reared chicken on roasted root vegetables, butternut squash, red onion and sage; roasted fillet of cod on a sauté of cherry tomato, garlic and basil; confit of duck on bubble and squeak with port and redcurrant sauce; and steak and Butcombe ale pie. Among the specials might be fish stew in saffron cream sauce; and roast leg of pork with cider and apple gravy. Vegetarians could well be tempted by linguini with spinach, garlic, cherry tomatoes and toasted pine nuts, while children should be happy with golden fried scampi, pasta with tomato and herb sauce. Lighter snacks include baguettes and sandwiches.

**Open** all day all wk 11-11 (Sun 12-10.30) Closed: 25-26 Dec **Bar Meals** L served Mon-Sat 12-2, Sun 12-9 booking required D served Mon-Sat 7-10, Sun 12-9 booking required Av main course £13.95 **Restaurant** L served Mon-Sat 12-2, Sun 12-9 booking required D served Mon-Sat 7-10, Sun 12-9 booking required Fixed menu price fr £23 Av 3 course à la carte fr £23.85 ⊕ BUCCANEER HOLDINGS ◀ Butcombe Bitter, Bath Gem, Sharps Doom Bar. ♀ 12 **Facilities** Children's menu Garden Parking

---

## STOKE ST GREGORY

# Rose & Crown ♀

**Woodhill TA3 6EW ☎ 01823 490296**
e-mail: info@browningpubs.com
dir: *M5 junct 25, A358 towards Langport, left at Thornfalcon, left again, follow signs to Stoke St Gregory*

This 18th-century building became a pub in 1867, has been run by the same family since 1979 and enjoys a well deserved reputation for good food, local produce and a warm reception.

Fresh fish features on the specials board, alongside grills and roasts with a choice of sauces, vegetarian options and poultry dishes such as sizzling tandoori chicken.

**Open** all wk **Bar Meals** L served all wk 12-2 booking required D served all wk 7-9 booking required Av main course £10 **Restaurant** L served all wk 12-2 booking required D served all wk 7-9 booking required ⊕ FREE HOUSE ◀ Exmoor Fox, Stag, Butcombe, Otter Ale, Exmoor Ale, guest ales ♻ Thatchers Gold. ☿ 8 **Facilities** Children's menu Garden Parking

## TRISCOMBE

### The Blue Ball ☿

**TA4 3HE ☎ 01984 618242 ▤ 01984 618371**
e-mail: info@blueballinn.co.uk
dir: *From Taunton take A358 past Bishops Lydeard towards Minehead*

A converted 18th-century thatched barn, the Blue Ball Inn is hidden away down a narrow lane in the Quantock Hills. Inside are A-frame wooden ceilings, solid beech furniture, and log fires. On fine days take a seat outside in the large beer garden or on the patio. Typical menu dishes are marinated Moroccan lamb with Mediterranean vegetables, lemon couscous and harissa sauce; five spice belly of pork with noodles and star anise broth; and corn-fed chicken with herb velouté and baby spring vegetables. Puddings are home-made and may include dark chocolate tart, lemon and thyme pannacotta, and rhubarb syllabub with crushed meringue and shortbread.

**Open** all day noon-3.30 6.30-11 (Fri-Sat 12-11 Sun 12-9) Closed: 25-26 Dec eve, 1 Jan eve **Bar Meals** L served Mon-Sat 12-2.30, Sun 12-6 D served all wk 7-9.30 Av main course £8.50 **Restaurant** L served Tue-Sat 12-2.30, Sun 12-6 booking required D served Tue-Sun 7-9.30 booking required ⊕ PUNCH TAVERNS ◀ Cotleigh Tawny, Exmoor Gold & Stag, St Austell, Tribute, Otter Head Ale. ☿ 8 **Facilities** Children's menu Dogs allowed Garden Parking

## WELLS

### The Fountain Inn & Boxer's Restaurant ☿

**1 Saint Thomas St BA5 2UU ☎ 01749 672317 ▤ 01749 670825**
e-mail: eat@fountaininn.co.uk
dir: *City centre, at A371 & B3139 junct. Follow signs for The Horringtons. Inn on junct of Tor St & Saint Thomas St*

Built during the 16th century to house builders working on nearby Wells Cathedral, the Fountain Inn & Boxer's Restaurant has earned a well-deserved reputation for good food and exciting wine. A family-run business since 1981, the front of house manager was born at the pub! Head chef Julie Pearce uses the finest local produce to create an impressive selection of quality home-cooked food for both the bar and the restaurant. Lunchtime favourites might include doorstep sandwiches with dressed salad and hand-cut chips; or oven-baked goats' cheese in Parma ham with tomato salad. Among the restaurant mains, try roasted cod with pesto and creamy

leek mash; roast guinea fowl with chestnut and sage stuffing; or filo parcel with chargrilled Mediterranean vegetables, basil pesto and Greek salad.

**Open** all wk noon-2 6-11 Closed: 25-26 Dec **Bar Meals** L served all wk 12-2 D served all wk 6-9 Av main course £9.95 **Restaurant** L served all wk 12-2 D served all wk 6-9 Av 3 course à la carte fr £21 ⊕ INNSPIRED ◀ Butcombe Bitter, Interbrew Bass, Courage Best. ☿ 23 **Facilities** Children's menu Parking

## WEST HUNTSPILL

### Crossways Inn ☿

**Withy Rd TA9 3RA ☎ 01278 783756 ▤ 01278 781899**
e-mail: crossways.inn@virgin.net
dir: *On A38 3.5m from M5*

The Crossways Inn is a 17th-century coaching inn that is an integral part of village life. A skittle alley and pool table are available and live music, themed meals, and unusual competitions are regular events. Produce comes from local sources wherever possible, and dishes are from the menu or specials blackboards, from snacks like deep-fried whitebait and traditional pies, to lasagne, grilled duck breast with grilled peaches, lemon butter chicken or mushroom and brie Wellington. There's a family room and secluded garden.

**Open** all wk 10-3.30 6-mdnt Closed: 25 Dec **Bar Meals** Av main course £7 food served all day **Restaurant** food served all day ⊕ FREE HOUSE ◀ Interbrew Bass, Flowers IPA, Fuller's London Pride, Exmoor Stag, Cotleigh Snowy, Butcombe Gold, Branscombe Bitter ♻ Ashton Press. ☿ 8 **Facilities** Children's menu Play area Family room Dogs allowed Garden Parking

## WEST MONKTON

### The Monkton Inn ♥

**Blundells Ln TA2 8NP ☎ 01823 412414**
web: www.themonkton.co.uk
dir: *M5 junct 25 to Taunton, right at Creech Castle for 1m, left into West Monkton Village*

This village pub has been completely rejuvenated by its owners, Eddie Street and Guy Arnold. The duo have refurbished the interior and kitchen, and added a stylish patio area. By serving freshly prepared, reasonably priced food they have built a loyal following, while taking good care of drinkers too. Lunch and dinner menus change daily, which makes for a great many possibilities. Randomly selected are medallions of local pork with bacon, leek and sausage mash, apple and honey cider sauce; poached chicken with sweet potato and butternut squash mash, rich tomato sauce and fresh asparagus; and fresh fillet of plaice deep-fried in tempura batter, with home-made chips and tartare sauce.

**Open** noon-3 6-11 (Sat-Sun noon-11) Closed: Sun eve, Mon L **Bar Meals** L served Tue-Sun 12-2 Av main course £6 **Restaurant** L served Tue-Sun 12-2 D served Mon-Sat 6.30-9.30 booking required Fixed menu price fr £14.50 ⊕ ENTERPRISE INNS ◀ Butcombe Bitter, Cotleigh Tawny Exmoor Ale, Exmoor Gold. ♥ 7 **Facilities** Children's menu Play area Garden Parking

## WHEDDON CROSS

### The Rest and Be Thankful Inn ★★★★ INN

**TA24 7DR ☎ 01643 841222   ▤ 01643 841813**
e-mail: stay@restandbethankful.co.uk
dir: *5m S of Dunster*

Years ago, travellers were grateful for a break at this coaching inn, nearly 1,000 feet up in Exmoor's highest village. Old world charm blends with friendly hospitality in the bar and spacious restaurant, where log fires burn in winter and home-cooked food is served. In addition to the restaurant menu there is a weekly specials board, a light lunch menu and a traditional Sunday carvery. The pub also has a skittle alley and pool table.

**Open** all wk 10-3 6-close **Bar Meals** L served all wk 12-2 D served all wk 7-9 **Restaurant** L served all wk 12-2 booking required D served all wk 7-9 booking required ⊕ FREE HOUSE ◀ Exmoor Ale, Proper Job, Tribute, Guinness. **Facilities** Children's menu Garden Parking **Rooms** 8

## WIVELISCOMBE

### White Hart ★★★★ INN ♥

**West St TA4 2JP ☎ 01984 623344   ▤ 01984 624748**
e-mail: reservations@whitehartwiveliscombe.co.uk
web: www.whitehartwiveliscombe.co.uk
dir: *M5 junct 26. Pub in town centre*

Facing the square in Wiveliscombe is this 350-year-old former coaching inn, transformed throughout by recent major renovations. Beers from both the village's breweries, Cotleigh and Exmoor, are normally served alongside each other in the vibrant, friendly bar. Its reputation for high quality, freshly cooked food using locally sourced produce has led to a number of prestigious accolades for its pub classics, such as steak and Tawny ale pie; and Beech Hayes Farm Olde English sausages with apple mash and rich onion gravy, as well as an ever-changing menu that includes the 'famous' White Hart burger with home-made chips. Other favourites are starters such as chargrilled local organic vegetable terrine with goats' cheese and pesto salad; River Exe mussels cooked in white wine and cream; main dishes like pan-fried free-range West Country duck breast on a confit of garlic mash with orange and rosemary sauce; fresh potato gnocchi with local organic Mediterranean vegetable and tomato sauce topped with glazed Exmoor Blue cheese; and for dessert, sticky toffee pudding; rhubarb strudel with fresh homemade custard; or the board of local cheeses. On offer at lunchtime is a selection of sandwiches, baguettes and omelettes, while Sundays bring traditional roasts using finest, 21-day topside with thyme-herbed Yorkshire pudding and goose fat-roasted potatoes.

Open all day all wk 10.30am-11pm (Fri-Sat 10am-mdnt) **Bar Meals** L served Tue-Sun 12-2 booking required D served all wk 6.30-9 booking required Av main course £8 **Restaurant** L served Tue-Sun 12-2 booking required D served all wk 6.30-9 booking required Av 3 course à la carte fr £22.50 ⊞ FREE HOUSE ◧ Cotleigh Tawny Owl, Exmoor Gold, Sharps Doom Bar, Fullers London Pride, Cotleigh Harrier ♂ Rattler. ♟ 10 **Facilities** Children's menu Dogs allowed Garden Parking **Rooms** 16

## YEOVIL

# The Masons Arms ★★★★ INN

**41 Lower Odcombe BA22 8TX ☎ 01935 862591**
📠 01935 862591

e-mail: paula@masonsarmsodcombe.co.uk
dir: *A3088 to Yeovil, right to Montacute, through village, 3rd right after petrol station to Odcombe*

Built of local hamstone, with four thatched 'eyebrows' above the upper windows, and dating back to the 15th century, this is the oldest building in the village. In the bar, sample a pint of Drew's (he's the co-owner and brewer) Odcombe No 1 from the pub's micro-brewery. Drew also runs the kitchen, producing freshly prepared traditional pub grub such as fish pie topped with chive mash; spicy meatball pasta; corned beef hash; and ham, egg and chips, while his daily-changing carte menu might feature lamb's liver and bacon, bubble 'n' squeak and onion gravy; sirloin steak with brandy, black pepper sauce and slow-cooked cabbage; cod fillet wrapped in prosciutto, provençale vegetables and pea purée; and red pepper and Parmesan risotto with oyster mushroom fritters.

Open all wk noon-3 6-mdnt **Bar Meals** L served all wk 12-2 booking required D served all wk 6.30-9.30 booking required Av main course £10 **Restaurant** L served all wk 12-2 booking required D served all wk 6.30-9.30 booking required ⊞ FREE HOUSE ◧ Drew's Odcombe ♂ Westons Bounds Brand. **Facilities** Children's menu Dogs allowed Garden Parking **Rooms** 6

## STAFFORDSHIRE

## ALSTONEFIELD

# The George ♟

**DE6 2FX ☎ 01335 310205**
e-mail: emily@thegeorgeatalstonefield.com
web: www.thegeorgeatalstonefield.com
dir: *7m N of Ashbourne, signed Alstonefield to left off A515*

The nearby Manifold Valley is a famous haunt for ramblers and many seek well-earned refreshment at this friendly 18th-century coaching inn. Run by three generations of the same family since the 1960s, the current landlady warmly welcomes all-comers, as long as muddy boots are left at the door. She has undertaken a sympathetic restoration of the dining room, which revealed many features including a Georgian fireplace hidden for over a century. The place oozes warmth and charm, with fires crackling in the grate, tiled floors gleaming,

and contented chatter from locals, walkers and diners. The appeal of this fine pub, other than the wonderful location and welcome, includes the cracking range real ales and wines by the glass, and the fantastic home-cooked food - the chef makes all his own jams, pickles and chutneys on the premises. The emphasis is on seasonal, regional and traditional dishes, with plenty of hearty options for walkers and fishermen: a range of sandwiches (roast beef and onion marmalade), steak and Guinness pie, home-made beef burger, and Tissington sausages with mash and gravy. By night, tuck into potted smoked mackerel or Devon crab with dill and radicchio risotto, and follow with roast duck breast with haricot bean casserole and kale, or whole baked bass with tomato salsa. Leave room for Bakewell pudding, dark chocolate tart with blueberry fool, and spotted Dick with honeyed figs and lashings of custard. Alternatively, round off with a plate of Hartington stilton with walnut and raisin loaf and a glass of port. A new vegetable patch supplies much of the produce. Allow time to visit Emily's farm shop, housed in the converted 18th-century coach house.

Open all wk Mon-Fri 11.30-3 6-11 (Sat 11.30-11 Sun 12-10) Closed: 25 Dec **Bar Meals** L served all wk 12-2.30 booking required D served Mon-Sat 7-9, Sun 6.30-8 booking required Av main course £12 **Restaurant** L served all wk 12-2.30 booking required D served Mon-Sat 7-9, Sun 6.30-8 booking required Av 3 course à la carte fr £25 ⊞ MARSTONS ◧ Marston's Bitter & Pedigree, Jennings Cumberland Ale, Brakspear Oxford Gold, Guest ale ♂ Thatchers. ♟ 8 **Facilities** Children's menu Dogs allowed Garden Parking

## CHEADLE

# The Queens At Freehay

**Counslow Rd, Freehay ST10 1RF ☎ 01538 722383**
📠 01538 723748
dir: *4m from Alton Towers*

Very much a family-run establishment, the pub dates from the 18th century and has a pretty setting surrounded by mature trees and garden. The interior is refreshingly modern in style, with elegant tables and chairs. The pub has established a good reputation for food, and dishes from the menu are supplemented by chef's specials from the fish or meat boards. Expect home-made beef and merlot pie; Moroccan lamb tagine; and fish and chips. Children have their own menu.

continued

England

**Open** all wk noon-3 6-11 (Sun noon-4 6.30-11) Closed: 25-26, 31 Dec-1 Jan **Bar Meals** L served all wk 12-2 booking required D served all wk 6-9.30 booking required **Restaurant** L served all wk 12-2 booking required D served all wk 6-9.30 booking required ⊕ FREE HOUSE ◄ Draught Burton, Peakstones Alton Abbey. **Facilities** Children's menu Garden Parking

## COLTON

### The Yorkshireman ♥

Colton Rd WS15 3HB ☎ 01889 583977
e-mail: theyorkshireman@btconnect.com
dir: *10m from Stafford*

To know why the former Railway Tavern changed its name, look no further than the fact that a Yorkshireman once owned it, and rechristened it in his own honour. John and Jo Ashmore saw no reason to change it when they bought the pub in 2007, but gave it a complete makeover. Beers are brewed by Blythe's just up the road, the most popular being Palmer's Poison, named after Rugeley's famous serial-murdering doctor. Curled up on his bed in the corner of the bar you'll probably find Dahl, the pub's lazy greyhound. Locally sourced food can change daily to include gammon with free-range egg, fresh pineapple and chips; poached smoked haddock with sautéed new potatoes and creamy mustard and white wine sauce; and roasted pepper stuffed with pilau rice, and vegetable and chickpea tandoori. The Deli sells the Yorkshireman's own sauces and dishes, including fishcakes and beefburgers, to take away, plus local cheeses and vegetables.

**Open** all wk noon-2.30 5.30-11 (Sun noon-6) **Bar Meals** L served Mon-Sat 12-2.30, Sun 12-6 D served Mon-Sat 6-9.30 Av main course £10 **Restaurant** L served Mon-Sat 12-2.30, Sun 12-6 booking required D served Mon-Sat 6-9.30 booking required ⊕ FREE HOUSE ◄ Blythes, Black Sheep. ♥9 **Facilities** Children's menu Dogs allowed Garden Parking

## STAFFORD

### The Holly Bush Inn ♥

Salt ST18 0BX ☎ 01889 508234 ▤ 01889 508058
e-mail: geoff@hollybushinn.co.uk
web: www.hollybushinn.co.uk
dir: *Telephone for directions*

The Holly Bush is well known for the quality of its food. The pub's comfortably old-fashioned interior contains all the vital ingredients: heavy carved beams, open fires, attractive prints and cosy alcoves. The team are more enthusiastic than ever in their attempts to reduce food miles and support local producers. At lunchtime there are a good selection of sandwiches, hot sandwiches, toasties and filled jacket potatoes. On the main menu are traditional Staffordshire oatcakes filled with spiced black pudding and a herby tomato sauce; and a centuries' old recipe of slow cooked venison casserole. Other typical dishes include Forest Blue stuffed pears with raspberry and poppy seed vinaigrette; home-made steak and kidney pudding with onion gravy; braised lamb and apples. Seafood dishes attest to the excellent relationships developed with Brixham's fishermen; while local award-winning cheeses and a great selection of locally farmed steaks complete the picture. The chalkboard displays the vegetarian options.

**Open** all wk 12-11 (Sun 12-10.30) **Bar Meals** Av main course £10.50 food served all day ⊕ FREE HOUSE ◄ Adnams, Pedigree, guest ales. ♥ 12 **Facilities** Children's menu Garden Parking

### The Moat House ★★★★ HL ⊛⊛ ♥

Lower Penkridge Rd, Acton Trussell ST17 0RJ
☎ 01785 712217 ▤ 01785 715344
e-mail: info@moathouse.co.uk
dir: *M6 junct 13 towards Stafford, 1st right to Acton Trussell*

A Grade II listed mansion dating back to the 14th century, standing on a mound, scheduled as an Ancient Monument, beside the Staffordshire and Worcestershire Canal. Inside are oak beams and an inglenook fireplace, the stylish Brasserie Bar, and the Conservatory Restaurant. The food, for which the AA has awarded two Rosettes, is listed on a variety of menus offering, for example, beef tomato and buffalo mozzarella salad with crushed basil and extra virgin olive oil; 28-day, dry-aged Staffordshire sirloin steak with thick-cut chips, onion rings, field mushroom, tomato and a pepper sauce; free-range Tamworth pork cutlet with mashed potatoes, mustard carrots and cider velouté; and seared fillet of salmon served on a bed of wilted spinach with a sauce vierge and new potatoes.

Open all day all wk 10am-11pm Closed: 25 Dec Bar Meals L served all wk 12-2.15 D served Sun-Fri 6-9 Av main course £10 Restaurant L served all wk 12-2 booking required D served all wk 6.30-9 booking required Av 3 course à la carte fr £40 ⊕ FREE HOUSE ◀ Old Speckled Hen, Greene King IPA, Guinness. ⚲ 16 Facilities Children's menu Family room Garden Parking Rooms 41

## WATERHOUSES

# Ye Olde Crown

**Leek Rd ST10 3HL ☎ 01538 308204  ▤ 01538 308204**
e-mail: kerryhinton@hotmail.co.uk
dir: *From Ashbourne take A52 then A523 towards Leek. Village in 8m*

A traditional village local, Ye Olde Crown dates from around 1647 when it was built as a coaching inn. Sitting on the bank of the River Hamps, and on the edge of the Peak District National Park and the Staffordshire moorlands, it's ideal for walkers. Inside are original stonework and interior beams, and open fires are lit in cooler weather. Food choices, all home-cooked, are found on the specials board and à la carte menu.

Open all day Sat (noon-11.20) & Sun (noon-10.30) Closed: Mon L Bar Meals L served Tue-Sun 12-2.30 D served all wk 6-8.30 booking required Av main course £5 Restaurant L served Tue-Sun 12-2.30 D served all wk 6-8.30 booking required ⊕ SCOTTISH & NEWCASTLE ◀ Guinness, Theakstons, Spitfire, Abbot Ale, Guest ales. Facilities Children's menu Parking

## WETTON

# Ye Olde Royal Oak

**DE6 2AF ☎ 01335 310287**
e-mail: brian@rosehose.wanadoo.co.uk
dir: *A515 towards Buxton, left in 4m to Manifold Valley-Alstonfield, follow signs to Wetton*

The stone-built inn dates back over 400 years and features wooden beams recovered from oak ships at Liverpool Docks. It was formerly part of the Chatsworth Estate, and the Tissington walking and cycling trail is close by. Look out for dishes such as home-made soup; large battered cod; and treacle sponge. Separate vegetarian and children's menus are available. The pub's moorland garden includes a campsite.

Open  Closed: Mon-Tue in winter Bar Meals L served Wed-Sun 12-2 D served Wed-Sun 7-9 Av main course £7.50 ⊕ FREE HOUSE Facilities Children's menu Family room Dogs allowed Garden Parking

## WRINEHILL

# The Hand & Trumpet ⚲

**Main Rd CW3 9BJ ☎ 01270 820048  ▤ 01270 821911**
e-mail: hand.and.trumpet@brunningandprice.co.uk
dir: *M6 junct 16 follow signs for Keele, continue onto A531, 7m on right*

A relaxed country pub, The Hand & Trumpet has a comfortable interior with original floors, old furniture, open fires and rugs. A deck to the rear overlooks the sizeable grounds, which include a large pond. There's a locally sourced menu of dishes such as braised lamb shoulder with honey roasted vegetables, rosemary and redcurrant gravy; or wild mushroom, celeriac, leek and thyme pie.

Open all day all wk 11.30-11 (Sun 11.30-10.30) Closed: 25 Dec Bar Meals L served all wk 12-10 booking required D served all wk 12-10 booking required Av main course £12.95 food served all day ⊕ FREE HOUSE ◀ Deuchars IPA, Hawkshead Lakeland Gold, Guest ales ♂ Stonehouse. ⚲ 22 Facilities Children's menu Family room Dogs allowed Garden Parking

## SUFFOLK

### BRANDESTON

# The Queens Head ⚲

**The Street IP13 7AD ☎ 01728 685307**
e-mail: thequeensheadinn@btconnect.com
dir: *From A14 take A1120 to Earl Soham, then S to Brandeston*

Originally four cottages, the pub has been serving ale to the villagers of Brandeston since 1811. A large open bar allows drinkers and diners to mix, and good use is made of the huge garden in summer. Local food is served, with dishes like herb-crusted and pressed shoulder of pork with wholegrain mustard; and confit duck leg with spring onion crushed potato and a rich berry jus.

Open noon-3 5-mdnt (Sun noon-5) Closed: Sun eve Bar Meals L served all wk 12-2 booking required D served Mon-Sat 6.30-9 booking required Restaurant L served all wk 12-2 booking required D served Mon-Sat 6.30-9 booking required ⊕ ADNAMS ◀ Adnams Broadside & Bitter, Explorer, seasonal ales ♂ Aspall. ⚲ 8 Facilities Children's menu Dogs allowed Garden Parking

### BURY ST EDMUNDS

# The Linden Tree

**7 Out Northgate IP33 1JQ ☎ 01284 754600**
e-mail: lindentree@live.com
dir: *Opposite railway station*

Built to serve the railway station, this is a big, friendly Victorian pub, with stripped pine bar, dining area, non-smoking conservatory and charming garden. The family-orientated menu ranges from beef curry, home-made pies, and liver and bacon, to crab thermidor, fresh sea bass, and mushroom and lentil moussaka. Youngsters will go for the burgers, scampi, or pork chipolatas. Freshly filled ciabattas at lunchtime.

Open all wk noon-11 (Fri-Sat 11-11 Sun noon-10) Closed: 25 Dec Bar Meals L served all wk 12-2.30 D served all wk 6-9.30 Restaurant L served all wk 12-2.30 booking required D served all wk 6-9.30 booking required ⊕ GREENE KING ◀ Greene King, IPA & Old Speckled Hen, guest. Facilities Children's menu Play area Dogs allowed Garden

England

**England**

## CHILLESFORD

# The Froize Inn ◉ ♀

**The Street IP12 3PU ☎ 01394 450282**
e-mail: dine@froize.co.uk
dir: *On B1084 between Woodbridge (8m) & Orford (3m)*

A former gamekeeper's cottage, this 15th-century free house and restaurant is a distinctive red-brick building standing on the site of Chillesford Friary. It is a thoroughly traditional pub with a modern dining room championing East Anglian growers and suppliers. The menu offers rustic English and French dishes, with plenty of fresh seafood in summer and game in winter. The pub stands on the popular Suffolk Coastal Path.

**Open** Closed: Mon **Restaurant** L served Tue-Sun 12-2 booking required D served Thu-Sat from 7pm booking required ⊕ FREE HOUSE ◢ Adnams ♂ Aspall. ♀ 14 **Facilities** Children's menu Garden Parking

## COTTON

# The Trowel & Hammer Inn

**Mill Rd IP14 4QL ☎ 01449 781234 ▤ 01449 781765**
dir: *From A14 follow signs to Haughley, then Bacton. Turn left for Cotton*

A herd of nine carved teak elephants trekking through the main hall way to the outdoor swimming pool gives you a clue that this is no ordinary pub. At first sight the well maintained, wisteria-clad building belies its 16th-century origins; but, inside, the old oak timbers and traditional fireplace give a better idea of its age. Contemporary needs haven't been forgotten, and licensee Sally Burrows has created secluded areas to cater for all age groups. In the summer, the garden, with its tropical theme and poolside umbrellas, is the place to relax. Menus are a blend of farmhouse cooking and international cuisine, so expect to find regular Sunday roast alongside crocodile and kangaroo.

**Open** all wk ⊕ FREE HOUSE ◢ Adnams Bitter & Broadside, Greene King IPA, Old Speckled Hen. **Facilities** Garden Parking

## DENNINGTON

# The Queens Head

**The Square IP13 8AB ☎ 01728 638241**
e-mail: queenshead123@yahoo.co.uk
dir: *From Ipswich A14 to exit for Lowestoft (A12), then B1116 to Framlingham then follow signs to Dennington*

Recently refurbished, this 500-year-old inn retains bags of old world charm including open fires, a resident ghost, a coffin hatch and a bricked-up tunnel to the neighbouring church. The menu centres around fresh food made with local produce and ingredients - perhaps cottage pie or fillet of plaice parcels.

**Open** all wk noon-3 6.30-11 Closed: 25-26 Dec **Restaurant** L served all wk 12-2 booking required D served all wk 6.30-9 booking required Fixed menu price fr £9 ⊕ FREE HOUSE ◢ Adnams, Elgoods, Mauldons ♂ Aspall. **Facilities** Children's menu Garden Parking

## ERWARTON

# The Queens Head

**The Street IP9 1LN ☎ 01473 787550**
dir: *From Ipswich take B1456 to Shotley*

This handsome 16th-century Suffolk free house provides a relaxed atmosphere in the bar with its bowed black oak beams, low ceilings and cosy coal fires, and magnificent views over the fields to the Stour estuary. The wide-ranging menu offers traditional hot dishes and snacks, while daily specials include pheasant casserole, spinach and red lentil curry, Guinness-battered cod and chips, and home-made fishcakes. Booking is advised at weekends.

**Open** all wk Closed: Sun eve **Bar Meals** L served all wk 12-2.30 booking required D served all wk 6.30-9 booking required **Restaurant** L served all wk 12-2.30 booking required D served Mon-Sat 6.30-9 booking required ⊕ FREE HOUSE ◢ Adnams Bitter & Broadside, Greene King IPA, Guinness ♂ Aspall. **Facilities** Children's menu Garden Parking

## GREAT BRICETT

# Red Lion

**Green Street Green IP7 7DD ☎ 01473 657799**
▤ 01473 658492
e-mail: janwise@fsmail.net
dir: *4.5m from Needham Market on B1078*

This charming 17th-century building may look like a traditional village pub and it was, arguably, just another hostelry until Jan Wise came along and turned it into East Anglia's only vegetarian pub. She has a fixed rule: nothing is served that means killing an animal, so there's no Sunday carvery, no mixed grill, no scampi in a basket. Wanting to 'celebrate the fantastic flavours that only vegetables can provide', Jan uses her 30 years' experience as a vegetarian caterer to create internationally-inspired starters such as dim sum, nachos or houmous, perhaps followed by oyster mushroom, leek and pine nut parcel; roasted vegetable and brie tart; or African sweet potato stew. She's back on more familiar territory with her desserts, which typically include chocolate brownies, rhubarb crumble and summer pudding. Not only is it advisable to book, you'll also need a healthy appetite.

**Open** Closed: Mon **Bar Meals** L served Tue-Sun 12-2 D served Tue-Sat 6-9 Av main course £7.90 ⊕ GREENE KING ◢ Greene King IPA, Old Speckled Hen. **Facilities** Children's menu Play area Dogs allowed Garden Parking

## HALESWORTH

# The Queen's Head ♀

**The Street, Bramfield IP19 9HT ☎ 01986 784214**
e-mail: qhbfield@aol.com
dir: *2m from A12 on A144 towards Halesworth*

A lovely old building in the centre of Bramfield on the edge of the Suffolk Heritage Coast near historic Southwold. The enclosed garden, ideal for children, is overlooked by the thatched village church which has an unusual separate round bell tower. The pub's interior welcomes with scrubbed pine tables, exposed beams, a vaulted ceiling in the bar and enormous fireplaces. In the same capable hands for over ten years, the landlord enthusiastically supports the 'local and organic' movement – reflected by the menu which proudly names the farms and suppliers from which the carefully chosen ingredients are sourced. Local produce notwithstanding, there's a definite cosmopolitan twist to many dishes, and vegetarian options are a particular strength: mushrooms baked in cream and garlic au gratin could be followed by fresh tagliatelle with pesto, roast red peppers and grilled goats' cheese. Local turkey, wild mushroom, bacon and chestnut pie or fillets of sea bass with rocket pesto mayonnaise are fine main course examples. Amanda's home-made desserts number half a dozen tempting options such as warm chocolate fudge cake or hot sticky toffee pudding. Look out for special dining evenings and live music.

Open all wk 11.45-2.30 6.30-11 (Sun noon-3 7-10.30) Closed: 26 Dec **Bar Meals** L served all wk 12-2 D served Mon-Fri 6.30-9.15, Sat 6.30-10, Sun 7-9 Av main course £10.95 **Restaurant** Av 3 course à la carte fr £20.95 ⊕ ADNAMS ◀ Adnams Bitter, Broadside. ₹ 8 **Facilities** Children's menu Family room Dogs allowed Garden Parking

## HITCHAM

# The White Horse Inn ₹

**The Street IP7 7NQ ☎ 01449 740981** 🖹 **01449 740981**
e-mail: lewis@thewhitehorse.wanadoo.co.uk
dir: *13m from Ipswich & Bury St Edmunds, 7m Stowmarket, 7m Hadleigh*

There's a warm, friendly atmosphere at this family-run free house. Parts of the Grade II listed building are estimated to be around 400 years old, and make a perfect setting for traditional pub games and regular live entertainment. Freshly-prepared meals are served in the bar and restaurant and, in summer, the beer garden is open for barbecues.

Open all wk **Bar Meals** L served all wk 12-2.30 D served all wk 6-9 Av main course £9.50 **Restaurant** L served all wk 12-2.30 D served all wk 6-9 booking required Av 3 course à la carte fr £20 ⊕ FREE HOUSE ◀ IPA, Adnams Best Bitter, Rattlesden Best, Stowmarket Porter, Adnams Fisherman. ₹ 8 **Facilities** Children's menu Dogs allowed Garden Parking

## HOLBROOK

# The Compasses

**Ipswich Rd IP9 2QR ☎ 01473 328332** 🖹 **01473 327403**
e-mail: compasses.holbrook@virgin.net
dir: *From A137 S of Ipswich, take B1080 to Holbrook, pub on left. From Ipswich take B1456 to Shotley. At Freston Water Tower right onto B1080 to Holbrook. Pub 2m right*

Holbrook is bordered by the rivers Orwell and Stour, and this traditional country pub, which dates from the 17th century, is on the Shotley peninsula. A good value menu includes

ploughman's, salads and jacket potatoes; pub favourites such as chilli con carne or chicken with cashew nuts; and a fish selection including seafood lasagne. Party bookings are a speciality, and look out for Wine of the Week deals. Pensioners' weekday lunches complete this pub's honest offerings.

Open all wk 11.30-2.30 6-11 (Sun noon-3 6-10.30) Closed: 25-26 Dec, 1 Jan, Tue eve **Bar Meals** L served all wk 12-2.15 booking required D served Wed-Mon 6-9.15 booking required **Restaurant** L served all wk 12-2.15 booking required D served Wed-Mon 6-9.15 booking required ⊕ PUNCH TAVERNS ◀ Greene King IPA, Adnams Bitter, Guinness ⊘ Aspall. **Facilities** Children's menu Play area Garden Parking

## IXWORTH

# Pykkerell Inn ₹

**38 High St IP31 2HH ☎ 01359 230398** 🖹 **01359 230398**
dir: *On A143 from Bury St Edmunds towards Diss*

This former coaching inn dates from 1530 and still retains most of its original beams, inglenook fireplace and other features. The wood-panelled library is just off the lounge, and the 14th-century barn encloses a patio and barbecue. The extensive menu includes vegetarian options and children's meals, as well as traditional Sunday roast lunch. Menu boards highlight a variety of fresh fish, and may include red snapper, monkfish and Dover sole.

Open noon 3 5.30-11.30 Closed: Mon L **Bar Meals** L served Tue-Sun 12-2 D served all wk 7-9 ⊕ GREENE KING ◀ Greene King IPA, Abbot Ale, Old Speckled Hen. ₹ 6 **Facilities** Children's menu Dogs allowed Garden Parking

## KETTLEBURGH

# The Chequers Inn

**IP13 7JT ☎ 01728 723760 & 724369** 🖹 **01728 723760**
e-mail: info@thechequers.net
dir: *From Ipswich A12 onto B1116, left onto B1078 then right through Easton*

The Chequers is set in beautiful countryside on the banks of the River Deben. The landlord serves a wide range of cask ales, including two guests. In addition to snack and restaurant meals, the menu in the bar includes local sausages and ham with home-produced free-range eggs. The riverside garden can seat up to a hundred people.

Open all wk **Bar Meals** L served all wk 12-2 D served all wk 7-9.30 Av main course £6.50 **Restaurant** L served all wk 12-2 D served all wk 7-9.30 Av 3 course à la carte fr £18 ⊕ FREE HOUSE ◀ Greene King IPA, Black Dog Mild, 3 guest ales ⊘ Aspall. **Facilities** Children's menu Play area Dogs allowed Garden Parking

## LAXFIELD

### The Kings Head ♀

**Gorams Mill Ln IP13 8DW ☎ 01986 798395**
e-mail: bob-wilson5505@hotmail.co.uk
dir: *On B1117*

Beautifully situated overlooking the river, the garden of this thatched 16th-century alehouse was formerly the village bowling green. Beer is still served straight from the cask in the original tap room, whilst high-backed settles and wooden seats add to the atmosphere. Home-cooked dishes complement the à la carte menu and chef's specials and, on warmer evenings, the rose gardens and arbour are perfect for al fresco dining.

Open all wk **Bar Meals** L served all wk 12-2.30 D served Mon-Sat 7-9.30 Av main course £7.50 **Restaurant** L served all wk 12-2.30 booking required D served Mon-Sat 7-9.30 booking required Fixed menu price fr £7.50 Av 3 course à la carte fr £15 ⊕ ADNAMS ◀ Adnams Best & Broadside, Adnams seasonal, guest ales ♻ Aspall. ♀ 8 **Facilities** Children's menu Play area Family room Dogs allowed Garden Parking

## LIDGATE

### The Star Inn

**The Street CB8 9PP ☎ 01638 500275 ▤ 01638 500275**
e-mail: tonyaxon@aol.com
dir: *From Newmarket clocktower in High St follow signs towards Clare on B1063. Lidgate 7m*

This pretty, pink-painted Elizabethan building is made of two cottages with gardens front and rear; inside, two traditional bars with heavy oak beams, log fires and pine furniture lead into the dining room. Yet the Star's English appearance holds a surprise, for here is a Spanish restaurant offering authentic Mediterranean cuisine. No mere gastro-pub, The Star provides a meeting place for local residents, and is also popular with Newmarket trainers on race days. The menu offers starters like Catalan spinach; and Mediterranean fish soup might precede Spanish meatballs; or hake a la vasca. Other tastes are also catered for, with dishes such as smoked salmon and avocado; roast lamb with garlic; and fillet steak in pepper sauce.

Open all wk noon-3 6-mdnt Closed: 25-26 Dec, 1 Jan **Bar Meals** L served Mon-Sat 12-3 booking required D served Mon-Sat 7-10 booking required Av main course £11.50 **Restaurant** L served all wk 12-3 booking required D served Mon-Sat 7-10 booking required Fixed menu price fr £14 Av 3 course à la carte fr £28 ⊕ GREENE KING ◀ Greene King IPA, Ruddles County, Abbot Ale. **Facilities** Children's menu Garden Parking

## MILDENHALL

### The Olde Bull Inn ★★★ HL ❀ ♀

**The Street, Barton Mills IP28 6AA ☎ 01638 711001 ▤ 01638 712003**
e-mail: bookings@bullinn-bartonmills.com
dir: *Off the A11 between Newmarket and Mildenhall, signed Barton Mills*

Refurbished in contemporary style, the Bull Inn stands on the Cambridge/Suffolk border. Rich in history and looking much the same as it did when it was a coaching inn in the 16th century, the pub is popular with travellers heading for Norwich or the Norfolk coast. Everything is freshly prepared on the premises, so look for Newmarket bangers and mash, ciabatta with home-baked ham and mustard, or Denham Estate wild boar casserole with dumplings. Linger over three courses in the Oak Room, perhaps following prawn and crayfish cocktail with braised lamb shank, and finishing with lemon tart.

Open all day all wk 8am-11pm **Bar Meals** L served all wk 12-9 D served all wk 12-9 Av main course £8.75 food served all day **Restaurant** L served Sun 12-3 D served all wk 6-9 Av 3 course à la carte fr £22 ⊕ FREE HOUSE ◀ Adnams Broadside, Greene King IPA, Brandon Brewery Rusty Bucket, Humpty Dumpty, Wolf. ♀ 8 **Facilities** Children's menu Family room Garden Parking **Rooms** 14

## MONKS ELEIGH

### The Swan Inn ❀❀ ♀

**The Street IP7 7AU ☎ 01449 741391**
e-mail: carol@monkseleigh.com
dir: *On B1115 between Sudbury & Hadleigh*

With its magnificent fireplace, the main restaurant in this thatched inn may once have been used as the local manorial court. The pub welcomed its first customers in the 16th century when the interior would have been open to the roof. Some of the original wattle and daub that was exposed during renovation work, can now be seen behind a glass panel. The regularly changing menus reflect local ingredients wherever possible. Look for game in season, local vegetables and fresh fish from the coast. Starters like creamy pea and asparagus soup and dressed Cromer crab precede main course options such as roast monkfish wrapped in Parma ham and sage leaves on buttered samphire, or chargrilled sirloin steak with aubergine, cherry tomato and basil compote.

Open noon-2.30 7-11 Closed: 25-26 Dec, 1-2 Jan, Mon-Tue (ex BH) **Bar Meals** L served Wed-Sun 12-2 D served Wed-Sat 7-9 Av main course £10 **Restaurant** L served Wed-Sun 12-2 D served Wed-Sat 7-9 Fixed menu price fr £13.50 Av 3 course à la carte fr £25 ⊕ FREE HOUSE ◀ Greene King IPA, Adnams Bitter, Broadside ♂ Aspall, Thatchers Katy. ♟ 20 **Facilities** Children's menu Garden Parking

## ST PETER SOUTH ELMHAM

## Wicked at St Peter's Hall ♟
**NR35 1NQ ☎ 01986 782288**
e-mail: mail@wickedlygoodfoodltd.co.uk
dir: *From A143/A144 follow brown signs to St Peter's Brewery*

This magnificent 13th-century moated hall is home to one of Suffolk's most unusual and romantic pub/restaurants. The building was enlarged in 1539 using materials salvaged from nearby Flixton Priory, and the conversion features period furnishings that make the most of original stone floors, Gothic windows and lofty ceilings. St Peter's brewery was established in 1996 in adjacent former agricultural buildings, and now produces traditional ales as well as some unusual varieties like honey porter and fruit beer. The full range of beers is available in the bar. Locally sourced free range and organic produce is the mainstay of the menus, which range through dishes like pan-fried Barbary duck with brandy and cassis jus; baked salmon with Dijon mustard and herb crust; and breast of local pheasant in pancetta with redcurrant and spiced apple jus.

Open noon-3 6-11 (Sun noon-4) Closed: 1-12 Jan, Mon **Bar Meals** L served Tue-Sat 12-3 booking required Av main course £8 **Restaurant** L served Sun 12-4 booking required D served Tue-Sat 6-10 booking required Av 3 course à la carte fr £25 ⊕ ST PETERS BREWERY ◀ Golden Ale, Organic Ale, Grapefruit ale, Cream Stout, Organic Best Bitter ♂ Aspalls. ♟ 20 **Facilities** Children's menu Garden Parking

## SNAPE

## The Crown Inn ♟
**Bridge Rd IP17 1SL ☎ 01728 688324**
e-mail: snapecrown@tiscali.co.uk
dir: *A12 N to Lowestoft, right to Aldeburgh, then right again in Snape at x-rds by church, pub at bottom of hill*

Visitors to Snape Maltings, home of the Aldeburgh Music Festival, will find this 15th-century former smugglers' inn perfect for a pre- or post-concert dinner. Set close to the River Alde, the pub has old beams, brick floors and, around the large inglenook, a very fine double Suffolk settle. Cooking with produce from local suppliers and his own allotment, the landlord also rears livestock on site. His modern British menus, with daily specials, include starters of potted smoked haddock

with green peppercorns and quail's egg salad; and pressed game terrine with pickled mushrooms. Main courses might be pheasant with pearl barley and root vegetable broth; home-reared pork sausages with mash and shallot gravy; and crisp battered cod and chips. For pudding, baked Seville orange marmalade cheesecake may be on the menu.

Open all wk **Bar Meals** L served all wk 12-2.30, Tue-Sun 12-2.30 (Nov-Apr) booking required D served all wk 6-9.30, Tue-Sat 6-9.30 (Nov-Apr) booking required Av main course £10.95 **Restaurant** L served all wk 12-2.30, Tue-Sun 12-2.30 (Nov-Apr) booking required D served all wk 6-9.30, Tue-Sat 6-9.30 (Nov-Apr) booking required Av 3 course à la carte fr £20 ⊕ ADNAMS ◀ Adnams Best, Broadside, Old Ale, Regatta, Explorer. ♟ 18 **Facilities** Children's menu Dogs allowed Garden Parking

## The Golden Key ♟
**Priory Ln IP17 1SQ ☎ 01728 688510**
e-mail: info@snape-golden-key.co.uk
dir: *Telephone for directions*

The 17th-century building has seen many changes over the last few years. Locally sourced food is key to the seasonal menus, which include fresh fish daily from Aldeburgh; Hogwarts Large Black rare-breed pork; and Simply Snape Jacob lamb. Typical dishes are dressed Aldeburgh crab; wild rabbit casserole; and Emmerdale Farm Suffolk Red Poll steak, mushroom and ale pie. A small shop has sells a range of local products.

Open all wk **Bar Meals** L served Mon-Sat 12-2, Sun 12-2.30 booking required D served Mon-Sat 6.30-9, Sun 7-9 booking required Av main course £10 **Restaurant** L served Mon-Sat 12-2, Sun 12-2.30 booking required D served Mon-Sat 6.30-9, Sun 7-9 booking required ⊕ ADNAMS ◀ Adnams Bitter, Broadside, Explorer, Old, Oyster Stout ♂ Aspall. ♟ 14 **Facilities** Children's menu Family room Dogs allowed Garden Parking

## SOUTHWOLD

## The Randolph ◉ ♟
**41 Wangford Rd, Reydon IP18 6PZ ☎ 01502 723603**
🖷 01502 722194
e-mail: reception@therandolph.co.uk
dir: *A1095 from A12 at Blythburgh 4m, Southwold 9m from Darsham train station*

This grand late-Victorian establishment with large gardens was built by Adnams and named after Lord Randolph Churchill, Sir Winston's father. There's a traditional bar but the interior has more of a gastro-pub ambience. Modern British menus offer simple dishes full of flavour, such as deep-fried cod in Adnams batter with hand-cut chips; and confit of duck legs served on an egg noodle and vegetable stir-fry with hoi sin sauce.

Open all wk **Bar Meals** L served all wk 12-2 D served all wk 6.30-9 Av main course £10.95 **Restaurant** L served all wk 12-2 booking required D served all wk 6.30-9 booking required Av 3 course à la carte fr £21.50 ⊕ ADNAMS PLC ◀ Adnams Bitter, Adnams Broadside, Explorer, Old Ale ♂ Aspall. ♟ 6 **Facilities** Children's menu Garden Parking

## STOKE-BY-NAYLAND

### The Crown ★★★ SHL ⊛⊛ ♟

**CO6 4SE ☎ 01206 262001  🗏 01206 264026**
e-mail: thecrown@eoinns.co.uk
dir: *Exit A12 signed Stratford St Mary/Dedham. Through Stratford St Mary 0.5m, left, follow signs to Higham. At village green turn left, left again 2m, pub on right*

This modernised and extended mid-16th century village inn enjoys views across the beautiful Box Valley. Wherever possible, local produce underpins dishes on the monthly-changing modern British menu, all of them freshly prepared by a team of eleven chefs. Being so close to the coast means there is an excellent selection of daily fish dishes on the blackboard – perhaps grilled lemon sole with cherry vine tomatoes, herb oil, new potatoes and fresh mixed salad or fish cakes with chips. Lunch brings full meals or light options such as goats' cheese and basil tart. An evening meal might take in venison carpaccio with rocket, crispy garlic and Parmesan; steak and kidney pudding with horseradish mash and spring greens; and fig tarte Tatin with clotted cream. A decent selection of ales sits alongside a superb wine list; the inn even has its own wine shop, offering wines to drink in or take away.

**Open** all day all wk 7.30am-11pm (Sun 8am-10.30pm) Closed: 25-26 Dec **Bar Meals** L served Mon-Sat 12-2.30, Sun 12-9 D served Mon-Thu 6-9.30, Fri-Sat 6-10, Sun 12-9 Av main course £13.50 **Restaurant** L served Mon-Sat 12-2.30, Sun 12-9 D served Mon-Thu 6-9.30, Fri-Sat 6-10, Sun 12-9 Av 3 course à la carte fr £25 ⊕ FREE HOUSE ◀ Adnams Best Bitter, Brewers Gold, Woodforde's Wherry, guest ales ♻ Aspalls. ♟ 34 **Facilities** Children's menu Dogs allowed Garden Parking **Rooms** 11

## STOWMARKET

### The Buxhall Crown ♟

**Mill Rd, Buxhall IP14 3DW ☎ 01449 736521**
e-mail: thebuxhallcrown@hotmail.co.uk
dir: *3m from Stowmarket and A14*

A 17th-century building, The Buxhall Crown has a classic old bar with intimate corners and an open fire, and a second bar with a lighter, more modern feel. The owners and staff pride themselves on the friendly family feel of the pub, and the high quality of the food they serve. Dishes are prepared from locally sourced produce, and breads, biscuits, ice creams and sorbets are all freshly made on the premises. Anything from a little nibble to a full four-course meal is catered for, with the likes of spring roll of duck confit, vegetables and oriental dressing; grilled fillet of mackerel with warm potato salad and salsa verde; and slow braised English lamb with rosemary, root vegetables and lemon sauce. A meat-free alternative might be tempura battered vegetables with sweet chilli dipping sauce. The menu changes regularly to suit the weather and the availability of ingredients.

**Open** noon-3 7-11 (Sat noon-3 6.30-11) Closed: Sun eve & Mon **Bar Meals** L served Tue-Sun 12-2 D served Tue-Fri 7-10, Sat 6.30-10 Av main course £11.95 **Restaurant** L served Tue-Sun 12-2 D served Tue-Fri 7-10, Sat 6.30-10 Av 3 course à la carte fr £20.85 ⊕ GREENE KING ◀ Greene King IPA, Old Trip, Old Speckled Hen. ♟ 12 **Facilities** Children's menu Dogs allowed Garden Parking

## THORPENESS

### The Dolphin Inn ♟

**Peace Place IP16 4NA ☎ 01728 454994**
e-mail: info@thorpenessdolphin.com
dir: *A12 onto A1094 & follow Thorpeness signs*

A traditional inn and village shop in the heart of Thorpeness, The Dolphin offers lots of local food, including fish. In summer, you can enjoy a barbeque in the sprawling garden. The pub's interior is equally inviting, with a large fireplace and pine furniture. A meal might include potted Orford shrimps with toast; Musks pork and leek sausages with butternut mash and onion gravy; and lemon cheesecake with fig compote.

**Open** Closed: Sun eve & Mon in winter **Bar Meals** L served all wk 12-2.30 booking required D served all wk 6.30-9.30 booking required **Restaurant** L served all wk 12-2.30 booking required D served all wk 6.30-9.30 booking required ⊕ FREE HOUSE ◀ Adnams Best, Adnams Broadside, Rusty Bucket, Nautilus, Mid Summer Gold ♻ Aspall. ♟ 8 **Facilities** Children's menu Dogs allowed Garden Parking

## WALBERSWICK

### The Anchor ⊛⊛ ♟

**Main St IP18 6UA ☎ 01502 722112  🗏 01502 724464**
e-mail: info@anchoratwalberswick.com
dir: *Please telephone for directions*

A 1920s Arts and Crafts building located within earshot of the sea and run with passion and personality by Sophie and Mark Dorber. Her zealous dedication to local ingredients, including vegetables from her allotment, and skill in the kitchen is more than matched by his vast knowledge of beer and wines, the short perfectly seasonal menu pairing each flavour-packed dish with a different suggestion for beer and wine by the glass. Cooking is unpretentious, striking an interesting modern note, yielding the likes of double-baked Green's cheddar soufflé with caramelised onions, braised Blythburgh pork belly with Savoy cabbage and cider jus, and Hoegaarden braised rabbit's legs and peppered loin with buttered leeks and turnip gratin. Expect a relaxed atmosphere and a contemporary feel to the spruced-up bar, with its blue, sand and stone décor reflecting its seaside location, and rear dining room. The splendid rear terrace and garden overlook a beach-hut-dotted horizon.

**Open** all wk **Bar Meals** L served all wk 12-3 D served all wk 6-9 Av main course £13.25 **Restaurant** L served all wk 12-3 booking required D served all wk 6-9 booking required Av 3 course à la carte fr £24.50 ◀ Adnams Bitter, Broadside, Seasonal ♻ Aspalls. ♟ 16 **Facilities** Children's menu Family room Dogs allowed Garden Parking

## Bell Inn ♟

**Ferry Rd IP18 6TN ☎ 01502 723109** 📄 **01502 722728**
e-mail: thebell@adnams.co.uk
dir: *From A12 take B1387, follow to beyond village green, bear right down track*

The inn dates back 600 years and is located near the village green, beach and the ancient fishing harbour on the River Blyth. The large garden has beach and sea views, while the building's great age is evident from the interior's low beams, stone-flagged floors, high wooden settles and open fires. Adnams furnishes the bar with Broadside and Spindrift among others, while Suffolk cyder maker Aspall is also well represented. (Aspall has spelt its cyder with a 'y' since the 1920s, reputedly to reflect the refined quality of the family firm's multi-award-winning product.) Food is all home cooked with local produce featuring strongly, particularly fresh fish. Specialities include starters of locally smoked sprats or Suffolk smokies – flaked smoked haddock in a creamy cheese sauce – both served with granary toast and a salad garnish. There are non-fish dishes too, like baked Suffolk ham or lamb burger in toasted ciabatta.

**Open** all wk **Bar Meals** L served all wk 12-2 D served all wk 7-9 🍺 ADNAMS 🍺 Adnams Bitter, Broadside, Regatta, Old Ale, Explorer, Spindrift 🍏 Aspall. ♟ 15 **Facilities** Children's menu Family room Dogs allowed Garden Parking

---

## WESTLETON

## The Westleton Crown ★★★ HL 🏵🏵 ♟

**The Street IP17 3AD ☎ 01728 648777** 📄 **01728 648239**
e-mail: reception@westletoncrown.co.uk
web: www.westletoncrown.co.uk
dir: *A12 N, turn right for Westleton just after Yoxford. Hotel opposite on entering Westleton*

Guests have been accommodated on the site of the Crown since the 12th century when a priest in charge of Sibton Abbey lived here and took in travellers, and in the 17th century it was a thriving coaching inn. Over the years this attractive brick-built pub, located opposite the parish church in a peaceful village close to the RSPB's Minsmere Reserve, has evolved through careful renovation and refurbishment into a well-appointed inn, combining historic character with contemporary charm, and providing a comfortable base for exploring Suffolk's glorious Heritage Coast. Inside you will find two crackling log fires, local real ales, a good list of wines (9 available by the glass), and an extensive menu that includes innovative daily specials and classic dishes with a twist, all freshly prepared from the best local produce available. You can eat in the cosy parlour, in the elegant dining room, or in the light and airy conservatory restaurant. Starters and lighter dishes may include free-range Blythburgh ham terrine with piccalilli, and baked butternut squash and onion tart. Main courses embrace braised shank of lamb with ratatouille, and local venison with sage creamed potatoes and blueberry sauce. Seafood lovers should look to the specials list for grilled bream with olive oil crushed potatoes and a clam and herb velouté; fresh battered haddock with tartare sauce, mushy peas and hand-cut chips; and the Crown's own smoked fish platter. Save some space for accomplished desserts like warm chestnut and chocolate brownie with marshmallow ice cream; and caramelised blackberry crème brûlée. Outside are large terraced gardens, floodlit in the evening.

**Open** all day all wk 7am-11pm (Sun 7.30am-10.30pm) **Bar Meals** L served all wk 12-2.30 D served all wk 7-9.30 Av main course £15 food served all day **Restaurant** L served all wk 12-2.30 D served all wk 7-9.30 🍺 FREE HOUSE 🍺 Adnams Bitter, range of real ales. ♟ 9 **Facilities** Children's menu Dogs allowed Garden Parking **Rooms** 25

---

# SURREY

## ABINGER

## The Stephan Langton ♟

**Friday St RH5 6JR ☎ 01306 730775**
e-mail: info@stephan-langton.co.uk
dir: *Exit A25 between Dorking & Guildford at Hollow Lane, W of Wootton. 1.5m then left into Friday St. At end of hill right at pond*

A brick and timber-built country pub, set in a tranquil valley, The Stephan Langton is named after a 13th-century local boy who later, as Archbishop of Canterbury, helped draw up the Magna Carta. The current building dates from the 1930s, though looks older, and replaces its predecessor which burnt down. The lunchtime food, like the decor, is unpretentious, but will go down well following a strenuous walk through some of Surrey's most challenging terrain, not least Leith Hill, the highest summit in south-east England. From the daily blackboard come toasted panini with home-made soup; pork pie with piccalilli; and pan-fried pollock with crushed potatoes and leaf salad. From the dinner menu expect the likes of Aberdeen Angus rib-eye steak with horseradish layered potatoes; or confit belly of pork with cumin, haricot beans and chorizo.

**Open** all wk 11-3 5-10.30 (Sat 11-11 Sun 11-9) **Bar Meals** L served Tue-Sun 12-30-2.30 D served Tue-Sat 7-9 Av main course £10 **Restaurant** L served Tue-Sun 12.30-2.30 D served Tue-Sat 7-9 booking required Fixed menu price fr £18.50 Av 3 course à la carte fr £28.50 🍺 FREE HOUSE 🍺 Fuller's London Pride, Hogsback TEA, Shere Drop 🍏 Stowford Press, Old Rosie Scrumpy. ♟ 14 **Facilities** Children's menu Dogs allowed Garden Parking

**England**

### BETCHWORTH

## The Red Lion ★★★ INN ♥

**Old Rd, Buckland RH3 7DS**
☎ **01737 843336** 🖹 **01737 845242**
e-mail: info@redlionbetchworth.co.uk
dir: *Telephone for directions*

The family-run Red Lion dates back to 1795 and is set in 18 acres with a cricket ground, a 230-year-old wisteria and rolling countryside views, all just 15 minutes from Gatwick Airport. The menu offers a pie of the week, fresh beer-battered pollack with hand cut chips, home-made burger, bangers and mash, and wild mushroom linguine. The area is ideal for walkers.

**Open** all day all wk 11am-11.30pm (Fri-Sat 11am-mdnt) **Bar Meals** L served Sun-Fri 12-2.30, Sat 12-4 **Restaurant** L served Mon-Fri 12-2.30, Sat-Sun 12-4 D served all wk 6-9 ⊕ PUNCH TAVERNS ◼ Fuller's London Pride, Adnams Broadside, Adnams Bitter, guest ale. ♥ 10 **Facilities** Children's menu Dogs allowed Garden Parking **Rooms** 6

### BRAMLEY

## Jolly Farmer Inn ♥

**High St GU5 0HB** ☎ **01483 893355** 🖹 **01483 890484**
e-mail: enquiries@jollyfarmer.co.uk
dir: *From Guildford take A281 (Horsham road). Bramley 3.5m S of Guildford*

The family that own this friendly 16th-century free house have a passion for cask ales, and you'll always find up to eight real ales and six lagers, as well as an impressive range of Belgian bottled beers. All meals are freshly cooked to order: expect the likes of chargrilled swordfish loin steak, coq au vin, and butternut squash risotto on the specials board, alongside old favourites such as local pork and herb sausages.

**Open** all day all wk 11-11 **Bar Meals** L served all wk 12-2.30 D served all wk 6-9.30 **Restaurant** L served all wk 12-2.30 D served all wk 6-9.30 ⊕ FREE HOUSE ◼ 8 continually changing cask ales ♻ Westons Stowford Press. ♥ 16 **Facilities** Children's menu Dogs allowed Garden Parking

### CHURT

## Pride of the Valley ♥

**Tilford Rd GU10 2LH** ☎ **01428 605799** 🖹 **01428 605875**
e-mail: reservations@prideofthevalleyhotel.com
dir: *4m from Farnham on outskirts of Churt Village. 3m from Haslemere*

Built in 1867, the Pride of the Valley is a former coaching inn with its own lovely garden set in the heart of the Surrey countryside. The inn was frequented by former Prime Minister David Lloyd George when he lived in the area, and then by Britain's first Formula One champion Mike Hawthorn. This association is celebrated with a number of period photos of Hawthorn in the bar. Locally brewed beers are served, and food is locally sourced from Surrey and Hampshire. The monthly changing menu reflects the current season, with dishes such as trout rillettes with mini toasts and beetroot dressing; slow roast organic mutton pudding with braised Savoy cabbage and red wine sauce; and hot chocolate fondant with cinnamon ice cream and chocolate sauce.

**Open** all wk **Bar Meals** L served Mon-Sat 12-2.30, Sun 12-3 D served all wk 6.30-9.30 Av main course £8.95 **Restaurant** L served Tue-Sun 12-2.30 booking required D served Tue-Sat 6.30-9.30 booking required Av 3 course à la carte fr £26 ⊕ FREE HOUSE ◼ Hogs Back TEA, Hogs Back Bitter, Ringwood 49er. ♥ 8 **Facilities** Children's menu Dogs allowed Garden Parking

### COMPTON

## The Withies Inn ♥

**Withies Ln GU3 1JA** ☎ **01483 421158** 🖹 **01483 425904**
dir: *Telephone for directions*

Set amid unspoiled country on Compton Common, just below the Hog's Back, this low-beamed, 16th-century pub has been carefully modernised to incorporate a small restaurant. There is also a splendid garden where meals are served in the pergola. Snacks are available in the bar, while in the restaurant there is a selection from the chargrill, and dishes such as poached halibut with prawns and brandy sauce; home-cooked steak, kidney and mushroom pie; and steak Diane flambé.

**Open** 11-3 6-11 (Fri 11-11) Closed: Sun eve **Bar Meals** L served all wk 12-2.30 D served Mon-Sat 7-10 **Restaurant** L served all wk 12-2.30 D served Mon-Sat 7-10 ⊕ FREE HOUSE ◼ TEA, Sussex, Adnams. ♥ 8 **Facilities** Children's menu Dogs allowed Garden Parking

### DUNSFOLD

## The Sun Inn ♥

**The Common GU8 4LE** ☎ **01483 200242**
🖹 **01483 201141**
e-mail: suninn@dunsfold.net
dir: *A281 through Shalford & Bramley, take B2130 to Godalming. Dunsfold on left after 2m*

A traditional 500-year-old family-run inn in a chocolate box village, set opposite the cricket green and village pond. Inside the welcome is warm, with blazing fires and an array of real ales. Home-made food includes the house speciality of Aberdeen Angus burgers, plenty of vegetarian options, and Sunday lunches brimming with fresh vegetables. Children have a menu of their favourites; alternatively many main courses can be served in smaller portions.

**Open** all wk 11-3 5-mdnt (Fri-Sun 11am-mdnt) **Bar Meals** L served all wk 12-2.30 D served Tue-Sat 5-9.15, Sun 6-8.30 Av main course £8.85 **Restaurant** L served all wk 12-2.30 D served Tue-Sat 7-9.15, Sun 7-8.30 Fixed menu price fr £5.95 ⊕ PUNCH TAVERNS ◀ Harveys Sussex, Adnams, Speckled Hen, Tribute, Guinness Ö Westons Old Rosie. ⏺ 9 **Facilities** Children's menu Dogs allowed Garden Parking

---

## ELSTEAD

# The Woolpack ⏺

**The Green GU8 6HD** ☎ 01252 703106 🖹 01252 705914
e-mail: woolpack.elstead@yahoo.co.uk
dir: *A3 S, take Milford exit, follow signs for Elstead on B3001*

Originally a wool exchange dating to the 17th century, The Woolpack has been many things, including a butcher's shop and a bicycle repairer's, before becoming a popular pub. The surrounding hundreds of acres of common land attract ramblers galore, especially at lunchtime, and their arrival in the bar is often heralded by the rustle of protective plastic shopping bags over their muddy boots. In the carpeted bar, weaving shuttles and other remnants of the wool industry make appealing features, as do the open log fires, low beams, high-backed settles, window seats and spindle-backed chairs. A good range of cask-conditioned beers is offered, and large blackboards display frequently changing main meals, sandwiches, ploughman's and burgers. Menus are planned around local produce, taking account of the seasons, and choices range from traditional sausages and mash to pan-fried sea bass with couscous. Leave room for home-made desserts.

**Open** all wk noon-3 5.30-11 (Sat-Sun noon-11) **Bar Meals** L served all wk 12.2.30 booking required D served all wk 7-9.30 booking required Av main course £12 **Restaurant** L served all wk 12-2.30 booking required D served all wk 7-9.30 booking required Av 3 course à la carte fr £24 ⊕ PUNCH TAVERNS ◀ Greene King Abbot Ale, Hobgoblin, Youngs, Spitfire, London Pride Ö Old English. ⏺ 40 **Facilities** Children's menu Family room Dogs allowed Garden Parking

---

## EPSOM

# White Horse ⏺

**63 Dorking Rd KT18 7JU** ☎ 01372 726622
e-mail: enquiries@whitehorseepsom.com
dir: *On A24 next to Epsom General Hospital*

The town's oldest surviving pub focuses on four areas - real ales, freshly cooked traditional British food, being family friendly and, as host of the Epsom Jazz Club on Tuesday evenings, live entertainment. Typical starters are hot smoked salmon pâté or creamy garlic mushrooms: mains include chef's own pie of the week, fresh fish of the week and curry of the day; or braised lamb shank on herb mash. A carvery is available on Saturday and Sunday.

**Open** Closed: Mon until 6pm **Bar Meals** Av main course £8 food served all day **Restaurant** food served all day ⊕ PUNCH TAVERNS ◀ guest ales. ⏺ 7 **Facilities** Children's menu Play area Family room Dogs allowed Garden Parking

---

## FARNHAM

# The Bat & Ball Freehouse ⏺

**15 Bat & Ball Ln, Boundstone GU10 4SA** ☎ 01252 792108
e-mail: info@thebatandball.co.uk
dir: *From A31 Farnham bypass follow signs for Birdworld. Left at Bengal Lounge into School Hill. At top over staggered x-rds into Sandrock Hill Rd. After 0.25m left into Upper Bourne Lane, signed*

Tucked down a lane in a wooded valley south of Farnham, this 150-year-old inn is worth hunting out. The interior features oak beams, a roaring fire on colder days, and plenty of cricketing memorabilia. Outside is a children's play area and a lovely garden with vine-topped pergola that backs onto the Bourne stream. Expect a varied selection of home-cooked food: perhaps Wensleydale, apple and walnut pâté followed by coq au vin, home-made pie or half duck slow roasted in orange, apricots and vermouth.

**Open** all wk 11-11 (Sun noon-10.30) **Bar Meals** L served Mon-Sat 12-2.15, Sun 12-3 booking required D served Mon-Sat 7-9.30, Sun 6-8.30 booking required Av main course £10.50 ⊕ FREE HOUSE ◀ Youngs Bitter, Tongham TEA, Triple FFF, Harvey's Sussex Bitter, Hop Back. ⏺ 8 **Facilities** Children's menu Play area Family room Dogs allowed Garden Parking

## GUILDFORD

### The Keystone ?

**3 Portsmouth Rd GU2 4BL ☎ 01483 575089**
e-mail: drink@thekeystone.co.uk
dir: *0.5m from Guildford train station. Turn right from station. Cross 2nd pedestrian crossing, follow road downhill. Past Savills Estate Agents. Pub 200yds on left*

From its outdoor seating areas to the wooden floors and leather sofas in the bar, this town pub has a stylish, well-kept feel. Themed nights, live music and a book swap facility are just some of the distinctive ideas to look out for. Expect fairly priced, modern pub food, with award-winning home-made pies a speciality. Other dishes include pan-fried sea bass with ratatouille and rice; cherry tomato, black olive and melted brie tart; and wild boar sausages with braised red cabbage.

**Open** all wk noon-11 (Fri-Sat noon-mdnt Sun noon-7) Closed: 25-26 Dec, 1 Jan **Bar Meals** L served Mon-Fri 12-3, Sat-Sun 12-5 D served Mon-Thu 6-9 Av main course £8.50 ◀ Black Sheep, 6X, Guinness, guest ale ♂ Westons Organic. ♀ 10 **Facilities** Children's menu Garden

## LEIGH

### The Plough ?

**Church Rd RH2 8NJ ☎ 01306 611348   📄 01306 611299**
e-mail: sarah@theploughleigh.wanadoo.co.uk
dir: *Telephone for directions*

This welcoming country pub stands opposite St Bartholomew's Church overlooking the village green. There is always a great atmosphere here and the low beams are conveniently padded! The comprehensive menu is supplemented by daily specials, and dishes range from nachos, jacket potatoes and salads like warm bacon, black pudding and potato in the bar to braised lamb shank in redcurrant and mint gravy, or sea bass fillet with champagne and asparagus sauce from the main menu in the restaurant area. Home-made pies go down well, as do puddings like Mars bar cheesecake.

**Open** all wk 11-11 (Sun noon-11) **Bar Meals** Av main course £9.50 food served all day **Restaurant** Av 3 course à la carte fr £22.50 food served all day ⊕ HALL & WOODHOUSE ◀ Badger Best , Tanglefoot, Sussex Bitter. ♀ 10 **Facilities** Children's menu Dogs allowed Garden Parking

## LONG DITTON

### The Ditton ?

**64 Ditton Hill Rd KT6 5JD ☎ 020 8339 0785**
e-mail: goodfood@theditton.co.uk
dir: *Please telephone for directions*

The old Plough & Harrow has been given a facelift to return the pub to its former glory and a trendy new name, the rambling village pub now sports a fresh, contemporary feel throughout the bar and interconnecting dining areas. The focus is on family dining and wide-ranging menus take in classic bar snacks, a mezze menu, home-made pies, roasts on Sundays, and more adventurous dishes like pan-fried pork with mash and sherry sauce. The barbecue menu draws the crowds to the large garden on warm summer days.

**Open** all day all wk noon-11 **Bar Meals** L served all wk 12-9 D served all wk 12-9 Av main course £8.95 food served all day **Restaurant** L served Sat-Sun 12-9 booking required D served Mon-Sat 12-9 booking required Av 3 course à la carte fr £22.50 ⊕ ENTERPRISE INNS ◀ Bombardier, Youngs, Tanglefoot. ♀ 8 **Facilities** Children's menu Play area Dogs allowed Garden Parking

## MICKLEHAM

### King William IV ?

**Byttom Hill RH5 6EL ☎ 01372 372590**
dir: *From M25 junct 9, A24 signed to Dorking, pub just before Mickleham*

The former ale house, built in 1790 for workers on Lord Beaverbrook's estate, has a panelled snug and larger back bar with an open fire, cast iron tables and grandfather clock. The terraced garden, ideal for summer dining, offers panoramic views of the Mole Valley. The chef proprietor serves good food alongside real ales, with specials such as roast pheasant breast with red wine jus; and seared king scallops on crayfish in tomato sauce. An ideal location for outstanding local walks.

**Open** all wk Closed: 25 Dec **Bar Meals** L served Mon-Fri 11.45-2, Sat 12-2, Sun 12-5 booking required D served Tue-Sat 7-9 booking required Av main course £10 **Restaurant** L served Mon-Fri 11.45-2, Sat 12-2, Sun 12-5 booking required D served Tue-Sat 7-9 booking required Av 3 course à la carte fr £17 ⊕ FREE HOUSE ◀ Hogs Back TEA, Adnams Best, guest ales ♂ Stowford Press. ♀ 11 **Facilities** Children's menu Garden Parking

## NEWDIGATE

### The Surrey Oaks ?

**Parkgate Rd RH5 5DZ ☎ 01306 631200   📄 01306 631200**
e-mail: ken@surreyoaks.co.uk
dir: *From A24 follow signs to Newdigate, at T-junct turn left, pub 1m on left*

Picturesque oak-beamed pub located one mile outside Newdigate. Parts of the building date back to 1570, and it became an inn around the middle of the 19th century. There are two bars, one with an inglenook fireplace, as well as a restaurant area, patio and beer garden with boules pitch. A typical specials board features Barnsley lamb chop with minted gravy, chicken and ham pie, and grilled plaice with parsley butter.

Open all wk 11.30-2.30 5.30-11 (Sat 11.30-3 6-11 Sun noon-10.30) Bar Meals L served Mon-Fri 12-2, Sat-Sun 12-2.15 D served Tue-Sat 6.30-9.30 Av main course £9 Restaurant L served Mon-Fri 12-2, Sat-Sun 12-2.15 D served Tue-Sat 6.30-9.30 ⊕ ADMIRAL TAVERNS ◀ Harveys Sussex Best, Surrey Hills Ranmore Ale, rotating guest ales ☼ Moles Black Rat, Weston's Country Perry. ♈ 8 Facilities Children's menu Play area Dogs allowed Garden Parking

## OCKLEY

## The Kings Arms Inn ♈

Stane St RH5 5TS ☎ 01306 711224
e-mail: enquiries@thekingsarmsockley.co.uk
dir: From M25 junct 9 take A24 through Dorking towards Horsham, A29 to Ockley

The many charms of this heavily-beamed 16th-century inn include welcoming log fires, a priest hole, a friendly ghost, and an award-winning garden. Set in the picturesque village of Ockley and overlooked by the tower of Leith Hill, it's an ideal setting in which to enjoy a pint and home-cooked food. Using the best of local produce where possible, expect dishes fillet of beef Stroganoff, pan-fried duck breast with honey and mustard sauce, or roast salmon fillet with cucumber and chorizo salad. Sunday roasts include whole hog roast, back by popular demand.

Open all wk noon-2.30 5-11 Bar Meals L served all wk 12-2.30 D served all wk 6.30-9.30 Av main course £11 Restaurant L served all wk 12-2.30 D served all wk 6.30-9.30 Av 3 course à la carte fr £25 ⊕ CROSSOAK INNS ◀ Horsham Best, Doom Bar, Old Speckled Hen. ♈ 10 Facilities Children's menu Garden Parking

## RIPLEY

## The Talbot Inn ★★★★ INN ◉

High St GU23 6BB ☎ 01483 225188    📄 01483 211332
e-mail: info@thetalbotinn.com
dir: Please telephone for directions

The latest addition to Merchant Inns impressive pub portfolio is this stunningly renovated 15th-century coaching inn. The classic beamed bar contrasts spectacularly with the chic dining room, with its copper ceiling and modern glass conservatory extension. Good food blends pub classics like liver and bacon with more innovative dishes like grilled bream with crab and spring onion risotto and shellfish sauce.

Open all day all wk noon-11 (Sun noon-10) Bar Meals D served all wk 6-11 booking required Av main course £10 food served all day Restaurant L served all wk 12-3 booking required D served all wk 6-9.30 booking required Fixed menu price fr £16 Av 3 course à la carte fr £35 ⊕ MERCHANT INNS ◀ Shere Drop, IPA, Abbot Ale ☼ Stowford Press. Facilities Children's menu Dogs allowed Garden Parking Rooms 39

## SOUTH GODSTONE

## Fox & Hounds ♈

Tilburstow Hill Rd RH9 8LY ☎ 01342 893474
dir: 4m from M25 junct 6

Parts of this cosy, traditional inn date back to 1368, though Thomas Hart first opened it as a pub in 1601. There's a large inglenook in the restaurant, and a real fire in the lower bar. Specialising in fish and seafood, regular visitors to the specials board might find supremes of marlin pan-fried in Cajun spices; home-made cheese-topped shepherd's pie; and brochettes of sole and tiger prawns. Outside is a large garden with pleasant rural views. The pub is said to have a resident ghost who might once have been a smuggler.

Open all day all wk noon-11 (25 Dec noon-2) Bar Meals food served all day Restaurant food served all day ⊕ GREENE KING ◀ All Greene King. ♈ 13 Facilities Children's menu Dogs allowed Garden Parking

## STAINES

## The Swan Hotel ♈

The Hythe TW18 3JB ☎ 01784 452494    📄 01784 461593
e-mail: swanhotel@fullers.co.uk
dir: Just off A308, S of Staines Bridge. 5m from Heathrow

This 18th-century inn stands just south of Staines Bridge and was once the haunt of river bargemen who were paid in tokens which could be exchanged at the pub for food and drink. It has a spacious, comfortable bar, and a menu based on traditional home-cooked food. Examples range from sausage and mash; pot-roast lamb shank; and steak and ale pie, to seafood risotto or vegetarian noodle bowl.

Open all wk 11-11 Bar Meals L served Mon-Sat 12-3, Sun 12-8 D served Mon-Sat 6-10, Sun 12-8 Restaurant L served Mon-Sat 12-3, Sun 12-8 D served Mon-Sat 6-10, Sun 12-8 ⊕ FULLER SMITH TURNER PLC ◀ Fuller's London Pride, ESB, Discovery. ♈ 10 Facilities Children's menu Dogs allowed Garden

## WEST HORSLEY

## The King William IV ♈

83 The Street KT24 6BG ☎ 01483 282318
📄 01483 282318
e-mail: kingbilly4th@aol.com
dir: On The Street off A246 (Leatherhead to Guildford)

When laws limiting the consumption of gin were passed in the 1830s, the King William IV began a swift trade in ale through its street-level windows. Fortunately, many of the original Georgian features have been preserved, giving this traditional countryside local a warm and welcoming atmosphere, augmented by open fires in winter and a light and airy conservatory restaurant. Today it's popular with walkers, not least for the large garden and terrace to the rear, with colourful tubs and floral baskets. Beers include several lagers, while the generously proportioned wine list proffers a good selection by

continued

**England**

the glass. The well-priced menu ranges over reliable starters such as deep-fried French brie or crispy garlic mushrooms, and leads on to equally popular mains like seared tuna, or marinated minty lamb rumps. Children can tuck into home-made lasagne and a shot of sugar-free 'safari juice'.

Open all day all wk 11.30am-mdnt (Sun noon-10.30) Bar Meals L served all wk 12-3 D served Mon-Sat 6.30-9.30 Av main course £9.50 Restaurant L served all wk 12-3 D served Mon-Sat 6.30-9.30 Fixed menu price fr £9.50 ⊕ ENTERPRISE INNS ◀ Shere Drop, Courage Best. ♀ 12 Facilities Children's menu Family room Dogs allowed Garden Parking

## EAST SUSSEX

### BLACKBOYS

## The Blackboys Inn ♀

**Lewes Rd TN22 5LG ☎ 01825 890283** 🖹 **01825 890283**
e-mail: blackboys-inn@btconnect.com
dir: *From A22 at Uckfield take B2102 towards Cross in Hand. Or from A267 at Esso service station in Cross in Hand take B2102 towards Uckfield. Village in 1.5m at junct of B2102 & B2192*

Set in 12 acres of beautiful countryside, the rambling, black-weatherboarded inn comprises two restaurant rooms and two cosy bar areas full of endearingly historic features but up to date with interior design. Menus offer freshly prepared food - fish, game, roasts and vegetarian specialities – with home-grown vegetables where possible; while the bar snack selection is known for its famous range of burgers. Grounds include a large duck pond, a secret garden for adults only and a separate party venue.

Open all wk noon-mdnt Bar Meals L served Mon-Fri 12-3, Sat 12-10, Sun 12-9 D served Sun-Mon 6-9, Tue-Sat 6-10 Av main course £8.50 Restaurant L served Mon-Fri 12-3, Sat 12-10, Sun 12-9 D served Sun-Mon 6-9, Tue-Sat 6-10 Av 3 course à la carte fr £22 ⊕ HARVEYS OF LEWES ◀ Harveys Sussex Best Bitter, Sussex Halow, Sussex XXXX Old Ale, seasonal ♂ Stowford Press. ♀ 8 Facilities Children's menu Dogs allowed Garden Parking

### CHAILEY

## The Five Bells Restaurant and Bar ♀

**East Grinstead Rd BN8 4DA ☎ 01825 722259**
🖹 **01825 723368**
e-mail: info@fivebellschailey.co.uk
dir: *5m N of Lewes on A275*

Handy for Sheffield Park, the Bluebell Railway, Plumpton racecourse and walks around Chailey. With origins in the 15th century and serving ale since the 17th, this country pub cum wine bar cum smart restaurant has many original features, including a large inglenook fireplace. The highly qualified kitchen team create modern European dishes rooted in English tradition from fresh, organic and free-range ingredients. Friday

evenings host live jazz, and in summer the large bar terrace and secluded restaurant garden come into their own.

Open all wk noon-3 6-11 (Sun-Mon noon-3) Closed: Sun & Mon eve Bar Meals L served all wk 12-2.30 D served Tue-Thu 6-9, Fri-Sat 6-9.30 Av main course £11.95 Restaurant L served all wk 12-2.30 D served Tue-Thu 6-9, Fri-Sat 6.9.30 ⊕ ENTERPRISE INNS ◀ Harvey's Best, Youngs Special ♂ Stowford Press. ♀ 7 Facilities Children's menu Dogs allowed Garden Parking

### COOKSBRIDGE

## The Rainbow Inn ♀

**Resting Oak Hill BN8 4SS ☎ 01273 400334**
🖹 **01273 401667**
e-mail: lwilson@sterlinggroupltd.com
dir: *3m outside Lewes on A275 towards Haywards Heath*

Built of brick and flint and making the most of its pretty corner site, the 17th-century Rainbow boasts a sun-trap enclosed rear terrace with views to the South Downs – a super spot to unwind with a cracking pint of Harveys on lazy summer days. On cooler days, head inside and cosy-up by the blazing fire in the rustic bar, or peruse the chalkboard specials and settle in one of three warmly decorated dining areas, all sporting wooden floors, an eclectic mix of tables and chairs, tasteful artwork, and a relaxing atmosphere. Look out for Newhaven fish (sea bass with herb butter), confit of Sussex pork belly with mixed bean cassoulet, and local estate game, perhaps roast saddle of venison with sweet potato rösti and port jus. Simpler, lighter bar meals take in filled rolls and ploughman's platters. Leave room for baked lemon and lime tart or the impressive cheese selection. Upstairs are two charming little private dining rooms.

Open all wk noon-3 5-11 (Sat-Sun noon-11) Bar Meals Av main course £6.50 food served all day Restaurant Fixed menu price fr £12.95 Av 3 course à la carte fr £21 food served all day ⊕ STERLING PUB COMPANY ◀ Harveys Best Bitter, Guinness ♂ Stowford Press. ♀ 10 Facilities Children's menu Dogs allowed Garden Parking

## DANEHILL

### The Coach and Horses 🍷

**RH17 7JF ☎ 01825 740369 📠 01825 740369**

dir: *From East Grinstead, S through Forest Row on A22 to junct with A275 (Lewes road), right on A275, 2m to Danehill, left onto School Lane, 0.5m, pub on left*

Set on the edge of Ashdown Forest, the Coach and Horses has provided hospitality since 1847. It was built as an ale house with stabling and a courtyard between two large country estates; these days the stables form part of a comfortable country-style restaurant, and the original bars remain busy with locals. Open fires and neatly tended gardens add colour to a characterful setting: expect half-panelled walls, highly polished wooden floorboards and vaulted beamed ceilings. Food plays a key role in its success. Typical choices include confit rabbit terrine with shallot chutney; spicy Portland crab and saffron risotto with Parmesan; and hot chocolate fondant with pistachio crème Anglaise. In addition to the main menu and blackboard dishes, sandwiches are available at lunchtime. The landlady now sells her own preserves under the name of Ladypots.

**Open** all wk 11.30-3 6-11 (Sat-Sun 11.30-11) **Bar Meals** L served all wk 12-2 D served Mon-Sat 7-9 Av main course £12.50 **Restaurant** L served all wk 12-2 D served Mon-Sat 7-9 Av 3 course à la carte fr £23.75 FREE HOUSE Harveys Best & Old Ale, Wadworth IPA, WJ King & Co, Hammerpot, Dark Star Stowford Press. 🍷 10 **Facilities** Children's menu Play area Dogs allowed Garden Parking

## EAST CHILTINGTON

### The Jolly Sportsman 🍷

**Chapel Ln BN7 3BA ☎ 01273 890400 📠 01273 890400**

e-mail: thejollysportsman@mistral.co.uk

dir: *From Lewes take A275, left at Offham onto B2166 towards Plumpton, take Novington Ln, after approx 1m left into Chapel Ln*

Secluded and romantic, this sympathetically upgraded dining inn is tucked away down a quiet no-through road surrounded by downland. The bar retains some of the character of a Victorian ale house, while the dining room strikes a cool, modern pose, and there is a terrace with Moroccan-tiled tables overlooking the garden. Typical dishes are mussel, tomato and herb risotto; roast partridge with cabbage, bacon and Lyonnaise potatoes; and almond custard fritter with roast plums.

**Open** Closed: 25-26 Dec, Mon ex BH **Bar Meals** L served Tue-Sat 12.15-2.30, Sun 12.15-3 D served Tue-Thu & Sun 7-9.30, Fri-Sat 7-10 booking required Av main course £13.50 **Restaurant** L served Tue-Sat 12.15-2.30, Sun 12.15-3 booking required D served Tue-Thu & Sun 7-9.30, Fri-Sat 7-10 booking required Fixed menu price fr £15.75 Av 3 course à la carte fr £25 FREE HOUSE Dark Star Hophead, guest ales. 🍷 9 **Facilities** Children's menu Play area Dogs allowed Garden Parking

## FLETCHING

### The Griffin Inn 🍷

**TN22 3SS ☎ 01825 722890 📠 01825 722810**

e-mail: info@thegriffininn.co.uk

dir: *M23 junct 10 to East Grinstead, then A22, then A275. Village signed on left, 15m from M23*

The Griffin's superbly landscaped gardens boast one of the best views in Sussex, looking out over the Ouse Valley towards Sheffield Park. In the summer months, the terrace forms an important part of the restaurant. The Grade II listed Griffin is reputedly the oldest licensed building in Sussex and is over 400 years old. Old beams, wainscotting, open fires and pews make up the character of the main bar. Menus change daily, with the emphasis on fresh Rye Bay fish and organic, locally sourced ingredients. Modern British dishes are given a Mediterranean twist, and a meal might start with spiced beef carpaccio with black olives and caper dressing; followed by roast rack of Sussex lamb, chargrilled courgette and cavalo nero. Puddings include roast apples and pears with mascarpone and pine nuts.

**Open** all wk noon-11 Closed: 25 Dec **Bar Meals** L served Mon-Fri 12-2.30, Sat-Sun 12-3 D served all wk 7-9.30 Av main course £11.50 **Restaurant** L served Mon-Fri 12-2.30, Sat-Sun 12-3 booking required D served Mon-Sat 7-9.30 booking required Fixed menu price fr £30 Av 3 course à la carte fr £30 FREE HOUSE Harvey Best, Kings of Horsham, Hepworths. 🍷 15 **Facilities** Children's menu Play area Garden Parking

## GUN HILL

### The Gun Inn 🍷

**TN21 0JU ☎ 01825 872361 📠 01622 851881**

e-mail: enquiries@thegunhouse.co.uk

dir: *5m S of Heathfield, 1m off A267 towards Gun Hill. 4m off A22 between Uckfield & Hailsham*

A lovely 17th-century building and former courthouse set in delightful East Sussex countryside, with extensive views from a pretty terrace and garden. Wood dominates the interior, with beams, and a beautiful wooden floor. A separate panelled dining room with stunning fireplace is ideal for private parties. Three deli board selections can be shared - the cold meat board, for example, includes garlic sausage, salami, chorizo, honey roast ham and farmhouse terrine. From the menu, starters of stuffed mushroom with stilton and bacon, and The Gun Sussex smokie – oven-baked smoked haddock with mozzarella and mustard sauce. Main dishes include home-made Dublin pie (beef, mushrooms and Guinness gravy), and chef's favourite Sussex beef cuts (rib-eye, sirloin) with sauce of your choice. Game dishes are available when in season. The Old Coach House behind the pub is now a farmers' market.

**Open** noon-3 6-11 (Sat-Sun noon-11) **Bar Meals** L served Mon-Fri 12-3, Sat-Sun 12-10 D served Mon-Fri 6-9.30, Sat-Sun 12-10 Av main course £9.95 **Restaurant** L served Mon-Fri 12-3, Sat-Sun 12-10 D served Mon-Fri 6-9.30, Sat-Sun 12-10 Fixed menu price fr £10 Av 3 course à la carte fr £19 FREE HOUSE Harveys, Guinness, Youngs. 🍷 13 **Facilities** Children's menu Play area Garden Parking

### HARTFIELD

## Anchor Inn

**Church St TN7 4AG** ☎ **01892 770424**
dir: *On B2110*

A 14th-century inn at the heart of Winnie the Pooh country, deep within the scenic Ashdown Forest. Inside are stone floors enhanced by a large inglenook fireplace. Sandwiches and salads are among the bar snacks, while for something more substantial you could try whole Dover sole; grilled pork loin on a bed of spaghetti; or medallions of beef fillet. Puddings include crème brûlée; ice cream gâteau; and orange marmalade bread and butter pudding.

Open all day all wk **Bar Meals** L served all wk 12-2 booking required D served all wk 6-10 booking required Av main course £8 **Restaurant** L served all wk 12-2 booking required D served all wk 6-10 booking required ⊕ FREE HOUSE ◀ Harveys Sussex Best Bitter, Larkins. **Facilities** Children's menu Family room Dogs allowed Garden Parking

### ICKLESHAM

## The Queen's Head ♉

**Parsonage Ln TN36 4BL**
☎ **01424 814552** 📄 **01424 814766**
dir: *Between Hastings & Rye on A259. Pub in village on x-rds near church*

A 17th-century tile-hung building, full of exposed oak beams, the pub has a magnificent view across the Brede valley to Rye. The traditional atmosphere has been conserved, with vaulted ceilings, large inglenook fireplaces, church pews, old farm implements, and a bar from an old Bank in Eastbourne. Typical of the home-made dishes are a choice of pies; Thai vegetable curry; steaks and grills; salads and snacks. Gardens include a playhouse, climbing frame and boule pitch.

Open all wk 11-11 (Sun 11-10.30) **Bar Meals** L served Mon-Fri 12-2.30, Sat-Sun 12-9.30 D served Mon-Fri 6-9.30, Sat-Sun 12-9.30 Av main course £8.95 ⊕ FREE HOUSE ◀ Rother Valley Level Best, Greene King Abbot Ale, Harveys Best, Dark Star, Ringwood 49r ⚥ Biddenden. ♉ 10 **Facilities** Children's menu Play area Garden Parking

### OFFHAM

## The Blacksmiths Arms ★★★★ INN ♉

**London Rd BN7 3QD** ☎ **01273 472971**
e-mail: blacksmithsarms@tiscali.co.uk
dir: *2m N of Lewes on A275*

An attractive, mid-18th-century free house popular with walkers and cyclists on the South Downs Way. Harvey's ales are served in the bar, where log fires burn in the inglenook. Bernard and Sylvia Booker's use of local produce is shown in dishes like Auntie Kate's crispy roast duckling with spiced orange and Cointreau sauce; rack of South Downs lamb with poached pear and apricot sauce; and locally caught seafood.

Open Closed: Mon **Bar Meals** L served Tue-Sun 12-2 Av main course £6 **Restaurant** L served Tue-Sun 12-2 booking required D served Tue-Sun 6.30-9 booking required Fixed menu price fr £10 Av 3 course à la carte fr £22.50 ⊕ FREE HOUSE ◀ Harveys Ales. ♉ 10 **Facilities** Children's menu Garden Parking **Rooms** 4

### RINGMER

## The Cock ♉

**Uckfield Rd BN8 5RX** ☎ **01273 812040** 📄 **01273 812040**
e-mail: matt@cockpub.co.uk
web: www.cockpub.co.uk
dir: *On A26 approx 2m N of Lewes just outside Ringmer*

Built in the 16th-century, this former coaching inn was a mustering point during the Civil War for the siege of Arundel. Original oak beams, flagstone floors and a blazing fire set a cosy scene. Frequent specials include pot roasted pheasant, organic sausage and onion pie, whole fresh brill, and vegetarian quiche. The west-facing restaurant and garden have views to the South Downs and some wonderful sunsets.

Open all wk 11-3 6-11.30 (Sun 11-11) Closed: 26 Dec **Bar Meals** L served Mon-Sat 12-2, Sun 12-9.30 D served Mon-Sat 6-9.30, Sun 12-9.30 Av main course £9.50 **Restaurant** L served Mon-Sat 12-2, Sun 12-9.30 booking required D served Mon-Sat 6-9.30, Sun 12-9.30 booking required Av 3 course à la carte fr £18.50 ⊕ FREE HOUSE ◀ Harveys Sussex Best Bitter, Sussex XXXX Old Ale, Fuller's London Pride, Dark Star Hophead ⚥ Westons 1st Quality. ♉ 9 **Facilities** Children's menu Play area Dogs allowed Garden Parking

## RYE

# Mermaid Inn ★★★ HL ◉ ⚲

**Mermaid St TN31 7EY ☎ 01797 223065**
🖷 01797 225069
e-mail: info@mermaidinn.com
dir: *A259, follow signs to town centre, then into Mermaid St*

Destroyed by the French in 1377 and rebuilt in 1420 (on foundations dating back to 1156), the Mermaid is steeped in history and stands among the cobbled streets of Rye. Once famous for its smuggling associations, the infamous Hawkhurst Gang used to meet here, it remains strong on romantic, old-world appeal, with beams hewn from ancient ships' timbers, antique furnishings, linenfold panelling, and huge fireplaces carved from French stone ballast rescued from the harbour. There is also a priest's hole in the lounge bar. Food is served in the bar and atmospheric restaurant, and in the summer you can relax under sunshades on the patio. Bar food ranges from sandwiches or baked fish pie, to smoked haddock and salmon fishcakes and sirloin steak with chips and blue cheese sauce.

**Open** all wk noon-11 **Bar Meals** L served all wk 12-2.30 D served all wk 6-9 Av main course £8.50 **Restaurant** L served all wk 12-2.30 booking required D served all wk 7.30-9.30 booking required Fixed menu price fr £24 Av 3 course à la carte fr £35 ⊕ FREE HOUSE ◖ Greene King Old Speckled Hen, Courage Best, Fuller's London Pride. ⚲ 11 **Facilities** Children's menu Garden Parking **Rooms** 31

## SHORTBRIDGE

# The Peacock Inn ⚲

**TN22 3XA ☎ 01825 762463**  🖷 01825 762463
e-mail: enquiries@peacock-inn.co.uk
dir: *Just off A272 (Haywards Heath to Uckfield road) & A26 (Uckfield to Lewes road)*

Mentioned in Samuel Pepys' diary, the Peacock dates from 1567 and is full of old world charm. Today it is renowned for its food (created by no fewer than three chefs), and also the resident ghost of Mrs Fuller. The large rear patio garden is a delightful spot in summer. Food choices include toasted ciabatta and toasted foccacia with a variety of fillings. For the hungry there are starters such as chicken and duck liver pâté, or crayfish tails and smoked salmon, followed by seafood crepe, pan-fried sea bass fillets; steak, Guinness and mushroom pie or fillet steak with garlic and stilton butter. For the non-meat eaters there's Mediterranean vegetable and mozzarella tartlet, or vegetarian tagine. Look out for chefs' specials.

**Open** all wk Mon-Fri 11-3 (Sat-Sun all day) Closed: 25-26 Dec **Bar Meals** L served Mon-Fri 12-3, Sat-Sun all day D served Mon-Fri 6-10, Sat-Sun all day ⊕ FREE HOUSE ◖ Abbot Ale, Harveys Best Bitter, Fuller's London Pride. ⚲ 8 **Facilities** Children's menu Dogs allowed Garden Parking

## THREE LEG CROSS

# The Bull ⚲

**Dunster Mill Ln TN5 7HH**
☎ 01580 200586  🖷 01580 201289
e-mail: enquiries@thebullinn.co.uk
dir: *From M25 at Sevenoaks toward Hastings, right at x-rds onto B2087, right onto B2099 thru Ticehurst, right for Three Legged Cross*

The Bull is based on a 14th-century Wealden hall house, set in a hamlet close to Bewl Water. The interior features oak beams, inglenook fireplaces, quarry tiled floors, and an intimate bar. The gardens are popular with families who enjoy the duck pond, petanque pitch, aviary and children's play area. Menus offer pub favourites ranging from freshly baked baguettes and bar snacks to hearty dishes full of comfort, such as bangers and mash and treacle tart.

**Open** all wk noon-11 Closed: 25-26 Dec eve **Bar Meals** L served Mon-Fri 12-2.30, Sat 12-3, Sun 12-8 D served Mon-Sat 6.30-9, Sun 6.30-8 **Restaurant** L served Mon-Fri 12-2.30, Sat 12-3, Sun 12-8 D served Mon-Sat 6.30-9, Sun 6.30-8 ⊕ FREE HOUSE ◖ Harveys, Sussex Best, Harveys Armada, Timothy Taylor, 1066, guest ales Ö Stowford Press. ⚲ 7 **Facilities** Children's menu Play area Dogs allowed Garden Parking

## WADHURST

# The Best Beech Inn ⚲

**Mayfield Ln TN5 6JH ☎ 01892 782046**
dir: *7m from Tunbridge Wells. On A246 at lights turn left onto London Rd (A26), left at mini rdbt onto A267, left then right onto B2100. At Mark Cross signed Wadhurst, 3m on right*

The unusually-named Best Beech Inn is going from strength to strength. The inn dates back to 1680, and has been sympathetically refurbished in recent years to preserve the essentially Victorian character of its heyday. The result is a place bursting with personality, characterised by comfy chairs, exposed brickwork and open fireplaces. Ideally situated near the Kent and Sussex border, in an Area of Outstanding Natural Beauty, the inn includes a fine à la carte restaurant offering excellent European cuisine with a French influence. For those who prefer a more informal atmosphere, there is the bar bistro with a comprehensive menu available from the blackboard. Dinner could begin with pork rillette and apricot chutney, move on to bouillabaisse with saffron new potatoes, and finish with tarte au chocolat, marmalade syrup and vanilla ice cream.

**Open** all day all wk noon-11pm **Bar Meals** L served Mon-Sat 12-3, Sun 12-4 booking required D served Mon-Sat 6-9.30 booking required **Restaurant** L served Mon-Sat 12-3, Sun 12-4 booking required D served Mon-Sat 6-9.30 booking required ⊕ SHEPHERD NEAME ◖ Kent Best, Master Brew. ⚲ 7 **Facilities** Children's menu Family room Dogs allowed Garden Parking

continued

England

## WARTLING

### The Lamb Inn ♟

**BN27 1RY ☎ 01323 832116**

web: www.lambinnwartling.co.uk
dir: *A259 from Polegate to Pevensey rdbt. Take 1st left to Wartling & Herstmonceux Castle. Pub 3m on right*

This family-run, classic country pub and restaurant was built in 1526, although it did not begin dispensing ale until 1640. Since then it has provided a welcome rest stop to everyone from 18th-century smugglers to today's birdwatchers, walkers and locals who enjoy the nearby Pevensey Levels and surrounding East Sussex countryside. Draw up one of the comfortable cream sofas to the fire and, as your well-behaved dog settles down at your feet, enjoy a real ale from Sussex breweries or a glass of wine. Aside from liquid refreshment, the pub is well known for its food. Everything is made on the premises, including the bread, and, as far as possible, makes use of top quality produce sourced locally from places like Chilley Farm, which specialises in raising Gloucester Old Spot pigs, Southdown and Kent Cross lamb, and Sussex beef without additives and in unhurried fashion. Fish makes the short journey from Hastings and Newhaven to become house specialities, offered daily on the specials board. An easy-to-assimilate menu offers plenty of variety, so that a meal might begin with pancake of creamy garlic mushrooms glazed with Stilton; smoked mackerel, prawn and crayfish terrine with horseradish cream and Melba toast; or grilled fresh figs. For a main course, there could be seafood platter; fillet of lemon sole stuffed with spinach and crab, dill and Champagne sauce; chargrilled Tottingworth Farm Barnsley chop with dauphinoise potatoes, garlic and parsley butter; rib-eye of Sussex Limousin beef with home-made wedges, mushrooms and fried onions; or, for vegetarians, risotto and dressed salad; or winter vegetable casserole with Parmesan and breadcrumb crust. Traditional home-made desserts are represented by iced chocolate and Tia Maria parfait, and lemon and sultana bread and butter pudding with clotted cream. Look out for year round events and special nights.

**Open** all wk Closed: Sun eve, Mon in winter **Bar Meals** L served all wk 12-2.15 booking required D served Tue-Sat 7-9 booking required Av main course £8.95 **Restaurant** L served all wk 12-2.15 booking required D served Tue-Sat 7-9 booking required Fixed menu price fr £11.95 Av 3 course à la carte fr £22.95 ◀ Harveys, Red River, Horsham Best, Toff's, Level Best. ♟ 8 **Facilities** Children's menu Dogs allowed Garden Parking

## AMBERLEY

### Black Horse ♟

**High St BN18 9NL ☎ 01798 831700**
dir: *Please telephone for directions*

A traditional 17th-century tavern with a lively atmosphere in a beautiful South Downs village. Look out for the display of sheep bells donated by the last shepherd to have a flock on the local hills. Food is served in the large restaurant and bar or in the beer garden complete with pond, and there's plenty of choice for everyone including a children's menu. Great beer, good local walks, and nice views of the South Downs. Dogs (on leads) are welcome in the bar.

**Open** all day all wk **Bar Meals** L served all wk 12-3 D served Sun-Thu 6-8.30, Fri-Sat 6-9.30 Av main course £10 **Restaurant** L served Sun only booking required D served Sun-Mon & Wed-Thu 6-8.30, Fri-Sat 6-9.30 booking required ⊕ ADMIRAL TAVERNS ◀ Greene King IPA, Harveys Sussex, guest ale. ♟ 9 **Facilities** Children's menu Dogs allowed Garden

### The Bridge Inn ♟

**Houghton Bridge BN18 9LR ☎ 01798 831619**
e-mail: bridgeamberley@btinternet.com
web: www.bridgeinnamberley.com
dir: *5m N of Arundel on B2139. Next to Amberley main line station*

Standing alongside the River Arun at the mid-point of the South Downs Way National Trail, this traditional free house dates from 1650. The pretty pub garden and patio are summer favourites, whilst the candle-lit bar and log fires come into their own on cold winter evenings. Daily chalkboard specials and an extensive range of pub classics sustain the heartiest appetites.

**Open** all day all wk noon-11 (Sun noon-10.30) **Bar Meals** L served Mon-Fri 12-2.30, Sat-Sun 12-4 D served Sun-Mon 6-8, Tue-Sat 6-9 Av main course £9 **Restaurant** Av 3 course à la carte fr £17 ⊕ FREE HOUSE ◀ Harveys Sussex, Fuller's London Pride, Hopback Summer Lightning, Sharps Cornish Coaster Ŏ Westons Stowford Press, Westons Old Rosie. ♟ 8 **Facilities** Children's menu Dogs allowed Garden Parking

## BALCOMBE

# The Cowdray

**RH17 6QD ☎ 01444 811280**
e-mail: alexandandy@hotmail.co.uk
dir: *Please telephone for directions*

Just a mile from the M23 (junct 10a), the once run-down village boozer has been transformed into cosy dining pub, with Alex and Andy Owen, who once worked for Gordon Ramsay, re-opening the doors in early 2008. Expect wood floors, a fresh, crisp decor, and a pub menu that's a cut above average and boasts 85% Sussex produce. Follow wild mushroom risotto with pan-fried squid with chorizo, prawns and clams, or Old Spot pork belly with root vegetables, and pear Tatin.

**Open** all wk noon-3 5.30-11 Closed: 25 Dec eve, 1 Jan eve **Bar Meals** L served Mon-Sat 12-3, Sun 12-4 D served Mon-Thu 6-9, Fri-Sat 6-10 Av main course £8.50 **Restaurant** L served Mon-Sat 12-3, Sun 12-4 D served Mon-Thu 6-9, Fri-Sat 6-10 booking required Av 3 course à la carte fr £25 ⊕ GREENE KING **Facilities** Children's menu Play area Family room Dogs allowed Garden Parking

---

## BURGESS HILL

# The Oak Barn ⚐

**Cuckfield Rd RH15 8RE ☎ 01444 258222**
📄 01444 258388
e-mail: enquiries@oakbarnrestaurant.co.uk
web: www.oakbarnrestaurant.co.uk
dir: *Please telephone for directions*

Beautifully restored six years ago, using old timbers salvaged from wooden ships, acres of oak flooring and fine stained glass, this 250-year-old barn has been transformed into a popular pub-restaurant. Lofty, raftered ceilings, a galleried restaurant, and leather chairs fronting a huge fireplace set the atmospheric scene for tucking into mussels in garlic, cream and white wine, pork belly with caramelised apples, and banoffee pie, or one of the all-day bar meals.

**Open** all day all wk 10am-11pm (Sun 11-11) **Bar Meals** L served all wk 12-2.30 D served all wk 6-9.30 Av main course £13 **Restaurant** L served all wk 12-2.30 booking required D served all wk 6-9.30 booking required Av 3 course à la carte fr £21 ⊕ FREE HOUSE ◀ Guinness, Harveys. ⚐ 12 **Facilities** Children's menu Garden Parking

## BURPHAM

# George & Dragon ◉

**BN18 9RR ☎ 01903 883131**
e-mail: sara.cheney@btinternet.com
dir: *Off A27 1m E of Arundel, signed Burpham, 2.5m pub on left*

Tucked away down a long 'no through road', Burpham looks across the Arun valley to the mighty Arundel Castle. There are excellent riverside and downland walks on the doorstep of this 300 year-old free house, and walkers and their dogs are welcome in the bar: but please, leave any muddy footwear in the porch. Inside you'll find beamed ceilings, modern prints, with worn stone flagstones. The original rooms have been opened out to form a large space that catches the late sunshine, but there are still a couple of alcoves with tables for an intimate drink. Look a little further, and you'll also discover a small bar hidden around a corner. This is very much a dining pub, attracting visitors from far and wide. The à la carte menu and specials board offer a good choice of dishes between them: for starters you could try caramelised red onion, fig and pear tartlet with stilton dressing, or game terrine with Arundel ale chutney. Main courses might include honey roasted Scotch salmon on citrus cous cous with pan-roasted vegetables and soy sauce; wild mushroom, garlic, leek and thyme crumble with Sussex Cheddar topping and side salad; or pan roasted English lamb rump on red onion confit with black pepper, red wine and cranberry sauce, served with dauphinoise potatoes and fresh vegetables. There are tables outside, ideal for whiling away an afternoon or evening in summer, listening to the cricket being played on the green a few steps away.

**Open** all wk 11.30-3 6-mdnt **Bar Meals** L served Mon-Fri 12-2, Sat-Sun 12-3 booking required D served all wk 6-9 booking required Av main course £13.95 **Restaurant** L served Mon-Sat 12-2 booking required D served Mon-Sun 6-9 booking required Av 3 course à la carte fr £24.95 ⊕ FREE HOUSE ◀ Brewery-on-Sea Spinnaker Bitter, Fuller's London Pride, Arundel Ales and guest ales ♻ Stowford Press. **Facilities** Children's menu Dogs allowed Garden Parking

## CHARLTON

### The Fox Goes Free ♟

**PO18 0HU ☎ 01243 811461** 📄 **01243 811712**
e-mail: enquiries@thefoxgoesfree.com
web: www.thefoxgoesfree.com
dir: *A286, 6m from Chichester towards Midhurst. 1m from Goodwood racecourse*

Nestling in unspoilt countryside, this lovely old brick and flint free house was a favoured hunting lodge of William III. With its three huge fireplaces, old pews and brick floors, the 16th-century building simply exudes charm and character. The pub, which hosted the first Women's Institute meeting in 1915, lies close to the rambling Weald and Downland open-air museum, where fifty historic buildings from around southern England have been reconstructed to form a unique collection. Goodwood estate is also close by, and The Fox attracts many a punter during the racing season and the annual Festival of Speed. Away from the high life, you can watch the world go by from the solid timber benches and tables to the front, or relax under the apples trees in the lawned rear garden. Everything is home-made and, whether you're looking for a quick bar snack or something more substantial, the daily changing menus offer plenty of choice. Baguettes filled with sausage and caramelised onions or smoked salmon with mascarpone will fill the odd corner, whilst fresh battered cod and chips; or steak and mushroom pie are tempting alternatives from the bar menu. À la carte choices include roast shoulder of lamb with braised red cabbage and olives; and pan-fried chicken with Parma ham, creamed leeks and red wine sauce.

**Open** all day all wk 11-11 (Sun noon-11) Closed: 25 Dec eve **Bar Meals** L served Mon-Fri 12-2.30, Sat-Sun 12-10 booking required D served Mon-Fri 6.30-10, Sat-Sun 12-10 booking required Av main course £8.50 **Restaurant** L served all wk 12-2.30 booking required D served all wk 6.30-10 booking required Av 3 course à la carte fr £25 ⊕ FREE HOUSE ◀ Ballards Best, The Fox Goes Free, Harveys Sussex. ♟ 8 **Facilities** Children's menu Dogs allowed Garden Parking

## CHICHESTER

### Royal Oak Inn ★★★★★ INN ◉ ♟

**Pook Ln, East Lavant PO18 0AX ☎ 01243 527434**
📄 **01243 775062**
e-mail: enquiries@royaloakeastlavant.co.uk
web: www.royaloakeastlavant.co.uk
dir: *A286 from Chichester signed Midhurst, 2m then right at mini-rdbt, pub over bridge on left*

Set just outside Chichester in the picturesque village of East Lavant, this coaching inn offers a friendly welcome, real ales and award-winning food all within reach of the rolling hills of Sussex. The Royal Oak was a regular pub for many years, but has been exceptionally well converted to offer stylish, sleekly furnished guest accommodation. The brick-lined restaurant and bar achieve a crisp, rustic brand of chic: details include fresh flowers, candles, and wine attractively displayed in alcoves set into the walls. Favourite dishes include tempura vegetables with teriyaki and sweet chilli dipping sauce; seared scallops on parsnip purée with crisp pancetta; risotto of wild mushrooms with marinated artichokes and shaved pecorino; and fillet steak with a creamy pepper sauce, chestnut mushrooms and bordelaise potatoes.

**Open** all day all wk 7am-11.30pm Closed: 25 Dec **Bar Meals** Av main course £15.50 **Restaurant** L served all wk 12-3 booking required D served all wk 6.30-11 booking required Av 3 course à la carte fr £30 ⊕ FREE HOUSE ◀ Ballards, HSB, Sussex, Arundel. ♟ 20 **Facilities** Children's menu Garden Parking **Rooms** 8

## CHILGROVE

### The Fish House ♟

**High St PO18 9HX ☎ 01243 519444**
e-mail: info@thefishhouse.co.uk
dir: *On B2141 between Chichester & Petersfield*

Low ceilings, beams and decorative brickwork combine with leather sofas in the bar of this recently refurbished wisteria-covered building. Here, too, you'll find a crustacean counter, Irish Marble topped bar and a 300 year-old French fireplace. Besides its signature Guinness and oysters, the Fish House offers a daily set lunch menu and Sunday roasts in the bar. Meanwhile the sumptuous fine dining restaurant features paintings by John Holt, as well as hand-made furniture and contrasting linen drapes. From their tables, diners can watch head chef Alan Gleeson preparing dishes from an à la carte menu where fish and seafood naturally top the bill. Typical dishes include whole baby plaice, baked mash and fine beans; steamed fillet of hake, glass noodles and enoki mushrooms; and local game pie, red cabbage and crushed parsnips.

**Open** all day all wk **Bar Meals** L served all wk 12-2.30 D served all wk 6-10 Av main course £12.50 **Restaurant** L served all wk 12-2.30 booking required D served all wk 6-10 booking required Fixed menu price fr £17 Av 3 course à la carte fr £40 ⊕ FREE HOUSE ◀ Black Sheep, Harveys Best Ŏ Westons Organic. ♀ 24 **Facilities** Children's menu Dogs allowed Garden Parking

## COMPTON

## Coach & Horses

**The Square PO18 9HA** ☎ 02392 631228
dir: *On B2146 S of Petersfield, to Emsworth, in centre of Compton*

The 16th-century pub is set quite remotely in the prettiest of Downland villages, a popular spot for walkers and cyclists. The front bar features two open fires and a bar billiards table, while the restaurant is in the oldest part of the pub, with many exposed beams. Up to five guest beers from independent breweries are usually available. There is an extensive menu of home-cooked dishes, all made to order.

**Open** all wk 11.30-3 6-11 **Bar Meals** L served all wk 12-2 D served all wk 7-9 Av main course £10 **Restaurant** L served all wk 12-2 booking required D served all wk 7-9 booking required Fixed menu price fr £17.75 Av 3 course à la carte fr £25 ⊕ FREE HOUSE ◀ Fuller's ESB, Ballard's Best, Dark Star Golden Gate, Oakleaf Brewery Nuptu'ale, Dark Star Hophead Ŏ Stowford Press, Thatchers. **Facilities** Children's menu Dogs allowed

## DUNCTON

## The Cricketers ♀

**GU28 0LB** ☎ 01798 342473
dir: *On A285, 3m from Petworth, 8m from Chichester*

Dating back to the 16th century, this attractive white-painted pub is situated in spectacular walking country at the western end of the South Downs. Rumoured to be haunted, the inn has changed little over the years. There is a delightful and very popular garden with extensive deck seating and weekend barbecues. The menus sometimes change four times a day, offering good hearty meals like beer-battered haddock or rib-eye steak, both with hand-cut chips. An ideal stop-off point for coach parties visiting Goodwood.

**Open** all day all wk **Bar Meals** L served Mon-Fri 12-2.30, Sat-Sun 12-6 D served Mon-Fri 6-9, Sat-Sun 12-9 **Restaurant** L served Mon-Fri 12-2.30, Sat-Sun 12-6 D served Mon-Fri 6-9, Sat-Sun 12-9 ⊕ FREE HOUSE ◀ Betty Stogs, Horsham Best, Arundel Gold, Guest ale Ŏ Thatchers Heritage. ♀ 8 **Facilities** Children's menu Play area Dogs allowed Garden Parking

## EAST ASHLING

## Horse and Groom ★★★★ INN ♀

**East Ashling PO18 9AX** ☎ 01243 575339
📄 01243 575560
e-mail: info@thehorseandgroomchichester.co.uk
dir: *3m from Chichester on B1278 between Chichester & Rowland's Castle. 2m off A27 at Fishbourne*

A substantially renovated 17th-century inn located at the foot of the South Downs. This is good walking country, and top tourist attractions lie within easy reach. The flagstone floor and beamed bar is cosy, with a working range at one end and an open fire at the other. The underground cellar keeps ales at a constant temperature, and there are bar snack, blackboard and full carte menus. The enclosed garden is great place for alfresco eating in warmer weather.

**Open** noon-3 6-11 (Sun noon-6) Closed: Sun eve **Bar Meals** L served all wk 12-2.15 D served Mon-Sat 6.30-9.15 Av main course £10.95 **Restaurant** L served all wk 12-2.15 D served Mon-Sat 6.30-9.15 booking required ⊕ FREE HOUSE ◀ Youngs, Harveys, Summer Lightning, Hop Head Ŏ Stowford Press. ♀ 6 **Facilities** Children's menu Dogs allowed Garden Parking Rooms 11

## EAST DEAN

## The Star & Garter ♀

**PO18 0JG** ☎ 01243 811318   📄 01243 811826
e-mail: thestarandgarter@hotmail.com
dir: *On A286 between Chichester & Midhurst. Exit A286 at Singleton. Village in 2m*

This pub is located in the pretty downland village of East Dean just above the village pond. Built in 1740 from traditional Sussex napped flint, the interior has been opened out to give a light and airy atmosphere, with original brickwork, oak flooring, antique panelling, scrubbed tables and a wood-burning stove. The menu changes almost daily, with a wide choice of fish and shellfish listed on a large blackboard above the fire. Shellfish platters are available from Easter to October, featuring Selsey crab, lobster, hand-carved salmon, crevettes and other shellfish as available. A Star Platter serves two and a Garter Platter serves four. A wide selection of meat, game and vegetarian dishes is also offered. Game grill is a popular choice, comprising a whole roasted partridge, pheasant breast, pigeon breasts and venison sausage with red wine jus.

continued

Open all wk **Bar Meals** Av main course £13 food served all day **Restaurant** Av 3 course à la carte fr £25 food served all day ⊕ FREE HOUSE ◀ Ballards Best, Guinness, Arundel Castle & Gold ☉ Westons 1st Quality, Westons Scrumpy, Stowford Press. ⬥ 10 **Facilities** Children's menu Dogs allowed Garden Parking

---

## FERNHURST

### The King's Arms ⬥

**Midhurst Rd GU27 3HA ☎ 01428 652005**
📄 01428 658970
dir: *On A286 between Haslemere & Midhurst, 1m S of Fernhurst*

A Grade II listed, 17th-century free house and restaurant set amidst rolling Sussex farmland, which can be seen at its best from the garden. The pub and its outbuildings are built from Sussex stone and decorated with hanging baskets, flowering tubs, vines and creepers. The L-shaped interior is very cosy, with beams, lowish ceilings, and a large inglenook fireplace, with the bar one side and restaurant and small dining room the other. Everything is home made and freshly prepared on the premises, from salad dressings to sorbets. Fish is an important commodity, and Michael regularly visits the south coast to buy direct from the boats, bringing back what later appears on the menu as, for instance, goujons of plaice with tartare sauce; monkfish loin in Parma ham with courgette ribbons, prawn and saffron sauce; or perhaps seared scallops with bacon and pea risotto. Alternatives to fish usually include Barbary duck breast with Savoy cabbage, baby roast potatoes and orange and port sauce; rack of English lamb with redcurrant and rosemary mash with lightly minted gravy; and fillet steak with dauphinoise potatoes, wild mushrooms and rich red wine jus. In addition to the monthly changing menu, there are daily changing specials such as steak, kidney and mushroom pudding. The large garden has some lovely trees, including a mature willow and pretty white lilacs, and views over surrounding fields.

Open all day all wk 11am-11pm (Sun noon-10.30pm) **Bar Meals** L served Mon-Sat 12-2.30, Sun 12-4 booking required D served Mon-Sat 6-9.30 booking required **Restaurant** L served Mon-Sat 12-2.30, Sun 12-4 booking required D served Mon-Sat 6-9.30 booking required ⊕ FREE HOUSE ◀ Hepworth Sussex, Skinners Betty Stogs. ⬥ 10 **Facilities** Children's menu Dogs allowed Garden Parking

---

## HALNAKER

### The Anglesey Arms at Halnaker ⬥

**PO18 0NQ ☎ 01243 773474** 📄 01243 530034
e-mail: angleseyarms@aol.com
web: www.angleseyarms.co.uk
dir: *From centre of Chichester 4m E on A285 (Petworth road)*

Whether you pop in for a quick drink or a full meal, you'll find a warm welcome in the wood-floored bar of this charmingly old-fashioned Georgian inn. The Anglesey stands in two acres of landscaped grounds on the Goodwood estate. Sandwiches, ploughman's with unpasteurised cheese, local sausages,

and other pub favourites fill the odd corner, or try the à la carte menu. The kitchen team makes skilful use of meat from organically raised animals, as well as locally-caught fish from sustainable stocks. The Anglesey has built a special reputation for its steaks, British beef hung for at least 21 days. Additional meats are supplied by the Estate's Home Farm, while vegetables come from Wayside Organics. The area is noted for shooting, so game birds and venison are also available. Dinner might begin with Sussex rarebit; toasted goats' cheese and red onion marmalade with salad leaves; or freshwater crayfish and mango salad with chilli dressing. Main course options include slow roasted English pork belly, plum sauce and cucumber salad; king prawns with Thai-style curry sauce and rice; and free range chicken breast on crushed new potatoes with seasonal greens, smoked bacon and mushroom sauce. Home-made puddings are listed on the blackboard, or choose hand-made cheeses with water biscuits and home-made chutney.

Open all wk 11-3 5.30-11 (Sat-Sun 11-11) **Bar Meals** L served Mon-Sun 12-2.30 D served Mon-Sat 6.30-9.30 Av main course £9.50 **Restaurant** L served Mon-Sun 12-2.30 booking required D served Mon-Sat 6.30-9.30 booking required Av 3 course à la carte fr £24 ⊕ PUNCH TAVERNS ◀ Young's Bitter, Bowman Swift One, Black Sheep Bitter ☉ Stowford Press. ⬥ 14 **Facilities** Children's menu Dogs allowed Garden Parking

---

## LICKFOLD

### The Lickfold Inn ⬥

**GU28 9EY ☎ 01798 861285**
e-mail: lickfold@evanspubs.co.uk
dir: *From A3 take A283, through Chiddingfold, 2m on right signed 'Lurgashall Winery', pub in 1m*

Dating back to 1460, this free house is in the capable hands of Camilla Hansen and Mark Evans. Period features include an ancient timber frame with herringbone-patterned bricks, and a huge central chimney. Inside are two restaurant areas with oak beamed ceilings, and a cosy bar dominated by a large inglenook fireplace, Georgian settles and moulded panelling. Look for the recurring garlic motif, reflecting the village's Anglo-Saxon name, 'leac fauld' - an enclosure where garlic grows. The pub offers lunchtime sandwiches, Sunday roasts, and seasonal dishes complemented by well-kept real ales and a good wine list. Expect Lickfold Inn fish pie; grilled aubergine with spinach and ricotta; and roast guinea fowl in bacon with potato rosti and redcurrant sauce. The large courtyard and rambling terraced gardens are ideal for alfresco dining. Fifty per cent of the pub's profits go to a children's hospice.

Open all day all wk noon-11 (Sun noon-5) Closed: 25 Dec **Bar Meals** Av main course £10 food served all day **Restaurant** Av 3 course à la carte fr £26 food served all day ⊕ FREE HOUSE ◖ Hogs Back TEA, Guinness, Old Speckled Hen. ♇ 12 **Facilities** Children's menu Dogs allowed Garden Parking

## LODSWORTH

# The Halfway Bridge Inn ♇

**Halfway Bridge GU28 9BP ☎ 01798 861281**
e-mail: enquiries@halfwaybridge.co.uk
web: www.halfwaybridge.co.uk
dir: *Between Petworth & Midhurst, next to Cowdray Estate & Golf Club on A272*

Midway between Petworth and Midhurst, hence its name, this mellow, red-brick inn was originally built as a coaching inn in 1740. Locally it is popular, not least because owners Paul and Sue Carter have made the inn an attractive destination for diners. Winter cosiness is guaranteed: rambling, tastefully furnished interconnecting rooms boast open fires, wooden floors, old beams and a casual and relaxed atmosphere, while in summer the sheltered patio and lawn is perfect for alfresco dining. Traditional pub dishes are given a modern twist and the emphasis is on local crab and Sussex pork, alongside fresh meats, fish and vegetables from the London markets. Daily specials are chalked up on the blackboards. The lunchtime bar menu consists of sandwiches - roast beef and horseradish, fresh crab - or a choice of appetizers from the main menu. These may include grilled mackerel with home-made foccacia bread and horseradish mousse; poached scallops with fennel, shallot and caper salad; and partridge and pheasant terrine with fruit chutney. Typical of the vegetarian main courses is chargrilled vegetable millefeuille layered with parmesan crisps and served with a Roquefort cream. Otherwise you may find game suet pudding with red wine jus; seafood risotto with rocket and parmesan salad; whole baked sea bass with roasted butternut squash, garlic and shallot butter; and roast pork belly with red wine jus. Puddings may include vanilla Cambridge burnt cream with chocolate chip cookie; and dark chocolate and pistachio nut tart with vanilla mascarpone.

Open all wk Mon-Sat 11-11, Sun 12-10.30 Closed: 25 Dec **Bar Meals** L served all wk 12-2.30 D served all wk 6.30-9.15 **Restaurant** L served all wk 12-2.30 D served all wk 6.30-9.15 ⊕ FREE HOUSE ◖ Skinners Betty Stogs, Ballards Best Bitter, Ringwood Best Bitter. ♇ 14 **Facilities** Children's menu Dogs allowed Garden Parking

# The Hollist Arms ♇

**The Street GU28 9BZ ☎ 01798 861310**
e-mail: george@thehollistarms.co.uk
dir: *0.5m between Midhurst & Petworth, 1m N of A272, adjacent to Country Park*

The Hollist Arms, a pub since 1823, is full of traditional charm and character. The 15th-century building overlooks a lawn where a grand old tree stands ringed by a bench. Step through the pretty entrance porch and you'll find roaring open fires, leather sofas and a blissful absence of fruit machines. You'll probably need to book to enjoy dishes such as tiger prawns and leek gratin with fresh bread; home-made steak, Guinness and mushroom pie; or hoi sin duck in soy sauce with ginger, mushrooms and spring onions. Bar snacks range from toasties to sausages and mash. Wash it down with real ales such as Timothy Taylor Landlord; Horsham Best or the locally-brewed Langham's Halfway to Heaven. The Hollist Arms is conveniently situated for Goodwood, Cowdray Park and Petworth House, and has its own business providing picnic hampers.

Open all day all wk 11am-11pm **Bar Meals** L served all wk 12-9 booking required D served all wk 12-9 booking required food served all day **Restaurant** L served all wk 12-9 booking required D served all wk 12-9 booking required food served all day ⊕ FREE HOUSE ◖ Langham, Timothy Taylor Landlord, Horsham Best ♂ Stowford Press. ♇ 7 **Facilities** Children's menu Dogs allowed Garden Parking

## LURGASHALL

# The Noah's Ark ♇

**The Green GU28 9ET ☎ 01428 707346**
e-mail: amy@noahsarkinn.co.uk
dir: *B2131 from Haslemere follow signs to Petworth/Lurgashall. A3 from London towards Portsmouth. At Milford take the A283 signed Petworth. Follow signs to Lurgashall*

Set in a picturesque village, beneath Blackdown Hill, this attractive 16th-century inn overlooks the cricket green. The revitalised interior is full of charm, with old beams and a large inglenook fireplace. Food is traditional British with a contemporary twist and the occasional French influence. Ingredients are carefully sourced from the best local suppliers for dishes ranging from Sussex beef bourguignon to Noah's ale battered cod and chips.

Open all day Closed: Mon (ex Summer) **Bar Meals** L served Tue-Sat 12-2.30 booking required D served Tue-Sat 7-9.30 booking required Av main course £13 **Restaurant** L served Tue-Sun 12-2.30 booking required D served Tue-Sat 7-9.30 booking required ⊕ GREENE KING ◖ Greene King IPA , Abbot, Guest ale ♂ Stowford Press. ♇ 8 **Facilities** Children's menu Family room Dogs allowed Garden Parking

# West Sussex

## NUTHURST

### Black Horse Inn ♀

**Nuthurst St RH13 6LH** ☎ **01403 891272**
e-mail: clive.henwood@btinternet.com
dir: *4m S of Horsham, off A281, A24 & A272*

Built of clay tiles and mellow brick, this one time smugglers' hideout is in a secluded backwater. It's a lovely old building, half masked by window boxes in summer, forming part of what was originally a row of workers' cottages on the Sedgwick Park estate. The building was first recorded as an inn in 1817, and inside you'll find stone-flagged floors, an inglenook fireplace and an exposed wattle and daub wall. The place has a warm and cosy atmosphere that's perfect for dining or just enjoying a drink. On sunny days, visitors can sit out on the terraces at the front and rear, or take their drinks across the stone bridge over a stream into the delightful back garden. Blackboard specials change regularly.

**Open** all wk **Bar Meals** L served all wk 12-2.30 booking required D served all wk 6-9.30 booking required **Restaurant** L served all wk 12-2.30 booking req D served all wk 6-9.30 booking req ⊕ FREE HOUSE ◖ Harveys Sussex, W J King, Fuller's London Pride, Hepworths, guest ales Ö Westons Stowford Press. ♀ 7 **Facilities** Children's menu Dogs allowed Garden Parking

## OVING

### The Gribble Inn ♀

**PO20 2BP** ☎ **01243 786893**  📄 **01243 786893**
e-mail: dave@thegribble.co.uk
dir: *From A27 take A259. After 1m left at rdbt, 1st right to Oving, 1st left in village*

Named after local schoolmistress Rose Gribble, the inn retains much 16th-century charm. Large open fireplaces, wood burners and low beams set the tone. There's no background music at this peaceful hideaway, which is the ideal spot to enjoy any of the half dozen real ales from the on-site micro-brewery. Liver and bacon; spinach lasagne with red peppers; and special fish dishes are all prepared and cooked on the premises.

**Open** all wk 11-3 5.30-11 (Fri-Sun 11-11) **Bar Meals** L served all wk 12-2.30 D served all wk 6.30-9.30 Av main course £9 **Restaurant** L served all wk 12-2.30 booking required D served all wk 6.30-9.30 booking required ⊕ HALL & WOODHOUSE ◖ Gribble Ale, Reg's Tipple, Fursty Ferret, Badger First Gold, Pigs Ear. ♀ 10 **Facilities** Children's menu Family room Dogs allowed Garden Parking

## PETWORTH

### The Grove Inn

**Grove Ln GU28 0HY** ☎ **01798 343659**
e-mail: steveandvaleria@tiscali.co.uk
dir: *On outskirts of town, just off A283 between Pullborough & Petworth. 0.5m from Petworth Park*

A 17th-century free house a stone's throw south of historic Petworth. Idyllically sited, it nestles in beautiful gardens with views to the South Downs; a patio area with shady pergola is ideal for alfresco drinks. Inside is a bar with oak-beamed ceilings and large fireplace, while the conservatory restaurant is the place to sample a seasonal menu revised every six to eight weeks. The pub is hosted by a husband and wife partnership: Valeria looks after front of house, warmly welcoming locals and visitors alike, while husband Stephen runs the kitchen operation. His simple objective is to serve quality dishes at prices that do not detract from their enjoyment. Typical starters include moules marinière and baked asparagus wrapped in Parma ham. Among the main courses you may find roasted lamb cannon with rosemary, or crayfish tail and penne pasta. Expect desserts along the lines of hot chocolate mousse or apple crumble.

**Open** Closed: Sun eve & Mon **Bar Meals** L served Tue-Sun 12-2.30 booking required D served Tue-Sat 6-9.15 booking required Av main course £9.20 **Restaurant** L served Tue-Sun 12-2.30 booking required D served Tue-Sat 6-9.15 booking required Av 3 course à la carte fr £26 ⊕ FREE HOUSE ◖ Youngs, Betty Stogs, Arundel Gold, Hogs Back TEA. **Facilities** Children's menu Dogs allowed Garden Parking

## POYNINGS

### Royal Oak Inn ♀

**The Street BN45 7AQ** ☎ **01273 857389**  📄 **01273 857202**
e-mail: ropoynings@aol.com
dir: *N on A23 just outside Brighton, take A281 signed Henfield & Poynings, then follow signs into Poynings*

Tucked away in a fold of the South Downs below the Devil's Dyke, the Royal Oak has eye-catching window blinds and cream-painted exterior and roaring winter fires within. Solid oak floors and old beams hung with hop bines blend effortlessly with contemporary decor and comfy sofas. In the bar, Sussex-bred Harveys real ales rub shoulders with offerings from Greene King and Morland, and a decent wine list includes a red and a white from a Sussex vineyard. The menu combines local and seasonal produce with sometimes ambitious international twists. Starters and light meals include sharing platters and sandwich platters, or more elaborate preparations such as potted Selsey crab with spring onion and garlic, lemon and lime toasts. For a main course you might choose hand-made Henfield sausages, creamed potato, rich gravy and red onion jam; or basil and pine nut risotto with a fried egg and balsamic syrup. Puddings are ordered at the bar – pear, apple and ginger crumble perhaps.

Open all day all wk 11-11 (Sun 11.30-10.30) Bar Meals food served all day Restaurant food served all day ⊕ FREE HOUSE ◀ Harveys Sussex, Abbot Ale, Greene King Morland Old Speckled Hen, Fuller's London Pride Ö Westons Herefordshire Country Perry, Old Rosie Scrumpy. ⏺ 12 Facilities Children's menu Play area Dogs allowed Garden Parking

---

### SHIPLEY

## George & Dragon ⏺

**Dragons Green RH13 7JE ☎ 01403 741320**
dir: *Signed from A272 between Coolham & A24*

Set amid beautiful Sussex countryside, this 17th-century cottage is a haven of peace and quiet, especially on balmy summer evenings when the garden is a welcome retreat. Its interior is all head-banging beams and inglenook fireplaces, with an excellent choice of real ales at the bar. Food-wise, expect pub classics such as local ham with egg and chips or a Yorkshire pudding filled with sausage, mash and gravy. Shipley is famous for its smock mill.

Open all wk Bar Meals L served all wk 12-2 booking required D served all wk 6-9 Av main course £7.50 Restaurant L served all wk 12-2 D served all wk 6-9 ⊕ HALL & WOODHOUSE ◀ Badger Best, Sussex Best, Hall and Woodhouse Fursty Ferret & Pickled Partridge, Guest ale Ö Westons Stowford Press. ⏺ 8 Facilities Children's menu Play area Family room Dogs allowed Garden Parking

---

### SLINDON

## The Spur ⏺

**BN18 0NE ☎ 01243 814216  ⬚ 01243 814707**
dir: *Off A27 on A29 outside Slindon*

Nestling on top of the South Downs, just outside the village of Slindon, sits this 17th-century pub. Inside this free house is an open-plan bar and restaurant, warmed by log fires that create a friendly atmosphere. If you book in advance you can use the skittle alley, or enjoy a game of pool or other pub games.

Open all wk 11.30-3 6-11 (Sun noon-3 7-10.30) Bar Meals L served all wk 12-2 D served Sun-Tue 7-9, Wed-Sat 7-9.30 Av main course £11.50 Restaurant L served all wk 12-2 booking required D served Sun-Tue 7-9, Wed-Sat 7-9.30 booking required Av 3 course à la carte fr £24 ⊕ FREE HOUSE ◀ Greene King IPA, Courage Directors. ⏺ 9 Facilities Children's menu Dogs allowed Garden Parking

---

### STEDHAM

## Hamilton Arms/Nava Thai Restaurant ⏺

**Hamilton Arms School Ln GU29 0NZ ☎ 01730 812555**
**⬚ 01730 817459**
e-mail: hamiltonarms@hotmail.com
web: www.thehamiltonarms.co.uk
dir: *Off A272 between Midhurst & Petersfield*

The Hamilton Arms is one of the first traditional English country pubs to serve authentic Thai food. The pub is set in a pretty village in beautiful South Downs countryside, and is also the base for a charitable trust to help prevent child prostitution in Thailand. The huge menu offers soups, curries, salads and speciality meat, seafood and vegetarian dishes, also available to takeaway. There is a patio to enjoy in warmer weather.

Open 11-3 6-11 (Sun noon-4 7-11, Fri-Sat 11am-11.30pm) Closed: Mon (ex BH) Bar Meals L served Tue-Sun 12-2.30 D served Tue-Sun 6-10 Restaurant L served Tue-Sun 12-2.30 D served Tue-Sun 6-10 booking required ⊕ FREE HOUSE ◀ Ballard's Best, Fuller's London Pride, Everards Tiger Best, Fuller's HSB, Wadworth 6X, Sussex King, Barnes Ö Westons Vintage. ⏺ 8 Facilities Children's menu Play area Dogs allowed Garden Parking

---

### WEST CHILTINGTON

## The Queens Head ⏺

**The Hollow RH20 2JN ☎ 01798 812244  ⬚ 01798 815039**
e-mail: enquiries@thequeenshead.info
dir: *Please telephone for directions*

A traditional, mainly 17th-century country pub with two bars, a restaurant and ample outside space. The interior has beams, low ceilings, an open fire and a bar. Mainly locally sourced, freshly cooked traditional dishes include beer-battered haddock and chips with mushy peas; Caesar salad with chicken and bacon; slow-roasted lamb shank with fresh herb mash; and mushroom Stroganoff with rice.

Open all day all wk noon-11 (Mon 5-11 ex BH noon-11 Sun noon-10.30) Bar Meals L served Tue-Sat 12-2.30, Sun & BH 12-4 D served Tue-Sat 6-9.30 Av main course £10.50 Restaurant L served Tue-Sat 12-2.30, Sun & BH 12-4 D served Tue-Sat 6-9.30 Av 3 course à la carte fr £18 ⊕ ENTERPRISE INNS PLC ◀ Harveys Sussex Best Bitter, Fuller's London Pride, Ballards Best Bitter, Itchen Valley Godfathers, Langhams Halfway to Heaven. ⏺ 7 Facilities Children's menu Dogs allowed Garden Parking

**England**

## TYNE & WEAR

### WHITLEY BAY

## The Waterford Arms ▼

**Collywell Bay Rd, Seaton Sluice NE26 4QZ**
☎ **0191 237 0450**
e-mail: les47@bt.connect.com
dir: *From A1 N of Newcastle take A19 at Seaton Burn then follow signs for A190 to Seaton Sluice*

The building dates back to 1899 and is located close to the small local fishing harbour, overlooking the North Sea. Splendid beaches and sand dunes are within easy reach, and the pub is very popular with walkers. Seafood dishes are the speciality, including seared swordfish, lemon sole, halibut, crab-stuffed plaice, and very large portions of fish and chips.

**Open** all wk noon-11.30 (Thu-Sat noon-mdnt Sun noon-10.30) **Bar Meals** Av main course £8 **Restaurant** L served Mon-Sat 12-9, Sun 12-4 booking required D served Mon-Sat 12-9, Sun 12-4 booking required food served all day ⊕ PUNCH ◀ Tetleys, John Smiths, Scotch, Guinness. ▼ 6 **Facilities** Children's menu Parking

## WARWICKSHIRE

### ALCESTER

## The Holly Bush

**37 Henley St B49 5QX** ☎ **01789 762482 & 0788 4342363**
e-mail: thehollybushpub@btconnect.com
dir: *M40 junct 15 for Warwick/Stratford, take A46 to Stratford*

Situated between Alcester's parish church and historic town hall, the 17th-century Holly Bush has been transformed from a one-bar boozer to a thriving pub serving great ales and delicious food by Tracey-Jane Deffley over the past six years. Menus blend traditional pub classics with contemporary dishes and an emphasis on using locally sourced ingredients, including herbs and vegetables from the pub's allotment garden. Extensive menus range from lunchtime sandwiches (bacon and stilton) ham, egg and chips, and beer-battered cod and chips, to chorizo and clam risotto, roast pork belly with apple mash and sweet cabbage, and monkfish wrapped in Parma ham with pea mash and red wine sauce. For pudding, choose perhaps chocolate mousse with fresh raspberries, or lemon tart with bitter chocolate sorbet. This is a cracking town centre pub run with passion and panache – and there's a great garden, too.

**Open** all day all wk noon-mdnt (Fri-Sat noon-1am) **Bar Meals** L served Mon-Sat 12-2.30, Sun 12-4 D served Tue-Sat 7-9.30 Av main course £7.50 **Restaurant** L served Mon-Sat 12-2.30, Sun 12-4 D served Tue-Sat 7-9.30 Av 3 course à la carte fr £23 ⊕ FREE HOUSE ◀ Sharpe's Doom Bar, Black Sheep, Purity Gold, Purity Mad Goose, Uley Bitter Õ Local farm cider. **Facilities** Children's menu Dogs allowed Garden

### ALDERMINSTER

## The Bell ▼

**CV37 8NY** ☎ **01789 450414** 🖹 **01789 450998**
e-mail: info@thebellald.co.uk
dir: *On A3400 3.5m S of Stratford-upon-Avon*

An 18th-century coaching inn whose interior blends modern touches with traditional charms. The spacious conservatory restaurant overlooks a delightful old courtyard with views of the Stour Valley beyond. A good selection of starters and 'little dishes' could include avocado and crayfish tails with tomato vinaigrette on mixed leaves; pan-fried duck livers with Grand Marnier, spiced apple and toasted brioche; and a platter of mixed hors d'oeuvres. Follow with pork fillet filled with apricots and lemongrass, wrapped in Parma ham and served with Madeira jus and vegetables; or fillet of beef mignon with green beans, cherry tomatoes and a Jack Daniels and gorgonzola sauce. If you prefer a snack, there is also a selection of baguettes and light bites including hot cheese and bacon bruschetta; smoked salmon and cream cheese baguette with mixed leaves; and bacon, lettuce and tomato baguette. Those fond of fresh fish should keep an eye on the blackboard.

**Open** 11.30-2.30 6-11 (Fri-Sat 11.30-11 Sun noon-4.30) Closed: Sun eve **Bar Meals** L served Mon-Fri 12-2, Sat 12-2.30, Sun 12-3 booking required D served Mon-Thu 7-9, Fri-Sat 6-9 booking required **Restaurant** L served Mon-Fri 12-2, Sat 12-2.30, Sun 12-3 booking required D served Mon-Thu 7-9, Fri-Sat 6-9 booking required ⊕ FREE HOUSE ◀ Hook Norton, Lady Godiva. ▼ 11 **Facilities** Children's menu Dogs allowed Garden Parking

### ALVESTON

## The Baraset Barn ▼

**1 Pimlico Ln CV37 7RF** ☎ **01789 295510**
🖹 **01789 292961**
e-mail: barasetbarn@lovelypubs.co.uk

Surrounded by glorious Warwickshire countryside close to Stratford-upon-Avon, the impressive Baraset Barn is part of Lovely Pubs, who now have six quality dining destinations in the area. Converted from an old barn, this is a unique gastro-pub, a light, modern venue with a distinct continental feel and a dramatic interior styled from granite, pewter and oak. The original flagstones remind customers of its 200-year history as a barn, but the glass-fronted kitchen introduces a stylish, up-to-the-minute visual appeal. From the bar, stone steps lead to the main dining area with high oak beams and brick walls, and the open mezzanine level makes for a perfect vantage point, while the luxurious lounge area sports sumptuous sofas for a relaxing morning coffee with the papers. The crowd-pleasing menu successfully blends classic British dishes with an eclectic Mediterranean choice, offering sharing plates, dishes from the stove and rotisserie, and a chalkboard listing daily fish dishes. Typically, begin with devilled kidneys on toast, or chilli, honey-seared tuna with fennel, rocket and lemon olive oil, or share a camembert, baked in its box and served with onion toast and pear chutney. For main course, try the spit-roast chicken with lemon and tarragon butter; lamb rump Provençal with fondant potato and basil jus; bouillabaisse; or a rib-eye steak with stilton cream sauce. Leave room for treacle tart with vanilla custard or share a hot chocolate and orange fondue, served with dipping strawberries, marshmallows and bananas.

**Open** all day 11am-mdnt Closed: 25 Dec & 1 Jan, Sun eve, Mon (Jan-Feb) **Bar Meals** L served all wk 12-2.30 D served Mon-Sat 6.30-9.30 Av main course £17 **Restaurant** L served Mon-Sat 12-2.30, Sun 12-3.30 booking required D served Mon-Sat 6.30-9.30 booking required Fixed menu price fr £10 Av 3 course à la carte fr £22 ◾ UBU. ⬥ 12 **Facilities** Children's menu Dogs allowed Garden Parking

## BARFORD

## The Granville @ Barford ⬥

**52 Wellesbourne Rd CV35 8DS** ☎ **01926 624236**
📄 **01926 624806**
e-mail: info@granvillebarford.co.uk
dir: *1m from M40 junct 15. Take A429 signed Stow. Located at furthest end of Barford village*

This friendly and stylish village dining pub in the heart of Shakespeare country is owned and run by Val Kersey. Everything on your plate here is made from local produce delivered daily, except for the bread, which arrives freshly-baked each morning from a neighbouring village. At lunchtime, try one of the larger size starters, such as warm black pudding with bubble and squeak, crispy bacon and stilton sauce; or a smoked salmon, dill and cucumber crème fraîche doorstop sandwich. In the evening, home in on crispy beer-battered fish of the day with chips, mushy peas and tartare sauce; home-made chicken Kiev with sauté potatoes and vegetables of the day; or butternut squash and herb risotto with Parmesan crisps. Enjoy alfresco dining in the spacious patio garden.

**Open** all wk noon-3 5.30-11 (Fri-Sat noon-11.30 Sun noon-11) **Bar Meals** Av main course £12 **Restaurant** Fixed menu price fr £14.50 Av 3 course à la carte fr £18 ⊕ ENTERPRISE INNS PLC ◾ Hooky Bitter, Purity Gold, Purity UBU. ⬥ 18 **Facilities** Children's menu Dogs allowed Garden Parking

## BROOM

## Broom Tavern ⬥

**High St B50 4HL** ☎ **01789 773656** 📄 **01789 773656**
e-mail: webmaster@broomtavern.co.uk
dir: *N of B439 W of Stratford-upon-Avon*

Once a haunt of William Shakespeare, this 16th-century brick and timber inn is smartly furnished, with a large beer garden where barbecues are held in summer. Very much at the heart of village life, it is home to the Broom Tavern Golf Society, and fun days, charity events and outings are a feature. The menu offers a large selection of vegetarian dishes and seafood.

**Open** all wk noon-3 5.30-11 **Bar Meals** L served all wk 12-2.30 D served all wk 6-9 Av main course £8.25 **Restaurant** L served all wk 12-2.30 booking required D served all wk 6-9 booking required ⊕ PUNCH TAVERNS ◾ Greene King IPA, Black Sheep, Timothy Taylor Landlord, Wells Bombardier. ⬥ 20 **Facilities** Children's menu Dogs allowed Garden Parking

## ETTINGTON

## The Houndshill ⬥

**Banbury Rd CV37 7NS** ☎ **01789 740267**
📄 **01789 740075**
dir: *On A422 SE of Stratford-upon-Avon*

Family-run inn situated at the heart of England, making it a perfect base for exploring popular tourist attractions such as Oxford, Blenheim, Stratford and the Cotswolds. The pleasant tree-lined garden is especially popular with families. Typical dishes range from poached fillet of salmon, and faggots, mash and minted peas, to supreme of chicken and ham and mushroom tagliatelle. Alternatively, try cold ham off the bone or home-made steak and kidney pie.

**Open** all wk Closed: 25-28 Dec **Bar Meals** L served all wk 12-2 D served all wk 7-9.30 Av main course £7.50 **Restaurant** L served all wk 12-2 D served all wk 7-9.30 Av 3 course à la carte fr £15 ⊕ FREE HOUSE ◾ Hook Norton Best, Spitfire. ⬥ 7 **Facilities** Children's menu Play area Dogs allowed Garden Parking

England

## LAPWORTH

### The Boot Inn 🍷

**Old Warwick Rd B94 6JU ☎ 01564 782464**
📠 **01564 784989**
e-mail: bootinn@hotmail.com
dir: *Telephone for directions*

Beside the Grand Union Canal, this lively 16th-century former coaching inn has a smartly refurbished interior, and an attractive garden with a canopy and patio heaters. The main draw is the brasserie-style food, with wide-ranging menus of home-produced dishes. A selection from the menu includes prawn, smoked haddock and spring onion fishcake, served with lemon gremolata and herb aioli; haddock in tempura batter with pea purée, sauce gribiche and frites; and fillet steak with smoked roast garlic, spinach and mascarpone mash.

Open all day all wk 11-11 (Thu-Sat 11am-mdnt Sun 11-10) Closed: 25 Dec Bar Meals L served all wk 12-2.30 D served Mon-Fri 7-9.30, Sat 6.30-9.30, Sun 7-9 Restaurant L served all wk 12-2.30 D served Mon-Fri 7-9.30, Sat 6.30-9.30, Sun 7-9 ⊕ LAUREL PUB PARTNERSHIPS ◀ Morland Old Speckled Hen, Fuller's London Pride, Hobgoblin. 🍷 8 Facilities Children's menu Dogs allowed Garden Parking

---

## NAPTON ON THE HILL

### The Bridge at Napton 🍷

**Southam Rd CV47 8NQ ☎ 01926 812466**
e-mail: info@thebridgeatnapton.co.uk
dir: *At Bridge 111 on Oxford Canal on A425, 2m from Southam & 1m from Napton on the Hill*

This is an ideal place to moor the narrow boat, though travellers by car or bike are equally welcome. Built as a stabling inn at Bridge 111 on the Oxford canal, the pub has a restaurant, three bars and a large garden, plus its own turning point for barges. There are some excellent ales, and food choices range from Aberdeen Angus beefburger with chips to the likes of honey-roasted belly pork with caramelised onions.

Open noon-3 6-11 (Sun noon-8) Closed: Mon (ex BH & summer school hols) Bar Meals L served Mon-Sat 12-2, Sun 12-7 booking required D served Mon-Sat 6-9, Sun 12-7 booking required Av main course £9 Restaurant L served Mon-Sat 12-2, Sun 12-7 booking required D served Mon-Sat 6-9, Sun 12-7 booking required ⊕ PUNCH TAVERNS ◀ Guinness, John Smith, Black Sheep, Guest ales. 🍷 6 Facilities Children's menu Play area Family room Dogs allowed Garden Parking

## RATLEY

### The Rose and Crown

**OX15 6DS ☎ 01295 678148**
e-mail: k.marples@btinternet.com
dir: *Follow Edgehill signs, 7m N of Banbury (13m SE of Stratford-upon-Avon) on A422*

Following the Battle of Edgehill in 1642, a Roundhead was discovered in the chimney of this 12th-century pub and beheaded in the hearth. His ghost reputedly haunts the building. Enjoy the peaceful village location and the traditional pub food, perhaps including beef and ale pie, scampi and chips, chicken curry and the Sunday roast, plus vegetarian options.

Open Closed: Mon L Bar Meals L served Tue-Sun 12-2.30 booking required D served Mon-Sat 6.30-9 booking required Av main course £9.95 ⊕ FREE HOUSE ◀ Wells Bombardier, Eagle IPA, Greene King Old Speckled Hen, Guest ale. Facilities Children's menu Family room Dogs allowed Garden Parking

## RED HILL

### The Stag at Redhill 🍷

**Alcester Rd B49 6NQ ☎ 01789 764634**   📠 **01789 764431**
e-mail: info@thestagatredhill.co.uk
web: www.thestagatredhill.co.uk
dir: *On A46 between Stratford-upon-Avon & Alcester*

A family-run business, The Stag is a 16th-century coaching inn, which has also been a court house and prison (you can still see a cell door in the court room restaurant). Food is freshly prepared and service begins with breakfast from 7.30am. From Mondays through to Saturday you might be tempted by the value 'Credit Crunch Lunch' (1, 2 or 3 courses). There is a large patio eating area, popular in fine weather. A helipad facility allows customers to fly in for a meal at their convenience.

Open all day all wk 7am-11pm Bar Meals L served all wk 12-5 D served all wk 5-9 Av main course £8.50 food served all day Restaurant L served all wk 12-5 D served all wk 5-9 Fixed menu price fr £12 food served all day ⊕ GREENE KING ◀ Greene King IPA, Abbot Ale, Old Speckled Hen, Ruddles, Morland Original ⊘ Stowford Press. 🍷 8 Facilities Children's menu Garden Parking

## RUGBY

# Golden Lion Hotel ★★★ HL ♟

**Easenhall CV23 0JA ☎ 01788 832265  📄 01788 832878**
e-mail: reception@goldenlionhotel.org
dir: *From Rugby take A426, take 1st exit Newbold road B4112. Through Newbold. At Harborough Parva follow brown sign, turn left, pub in 1m*

This charming 16th-century free house with low oak-beamed ceilings and narrow doorways was built on the trading route between London and the Welsh borders. James and Claudia are the third generation of the Austin family at the helm. You'll find traditional ales, roaring winter fires and an extensive wine list, as well as excellent food and service. Almost a dozen varieties of sandwich and baguette are served at lunchtime, or from the main menu you can choose the likes of fresh melon and Parma ham; pan-seared fillet of sea bream with ratatouille and crushed new potatoes; and lemon meringue pie with double cream. The pub is set amidst idyllic countryside in one of Warwickshire's best-kept villages.

**Open** all day all wk 11-11 (Sun noon - 11) **Bar Meals** L served Mon-Sat 12-2, Sun 12-2.30 D served Mon-Sat 4.30-9.30, Sun 3-8.45 Av main course £10.95 **Restaurant** L served Mon-Sat 12-2, Sun 12-2.30 D served Mon-Sat 4.30-9.30, Sun 3-8.45 Av 3 course à la carte fr £20 ⊕ FREE HOUSE ◄█ Guinness, Ruddles Best, 2 real ales. ♟ 7 **Facilities** Children's menu Garden Parking **Rooms** 20

# Old Smithy ♟

**1 Green Ln, Church Lawford CV23 9EF ☎ 02476 542333**
e-mail: smithy@king-henry-taverns.co.uk
dir: *Take the Coventry to Rugby Road, The Old Smithy is on the green in Church Lawford*

Anyone asked to draw their idyllic 'roses round the door' village pub might produce something looking like The Old Smithy. As with all King Henry's Taverns pubs, the menu features a huge choice of traditional favourites, such as gammon steak, fish and seafood, to haddock in batter; chicken dishes, and a selection for those with larger appetites, including Brontosaurus lamb shank. Vegetarians will welcome a six-way choice, including tomato and basil penne pasta.

**Open** all day all wk noon-11 **Bar Meals** Av main course £3 food served all day **Restaurant** food served all day ⊕ KING HENRY'S TAVERN ◄█ Guinness, IPA, Marstons Pedigree. ♟ 15 **Facilities** Children's menu Play area Family room Garden Parking

## SHIPSTON ON STOUR

# The Cherington Arms ♟

**Cherington CV36 5HS ☎ 01608 686233**
dir: *12m from Stratford-upon-Avon. 14m from Leamington & Warwick. 10m from Woodstock. 4m from Shipston on Stour*

An attractive 17th-century inn with exposed beams and Cotswold stone walls, stripped wood furniture and roaring log inglenook fire. The carte menu includes crab fishcakes with mango and chilli salsa; or breast of chicken stuffed with sun-dried tomato and cream pesto, all washed down with a pint of

Hook Norton. There's also a snack menu and specials board. Outside there are large riverside gardens with a mill race, ideal for alfresco dining. Horse riders and walkers are welcome.

**Open** all wk **Bar Meals** L served Mon-Fri 12-2, Sat-Sun 12-2.30 D served Sun, Tue-Thu 7-9, Fri-Sat 7-9.30 **Restaurant** L served Mon-Fri 12-2, Sat-Sun 12-2.30 D served Sun, Tue-Thu 7-9, Fri-Sat 7-9.30 ⊕ HOOK NORTON BREWERY ◄█ Hook Norton Best Bitter, guest ales ♺ Stowford Press. ♟ 11 **Facilities** Children's menu Dogs allowed Garden Parking

# The Red Lion ★★★★ INN ◉ ♟

**Main St, Long Compton CV36 5JS ☎ 01608 684221  📄 01608 684968**
e-mail: info@redlion-longcompton.co.uk
web: www.redlion-longcompton.co.uk
dir: *On A3400 between Shipston on Stour & Chipping Norton*

The newly refurbished interior of this Grade II listed free house blends old-world charm with a smart contemporary feel. High backed settles, stone walls and oak beams set the scene, with warming log fires in winter. Originally built as a coaching inn in 1748, the Red Lion stands in an Area of Outstanding Natural Beauty. The pub's walls are decorated with original paintings, and there are several distinct areas in which to dine or simply relax with a good pint. The bar is full of atmosphere, and visitors can eat there or in the restaurant area. In summer, it's a real treat to sit out in the garden, or take a leisurely lunch on the pretty, flower-bordered patio. The menu and blackboard specials cater for all tastes, from interesting sandwiches like crayfish, rocket and lemon mayonnaise on ciabatta to an open goats' cheese omelette with caramelised onions, spinach and salad. The adventurous starters include wild boar terrine with spiced pear chutney, whilst main course dishes range from venison with roasted winter vegetables to pan-fried scallops with creamed parsnips, crisp pancetta and a vermouth and chive sauce. Round off with warm treacle tart and clotted cream, or hazelnut cream and raspberry Pavlova with raspberry sauce.

**Open** all wk 11-11 **Bar Meals** L served Mon-Thu 12-2.30, Fri-Sun 12-9.30 D served Mon-Thu 6-9, Fri-Sun 12-9.30 Av main course £15.95 **Restaurant** L served Mon-Thu 12-2.30, Fri-Sun 12-9.30 D served Mon-Thu 6-9, Fri-Sun 12-9.30 Fixed menu price fr £11.95 ⊕ FREE HOUSE ◄█ Hook Norton Best, Adnams, Timothy Taylor. ♟ 7 **Facilities** Children's menu Play area Dogs allowed Garden Parking **Rooms** 5

## STRATFORD-UPON-AVON

### The One Elm ♀

**1 Guild St CV37 6QZ ☎ 01789 404919**
e-mail: theoneelm@peachpubs.com
dir: *In town centre*

Standing on its own in the heart of town, the One Elm has two dining rooms: downstairs is intimate, even with the buzzy bar close by, while upstairs feels grander. The menu features chargrilled côte de boeuf for two, Aberdeen Angus rump steak, and tuna, as well as other main courses. The deli board offers all-day nuts and seeds, cheeses, charcuterie and antipasti. The secluded terrace induces in some a feeling of being abroad.

Open all wk 11-11 (Thu-Sat 11am-mdnt) Closed: 25 Dec **Bar Meals** Av main course £11 food served all day **Restaurant** Av 3 course à la carte fr £18 food served all day ⊕ PEACH PUB CO ◀ London Pride, UBU Purity, Purity Gold. ♀ 9 **Facilities** Children's menu Dogs allowed Garden Parking

## STRETTON ON FOSSE

### The Plough Inn ♀

**GL56 9QX ☎ 01608 661053**
e-mail: saravol@aol.com
dir: *From Moreton-in-Marsh, 4m on A429 N. From Stratford-upon-Avon, 10m on A429 S*

A classic village pub built from mellow Cotswold stone, The Plough has the requisite bare beams and real fire, plus a friendly resident cat, Alfie. It's a family-run affair, with French chef and co-owner Jean Pierre in charge of the kitchen. Expect traditional French cooking from the specials board, while other choices might include beer-battered cod with chips and salad.

Open all wk 11.30-2.30 6-11.30 (Sun 12-2.30 7-11) Closed: 25 Dec eve **Bar Meals** L served all wk 12-2 D served Mon-Sat 7-9 Av main course £9.95 ⊕ FREE HOUSE ◀ Hook Norton, Ansells Mild, Spitfire, Purity, local ales Ó Old Katy, Black Rat, Thatchers Traditional. ♀ 9 **Facilities** Children's menu Play area Garden Parking

## TEMPLE GRAFTON

### The Blue Boar Inn ♀

**B49 6NR ☎ 01789 750010 ▤ 01789 750635**
e-mail: info@theblueboar.co.uk
dir: *From A46 (Stratford to Alcester) turn left to Temple Grafton. Pub at 1st x-rds*

The oldest part of the inn is 17th century, and has been an alehouse since that time. The restaurant features a 35-foot glass-covered well, home to a family of koi carp. There are four open fires in the bar and restaurant areas, and a patio garden with views of the Cotswold Hills. A menu of traditional dishes is served, with variety provided by daily specials prepared from local produce, game in particular.

Open all day all wk **Bar Meals** L served all wk 12-3 D served all wk 6-10 **Restaurant** L served all wk 12-3 D served all wk

6-10 ⊕ MARSTONS PUB COMPANY ◀ Marstons Banks Original, Pedigree, Guinness Ó Thatchers Gold. ♀ 6 **Facilities** Children's menu Garden Parking

## WELFORD-ON-AVON

### The Bell Inn ♀

**Binton Rd CV37 8EB ☎ 01789 750353 ▤ 01789 750893**
e-mail: info@thebellwelford.co.uk
dir: *Please telephone for directions*

In the heart of Warwickshire countryside, this 17th-century inn has all the classic touches, including open fires, flagstone floors, exposed beams and oak furniture. Legend has it that William Shakespeare contracted fatal pneumonia after stumbling home from here in the pouring rain. At least five real ales are always on offer, including local brews from the Purity Brewing Company just a few miles away. Food is taken seriously here and the local suppliers of quality ingredients are credited on the menu. In addition to the main menu, a specials carte tempts with prawn and ginger fritters in a sweet chilli and smoked garlic sauce; pan-roasted partridge on sautéed cabbage and potato with a sun blush tomato jus; and sticky fig and date pudding with butterscotch and walnut sauce.

Open all wk Sat 11.30-11 Sun noon-10.30 **Bar Meals** L served Mon-Sat 11.30-2.30, Sun all day booking required D served Mon-Thu 6-9.30, Fri-Sat 6-10, Sun all day booking required Av main course £12 **Restaurant** L served Mon-Sat 11.30-2.30, Sun all day booking required D served Mon-Thu 6-9.30, Fri-Sat 6-10, Sun all day booking required Av 3 course à la carte fr £22.95 ⊕ ENTERPRISE INNS ◀ Hook Norton (various), Flowers Original, Hobsons Best, Wadworth 6X, Flowers Best, Purity Gold, UBU. ♀ 16 **Facilities** Children's menu Garden Parking

## WITHYBROOK

### The Pheasant ♀

**Main St CV7 9LT ☎ 01455 220480 ▤ 01455 221296**
e-mail: thepheasant01@hotmail.com
dir: *7m from Coventry*

This well-presented 17th-century free house stands beside the brook where withies were once cut for fencing. An inglenook fireplace, farm implements and horse-racing photographs characterise the interior. Under the same ownership since 1981, the pub has a varied menu with a wealth of popular choices. Alongside a blackboard of specials, a typical menu includes pan-fried pork cutlets, fisherman's pie, braised faggots, and chicken and mushroom pie. Outside tables overlook the Withy Brook.

**Open** all wk 11-3 6-11.30 (Sun & BH 11-11) Closed: 25-26 Dec **Bar Meals** L served Mon-Sat 12-2, Sun 12-9 booking required D served Mon-Sat 6-10, Sun 12-9 booking required **Restaurant** L served Mon-Sat 12-2, Sun 12-9 booking required D served Mon-Sat 6-10, Sun 12-9 booking required ⊕ FREE HOUSE ◖ Courage Directors, Theakstons Best, John Smiths Smooth. ♀ 9 **Facilities** Children's menu Dogs allowed Garden Parking

## WEST MIDLANDS

### CHADWICK END

## The Orange Tree ♀

**Warwick Rd B93 0BN ☎ 01564 785364** 📄 **01564 782988** e-mail: theorangetree@lovelypubs.co.uk dir: *3m from Knowle towards Warwick*

Relaxation is the name of the game at this pub/restaurant in peaceful countryside. The interior is light, airy and warm with open kitchens, stone-fired ovens and log burning fires. Real ales are backed by Thatchers Gold cider on tap, so settle with a pint while choosing from the menu. Comfort springs to mind here too, where sharing plates of antipasti or Greek mezze can be followed by fired pizzas – try the sloppy Guiseppe with hot spiced beef and green peppers. Alternatively half a dozen different pastas range from tagllatelle bolognese to macaroni with smoked haddock and cauliflower cheese. Other sections on the carte promise grills, spit-roast chicken from the rotisserie, salads and dishes such as braised beef in Barolo from the oven. The sunny lounge area opens up through oversized French doors to the patio.

**Open** all day all wk 11-11 Closed: 25 Dec **Bar Meals** L served all wk 12-2.30 D served all wk 6-9.30 Av main course £13.50 **Restaurant** L served all wk 12-2.30 booking required D served all wk 6-9.30 booking required Av 3 course à la carte fr £25 ⊕ FREE HOUSE ◖ IPA, Old Hooky, Black Sheep ♻ Thatchers. ♀ 8 **Facilities** Children's menu Play area Dogs allowed Garden Parking

## ISLE OF WIGHT

### ARRETON

## The White Lion

**PO30 3AA ☎ 01983 528479** e-mail: chrisandkatelou@hotmail.co.uk dir: *B3056 (Newport to Sandown road)*

Sited in an outstandingly beautiful conservation area, this 300-year-old former coaching inn offers a genuinely hospitable welcome. Oak beams, polished brass and open fires set the cosy tone inside, while a safe outside seating area enjoys views of the Arreton scenery. Well-priced pub grub is served all day, ranging from traditional snacks to specials such as nasi goreng - Indonesian spicy rice with chicken and prawns. Favourite puddings of spotted dick and jam roly poly sell out quickly.

**Open** all day all wk **Bar Meals** Av main course £7.95 food served all day **Restaurant** Av 3 course à la carte fr £10 food served all day ⊕ ENTERPRISE INNS ◖ Badger Best, Fuller's London Pride, Timothy Taylor Landlord, John Smiths Smooth, Flowers Best. **Facilities** Children's menu Play area Family room Dogs allowed Garden Parking

### BEMBRIDGE

## The Crab & Lobster Inn ★★★★ INN ♀

**32 Foreland Field Rd PO35 5TR** **☎ 01983 872244** 📄 **01983 873495** e-mail: crab.lobster@bluebottle.com dir: *From Bembridge Village, 1st left after Boots down Forelands Rd to the Windmill Hotel. Left into Lane End Rd, 2nd right into Egerton Rd, left into Forelands Rd & immediately right into Foreland Field Rd*

Originally a fisherman's cottage, this award-winning beamed pub sits just yards from the popular 65-mile coastal path. A raised deck and patio area offer superb sea views. Locally caught seafood is one of the pub's great attractions; typical choices include a pint of prawns; lobster salad; home-made crab cakes; and seafood platters. For meat eaters there are pub classics such as steaks or ham, egg and chips.

**Open** all wk summer 11-11 (Sun 11-10.30) winter 11-3 6-11 (Sun 6-10.30) **Bar Meals** L served all wk 12-2.30 booking required D served Sun-Thu 6-9, Fri-Sat 6-9.30 booking required Av main course £8.50 **Restaurant** L served all wk 12-2.30 booking required D served Sun-Thu 6-9, Fri-Sat 6-9.30 booking required ⊕ ENTERPRISE INNS ◖ Interbrew Flowers Original, Goddards Fuggle-Dee-Dum, Greene King IPA, John Smiths. ♀ 12 **Facilities** Children's menu Dogs allowed Garden Parking **Rooms** 5

### BONCHURCH

## The Bonchurch Inn

**Bonchurch Shute PO38 1NU** **☎ 01983 852611** 📄 **01983 856657** e-mail: gillian@bonchurch-inn.co.uk dir: *Off A3055 in Bonchurch*

In its quiet, off the road location, this small family-run free house inn lies tucked away in a secluded Dickensian-style courtyard. You won't be disturbed by juke boxes or gaming machines, for little has changed here since this former coaching inn and stables was granted its first licence in the 1840s. Food is available lunchtime and evenings in the bar; choices range

continued

from sandwiches and ploughman's to fresh fish, juicy steaks and Italian specialities.

Open all wk 11-3 6.30-11 Closed: 25 Dec **Bar Meals** L served all wk 12-2 D served all wk 6.30-9 booking required Av main course £10 **Restaurant** D served all wk 7-8.45 booking required ⊕ FREE HOUSE ◀ Courage Directors, Best. **Facilities** Children's menu Family room Dogs allowed Garden Parking

## COWES

## The Folly ♥

**Folly Ln PO32 6NB ☎ 01983 297171**
dir: *Telephone for directions*

Reached by land and water, and very popular with the boating fraternity, the Folly is one of the island's more unusual pubs. Timber from an old sea-going French barge was used in the construction, and wood from the hull can be found in the bar. The menus are wide ranging with something for everyone. House specialities include venison Wellington, prime British beef ribs and slow cooked lamb.

Open all wk **Bar Meals** Av main course £8 food served all day **Restaurant** food served all day ⊕ GREENE KING ◀ Greene King IPA, Old Speckled Hen, Goddards Best Bitter. ♥ 10 **Facilities** Children's menu Dogs allowed Garden Parking

## GODSHILL

## The Taverners ♥

**High St PO38 3HZ ☎ 01983 840707**
web: www.thetavernersgodshill.co.uk
dir: *Please telephone for directions*

Tucked away in picture-perfect Godshill, the Island's 'honeypot' village, the Taverners has been wowing locals and tourists with top-notch pub food since locals Roger Serjent and Lisa Choi took over in May 2008. Changing menus champion local seasonal produce, from local allotment fruit and vegetables and Bembridge crab to village-reared organic pork and lamb. Take baked crab pot, braised ox cheek with horseradish mash, finishing with treacle tart, with roast rib of beef for Sunday lunch. One to watch!

Open all day all wk 11-11 (Fri 11am-mdnt Sun 11-10.30) Closed: 1st 2wks Jan **Bar Meals** L served all wk summer 11.30-3.30, Mon-Sat 12-3, Sun 12-4 winter D served all wk summer 6-9.30, Mon-Sat winter 6-9 Av main course £10 **Restaurant** L served all wk summer 12-3.30, Mon-Sat 12-3, Sun 12-4 winter booking

required D served Sun-Thu 6-9.30, Fri-Sat 6-10 summer, Sun-Thu 6-9, Fri-Sat 6-9.30 winter booking required Av 3 course à la carte fr £20 ⊕ PUNCH ◀ Undercliff, London Pride, John Smiths ♂ Stowford Press, Old Rosie. ♥ 8 **Facilities** Children's menu Play area Family room Dogs allowed Garden Parking

## NITON

## Buddle Inn ♥

**St Catherines Rd PO38 2NE ☎ 01983 730243**
dir: *Take A3055 from Ventnor. In Niton take 1st left signed 'to the lighthouse'*

A spit away from the English Channel one way and the Coastal Path the other, this 16th-century, former cliff-top farmhouse can claim to be one of the island's oldest hostelries. Popular with hikers and ramblers (and their muddy boots and dogs), the interior has the full traditional complement - stone flags, oak beams and large open fire, as well as great real ales on tap. Simple but well prepared food is served, including beef Wellington and venison casserole. Recent change of hands.

Open all day all wk 11-11 (Fri-Sat 11-mdnt Sun noon-10.30) **Bar Meals** L served all wk 12-2.45 D served all wk 6-9 **Restaurant** L served all wk 12-2.45 D served all wk 6-9 ⊕ ENTERPRISE INNS ◀ Bombardier, Fortyniner, Spitfire. ♥ 8 **Facilities** Children's menu Family room Dogs allowed Garden Parking

## NORTHWOOD

## Travellers Joy

**85 Pallance Rd PO31 8LS ☎ 01983 298024**
e-mail: tjoy@globalnet.co.uk

Ruth and Derek Smith run this 300-year-old alehouse, just a little way inland from Cowes. They keep eight real ales on hand pump all year round. Don't expect dishes described on the menu as 'drizzled' or 'pan-roasted' here because the food is home cooked and uncomplicated but with all the trimmings - grilled gammon steak, salmon steak, breaded plaice, double sausage with egg, chips and beans, honey-roast ham, home-made steak and kidney pie, and children's meals. Outside is a pétanque terrain, pets' corner and play area.

Open all wk **Bar Meals** L served all wk 12-2 D served all wk 6.30-9.30 Av main course £6.45 ⊕ FREE HOUSE ◀ Goddards Special Bitter, Courage Directors, Ventnor Golden Bitter, Deuchars IPA, St Austell Tribute. **Facilities** Children's menu Play area Family room Dogs allowed Garden Parking

England

## SEAVIEW

# The Seaview Hotel & Restaurant ★★★ HL ◎◎

**High St PO34 5EX** ☎ **01983 612711** 📄 **01983 613729**
e-mail: reception@seaviewhotel.co.uk
dir: *B3330 (Ryde to Seaview road), left via Puckpool along seafront road, hotel on left*

The Pump Bar is a unique English pub situated at the heart of a hotel that for many years has been welcoming locals and visitors alike in traditional style. Even a log fire blazes to keep out the winter chill. In a sailing-mad village this smart, sea-facing hotel is crammed with nautical associations. Amidst the lobster pots, oars, masts and other nautical memorabilia in the bar you'll find traditional and local real ales, complemented by wines and an extensive menu of traditional and innovative dishes from the bar menu. In summer, the terrace or the Front Bar are the places to relax and watch the world go by. Modelled on a naval wardroom, the Front Bar is home to a magnificent collection of naval pictures, photographs and artefacts – one of the most extensive private collections to be found on the Island. The hotel offers a choice of dining venues; there's the small Victorian dining room, and the more contemporary Sunshine restaurant, complete with its own conservatory. Both dining rooms offer the same menu, which reflects the hotel's close relationship with the Island's farmers and fishermen, ensuring that the chefs are always working with the very best seasonal produce. Polish up your taste-buds with Isle of Wight crab with green chilli, lime and coriander tagliatelle, or wild mushroom soup with truffle jelly; before moving on to the main course. Options might encompass New Close Farm venison with braised red cabbage, creamed potato and sultana and thyme sauce, or pan-fried pollack with beetroot mash, spinach and lemon balm. For dessert, choose chocolate mousse, or apple crumble with home-made custard.

Open all wk **Bar Meals** L served all wk 12-2.30 D served all wk 6.30-9.30 **Restaurant** L served all wk 12-2 (summer), Sat-Sun 12-2 (winter) booking required D served all wk 6.30-9.30 booking required ⊕ FREE HOUSE ◀ Goddards, Ventnor Bitter, guest ale. **Facilities** Children's menu Dogs allowed **Rooms** 28

## SHORWELL

# The Crown Inn

**Walkers Ln PO30 3JZ** ☎ **01983 740293** 📄 **01983 740293**
e-mail: info@crowninnshorwell.co.uk
dir: *Turn left at top of Carisbrooke High Street, Shorwell approx 6m*

Set in a pretty village in picturesque West Wight, with thatched cottages, a small shop, three manor houses, and the church opposite. In summer, arum lilies decorate the garden stream, and a Wendy house, slide and swings keep youngsters amused. The building dates in part from the 17th century, and different floor levels attest to many alterations. Log fires, antique furniture and a friendly female ghost, who disapproves of card playing, complete the picture of this traditional family-run pub. Beers on tap include an island brew, and food consists of home-made favourites based on locally sourced lamb, beef, plus game in winter and fish in summer. Tempting pub grub, plus an award-winning specials board offer cottage pie, steak and kidney pie, and game dishes when in season. There are also great fish, pasta and vegetarian dishes too.

Open all wk **Bar Meals** food served all day ⊕ ENTERPRISE INNS ◀ Goddards (local), Ringwood Fortyniner, Ringwood Best, Doom Bar, Adnams Broadside. **Facilities** Children's menu Play area Family room Dogs allowed Garden Parking

## VENTNOR

# The Spyglass Inn ♟

**The Esplanade PO38 1JX** ☎ **01983 855338**
📄 **01983 855220**
e-mail: info@thespyglass.com
dir: *Telephone for directions*

For centuries this area was a haunt of smugglers, and echoes of these activities can be seen in the huge collection of nautical memorabilia on the walls of this famous 19th-century inn. It has a superb position, right at the end of Ventnor Esplanade. Much of the food here is, naturally, fish, including home-made fish chowder, Ventnor crab and lobster, but other dishes might include several varieties of pie; local sausages; or ham and leek

continued

bake.

**Open** all day all wk 10.30am-11pm **Bar Meals** L served all wk 12-9.30 D served all wk 12-9.30 food served all day **Restaurant** L served all wk 12-9.30 D served all wk 12-9.30 food served all day ⊕ FREE HOUSE ◀ Ventnor Golden, Goddards Fuggle-Dee-Dom, Yates Undercliff Experience, Ringwood Best, Ringwood Fortyniner. ♀ 8 **Facilities** Children's menu Family room Dogs allowed Garden Parking

## WILTSHIRE

### ALDBOURNE

## The Crown at Aldbourne ★★★★ INN ♀

**The Square SN8 2DU ☎ 01672 540214** 🖹 **01672 541050**
e-mail: info@crownataldbourne.co.uk
dir: *M4 Junct 15 go N on A419 direction of Swindon. At first junct Aldbourne is signed on B4192. The Crown is situated in centre of village opposite the pond*

Overlooking the village square and duck pond, the Crown is a spick-and-span 18th-century inn with a cosy, traditional beamed bar and a wooden-floored dining room. Very much the village inn, smartly refurbished and with local Ramsbury Gold on tap, it offers a good selection of home-cooked dishes, from soup and sandwiches to Sunday roasts and a popular tapas menu. The courtyard is a pleasant spot for summer sipping.

**Open** all wk noon-3 6-11 (Sat-Sun noon-11) **Bar Meals** L served all wk 12-3 D served Mon-Sat 7-9.30 **Restaurant** L served all wk 12-3 D served Mon-Sat 7-9.30 ⊕ ENTERPRISE INNS ◀ Spitfire Shepherds Neame, Sharp's Cornish Coaster, Ramsbury Gold ♂ Westons Stowford Press. ♀ 8 **Facilities** Children's menu Play area Dogs allowed Garden Parking **Rooms** 4

### ALDERBURY

## The Green Dragon ♀

**Old Rd SP5 3AR ☎ 01722 710263**
dir: *1m off A36 (Southampton to Salisbury road)*

There are fine views of Salisbury Cathedral from this 15th-century pub, which is probably named after the heroic deeds of Sir Maurice Berkeley, the Mayor of Alderbury, who slew a green dragon in the 15th century. Dickens wrote Martin Chuzzlewit here, and called the pub the Blue Dragon. An interesting and daily changing menu features home-made meat and vegetarian dishes using locally sourced produce.

**Open** all wk **Bar Meals** L served all wk 12-2 D served all wk 6.30-9.30 **Restaurant** L served all wk 12-2 D served all wk 6.30-9.30 ⊕ HALL & WOODHOUSE ◀ Badger First Gold, Tanglefoot, Fursty Ferret ♂ Stowford Press. ♀ 14 **Facilities** Children's menu Dogs allowed Garden Parking

### AXFORD

## Red Lion Inn ♀

**SN8 2HA ☎ 01672 520271**
e-mail: info@redlionaxford.com
web: www.redlionaxford.com
dir: *M4 junct 15, A246 Marlborough centre. Follow Ramsbury signs. Inn 3m*

A pretty, 16th-century brick and flint pub with fine views over the Kennet Valley. In the bar there's a large inglenook, and a mix of seating. The inn specialises in seasonal game and fish dishes, and in addition to bar snacks, the regularly-changing menus offer plenty of choice. Perhaps a starter of warm salad of wood pigeon with smoked bacon lardons and black pudding; or seared scallops with sauce vièrge, sweet and sour greens to begin. Mains might be a classic lobster thermidor; oven-roasted cod pavé with shellfish bisque; fillet of venison with Cumberland sauce; or roast rump of lamb with redcurrant, red wine and port wine reduction. Vegetarians can look forward to dishes like the sweet potato, blue cheese and leek tart.

**Open** 12-3 6-11 Closed: Sun eve, Mon **Bar Meals** L served Tue-Sat 12-2.30 D served Tue-Fri 6-9 **Restaurant** L served Tue-Sun 12-2.30 D served Tue-Sun 12-9 ⊕ FREE HOUSE ◀ Axford Ale, Ramsbury Gold, Guest ales ♂ Stowford Press. ♀ 16 **Facilities** Children's menu Garden Parking

### BARFORD ST MARTIN

## Barford Inn ♀

**SP3 4AB ☎ 01722 742242** 🖹 **01722 743606**
e-mail: thebarfordinn@btconnect.com
dir: *On A30 5m W of Salisbury 1.5m from Wilton*

There's been a recent change of management at this 16th-century former coaching inn five miles outside Salisbury, but the welcoming lounge, lower bar area and intimate snug

England

have greeted visitors for generations. During World War II the Wiltshire Yeomanry dedicated a tank to the pub, known then as The Green Dragon. Meals are served in the bar or restaurant, and in warmer months in the garden or patio area. Alongside ploughman's, hot baguettes, jackets and sandwiches, you'll find gammon steak, sausage and mash, beef stroganoff or grilled sea bass fillet.

Open all day all wk Bar Meals L served all wk 12-2.30 D served Sun-Thu 6-9, Fri-Sat 6-9.30 Restaurant L served all wk 12-2.30 booking required D served Sun-Thu 6-9, Fri-Sat 6-9.30 booking required ⊕ HALL & WOODHOUSE ◀ Badger Dorset Best, Fursty Ferret, Festive. ♀ 6 Facilities Children's menu Dogs allowed Garden Parking

## BOX

## The Northey ♀

**Bath Rd SN13 8AE ☎ 01225 742333**
e-mail: office@ohhcompany.co.uk
dir: *4m from Bath on A4 towards Chippenham. Between M4 juncts 17 & 18*

Following a magnificent transformation, this former station hotel is a favourite in the area for food and drink. Designed throughout by owner Sally Warburton, the interior makes good use of wood and flagstone flooring, high-backed oak chairs, leather loungers and handcrafted tables around the bar, where interesting sandwiches, ciabattas and Italian platters hold sway. The main menu ranges from pork, duck and Toulouse sausage cassoulet to aromatic tagine of salmon and cod with curried potatoes and spinach.

Open all wk Bar Meals L served all wk 11-3 D served all wk 6-10 Av main course £11 Restaurant L served all wk 11-3 D served all wk 6-10 Fixed menu price fr £10 Av 3 course à la carte fr £15 ⊕ WADWORTH ◀ Wadworth 6X, IPA, Malt 'n' Hops, Old Father Timer. ♀ 10 Facilities Children's menu Dogs allowed Garden Parking

## The Quarrymans Arms ♀

**Box Hill SN13 8HN ☎ 01225 743569  📄 01225 742610**
e-mail: john@quarrymans-arms.co.uk
dir: *Telephone for directions*

Built above Brunel's famous Box railway tunnel, this 300-year-old pub is packed with stone-mining memorabilia (take a tour of the old mine workings). Great views through the restaurant window of the valley, abundantly laced with marked paths and trails. In addition to the regular menu – sizzling stir-fry, pork Dijonnaise, tuna niçoise – look out for the vegetarian menu and specials board.

Open all wk 11am-11.30pm Bar Meals L served all wk 11-3 booking required D served all wk 6- last booking booking required Av main course £10 Restaurant L served all wk 11-last booking booking required D served all wk 6-last booking booking required Av 3 course à la carte fr £19 ⊕ FREE HOUSE ◀ Butcombe Bitter, Wadworth 6X, Moles Best, Local guest ales Ö Stowford Press. ♀ 12 Facilities Children's menu Family room Dogs allowed Garden Parking

## BRADFORD-ON-AVON

## The Dandy Lion ♀

**35 Market St BA15 1LL ☎ 01225 863433**
📄 **01225 869169**
e-mail: Dandylion35@aol.com
dir: *Telephone for directions*

The owners have refurbished this 17th-century town centre pub, but its original spirit lives on through its well-kept ales and a mix of English and European food. The café-bar menu offers grazing boards ideal for sharing, hot-filled flatbreads, and thick-cut sandwiches alongside old comforts like home-baked Wiltshire ham with double free-range eggs and rustic chips. A meal in the restaurant could start with deep fried baby squid with chilli and garlic mayonnaise, and continue with braised lamb shank with root vegetables and creamy mash. Desserts are home made and shown on the blackboard.

Open all wk 11-3 6-11 (Fri-Sat 11-11 Sun 11.30-10.30) Bar Meals L served all wk 12-2.30 D served all wk 6-9 Av main course £8.95 Restaurant D served Fri-Sat 7-9.30 booking required Av 3 course à la carte fr £21.50 ⊕ WADWORTH ◀ Wadworth 6X, Henrys IPA, Wadworth Seasonal Ö Stowford Press, Westons Organic. ♀ 11 Facilities Children's menu

## The Swan ♀

**1 Church St BA15 1LN ☎ 01225 868686**
📄 **01225 868681**
e-mail: theswan-hotel@btconnect.com
web: www.theswan-hotel.com
dir: *From train station turn left, over bridge, on left adjacent to river*

Set beside the medieval bridge that spans the River Avon, the Swan is a striking, 15th-century honey-stoned inn that has been refurbished with style and flair. Bar and dining areas exude an elegant, contemporary feel, with rugs on stripped boards and flagged floors and comfy sofas fronting blazing log fires. The short menus range from a lunchtime deli board to ham hock terrine with piccalilli crostinis and seared tuna with crab risotto at dinner. A sunny terrace completes the picture.

Open all day all wk 7am-11pm (Sun 7am-10.30pm) Bar Meals L served all wk 12-2.30 booking required D served all wk 6.30-9.30 booking required Av main course £12 Restaurant L served all wk 12-2.30 booking required D served all wk 6.30-9.30 booking required Fixed menu price fr £12 Av 3 course à la carte fr £20 ⊕ GREENE KING ◀ Old Speckled Hen, Old Trip Ö Stowford Press. ♀ 8 Facilities Children's menu Garden Parking

**England**

### Bradford-on-Avon continued

## The Tollgate Inn ★★★★ INN ◉◉ ♈

**Holt BA14 6PX ☎ 01225 782326** 📠 01225 782805

e-mail: alison@tollgateholt.co.uk

dir: *M4 junct 18, A46 towards Bath, then A363 to Bradford-on-Avon, then B3107 towards Melksham, pub on right*

Built in the 16th century, The Tollgate, as with many old buildings, has a chequered history, having been part weaving mill, part Baptist chapel, and even the village school. You can eat in a small adjoining room with wood-burning stove and country-style decoration. The restaurant proper is up wooden stairs in what was originally the chapel for the weavers working below. Regular customers are attracted by modern British cooking with Mediterranean influences, locally sourced and supplied whenever possible. For example, hand-reared beef comes from the lush pastures of nearby Broughton Gifford; the lamb from Limpley Stoke; pork from Woolley Farm and village shoots provide the game; vegetables are grown in the surrounding fertile soils; and fish is delivered daily from Brixham. Lunchtime light bites (Tuesday to Saturday only) include corned beef hash with fried egg; Church Farm sausages with Dijon mash; eggs Benedict. The carte menu is full of temptation – Cornish crab ravioli on a pea and mint velouté; goats' cheese bruschetta with figs and local honey to start; with mains such as oven roasted Brixham halibut; risotto of local squashes; and rack of lamb with dauphinoise potatoes and rosemary sauce. The well-established garden and terrace (out of bounds to children under 12) is a tranquil and delightful place to eat when the weather permits.

**Open** 11.30-3 5.30-11 (Sun 11.30-3) Closed: Mon **Bar Meals** L served Tue-Sun 12-2 D served Tue-Sat 7-9 Av main course £13.50 **Restaurant** L served Tue-Sun 12-2 D served Tue-Sat 7-9 Fixed menu price fr £18.75 Av 3 course à la carte fr £22 ⊕ FREE HOUSE ◀ Exmoor Gold, Glastonbury Ales Mystery Tor, York Ales, Sharp's Doom Bar, Eden, Yorkshire Terrier ♂ Thatchers Gold, Thatchers Scrumpy. ♈ 9 **Facilities** Children's menu Dogs allowed Garden Parking **Rooms** 4

## The Three Crowns ♈

**SN15 5AF ☎ 01666 510366**

dir: *From Swindon take A3102 to Wootton Bassett, then B4042, 5m to Brinkworth*

Facing the church across the village green, the Three Crowns has been run by the same licensees for over 20 years. The building extends into a large, bright conservatory and garden room, then out onto a heated patio and garden that offers extensive views of the Dauntsey Vale. In winter, a welcoming log fire burns in the lounge. The Drinkers' Bar is dominated by two giant forge bellows and a wheelwright's bellow, all now converted into tables; settle there for a pint of Wadworth 6X or Abbey Ales Bellringer, and perhaps a game of cribbage or chess. When it's time to eat, the imaginative blackboard menus may offer locally smoked chicken with sherry and cream sauce; rack of English lamb with garlic breadcrumbs; poached halibut in white wine with a julienne of crispy leeks and seared scallops; or a baked vegetarian parcel with fresh tomato and basil sauce. The home-made dessert selection could feature strawberry shortbread; melon sorbet; or tangy lemon and Cointreau cheesecake.

**Open** all day all wk 10am-mdnt Closed: 25-26 Dec **Bar Meals** L served Mon-Sat 12-2, Sun 12-3 **Restaurant** L served Mon-Sat 12-2, Sun 12-3 D served all wk 6-9.30 ⊕ ENTERPRISE INNS ◀ Wadworth 6X, Greene King IPA, Wells Bombardier, Abbey Ales Bellringer ♂ Stowford Press. ♈ 20 **Facilities** Children's menu Play area Dogs allowed Garden Parking

### BROAD CHALKE

## The Queens Head Inn ♈

**1 North St SP5 5EN ☎ 01722 780344 & 0870 770 6634**

dir: *A354 from Salisbury towards Blandford Forum, at Coombe Bissett right towards Bishopstone, pub in 4m*

Attractive 15th-century-inn with friendly atmosphere and low-beamed bars, once the village bakehouse. On sunny days, enjoy the flower-bordered courtyard, whilst in colder weather the low beams and wood burner in the bar provide a cosy refuge. Menus include light snacks such as sandwiches, ploughman's lunches and home-made soups, as well as more substantial main courses: perhaps grilled trout with almonds, sirloin steak with a choice of vegetables, or wild game casserole.

**Open** all wk noon-3 6-11.30 (Fri-Sat 6-mdnt Sun noon-10.30)

Bar Meals L served Mon-Sat 12-2.30, Sun 12-6 D served Mon-Sat 6-9, Sun 12-6 Restaurant L served Mon-Sat 12-2.30, Sun 12-6 D served Mon-Sat 6-9, Sun 12-6 ⊕ Hall & Woodhouse ⌑ Badgers Best, Badger Tanglefoot, Hopping Hare ♂ Stowford Press. ♥ 7 Facilities Children's menu Family room Dogs allowed Garden Parking

## BURCOMBE

### The Ship Inn ♥

**Burcombe Ln SP2 0EJ ☎ 01722 743182  ▤ 01722 743182**
e-mail: theshipburcombe@mail.com
dir: *In Burcombe, off A30, 1m from Wilton & 5m W of Salisbury*

A 17th-century village pub with low ceilings, oak beams and a large open fire. In summer the riverside garden is a great place to enjoy a leisurely meal in the company of the resident ducks. Seasonal menu examples include home-made fishcakes; braised lamb shank with mustard mash and Savoy cabbage; grilled field mushroom with talegio; stuffed chicken supreme with brie and basil; or pumpkin curry with chickpeas and spinach. Daily changing specials, sandwiches and light bites are also available.

Open all wk Bar Meals L served all wk 12-2.30 D served all wk 6-9 Av main course £9 Restaurant L served all wk 12-2.30 D served all wk 6-9 Av 3 course à la carte fr £25 ⌑ Wadworth 6X, Courage Best, Butcombe. ♥ 10 Facilities Children's menu Dogs allowed Garden Parking

## CORSHAM

### The Flemish Weaver ♥

**63 High St SN13 0EZ ☎ 01249 701929**
dir: *Next to town hall on Corsham High St*

Standing opposite the historic Corsham Court, this stone-built town centre inn takes its name from a nearby row of original Flemish weavers' cottages. Drinkers and diners are all welcome to enjoy the winter log fires and candlelit interior - though it's advisable to book a table. Thatchers Gold and Stowford Press ciders complement a good range of real ales, some of which are served straight from the barrel. There's also an extensive wine list, with many choices available by the glass. Menus are changed daily, and you might start with hand-crumbed Somerset brie and cranberry compote before making the choice between tagliatelle in dolcelatte cream sauce with spinach and toasted pine nuts; and cod with leek and potato gratin. Typical desserts include bread and butter pudding laced with Bailey's;

and summer fruits and jelly terrine. Enjoy them in the large outdoor eating area on warmer days.

Open 11-3 5.30-11 (Sun noon-3) Closed: Sun eve Bar Meals L served Mon-Sat 11.30-2.30 booking required Av main course £5 Restaurant L served Mon-Sat 11.30-2.30, Sun 12-2.30 booking required D served Mon-Sat 6.30-9.30 booking required Fixed menu price fr £7.20 Av 3 course à la carte fr £14.95 ⊕ ENTERPRISE INNS ⌑ Bath Spa, Doom Bar, Bath Gem, Bob, HPA Wye Valley, Hook Norton ♂ Thatchers Gold, Stowford Press. ♥ 10 Facilities Children's menu Dogs allowed Garden Parking

## CORTON

### The Dove Inn ★★★ INN ◉ ♥

**BA12 0SZ ☎ 01985 850109  ▤ 01985 851041**
e-mail: info@thedove.co.uk
dir: *A36 (Salisbury towards Warminster), in 14m turn left signed Corton & Boyton. Cross rail line, right at T-junct. Corton approx 1.5m, turn right into village*

Tucked away in a lovely Wiltshire village near the River Wylye, this thriving traditional pub is a haven of tranquillity. A striking central fireplace is a feature of the refurbished bar, and the spacious garden is the perfect spot for barbecues or a drink on long summer days. The award-winning menu is based firmly on West Country produce, with many ingredients coming from within just a few miles. Popular lunchtime bar snacks give way to a full evening carte featuring a classy but hearty take on pub food. Typical starters include pan-fried pigeon breast with a redcurrant jus; and garlic king prawns with a sweet chilli dip. Main courses range from oven-baked sea bass stuffed with fresh herbs to spicy chicken curry with basmatic rice.

Open all wk noon-2.30 6-11 Bar Meals L served all wk 12-2 D served Sun-Thu 7-9, Fri-Sat 7-9.30 Av main course £6 Restaurant L served all wk 12-2 D served Sun-Thu 7-9, Fri-Sat 7-9.30 Av 3 course à la carte fr £18 ⊕ FREE HOUSE ⌑ Spitfire, Youngs, Butcombe, Hop Back GFB ♂ Stowford Press. ♥ 10 Facilities Children's menu Dogs allowed Garden Parking Rooms 5

## DONHEAD ST ANDREW

### The Forester ▼

**Lower St SP7 9EE ☎ 01747 828038**
e-mail: possums1@btinternet.com
dir: *4.5m from Shaftesbury off A30 towards Salisbury*

The Forester is a lovely old country pub located in the Donheads close to Wardour Castle in beautiful walking country. Traditional in style, it has warm stone walls, a thatched roof, original beams and an inglenook fireplace. An extension provides a restaurant and a restaurant/meeting room, with double doors opening on to the lower patio area. The garden and large patio area are furnished with hardwood chairs and tables as well as bench seating. The restaurant has a good reputation for its freshly cooked food and specialises in Cornish seafood, with deliveries five times a week. A Taste of the Sea lunch might offer pan-fried herring roes with smoked bacon, capers and parsley, followed by fillet of plaice with herb butter and new potatoes. Alternatives might be Kashmiri-style duck leg curry, or rump of local lamb with goats' cheese gnocchi, tomato and black olive jus.

Open noon-2 6.30-11 Closed: Sun eve **Bar Meals** L served all wk 12-2 booking required D served Mon-Sat 7-9 booking required Av main course £12.50 **Restaurant** L served all wk 12-2 D served Mon-Sat 7-9 booking required Fixed menu price fr £15.50 Av 3 course à la carte fr £20 ⊕ FREE HOUSE ◀ Ringwood, Butcombe, Butts ♂ Stowford Press, Ashton Press. ▼ 17 **Facilities** Children's menu Dogs allowed Garden Parking

## EAST KNOYLE

### The Fox and Hounds ▼

**The Green SP3 6BN ☎ 01747 830573 📄 01747 830865**
e-mail: pub@foxandhounds-eastknoyle.co.uk
web: www.foxandhounds-eastknoyle.co.uk
dir: *1.5m off A303 at the A350 turn off, follow brown signs*

East Knoyle and this picturesque, late-15th-century thatched and beamed, black and white free house are situated on a greensand ridge, from which there are magnificent views of Blackmore Vale. Add an imaginative menu and you have an ideal lunch or dinner venue. The village was where Sir Christopher Wren grew up, his father the local vicar. The pub's interior is quaint and comfortable, with wooden flooring, natural stone walls, flagstones, and sofas within toasting distance of a winter fire. A varied specials menu points out that all meat, chicken and game is sourced from local farms and

suppliers. In it, depending on daily availability, you can expect dishes such as Lizzie's lamb chump on mash and bacon with a rosemary/mint jus; aubergine filled with spinach, tomato, pecorino and mozzarella cheeses; chicken salad with basil and mango dressing; Moroccan vegetable tagine; fresh haddock in beer batter; crab and prawn risotto; slow-cooked lamb shanks in red wine; pan-fried calf's liver and bacon on mash with onion gravy; venison haunch steak with port and cranberry sauce; and Thai green chicken curry. You'll also find a range of ploughman's, and pizzas from a clay oven. If you're ready for more, desserts include chocolate lumpy bumpy and cream; apple and caramel pancake stack with vanilla ice cream; and bread and butter pudding laced with Bailey's.

Open all wk 11.30-3 5.30-11 **Bar Meals** L served all wk 12-2.30 D served all wk 6-9 **Restaurant** L served all wk 12-2.30 D served all wk 6-9 ⊕ FREE HOUSE ◀ Durdle Door, Cheer up, Copper Ale, Golden Arrow ♂ Thatchers Cheddar Valley. ▼ 10 **Facilities** Children's menu Dogs allowed Garden Parking

## GREAT CHEVERELL

### The Bell Inn ▼

**High St SN10 5TH ☎ 01380 813277**
e-mail: gillc@clara.co.uk
dir: *N side of Salisbury plain. A360 from Salisbury through West Lavington, 1st left after black & yellow striped bridge to Great Cheverell*

This former coaching inn stands on the northern edge of Salisbury Plain. There's a log fire in the 18th-century bar, and home-cooked West Country food is served in the elegantly styled restaurant. The imaginative and varied menu makes use of the best local ingredients where possible. Lunchtime brings filled ciabattas and baguettes, as well as old favourites like ham, eggs and chips. Main course dishes include baked sea bass with dill and white wine sauce; slow-cooked lamb shank with spring onion mash; and roasted vegetable, sun-dried tomato and goats' cheese parcel. The sunny, secluded garden is set in tranquil surroundings with lots of wooden benches and a patio area.

Open Closed: 26 Dec, 1 Jan **Bar Meals** L served all wk 12-2.30 D served all wk 6-9 Av main course £10 **Restaurant** L served all wk 12-2.30 D served all wk 6-9 Fixed menu price fr £13 Av 3 course à la carte fr £17 ⊕ FREE HOUSE ◀ 6X, IPA, Doom Bar, guest ale. ▼ 9 **Facilities** Children's menu Dogs allowed Garden Parking

## GREAT HINTON

### The Linnet ▼

**BA14 6BU ☎ 01380 870354 📄 01380 870354**
dir: *Just off A361 (Devizes to Trowbridge road)*

A former woollen mill in a picturesque setting, The Linnet was converted into a village local circa 1914. The pub prides itself on using the best of local produce and serving freshly prepared food at an honest price. Everything is made on the premises - bread, ice cream, pasta and sausages. The lunch menu offers a daily soup, warm salads and a good choice of steaks. A signature dish from the evening menu is baked tenderloin of pork filled with prunes and spinach wrapped in smoked bacon on a wild mushroom sauce and dauphinoise potatoes. A vegetarian alternative might be wild mushroom and tarragon risotto cake with tomato sauce, rocket salad and shaved parmesan. In summer sit on the large front patio area.

Open 11-2.30 6-11 Closed: 25-26 Dec, 1 Jan, Mon Bar Meals L served Tue-Sat 12-2, Sun 12-2.30 booking required D served Sun, Tue-Thu 6.30-9, Fri-Sat 6.30-9.30 booking required Av main course £8.50 Restaurant L served Tue-Sat 12-2, Sun 12-2.30 booking required D served Tue-Sun 6.30-9 booking required Fixed menu price fr £14.95 Av 3 course à la carte fr £26.95 ⊕ WADWORTH ◄ Wadworth 6X, Henrys IPA ♂ Stowford Press. ♀ 11 Facilities Children's menu Dogs allowed Garden Parking

## HINDON

### The Lamb at Hindon ★★★★ INN ⊛ ♀

**High St SP3 6DP ☎ 01747 820573 ▤ 01747 820605**
e-mail: info@lambathindon.co.uk
dir: *From A303 follow signs to Hindon. At Fonthill Bishop right onto B3089 to Hindon. Pub on left*

Wisteria clings to one corner of the mellow 17th-century coaching inn, tucked away in a charming village. At its height, 300 post horses were kept here to supply the coaches travelling between London and the West Country. Inside, the long bar is divided into several cosy areas, with sturdy period furnishings, flagstone floors, terracotta walls hung with old prints and paintings, and a splendid old stone fireplace with a crackling log fire. The chalkboard menu offers hearty modern pub dishes. Typically, tuck into lambs' kidneys with balsamic shallots and red wine jus, followed by roast salmon with Jerusalem artichokes and Puy lentils, or slow-cooked salt beef with horseradish dumplings, and butterscotch tart for pudding.

Open all day all wk 7.30am-mdnt Bar Meals L served all wk 12-2.30 D served all wk 6.30-9.30 booking required Av main course £10 Restaurant L served all wk 12-2.30 D served all wk 6.30-9.30 booking required Av 3 course à la carte fr £25 ⊕ BOISDALE ◄ Youngs Bitter, Wells Bombardier, 2 guest ales. ♀ 6 Facilities Children's menu Family room Dogs allowed Garden Parking Rooms 14

## HORNINGSHAM

### The Bath Arms ★★★ HL ⊛ ♀

**BA12 7LY ☎ 01985 844308 ▤ 01985 845187**
e-mail: enquiries@batharms.co.uk
dir: *Off B3092 S of Frome*

This impressive, creeper-clad stone inn is situated by one of the entrances to Lord Bath's Longleat Estate. It was built in the 17th century, becoming a public house with rooms in 1732. It has been comfortably refurbished and features a fine beamed bar with settles and old wooden tables, and a terracotta-painted dining room with an open fire. The lunch and bar menu offers Wiltshire ham and piccalilli sandwich; tuna niçoise; and sirloin steak with tarragon sauce and thick chips, while in the

evening a short menu might suggest chump of Dorset lamb with roast shallot purée and grilled courgettes; rolled saddle of rabbit with garden peas wrapped in pancetta; and grilled lemon sole with white truffle mash and saffron sauce. Finish with raspberry crème brûlée or South West Country cheeses.

Open all day all wk Bar Meals L served all wk 12-2.30 D served all wk 7-9 Av main course £9.50 Restaurant L served all wk 12-2.30 booking required D served all wk 7-9 booking required Fixed menu price fr £9.50 Av 3 course à la carte fr £29.50 ⊕ HILLBROOKE HOTELS ◄ Horningsham Pride, guest ales ♂ Stowford Press. ♀ 9 Facilities Children's menu Dogs allowed Garden Parking Rooms 15

## HORTON

### The Bridge Inn ♀

**Horton Rd SN10 2JS ☎ 01380 860273**
e-mail: bridge.innhorton@talktalkbusiness.net
dir: *A361 from Devizes, right at 3rd rdbt. Follow brown signs*

This waterside pub, built around 1800, pre-dates the neighbouring Kennet and Avon Canal. Situated in an idyllic setting, the interior is cosy with open fires and the canal-side garden is the perfect place to enjoy a pint while watching the narrow boats cruise by. The pub keeps excellent cask ales, some served straight from the wood. Menus offer traditional home-made English food, from filled rolls to hearty hot meals.

Open 11.30-3 6-11 (summer Sat-Sun & BH 11.30-11) Closed: Mon Oct-Mar Bar Meals L served all wk 12-2 (ex Mon winter) D served Mon-Sat 6-9 Av main course £8 Restaurant L served all wk 12-2 (ex Mon winter) D served Mon-Sat 6-9 Av 3 course à la carte fr £17 ⊕ WADWORTH ◄ Wadworth Henry's original IPA, 6X, Old Father Timer ♂ Stowford Press. ♀ 8 Facilities Children's menu Dogs allowed Garden Parking

## LACOCK

### Red Lion Inn ♀

**1 High St SN15 2LQ ☎ 01249 730456 ▤ 01249 730766**
e-mail: redlionlacock@wadworth.co.uk
dir: *Just off A350 between Chippenham & Melksham. Follow Lacock signs*

This historic 18th-century inn has kept its original features intact, from the large open fireplace to the flagstone floors and Georgian interior. Lunchtime menu offers sandwiches or organic baguettes, small plates like breaded whitebait, home comforts, and ploughman's boards, whilst more substantial evening dishes include goats' cheese and cheddar terrine; braised shoulder of lamb, port and redcurrant sauce; beef and garlic casserole; and butternut squash and parmesan risotto.

Open all day all wk 11-11 (Sun 11-10.30) Bar Meals L served Mon-Sat 12-2.30, Sun 12-3 D served all wk 6-9.30 Av main course £10.50 Restaurant L served Mon-Sat 12-2.30, Sun 12-3 D served all wk 6-9.30 Av 3 course à la carte fr £20 ⊕ WADWORTH ◄ Wadworth 6X, Henrys IPA, seasonal ales ♂ Stowford Press, Thatchers Gold. ♀ 15 Facilities Children's menu Dogs allowed Garden Parking

**Lacock continued**

## The Rising Sun ♀

**32 Bowden Hill SN15 2PP ☎ 01249 730363**
e-mail: the.risingsun@btinternet.co.uk

The pub is located close to the National Trust village of Lacock, on a steep hill, providing spectacular views over Wiltshire from the large garden. Beer festivals, live music, hog roasts and barbecues are a regular feature, and games and reading material are provided in the bar. Thai curries and stir-fries are popular options, alongside traditional liver, bacon and onions, steaks, and beef, ale and Stilton pie.

Open all wk noon-3 6-11 Bar Meals L served all wk 12-2 booking required D served all wk 6-9 booking required Restaurant L served all wk 12-2 booking required D served all wk 6-9 booking required ∰ MOLES BREWERY ◀ Moles Best, Molecatcher, Tap Bitter, Rucking Mole, guest ale ⚭ Thatchers Gold, Black Rat. ♀ 10 Facilities Children's menu Play area Dogs allowed Garden Parking

## LITTLE CHEVERELL

## The Owl

**Low Rd SN10 4JS ☎ 01380 812263**
dir: *A344 from Stonehenge, then A360, after 10m left onto B3098, right after 0.5m. Pub signed*

Sit in the pretty garden after dark and you'll discover that this pub is aptly named. As well as the hoot of owls, woodpeckers can be heard in summer. A brook runs at the bottom of the garden and there are views of Salisbury Plain. The pub itself is a cosy hideaway with oak beams and a fire in winter. Typical dishes include lasagne; Thai chicken curry; sizzling beef Szechwan; and stilton and mushroom pork.

Open all day all wk noon-11 Bar Meals L served all wk 12-9 D served all wk 12-9 food served all day ∰ ENTERPRISE INNS ◀ Hop Back Summer Lightning, Bath Gem. Facilities Children's menu Play area Dogs allowed Garden Parking

## LOWER CHICKSGROVE

## Compasses Inn ★★★★ INN ⊛ ♀

**SP3 6NB ☎ 01722 714318**
e-mail: thecompasses@aol.com
dir: *On A30 (1.5m W of Fovant) take 3rd right to Lower Chicksgrove. In 1.5m turn left into Lagpond Lane, pub 1m on left*

This picture-perfect 14th-century thatched inn is full of character and stands in a tiny hamlet on the old drovers' track from Poole to Birmingham - a route that can still be traced today. The rolling countryside that unfolds around is part of a designated Area of Outstanding Natural Beauty. Inside there's a long, low-beamed bar with stone walls, worn flagstone floors and a large inglenook fireplace with a wood-burning stove for colder days. Be sure to try the food: the kitchen team have won an AA rosette for their efforts. Dishes from the ever-changing blackboard menu are freshly made using seasonal produce. A meal might take in potted crab and avocado; venison steak

with mixed berry sauce and dauphinoise potatoes; and brioche bread and butter pudding with banana and rum. The garden has a large grassed area with some lovely views.

Open all wk noon-3 6-11 (Sun noon-3 7-10.30) Closed: 25-26 Dec Bar Meals L served all wk 12-2 D served all wk 6.30-9 Av main course £15 ∰ FREE HOUSE ◀ Keystone Large One & Solar Brew, Hidden Potential, Bass ⚭ Stowford Press. ♀ 8 Facilities Children's menu Dogs allowed Garden Parking Rooms 5

## LUDWELL

## The Grove Arms ♀

**SP7 9ND ☎ 01747 828328 ▤ 01747 828960**
e-mail: info@grovearms.com
dir: *On A30 (Shaftesbury to Salisbury road), 3m from Shaftesbury*

The Grove Arms is a 16th century village inn once owned by the aristocratic Grove family. David Armstrong-Reed, chef and owner, is passionate about local produce, which is sourced from local farms and estates. Dishes are freshly made, including the popular home-made breads and chutneys, and fresh fish features strongly. Popular dishes, such as meat pies, chicken curry, and Badger beer battered haddock with tartare sauce are also available to take away during the week.

Open all day all wk Bar Meals L served all wk 12-3 D served all wk 6-9.30 Av main course £7 Restaurant L served Mon-Fri 12-3, Sat-Sun 12-9.30 booking required D served Mon-Fri 6-9.30, Sat-Sun 12-9.30 booking required ∰ HALL & WOODHOUSE ◀ Badger Gold, Festive Feasant, Hopping Hare. ♀ 6 Facilities Children's menu Family room Dogs allowed Garden Parking

## MALMESBURY

## The Horse & Groom Inn ♀

**The Street, Charlton SN16 9DL ☎ 01666 823904**
e-mail: info@horseandgroominn.com
web: www.horseandgroominn.com
dir: *M4 junct 17 follow signs to Cirencester on A429. Through Corston & Malmesbury. Straight on at Priory rdbt, at next rdbt take 3rd exit to Cricklade, then to Charlton*

Owned by a small, private pub company, and with a new landlord holding the reins, this Cotswold stone, 16th-century coaching inn stands well back from the road from Malmesbury to Cricklade, fronted by a tree-sheltered lawn. A refurbishment a little while back ensured that it lost none of its charm and character, which is why you will still find the original stone flags and fireplaces in the popular Charlton Bar, and in the dining room furnishings that include solid oak tables and a rug-strewn wooden floor. Outside space is plentiful including a lovely walled garden and separate play area. In the dog-friendly indoor bar, a weekly guest ale is chosen by customers. Snacks include tempting sandwiches, deli platters to share, ploughman's and salads, and the more substantial home-made crab cakes with dill mayonnaise; double-cooked Cotswold lamb with whole-grain mustard mash; fresh battered pollack with hand-cut chips and crushed peas; and pan-fried liver with smoked bacon, mash and shallot sauce. The focus on sensibly priced, modern British cooking continues on the carte menu which offers St George's mushroom risotto with Parmesan and chives; roasted Cotswold chicken breasts marinated in lemon and thyme with truffle mash and Evesham asparagus; and grilled fillet of wild brown trout, herb-crushed potatoes and cherry tomato and fennel salad. Resident chef Paul Nicholson is passionate about flying the flag for Wiltshire produce, such as the beef, which comes from a family butcher's that recently celebrated its 200th anniversary, and the pork belly, which comes from nearby Bromham. The wine list may not be that long, but it is comprehensive and offers a good number by the glass.

**Open** all wk 11-11 (Sun 11-10.30) **Bar Meals** L served Mon-Sat 12-2.30 D served Sun-Thu 6.30-9, Fri-Sat 6.30-9.30 Av main course £11 **Restaurant** L served Mon-Sat 12-2.30, Sun 12-3 D served Sun-Thu 6.30-9, Fri-Sat 6.30-9.30 Av 3 course à la carte fr £25 ◪ Archers, Morland Original, Old Speckled Hen, guest ales. ♟ 8 **Facilities** Children's menu Play area Dogs allowed Garden Parking

## MARDEN

### The Millstream ♟

**SN10 3RH** ☎ 01380 848308 ▤ 01380 848337
e-mail: mail@the-millstream.net
dir: *Signed from A342*

The Millstream sits in lovely countryside in the Vale of Pewsey, within sight of both Salisbury Plain and the Marlborough Downs. It was tastefully refurbished a few years ago without losing its traditional feel: wooden floors, beamed ceilings, log fires and pretty muted colours create a cosy, welcoming interior. Books, games and comfy sofas add their own homely touch. The contemporary menu makes good us of locally sourced seasonal produce, plus fish from Cornwall. Look out for braised lamb shank, and spatchcock poussin, with all the trimmings.

**Open** noon-3 6-late (Fri-Sun noon-late) Closed: Mon (ex BH) **Bar Meals** L served Tue-Sat 12-3, Sun 12-4 booking required D served Tue-Sat 6.30-10 booking required **Restaurant** L served Tue-Sat 12-3, Sun 12-4 booking required D served Tue-Sat 6.30-10 booking required ⊕ WADWORTH ◪ 6X, Henry's IPA, Bishops Tipple, Malt & Hops Ŏ Stowford Press. ♟ 14 **Facilities** Children's menu Play area Family room Dogs allowed Garden Parking

MINETY

## Vale of the White Horse Inn ♟

**SN16 9QY** ☎ 01666 860175 ▤ 01666 860175
dir: *On B4040 (3m W of Cricklade, 6m & E of Malmesbury)*

This eye-catching inn overlooks its own lake. In summer, sitting out on the large raised terrace surrounded by rose beds, it's hard to think of a better spot. The lower ground floor originally provided stabling for horses. Here you'll find a good selection of real ales and a range of sandwiches and simple bar meals. Upstairs, lunch and dinner are served in the stone-walled restaurant with its polished tables and bentwood chairs. The menus offer something for most tastes, with starters including leek, stilton and sun-dried tomato quiche, and crayfish tail and king prawn cocktail. Main courses range from beer-battered cod and chips to confit duck leg on braised red cabbage with mustard mash and Madeira sauce. Finish with crumble or treacle tart with ice cream.

**Open** all day all wk 11-11 **Bar Meals** L served all wk 12-2.30 D served all wk 6-9.15 Av main course £8 **Restaurant** L served all wk 12-2.30 D served all wk 6-9.15 Av 3 course à la carte fr £16.50 ⊕ FREE HOUSE ◪ Wadworth, Henrys IPA, Three Castle Vale Ale, Hancocks, Archers Chrystal Clear Ŏ Stowford Press. ♟ 12 **Facilities** Children's menu Family room Dogs allowed Garden Parking

## NUNTON

### The Radnor Arms ♟

**SP5 4HS** ☎ 01722 329722
dir: *From Salisbury ring road take A338 to Ringwood. Nunton signed on right*

A popular pub in the centre of the village dating from around 1750. In 1855 it was owned by the local multi-talented brewer/baker/grocer, and bought by Lord Radnor in 1919. Bar snacks are supplemented by an extensive fish choice and daily specials, which might include braised lamb shank, wild mushroom risotto, tuna with noodles, turbot with spinach or Scotch rib-eye fillet, all freshly prepared. Fine summer garden with rural views. Hosts an annual local pumpkin competition.

**Open** all wk **Bar Meals** L served all wk 12-2.15 D served all wk 7-9 Av main course £8.95 **Restaurant** L served all wk 12-2.15 D served all wk 7-9 Av 3 course à la carte fr £25 ⊕ HALL & WOODHOUSE ◪ Badger Tanglefoot, Best, Golden Champion. ♟ 6 **Facilities** Children's menu Play area Family room Dogs allowed Garden Parking

## OAKSEY

### The Wheatsheaf Inn ⊛⊛ ♚

**Wheatsheaf Ln SN16 9TB ☎ 01666 577348**
e-mail: info@thecompletechef.co.uk
dir: *Off A419, 6m S of Cirencester*

A 14th-century village inn built of mellow Cotswold stone, the Wheatsheaf has a traditional feel, with a big inglenook fireplace, flagstone floors and dark beams. It also has something rather bizarre - an 18th-century 'royal' coffin lid displayed above the fireplace. The restaurant is light and modern, with a sisal carpet, wooden tables and painted walls decorated with wine racks and jars of preserved vegetables. Modern British food - all made on the premises from fresh local produce, and behind the award of two AA Rosettes – is displayed on daily blackboards that may include delicately flavoured chestnut soup; followed by succulent belly pork with braised red cabbage, creamy mash and shallot jus; and baked rice pudding with cinnamon and cranberry jam to finish. On Fridays fish and chips are available to eat in or take away. Look out too for the Britain's Best Burger menu.

**Open** all wk **Bar Meals** L served Tue-Sun 12-2 D served Tue-Sat 6.30-9 **Restaurant** L served Tue-Sun 12-2 D served Tue-Sat 6.30-9 ⊕ FREE HOUSE ◀ Sharp's Doom Bar, Hook Norton, Bath Gem. ♚ 9 **Facilities** Children's menu Dogs allowed Garden Parking

## PEWSEY

### The Seven Stars ♚

**Bottlesford SN9 6LU ☎ 01672 851325 ▤ 01672 851583**
e-mail: info@thesevenstars.co.uk
dir: *Off A345*

This thatched 16th-century free house stands in a splendid seven acre garden. Its front door opens straight onto the low-beamed, oak-panelled bar, now tastefully refurbished. Expect well-kept ales and an extensive menu of home-cooked food. With pheasant and pigeon on the menu when available, typical dishes include roast pork belly; smoked haddock risotto; and mutton shepherd's pie with greens. Finish with rice pudding with Bramley compote and crumble topping, then walk it off with a stroll in the garden.

**Open** noon-3 6-11 Closed: Mon **Bar Meals** food served all day **Restaurant** food served all day ⊕ FREE HOUSE ◀ Wadworth 6X, Brakspear, London Pride, Guest ales ♂ Stowford Press. ♚ 6 **Facilities** Children's menu Dogs allowed Garden Parking

## ROWDE

### The George & Dragon ★★★★ RR ⊛⊛ ♚

**High St SN10 2PN ☎ 01380 723053**
e-mail: thegandd@tiscali.co.uk
dir: *1m from Devizes, take A342 towards Chippenham*

Winter log fires warm the panelled bars and dining room of this 15th-century free house, not far from the Caen Hill lock flight on the Kennet and Avon Canal. Real ales dispensed at the bar are several in number, while wine lovers will have nearly a dozen by the glass to choose from. Rooms are cosy, welcoming and full of character. Bearing witness to the pub's age, a Tudor rose is carved on one of the beams in the restaurant, where tables are replete with crisp white linen and glowing candles. The pub specialises in seafood from Cornwall, so take your pick from the catch of the day chalked up on the blackboard. The list of starters is augmented by half a dozen dishes that can be served either as starters or as main courses, such as Cajun spiced fishcakes with hollandaise, or from the main course selection chargrilled tuna steak with an olive, green bean and soft-boiled egg salad. Home-made puddings may include glazed creamy rice pudding with apple compote.

**Open** Closed: Sun eve **Bar Meals** L served Mon-Sat 12-3, Sun 12-4 booking required D served Mon-Fri 7-10, Sat 6.30-10 booking required Av main course £12.50 **Restaurant** L served Mon-Sat 12-3, Sun 12-4 booking required D served Mon-Fri 7-10, Sat 6.30-10 booking required Fixed menu price fr £15.50 Av 3 course à la carte fr £26.50 ⊕ FREE HOUSE ◀ Butcombe Bitter, Milk Street Brewery Ales, Bath Ales Gem, ESB, London Pride, Ringwood 49er. ♚ 11 **Facilities** Children's menu Dogs allowed Garden Parking **Rooms** 3

## SEMINGTON

### The Lamb on the Strand ♚

**99 The Strand BA14 6LL ☎ 01380 870263 & 870815 ▤ 01380 871203**
e-mail: lamb@eyno.co.uk
dir: *1.5m E on A361 from junct with A350*

An 18th-century farmhouse that later became a beer and cider house. Today's popular dining pub typically offers starters of grilled goats' cheese with spiced beetroot; and grilled fig, chorizo and parmesan salad. Almost sure to be found on the generous list of main courses are sausages, mash and onion gravy; fillet of cod with herb crust, leeks and new potatoes; medallions of venison, parsnip purée, vegetables and Madeira jus; and cheesy pudding, salad and sauté potatoes.

**Open** noon-3 6.30-11 Closed: 25-26 Dec & 1 Jan, Sun eve **Bar Meals** L served all wk 12-2.30 D served Mon-Sat 6.30-9 Av main course £11 **Restaurant** L served all wk 12-2.30 D served Mon-Sat 6.30-9 ⊕ FREE HOUSE ◀ Butcombe Bitter, Ringwood Bitter, Shepherd Neame Spitfire, Guinness ♂ Thatchers. ♚ 12 **Facilities** Children's menu Dogs allowed Garden Parking

## SHERSTON

# The Rattlebone Inn ♟

**Church St SN16 0LR ☎ 01666 840871**
e-mail: eat@therattlebone.co.uk
dir: *M4 junct 17 go N to Malmesbury. 2m N after passing petrol station at Stanton St. Quentin, take rd to left signed Sherston*

Named after the legendary Saxon hero John Rattlebone, this lovely 16th-century pub boasts roaring winter fires and bags of character. A lively drinkers' pub serving real ales and organic cider, the Rattlebone also has a reputation for its country bistro menu. Expect locally sourced ingredients, summer spit roasts, and seasonal game, featuring dishes like venison marinated with port and juniper berries. The pub has two garden areas, two boules pistes and a well-used skittles alley.

Open all wk noon-3 5-11 ( Fri noon-3 5-mdnt Sat noon-mdnt Sun noon-11) Bar Meals L served Mon-Sat 12-3 D served Mon-Sat 6-7.30 Av main course £8 Restaurant L served all wk 12-3 D served Mon-Sat 6-9.30 Fixed menu price fr £10.95 Av 3 course à la carte fr £18 ⊕ YOUNG & CO ◖ Youngs Bitter, Bombardier, St Austell Tribute ♂ Stowford Press, Westons Organic. ♟ 14 Facilities Children's menu Dogs allowed Garden

---

## STOFORD

# The Swan Inn ★★★ INN ♟

**Warminster Rd SP2 0PR ☎ 01722 790236**
📠 01722 444972
e-mail: info@theswanatstoford.co.uk
dir: *From Salisbury take A36 towards Warminster. Stoford on right 4m from Wilton*

The Swan is a landmark coaching inn, close to the cathedral city of Salisbury, with attractive gardens overlooking the River Wylye to meadow and farmland. There is a welcoming log fire, four cask ales and a popular wine and cocktails selection. Traditional home cooked food includes Wiltshire pork sausages with mash and onion gravy, Lancashire hot pot, and oven baked whole sea bass with dill butter sauce.

Open all day all wk 8am-11pm (Sun 9am-10.30pm) Bar Meals Av main course £10 food served all day Restaurant Fixed menu price fr £10 Av 3 course à la carte fr £17 food served all day ⊕ FREE HOUSE ◖ Ringwood Best, Fuller's London Pride, Odyssey Best Bitter, Old Speckled Hen. ♟ 7 Facilities Children's menu Dogs allowed Garden Parking Rooms 9

## UPPER WOODFORD

# The Bridge Inn ♟

**SP4 6NU ☎ 01722 782323**
e-mail: enquiries@thebridgewoodford.co.uk
dir: *5m N of Salisbury, situated in the Woodford Valley, off the A360*

Hidden away beside the Wiltshire Avon just north of Salisbury, this charming pub has been completely refurbished to include a modern, theatre-style kitchen. As well as a riverside garden and winter fires, you'll find flowers and candles on the tables at any time of year. Seasonal menu choices might include braised lamb shank with gruyère mash; or home-made fish cakes with herbed chips, mixed leaves and tartare sauce.

Open all wk 11-3 6-11 (Sun 11-11 summer) Bar Meals L served all wk 12-2.30 D served all wk 6-9 Av main course £13 Restaurant L served all wk 12-2.30 D served all wk 6-9 Av 3 course à la carte fr £24 ⊕ ENTERPRISE INNS ◖ Summer Lightning, Wadworth 6X, Ringwood Best. ♟ 10 Facilities Children's menu Dogs allowed Garden Parking

---

## WARMINSTER

# The Angel Inn ♟

**Upton Scudamore BA12 0AG ☎ 01985 213225**
📠 01985 218182
e-mail: mail@theangelinn.co.uk
dir: *From Warminster take A350 towards Westbury or A36 towards Bath*

The Angel is a restored 16th-century coaching inn located in a village close to Warminster. Access to the pub is via a walled garden and terrace, where meals and drinks can be served in fine weather. Inside, open fires and natural wood flooring create a relaxed atmosphere. Dishes from the lunch menu vary from modern to traditional – you might, for example, find a starter of sesame crusted tuna loin, mango and chilli salsa, with mango purée and wasabi dressing; and a main course of braised lamb shank on a tomato and thyme cassoulet. For dinner the eclectic range of flavours continues in such dishes as confit guinea fowl terrine with an orange vinaigrette and toasted brioche; and roast fillet of pollack on wilted greens, with a mussel, lemongrass and coconut broth. Desserts, including ice creams and sorbets, are freshly made on the premises by the kitchen team.

Open all wk Closed: 25-26 Dec, 1 Jan Bar Meals Av main course £16 Restaurant Av 3 course à la carte fr £25 ⊕ FREE HOUSE ◖ Wadworth 6X, Butcombe, John Smith's Smooth, guest ales. ♟ 8 Facilities Children's menu Garden Parking

England

## WHITLEY

### The Pear Tree Inn ★★★★★ RR 🏵🏵 ☝

Top Ln SN12 8QX ☎ 01225 709131 📄 01225 702276

e-mail: enquries@thepeartreeinn.com

dir: A365 from Melksham towards Bath, at Shaw right onto B3353 into Whitley, 1st left in lane, pub at end

No great stretch of the imagination is required to picture the Pear Tree, surrounded by acres of wooded farmland, as the farmhouse it once was. The agricultural antiques that adorn its interior help to maintain a connection with those very different times, while its laid-back, comfortable feel comes from the flagstone floors, two log fires, and a bar that's open all day. Like other establishments in the Maypole Group, it cares deeply about its real ales and a carefully selected worldwide wine list that features many by the glass. The home-made food on its popular menu of hearty, traditional British dishes has earned generous praise, not least from the AA, which has awarded two Rosettes for the obvious attention paid to the quality and selection of ingredients. Indeed, everything comes from locally based suppliers - nearby farms and growers for the top quality fruit and vegetables - but some things have to come from further afield, such as the lemons from the Amalfi coast that provide the basis for the delicious lemon tart. There is also a healthy children's menu. Food is served throughout the pub, giving customers the option to choose a dining style to suit their mood and dress. Outside, an extensive patio area and a cottage garden make alfresco relaxation particularly agreeable.

Open all day all wk breakfast - 11pm Bar Meals L served all wk 12-2.30 D served all wk 6.30-9.30 Av main course £13.95 Restaurant L served all wk 12-2.30 D served all wk 6.30-9.30 Fixed menu price fr £12 🍺 Wadworth 6X, Sharps Doom Bar, London Pride. ☝ 19 Facilities Children's menu Dogs allowed Garden Parking Rooms 8

## WINTERBOURNE BASSETT

### The White Horse Inn ☝

SN4 9QB ☎ 01793 731257 📄 01793 739030

e-mail: ckstone@btinternet.com

dir: 5m S of Swindon on A4361 (Devizes road)

Lying just two miles north of the mysterious Avebury stone circle, the White Horse is an ideal base for walks on the historic Ridgeway path. Food is served in the bar and conservatory restaurant, as well as in the safe, lawned garden. Budget lunches and snacks are supported by a full menu and daily specials: look out for baked cod topped with tomato, herbs and mozzarella; mushroom Stroganoff; and beef, ale and mushroom pie.

Open all wk 11.30-3 6-11 Bar Meals L served all wk 12-2 D served all wk 6-7.30 Restaurant L served all wk 12-2 D served all wk 6-9.30 ⊕ WADWORTH 🍺 Wadworth 6X, IPA, Hophouse Brews ⍥ Stowford Press. ☝ 20 Facilities Children's menu Garden Parking

# WORCESTERSHIRE

## ABBERLEY

### The Manor Arms at Abberley ★★★ INN ☝

WR6 6BN ☎ 01299 896507 📄 01299 896723

e-mail: themanorarms@btconnect.com

dir: Signed from A443, Abberley B4202 towards Clows Top, right at village hall

Set in the historic village of Abberley overlooking a picturesque valley, this 300-year-old inn has plenty of original features, including oak beams and a log-burning fire. Food options range from bar snacks to a full à la carte menu. Themed evenings include home-made curries on Monday nights and fresh fish and chips on Fridays. Fish and chips are also available to take away on Monday to Saturday evenings.

Open noon-3 6-11.30 (Sat-Sun noon-11.30) Closed: Mon L Bar Meals L served Tue-Sun 12-2.30 booking required D served Mon-Sat 6-9 booking required Av main course £8.95 Restaurant L served Tue-Sun 12-2.30 D served Mon-Sat 6-9 Fixed menu price fr £10 ⊕ ENTERPRISE INNS 🍺 Timothy Taylor, Hooky Bitter, Hereford HPA, Flowers IPA. ☝ 11 Facilities Children's menu Dogs allowed Garden Parking Rooms 10

## BECKFORD

### The Beckford ★★★★ INN 🍷

**Cheltenham Rd GL20 7AN ☎ 01386 881532**
**📠 01386 882021**
e-mail: norman@thebeckford.com
dir: *On A46 (Evesham to Cheltenham road) 5m from M5 junct 9*

Parts of this traditional, family-run coaching inn date back to the 18th century, but extensive refurbishment has made sure things keep up to date without losing their charm. Field Marshall Montgomery was a welcome guest here in the 1960s when his niece was landlord. There's a pleasant bar area with a real fire, an attractive formal dining room and beautiful gardens. Menu choices include grilled seabass fillet in a seafood broth; venison steak on a confit of leeks; and wild mushroom risotto.

**Open** all wk 11-11 (Sat-Sun 11am-11.30pm) Closed: 25 Dec eve & 26 Dec eve **Bar Meals** L served Mon-Fri 12-2.30, Sat-Sun 12-9.40 booking required D served Mon-Fri 6.30-9.40, Sat-Sun 12-9.40 booking required Av main course £13 **Restaurant** L served Mon-Fri 12-2.30, Sat-Sun 12-9.40 booking required D served Mon-Fri 6.30-9.40, Sat-Sun 12-9.40 booking required Fixed menu price fr £10 Av 3 course à la carte fr £13.95 🛢 FREE HOUSE ◀ London Pride, Greene King Abbot, Marstons Pedigree 🍎 Stowford Press. 🍷 8 **Facilities** Children's menu Dogs allowed Garden Parking **Rooms** 10

## BEWDLEY

### Little Pack Horse 🍷

**31 High St DY12 2DH ☎ 01299 403762 📠 01299 403762**
e-mail: enquires@littlepackhorse.co.uk
dir: *From Kidderminster follow ring road & signs for Safari Park. Then follow signs for Bewdley over bridge, turn left, then right, right at top of Lax Lane. Pub in 20mtrs*

The interior of this historic timber-framed inn is warmed by cosy log fires and lit by candles at night. There are low beams, an elm bar, and a small outside patio for alfresco summer dining. The finest, local produce is sourced with an emphasis on seasonality. Expect an impressive range of roasts like Packhorse mix roast using lamb, beef, pork, turkey and slow roasted duck leg.

**Open** all wk noon-2.30 6-11.30 (Sat-Sun noon-mdnt) **Bar Meals** food served all day **Restaurant** food served all day 🛢 PUNCH TAVERNS ◀ Theakstons Best Wye Valley HPA, Dorothy Goodbodies Golden Ale, Black Sheep Bitter, Shepherd Neame Spitfire 🍎 Stowford Press, Westons Organic, Thatchers Katy. 🍷 21 **Facilities** Children's menu Family room Dogs allowed Garden

### Woodcolliers Arms ★★★ INN

**76 Welch Gate DY12 2AU ☎ 01299 400589**
e-mail: roger@woodcolliers.co.uk
dir: *2mins walk from No2 bus stop in Load Street, Bewdley. 3m from Kidderminster*

Dating from before 1780, this family-run free house is close to the centre of Bewdley and just across the river from the Severn Valley steam railway. Russian trained chef Boris Rumba serves a unique blend of freshly-prepared pub favourites and authentic Russian dishes. The regularly changing menu might offer mustard and herb crusted rack of lamb; steak and ale pie; Boyarsky salmon; or Sidrovka (loin of pork in cider and onion sauce). In winter try a bowl of Borsch or Imperial soup.

**Open** all wk 5-12.30 (Sat 12.30pm-12.30am Sun 12.30-11) **Bar Meals** L served Sat-Sun 12.30-3 D served all wk 6-9 booking required Av main course £8.95 **Restaurant** L served Sat-Sun 12.30-3 booking required D served all wk 6-9 booking required Fixed menu price fr £8.95 Av 3 course à la carte fr £15 🛢 OLIVERS INNS LTD ◀ Ludlow Gold, Hobsons Bitter, St George Friar Tuck 🍎 Thatchers Gold. **Facilities** Children's menu Dogs allowed Garden Parking **Rooms** 5

## CLOWS TOP

### The Colliers Arms 🍷

**Tenbury Rd DY14 9HA ☎ 01299 832242**
e-mail: thecolliersarms@aol.com
dir: *On A456.11 Pub 4m from Bewdley & 7m from Kidderminster*

This is a popular, family-owned, traditional country free house with a bar, lounge area and separate restaurant. From the outside patio and beer garden you can enjoy the views of the largest Norman church in England. The Colliers Arms has earned an excellent reputation for the quality of its freshly prepared, home-made food. At least half the ingredients used in cooking are sourced locally, a proportion that will increase with the pub's addition of a hugely productive vegetable, herb and fruit garden. On the lunch menu are beef Stroganoff with wild rice; and pork, apple and Shropshire Blue pie, while at dinner you might wish to order lamb cutlets with croquette potatoes and rosemary reduction; battered cod with coarse pea purée and home-made chips; papillote of gilthead bream with orange and fennel; and potato, spinach and cauliflower ragout.

**Open** noon-3 6-11 (Sat 11-11 Sun noon-4) Closed: Sun eve **Bar Meals** L served Mon-Fri 12-2, Sat 12-2.30, Sun 12-3 booking required D served Mon-Fri 6.30-9, Sat 6.30-9.30 booking required Av main course £10.95 **Restaurant** L served Mon-Fri 12-2, Sat 12-2.30, Sun 12-3 booking required D served Mon-Fri 6.30-9, Sat 6.30-9.30 booking required Fixed menu price fr £10.50 Av 3 course à la carte fr £20 🛢 FREE HOUSE ◀ Hobsons Best, Town Crier, Guinness, guest ale. 🍷 14 **Facilities** Children's menu Dogs allowed Garden Parking

## DROITWICH

### The Chequers ♥

**Cutnall Green WR9 0PJ ☎ 01299 851292**
📄 **01299 851744**
dir: *Telephone for directions*

A display of football memorabilia on the bar wall reveals that this is the home of Roger Narbett, chef to the England football team. He runs the Chequers with his wife Joanne, retaining its charming and traditional village pub atmosphere with open fire, panelled bar and richly coloured furnishings. Next to the bar is the Garden Room with warmly painted walls, a plush sofa and hanging tankards. Lunchtime sandwiches and toasted paninis are backed by classics such as Scotch beef steak pie with neeps, mash and onion gravy; and slow braised lamb with herb dumplings and root vegetables. The carte includes starters of carrot, sweet potato and red lentil soup with garlic toasty. Typical main courses may proffer breast of pot roast Jimmy Butler's belly of pork, while desserts like treacle tart with granny's thick custard should not be missed.

Open all wk Closed: 25 Dec, 1 Jan **Bar Meals** L served Mon-Sat 12-2, Sun 12-2.30 D served Mon-Sun 6.30-9.15 Av main course £10.75 **Restaurant** L served Mon-Sat 12-2, Sun 12-2.30 booking required D served Mon-Sun 6.30-9.15 booking required Fixed menu price fr £11.50 Av 3 course à la carte fr £18.50 ⊕ ENTERPRISE INNS ◀ Timothy Taylor, Enville Ale, Banks Bitter, Banks Mild, Hook Norton, Ruddles. ♥ 11 **Facilities** Children's menu Family room Dogs allowed Garden Parking

### The Honey Bee ♥

**Doverdale Ln, Doverdale WR9 0QB ☎ 01299 851620**
e-mail: honey@king-henrys-taverns.co.uk
dir: *Please telephone for directions*

'It's buzzin' at The Honey Bee but you won't get stung!' So say King Henry's Taverns, which owns this beekeeping-themed pub, with working beehives and a children's area containing an enormous beehive plaything. All the group's establishments offer a standard menu that covers most pub grub eventualities - steak and ale pie; whole roast chicken; pan-fried fillets of plaice; rump, fillet and rib steaks; lamb rogan josh; vegetarian balti; and broccoli and cream cheese bake.

Open all day all wk noon-10 **Bar Meals** Av main course £3 food served all day **Restaurant** food served all day ⊕ KING HENRY TAVERNS ◀ Guinness, Greene King IPA, Marstons Pedigree. ♥ 15 **Facilities** Children's menu Play area Family room Garden Parking

## FLADBURY

### Chequers Inn

**Chequers Ln WR10 2PZ ☎ 01386 860276**
e-mail: chequersinn@btinternet.com
dir: *Off A4538 between Evesham & Pershore*

The Chequers is a 14th-century inn with plenty of beams and an open fire, tucked away in a pretty village with views of the glorious Bredon Hills. Local produce from the Vale of Evesham provides the basis for home-cooked dishes offered from the monthly-changing menu, plus a choice of daily specials. There is also a traditional Sunday carvery. The pretty walled garden enjoys outstanding views, and the nearby River Avon is ideal for walking.

Open all wk 11.30-2.30 6-11 (Sun 11.30-3.30) **Bar Meals** L served all wk 12-2 D served Mon-Sat 6-9 ⊕ Enterprise Inns ◀ Purity, Bombardier Real Ales. **Facilities** Children's menu Garden Parking

## FLYFORD FLAVELL

### The Boot Inn ★★★★ INN ♥

**Radford Rd WR7 4BS ☎ 01386 462658 📄 01386 462547**
e-mail: enquiries@thebootinn.com
web: www.thebootinn.com
dir: *From Worcester take A422 towards Stratford. Turn right to village*

Parts of this family-run coaching inn date back to the 13th century, as heavy beams and slanting doorways attest. The large bar area is comfortable, with pool table and TV in a separate room. Good food is served by friendly staff, and may include mains like minted lamb and spinach curry or grilled swordfish steak with pink peppercorn sauce. Outside are gardens front and back, with a heated patio and sheltered smoking area.

Open all wk noon-mdnt (25 Dec noon-2) **Bar Meals** L served all wk 12-2 D served all wk 6.30-10 **Restaurant** L served all wk 12-2 D served all wk 6.30-10 ⊕ PUNCH TAVERNS ◀ Old Speckled Hen, London Pride, John Smith's Tribute. ♥ 8 **Facilities** Children's menu Dogs allowed Garden Parking **Rooms** 5

## KNIGHTWICK

## The Talbot 🍷

**WR6 5PH ☎ 01886 821235** 📠 **01886 821060**
e-mail: admin@the-talbot.co.uk
dir: *A44 (Leominster road) through Worcester, 8m W right onto B4197 at River Teme bridge*

The late 14th-century coaching inn has been owned by the Clift family for over 25 years and is run by Annie Clift and her team. Over the years they have developed their own style and are firmly rooted in the traditions and produce of the Teme Valley. Nearly everything is made in house, including bread, preserves, black pudding, raised pies and so on. The inn has a large kitchen garden run on organic principles, which produces a wide range of salads, herbs and, of course, vegetables. Sausages, hams, bacon and cheeses are sourced from local suppliers. The Talbot is the home of The Teme Valley Brewery, which uses hops grown in the parish. The cask conditioned ales are called This, That, T'Other and Wot. Wot is a seasonal brew, so there is Spring Wot, Wassail Wot, and Wotever Next.

**Open** all day all wk 7.30am-11.30pm Closed: 25 Dec pm **Bar Meals** L served all wk 12-2 D served all wk 6.30-9 Av main course £16 **Restaurant** D served all wk 6.30-9 booking required Fixed menu price fr £27 Av 3 course à la carte fr £38 ⊕ FREE HOUSE ◾ Teme Valley This, That , T'Other & Wot, Hobsons Best Bitter Choice. 🍷 9 **Facilities** Children's menu Dogs allowed Garden Parking

## MALVERN

## The Anchor Inn 🍷

**Drake St, Welland WR13 6LN ☎ 01684 592317**
e-mail: theanchor13@hotmail.com
dir: *M50 junct 1, A38 follow signs for Upton upon Severn. Left onto A4104, through Upton upon Severn, 2.5m. Pub on right*

The attractive 17th-century Anchor Inn has spectacular views of the Malvern Hills. There's a garden for warmer weather and a welcoming winter fire in the dining room. Fresh, quality food is cooked to order. Light bites and main meals are marked up on the chalkboard, with dishes such as pork loin stuffed with apple in stilton sauce, steak and kidney pie, and shank of lamb simmered in mint and rosemary gravy.

**Open** Closed: Sun eve **Bar Meals** L served all wk 12-2 D served Mon-Sat 7-9 booking required Av main course £9.99 **Restaurant** L served all wk 12-2 D served Mon-Sat 7-9 booking required ⊕ FREE HOUSE ◾ Black Sheep, Woods, Hook Norton,

Greene King, Malvern Hills. 🍷 20 **Facilities** Children's menu Family room Garden Parking

## MARTLEY

## Admiral Rodney Inn ★★★★ INN

**Berrow Green WR6 6PL ☎ 01886 821375**
e-mail: rodney@admiral.fslife.co.uk
web: www.admiral-rodney.co.uk
dir: *M5 junct 7, A44 signed Leominster. Approx 7m at Knightwick right onto B4197. Inn 2m on left at Berrow Green*

This early 17th-century farmhouse-cum-alehouse stands in the heart of the countryside on the Worcester Way footpath. The stylishly traditional interior includes a split-level restaurant housed in an old barn. Herefordshire steaks feature strongly, along with dishes like lamb shank with mustard mash, home-made pies, fish and chips, and a choice of vegetarian fare. A skittle alley is also available.

**Open** all wk noon-3 5-11 (Mon 5-11 Sat noon-11 Sun noon-10.30) **Bar Meals** L served Tue-Sat 12.30-2.30, Sun 12-4 D served all wk 6.30-9 Av main course £10 **Restaurant** L served Tue-Sat 12.30-2.30, Sun 12-4 D served all wk 6.30-9 Fixed menu price fr £7.95 ⊕ FREE HOUSE ◾ Wye Valley Bitter, local guest ales eg Black Pear, Malvern Hills Brewery, Muzzle Loader, Cannon Royal. **Facilities** Children's menu Dogs allowed Garden Parking Rooms 3

## The Crown Inn

**Berrow Green Rd WR6 6PA ☎ 01886 888840**
dir: *7m W of Worcester on B4204*

Once the scene of an unlikely gig by Eric Clapton, the Crown is a Victorian village pub with a large extension formed from redundant outbuildings, which now houses the dining area. In one bar is an open fire, Sky TV, pool table and jukebox, while the other has dining tables and French windows to the garden. This community pub is on the Worcester Way, so many visitors tend to be walkers. Locally sourced, freshly cooked food includes 10oz Kobe beefburger; lamb and mint sausages; Thai fish curry; and penne pasta with creamy goats' cheese sauce.

**Open** all wk noon-11 (Fri-Sat noon-mdnt Sun noon-10.30) **Bar Meals** L served Mon-Sat 12-2, Sun 12-3 D served Mon-Sat 6-9 Av main course £8.50 **Restaurant** L served Mon-Sat 12-2, Sun 12-3 D served Mon-Sat 6-9 Av 3 course à la carte fr £17.65 ⊕ MARSTONS ◾ Banks Bitter, Banks Mild. **Facilities** Children's menu Play area Dogs allowed Garden Parking

## OMBERSLEY

### Crown & Sandys Arms �

**Main Rd WR9 0EW ☎ 01905 620252** 📄 **01905 620769**
e-mail: enquiries@crownandsandys.co.uk
dir: *3m from Droitwich, off A449, 6m off junct 6 & junct 5 of M5*

After being closed for nearly a year for refurbishment, this classy establishment run by Richard and Rachael Everton reopened its doors in May 2009. The decor is bang up-to-date, yet the original beams and fireplaces seem to blend effortlessly with the trendy furnishings. Expect the same focus on well-kept real ales, a smoothly managed food operation and excellent service. Regular 'wine dinners' and themed evenings continue, complementing modern menus which burst with the latest flavours. The full carte is backed by a weekly specials list, and customers can choose between three dining areas: the Orangery, the Bistro and the Bar. Starters may include potted salmon and crab with hot toasted crumpets. Main dishes offer favourites like fish and home-cut chips; steak and kidney pudding; and steaks of best Scottish beef. Try a desserts such as lemon, sultana and treacle steamed sponge with custard.

**Open** all wk noon-3 5-11 (ex BH) **Bar Meals** L served all wk 12-2.30 D served all wk 6-9.30 booking required Av main course £10 **Restaurant** L served all wk 12-2.30 booking required D served all wk 6-9.30 booking required Av 3 course à la carte fr £20 ⊕ FREE HOUSE ◀ Sadlers Ale, Marstons, Woods Shropshire Lad, Burtons Bitter, Marstons Pedigree, Greene King IPA Ò Thatchers, Aspall. ♟ 16 **Facilities** Children's menu Garden Parking

## TENBURY WELLS

### The Peacock Inn

**WR15 8LL ☎ 01584 810506**
e-mail: info@the-peacock-at-boraston.co.uk
dir: *On A456 (Kidderminster to Tenbury Wells)*

A 14th-century coaching inn with a sympathetic extension overlooking the River Teme. A patio eating area means you can relax outside and enjoy the views in summer. The inviting bars and oak-panelled restaurant are enhanced by oak beams, dried hops and open log fires, while upstairs the ghost of Mrs Brown, a former landlady, does her best to make her presence felt. Produce from local markets and specialist suppliers is used for the menus, which cover an eclectic mix of reasonably priced dishes. The bar menu ranges from a three-egg omelette with choice of fillings and served with chips; to chilli con carne; or rendang pedis - a home-made Indonesian beef curry made to a family recipe. Other main courses tend towards the more usual: spicy meatballs; wholetail scampi; creamy pasta bake; and barbecued chicken fillet are among the choices.

**Open** noon-3 6-11 Closed: Sun eve **Bar Meals** L served all wk 12-2.30 D served Mon-Sat 6.30-8.30 **Restaurant** L served all wk 12-2.30 booking required D served Mon-Sat 7-8.30 booking required ⊕ PUNCH TAVERNS ◀ Hobsons Best Bitter, Spitfire, guest ale Ò Stowford Press, Westons Organic. **Facilities** Children's menu Dogs allowed Garden Parking

## EAST RIDING OF YORKSHIRE

### HOLME UPON SPALDING MOOR

### Ye Olde Red Lion Hotel ♟

**Old Rd YO43 4AD ☎ 01430 860220** 📄 **01430 861471**
dir: *Off A1079 (York to Hull road). At Market Weighton take A614. Right at painted rdbt in village centre, 100yds, right then 1st left*

A historic 17th-century coaching inn that once provided hospitality for weary travellers who were helped across the marshes by monks. It's still a great refuge, with a friendly atmosphere, oak beams and a cosy fire. The inspiring menu could include oven-baked duck breast with star anise sauce, corn fed chicken coq-au-vin or pan-seared sea bass with wilted greens and vièrge sauce.

**Open** 11-3 5-11 (Mon 5-11) Closed: Mon until 5pm **Bar Meals** L served Tue-Sun 12-2 D served Tue-Sun 5.30-9 ⊕ Enterprise Inns ◀ John Smiths, Black Sheep, Guinness. ♟ 9 **Facilities** Children's menu Garden Parking

### HUGGATE

### The Wolds Inn ★★★ INN ♟

**YO42 1YH ☎ 01377 288217**
e-mail: huggate@woldsinn.freeserve.co.uk
dir: *S off A166 between York & Driffield*

Probably the highest inn on the Yorkshire Wolds, this family-run hostelry is 16th century in origin, with tiled roofs and white-painted chimneys, and a wood-panelled interior with open fires and gleaming brassware. The robust menu includes dishes such as steak pie, fillet of plaice, chicken breast wrapped in bacon, grills, or a selection of jackets, baguettes and sandwiches. For a "mixed grill to remember", try the Wolds Topper.

**Open** noon-2 6.30-11 (Fri-Sat 5-11 Sun 5-10.30) Closed: Mon (ex BH) **Bar Meals** L served Tue-Sun 12-2 D served Tue-Thu 6.30-9, Fri-Sun 5-9 booking required Av main course £8 **Restaurant** L served Sun 12-2 booking required D served Tue-Thu 6.30-9, Fri-Sun 5-9 booking required Av 3 course à la carte fr £18 ⊕ FREE HOUSE ◀ Tetley Bitter, Timothy Taylor Landlord. ♟ 10 **Facilities** Children's menu Garden Parking **Rooms** 3

### KILHAM

### The Old Star Inn ♟

**Church St YO25 4RG ☎ 01262 420619**
e-mail: oldstarkilham@hotmail.com
dir: *Between Driffield & Bridlington on A164. 6m from Driffield. 9m from Bridlington*

Situated in the historic village of Kilham, with easy access to Bridlington, Scarborough and the Yorkshire Wolds, this quaint pub offers home-cooked food, a good selection of real ales and a warm welcome. Food is sourced from local suppliers, with particular attention to reducing the travelling time of ingredients. Special diets are catered for, and children have half price portions.

Smiths, regular guest, Copper Dragon. 🍷 8 **Facilities** Children's menu Garden Parking

---

SOUTH DALTON

## The Pipe & Glass Inn 🏵🏵 🍷

**West End HU17 7PN ☎ 01430 810246**
e-mail: email@pipeandglass.co.uk
web: www.pipeandglass.co.uk
dir: *Just off B1248 (Beverley to Malton road). 7m from Beverley*

**Open** all wk 5-11 (Mon 6-11 Fri noon-2 4-11 Sat noon-2.30 5.30-11 Sun noon-10.30) Closed: Mon-Thu L **Bar Meals** L served Fri-Sat 12-2, Sun 12-5 D served Tue-Fri 5-8.30, Sat 5.30-8.30 Av main course £8 **Restaurant** L served Sun 12-5 booking required booking required Av 3 course à la carte fr £20 ∰ FREE HOUSE ◀ John Smiths Cask, Deuchars, Theakstons, Black Sheep, Daleside, guest ales. 🍷 7 **Facilities** Children's menu Dogs allowed Garden Parking

---

## LOW CATTON

# The Gold Cup Inn 🍷

**YO41 1EA ☎ 01759 371354**
dir: *1m S of A166 or 1m N of A1079, E of York*

Solid tables and pews - reputedly made from a single oak tree - feature in the restaurant of this 300-year-old, family-run free house. There's a large beer garden, and the adjoining paddock drops down to the River Derwent. On the menu expect to find braised beef in red wine gravy on mashed potato; grilled gammon with port and mushroom sauce; baked cod loins with herb crust; and deep-fried brie with cranberry and orange dip.

**Open** noon-2.30 6-11 (Sat-Sun noon-11) Closed: Mon L **Bar Meals** L served Tue-Fri 12-2.30, Sat-Sun 12-6 D served all wk 6-9 Av main course £8.25 **Restaurant** L served Sun 12-5.30 booking required D served all wk 6-9 booking required Fixed menu price fr £12.5 Av 3 course à la carte fr £20 ∰ FREE HOUSE ◀ John Smiths, Theakstons. 🍷 15 **Facilities** Children's menu Play area Dogs allowed Garden Parking

---

## LUND

# The Wellington Inn 🍷

**19 The Green YO25 9TE ☎ 01377 217294**
🖺 01377 217192
dir: *On B1248 NE of Beverley*

Situated opposite the picture-postcard village green, the Wellington Inn is popular with locals and visitors alike. You can choose to eat from the bar menu or à la carte, and there's an extensive wine list. Expect king scallops with bacon and garlic risotto; or perhaps beef, mushroom and red onion suet pudding.

**Open** Closed: Mon L **Bar Meals** L served Tue-Sun 12-2 D served Tue-Sat 6.30-9 Av main course £13.95 **Restaurant** D served Tue-Sat 7-9 booking required Av 3 course à la carte fr £26 ∰ FREE HOUSE ◀ Timothy Taylor Landlord, Black Sheep Best, John

The present building, part 15th century, part 17th, stands on the site of the original gatehouse to Dalton Hall, the family seat of Lord Hotham. It was where visitors to the 'great house' stayed. When James and Kate Mackenzie took over in 2006, they undertook a full refurbishment, making sure they kept a country pub feel in the bar, while giving the restaurant a more contemporary look. A large conservatory looking out over the garden houses a magnificent long table seating twenty-four, and there is also plenty more room for dining in the garden. James uses as much local and seasonal produce as possible for his regularly changing menus, from which come starters of oak-smoked salmon with smoked eel, potato and horseradish salad; and potted spiced Gloucester Old Spot pork with sticky apples and crackling salad. Mains include roast Burdass lamb (from the Yorkshire Wolds) with braised mutton and kidney faggot, champ potato, broad beans and nettle and mint sauce; grilled sirloin steak with sautéed sea salt and thyme potatoes, green peppercorn sauce, ox tongue and shallot salad; fillet of Filey Bay sea bass with braised gem lettuce, ceps and oyster sauce; and baked Yorkshire field mushroom and spinach tart with 'Lincolnshire poacher' rarebit, poached egg and hazelnut pesto. Desserts are equally tempting, with lemon verbena burnt cream and spiced summer berries; sticky toffee pudding with stout ice cream and walnut praline; and fresh strawberries, syllabub and sorbet with elderflower shortbread. The wines are sourced entirely from small producers, so there's an interesting story behind every one.

**Open** noon-3 6.30-11 (Sun noon-10.30) Closed: 1wk Jan, Mon (ex BH) **Bar Meals** L served Tue-Sat 12-2, Sun 12-4 D served Tue-Sat 6.30-9.30 Av main course £14.95 **Restaurant** L served Tue-Sat 12-2, Sun 12-4 booking required D served Tue-Sat 6.30-9.30 booking required Av 3 course à la carte fr £29 ∰ FREE HOUSE ◀ Wold Top, Copper Dragon, Black Sheep, Cropton, John Smiths ♂ Old Rosie. 🍷 10 **Facilities** Children's menu Garden Parking

England

## NORTH YORKSHIRE

### AKEBAR

## The Friar's Head ☂

**Akebar Park DL8 5LY** ☎ **01677 450201 & 450591**
🖹 **01677 450046**
e-mail: info@akebarpark.com
dir: *From A1 at Leeming Bar onto A684, 7m towards Leyburn. Entrance at Akebar Park*

A typical stone-built Dales pub at the entrance to a stunning, peaceful holiday park, The Friar's Head overlooks beautiful countryside and grounds, where bowls or croquet can be played on the lawn. The large south-facing conservatory dining room called The Cloister is a stunning feature, particularly by candlelight, with its stone flags, lush planting and fruiting vines. Hand-pulled local ales are served, and typical dishes include beef and mushrooms in Dijon mustard cream sauce, and halibut steak with white wine cream sauce.

**Open** all wk 10-3 6-11.30 (Fri-Sun 10am-11.30pm Jul-Sep) Closed: 25 Dec, 26 Dec eve & 1 Jan **Bar Meals** L served all wk 12-2.30 D served all wk 6-9.30 **Restaurant** L served all wk 12-2.30 booking required D served all wk 6-9.30 booking required ⊕ FREE HOUSE ◧ John Smiths & Theakston Best Bitter, Black Sheep Best, Timothy Taylor Landlord. ☂ 14 **Facilities** Children's menu Garden Parking

### APPLETON-LE-MOORS

## The Moors Inn

**YO62 6TF** ☎ **01751 417435**
e-mail: enquiries@moorsinn.co.uk
dir: *On A170 between Pickering & Kirbymoorside*

Whether you're interested in walking or sightseeing by car, this family-run inn is a good choice for its location and good home-cooked food. Set in a small moors village with lovely scenery in every direction, in summer you can sit in the large garden and enjoy the splendid views. Dishes include pheasant casserole and fish pie, and in addition to hand-pumped Black Bull and Black Sheep, there is a selection of 50 malt whiskies.

**Open** 7-close (Sun noon-2 7-close) Closed: Mon **Bar Meals** L served Sun 12-2 booking required D served Tue-Sun 7-9 booking required **Restaurant** L served Sun 12-2 booking required D served Tue-Sun 7-9 booking required ⊕ FREE HOUSE ◧ Black Sheep, Black Bull ♂ Stowford Press. **Facilities** Children's menu Dogs allowed Garden Parking ♨

### APPLETREEWICK

## The Craven Arms ☂

**BD23 6DA** ☎ **01756 720270**
e-mail: thecravenarms@ukonline.co.uk
dir: *From Skipton take A59 towards Harrogate, B6160 N. Village signed on right. Pub just outside village*

This 16th-century Dales pub, with spectacular views of the River Wharfe and Simon's Seat, was originally a farm and later used as a weaving shed and courthouse. The village stocks are still outside. The building retains its original beams, flagstone floors and magnificent fireplace. Ten cask beers are served all year round, and the menu changes frequently. A cruck barn to the rear serves as restaurant and function room.

**Open** all day all wk **Bar Meals** L served all wk 12-2.30 D served all wk 6.30-8.30 Av main course £12 **Restaurant** L served all wk 12-2.30 D served all wk 6.30-8.30 ⊕ FREE HOUSE ◧ Timothy Taylor, Golden Best, Hetton Pale Ale, Wold Top Bitter. ☂ 8 **Facilities** Children's menu Dogs allowed Garden Parking

### ASENBY

## Crab & Lobster ◉◉ ☂

**Dishforth Rd YO7 3QL** ☎ **01845 577286**
🖹 **01845 577109**
e-mail: reservations@crabandlobster.co.uk
web: www.crabandlobster.co.uk
dir: *From A1(M) take A168 towards Thirsk, follow signs for Asenby*

Amid seven acres of garden, lake and streams stands this unique 17th-century thatched pub and adjacent small hotel. It is an Aladdin's cave of antiques and artefacts from around the world. Equally famous for its innovative cuisine and special gourmet extravaganzas, the menus show influences from France and Italy, with occasional oriental spices too. Starters leave no doubt you are in seafood heaven: crispy fishcakes of local codling and oak-smoked salmon, with creamed greens and poached hen's egg; a classic prawn cocktail with lobster and langoustine; and steamed Shetland mussels. The theme continues into main courses with the likes of lobster, scallop and prawn thermidor; and crab-crusted Wester Ross salmon. For those who prefer meat, the range of locally-sourced ingredients will not disappoint: prime Yorkshire fillet steak; herb-crusted loin of lamb; and roasted loin of venison are typical offerings.

**Open** all wk 11-11 **Bar Meals** L served all wk 12-2.30 D served Sun- Mon 7-9, Sat 6.30-9.30 Av main course £15 **Restaurant** Fixed menu price fr £16 Av 3 course à la carte fr £35 ⊕ FREE HOUSE ◀ John Smiths, Scots 1816, Golden Pippin, Guinness. ⬥ 16 **Facilities** Children's menu Garden Parking

## BAGBY

### The Roebuck Inn ⬥

**Main St YO7 2PF ☎ 01845 597315**
e-mail: info@roebuckinn.bagby.co.uk
dir: *2m SE of Thirsk. Easily accessed from A19 & A170. Follow signs for Bagby, Balk & Kilburn*

Owners Nicholas Stanley and Paul Taylor have recently refurbished this 18th century whitewashed free house. Yorkshire flavours predominate here, as Chef Helen Green relies on local suppliers to create dishes such as ocean medley pancakes with Yorkshire Blue sauce; and pork belly with apricot and cider sauce. As you'd expect, the Sunday roast beef comes with Yorkshire pudding as standard!

**Open** noon-2.30 6-11 (Fri-Sat noon-2.30 6-mdnt Sun noon-10.30) Closed: 25 Dec, Mon L **Bar Meals** L served Tue-Sat 12-2.30, Sun 12-4.30 D served Tue-Sat 6-9, Sun 5-8 **Restaurant** L served Tue-Sat 12-2.30, Sun 12-4.30 booking required D served Tue-Sat 6-9, Sun 5-8 booking required ⊕ FREE HOUSE ◀ John Smiths Cask, Black Sheep Best, guest ales. ⬥ 7 **Facilities** Children's menu Garden Parking

## BOROUGHBRIDGE

### The Black Bull Inn ⬥

**6 St James Square YO51 9AR ☎ 01423 322413**
🖷 01423 323915
web: www.blackbullboroughbridge.co.uk
dir: *From A1(M) junct 48 take B6265 E for 1m*

Standing in a quiet corner of the market square, the Black Bull was one of the main watering holes for travellers on the long road between London and the north of England. Today you have to turn off the A1(M), but it's worth it to discover an inn built in 1258 that retains its ancient beams, low ceilings and roaring open fires, not to mention one that also gives houseroom to the supposed ghosts of a monk, a blacksmith and a small boy. Tony is the landlord, the man responsible for setting and maintaining the high standards you'll enjoy at this popular place. Traditional pub fare is the order of the day, with

a menu listing 10oz fillet steak in creamy whisky sauce with wild mushroom and smoked bacon lardons; chicken breast wrapped in Parma ham with pan-fried wild mushrooms in port and garlic sauce; and salmon steak on a bed of fried noodles with spicy oriental sauce. On the Sizzlers menu are Mexican spiced vegetables in a hot sweet salsa sauce; and pan-fried duck breast topped with water chestnuts, peppers, mushrooms and bamboo shoots, with a sweet and sour sauce. Frequently changing blackboard specials widen the choice even more. What could possibly follow but chocolate fudge cake and cream; baked jam sponge with hot custard sauce; or mixed ice creams, brandy snaps and fruit purées.

**Open** all day all wk 11-11 (Fri-Sat 11am-mdnt, Sun noon-11) **Bar Meals** L served all wk 12-2 D served all wk 6-9 Av main course £7.50 food served all day **Restaurant** L served all wk 12-2 booking required D served all wk 6-9 booking required Av 3 course à la carte fr £18.65 ⊕ FREE HOUSE ◀ Black Sheep, John Smiths, Timothy Taylor Best Bitter, Cottage Brewing, Wells Bombardier Premium Bitter, guest. ⬥ 10 **Facilities** Children's menu Dogs allowed Parking

## BREARTON

### Malt Shovel Inn ⬥

**HG3 3BX ☎ 01423 862929**
e-mail: bleikers@themaltshovelbrearton.co.uk
dir: *From A61 (Ripon/Harrogate) onto B6165 towards Knaresborough. Left & follow Brearton signs. In 1m right into village*

The Bleiker family took over this 16th-century beamed free house in 2006, having previously run the Old Deanery in Ripon and established the hugely successful Bleiker's Smokehouse. Swiss-born Jurg's fine cooking specialises in fresh fish, classic sauces and well-sourced local produce. He and his wife Jane draw on their wealth of experience in food, hospitality and entertainment to create an ambience that combines elegance and theatricality. Their son and daughter-in-law are international opera soloists, and the pub's 'Dinner with Opera' evenings are a unique and thrilling part of life at the Malt Shovel. However it's their commitment to great food and wine, impeccable service and the warmest of welcomes that brings customers back again and again. Lunch from the popular new bistro menu, which features dishes like oxtail and kidney pudding; calves' liver and bacon; and fresh fish cakes may suffice for some. Others may plump for the authentic Thai dishes served in the conservatory on Wednesday to Saturday evenings: the choices include salt and chilli squid with sweet

continued

chilli sauce; and fresh crab and mango on fine herb salad. There are also lunchtime and evening cartes, when Jurg's sophisticated cooking techniques are given full rein: Dover sole meunière, for instance, or rösti with Gruyère cheese and green salad. With its open winter fires, flagstoned floors and pianos, the Malt Shovel exudes both atmosphere and character. The rural setting has some good examples of ancient strip farming, and although the pub is surrounded by rolling farmland, it's just fifteen minutes from Harrogate and within easy reach of both Knaresborough and Ripon.

**Open** Closed: Mon-Tue, Sun eve **Bar Meals** L served Wed-Sat 12-2, Sun 12-3 booking required D served Wed-Sat 6-9 booking required Av main course £12.95 **Restaurant** L served Wed-Sat 12-2, Sun 12-3 booking required D served Wed-Sat 6-9 booking required Av 3 course à la carte fr £30 ⊕ FREE HOUSE ◀ Black Sheep Best, Timothy Taylor Landlord, guest beer. ♀ 21 **Facilities** Children's menu Garden Parking

## BROMPTON-BY-SAWDON

### The Cayley Arms ♀

**YO13 9DA ☎ 01723 859372**
e-mail: joannabou@hotmail.co.uk
dir: *Situated on the A170 in Brompton-by-Sawdon between Pickering and Scarborough*

Standing in the heart of picturesque Brompton-by-Sawdon, the pub is named after pioneering aviator Sir George Cayley. Its cosy log fire and friendly atmosphere has been the centre of village life for over a century, and is well-known to travellers between Pickering and Scarborough. Chunky lunchtime sandwiches with home-made crisps and hot baguettes are supplemented by hot dishes like Yorkshire pudding and boozey beef. In the evening expect spinach and ricotta tortellini; fisherman's pie with potato topping; or oven-baked chicken with leek and blue cheese sauce.

**Open** noon-3 5-close (Mon 6-close) Closed: Mon L **Bar Meals** L served Tue-Sun 12-2 D served Mon-Sat 6-9 **Restaurant** L served Tue-Sat 12-2 D served Mon-Sat 6-9 ⊕ PUNCH TAVERNS ◀ Tetley Cask, Black Sheep Cask. ♀ 20 **Facilities** Children's menu Play area Dogs allowed Garden Parking

## BROUGHTON

### The Bull ♀

**BD23 3AE ☎ 01756 792065**
e-mail: enquiries@thebullatbroughton.com
web: www.thebullatbroughton.com
dir: *3m from Skipton on A59*

Like the village itself, the pub is part of the 3,000-acre Broughton Hall estate, owned by the Tempest family for 900 years. Named after the estate's famous herd of shorthorns, it is now part of Ribble Valley Inns, whose philosophy is to obtain the finest local ingredients for traditional fare with modern twists, the finest local ales and a great atmosphere. The locally brewed ales are backed by a dozen wines served by the glass. Head chef Neil Butterworth has been working with acclaimed chef Nigel Haworth to create a unique Yorkshire menu. Summer offers alfresco dining on the craggy terraces and there are welcoming log fires in winter.

**Open** all wk Mon-Sat noon-11pm, Sun noon-10.30pm **Bar Meals** Av main course £15 **Restaurant** L served Mon-Sat noon-2, Sun noon-8.30 booking required D served Mon-Fri 6-9, Sat 5.30-9, Sun noon-8.30 booking required ⊕ FREE HOUSE ◀ Timothy Taylor, Copper Dragon, Saltaire Raspberry Blonde. ♀ 12 **Facilities** Children's menu Dogs allowed Garden Parking

## BYLAND ABBEY

### Abbey Inn ★★★★★ RR ◉ ♀

**YO61 4BD ☎ 01347 868204 📄 01347 868678**
e-mail: abbeyinn@english-heritage.org.uk
web: www.bylandabbeyinn.com
dir: *From A19 Thirsk/York follow signs to Byland Abbey/Coxwold*

The ivy-clad Abbey Inn was built as a farmhouse in 1845 by Fr Alban Molyneux and a team of monks, using 'borrowed' stones from the ruined Cistercian monastery just across the road. In its day, Byland Abbey was probably Europe's largest ecclesiastical building; but, thanks to Henry VIII, it is now just a beautiful ruin in the shadow of the Hambleton Hills. Perhaps unconsciously, Fr Molyneux chose an appropriate location for his building – for the medieval abbey guesthouse where monks once entertained King Edward II was recently discovered beneath the foundations of the inn. Be sure to reserve a table well in advance, as Sunday lunch is often booked up to four weeks ahead. Two dining rooms at the front overlook the abbey itself; a third, known as the Piggery, stands on the site of the original back yard. The award-winning gastro-pub uses only fresh seasonal Yorkshire produce, and the daily-changing menu might offer starters and light bites such as organic parsnip and honey soup; Gloucester Old Spot and chestnut sausages with creamed mash; or potted brown shrimps in blade mace butter with lemon and home-made granary bread. Main course dishes include braised wild rabbit in red wine with creamed mash and wilted curly kale; crispy feta and spinach pastries with tomato and chickpeas; and pan-fried black bream with potato tartiflette, clams and samphire. Leave room for dessert: Yorkshire Parkin with black treacle ice cream is a typical choice. Children are offered the same healthy food but in half-size portions, whilst early evening diners may choose a three-course set menu.

Open noon-2.30 6-11 (Sun noon-3) Closed: 25-26 Dec, 24 & 31 Dec eve, 1 Jan, Sun eve, Mon-Tue **Bar Meals** Av main course £14.50 **Restaurant** L served Wed-Sat 12-2.30, Sun 12-3 D served Wed-Sat 6-11 Fixed menu price fr £12.50 Av 3 course à la carte fr £20.95 ⊕ FREE HOUSE ◀ Black Sheep Best, Timothy Taylor. ♀ 8 **Facilities** Children's menu Garden Parking **Rooms** 3

## CHAPEL LE DALE

# The Old Hill Inn

LA6 3A4 ☎ 015242 41256
dir: *From Ingleton take B6255 4m, on right*

Parts of this ancient inn date from 1615. Built as a farm it later served as a stopping place for drovers. It is run by a family of chefs, three prepare the savoury dishes and one, a pastry chef, is renowned for his spectacular sugar sculptures. Lunch includes hot or cold home-cooked ham and local sausages. From the main menu, try beetroot and mascarpone risotto topped with Wensleydale cheese or beef and ale casserole, finishing with chocolate indulgence. Lovely Dales views are offered, with good walks from the pub.

Open Closed: 24-25 Dec, Mon (ex BH) **Bar Meals** L served Tue-Sun 12-2.30 booking required D served Tue-Sun 6.30-8.45, Sat 6-8.45 booking required **Restaurant** L served Tue-Sun 12-2.30 booking required D served Tue-Sun 6.30-8.45, Sat 6-8.45 booking required ⊕ FREE HOUSE ◀ Black Sheep Best & Ale, Timothy Taylor Landlord, Theakstons Best, Dent Aviator Ö Thatchers Gold. **Facilities** Children's menu Dogs allowed Garden Parking

## CLAPHAM

# New Inn ♀

LA2 8HH ☎ 01524 251203  📄 01524 251496
e-mail: info@newinn-clapham.co.uk
dir: *On A65 in Yorkshire Dale National Park*

Set in the charming village of Clapham beneath the famous summit of Ingleborough, this 18th-century inn offers a delightful blend of old and new. Expect a warm welcome from outdoors enthusiasts Keith and Barbara Mannion, who have run the inn since 1987. The honest, wholesome food ranges from traditional crusty steak pie with vegetables and mash to the likes of Vietnamese chilli chicken with stir-fried vegetables and noodles. This is a popular base for walking holidays.

Open all day all wk 11am-mdnt (Fri-Sat 11am-1am) **Bar Meals** L served all wk 12-2 D served all wk 6.30-8.30 Av main course £9 **Restaurant** L served all wk 12-1.30 booking required D served all wk 6.30-8 Fixed menu price fr £10 Av 3 course à la carte fr £22 ⊕ ENTERPRISE INNS ◀ Black Sheep Best, Timothy Taylor Landlord, Copper Dragon Pippin, Copper Dragon Best, Bowland Hen Harrier. ♀ 18 **Facilities** Children's menu Dogs allowed Garden Parking

## COLTON

# Ye Old Sun Inn ♀

Main St LS24 8EP ☎ 01904 744261  📄 01904 744261
e-mail: kelly.mccarthy@btconnect.com
dir: *3-4m from York, off A64*

Dating from the 18th-century, this whitewashed local stands at the heart of the village with tables and chairs on the lawn overlooking rolling countryside. The pub prides itself on serving fine local food and ales – restaurant-style dishes without the fuss. Ingredients are locally sourced and mentioned on the menu and everything is cooked from fresh. Typical dishes

continued

are lime and ginger chicken, smoked venison and beetroot, haddock with Yorkshire Blue cheese, and mixed bean fricassee topped with a herb scone; all dishes come with a wine recommendation.

**Open** Closed: 1-26 Jan, Mon **Bar Meals** L served Tue-Sat 12-2, Sun 12-4 booking required D served Tue-Sat 6-9.30 booking required Av main course £13.50 **Restaurant** Fixed menu price fr £17.95 ⊕ ENTERPRISE INNS ◀ Timothy Taylor Landlord, Timothy Taylor Golden Best, Black Sheep, guest ale. ♀ 18 **Facilities** Children's menu Garden Parking

## FADMOOR

### The Plough Inn ♀

**Main St YO62 7HY** ☎ **01751 431515** 🖹 **01751 432492**
**e-mail:** enquiries@theploughfadmoor.co.uk
**web:** www.ploughrestaurant.co.uk

**dir:** *1m N of Kirkbymoorside on A170 (Thirsk to Scarborough road)*

With dramatic views over Ryedale and the Wolds, the setting of this stylish country pub and restaurant overlooking the village green could hardly be more idyllic. Lovingly restored a few years ago, the inn's 18th-century feel is strongly conveyed by its low, beamed ceilings, comfortable wall benches and log fires in winter. Neil Nicholson is head chef and creator of an extensive and varied menu reliant on local meats, vegetables, herbs and salad crops, and fish straight from East Coast quaysides. His wife Rachael looks after front of house, with a team of staff providing a level of service that encourages people to come back again and again. The Plough has built up a reputation for good food served either in the bar, in one of the intimate dining rooms, or on the terrace. Lunch and dinner menu starter options include creamy button mushroom and blue Stilton pot with toasted onion bread; and timbale of fresh Scottish salmon and Greenland prawns with home-made Marie Rose sauce. These could be followed by slow-roasted boneless half Gressingham duckling with orange, mandarin and brandy sauce; paupiette of plaice, stuffed with fresh spinach and prawns with tarragon, white wine and cream sauce; or Thai green vegetable curry with steamed, flavoured basmati rice. Desserts made on the premises offer choices of Neapolitan parfait with fresh fruit; baked American cheesecake with fresh raspberries; and warm treacle tart with white chocolate ice cream. The Sunday lunch menu goes way beyond traditional roasts to include lamb and vegetable casserole, and mushroom and Brie Wellington.

**Open** noon-2.30 6.30-11 (Sun noon-5) Closed: 25-26 Dec, 1 Jan,

Mon-Tue (ex BH), Sun eve **Bar Meals** L served Wed-Sat 12-2, Sun 12-2.30 booking required D served Wed-Sat 6.30-8.45 booking required Av main course £10.50 **Restaurant** L served Wed-Sat 12-2, Sun 12-3.30 booking required D served Wed-Sat 6.30-8.45 booking required Fixed menu price fr £13.75 Av 3 course à la carte fr £22 ⊕ FREE HOUSE ◀ Black Sheep Best, John Smith's, Tetley Cask, guest ales Ö Stowford Press. ♀ 8 **Facilities** Children's menu Garden Parking

## GREAT AYTON

### The Royal Oak ★★★ INN ♀

**123 High St TS9 6BW** ☎ **01642 722361** 🖹 **01642 724047**
**e-mail:** info@royaloak-hotel.co.uk
**dir:** *Telephone for directions*

Real fires and a relaxed atmosphere are part of the attraction at this traditional 18th-century former coaching inn now corner pub, run by the Monaghan family since 1978. The public bar and restaurant retain many original features and offer a good selection of real ales, and an extensive range of food is available all day.

**Open** all wk Closed: 25 Dec **Bar Meals** L served Mon-Sat 12-2, Sun 12-6 D served Mon-Sat 6.30-9.30 **Restaurant** L served Mon-Sat 12-2, Sun 12-6 booking required D served Mon-Sat 6.30-9.30 ⊕ SCOTTISH & NEWCASTLE ◀ Theakstons, John Smiths Smooth, Directors. ♀ 10 **Facilities** Children's menu Garden **Rooms** 5

## HAROME

### The Star Inn ⊛⊛

**YO62 5JE** ☎ **01439 770397** 🖹 **01439 771833**
**dir:** *From Helmsley take A170 towards Kirkbymoorside 0.5m. Turn right for Harome*

A fine 14th-century cruck-framed longhouse is home to this award-winning gastro-pub with a bar full of Mousey Thompson hand-carved oak furniture. Recent additions to the inn include a new dining area, a chef's table, a private dining room upstairs, a summer dining terrace and a kitchen garden. A further new property comprises an indoor swimming pool and a 40-seater dining room within 200 yards of the inn. Produce sourced directly from nearby farms and estates, and fish and shellfish from Whitby and Hartlepool, are used to good effect in the regional menu. Dishes might include risotto of red-legged partridge with yellow chanterelles, white truffle oil and wilted garden rainbow chard; and pan-roasted Duncombe Park roe deer with little venison cottage pie, York ham lardons, girolle mushrooms and tarragon juices.

**Open** 11.30-3 6-11 (Sun noon-11) Closed: 25 Dec, Mon L **Bar Meals** L served Tue-Sun 11.30-2 D served Mon-Sat 6-9.30 Av main course £20 **Restaurant** L served Tue-Sun 11.30-2 booking required D served Mon-Sat 6-9.30 booking required Av 3 course à la carte fr £40 ⊕ FREE HOUSE ◀ Black Sheep Special, Copper Dragon, Hambleton Ales, John Smith's, Theakstons Best. **Facilities** Children's menu Garden Parking

## HARROGATE

### The Boars Head Hotel ★★★ HL ◉◉ ♟

**Ripley Castle Estate HG3 3AY ☎ 01423 771888**
📄 **01423 771509**
e-mail: reservations@boarsheadripley.co.uk
dir: *On A61 (Harrogate/Ripon road). Hotel in village centre*

Dating back to 1830 when the Lord of the Manor rebuilt the village next to his castle, this old coaching inn, originally called The Star, was refurbished by the present Lord (Sir Thomas Ingilby) in 1990 and turned into an impressive hotel. Sir William Ingilby closed all three of Ripley's inns when he inherited the estate soon after the First World War, and Ripley remained dry until the Star was re-opened as the Boar's Head Hotel. Oil paintings and furniture from the castle help to create the country-house feel in tranquil drawing and morning rooms. Stable partitions in the pubby bar and bistro bring intimacy to the relaxed, candlelit atmosphere, where an array of handpumps dispense some cracking Yorkshire ales. Food options begin with classic sandwiches (poached salmon with lemon and dill crème fraiche), and starters like goats' cheese and pepper terrine, or chicken liver parfait. For main course, choose pork and leek sausages on crushed potatoes, breast of estate pheasant wrapped in bacon with herb potatoes, and haddock with butterbean and tomato salad. In the restaurant, main course prices are inclusive of a starter, dessert and coffee, so the price of your meal depends on your choice of main course. Mains range from roast duck breast with confit shallots to pan-seared sea bass with crab beignet and braised fennel.

Open all wk Bar Meals L served all wk 12-2 D served all wk 6-9.30 Restaurant L served all wk 12-2 D served all wk 7-9 booking required ⊕ FREE HOUSE ◀ Theakston Best & Old Peculier, Daleside Crackshot, Hambleton White Boar, Black Sheep Best. ♟ 10 Facilities Children's menu Dogs allowed Garden Parking Rooms 25

## HAWES

### The Moorcock Inn ♟

**Garsdale Head LA10 5PU ☎ 01969 667488**
📄 **01969 667488**
e-mail: admin@moorcockinn.com
dir: *On A684 5m from Hawes, 15m from Sedbergh at junct for Kirkby Stephen (10m). Garsdale Station 1m*

A heart-warming 18th-century hostelry, where owners Caz and Simon welcome weary walkers with or without muddy boots and dogs. Candles glow in the windows, while inside fairy lights pick out a cosy blend of original stonework and bright colours, furnished with comfy sofas and traditional wooden chairs. Savour the pub's local ales around the wood-burning stove, or enjoy the spectacular views from the garden. Traditional fare ranges from Whitby scampi; lamb and root vegetable hotpot; to steak, mushroom and ale pie. Vegetarians and children are not forgotten with their own choices.

Open all day all wk 11am-mdnt Bar Meals food served all day Restaurant food served all day ⊕ FREE HOUSE ◀ Black Sheep, Copper Dragon, Boddingtons Cask, guest ales. ♟ 7 Facilities Children's menu Family room Dogs allowed Garden Parking

## HELMSLEY

### The Crown Inn Ⓐ ★★★★ INN

**Market Square YO62 5BJ ☎ 01439 770297**
e-mail: info@tchh.co.uk
dir: *Please telephone for directions*

The family-run 16th-century inn overlooking Helmsley's beautiful square has been refurbished with style and taste, without losing the inn's historic charm. You can order a pint of Black Sheep and tuck into some fresh home-made food using local produce in the cosy bar and lounge, each warmed by an open log fire.

Open all day all wk 7.30am-11.30pm Bar Meals Av main course £9 food served all day Restaurant Fixed menu price fr £14.95 Av 3 course à la carte fr £20 ⊕ FREE HOUSE ◀ Black Sheep, John Smith Cask, Guest ale. Facilities Children's menu Family room Dogs allowed Garden Parking Rooms 19

## HETTON

### The Angel ♟

**BD23 6LT ☎ 01756 730263** 📄 **01756 730363**
e-mail: info@angelhetton.co.uk
dir: *A59 onto B6265 towards Grassington. Left at Rylstone Pond (signed) then left at T-junct*

Much loved for its modern British food, this ivy-clad Dales inn has a long and interesting history. Built in the 15th century, it welcomed drovers in the early 1800s, and some local residents remember it as a traditional farmhouse pub in the 1950s. Denis and Juliet Watkins took the reins in 1985 and made it a landmark gastro-pub; since Denis' death in 2004, Juliet and her dedicated team, with chef Bruce Elsworth, have stayed true to his vision of 'good food and great value'. The interior is all oak beams, nooks and crannies, and winter log fires; in summer you can sit on the flagged forecourt and enjoy views of Cracoe Fell. Locally-sourced meats, seasonal game and fresh Fleetwood fish are the foundation of the varied menus. The brasserie blackboard menu might offer pea and prosciutto risotto followed by Lancashire hotpot, whilst à la carte diners might enjoy goats' cheese soufflé; and monkfish roasted in Parma ham.

Open all wk noon-3 6-11 Closed: 25 Dec & 1wk Jan Bar Meals L served all wk 12-2.15 D served all wk 6-9.30 (6-9 in winter) Restaurant L served Sun 12-1.45 booking required D served Mon-Fri 6-9, Sat 6-9.30 booking required Fixed menu price fr £25 Av 3 course à la carte fr £29 ⊕ FREE HOUSE ◀ Blacksheep Bitter, Timothy Taylor Landlord, Hetton Pale Ale. ♟ 24 Facilities Children's menu Garden Parking

## HOVINGHAM

### The Malt Shovel

**Main St YO62 4LF** ☎ **01653 628264**  📄 **01653 628264**
e-mail: info@themaltshovelhovingham.co.uk
dir: *18m NE of York, 5m from Castle Howard*

Tucked away in the Duchess of Kent's home village, the stone-built 18th-century Malt Shovel offers a friendly atmosphere with good value food prepared from quality local ingredients. Popular options include Whitby wholetail scampi, vegetarian pancake, chicken stroganoff and steak pie. Fresh vegetables, hand-cut chips and daily specials board featuring game dishes complete the picture. Recent change in ownership.

Open all wk 11.30-2 6-11 (winter), 11.30-2.30 5.30-11 (summer) Bar Meals L served Mon-Sat 11.30-2 (winter) 11.30-2.30 (summer), Sun 12-2.30 D served Mon-Sat 6-9 (winter) 5.30-9 (summer), Sun 5.30-8 Av main course £8.50 Restaurant L served Mon-Sat 11.30-2 (winter) 11.30-2.30 (summer), Sun 12-2.30 booking required D served Mon-Sat 6-9 (winter) 5.30-9 (summer), Sun 5.30-8 booking required Fixed menu price fr £8.75 ⊕ PUNCH TAVERNS ◀ Tetley's, Black Sheep, Guest Ale. Facilities Children's menu Garden Parking

### The Worsley Arms Hotel ★★★ HL ♟

**Main St YO62 4LA** ☎ **01653 628234**  📄 **01653 628130**
e-mail: enquiries@worsleyarms.co.uk
dir: *On B1257 between Malton & Helmsley*

In 1841 Sir William Worsley thought he would turn the village of Worsley into a spa to rival Bath, and built a spa house and a hotel. However, he reckoned without the delicate nature of his guests who disliked the muddy track between the two. Inevitably the spa failed, but the hotel survived and, together with the separate pub, forms part of the Worsley family's historic Hovingham Hall estate, birthplace of the Duchess of Kent, and currently home to her nephew. You can eat in the restaurant or the Cricketer's Bar (the local team has played on the village green for over 150 years). Hambleton Stallion beer from nearby Thirsk is on tap, and food choices include seared Gressingham duck with celeriac and potato dauphinoise, Worsley Arms fishcakes with lemon fish cream, Waterford Farm sausages with mash and red onion confit, or rack of North Yorkshire lamb with fondant potato, roast garlic and fresh mint.

Open all day all wk Bar Meals L served all wk 12-2 booking required D served all wk 6.30-9 booking required Av main course £11 Restaurant L served Sun 12-2 booking required D served all wk 6.30-9 booking required Fixed menu price fr £29.50 Av 3 course à la carte fr £23.50 ⊕ FREE HOUSE ◀ Tetleys, Hambleton Ales. ♟ 20 Facilities Children's menu Dogs allowed Garden Parking Rooms 20

## HUBBERHOLME

### The George Inn

**BD23 5JE** ☎ **01756 760223**
dir: *From Skipton take B6265 to Threshfield. B6160 to Buckden. Follow signs for Hubberholme*

To check if the bar is open, look for a lighted candle in the window. Another old tradition is the annual land-letting auction on the first Monday night of the year, when local farmers bid for 16 acres of land owned by the church. Stunningly located beside the River Wharfe, this pub has flagstone floors, stone walls, mullioned windows, an open fire and an inviting summer terrace. Lunches include chicken and cheese melt and maybe a pint of Black Sheep; evening choices include pork escalope topped with spiced cheese and Wensleydale cheese.

Open noon-3 7-11 Closed: 1st 2wks Dec, Mon Bar Meals L served Tue-Sun 12-2 D served Tue-Sun 7-8.30 booking required Av main course £9 ⊕ FREE HOUSE ◀ Black Sheep Best, Black Sheep Special, Skipton Brewery ♂ Thatchers Gold. Facilities Children's menu Garden Parking

## KILBURN

### The Forresters Arms Inn ♟

**YO61 4AH** ☎ **01347 868386**
e-mail: admin@forrestersarms.com
dir: *From Thirsk take A170, after 3m turn right signed Kilburn. At Kilburn Rd junct, turn right, Inn on left in village square*

A sturdy stone-built former coaching inn still catering for travellers passing close by the famous White Horse of Kilburn on the North York Moors. Next door is the famous Robert Thompson workshop; fine examples of his early work, with the distinctive mouse symbol on every piece, can be seen in both bars. Visiting coachmen would undoubtedly have enjoyed the log fires, cask ales and good food as much as today's visitors.

Open all day all wk 9am-11pm Bar Meals L served all wk 12-3 booking required D served all wk 6-9 booking required Av main course £7.95 Restaurant L served all wk 12-3 booking required D served all wk 6-9 booking required ⊕ ENTERPRISE INNS ◀ John Smiths Cask, Guinness, Hambleton Bitter, Guest ales. ♟ 6 Facilities Children's menu Dogs allowed Garden Parking

## KIRKBYMOORSIDE

### George & Dragon Hotel ♟

**17 Market Place YO62 6AA** ☎ **01751 433334**  📄 **0870 7060004**
e-mail: reception@georgeanddragon.net
dir: *Just off A170 between Scarborough & Thirsk. In town centre*

A former cornmill, rectory and 17th-century coaching inn have been seamlessly combined to make this welcoming hotel in the heart of Kirkbymoorside. Its beamed, olde worlde interior is full of character and comfy chairs. Visitors can sit by the log fire and sample hand-pulled real ales, wines by the glass and a choice of 30 malt whiskies. Food is served all day using fresh local produce, and includes a bar lunchtime menu, à la carte and specials board. Dishes range from pub food favourites (fried Whitby scampi, steak and stilton pie) to classy offerings such as duck liver pâté with home-made chutney or fillets of east coast bass and red mullet with mussel and prawn risotto and asparagus. Light options include filled baguettes; mussel cassoulet; and home-made soup with home-made bread.

Open all day all wk 10.30am-11pm **Bar Meals** Av main course £12 food served all day **Restaurant** Av 3 course à la carte fr £20 food served all day ⊕ FREE HOUSE ◼ Black Sheep Best, Tetley, Copper Dragon, Guest ale. ♀ 10 **Facilities** Children's menu Dogs allowed Garden Parking

## KNARESBOROUGH

## The General Tarleton Inn ★★★★★ RR ⊗⊗ ♀

**Boroughbridge Rd, Ferrensby HG5 0PZ ☎ 01423 340284** 🖹 **01423 340288**
e-mail: gti@generaltarleton.co.uk
web: www.generaltarleton.co.uk
dir: *A1(M) junct 48 at Boroughbridge, take A6055 to Knaresborough. Inn 4m on right*

What started in the 18th-century as a coaching inn is now known for its contemporary comforts, unstuffy atmosphere, and top-class dining, endorsed by two AA Rosettes. The 'Butcher General' himself, Sir Banastre Tarleton, distinguished himself during the American War of Independence, and a member of his platoon probably asked to name the inn in his honour. Step inside to find a reception lounge with large sofas, daily papers, glossy magazines and a warm and welcoming, low-beamed bar with log fires and cosy corners, the perfect setting in which to enjoy some Yorkshire real ales. Menus subtitled 'Food with Yorkshire Roots' change daily to reflect the seasons and the day's pick of the crop or catch. The chef gets a call most days from the fishing boats as they return to ports on both coasts and within hours the fish is in the kitchen. In the Bar Brasserie, from where you can spill out into the light and airy covered courtyard, try The General's home-made black pudding with crispy bacon, lightly poached egg and sherry vinegar reduction; hotch-potch of Yorkshire pork with mock goose pie; or the signature dish of seafood parcels in lobster sauce, known as Little Moneybags. In the chic Tarleton restaurant start with warm shredded duck with chorizo, pancetta, croutons and salad leaves; follow with grilled fillet

of brill with pak choi, fondant potato, brown shrimp and sauce vièrge; and end with iced nougatine parfait, passionfruit sorbet and raspberry coulis. The wine list features some fine bottles at bargain prices, as well as an impressive selection of house wines. Children are very welcome, as the menu of home-made dishes road-tested by the owners' three offspring testifies.

Open all wk 12-3 6-11 **Bar Meals** L served all wk 12-2 booking required D served all wk 6-9.15 booking required Av main course £13.95 **Restaurant** L served Sun 12-1.45 booking required D served Mon-Sat 6-9.15 booking required Av 3 course à la carte fr £30 ⊕ FREE HOUSE ◼ Black Sheep Best, Timothy Taylor Landlord. ♀ 8 **Facilities** Children's menu Garden Parking **Rooms** 14

## LASTINGHAM

## Blacksmiths Arms ♀

**YO62 6TL ☎ 01751 417247** 🖹 **01751 417247**
e-mail: pete.hils@blacksmithslastingham.co.uk
dir: *7m from Pickering & 4m from Kirbymoorside. A170 (Pickering to Kirbymoorside road), follow Lastingham & Appleton-le-Moors signs*

This 17th-century pub stands opposite St Mary's Church (renowned for its Saxon crypt) in the National Park area. The stone-built free house retains its original low-beamed ceilings and open range fireplace, and outside there's a cottage garden and decked seating area. Home-cooked dishes prepared from locally supplied ingredients include lamb casserole served with Yorkshire pudding, and beer-battered jumbo cod. Snacks range through panini, luxury salad, filled roll platters and buckets of chips. Look out for daily specials.

Open all day noon-11.30 Closed: Tue L (Nov-May) **Bar Meals** L served all wk (not Tue Nov-May) 12-5 D served all wk 6.30-8.45 Av main course £8.50 **Restaurant** L served Mon-Sat 12-2 (not Tue Nov-May), Sun 12-5 booking required D served all wk 6.30-8.45 booking required ⊕ FREE HOUSE ◼ Theakstons Best Bitter, 2 rotating guest ales. ♀ 10 **Facilities** Children's menu Family room Garden

## LEYBURN

### Sandpiper Inn ♥

**Market Place DL8 5AT ☎ 01969 622206**
📄 **01969 625367**
e-mail: hsandpiper99@aol.com
dir: *From A1 take A684 to Leyburn*

Although it has been a pub for only 30 years, the building that houses the Sandpiper Inn in is the oldest in Leyburn, dating back to around 1640. It has a beautiful summer garden, and inside, a bar where you can enjoy a pint of Black Sheep or Copper Dragon, a snug and dining room where an exciting and varied mix of traditional and more unusual dishes is served. Lunch brings sandwiches (brie, salami and rocket for example); and Masham sausage and mash with onion gravy. An evening meal could start with warm pigeon on a butternut squash risotto or terrine of game with apple chutney, and continue with fish pie topped with Berwick Edge cheese or slow-cooked Dales lamb with winter vegetables and dauphinoise potatoes. Sunday lunch includes roasted rib of Dales beef with onion gravy and Yorkshire pudding.

**Open** 11.30-3 6.30-11 (Sun noon-2.30 7-10.30) Closed: Mon & occasionally Tue **Bar Meals** L served all wk 12-2.30 Av main course £8.50 **Restaurant** L served all wk 12-2.30 booking required D served all wk 6.30-9.30 booking required ⊕ FREE HOUSE ◀ Black Sheep Best, Black Sheep Special, Daleside, Copper Dragon, Archers. ♥ 8 **Facilities** Children's menu Family room Dogs allowed Garden

## MASHAM

### The Black Sheep Brewery

**HG4 4EN ☎ 01765 689227 & 680100 📄 01765 689746**
e-mail: sue.dempsey@blacksheep.co.uk
dir: *Off A6108, 9m from Ripon & 7m from Bedale*

Paul Theakston, of Masham's famous brewing family, founded the Black Sheep Brewery in the early nineties according to traditional brewing principles. The complex boasts a visitor centre where you can enjoy a 'shepherded' tour of the brewhouse, before popping into the cosy bistro and 'baa...r' to sample the ales. The beers also find their way into a range of hearty dishes, including steak and Riggwelter casserole served with jacket potato.

**Open** all wk 10.30-4.30 (Thu-Sat 10.30-late) **Bar Meals** food served all day **Restaurant** food served all day ⊕ BLACK SHEEP BREWERY ◀ Black Sheep Best Bitter, Riggwelter, Black Sheep Ale. **Facilities** Children's menu Family room Garden Parking

## MIDDLEHAM

### The White Swan ♥

**Market Place DL8 4PE ☎ 01969 622093**
📄 **01969 624551**
e-mail: enquiries@whiteswanhotel.co.uk
dir: *From A1, take A684 towards Leyburn then A6108 to Ripon, 1.5m to Middleham*

Overlooking the town's picturesque market square and boasting lovely rural views, the White Swan has recently been extended and refurbished. An old-fashioned flagstone floor adds to the atmosphere of the cosy public bar, with its welcoming winter fire. A range of hand-pulled Yorkshire ales, Thatchers cider and quality wines complement the very best modern cuisine, from pizzas and pasta dishes to seasonal game, daily fresh fish and tempting puddings. All meals are freshly prepared using mostly Yorkshire ingredients.

**Open** all day all wk 10.30am-11pm (mdnt at wknds) **Restaurant** L served all wk 12-2.15 booking required D served all wk 6.30-9.30 booking required ⊕ FREE HOUSE ◀ Black Sheep Best, John Smith's, Theakstons ♂ Thatchers Gold. ♥ 10 **Facilities** Children's menu Family room Dogs allowed Parking

## NUNNINGTON

### The Royal Oak Inn 🍷

**Church St YO62 5US** ☎ **01439 748271** 📄 **01439 748271**
dir: *Village centre, close to Nunnington Hall*

A short walk through the village from Nunnington Hall brings you to this Grade II listed country inn. The sign on the front door says it all – 'Real ale, real food, real people'. Traditional decor, with open fires in winter and fresh flowers in summer, make for a welcoming atmosphere, and the patio garden is a welcome recent addition. Hearty home-cooked meals are prepared from seasonal vegetables, locally reared meats and game from local farms and estates. Expect main dishes like Fisherman's pot or steak and kidney casserole. Home-made desserts such as sticky toffee pudding or triple chocolate mousse are a proper treat.

**Open** 11.45-2.30 6.30-11 (Sun noon-2.30 7-11) Closed: Mon **Bar Meals** L served Tue-Sun 12-2 Av main course £11 **Restaurant** D served Tue-Sun 6.30-9 ⊕ FREE HOUSE ◀ Black Sheep, Wold Top, John Smiths, Theakstons XB. 🍷 11 **Facilities** Children's menu Dogs allowed Garden Parking

## OLDSTEAD

### The Black Swan ★★★★★ RR ◉◉ 🍷

**Main St YO61 4BL** ☎ **01347 868387**
e-mail: enquiries@blackswanoldstead.co.uk
dir: *A1 junct 49, A168, A19S of A19N to Coxwold then Byland Abbey. In 2m left for Oldstead, pub 1m on left*

The Black Swan, which dates from the 16th century, is owned and run by the Banks family, who have lived and farmed in the village for generations. The bar is full of character with a log fire, flagstone floor, window seats, antique furniture and oak fittings by Robert 'Mousey' Thompson. Choice at the bar includes real ales, good wines by the glass, malt whiskies and old port. Both lunch and evening menus offer home-made fare including traditional and more sophisticated dishes. Options include pub classics (fish and chips; beef casserole; steak and chips) plus starters such as celeriac velouté with grilled pancetta, capers and shallots; followed by fillet of turbot with salmon and crab ravioli; or haunch of venison with button onion tart. Ingredients are fresh, and the beef, pork and lamb comes from local farms. Printed details of walks from the pub are available at the bar, and you are welcome to leave your vehicle in the car park while you enjoy your walk.

**Open** all wk noon-3 6-11 **Bar Meals** L served all wk 12-2 D served all wk 6-9 Av main course £11.50 **Restaurant** L served all wk 12-2 booking required D served all wk 6-9 booking required Av 3 course à la carte fr £21.95 ⊕ FREE HOUSE ◀ Black Sheep, Copper Dragon, Guinness Ő Thatchers Gold. 🍷 19 **Facilities** Children's menu Garden Parking **Rooms** 0

## PICKERING

### Fox & Hounds Country Inn ★★ HL ◉ 🍷

**Sinnington YO62 6SQ** ☎ **01751 431577** 📄 **01751 432791**
e-mail: foxhoundsinn@easynet.co.uk
dir: *3m W of town, off A170 between Pickering & Helmsley*

This handsome 18th-century coaching inn lies in Sinnington, on a quiet road between Pickering and Kirkbymoorside. A gentle walk from the pub passes the village green to the pretty riverside where ducks swim in the shallows and an ancient packhorse bridge leads to more footpaths through the woods. Proprietors Andrew and Catherine Stephens and friendly efficient staff ensure a warm welcome. As you settle down with a pint of Theakstons or Black Sheep, you can relax and enjoy the oak-beamed ceilings, old wood panelling and open fires. The menu is full of locally farmed produce, and many of the starters are also available as main courses. Expect the likes of pan-crisp braised belly pork with ginger and honey noodles; Gressingham duck leg, roast beetroot and rocket; and Swaledale 'Old Peculiar' cheese soufflé.

**Open** all wk noon-2 6.30-9 Closed: 25-26 Dec **Bar Meals** L served all wk 12-2 booking required D served all wk 6.30-9 booking required Av main course £13.95 **Restaurant** L served all wk 12-2 booking required D served all wk 6.30-9 booking required Av 3 course à la carte fr £25 ⊕ FREE HOUSE ◀ Theakstons Best, Black Sheep Special, Worthingtons Creamflow. 🍷 7 **Facilities** Children's menu Dogs allowed Garden Parking **Rooms** 10

**Pickering continued**

## Horseshoe Inn ⚲

**Main St, Levisham YO18 7NL ☎ 01751 460240**
🖹 01751 460052
e-mail: info@horseshoelevisham.co.uk
dir: *A169, 5m from Pickering. 4m, pass Fox & Rabbit Inn on right. In 0.5m left to Lockton. Follow steep winding road to village*

At the head of a tranquil village deep in Heartbeat country on the edge of the North York Moors National Park, this spruced-up 16th-century inn makes an ideal pit-stop or base for walking, cycling and touring the moors – don't miss a trip on the nearby steam railway. Charles and Toby Wood have created in inviting atmosphere in the beamed bar, with its polished plank floor and roaring log fire, offering tip-top Yorkshire ales and hearty country cooking – pork belly with cider gravy, steak and mushroom pie, roast beef and horseradish sandwiches.

Open all wk **Bar Meals** L served all wk 12-2 booking required D served all wk 6-8.30 booking required Av main course £11 **Restaurant** L served all wk 12-2 booking required D served all wk 6-8.30 booking required Av 3 course à la carte fr £19 ⊕ FREE HOUSE ◾ Black Sheep Best, Timothy Taylor Landlord Ŏ Thatchers. ⚲ 9 **Facilities** Children's menu Dogs allowed Garden Parking

## PICKHILL

## Nags Head Country Inn ★★ HL ◉ ⚲

**YO7 4JG ☎ 01845 567391** 🖹 01845 567212
e-mail: enquiries@nagsheadpickhill.co.uk
dir: *1m E of A1. 4m N of A1/A61 junct*

This region of Yorkshire is known as 'Herriot country', after the books by the famous country vet. A direct descendant of the coaching inn tradition, the Nag's Head is a 200-year-old free house set in the village of Pickhill. It's perfectly situated for exploring the local fells, playing a round of golf, fishing or having a flutter at nearby Thirsk, Ripon and Catterick races. Once you've worked up an appetite, head inside where beamed ceilings, stone-flagged floors and winter fires make for a most welcoming atmosphere. A lengthy but thoughtful menu is equally appealing. Starters like potted brown shrimps with five spice and lime herb croutons precede main course options that include luxury fish pie; saddle of Pickhill hare with confit leg; and pan-fried calves' liver with crispy bacon. Desserts too rise above the usual; individual apple tarte Tatin, for example, is served with blackberry ice cream.

Open all wk 11-11 (Sun 11-10.30) Closed: 25 Dec **Bar Meals** L served Mon-Sat 12-2, Sun 12-2.30 booking required D served Mon-Sat 6-9.30, Sun 6-9 booking required Av main course £12.95 **Restaurant** L served Mon-Sat 12-2, Sun 12-2.30 booking required D served Mon-Sat 6-9.30, Sun 6-9 booking required Av 3 course à la carte fr £22.50 ⊕ FREE HOUSE ◾ Black Sheep Best, Old Peculier, Theakstons Best Bitter, Black Bull, York Brewery Guzzler Ŏ Thatchers Gold. ⚲ 8 **Facilities** Children's menu Dogs allowed Garden Parking **Rooms** 14

## PICTON

## The Station Hotel ⚲

**TS15 0AE ☎ 01642 700067**
dir: *1.5m from A19*

'Hotel' by name only, this is family-run and family-friendly village pub has had the same owner for 20 years. Offering real food at reasonable prices, just about everything is home made from locally sourced produce, with one menu serving both bar and dining room. While the children enjoy the outdoor play area in the beer garden, parents can relax in front of the open fire and scan the extensive specials board over a pint of John Smiths.

Open all wk 6-11.30 (Sat noon-2.30 6-11.30 Sun noon-4 6-11.30) **Bar Meals** L served Sat 12-2.30, Sun 12-4 booking required D served all wk ⊕ FREE HOUSE ◾ John Smiths Cask, John Smiths Smooth, Guinness. ⚲ 6 **Facilities** Children's menu Play area Garden Parking

## REETH

## Charles Bathurst Inn ★★★★ INN ⚲

**Arkengarthdale DL11 6EN ☎ 01748 884567**
🖹 01748 884599
e-mail: info@cbinn.co.uk
web: www.cbinn.co.uk
dir: *From A1 leave at Scotch Corner, take A6108 to Richmond then B6270 to Reeth. At Buck Hotel turn N to Langthwaite, pass church on right, Inn 0.5m on right*

Cosy fires and antique pine furniture greet customers entering this 18th-century free house. Strategically located on the edge of the Pennine Way and close to the mid-point of the coast-to-coast walk, the inn is set in remote and beautiful Arkengarthdale. The building was formerly a bunkhouse for lead miners employed by Charles Bathurst, an 18th-century lord of the manor and son of Oliver Cromwell's physician. Today, the owners pride themselves on knowing the provenance of all their food, and the daily menu is written up on an imposing mirror hanging at the end of the bar. Starters might include butternut squash and Parmesan risotto; and pan-fried mackerel on Greek salad. For a hearty lunch try steamed steak and red wine suet pudding with parsnip mash; or the lighter goats' cheese, tomato and red onion tartlet; followed, perhaps, by plum crumble with crème Anglaise.

Open all wk 11am-mdnt Closed: 25 Dec **Bar Meals** L served all wk 12-2 booking required D served all wk 6.30-9 booking required Av main course £11.95 **Restaurant** L served all wk 12-2 booking required D served all wk 6.30-9 booking required Av 3 course à la carte fr £22 ⊕ FREE HOUSE ◀ Theakstons, John Smiths Bitter, John Smiths Smooth, Black Sheep Best, Riggwelter. ⛉ 12 **Facilities** Children's menu Play area Garden Parking **Rooms** 19

---

## SAWDON

# The Anvil Inn ⛉

**Main St YO13 9DY** ☎ **01723 859896**
e-mail: theanvilinnsawdon@btinternet.com
web: www.theanvilinnsawdon.co.uk
dir: *1.5m N of Brompton-by-Sawdon, on A170 8m E of Pickering & 6m W of Scarborough*

Set on the edge of Dalby Forest, this is a walkers' and birdwatchers' paradise. It was a working forge for over 200 years until 1985; many artefacts remain, including the original furnace. Local produce, nicely handled and well priced, appears in dishes such as fresh crab and leek terrine with avocado dressing; pan-roasted lamb loin with a ragout of chorizo, beans, tomatoes and olives; and steamed marmalade sponge pudding. Two self-catering cottages are available.

**Open** Closed: 26 Dec & 1 Jan, Mon **Bar Meals** L served Tue-Sat 12-2, Sun 12-3 booking required D served Tue-Sat 6.30-9 booking required Av main course £13.75 **Restaurant** L served Tue-Sat 12-2, Sun 12-3 booking required D served Tue-Sat 6.30-9 booking required Av 3 course à la carte fr £19 ⊕ FREE HOUSE ◀ Daleside Blonde, Hobgoblin Ale, Copper Dragon, Wold Top, Daleside Old Leg Over ⟳ Stowford Press. ⛉ 11 **Facilities** Children's menu Dogs allowed Garden Parking

---

## SAWLEY

# The Sawley Arms ⛉

**HG4 3EQ** ☎ **01765 620642**
e-mail: junehawes1@aol.co.uk
dir: *A1(M) junct 47, A59 to Knaresborough, B6165 to Ripley, A61 towards Ripon, left for Sawley. Or from Ripon B6265 towards Pateley Bridge, left to Sawley. Pub 1m from Fountains Abbey*

This delightful 200-year-old pub stands just a mile from Fountains Abbey. Run by the same owners for 40 years, it was a frequent haunt of the late author and vet James Herriot. Surrounded by its own stunning gardens, the pub is big on old world charm. The menu is suitably traditional, with dishes ranging from pies and casseroles to fresh plaice mornay with sautéed leeks, creamed potatoes and a rich cheese glaze.

**Open** 11.30-3 6-10.30 Closed: 25 Dec, Sun eve & Mon eve in winter **Bar Meals** L served all wk 12-2.30 booking required D served all wk 6.30-9.30 booking required **Restaurant** L served all wk 12-2.30 booking required D served all wk 6.30-9.30 booking required ⊕ FREE HOUSE ◀ Theakston Best, John Smiths. ⛉ 8 **Facilities** Children's menu Garden Parking

---

## SNAINTON

# Coachman Inn ⛉

**Pickering Road West YO13 9PL** ☎ **01723 859231**
📄 **01723 850008**
e-mail: james@coachmaninn.co.uk
dir: *5m from Pickering, off A170 onto B1258*

The Coachman is an imposing Grade II listed Georgian coaching inn, run by James and Rita Osborne. It was once the last staging post before Scarborough for the York mail. As well as the varied main menu, there is a daily specials board including dishes like smoked local venison with asparagus and quail egg; and seared scallops with gruyère and chive mash, grilled pancetta and lemon oil. Outside is a large lawned area with flowers, trees and seating.

**Open** Closed: Mon **Bar Meals** L served Wed-Sun 12-2 D served Tue-Sun 6.30-9 **Restaurant** L served Wed-Sun 12-2 booking required D served Tue-Sat 7-9 booking required ⊕ FREE HOUSE ◀ John Smiths, Wold Top, Guinness ⟳ Stowford Press. ⛉ 7 **Facilities** Children's menu Garden Parking

## STARBOTTON

### Fox & Hounds Inn ☂

**BD23 5HY ☎ 01756 760269 & 760367**

e-mail: starbottonfox@aol.com
dir: *Telephone for directions*

Situated in a picturesque limestone village in Upper Wharfedale in the heart of the Yorkshire Dales, this ancient pub was originally built as a private house, but has been a pub for more than 160 years. Make for the cosy bar, with its solid furnishings and flagstones, and enjoy a pint of Black Sheep or one of the guest ales. The menu offers steak and ale pie, minted lamb shank, pork medallions in brandy and mustard sauce, and a selection of steaks.

**Open** noon-3 6-11 (Sun noon-3.30 5.30-10.30) Closed: 1-22 Jan, Mon **Bar Meals** Av main course £10.45 ⊕ FREE HOUSE ◀ Black Sheep, Timothy Taylor Landlord, Moorhouse, guest ales. ☂ 8 **Facilities** Children's menu Garden Parking

## SUTTON-ON-THE-FOREST

### The Blackwell Ox Inn ★★★★ INN ◉ ☂

**Huby Rd YO61 1DT ☎ 01347 810328 📄 01347 812738**

e-mail: enquiries@blackwelloxinn.co.uk
dir: *7m from centre of York off A1237. Take B1363, at T-junct left. Pub on right*

Set in the picturesque village of Sutton-on-the-Forest, the Blackwell Ox blends modern elegance with period charm. Visitors will find hand-pulled ales and an open fire in the bar, as well as a terrace for sitting out in the warmer months. Meanwhile, restaurant diners can relax in the lounge area before or after their meal. The chef believes in simple, honest cooking, and sources local North Yorkshire produce to create his dishes. Substantial 'knife and fork' sandwiches appear at lunchtime, alongside a fixed price menu that might include salmon fritters with aïoli; or confit of pork with cassoulet. A typical evening meal might start with pea and mint soup, followed by sea bass with braised endive, and finishing with lemon posset and butter shortbread.

**Open** all wk noon-3 5.30-11 (Sun close 10.30) **Bar Meals** Av main course £11.45 food served all day **Restaurant** Fixed menu price fr £10.95 Av 3 course à la carte fr £25 food served all day ⊕ FREE HOUSE ◀ Black Sheep, John Smiths Cask, Guinness, Timothy Taylor Landlord, Copper Dragon. ☂ 9 **Facilities** Children's menu Garden Parking **Rooms** 7

## THORNTON WATLASS

### The Buck Inn ★★★ INN ☂

**HG4 4AH ☎ 01677 422461 📄 01677 422447**

e-mail: innwatlass1@btconnect.com
web: www.buckwatlass.co.uk
dir: *From A1 at Leeming Bar take A684 to Bedale, then B6268 towards Masham. Village 2m on right, by cricket green*

The Buck Inn doesn't just overlook the village green and cricket pitch; players score four runs for hitting the pub wall, and six if the ball goes over the roof! Very much the quintessential village scene in beautiful Thornton Watlass, Bedale is where Wensleydale, gateway to the Yorkshire Dales National Park, begins, and this glorious area is where much of the television programme Heartbeat was filmed. The pub is a traditional, well run, friendly institution that has been in experienced hands of Michael and Margaret Fox for over 20 years, so they have no trouble in maintaining its welcoming and relaxed atmosphere. There are three separate dining areas - the bar for informality, the restaurant for dining by candlelight, and on busy days the large function room is opened. The menu ranges from traditional, freshly prepared pub fare to exciting modern cuisine backed by daily changing blackboard specials. Typical bar favourites are Masham rarebit (Wensleydale cheese with local ale topped with bacon and served with pear chutney); steak and ale pie; oven-baked lasagne; lamb cutlets with rosemary and redcurrant sauce, and beer-battered fish and chips. Hearty and wholesome daily specials may take in chicken liver parfait with red onion marmalade; beef Wellington with Madeira sauce; game casserole, and roast cod with mash and saffron cream.

**Open** all wk 8am-mdnt Closed: 25 Dec eve **Bar Meals** L served Mon-Sat 12-2, Sun 11-3 D served all wk 6.30-9.30 Av main course £12.75 **Restaurant** L served Mon-Sat 12-2, Sun 11-3 D served all wk 6.30-9.30 ⊕ FREE HOUSE ◀ Theakston Best, Black Sheep Best, Theakston Black Bull, guest ales. ☂ 7 **Facilities** Children's menu Play area Family room Dogs allowed Garden Parking **Rooms** 7

## TOPCLIFFE

### The Angel Inn ♥

**YO7 3RW** ☎ **01845 577237** 📄 **01845 578000**
e-mail: kevin@topcliffeangelinn.co.uk
web: www.topcliffeangelinn.co.uk
dir: *On A168(M), 3m from A1*

A refurbishment has given this old country inn a more contemporary feel, but with more than a nod to tradition. The restaurant has a good local reputation for creative dishes such as fillet of red mullet with warm potato, celeriac and beetroot salad; pheasant pot au feu with stuffed cabbage and spätzle; and, for two, seafood casserole under puff pastry.

**Open** all day all wk 9am-11pm (Fri-Sat 9am-mdnt) **Bar Meals** L served all wk 12-3 booking required D served all wk 5-9 booking required ⊕ CAMERONS ◖ John Smith, Black Sheep, Timothy Taylor. ♥ 8 **Facilities** Children's menu Dogs allowed Garden Parking

## WASS

### Wombwell Arms ♥

**YO61 4BE** ☎ **01347 868280**
e-mail: wombwellarms@btconnect.com
web: www.wombwellarms.co.uk
dir: *From A1 take A168 to A19 junct. Take York exit, then left after 2.5m, left at Coxwold to Ampleforth. Wass 2m*

Ian and Eunice Walker recently took over this character country pub in breathtaking surroundings on the southern edge of the North York Moors National Park. The building was constructed around 1620 as a granary, probably using stone from nearby Byland Abbey, but 25 years or so later it had became an alehouse. There are two bars, one with a huge open fire, and the Poachers, with a wood-burning stove, where dogs are welcome to sprawl across the floor, no doubt wondering why it takes their owners so long to put away a pint of Timothy Taylor Landlord, Theakston's Black Bull or Old Peculier. High quality, freshly prepared meals are available in both bars, as well as in the two restaurants, and the Walkers have established North Yorkshire suppliers for most of the produce used. Light lunches include tempting filled ciabatta and granary bread sandwiches, salads, ploughman's and smoked salmon and scrambled eggs. On a very manageable menu, starters such as pigeon bruschetta with mushrooms; trio of smoked fish; and twice-baked cheese soufflé could be followed with king prawn risotto and pan-fried scallops; roasted chicken breast with creamy leek and stilton sauce; poacher's casserole; orvegetarian chickpea curry. Then there are the Wombwell Classics, including Wass steak pie; a 10-oz sirloin steak; or haddock, chips and garden or mushy peas. Children get their look-in too with home-made fish fingers and chips with peas and beans; pizza Margherita; and pasta Bolognaise with salad. This is a great location for those planning to walk the Cleveland Way.

**Open** all wk noon-3 6-11 (Sat noon-11 Sun noon-4) **Bar Meals** L served Mon-Thu 12-2, Fri-Sat 12-2.30, Sun 12-3 D served Mon-Thu 6.30-9, Fri-Sat 6.30-9.30 Av main course £10.95 **Restaurant** L served Mon-Thu 12-2, Fri-Sat 12-2.30, Sun 12-3 booking required D served Mon-Thu 6.30-9, Fri-Sat 6.30-9.30 booking required Av 3 course à la carte fr £17.15 ⊕ FREE HOUSE ◖ Timothy Taylor Landlord, Theakstons Black Bull, Theakstons Old Peculier. ♥ 9 **Facilities** Children's menu Dogs allowed Garden Parking

## WEAVERTHORPE

### The Star Country Inn

**YO17 8EY** ☎ **01944 738273** 📄 **01944 738273**
e-mail: starinn.malton@btconnect.com
dir: *From Malton take A64 towards Scarborough. 12m, at Sherborn right at lights. Weaverthorpe 4m, inn opposite junct*

Situated in the village of Weaverthorpe in the heart of the Yorkshire Wolds, this 200-year-old inn has a rustic interior with large winter fires and a welcoming, convivial atmosphere. Food is fresh and locally sourced where possible, and pride is taken in everything from fresh-baked breads to home-made ice cream. Even the tomato ketchup is made on site! A meal might include ham hock terrine followed by beer battered Whitby fish with hand cut chips, mushy peas and tartare sauce, while spicier options include vegetable balti with pilau rice or green Thai prawn curry. A classy selection of specials might include pan-fried pigeon breast with watercress salad and walnut dressing; or pan-seared Shetland king scallops with curried parsnip purée and parsnip chips. The Star is an ideal base for visiting local attractions such as Castle Howard, and the area is also popular with cyclists and bird-watchers.

**Open** all day noon-mdnt Closed: Mon **Bar Meals** L served Tue-Sat 12-6, Sun 12-3 booking required Av main course £8 food served all day **Restaurant** L served Sun 12-3 booking required D served Tue-Sun 6-9 booking required ⊕ FREE HOUSE ◖ Bitter, John Smiths, Wold Top, Theakstons. **Facilities** Children's menu Garden Parking

## WEST BURTON

# Fox & Hounds

**DL8 4JY ☎ 01969 663111** 📄 **01969 663279**
web: www.fhinn.co.uk
dir: *A468 between Hawes & Leyburn, 0.5m E of Aysgarth*

The Fox and Hounds is a traditional pub in a beautiful Dales setting overlooking the village green, which has swings and football goals for children, and its own hidden waterfalls. The pub is a proper local, hosting men's and women's darts teams and a dominoes team. In summer customers play quoits out on the green. Home-made food prepared from fresh ingredients is served. Dishes include chicken curry, steak and kidney pie, lasagne, steaks and other pub favourites.

**Open** all day all wk **Bar Meals** L served all wk 12-2 D served all wk 6-8.30 Av main course £7.95 **Restaurant** L served all wk 12-2 booking required D served all wk 6-8.30 booking required Av 3 course à la carte fr £16 ⊕ FREE HOUSE ◗ Black Sheep, John Smiths, Theakstons Best, Copper Dragon ♺ Stowford Press. **Facilities** Children's menu Family room Dogs allowed Parking

# SOUTH YORKSHIRE

## BRADFIELD

# The Strines Inn

**Bradfield Dale S6 6JE ☎ 0114 2851247**
dir: *N off A57 between Sheffield & Manchester*

Nestled amid the breathtaking moorland scenery of the Peak District National Park, overlooking Strines Reservoir, this popular free house feels a world away from nearby Sheffield but is in fact within its border. Although it was built as a manor house in the 13th century, most of the present building is 16th century. It has been an inn since 1771. Traditional home-made fare ranges from sandwiches, salads and jacket potatoes, to substantial Yorkshire puddings with a choice of fillings, plus grilled steaks, mammoth mixed grill, or pie of the day.

**Open** all wk 10.30-3 5.30-11 (Sat-Sun 10.30am-11pm) Closed: 25 Dec **Bar Meals** L served all wk 12-2.30 D served all wk 5.30-9 Av main course £8.25 ⊕ FREE HOUSE ◗ Marston's Pedigree, Kelham Island, Mansfield Cask, Bradfield Bitter, Old Speckled Hen. **Facilities** Children's menu Play area Dogs allowed Garden Parking

## CADEBY

# Cadeby Inn ▾

**Main St DN5 7SW ☎ 01709 864009**
e-mail: info@cadeby-inn.co.uk

Before being converted into a picturesque whitewashed pub, with a stone-walled traditional bar and a more contemporary restaurant with stylish yet comfortable chairs, this was a farmhouse. Sandstone walls enclose the large front garden, while a patio and smaller garden lie at the rear; ideal for enjoying a meal or a pint of John Smiths in the warmer weather. The lunch menu offers interesting sandwiches like classic minute steak and onion, or open sandwich of smoked salmon, prawn and lemon mayonnaise; or crisp warm brie with Waldorf salad and cranberry sauce. In the evening you might start with creamy parsnip and apple soup, followed by main courses such as Whitby cod fillet, creamy mash, parsley sauce and crisp bacon; confit duck leg, stew of white beans, Savoy cabbage, shallots and thyme; and simple wild mushroom and parmesan risotto.

**Open** all wk noon-11 **Bar Meals** L served all wk 12-5.30 food served all day **Restaurant** L served all wk 12-9.30 D served Mon-Sat 12-9.30, Sun 12-8 food served all day ⊕ FREE HOUSE ◗ John Smiths Cask, Black Sheep Best Bitter, Guinness. ▾ 6 **Facilities** Children's menu Garden Parking

## DONCASTER

# Waterfront Inn ▾

**Canal Ln, West Stockwith DN10 4ET ☎ 01427 891223**
dir: *From Gainsborough take either A159 N, then minor road to village. Or A631 towards Bawtry/Rotherham, then right onto A161, then minor road*

Built in the 1830s overlooking the Trent Canal basin and the canal towpath, the pub is now popular with walkers and visitors to the nearby marina. Real ales and good value food are the order of the day, including pasta with home-made ratatouille, broccoli and cheese bake, deep fried scampi, half honey-roasted chicken, and lasagne.

**Open** noon-2.30 6-11 (Sat noon-11 Sun noon-9) Closed: Mon (ex BH) **Bar Meals** L served Tue-Sun, 12-2.30 D served Tue-Sun 6.30-9 Av main course £7.99 **Restaurant** L served Tue-Sun 12-2.30 D served Tue-Sun 6.30-9 ⊕ ENTERPRISE INNS ◗ John Smiths Cask, Greene King Old Speckled Hen. ▾ 9 **Facilities** Children's menu Play area Dogs allowed Garden Parking

## PENISTONE

# Cubley Hall ♀

**Mortimer Rd, Cubley S36 9DF ☎ 01226 766086**
📠 **01226 767335**
e-mail: info@cubleyhall.co.uk
dir: *M1 junct 37, A628 towards Manchester, or M1 junct 35a, A616. Hall just S of Penistone*

Please say hello to Flo if you see her wandering about; she'll be dressed in Edwardian clothes and may not reply. Flo, or Florence Lockley to be precise, married here in 1904 and has become the resident ghost in this fine-looking mansion. Since the 1700s it has been used for a variety of purposes, from moorland farm to today's freehouse pub, by way of gentleman's residence and, for 50 years, a children's home. Despite those decades of youthful assault, many original features such as mosaic floors, ornate plasterwork, oak panelling and stained glass have somehow survived. The restaurant, massively oak-beamed and solidly slate-floored, was once the barn; old pine tables, chairs and pews add to the ambience. There are plenty of snacks and light meals, such as creamy garlic mushrooms; pork and leek sausage with creamy mash and rich onion gravy; a 'sizzlin' platter of spicy chicken wings; pizzas and pastas; and chargrilled beefburger, rump steak; gammon and chicken fajitas. Main courses include chilli con carne with rice, sour cream and nachos; 'classic British' pie of the day with shortcrust pastry, salted steak fries and a panache of vegetables; pan-fried lamb's liver with onions and lardons; chargrilled chicken breast marinated in cumin and coriander with steamed rice, sultanas and pinenuts, topped with natural yoghurt; Whitby wholetail breaded scampi with homemade tartare sauce; risotto with mixed beans, fresh herbs, Parmesan and pesto; and seasonal salads. Ten daily specials on blackboards, several 'credit munch' options and a children's menu complete the picture. The hotel, particularly its garden pavilion, is a popular wedding venue.

**Open** all wk **Bar Meals** D served Mon-Fri until 9.30, Sat-Sun until 10 Av main course £8 food served all day **Restaurant** L served Sun 12.30-3.30 booking required D served Sun, last orders at 5.45 booking required Fixed menu price fr £9.75 Av 3 course à la carte fr £21 ⊕ FREE HOUSE ◼ Tetley Bitter, Burton Ale, Greene King Abbot Ale, Young's Special. ♀ 7 **Facilities** Children's menu Play area Family room Garden Parking

## SHEFFIELD

# The Fat Cat

**23 Alma St S3 8SA ☎ 0114 249 4801** 📠 **0114 249 4803**
e-mail: info@thefatcat.co.uk
dir: *Telephone for directions*

This reputedly haunted three-storey, back street pub was built in 1832, and is Grade II listed. A constantly changing range of guest beers from across the country, especially from micro-breweries, makes for a real ale heaven. Two hand-pumped ciders, unusual bottled beers and 21 country wines are also sold, while the Kelham Island Brewery, owned by the pub, accounts for at least four of the ten traditional draught real ales on offer. The number of different beers sold since the concept was introduced now exceeds 4,500. The smart interior is very much that of a traditional, welcoming city pub; outside there's an attractive walled garden complete with Victorian-style lanterns, bench seating and shrubbery. Real fires in winter complete the cosy feel. Home-cooked food from a simple weekly menu is available except on Sunday evenings – nutty mushroom pie or Mexican chicken casserole. Look out for special events such as beer and food evenings.

**Open** all wk noon-11 (Sat-Sun noon-mdnt) Closed: 25 Dec **Bar Meals** L served all wk 12-2.30 D served Mon-Sat 6-8 ⊕ FREE HOUSE ◼ Timothy Taylor Landlord, Kelham Island Bitter, Pale Rider, Pride of Sheffield, Kelham Island Gold ↻ Stowford Press, Guest ciders. **Facilities** Children's menu Family room Dogs allowed Garden Parking

## TOTLEY

# The Cricket Inn ♀

**Penny Ln, Totley Bents S17 3AZ ☎ 0114 236 5256**
e-mail: info@brewkitchen.co.uk
dir: *Follow A621 from Sheffield 8m. Turn right onto Hillfoot Rd, 1st left onto Penny Ln*

Being so close to the Peak District means that The Cricket is a natural choice for sustenance when you have completed your ten-mile tramp or fell run. Muddy running shoes, walking boots, children and dogs are all welcome. The pub is owned by the Thornbridge Brewery, so expect to find four of its ales on tap as well as a small selection of bottled Belgians. The building was originally a farmhouse which started selling beer to navvies building the Totley Tunnel on the nearby Sheffield to Manchester railway. It opened for business in its current guise

continued

in 2007 and today it's a forward-looking venture that links the innovative beers with great pub food. Fill the odd corner with tasty snacks like fresh (rather than frozen) whitebait; main course offerings include steak and kidney pie with home-made ham hock. Whatever you order, the chips, fried in beef dripping the way nature intended, are not to be missed.

**Open** all wk 11-11 **Bar Meals** L served Mon-Fri 12-2.30, Sat-Sun all day D served Mon-Fri 5-8.30, Sat-Sun all day Av main course £12 **Restaurant** L served Mon-Fri 12-2.30, Sat-Sun all day D served Mon-Fri 5-8.30, Sat-Sun all day Fixed menu price fr £12 Av 3 course à la carte fr £20 ⊕ BREWKITCHEN LTD ♀ 8 **Facilities** Children's menu Dogs allowed Garden Parking

## WEST YORKSHIRE

### HAWORTH

## The Old White Lion Hotel ★★ HL ♀

**Main St BD22 8DU ☎ 01535 642313** 🖹 **01535 646222**
e-mail: enquiries@oldwhitelionhotel.com
dir: *A629 onto B6142, hotel 0.5m past Haworth Station*

This traditional 300-year-old coaching inn is set in the famous Brontë village of Haworth, looking down onto the famous cobbled Main Street. In the charming bar the ceiling beams are held up by timber posts. Bar food includes all the usual favourites plus a great selection of filled giant Yorkshire puddings. From the carte in the candlelit restaurant choose between game casserole of rabbit, venison, wild boar and pigeon in red wine; and mango, stilton and sweet chilli topped chicken.

**Open** all wk 11-11 (Sun noon-10.30) **Bar Meals** L served Mon-Fri 12-2.30, Sat-Sun all day D served Mon-Fri 6-9.30, Sat-Sun all day Av main course £8.30 **Restaurant** L served Sun 12-2.30 booking required D served all wk 7-9.30 booking required Fixed menu price fr £17 Av 3 course à la carte fr £17.90 ⊕ FREE HOUSE ◀ Theakstons Best (Green Label), Tetley Bitter, John Smiths, Websters, guest beer. ♀ 6 **Facilities** Children's menu Parking **Rooms** 15

### LEEDS

## The Cross Keys ♀

**107 Water Ln LS11 5WD ☎ 0113 243 3711**
e-mail: info@the-crosskeys.com
dir: *0.5m from Leeds Station: right onto Neville St, right onto Water Lane. Pass Globe Rd, pub on left*

Just across the river from Leeds city station, the Cross Keys stands huddled between converted industrial buildings enjoying a second lease of life as fashionable offices. So if the open fires, exposed brick walls and beamed ceilings put you in mind of some old-world rural backwater, think again. For this cosy city pub with its fine outdoor courtyard is firmly geared towards the Wi-Fi generation. Yet with ales from local independent breweries, Weston's organic cider, and a menu that captures long lost recipes and traditional British classics,

it is well worth a visit. Lunchtime brings salt beef sandwiches with English mustard and pickles; devilled mushrooms on toast; and a range of hot dishes like home-made faggots with bubble and squeak. In the evenings, fresh seafood and herb broth might precede slow-cooked wild rabbit with herb dumplings and colcannon, followed by rice pudding with caramelised apples.

**Open** all wk noon-11 (Fri-Sat noon-mdnt, Sun noon-10.30) **Bar Meals** L served Mon-Sat 12-4, Sun 12-8 D served Mon-Sat 6-10 Av main course £7.50 **Restaurant** L served Mon-Sat 12-4, Sun 12-8 D served Mon-Sat 6-10 Fixed menu price fr £14 Av 3 course à la carte fr £17.95 ⊕ FREE HOUSE ◀ Roosters, Duvel, Liefmans Frambogen ⍥ Westons Organic, Westons Medium Dry. ♀ 13 **Facilities** Children's menu Dogs allowed Garden

### LINTON

## The Windmill Inn ♀

**Main St LS22 4HT ☎ 01937 582209** 🖹 **01937 587518**
web: www.thewindmillinnwetherby.co.uk
dir: *From A1 exit at Tadcaster/Otley junct, follow Otley signs. In Collingham follow Linton signs*

A coaching inn since the 18th century, the building actually dates back to the 14th century, and originally housed the owner of the long-disappeared windmill. Stone walls, antique settles, log fires, oak beams and lots of brass set the scene in which to enjoy good bar food prepared by enthusiastic licensees. Expect the likes of chicken breast on mustard mash with onion jus, sea bass on pepper mash with tomato and basil sauce, baked salmon on Italian risotto, or king prawns in lime and chilli butter. While you're there, ask to take a look at the local history scrapbook.

**Open** all wk 11-3 5.30-11 (Sat-Sun 11-11) Closed: 1 Jan **Bar Meals** L served Mon-Fri 12-2, Sat 12-2.30, Sun 12-5.45 Av main course £8.95 **Restaurant** L served Mon-Fri 12-2, Sat 12-2.30, Sun 12-5.45 D served Mon-Tue 5.30-8.30, Wed-Sat 5.30-9, Sun 12-5.45 Fixed menu price fr £9.95 Av 3 course à la carte fr £13.95 ⊕ SCOTTISH COURAGE ◀ John Smiths, Theakston Best, Daleside, Greene King Ruddles County. ♀ 12 **Facilities** Children's menu Dogs allowed Garden Parking

## MYTHOLMROYD

### Shoulder of Mutton ▾

**New Rd HX7 5DZ ☎ 01422 883165**
dir: *A646 Halifax to Todmorden, in Mytholmroyd on B6138, opposite rail station*

Award-winning Pennines' pub situated by a trout stream in the village where Ted Hughes was born. Popular with walkers, cyclists and families, the pub's reputation for real ales and hearty fare using locally sourced ingredients is strong. The menu ranges from snacks and sandwiches to vegetarian quiche; filled giant Yorkshire pudding; Cumberland sausages; and beef in ale. Look out for the 17th-century counterfeit golden guineas on display in the bar.

Open Closed: Tue L Bar Meals L served Wed-Mon 11.30-2 D served Wed-Sun 7-8.15 Av main course £4.50 ⊕ ENTERPRISE INNS ◀ Black Sheep, Copper Dragon, Greene King IPA, Timothy Taylor Landlord, Castle Eden. ▾ 10 Facilities Children's menu Play area Family room Dogs allowed Garden Parking  ◉

## SOWERBY

### The Travellers Rest ▾

**Steep Ln HX6 1PE ☎ 01422 832124   📄 01422 831365**
dir: *M62 junct 22 or 24*

The stone-built Travellers Rest was built in 1730 and sits high on a steep hillside with glorious views, a dining terrace, duck pond, huge car park and helipad. The cosy stone-flagged bar boasts fresh flowers and an open fire, while the restaurant has beams, animal print sofas, a wood-burning stove, and exposed stonework. Dishes cooked to order from local produce are rooted in Yorkshire tradition yet refined with French flair, yielding a happy mix of classic and contemporary cooking. Start with ham hock terrine with home-made piccalilli, belly pork with truffled new potatoes, or salmon tapas; continue with lamb loin with cabbage and Parma ham, breast of pigeon with bacon and thyme risotto, or venison with sweet potato crisps. Resist the sticky toffee pudding if you can.

Open Closed: Mon-Tue Bar Meals L served Sat 12-2, Sun 12-7 D served Wed-Thu 5-9, Fri 5-9.30, Sat 5.30-9.30, Sun 12-7 Restaurant L served Sat 12-2, Sun 12-7 D served Wed-Thu 5-9, Fri 5-9.30, Sat 5.30-9.30, Sun 12-7 ⊕ FREE HOUSE ◀ Timothy Taylor Landlord, Timothy Taylor, Best Bitter. ▾ 8 Facilities Children's menu Dogs allowed Garden Parking

## SOWERBY BRIDGE

### The Alma Inn

**Cotton Stones HX6 4NS ☎ 01422 823334**
e-mail: info@almainn.com
dir: *Turn off A58 at Triangle Twixt Sowerby Bridge & Ripponden. Follow signs for Cotton Stones*

The old stone inn stands in a dramatic rural location in the heart of Calderdale with views across the glorious Rydale Valley from its terrace and garden. Inside, stone-flagged floors, oak beams, glowing fires, and rustic pine tables set the informal, traditional scene for supping pints of Taylor Landlord and, surprisingly, for tucking into Italian-inspired dishes. Expect great value pizzas and pasta dishes, or fillet steak Rossini, and pubby bar meals, from the Alma burger to fish pie.

Open all day all wk noon-11 Bar Meals Av main course £8 food served all day Restaurant Fixed menu price fr £7.50 Av 3 course à la carte fr £14 food served all day ⊕ FREE HOUSE ◀ Tetley Bitter, Timothy Taylor Landlord, Timothy Taylor Golden Best. Facilities Children's menu Dogs allowed Garden Parking

## THORNTON

### Ring O'Bells Country Pub & Restaurant ▾

**212 Hilltop Rd BD13 3QL ☎ 01274 832296**
📄 **01274 831707**
e-mail: enquiries@theringobells.com
web: www.theringobells.com
dir: *From M62 take A58 for 5m, right onto A644. 4.5m follow Denholme signs, onto Well Head Rd into Hilltop Rd*

On a clear day, views from the Ring O'Bells stretch up to 30 miles across rugged Pennine moorland. The pub was converted from a Wesleyan chapel, and the restaurant was formerly two mill workers' cottages. The wood-panelled and welcoming bar and dining area serves cask-conditioned ales and a fine selection of malt whiskies. The fully air-conditioned Brontë restaurant has a contemporary look; a conservatory running its whole length rewards diners with stunning valley views. Produce is sourced from local farmers and suppliers, so the à la carte menu and daily specials board offer British dishes with European influences. Expect starters such as lamb and spinach meatballs on a tsatziki sauce; turkey, lemon and rice soup; and leek and mushroom tart with creamy blue cheese sauce. Main courses may include poached haddock with prawn mornay sauce; chicken breast filled with garlic wild mushrooms; diced pork with apricots and celery casserole; or pork, coriander and plum sausages with mustard mash. Imaginative vegetarian options are on the blackboard, and all dietary requirements can be catered for. A range of desserts is made to order, from chef's creative crème brûlée to traditional warm lattice apple pie served with vanilla ice cream and toffee sauce.

Open all wk 11.30-4 5.30-11.30 (Sat-Sun 6.15-11.30) Closed: 25 Dec Bar Meals Av main course £10.95 Restaurant Fixed menu price fr £7.95 Av 3 course à la carte fr £19.95 food served all day ⊕ FREE HOUSE ◀ John Smiths, Courage Directors, Black Sheep ales. ▾ 12 Facilities Children's menu Parking

## CHANNEL ISLANDS

## GUERNSEY

### CASTEL

## Hotel Hougue du Pommier ★★★ HL

**Hougue du Pommier Rd GY5 7FQ ☎ 01481 256531**
📠 01481 256260
e-mail: hotel@houguedupommier.guernsey.net
dir: *Telephone for directions*

An 18th-century Guernsey farmhouse with the only feu du bois (literally 'cooking on the fire') in the Channel Islands. Eat in the beamed Tudor Bar with its open fire or the more formal restaurant. Menu options may include dishes from the spit-roast menu, baked aubergine and Mediterranean vegetable ragout; chargrilled supreme of chicken; or Chef's seafood fishcake. The 8-acre gardens have a swimming pool, barbecue and medieval area, where banquets are held the first Saturday of the month.

Open all day all wk **Bar Meals** L served all wk 12-2 booking required D served all wk 6.30-9 booking required Av main course £9.50 **Restaurant** L served all wk 12-2 booking required D served all wk 6.30-9 booking required Fixed menu price fr £19.50 Av 3 course à la carte fr £25 ⊕ FREE HOUSE ◀ John Smiths, Extra Smooth, Guernsey Best Bitter, Guinness. **Facilities** Children's menu Dogs allowed Garden Parking **Rooms** 40

## JERSEY

### ST AUBIN

## Old Court House Inn ♟

**St Aubin's Harbour JE3 8AB ☎ 01534 746433**
📠 01534 745103
e-mail: info@oldcourthousejersey.com
dir: *From Jersey Airport, right at exit, left at lights, 0.5m to St Aubin*

The original courthouse at the rear of the property dates from 1450 and was first restored in 1611. Beneath the front part are enormous cellars where privateers stored their plunder. Three bars offer food, and there are two restaurants, the Granite and the Mizzen, with terrific views over the harbour, plus an attractive courtyard. There's lots of locally caught fish on the menus of course.

Open Closed: 25 Dec, Mon Jan-Feb **Bar Meals** L served all wk 12.30-2.30 D served Mon-Sat 7-10 Av main course £8 **Restaurant** L served all wk 12.30-2.30 D served all wk 7-10.30 Fixed menu price fr £10 Av 3 course à la carte fr £20 ⊕ FREE HOUSE ◀ Directors, Theakstons, John Smiths, Jersey Brewery. ♟ 8 **Facilities** Children's menu Dogs allowed Garden

### ST MARTIN

## Royal Hotel ♟

**La Grande Route de Faldouet JE3 6UG ☎ 01534 856289**
📠 01534 857298
e-mail: johnbarker@jerseymail.co.uk
dir: *2m from Five Oaks rdbt towards St Martyn. Pub on right next to St Martin's Church*

A friendly atmosphere, value for money, and great food and drink are the hallmarks of this friendly local in the heart of St Martin. John Barker, the landlord, has been extending a welcome for 23 years at this former coaching inn. Roaring log fires warm winter visitors, and there's a sunny beer garden to relax in during the summer months. Among the traditional home-made favourites are steak and ale pie, fresh grilled trout, monkfish and prawn Thai curry, and vegetarian lasagne. Ploughman's lunches, filled jacket potatoes, grills and children's choices are also on offer.

Open all day all wk **Bar Meals** L served Mon-Sat 12-2.15 D served Mon-Sat 6-8.30 Av main course £8.50 **Restaurant** L served Mon-Sat 12-2.15 D served Mon-Sat 6-8.30 ⊕ RANDALLS VAUTIER ◀ John Smiths Smooth, Theakstons Cool, Guinness, Ringwood Real Ale. ♟ 9 **Facilities** Children's menu Play area Garden Parking

## ISLE OF MAN

### PORT ERIN

## Falcon's Nest Hotel ★★ HL

**The Promenade, Station Rd IM9 6AF ☎ 01624 834077**
📠 01624 835370
e-mail: falconsnest@enterprise.net

A popular hotel overlooking a beautiful, sheltered harbour and beach. In 1865 Gladstone, then prime minister, stayed here with his son, and was responsible for what he called 'an amusing incident' involving a teapot. The lounge and saloon bars serve local beers, over 150 whiskies, snacks and meals, although there is also a restaurant with carvery option. Fish include local crab, prawns, sea bass, lobster and local scallops known as 'queenies'.

Open all wk **Bar Meals** L served all wk 12-2 D served all wk 6-9 Av main course £8 **Restaurant** L served all wk 12-2 D served all wk 6-9 Fixed menu price fr £15 Av 3 course à la carte fr £21 ⊕ FREE HOUSE ◀ Manx guest ale, Guinness, John Smiths, guest ales. **Facilities** Children's menu Family room Dogs allowed Parking **Rooms** 35

## SCOTLAND

## CITY OF ABERDEEN

### ABERDEEN

## Old Blackfriars ♟

**52 Castle St AB11 5BB ☎ 01224 581922**
📄 **01224 582153**
dir: *From train station down Deeside to Union St. Turn right. Pub at end on right*

Stunning stained glass and a warm, welcoming atmosphere are features of this traditional city centre pub, situated in Aberdeen's historic Castlegate. It is built on the site of property owned by Blackfriars Dominican monks, hence the name. The menu runs from sandwiches and filled potatoes through to hearty dishes such as bangers and mash; chicken tikka masala; and beef au poivre. Finish with sticky toffee pudding or pancakes in maple syrup.

**Open** all wk Closed: 25 Dec, 1 Jan ⊕ BELHAVEN ◀ Abbot Ale, Deuchars IPA, Caledonian 80/-, Inveralmond, Ossian, Guest ales. ♟ 12

## ABERDEENSHIRE

### MARYCULTER

## Old Mill Inn

**South Deeside Rd AB12 5FX ☎ 01224 733212**
📄 **01224 732884**
e-mail: Info@oldmillinn.co.uk
dir: *5m W of Aberdeen on B9077*

This delightful family-run 200-year-old country inn stands on the edge of the River Dee, five miles from Aberdeen city centre. A former mill house, the 18th-century granite building has been tastefully modernised to include a restaurant where the finest Scottish ingredients feature on the menu: venison stovies, peppered carpaccio of beef, cullen skink, and chicken and venison terrine are typical.

**Open** all wk **Bar Meals** L served all wk 12-2 D served all wk 5.30-9 **Restaurant** L served all wk 12-2 D served all wk 5.30-9 ⊕ FREE HOUSE ◀ Interbrew Bass, Caledonian Deuchars IPA, Timothy Taylor Landlord. **Facilities** Children's menu Garden Parking

### NETHERLEY

## The Lairhillock Inn ♟

**AB39 3QS ☎ 01569 730001** 📄 **01569 731175**
e-mail: info@lairhillock.co.uk
dir: *From Aberdeen take A90. Right towards Durris on B9077 then left onto B979 to Netherley*

Set in beautiful rural Deeside yet only 15 minutes drive from Aberdeen, this award-winning 200-year-old former coaching inn offers real ales in the bar and real fires in the lounge to keep out the winter chill. Dishes are robust and use a bounty of fresh, quality, local and regional produce such as langoustines from Gourdon, mussels from Shetland, scallops from Orkney, wild boar and venison from the Highlands and salmon from the Dee and Don, not forgetting certified Aberdeen Angus beef. For lunch, try the Lairhillock lasagne which layers pasta with minced venison, beef and pork topped with wild mushroom sauce. For a more formal dining option, the atmospheric Crynoch restaurant menu might feature shredded confit duck leg and beetroot timbale, followed by chicken supreme filled with sage and sausagemeat. Quality abounds on the children's menu too, where spicy spare ribs and Finnan haddock fishcakes can be found.

**Open** all wk 11am-mdnt Closed: 25-26 Dec, 1-2 Jan **Bar Meals** L served all wk 12-2 booking required D served all wk 6-9.30 booking required Av main course £9.95 **Restaurant** D served Tue-Sat 7-9.30 booking required Av 3 course à la carte fr £27.50 ⊕ FREE HOUSE ◀ Timothy Taylor Landlord, Courage Directors, Cairngorm, Tradewinds, Greene King IPA. ♟ 7 **Facilities** Children's menu Dogs allowed Garden Parking

## ARGYLL & BUTE

### ARDUAINE

## Loch Melfort Hotel ★★★ HL 🌐🌐 ♟

**PA34 4XG ☎ 01852 200233**
e-mail: reception@lochmelfort.co.uk
web: www.lochmelfort.co.uk
dir: *On A816, 20m s of Oban*

Standing in 26 acres of grounds next to the National Trust for Scotland's Arduaine Gardens, this award–winning hotel and restaurant offers the perfect place for a relaxing holiday or short break at any time of year. The hotel is framed by woodlands and the magnificent mountains of Argyll and, from its waterside location on the Scottish west coast, guests can enjoy spectacular views across Asknish Bay and the Sound of Jura. There's a uniquely informal and relaxed atmosphere as you step into the warmth and tranquillity of this comfortable country house with its cosy bar, welcoming sitting rooms and squashy sofas beside the log fire. The main house is principally Victorian, built by J. Arthur Campbell in 1896; some of the beautiful original features remain, including oak panelling and 19th-century family portraits. Fresh scented flowers adorn the treasured occasional tables and bookcases, whilst the latest lifestyle magazines are available in the lounges. Choose to dine in the formal Arduaine Restaurant, where tian of Asknish Bay crab with apple and sweet pepper sauce; or marinated Islay scallops with pea pesto, lime and chilli dressing might introduce main courses like pan-fried loin of Argyll venison with dauphinoise potatoes, creamed leeks and a thyme and juniper jus; or sea trout fillet with braised fennel, and pea and chervil risotto. The more relaxed atmosphere of the modern Chartroom 2 bar and bistro is the place to enjoy all-day drinks, teas, coffees and home baking, as well as light lunches and suppers. It has the finest views on the West Coast and serves home-made Scottish fare including plenty of locally landed seafood. You can sit outside and enjoy a drink in warmer weather or crowd around the cosy fire in winter and watch the waves crashing against the rocks.

Open all wk 11-11 Bar Meals L served all wk 12-2.30 D served all wk 6-8.30 Av main course £8.95 ⊕ FREE HOUSE ◀ 80/- Ale Belhaven, Fyne Ale. ♟ 8 Facilities Children's menu Play area Dogs allowed Garden Parking Rooms 25

### CONNEL

## The Oyster Inn

**PA37 1PJ ☎ 01631 710666  📄 01631 710042**
e-mail: stay@oysterinn.co.uk
dir: *Please telephone for directions*

A comfortable, informal hotel overlooking the tidal whirlpools and white water of the Falls of Lora, and enjoying glorious views of the mountains of Mull. It was built in the 18th century to serve ferry passengers, but the ferry is no more, superseded by the modern road bridge. Years ago it was known as The Glue Pot, because canny locals knew they could be 'stuck' here between ferries, and thus get round complicated Sunday licensing laws. Food is served all day, using locally-sourced, quality produce, particularly from the sea and lochs, such as West Coast mussels marinière; Ferryman's ocean pie; and seafood pancakes. Other dishes include steak and ale pie; bangers and mash; local lamb shank; and tempura battered vegetables. There's a log fire in the bar, where regular live music is performed, and where your companions are reasonably certain to be walkers, divers, canoeists, fishermen or yachting enthusiasts.

Open all wk noon-mdnt Bar Meals L served all wk 12.30-2.30 D served all wk 5.30-8.30 Av main course £9.95 Restaurant D served all wk 6-8.30 booking required ⊕ FREE HOUSE ◀ Guinness. Facilities Children's menu Dogs allowed Garden Parking

### KILFINAN

## Kilfinan Hotel Bar

**PA21 2EP ☎ 01700 821201  📄 01700 821205**
e-mail: kilfinanhotel@btconnect.com
dir: *8m N of Tighnabruaich on B8000*

The hotel, on the eastern shore of Loch Fyne set amid spectacular Highland scenery on a working estate, has been welcoming travellers since the 1760s. The bars are cosy with log fires in winter, and offer a fine selection of malts. There are two intimate dining rooms, with the Lamont room for larger parties. Menus change daily and offer the best of local produce: Loch Fyne oysters, of course, and langoustine grilled in garlic butter; cullen skink soup; and moules marinière, plus game, Aberdeen Angus beef and a variety of Scottish sweets and cheeses. Enjoy the views from the garden on warmer days.

Open all wk Bar Meals L served all wk 12.30-4 D served all wk 6.30-9.30 Av main course £7.95 Restaurant L served all wk 12.30-4 booking required D served all wk 6.30-9.30 booking required Av 3 course à la carte fr £22 ⊕ FREE HOUSE ◀ McEwens 70/-, McEwens 80/-. Facilities Children's menu Family room Dogs allowed Garden Parking

## PORT APPIN

### The Pierhouse Hotel & Seafood Restaurant ★★★ SHL 🏵

**PA38 4DE** ☎ **01631 730302** 📄 **01631 730509**
e-mail: reservations@pierhousehotel.co.uk
dir: *A828 from Ballachulish to Oban. In Appin right at Port Appin & Lismore ferry sign. After 2.5m left after post office, hotel at end of road by pier*

Situated in a quiet village on the shores of Loch Linnhe, this family-run hotel, bar and renowned seafood restaurant is surrounded by Scotland's magnificent West Coast. You arrive along a narrow road from Appin, or by boat, tying up to one of the hotel's ten moorings near the pier. The Pierhouse prides itself on the freshness and quality of its seafood, game and meats, and sources virtually all such produce locally. Once the piermaster's home, it now houses a popular bar, pool room, terrace and dining area, and offers a selection of menus featuring oysters hand-picked from the Lismore beds; mussels and langoustines harvested from Loch Linnhe and Loch Etive; and lobsters and crab kept mouth-wateringly fresh in creels at the end of the pier. As well as fish of the day, there are several seafood platters – the Pierhouse, for example, consists of those local langoustines and mussels, as well as plump grilled Mull scallops, oysters, fresh and smoked salmon and a roll mop. There are alternatives to seafood, such as Highland fillet steak served on creamy herb mash with a whisky and peppercorn sauce; and pappardelle with fresh mushrooms, herbs, white wine, garlic and cream topped with Gruyère cheese.

Open all wk 11-11 Closed: 25-26 Dec Bar Meals L served all wk 12.30-2.30 D served all wk 6.30-9.30 Av main course £9 Restaurant L served all wk 12.30-2.30 booking required D served all wk 6.30-9.30 booking required Fixed menu price fr £35 Av 3 course à la carte fr £23 ⊕ FREE HOUSE ◀ Calders 80/-, Belhaven Best, Guinness. **Facilities** Children's menu Family room Dogs allowed Garden Parking **Rooms** 12

## STRACHUR

### Creggans Inn ★★★ HL 🏵🏵 ☴
**PA27 8BX** ☎ **01369 860279** 📄 **01369 860637**
e-mail: info@creggans-inn.co.uk
dir: *A82 from Glasgow, at Tarbet take A83 towards Cairndow, left onto A815 to Strachur*

From the hills above this informal family-friendly free house on the shores of Loch Fyne, you can gaze across the Mull of Kintyre to the Western Isles beyond. It has been a coaching inn since the days of Mary Queen of Scots. Current proprietors Archie and Gill MacLellan were preceded years ago by Sir Fitzroy Maclean, reputedly the man upon whom Ian Fleming based his most famous character. A good selection of real ales, wines by the glass and malt whiskies are all served at the bar. There's a formal terraced garden and patio for alfresco summer enjoyment, and regional produce plays a key role in the seasonal menus: the famed Loch Fyne oysters of course, but also salmon from the same waters, smoked or grilled. Robust main courses may feature fillet of Aberdeenshire beef; haddock in a crisp beer batter; or pot-roasted chicken. Apple and bramble tart with home-made cinnamon ice cream makes a fulfilling conclusion.

Open all wk 11am-mdnt Bar Meals L served all wk 12-2.30 D served all wk 6-8.30 Av main course £9.50 Restaurant D served all wk 7-8.30 booking required Fixed menu price fr £37.50 ⊕ FREE HOUSE ◀ Fyne Ales Highlander, Atlas Latitude, Deuchars IPA, Harviestoun Bitter & Twisted. ☴ 7 **Facilities** Children's menu Dogs allowed Garden Parking **Rooms** 14

## TAYVALLICH

### Tayvallich Inn
**PA31 8PL** ☎ **01546 870282**
dir: *From Lochgilphead take A816 then B841/B8025*

Following a change of hands in recent times, the Tayvallich Inn is now run by Glen and Lynne Hyde. The property was converted from an old bus garage in 1976. The name translates as 'house in the pass' and it has the most spectacular setting. The inn stands by a natural harbour at the head of Loch Sween with stunning views over the anchorage, particularly from the outside area of decking, where food and drinks can be enjoyed. Those seated inside can gaze out over the village and Tayvallich Bay from the large picture windows. A selection of fine wines and single malts are served as well as Loch Fyne Ales. Not surprisingly given the location, fresh seasonal seafood is the house speciality, available along with good quality pub food. Those interested in the works of 19th-century engineer Thomas Telford will find plenty of bridges and piers in the area.

Open Closed: 25-26 Dec, Mon (Nov-Mar) Bar Meals L served all wk 12-2.15 D served all wk 6-8.45 Restaurant L served all wk 12-2.15 booking required D served all wk 6-8.45 booking required ⊕ FREE HOUSE ◀ Tennents, Guinness, Loch Fyne Ales. **Facilities** Children's menu Dogs allowed Garden Parking

## DUMFRIES & GALLOWAY

### KIRKCUDBRIGHT

### Selkirk Arms Hotel ★★★ HL ♍

**Old High St DG6 4JG ☎ 01557 330402**  📠 **01557 331639**
e-mail: reception@selkirkarmshotel.co.uk
web: www.selkirkarmshotel.co.uk
dir: *M74 & M6 to A75, halfway between Dumfries & Stranraer on A75*

Robert Burns is reputed to have written the Selkirk Grace at this privately owned hotel, and the proprietors have created their own real ale, The Selkirk Grace, in conjunction with Sulwath Brewers. There are two bars, and a great choice of dishes is offered in The Bistro or more intimate Artistas Restaurant, including pan-seared Kirkcudbright king scallops; slow roast lamb shank; and Eccelfechan butter tart.

**Open** all wk **Bar Meals** L served all wk 12-2 D served all wk 6-9 Av main course £9.95 **Restaurant** L served Sun 12-2 booking required D served all wk 7-9 booking required Fixed menu price fr £19 Av 3 course à la carte fr £30 ⊕ FREE HOUSE ◀ Youngers Tartan, John Smiths Bitter, Criffel, Timothy Taylor Landlord, The Selkirk Grace. ♍ 8 **Facilities** Children's menu Dogs allowed Garden Parking **Rooms** 17

### NEW ABBEY

### Criffel Inn

**2 The Square DG2 8BX ☎ 01387 850305  & 850244**
📠 **01387 850305**
e-mail: criffelinn@btconnect.com
dir: *A74/A74(M) exit at Gretna, A75 to Dumfries, A710 to New Abbey*

A former 18th-century coaching inn set on the Solway Coast in the historic conservation village of New Abbey close to the ruins of the 13th-century Sweetheart Abbey. Expect a warm welcome and excellent home-cooked food using local produce. There's a lawned beer garden overlooking the corn-mill and square; ideal for touring Dumfries and Galloway.

**Open** all wk noon-2.30 5-11 (Mon-Tue 5-11 Fri-Sat noon-2.30 5-mdnt) **Bar Meals** L served Wed-Sun 12-2 D served Wed-Sun

5-8 Av main course £7.95 **Restaurant** L served Wed-Sun 12-2 D served Wed-Sun 5-8 ⊕ FREE HOUSE ◀ Belhaven Best, McEwans 60-, Guinness. **Facilities** Children's menu Family room Dogs allowed Garden Parking

### NEWTON STEWART

### The Galloway Arms ★★★ INN ♍

**54-58 Victoria St DG8 6DB ☎ 01671 402653**
📠 **01671 401202**
e-mail: info@gallowayarmshotel.com
dir: *In the centre of Newton Stewart opposite town clock*

Established in 1750, the Galloway Arms is older than the town of Newton Stewart, which was built around it. The newly refurbished Earls Room lounge offers a range of over 100 malt whiskies, as well as real ale and traditional Scottish beers. Local produce from a 20-mile radius is the foundation of most dishes, which might feature fresh Kirkcudbright scallops, beef sourced from only five local farms or Galloway venison.

**Open** all day all wk 11am-mdnt (Fri-Sat 11am-1am) **Bar Meals** L served all wk 12-2 D served all wk 6-9 Av main course £8 **Restaurant** D served all wk 6-9 Av 3 course à la carte fr £17.95 ⊕ FREE HOUSE ◀ Belhavan Best, Guinness, Caledonian Deuchars IPA. ♍ 11 **Facilities** Children's menu Dogs allowed Garden Parking **Rooms** 17

## DUNDEE, CITY OF

### BROUGHTY FERRY

### The Royal Arch Bar ♍

**285 Brook St DD5 2DS ☎ 01382 779741**
📠 **01382 739174**
dir: *3m from Dundee. 0.5 min from Broughty Ferry rail station*

In Victorian times, the jute industry made Broughty Ferry the 'richest square mile in Europe'. Named after a Masonic lodge which was demolished to make way for the Tay road bridge, the pub dates from 1869. Look forward to a nice pint in the bar with its original hand-carved oak bar, sideboard and counter. An extensive selection of meals range from light snacks to three-course meals, served in the bar, lounge, restaurant or pavement café.

**Open** all wk Closed: 1 Jan **Bar Meals** L served Mon-Fri 12-2.15, Sat-Sun 12-5 booking required D served All wk 5-7.30 booking required Av main course £8 ⊕ FREE HOUSE ◀ McEwans 80/-,

Scotland

Belhaven Best, Guinness, Caledonian, Deuchars IPA. ♀ 12
**Facilities** Children's menu Family room Dogs allowed Garden

## GATEHEAD

### The Cochrane Inn

**45 Main Rd KA2 0AP ☎ 01563 570122**
dir: *From Glasgow A77 to Kilmarnock, then A759 to Gatehead*

There's a friendly, bustling atmosphere inside this traditional
village centre pub, which sits just a short drive from the
Ayrshire coast. The menus combine British and international
flavours. At lunch this might translate as cullen skink with
crayfish tails followed by penne Arrabiata or spicy lamb curry.
In the evening, maybe crispy bacon and houmous on toast
ahead of a hearty steak pie with carrots and mash.

**Open** all wk noon-2.30 5.30 onwards (Sun noon-9) **Bar Meals**
food served all day **Restaurant** food served all day ⊕ FREE
HOUSE ◀ John Smiths. **Facilities** Children's menu Garden Parking

## EDINBURGH, CITY OF

### EDINBURGH

### Bennets Bar ♀

**8 Leven St EH3 9LG ☎ 0131 229 5143**
e-mail: knight@hotmail.com
dir: *Next to Kings Theatre. Please phone for more detailed directions*

Bennets is a friendly pub, popular with performers from the
adjacent Kings Theatre, serving real ales and over 120 malt
whiskies. It's a listed property dating from 1839 with hand-
painted tiles and murals on the walls, original stained glass
windows and brass beer taps. Reasonably priced home-made
food ranges from toasties, burgers and salads to stovies,
steak pie, and macaroni cheese. There's also a daily roast and
traditional puddings.

**Open** all wk 11-11 (Sun noon-1am) Closed: 25 Dec **Bar Meals** L
served Mon-Sat 12-2 D served Mon-Sat 5-8.30 Av main course
£6.25 ⊕ IONA PUB ◀ Caledonian Deuchars IPA, Guinness,
Caledonian 80/-. ♀ 14 **Facilities** Children's menu Family room

## RATHO

### The Bridge Inn ♀

**27 Baird Rd EH28 8RA ☎ 0131 333 1320**
📄 0131 333 3480
e-mail: info@bridgeinn.com
dir: *From Newbridge at B7030 junct, follow signs for Ratho and
Edinburgh Canal Centre*

An 18th-century former farmhouse was converted to create this
canal-side pub in 1820 with the opening of the Union Canal.
It was once owned by the family of the last man to be hanged
in public in Edinburgh, and his ghost is reputed to haunt the
building. In addition to the restaurant and two bars, The Bridge
Inn also has a restaurant barge on the canal, providing the

perfect venue for wedding parties, birthdays and other special
events. Dishes range from bar snacks and light bites, such as
mushrooms stuffed with haggis and black pudding, battered,
deep-fried and served with red onion marmalade, to main
courses of smoked haddock fishcakes with lime and tarragon
dressing, or pork and beef medallions with wholegrain mustard
sauce and crushed potatoes.

**Open** all day all wk 11-11 (Fri-Sat 11am-mdnt) Closed: 25-26
Dec, 1-2 Jan **Bar Meals** L served Mon-Sat 11-9, Sun 12-30-9
D served Mon-Sat 11-9, Sun 12-30-9 Av main course £9 food
served all day **Restaurant** L served Mon-Sat 12-2.30, Sun
12.30-8.30 booking required D served Mon-Sat 6.30-9.30, Sun
12.30-8.30 booking required Fixed menu price fr £9.50 Av 3
course à la carte fr £16 ⊕ FREE HOUSE ◀ Belhaven, Deuchars
IPA, Tennents, Stewarts Pentland. ♀ 6 **Facilities** Children's menu
Family room Garden Parking

## FIFE

### ANSTRUTHER

### The Dreel Tavern ♀

**16 High Street West KY10 3DL ☎ 01333 310727**
📄 01333 310577
e-mail: dreeltavern@aol.com
dir: *From Anstruther centre take A917 towards Pittenweem*

Complete with a local legend concerning an amorous
encounter between James V and a local gypsy woman,
the welcoming 17th-century Dreel Tavern has plenty of
atmosphere. Its oak beams, open fire and stone walls retain
much of the distant past, while home-cooked food and cask-
conditioned ales are served to hungry visitors of the present.
Peaceful gardens overlook Dreel Burn.

**Open** all wk 11am-mdnt **Bar Meals** L served all wk 12-3 D served
all wk 5.30-9.30 **Restaurant** L served all wk 12-3 D served all wk
5.30-9.30 ⊕ FREE HOUSE ◀ Deuchars IPA, 2 guest ales. ♀ 20
**Facilities** Children's menu Family room Dogs allowed Garden
Parking

## CRAIL

### The Golf Hotel ♀

**4 High St KY10 3TD ☎ 01333 450206   📄 01333 450795**
e-mail: enquiries@thegolfhotelcrail.com
dir: *At the end of High Street opposite Royal Bank*

The present day Golf Hotel occupies a striking 18th-century
Grade I listed building, but the first inn on the site opened
its doors 400 years earlier. The characterful bars have an old
world atmosphere. Well known for its traditional Scottish
high tea with home-made pancakes and cakes, the inn is also
popular for its home cooking. Choices range from fresh Crail
crab salad and macaroni cheese through to steak and Deuchars
ale pie or grilled fresh haddock in garlic butter from the carte
menu.

continued

**Scotland**

Open all day all wk 11am-mdnt (Sun noon-mdnt) Bar Meals Av main course £6.50 food served all day Restaurant Av 3 course à la carte fr £15 food served all day ⊕ FREE HOUSE ◀ McEwans 60/-, 80/-, 70/-, Belhaven Best, real ale. ♀ 6 Facilities Children's menu Dogs allowed Garden Parking

## ST ANDREWS

### The Inn at Lathones ★★★★ INN ◉◉ ♀
Largoward KY9 1JE ☎ 01334 840494  📄 01334 840694
e-mail: lathones@theinn.co.uk
dir: 5m from St Andrews on A915

St Andrews' oldest coaching inn – parts of the building date back over 400 years. Belhaven Best on tap is backed by eleven bottled Orkney beers served in pewter tankards in the bar lounge, which welcomes with leather sofas and log burning fires; the pewter theme continues with the restaurant's water goblets. A consistent winner of AA rosettes, the kitchen team prepares the best fresh local produce in seasonal menus. A typical carte selection could start with hare fillet and scallops on a rocket salad; and follow with a tempura of salmon, halibut and haddock with home-made chips and tartare sauce. Puddings of the day are usually old favourites, but more exotic options also tempt. The inn is an award-winning live music venue, a considerable achievement when maximum capacity is limited to just 50 people; the walls of the inn display one of the best collections of music memorabilia in the country.

Open all wk Closed: 2wks Jan Bar Meals Av main course £10.50 food served all day Restaurant L served all wk 12-2.30 D served all wk 6-9.30 Av 3 course à la carte fr £25 ⊕ FREE HOUSE ◀ Dark Island, Three Sisters, Belhaven Best. ♀ 11 Facilities Children's menu Dogs allowed Garden Parking Rooms 13

### The Jigger Inn ♀
The Old Course Hotel KY16 9SP ☎ 01334 474371
📄 01334 477688
dir: Please telephone for directions

Once the stationmaster's lodge on a railway line that disappeared many years ago, the Jigger is in the grounds of the Old Course Hotel. St Andrew's is renowned throughout the world as the Home of Golf, so don't be surprised by the golfing memorabilia, or by sharing bar space with a caddy or two. Open-hearth fires are the backdrop for a selection of Scottish beers. All-day availability is one advantage of a short, simple menu that lists soup, sandwiches and barbecued chicken salad wrap with honey mustard dressing as starters, and continues with beer-battered fish and chips; sausage and mash with onion gravy; warm sunblushed tomato with goats' cheese and rocket tart, and gremolata dressing; and grilled Speyside steak with seasoned fries and onion rings.

Open all day all wk 11-11 (Sun noon-11) Closed: 25 Dec Bar Meals L served all wk 12-9.30 Av main course £11 food served all day Restaurant D served all wk 12-9.30 booking required ⊕ FREE HOUSE ◀ Guinness, St Andrews Best. ♀ 8 Facilities Children's menu Garden Parking

### GLASGOW

### Ubiquitous Chip ◉◉ ♀
12 Ashton Ln G12 8SJ ☎ 0141 334 5007
📄 0141 337 6417
e-mail: mail@ubiquitouschip.co.uk
dir: In West End of Glasgow, off Byres Rd. Beside Hillhead subway station

Situated in a unique, glass-covered mews, with cobbled floors, water fountains and a fabulous array of lush green plants, this culinary legend combines Scottish tradition with an imaginative touch. Glasgow residents have been treated to some top-notch Scottish cooking for 38 years and the place is as popular as ever. Traditional draught beers, over a hundred malt whiskies and excellent wines are served from three bars; the stunning roof terrace is a quiet space in which to enjoy them. The original upper level bar with its coal fire and the sound of no music is a regular haunt for the city's media types. The Wee bar, reputed to be the smallest in Scotland, is intimate and cosy. Finally the Corner bar boasts an imported tin ceiling and a granite bar top reclaimed from a mortuary. The food continues to showcase the best of Scotland's produce, take Orkney organic salmon with spinach sauce, Angus fillet steak au poivre, Seil Island crab salad, and Scrabster ling on clapshot with chillied seaweed.

Open all wk 11am-mdnt Closed: 25 Dec, 1 Jan Bar Meals L served all wk 12-11 D served all wk 12-11 Av main course £5.50 food served all day Restaurant L served Mon-Sat 12.30-2.30, Sun 12.30-3 booking required D served all wk 5.30-11 booking required Fixed menu price fr £23.85 Av 3 course à la carte fr £15 food served all day ⊕ FREE HOUSE ◀ Deuchars IPA, The Chip 71 Ale. ♀ 21 Facilities Children's menu

### AVIEMORE

### The Old Bridge Inn ♀
Dalfaber Rd PH22 1PU ☎ 01479 811137
e-mail: nigel@oldbridgeinn.co.uk
dir: Exit A9 to Aviemore, 1st left to Ski Rd, then 1st left again 200mtrs

Set in the spectacular Scottish Highlands, in an area well-known for its outdoor pursuits, this friendly Aviemore pub overlooks the River Spey. Dine in the relaxing bars with roaring log fire, the comfortable restaurant, or in the attractive riverside garden. A tempting chargrill menu includes lamb chops in redcurrant jelly, Aberdeen Angus sirloin or rib-eye steaks, and butterflied breast of chicken marinated in yoghurt, lime and coriander. Other choices include braised guinea fowl with brandy or potato gnocchi with butternut squash in a filo basket.

Open all wk 11-11 (Fri-Sat 11am-mdnt Sun 12.30-11) Bar Meals L served all wk 12-2 D served all wk 6-9 Restaurant L served all wk 12-2 booking required D served all wk 6-9 booking required ⊕ FREE HOUSE ◀ Caledonian 80/-, Cairngorm Highland IPA, Deuchars IPA, Timothy Taylor, Atlas Avalanche. ♥ 18 **Facilities** Children's menu Play area Family room Garden Parking

## CARRBRIDGE

### The Cairn ⚘ ★★★ INN ♥

**PH23 3AS** ☎ **01479 841212** 📄 **01479 841362**
e-mail: info@cairnhotel.co.uk
dir: *Village centre on old A9 close to historic 1717 Pack Horse bridge*

The Highland village of Carrbridge and this family-run inn make the perfect base for exploring the Cairngorms, the Moray coast and the Malt Whisky Trail. In the homely, tartan-carpeted bar, you'll find blazing winter log fires, all-day sandwiches, and hearty bar meals, including sweet marinated herring with oatcakes, venison sausage casserole, and sticky toffee pudding.

**Open** all day all wk 11-11 (Fri-Sat 11am-1am) **Bar Meals** L served all wk 12-2 D served all wk 6-8.30 Av main course £7 ⊕ FREE HOUSE ◀ Cairngorm, Orkney. ♥ 8 **Facilities** Children's menu Dogs allowed Garden Parking **Rooms** 7

## CAWDOR

### Cawdor Tavern ♥

**The Lane IV12 5XP** ☎ **01667 404777** 📄 **01667 404777**
e-mail: enquiries@cawdortavern.info
dir: *From A96 (Inverness-Aberdeen) take B9006 & follow Cawdor Castle signs. Tavern in village centre*

Standing close to the famous castle in a beautiful conservation village, the tavern was formerly a joinery workshop for the Cawdor Estate. Oak panelling from the castle, gifted by the late laird, is used to great effect in the lounge bar. Roaring log fires keep the place cosy and warm on long winter evenings, while the garden patio comes into its own in summer. A single menu is offered for both restaurant and bar, where refreshments include a choice of real ales and 100 malt whiskies. The pub's reputation for seafood draws diners from some distance for dishes like fresh Wester Ross salmon with potatoes and parsley butter. Other favourites include smooth chicken liver pâté with home-made apple jelly and crostini; a trio of Scottish puddings – black pudding, white pudding and haggis served with home-made chutney; and prime beef steak pie and mash.

**Open** all wk 11-3 5-11 (Sat 11am-mdnt Sun 12.30-11) Closed: 25 Dec, 1 Jan **Bar Meals** L served Mon-Sat 12-2, Sun 12.30-3

D served all wk 5.30-9 booking required Av main course £8.95 **Restaurant** D served all wk 5.30-9 booking required Av 3 course à la carte fr £18.95 ⊕ FREE HOUSE ◀ Red McGregor, 3 Sisters, Orkney Dark Island, Raven Ale, Latitude Highland Pilsner. ♥ 8 **Facilities** Children's menu Family room Dogs allowed Garden Parking

## GAIRLOCH

### The Old Inn ♥

**IV21 2BD** ☎ **01445 712006** 📄 **01445 712933**
e-mail: info@theoldinn.net
dir: *Just off A832, near harbour at south end of village*

Gairloch's oldest hostelry enjoys a fabulous setting at the foot of the Flowerdale Valley by the harbour, looking out across Gairloch Harbour to the isles of Rona, Raasay and Skye, and was built by the estate in 1750. On a good day, you might be able to spy the Outer Hebrides from this attractive inn, which makes a popular base for the many local activities - walking, fishing, golf, bird-watching and boat trips to see whales and bottlenose dolphins – or for simply resting and lolling. In the two bars you'll find the inn's own beer, the Blind Piper of Gairloch, which was created by the landlord and locals, alongside a good range of real ales. If you fancy a wee dram, then you have an extensive range of Highland malts to choose from. Seafood is the main draw in an area where Gairloch lobster, Loch Ewe scallops, Minch langoustines, mussels, brown crab and fresh fish are regularly landed. Tuck into Cullen skink, a soup of smoked haddock, potato and cream, or crispy-fried squid, before launching into smoked haddock risotto; pan-seared scallops with smoked bacon mash and tamarind sauce, or Cajun-spiced cod. Carnivores will not be disappointed with pork belly served with herb-roasted vegetables, or venison steak with braised red cabbage, garlic confit, basil mash, and Highland blue cheese and whisky cream. A large grassy area by the pretty stream with picnic tables is an attractive place to eat and enjoy the views. Dogs are more than welcome, with bowls, baskets and rugs to help them feel at home.

**Open** all day all wk 11am-mdnt (Sun noon-mdnt) **Bar Meals** L served all wk 12-2.30 (summer 12-4.30) D served all wk 5-9.30 Av main course £9.50 food served all day **Restaurant** D served all wk 6-9.30 booking required Fixed menu price fr £25 Av 3 course à la carte fr £17.50 ⊕ FREE HOUSE ◀ Adnams Bitter, Isle of Skye Red Cullin, Blind Piper, An Teallach, Deuchars IPA, Wildcat. ♥ 8 **Facilities** Children's menu Play area Family room Dogs allowed Garden Parking

## INVERIE

### The Old Forge

**PH41 4PL ☎ 01687 462267** 📄 **01687 462267**
e-mail: info@theoldforge.co.uk
dir: *From Fort William take A830 (Road to the Isles) towards Mallaig. Take ferry from Mallaig to Inverie (boat details on website)*

Britain's most remote mainland pub, The Old Forge is accessible only by boat, and stands literally between heaven and hell (Loch Nevis is Gaelic for heaven and Loch Hourn is Gaelic for hell). It's popular with everyone from locals to hillwalkers, and is renowned for its impromptu ceilidhs. It is also the ideal place to sample local fish and seafood, and other specialities such as haunch of estate venison. There are nine boat moorings and a daily ferry from Mallaig.

**Open** all wk **Bar Meals** L served all wk 12-3 D served all wk 6-9.30 Av main course £10 food served all day **Restaurant** L served all wk 12-3 D served all wk 6-9.30 ⊕ FREE HOUSE 🍺 80 Shilling, Guinness, Red Cuillin, real ales. **Facilities** Children's menu Play area Family room Dogs allowed Garden Parking

## LYBSTER

### Portland Arms ★★★★ INN 🍷

**KW3 6BS ☎ 01593 721721** 📄 **01593 721722**
e-mail: manager.portlandarms@ohiml.com
dir: *Exit A9 signed Latheron, take A99 to Wick. Then 4m to Lybster*

A former coaching inn, just half a mile from the North Sea coastline, the welcoming Portland Arms has evolved into a comfortable modern hotel. The bar and dining areas serve fresh local produce and extensive menus cater for all tastes, with everything from home-made soup with freshly baked baguette to flash-fried langoustine in garlic and brandy butter. Look out for delicious desserts and home baking with morning coffee and afternoon tea. Sunday lunch is a speciality.

**Open** all day all wk 7am-11pm **Bar Meals** food served all day **Restaurant** food served all day ⊕ FREE HOUSE 🍺 McEwans 70/-, Guinness. 🍷 6 **Facilities** Children's menu Parking **Rooms** 22

## NORTH BALLACHULISH

### Loch Leven Hotel

**Old Ferry Rd PH33 6SA ☎ 01855 821236**
📄 **01855 821550**
e-mail: reception@lochlevenhotel.co.uk
dir: *Off A82, N of Ballachulish Bridge*

With its relaxed atmosphere, beautiful loch-side setting, and dramatic views, this privately owned hotel lies in the heart of Lochaber, 'The Outdoor Capital of the UK', and is popular with walkers and climbers. It began life over 300 years ago, accommodating travellers using the Ballachulish Ferry. Food is available in the restaurant and the bar, both of which offer spectacular views over the fast-flowing narrows to the mountains. Home-cooked meals use local produce, especially fresh seafood, game and other traditional Scottish dishes.

**Open** 11-11 (Thu-Sat 11am-mdnt Sun 12.30-11) Closed: afternoons in winter **Bar Meals** L served all wk 12-3 D served all wk 6-9 Av main course £8.95 **Restaurant** L served all wk 12-3 D served all wk 6-9 Fixed menu price fr £12.95 Av 3 course à la carte fr £15 ⊕ FREE HOUSE 🍺 John Smith's Extra Smooth, MacEwans 80%. **Facilities** Children's menu Play area Family room Dogs allowed Garden Parking

## PLOCKTON

### The Plockton Hotel ★★★ SHL 🍷

**Harbour St IV52 8TN ☎ 01599 544274** 📄 **01599 544475**
e-mail: info@plocktonhotel.co.uk
web: www.plocktonhotel.co.uk
dir: *On A87 to Kyle of Lochalsh take turn at Balmacara. Plockton 7m N*

The Pearson family's uniquely converted inn stands on the shores of Loch Carron, with stunning views of the loch to the surrounding Applecross hills – it's a location to die for. It was built in 1827 and later became a ship's chandlery from which it was converted into a hotel in 1913 and has now been run by the Pearson family for 20 years, who are fully committed to caring for their guests with good old-fashioned Highland hospitality. Menus are based on the very best of Highland produce, with seafood a major strength: locally caught langoustines and fresh fish landed at Gairloch and Kinlochbervie. This translates to smoked fish soup, roast monkfish wrapped in bacon, and traditional battered haddock and chips. Meat-eaters will not be disappointed with the Aberdeen Angus rib-eye steak platter served with a peppered whisky sauce. A fine range of malts is available to round off that perfect Highland day.

**Open** all day all wk 11am-mdnt (Sun 12.30pm-11pm) **Bar Meals** L served all wk 12-2.15 D served all wk 6-10 Av main course £9.75 **Restaurant** L served all wk 12-2.15 D served all wk 6-10 booking required Av 3 course à la carte fr £20 ⊕ FREE HOUSE 🍺 Caledonian Deuchars IPA, Hebridean Gold - Isle of Skye Brewery, Harviestoun Blonde Ale, Crags Ale. 🍷 6 **Facilities** Children's menu Family room Garden **Rooms** 15

## Plockton Inn & Seafood Restaurant

**Innes St IV52 8TW** ☎ **01599 544222** 📄 **01599 544487**
e-mail: info@plocktoninn.co.uk
dir: *On A87 to Kyle of Lochalsh take turn at Balmacara. Plockton 7m N*

Mary Gollan and her brother Kenny, the proprietors of this attractive stone-built free house, were born and bred in Plockton. Their great grandfather built this property as a manse, just 100 metres from the harbour in the fishing village where BBC Scotland's Hamish Macbeth series was filmed in the mid-1990s. Mary, Kenny and his partner, Susan Trowbridge, bought the inn over ten years ago, Mary and Susan doing the cooking, Kenny running the bar. The atmosphere is relaxed and friendly, with winter fires in both bars, and a selection of more than 50 malt whiskies. Taking pride of place on the regular and daily-changing specials menus in the dining room and the lounge bar are fresh West Coast fish and shellfish and West Highland beef, lamb and game. Starters include fish-based soup of the day; hot Plockton prawns (landed by the barman himself) with garlic butter; and roasted red pepper pâté. Haggis and clapshot is a particular speciality (including a vegetarian version), served with neeps, tatties and home-made pickled beetroot. Seafood main dishes take in creel-caught langoustines from the waters of Loch Carron, served cold with Marie Rose sauce; and hake fillet with pesto crust, as well as the famous seafood platter. The finest seafood is taken to the smokehouse on the premises and can later be enjoyed from the menu. Other dishes include braised lamb shank; venison in ale; chicken Caesar salad; and aubergine parmigiana. Among some truly mouth-watering desserts is lemon and ginger crunch pie, as well as a selection of Scottish cheeses served with Orkney oatcakes. The National Centre of Excellence in Traditional Music is based in Plockton, which is why the inn's public bar resonates with fantastic live sounds on Tuesdays and Thursdays.

**Open** all day all wk **Bar Meals** L served all wk 12-2.30 D served all wk 6-9 **Restaurant** D served all wk 6-9 booking required Av 3 course à la carte fr £18 ⊕ FREE HOUSE ◀ Greene King Abbot Ale, Fuller's London Pride, Isle Of Skye Blaven, Caledonian 80/-, Plockton Crag Ale. **Facilities** Children's menu Play area Dogs allowed Garden Parking

## TORRIDON

## The Torridon Inn ♀

**IV22 2EY** ☎ **01445 791242** 📄 **01445 712253**
e-mail: Inn@thetorridon.com
web: www.thetorridon.com
dir: *From Inverness take A9 N, then follow signs to Ullapool. Take A835 then A832. In Kinlochewe take A896 to Annat. Pub 200yds on right after village*

Once a grand shooting lodge, built for the first Earl of Lovelace in 1887, The Torridon enjoys one of the most impressive coastal positions in the Scottish Highlands. The inn was created by converting the stable block, buttery and farm buildings of nearby Ben Damph House, now known as The Torridon Hotel. Whether you use it as a base to enjoy some of the many activities on offer, or simply want to unwind with a warm fire and relaxing pint from the good selection of local real ales after a hard day's walking, you can be sure of a memorable visit. Newly refurbished, the cosy bar offers a Highland welcome from both staff and locals: choose from a range of over 60 malt whiskies, or recount the day's adventures over a pint of local real ale. Entertainment ranges from indoor games to regular traditional live music sessions. The inn has its own restaurant, also refurbished, where you can sample high quality, locally sourced food at any time. Hearty soups, sandwiches and bar meals are available during the day, and in the evening there's a delicious choice of starters, main courses and desserts. Local produce drives menus that might feature venison, salmon, haggis and home-made specials. Dinner could begin with caramelised onion tart with fresh rocket and olive oil, or double-baked Beauly wild boar belly with Loch Ewe scallops and caramelised apple. Typical main course choices include game casserole served with creamy mashed potatoes and seasonal baby vegetables; butternut squash, ricotta and pine nut pasta parcels in a creamy pesto sauce; and whole baked trout with almond, breadcrumb and spring onion stuffing, served with new potatoes and garden salad. Tea and coffee is available throughout the day.

**Open** all wk Closed: Nov-27 Mar **Bar Meals** L served all wk, all day D served all wk 6-9 Av main course £13.50 food served all day **Restaurant** Av 3 course à la carte fr £22 ◀ Isle of Skye Brewery - Red Cuillin, Blaven, Torridon Ale, Cairngorm Brewery - Stag, Tradewinds. ♀ 8 **Facilities** Children's menu Play area Dogs allowed Garden Parking

Scotland

**Scotland**

## MIDLOTHIAN

### PENICUIK

## The Howgate Restaurant ▼

**Howgate EH26 8PY ☎ 01968 670000 ▤ 01968 670000**
e-mail: peter@howgate.com
dir: *10m N of Peebles. 3m E of Penicuik on A6094 between Leadburn junct & Howgate*

A short drive from Edinburgh, the Howgate was once a racehorse stables and a dairy. These days this long, low building makes a warm and welcoming bar and restaurant, overseen by chefs Steven Worth and Sean Blake. There is an impressive wine list from all the corners of the world, great real ales, a regularly changing menu, and a 'dishes of the moment' selection. Options might include Borders venison and cranberry pie, pan-fried duck breast with asparagus, pan-fried trio of sea bass, salmon and king prawns, or mushroom and red pepper stroganoff.

Open all wk Closed: 25-26 Dec, 1 Jan Bar Meals L served all wk 12-2 D served all wk 6-9.30 Av main course £9.95 Restaurant L served all wk 12-2 booking required D served all wk 6-9.30 booking required Fixed menu price fr £15 Av 3 course à la carte fr £25 ⊕ FREE HOUSE ◖ Belhaven Best, Hoegaarden Wheat Biere. ▼ 12 Facilities Children's menu Garden Parking

## NORTH LANARKSHIRE

### CUMBERNAULD

## Castlecary House Hotel ★★★ HL ▼

**Castlecary Rd G68 0HD ☎ 01324 840233**
▤ 01324 841608
e-mail: enquiries@castlecaryhotel.com
dir: *A80 onto B816 between Glasgow & Stirling. 7m from Falkirk, 9m from Stirling*

Run by the same family for over 30 years, this friendly hotel is located close to the historic Antonine Wall and Forth and Clyde Canal. Meals in the lounge bars plough a traditional furrow with options such as home-made steak pie; oven-baked Scottish salmon fillet with a sun-dried tomato and herb brioche crust; and a range of flame-grilled steaks. More formal restaurant fare is available in Camerons Restaurant.

Open all wk Bar Meals Av main course £8.50 food served all day Restaurant Av 3 course à la carte fr £22 ⊕ FREE HOUSE ◖ Arran Blonde, Harviestoun Brooker's Bitter & Twisted, Inveralmond Ossian's Ale, Housten Peter's Well, Caledonian Deuchars IPA. ▼ 8 Facilities Children's menu Dogs allowed Garden Parking Rooms 60

## PERTH & KINROSS

### GLENFARG

## The Famous Bein Inn ★★ SHL ⊛

**PH2 9PY ☎ 01577 830216 ▤ 01577 830211**
e-mail: enquiries@beininn.com
dir: *On the intersection between A912 & B996. 2m N of Glenfarg just off junct 8, M90*

Situated in a wooded glen overlooking the river, the inn is now owned by a local farming family, well known for the quality of their beef, and maintains a nearly 150-year-old tradition of catering for travellers between Perth and Edinburgh. Locally sourced and freshly prepared food is served in the restaurant or bistro. Expect dishes such as North Sea mackerel fillet with Arran wholegrain mustard potato salad, or pan roast rump of black face Perthshire lamb with bacon and cabbage and sesame potatoes. Visitors might also enjoy coffee and a scone by a log fire or a refreshing pint of Belhaven Best on the sundeck.

Open all day all wk Closed: 25 Dec Bar Meals Av main course £9.95 food served all day Restaurant Fixed menu price fr £17.95 Av 3 course à la carte fr £21.95 food served all day ⊕ FREE HOUSE ◖ Belhaven Best, Inveralmond Ale, Guinness. Facilities Children's menu Parking Rooms 11

### GUILDTOWN

## Anglers Inn ★★★ INN ⊛ ▼

**Main Rd PH2 6BS ☎ 01821 640329**
e-mail: info@theanglersinn.co.uk
dir: *6m N of Perth on A93*

Refurbished by Shona and Jeremy Wares, formerly of 63 Tay Street (an AA-Rosetted restaurant in Perth), as a contemporary gastro-pub, the Anglers provides a relaxing venue in a country setting just six miles from Perth. Comfortable leather chairs and a log fire maintain a homely atmosphere. Jeremy is the accomplished chef, offering the likes of Angler's fishcakes with chilli jam and herb salad; and roast marinated rump of lamb with haggis haché, spinach and rosemary vinaigrette. This is the perfect stop before or after the races at Perth Race Course.

Open all day all wk 11am-mdnt Bar Meals L served all wk 12-2 D served all wk 6-9 Av main course £13 Restaurant L served all wk 12-2 booking required D served all wk 6-9 booking required Fixed menu price fr £15 Av 3 course à la carte fr £25 ⊕ FREE HOUSE ◖ Ossian, Liafail, Boddingtons. ▼ 13 Facilities Children's menu Dogs allowed Garden Parking Rooms 5

## KINNESSWOOD

# Lomond Country Inn ♀

**KY13 9HN ☎ 01592 840253** 📄 **01592 840693**
e-mail: info@lomondcountryinn.co.uk
dir: *M90 junct 5, follow signs for Glenrothes then Scotlandwell, Kinnesswood next village*

A small, privately owned hotel on the slopes of the Lomond Hills that has been entertaining guests for more than 100 years. It is the only hostelry in the area with uninterrupted views over Loch Leven to the island where Mary Queen of Scots was imprisoned. The cosy public areas offer log fires, a friendly atmosphere, real ales and a fine collection of single malts. If you want to make the most of the loch views, choose the restaurant, a relaxing room freshly decorated in country house style. The focus is on serving well kept real ales such as Orkney Dark Island, and a mix of traditional and favourite pub dishes which are all competitively priced. Starters may feature home-made pâté; sautéed mushrooms; and North Atlantic prawn cocktail. Main courses include steak and Guinness pie; mince and tatties; Cajun chicken breast; and home-made locally sourced game stew.

Open all day all wk 7am-1am Bar Meals L served all wk 7am-9pm D served all wk 5-9 Av main course £5.95 food served all day Restaurant L served all wk 7am-9pm D served all wk 5-9 Fixed menu price fr £9.95 Λv 3 course à la carte fr £18.95 food served all day ⊕ FREE HOUSE ◀ Deuchars IPA, Calders Cream, Tetleys, Orkney Dark Island, Bitter & Twisted. ♀ 6 Facilities Children's menu Play area Family room Dogs allowed Garden Parking

## PITLOCHRY

# Moulin Hotel ★★★ HL ♀

**11-13 Kirkmichael Rd, Moulin PH16 5EH**
**☎ 01796 472196** 📄 **01796 474098**
e-mail: enquiries@moulinhotel.co.uk
web: www.moulinhotel.co.uk
dir: *From A924 at Pitlochry take A923. Moulin 0.75m*

Built in 1695 at the foot of Ben Vrackie on the old drove road from Dunkeld to Kingussie, the inn faces Moulin's square, a rewarding three-quarters of a mile from the busy tourist centre of Pitlochry. A great all-round inn, popular as a walking and touring base, it offers comfortable accommodation, extensive menus, and conference and function room facilities. A major refurbishment of the building in the 1990s opened up old fireplaces and beautiful stone walls that had been hidden for many years, and lots of cosy niches were created using timbers from the old Coach House (now the brewery). The courtyard garden is lovely in summer, while blazing log fires warm the Moulin's rambling interior in winter. Menus partly reflect the inn's Highlands location, and although more familiar dishes are available such as seafood pancake, lamb shank and fish and chips, you also have the opportunity to try something more local, such as haggis, neeps and tatties; venison Braveheart; Scotsman's bunnet, which is a meat and vegetable stew-filled batter pudding; or game casserole. You might then round off your meal with ice cream with Highland toffee sauce, or bread-and-butter pudding. A specials board broadens the choice further. Around 20 wines by the glass and more than 30 malt whiskies are available. Moulin may look like a French word but it is actually derived from the Gaelic 'maohlinn', meaning either smooth rocks or calm water.

Open all day all wk 11-11 (Fri-Sat 11am-11.45pm Sun noon-11) Bar Meals L served all wk 12-9.30 D served all wk 12-9.30 Av main course £9.50 food served all day Restaurant D served all wk 6-9 booking required Fixed menu price fr £23.50 Av 3 course à la carte fr £27 ⊕ FREE HOUSE ◀ Moulin Braveheart, Old Remedial, Ale of Atholl, Moulin Light. ♀ 20 Facilities Children's menu Garden Parking Rooms 15

## RENFREWSHIRE

### HOUSTON

## Fox & Hounds ☼

**South St PA6 7EN ☎ 01505 612448 & 612991**
📠 **01505 614133**
e-mail: jonathon.wengel@btconnect.com
dir: *A737, W from Glasgow. Take Johnstone Bridge off Weir exit, follow signs for Houston. Pub in village centre*

Run by the same family for over thirty years, this charming 18th-century village inn is home to the award-winning Houston Brewing Company. Sample a pint of Jock Frost or Warlock Stout in one of the three bars. There is a micro-brewery malt of the month, wine of the week to sample too. From the appealing bar or restaurant menus, choose from charred sausage du jour with creamy mash and onion gravy, tagliatelle with fresh peas and courgette, Houston ale-battered haddock, or slow braised game casserole. Look out for gourmet evenings and live music nights.

Open all day all wk 11am-mdnt ( Fri-Sat 11am-1am Sun from 12.30) Bar Meals Av main course £8 food served all day Restaurant Av 3 course à la carte fr £25 food served all day ⊕ FREE HOUSE ◖ Killelan, Warlock Stout, Texas, Jock Frost, Peter's Well. ☼ 10 Facilities Children's menu Dogs allowed Garden Parking

## SCOTTISH BORDERS

### ETTRICK

## Tushielaw Inn

**TD7 5HT ☎ 01750 62205 📠 01750 62205**
e-mail: robin@tushielaw-inn.co.uk
dir: *At junct of B709 & B711(W of Hawick)*

An 18th-century former toll house and drovers' halt on the banks of Ettrick Water, this is a good base for touring the Borders, fishing, and tackling the Southern Upland Way. An extensive menu is always available with daily-changing specials. Fresh produce is used in season, with local lamb and Aberdeen Angus beef regular specialities. Home-made steak and stout pie and sticky toffee pudding are popular choices.

Open all wk Bar Meals Av main course £10 ⊕ FREE HOUSE Facilities Children's menu Dogs allowed Parking

### LEITHOLM

## The Plough Hotel ☼

**Main St TD12 4JN ☎ 01890 840252 📠 01890 840252**
e-mail: theplough@leitholm.wanadoo.co.uk
dir: *5m N of Coldstream on A697. Take B6461, Leitholm in 1m*

The only pub remaining in this small border village (there were originally two), the Plough dates from the 17th century and was once a coaching inn. Food is traditional with the likes of parsnip soup or pâté and Melba toast followed steak and Guinness pie; home-made lasagne; or local sausages with Yorkshire pudding. Tuesdays and Fridays are fish and chip nights.

Open all day all wk noon-mdnt Bar Meals Av main course £12 food served all day Restaurant food served all day ⊕ FREE HOUSE ◖ Guinness. ☼ 8 Facilities Children's menu Garden Parking

### TIBBIE SHIELS INN

## Tibbie Shiels Inn

**St Mary's Loch TD7 5LH ☎ 01750 42231 📠 01750 42302**
dir: *From Moffat take A708. Inn 14m on right*

On the isthmus between St Mary's Loch and the Loch of the Lowes, this waterside hostelry is named after the woman who first opened it in 1826. Isabella 'Tibbie' Shiels expanded the inn from a small cottage to a hostelry capable of sleeping around 35 people, many of them on the floor! Famous visitors during her time included Walter Scott, Thomas Carlyle and Robert Louis Stevenson. Tibbie Shiels herself is rumoured to keep watch over the bar, where the selection of over 50 malt whiskies helps sustain long periods of ghost watching. Now under new ownership, meals can be enjoyed in either the bar or the dining room. The inn will also prepare packed lunches for your chosen activity – be it walking (the inn now lies on the coast-to-coast Southern Upland Way walking trail), windsurfing or fishing (residents fish free of charge).

Open all day all wk 9am-mdnt Bar Meals Av main course £10 food served all day Restaurant Fixed menu price fr £16 Av 3 course à la carte fr £20 food served all day ⊕ FREE HOUSE ◖ Broughton Greenmantle Ale, Belhaven 80/- ♂ Stowford Press. Facilities Children's menu Play area Dogs allowed Garden Parking

## WEST LINTON

## The Gordon Arms ♥

**Dolphinton Rd EH46 7DR ☎ 01968 660208**
📄 01968 661852
e-mail: info@thegordon.co.uk

Set in the pretty village of West Linton but within easy reach of the M74, this 17th-century inn has a real log fire in the cosy lounge bar, and a lovely sun-trap beer garden. Enjoy a local ale alongside your meal, which may start with feta cheese and cous cous fritters with a spicy red schoog, or cullen skink; continue with steak and ale pie, haggis, or collops of venison with a rustic butternut squash and sweet potato purée; and finish with sticky toffee pudding.

Open all day all wk 11-11 (Fri-Sat 11-1am Tue 11-mdnt) **Bar Meals** L served Mon-Fri 12-3, Sat-Sun all day D served Mon-Fri 6-9, Sat-Sun all day **Restaurant** L served Mon-Fri 12-3, Sat-Sun all day D served Mon-Fri 6-9, Sat-Sun all day ⊕ SCOTTISH & NEWCASTLE ◀ John Smiths, Guinness, real ales. ♥ 7 **Facilities** Children's menu Play area Dogs allowed Garden Parking

## STIRLING

## KIPPEN

## Cross Keys Hotel

**Main St FK8 3DN ☎ 01786 870293**
e-mail: info@kippencrosskeys.co.uk
dir: *10m W of Stirling, 20m from Loch Lomond off A811*

Refurbished by owners Debby and Brian, this cosy inn now serves food and drink all day. Nearby Burnside Wood is managed by a local community woodland group, and is perfect for walking and nature trails. The pub's interior, warmed by three log fires, is equally perfect for resting your feet afterwards. Regular events include a weekly Tuesday folk night.

Open all day noon-11 (Fri-Sat noon-1am Sun noon-11) Closed: 25 Dec, 1-2 Jan, Mon **Bar Meals** L served Tue-Sun 12-9 D served Tue-Sun 12-9 food served all day **Restaurant** L served Tue-Sun 12-9 D served Tue-Sun 12-9 food served all day ⊕ FREE HOUSE ◀ Belhaven Best, Harviestoun Bitter & Twisted, Guinness. **Facilities** Children's menu Family room Dogs allowed Garden Parking

## WEST LOTHIAN

## LINLITHGOW

## Champany Inn - The Chop and Ale House ◉◉

**Champany EH49 7LU ☎ 01506 834532** 📄 01506 834302
e-mail: reception@champany.com
dir: *2m N.E of Linlithgow on corner of A904 & A803*

At Champany Corner a collection of buildings, some 16th century, has been turned into two splendid restaurants. The more informal is the easy chair and couch-strewn Chop and Ale House bar, where your eyes will alight on the rock pond, where you'll find fresh Loch Gruinart oysters and lobsters before preparation for the pot. In the elegant, octagonal restaurant starters include Highland black pudding with onion marmalade; triple-smoked rump of beef with single-vineyard olive oil and fresh oregano; and fillet of salmon hot smoked over woodchips. In winter try cullen skink, a soup made from smoked haddock. Walking from the bar to the restaurant takes you past a chilled counter filled with a selection of steaks for the charcoal grill. Although Aberdeen Angus holds centre-stage, the two-AA Rosette menu also offers baked chicken filled with smoked bacon and tarragon mousse; and grilled salmon, langoustines and deep-fried organic cod.

Open all wk noon-2 6.30-10 (Fri-Sun noon-10) Closed: 25-26 Dec, 1 Jan **Bar Meals** food served all day **Restaurant** food served all day ⊕ FREE HOUSE ◀ Belhaven. **Facilities** Children's menu Garden Parking

Scotland

**Wales**

## WALES

## ISLE OF ANGLESEY

### BEAUMARIS

## Ye Olde Bulls Head
## Inn ★★★★★ INN ◎◎ ♥

**Castle St LL58 8AP ☎ 01248 810329  📄 01248 811294**
e-mail: info@bullsheadinn.co.uk
web: www.bullsheadinn.co.uk
dir: *From Britannia Road Bridge follow A545. Inn in town centre*

Situated a stone's throw from the gates of imposing Beaumaris castle, The Bull (as it is commonly known) is inextricably linked to Anglesey's history. Built in 1472 as a coaching house, it has welcomed such distinguished guests as Samuel Johnson and Charles Dickens. Inside there's a traditional bar leading on to the popular brasserie which offers modern European cuisine - perhaps shredded duck salad with plum sauce, followed by pork saltimbocca with celeriac purée and Marsala sauce. Or it's up the stairs to the smartly modern, first-floor Loft restaurant which offers a more formal menu. Try a terrine of wild rabbit, foie gras and Parma ham, followed by fillet of Anglesey black beef with spinach, red wine, shallots, ceps, fine beans, pancetta, fondant potatoes and Madeira jus. Delectable desserts like caramelised hazelnut and sweet apple semifreddo with Bramley apple fritters and hazelnut tuile will be hard to resist. If you'd like to stay and explore the area, there are richly decorated guest rooms available.

Open all wk Mon-Sat 11am-11pm (Sun noon-10.30pm) Closed: 25 Dec Bar Meals L served Mon-Sat 12-2, Sun 12-3 D served Mon-Sat 6-9, Sun 6.30-9.30 Restaurant D served Mon-Sat 7-9.30, Sun 6.30-9.30 booking required ⊕ FREE HOUSE ◀ Bass, Hancocks, Worthingtons, guest ales. ♥ 16 Facilities Children's menu Parking Rooms 13

### RED WHARF BAY

## The Ship Inn ♥

**LL75 8RJ ☎ 01248 852568  📄 01248 851013**
dir: *Telephone for directions*

Wading birds in their hundreds flock to feed on the extensive sands of Red Wharf Bay, making The Ship's waterside beer garden a birdwatcher's paradise on warm days. Before the age of steam, sailing ships landed cargoes here from all over the world; now the boats bring fresh Conwy Bay fish and seafood to the kitchens of this traditional free house. A single menu covers the bars and the restaurant, and specials always include a catch of the day. Lunchtime sandwiches are a cut above the usual: choose from the likes of open prawn on granary bloomer with lemon and dill mayonnaise; or a baguette of roast turkey with sage and apricot stuffing. Starters range from salmon fishcakes to hot-smoked duck and spring onion salad with teriyaki dressing. A main course of baked half shoulder of Welsh spring lamb with celeriac dauphinoise could be rounded off by lemon tart with fruit compote.

Open all wk Bar Meals L served all wk 12-2.30 D served all wk 6-9 booking required Av main course £10 Restaurant D served Sat-Sun booking required Fixed menu price fr £17.50 Av 3 course à la carte fr £20 ⊕ FREE HOUSE ◀ Brains SA, Adnams, guest ales. ♥ 16 Facilities Children's menu Play area Family room Garden Parking

## CARDIFF

### CREIGIAU

## Caesars Arms ♥

**Cardiff Rd CF15 9NN ☎ 029 2089 0486**
📄 **029 2089 2176**
e-mail: caesarsarms@btconnect.com
dir: *1m from M4 junct 34*

Just ten miles outside Cardiff, Caesars Arms sits tucked away down winding lanes. A whitewashed building that is probably older than it looks, it has an appealing interior. With fine views of the surrounding countryside from its heated patio and terrace, it attracts a well-heeled clientele. And it is little wonder, as its restaurant has a vast selection of fresh fish, seafood, meat and game taking pride of place. The emphasis here is on locally sourced food, displayed on shaven ice. Starters might include imaginative choice such as Bajan fishcakes, scallops with leek julienne or cherry-smoked duck breast with organic beetroot. Main courses take in hake, halibut, Dover sole and lobster, as well as a show-stopping Pembrokeshire sea bass baked in rock salt, which is cracked open and filleted at your table. But is not all about fish - other choices include steak from slow-reared, dry-aged pedigree Welsh Blacks plus lamb and venison from the Brecon Beacons, and free-range chickens from the Vale of Glamorgan. Home-grown organic herbs, salads and vegetables are all used as much as possible, and the inn has its own smokery. Another attraction is the farm shop, which provides a range of home-produced honey, free-range eggs, Welsh cheeses, home-baked bread and chef's ready-prepared meals to take away.

Open all wk noon-2.30 6-10 (Sun noon-4) Closed: 25 Dec, 1 Jan, Sun eve **Bar Meals** L served Mon-Sat 12-2.30 Av main course £6.95 **Restaurant** L served Mon-Sat 12-2.30, Sun 12-4 D served Mon-Sat 6-10 Fixed menu price fr £6.95 Av 3 course à la carte fr £25 ⊕ FREE HOUSE ◂ Felinfoel Double Dragon, Guinness. ⬥ 8 **Facilities** Children's menu Dogs allowed Garden Parking

## Gwaelod-y-Garth Inn ⬥

**Main Rd, Gwaelod-y-Garth CF15 9HH**
☎ 029 2081 0408 & 07855 313247
dir: *From M4 junct 32, N on A470, left at next exit, at rdbt turn right 0.5m. Right into village*

Meaning 'foot of the garth (mountain)', this welcoming pub was originally part of the Marquess of Bute's estate. Every window of the pub offers exceptional views, and it's a much favoured watering hole for ramblers, cyclists and hang-gliders as well as some colourful locals. Real ales change every week, and the pub offers Gwynt y Ddraig award-winning ciders. Starters might include mussels in a tomato and garlic sauce; and main courses like rack of lamb with a herb crust, or duck breast with a kumquat and blackcurrant sauce.

Open all wk 11am-mdnt (Sun noon-11) **Bar Meals** food served all day **Restaurant** L served Mon-Thu 12-2, Fri-Sat 11am-mdnt, Sun 12-3 booking required D served Mon-Sat 6.30-9 booking required ⊕ FREE HOUSE ◂ HPA (Wye Valley), Otley OI, RCH Pitchfork, Vale of Glamorgan, Crouch Vale Brewers Gold ♆ Local cider. ⬥ 7 **Facilities** Children's menu Family room Dogs allowed Garden Parking

### ABERGORLECH

## The Black Lion

**SA32 7SN ☎ 01558 685271**
e-mail: georgerashbrook@hotmail.com
dir: *A40 E from Carmarthen, then B4310 signed Brechfa & Abergorlech*

A family-run establishment in the Brechfa Forest, this 16th-century former coaching inn has an award-winning beer garden overlooking the Cothi River and an ancient stone-built Roman bridge. Flagstone floors, settles and a grandfather clock grace the antique-furnished bar, while the dining room is more modern in style. Lots of home-made food and puddings are served, prepared from locally sourced produce, with Welsh steaks as a speciality.

Open all day Closed: Mon (ex BH) **Bar Meals** L served Tue-Sun 12-2.30 D served Tue-Sun 7-9 booking required Av main course £7.50 **Restaurant** D served Tue-Sun 7-9 booking required ⊕ FREE HOUSE ◂ Rhymney ♆ Stowford Press. **Facilities** Children's menu Dogs allowed Garden Parking

### LLANDDAROG

## White Hart Thatched Inn & Brewery

**SA32 8NT ☎ 01267 275395**
e-mail: bestpubinwales@aol.com
web: www.thebestpubinwales.co.uk
dir: *6m E of Carmarthen towards Swansea, just off A48 on B4310, signed Llanddarog*

The Coles family invites you to try a pint from the micro-brewery that adjoins their ancient thatched free house. Built in 1371, the pub's thick stone walls and heavy beams enclose a cosy log fire and converted barn restaurant. The menu ranges far and wide, using the best of local produce. Expect Welsh lamb chops and Black Beef steaks from the grill; duck sizzling in orange sauce; and swordfish in Spanish sauce. In summer, the flower-filled patio garden is perfect for alfresco dining.

Open all wk 11.30-3 6.30-11 (Sun noon-3 7-10.30) **Bar Meals** L served all wk 11.30-3 D served all wk 6.30-11 **Restaurant** L served all wk 11.30-3 D served all wk 6.30-11 ⊕ FREE HOUSE ◂ Roasted Barley Stout, Llanddarog Ale, Bramling Cross. **Facilities** Children's menu Play area Garden Parking

**Wales**

## LLANDEILO

### The Angel Hotel ♥

**Rhosmaen St SA19 6EN ☎ 01558 822765**
📠 **01558 824346**
e-mail: capelbach@hotmail.com
dir: *In town centre next to post office*

This popular pub in the centre of Llandeilo has something for everyone. Real ales are available in the bar area, which hosts regular live music nights. Upstairs, the Yr Eglwys function room ceiling is decorated with soaring frescoes inspired by Michelangelo's Sistine Chapel, and at the rear is an intimate bistro with warm terracotta walls, where dishes might include warm chorizo and potato salad, followed by slowly roasted Welsh beef in a sweet baby onion gravy.

**Open** 11.30-3 6-11 Closed: Sun **Bar Meals** L served Mon-Sat 11.30-2.30 D served Mon-Sat 6-9 Av main course £5 **Restaurant** L served Mon-Sat 11.30-2.30 booking required D served Mon-Sat 6-9 booking required Fixed menu price fr £9.95 Av 3 course à la carte fr £16 ⊕ FREE HOUSE ◀ Evan Evans Ales, Tetleys, Butty Bach. ♥ 12 **Facilities** Children's menu Garden

## LLANWRDA

### The Brunant Arms ♥

**Caio SA19 8RD ☎ 01558 650483** 📠 **01558 650832**
e-mail: thebrunantarms@yahoo.co.uk
dir: *1.4m of the main A482*

Tucked away at the foot of a small valley, the village of Caio lies safely off the road from Lampeter to Llandovery. Here, the Brunant Arms offers a relaxed welcome with some unusual real ales and good food. The menu features soft floured baps and filled jacket potatoes, as well as daily choices that might include Welsh cawl with herb dumplings; locally sourced venison steaks; sweet potato and butternut korma; or home-cooked Carmarthen ham, egg and chips.

**Open** noon-3 6-11 (Fri-Sat noon-3 6-1am Sun noon-11) Closed: Mon **Bar Meals** L served Tue-Sun 12-2 D served Tue-Sun 6.30-9 Av main course £4.95 **Restaurant** L served Tue-Sun 12-2 D served Tue-Sun 6.30-9 Av 3 course à la carte fr £18.50 ⊕ FREE HOUSE ◀ Ramblers Ruin, Wolvers Ale, Cribyn, Jacobi Dark Ale Ŏ Taffy Apples. ♥ 30 **Facilities** Children's menu Dogs allowed Garden Parking

## LLWYNDAFYDD

### The Crown Inn & Restaurant ♥

**SA44 6BU ☎ 01545 560396**
e-mail: www.the-crown-inn.moonfruit.com
dir: *Off A487 NE of Cardigan*

A Welsh longhouse dating from 1799, with original beams, open fireplaces and a pretty restaurant. Rob and Monique, the young owners, have been there for 18 months now, and are having a great time. A varied menu offers a good selection of dishes, including lamb and root vegetable casserole with rosemary cobbler; or whole trout stuffed with pine nuts and bacon with rosemary and lemon butter. Blackboard specials and bar meals are available lunchtimes and evenings. Outside is a delightful, award-winning garden. An easy walk down the lane leads to a cove with caves and National Trust cliffs.

**Open** all day all wk noon-11 **Bar Meals** L served all wk 12-3 D served all wk 6-9 Av main course £8.95 **Restaurant** L served all wk 12-3 D served all wk 6-9 ⊕ FREE HOUSE ◀ Flowers IPA , Greene King Old Speckled Hen, Honey Ales, Envill Ale, Fuller's London Pride, guest ale. ♥ 11 **Facilities** Children's menu Play area Family room Dogs allowed Garden Parking

## BETWS-Y-COED

### White Horse Inn

**Capel Garmon LL26 0RW ☎ 01690 710271**
📠 **01690 710721**
e-mail: r.alton@btconnect.com
web: www.whitehorseinnsnowdonia.co.uk
dir: *Telephone for directions*

Picturesque Capel Garmon perches high above Betws-y-Coed, with spectacular views of the Snowdon Range, a good 20 kilometres away. To make a detour to find this cosy 400-year-old inn with its original exposed timbers, stone walls, and log fires, is to be rewarded by a menu featuring fresh local produce. Home-cooked food is available in the bars and cottage-style restaurant.

**Open** all wk 6-11pm Closed: 25 Dec **Bar Meals** L served Sun 12-2 D served all wk 6-9 **Restaurant** L served Sun 12-2 D served all wk 6-9 ⊕ FREE HOUSE ◀ Tetley Smoothflow, Rev James Ŏ Old

English. **Facilities** Children's menu Family room Dogs allowed Parking

## BETWS-YN-RHOS

### The Wheatsheaf Inn ♥

LL22 8AW ☎ 01492 680218 🖹 01492 680666
e-mail: wheatsheafinn@hotmail.co.uk
web: www.thewheatsheafinn.org.uk
dir: *A55 to Abergele, take A548 to Llanrwst from High Street. 2m turn right B5381, 1m to Betws-yn-Rhos*

The Wheatsheaf, licensed as a coaching inn during the 17th century, stands in the village of Betws-Yn-Rhos opposite the twin towered church of St Michael. The inn has plenty of character with splendid oak beams adorned with brasses, stone pillars and plenty of cosy, old world charm. Bar snacks are served in addition to the restaurant menu where choices range from local Welsh Black beef steaks or pork medallions with black pudding and Stilton sauce, to a house speciality: Welsh lamb joint slow roasted with rosemary and thyme.

**Open** all day all wk noon-11 (Fri-Sat noon-mdnt) **Bar Meals** L served all wk 12-2 booking required D served all wk 6-9 booking required Av main course £10 **Restaurant** L served all wk 12-2 booking required D served all wk 6-9 booking required ⊕ ENTERPRISE INNS ◀ John Smiths, Brains, Hobgoblin, Old Speckled Hen, Guinness. ♥ 6 **Facilities** Children's menu Dogs allowed Garden Parking

## COLWYN BAY

### Pen-y-Bryn ♥

Pen-y-Bryn Rd LL29 6DD ☎ 01492 533360
e-mail: pen.y.bryn@brunningandprice.co.uk
dir: *1m from A55. Follow signs to Welsh Mountain Zoo, estab at top of hill*

Don't be put off by the simple exterior of this 1970s building – the interior has character in spades, with oak floors, open fires, rugs and old furniture. The atmosphere is friendly and chatty, with local ales and good, straightforward food cooked and served throughout the day. Outside, the rear garden and terrace have panoramic views over the sea and the Great Orme headland. The modern British menu offers a great choice of sandwiches, rolls and wraps like sausage bap with mustard fried onions; warm crispy lamb and feta cheese wrap; and a simple smoked salmon sandwich with lemon and chive cream cheese. Main course options range from green pea and mint risotto with char-grilled asparagus and Parmesan, to slow-

roasted belly pork with roasted sweet potatoes, chorizo and spiced apple sauce. Leave space for strawberries with vanilla cream and shortbread, or white chocolate and raspberry trifle.

**Open** all day all wk noon-11pm (Sun noon-10.30pm) **Bar Meals** D served Mon-Sat 12-9.30, Sun 12-9 Av main course £9.95 food served all day **Restaurant** D served Mon-Sat 12-9.30, Sun 12-9 food served all day ⊕ BRUNNING & PRICE ◀ Timothy Taylor Landlord, Thwaites Original, Ormes Best, Flowers Original, ♂ Stonehouse. ♥ 17 **Facilities** Children's menu Dogs allowed Garden Parking

## DOLWYDDELAN

### Elen's Castle

LL25 0EJ ☎ 01690 750207
e-mail: stay@hotelinsnowdonia.co.uk
dir: *5m S of Betws-Y-Coed, follow A470*

Once an 18th-century coaching inn and a part of the Earl of Ancaster's Welsh Estate, this family-run free house now boasts an old world bar with a wood-burning stove. The intimate restaurant offers breathtaking views of the mountains and Lledr River, which can also be enjoyed from the garden. Sample dishes include wild rice, spinach and honey roast with summer vegetable ratatouille; and Conwy valley lamb shank on mashed potato and leek with rosemary jus.

**Open** vary by season Closed: 2wks Jan, wk days in quiet winter periods **Bar Meals** L served all wk 12-2 (summer holidays) D served all wk 6.30-9 Av main course £7.95 **Restaurant** D served all wk 6.30-9 Fixed menu price fr £17.50 Av 3 course à la carte fr £20 ⊕ Free House ◀ Brains, Worthington, Black Sheep, Spitfire ♂ Stowford Press. **Facilities** Children's menu Play area Family room Dogs allowed Garden Parking

## DENBIGHSHIRE

## PRESTATYN

### Nant Hall Restaurant & Bar ♥

Nant Hall Rd LL19 9LD ☎ 01745 886766
🖹 01745 886998
e-mail: mail@nanthall.com
dir: *E towards Chester, 1m on left opposite large car garage*

Nant Hall, a Grade II listed Victorian country house in seven acres of grounds, operates as a gastro-pub with a great variety of food, beers and wines. The menu offers local and regional dishes alongside recipes from around the world: Thai green chicken curry, pan-seared fillet of salmon with a creamy herb risotto, chargrilled steaks, Chinese chicken and vegetable satay, or creamy fish pie in a parsley sauce. The large outdoor eating area is great in summer.

**Open** all day noon-11pm Closed: Mon **Bar Meals** Av main course £9.95 food served all day **Restaurant** Fixed menu price fr £10.95 Av 3 course à la carte fr £15 food served all day ⊕ FREE HOUSE ◀ Bass Smooth, Boddingtons. ♥ 14 **Facilities** Children's menu Family room Garden Parking

**Wales**

## RHEWL

## The Drovers Arms, Rhewl ♟

**Denbigh Rd LL15 2UD ☎ 01824 703163**
📄 **01824 703163**
dir: *1.3m from Ruthin on A525*

A small village pub whose name recalls a past written up and illustrated on storyboards displayed inside. Main courses are divided on the menu into poultry, traditional meat, fish, grills and vegetarian; examples from each section are chicken tarragon; Welsh lamb's liver and onions; Vale of Clwyd sirloin steak; home-made fish pie; and mushroom stroganoff. Desserts include treacle sponge pudding.

**Open** all wk noon-3 5.30-11 (Sat noon-3 5.30-mdnt Sun noon-11pm Open all day Jun-Sep) Closed: Tue L **Bar Meals** L served all wk 12-2 booking required D served all wk 6-9 booking required **Restaurant** L served all wk 12-2 booking required D served all wk 6-9 booking required ⊕ J W Lees ◀ J W Lees bitter. ♟ 6 **Facilities** Children's menu Play area Garden Parking

## FLINTSHIRE

## BABELL

## Black Lion Inn ♟

**CH8 8PZ ☎ 01352 720239**
e-mail: theblacklioninn@btinternet.com
dir: *A55 junct 31 to Caerwys turn left at crossroads signed Babell. Travel 3m turn right at fork*

Ancient inns spawn ghost stories, but the 13th-century Black Lion boasts more than its fair share. Ask about them when you visit, but don't be put off savouring a local real ale on the outside decking while the children enjoy the play area. Alternatively tuck into good home-cooked dishes like black pudding layered with crisp back bacon; and pork escalope with fresh asparagus sauce. Irish music keeps the spirits awake on the last Wednesday of the month.

**Open** all wk 6pm-close (Sat-Sun noon-close) **Bar Meals** L served Sat-Sun 12-9 D served Thu-Sun 6-9 Av main course £12.95 **Restaurant** L served Sat-Sun 12-9 D served Thu-Sun 6-9 Av 3 course à la carte fr £22 ⊕ FREE HOUSE ◀ Thwaites Lancaster Bomber, Thwaites Smooth Bitter, Purple Moose Brewery - Traeth Mawr, Thirstquencher Spitting Feathers. ♟ 7 **Facilities** Children's menu Play area Garden Parking

## MOLD

## Glasfryn ♟

**Raikes Ln, Sychdyn CH7 6LR ☎ 01352 750500**
📄 **01352 751923**
e-mail: glasfryn@brunningandprice.co.uk
dir: *From Mold follow signs to Theatr Clwyd, 1m from town centre*

Built as a judge's residence in around 1900, later a farm and then divided into bedsits, this building was rescued by the present owners ten years ago and transformed into a wonderful pub. It attracts a variety of visitors from farmers and business people to holidaymakers along the north Wales coast. Outside, the newly landscaped garden is maturing well, while inside is a bright open space with lots of polished wooden tables and chairs. The comprehensive daily menu runs from sandwiches and snacks through to meals such as Pen Llyn bacon with roasted sweet potato and honey mustard dressing, followed by smoked haddock and salmon fishcakes with chive mayonnaise; or perhaps smoked duck with rhubarb and ginger chutney, followed by Edwards of Conwy lamb and leek sausages with mash and gravy. Puddings and cheeses are not to be missed.

**Open** all day noon-11 Closed: 25 Dec, Sun **Bar Meals** Av main course £9 food served all day **Restaurant** food served all day ⊕ BRUNNING & PRICE ◀ Timothy Taylor, Thwaites, Snowdonia Ale. ♟ 20 **Facilities** Children's menu Dogs allowed Garden Parking

## GWYNEDD

## ABERDYFI

## Penhelig Arms Hotel & Restaurant ♟

**Terrace Rd LL35 0LT ☎ 01654 767215   📄 01654 767690**
e-mail: info@penheligarms.com
dir: *On A493 W of Machynlleth*

The Penhelig Arms has been in business since the late 18th century. It enjoys glorious views over the tidal Dyfi estuary, and is idyllically placed for breezy sea strolls or hill walks. Cader Idris and a variety of majestic mountains and historic castles are within easy reach. In the summer months many customers relax on the sea wall opposite the pub. Locals and visitors alike experience a warm welcome in the wood-panelled Fisherman's bar, where traditional ales and home-cooked bar meals are served. Alternatively take a seat in the popular waterfront restaurant, and relax as your decision-making skills are put to the test: will it be half a dressed Aberdyfi lobster with salad and mayonnaise, or melon and crayfish tails with chilli and lime dressing? Follow up with the likes of grilled monkfish wrapped in pancetta; or roast rump of lamb with root vegetable mash and rosemary gravy.

**Open** all day all wk 11-11 Closed: 25-26 Dec **Bar Meals** L served all wk 12-2 D served all wk 6-9 booking required Av main course £12.50 **Restaurant** L served all wk 12-2 booking required D served all wk 7-9 booking required Fixed menu price fr £29 Av 3 course à la carte fr £25 ⊕ S A BRAIN & CO LTD ◀ Adnams Broadside, Brains Reverend James & SA, Brains SA, Everards Toger. ♟ 22 **Facilities** Children's menu Dogs allowed Garden Parking

# Monmouthshire

## CHEPSTOW

### Castle View Hotel ★★★ HL ♀

16 Bridge St NP16 5EZ ☎ 01291 620349
📠 01291 627397
e-mail: castleviewhotel@btconnect.com
dir: *Opposite Chepstow Castle*

Standing opposite Chepstow Castle and built as a private house in the 17th-century, the inn boasts walls that are five feet thick and a delightful secluded walled garden. Using quality ingredients from local suppliers the menus may list moules marinière, braised lamb shank with redcurrant and rosemary jus, wild mushrooms risotto, and traditional bar snacks like sandwiches, ploughman's lunches and omelettes.

Open all wk Bar Meals L served all wk 12-3 D served all wk 6.30-9.30 Av main course £12 Restaurant L served all wk 12-3 D served all wk 6.30-9.30 Av 3 course à la carte fr £20 ⊕ FREE HOUSE ◀ Wye Valley Real Ale, Double Dragon, Felinfoel Best Bitter ♻ Stowford Press. ♀ 6 Facilities Children's menu Dogs allowed Garden Parking Rooms 13

## LLANTRISANT

### The Greyhound Inn ⓐ ★★★ INN ♀

NP15 1LE ☎ 01291 672505 & 673447 📠 01291 673255
e-mail: enquiry@greyhound-inn.com
dir: *M4 junct 24, A449 towards Monmouth, exit at 1st junct signed Usk. 2nd left for Llantrisant. Or from Monmouth A40, A449 exit for Usk. In Usk left into Twyn Sq follow Llantrisant signs. 2.5m under A449 bridge. Inn on right*

A traditional 17th-century Welsh longhouse, once part of a 400-acre farm. In 1845 the milk parlour was converted into an inn, and over the years the land was sold off. By 1980, the whole complex was in a sorry state, as pictures hanging in the Cocktail and Llangibby lounges bear witness. Today,

after 27 years in the same family's hands, the Greyhound has two acres of award-winning gardens, a four-acre paddock, accommodation and an array of restored outbuildings. Owner Nick Davies heads the kitchen team, serving customers in the four eating areas, one of which is a candlelit dining room. The regular menu ranges over old favourites such as prawn cocktail, home-made curries, pies and lasagne. It is complemented by a daily specials blackboard offering unusual and seasonal dishes: chicken veronique; local pheasant; pork roberto; and Usk salmon. The vegetarian selection, with eight choices, is particularly notable. Home-made sweets include hazelnut meringue gateau, peach Melba and profiteroles.

Open all day 11-11 Closed: 25 & 31 Dec, 1 Jan, Sun eve Bar Meals L served all wk 12-2.15 D served Mon-Sat 6-10 Av main course £11 Restaurant L served all wk 12-2.15 D served Mon-Sat 6-10 ⊕ FREE HOUSE ◀ Interbrew Flowers Original & Bass, Greene King Abbot Ale, guest ale. ♀ 10 Facilities Children's menu Family room Dogs allowed Garden Parking Rooms 10

## LLANVAIR DISCOED

### The Woodland Tavern Country Pub & Dining ♀

NP16 6LX ☎ 01633 400313 📠 01633 400313
e-mail: info@thewoodlandtavern.co.uk
dir: *5m from Caldicot & Magor*

This old inn has been extended to accommodate a growing number of diners, but remains at heart a friendly family-run village local. The pub is located close to the Roman fortress town of Caerwent and Wentworth's forest and reservoir; it was nicknamed 'the war office' when Irish navvies held bare-knuckle fights here while building the reservoir. A patio area with seating ensures that food and drink can be served outside in fine weather. A short fixed-price lunch menu offers a couple of choices at each stage: tomato, basil and mozzarella salad; deep-fried fillet of haddock; and creamed rice pudding with apple compote would be typical. The more extensive restaurant menu proffers the likes of baked flat mushrooms with red onion marmalade topped with goats' cheese; followed by roast rump of Welsh lamb served on mash.

Open Closed: Mon, Sun eve Bar Meals L served Tue-Sat 12-2, Sun 12-3 D served Tue-Fri 6-9, Sat 6-9.30 Av main course £11.50 Restaurant L served Tue-Sat 12-2, Sun 12-3 booking required D served Tue-Fri 6-9, Sat 6-9.30 booking required Fixed menu price fr £9.95 Av 3 course à la carte fr £20 ⊕ FREE HOUSE ◀ Brains, Felinfoel Double Dragon, Tomas Watkins OSB, Guest ales. ♀ 8 Facilities Children's menu Dogs allowed Parking

## MAMHILAD

### Horseshoe Inn ♀

NP4 8QZ ☎ 01873 880542
e-mail: horseshoe@artizanleisure.com
dir: *A4042 (Pontypool to Abergavenny road), at Mamhilad Estate rdbt take 1st exit onto Old Abergavenny road. 2m over canal bridge on right*

Bordering the Brecon to Monmouth canal and sited on the Pontypool to Abergavenny turnpike, the Horseshoe started providing welcome sustenance for canal navigators and horse-drawn coach passengers over 200 years ago. The ambience of its history is recalled in its original oak beams, stone walls and huge fireplaces. Today it continues the tradition of serving fine real ales, good value wines and tasty locally produced food in the relaxed surroundings of crackling wood fires, cosy armchairs and informal dining rooms. Rymney Bitter and Butty Bach are among the beer choices, while wine lovers can choose between ten served by the glass. Typical starters are home-cured gravadlax with citrus crème fraîche; haddock and spring onion fishcakes with tomato butter sauce; and blue cheese panacotta with redcurrant syrup and rocket salad. Main courses vary from chorizo sausage cassoulet to trio of Gloucester Old Spot sausages with bubble and squeak and onion gravy. Desserts are all home made.

Open all wk Bar Meals L served all wk 12-2.30 D served all wk 6.30-9.30 Av main course £9 Restaurant L served all wk 12-2.30 D served all wk 6.30-9.30 Av 3 course à la carte fr £25 ⊕ FREE HOUSE ◀ Abbot Ale, London Pride, Rymney Bitter, Butty Bach, Guest Ales. ♀ 10 Facilities Children's menu Dogs allowed Garden Parking

## PANTYGELLI

# The Crown ♀

**Old Hereford Rd NP7 7HR ☎ 01873 853314**
e-mail: crown@pantygelli.com
dir: *Please telephone for directions*

Reputedly an old coaching inn dating back to the 16th century, this charming family-run free house is a genuine community local. Located on the edge of the Brecon Beacons National Park, it's popular with walkers, cyclists and general visitors. Stowford Press cider supports the range of local ales, and the food offering ranges from hot roast pork and apple sauce ciabattas to herb-crusted baked mussels; or Welsh black beef with bubble and squeak.

Open noon-2.30, 6-11 (Sat-Sun noon-3, Sun 6-10.30) Closed: Mon lunch Bar Meals L served Tue-Sun 12-2 booking required D served Tue-Sat 7-9 booking required Restaurant L served Tue-Sun 12-2 booking required D served Tue-Sat 7-9 booking required ⊕ FREE HOUSE ◀ Rhymney Bitter, Wye Valley HPA Ŏ Westons Stowford Press. ♀ 7 Facilities Children's menu Dogs allowed Garden Parking

# The Beaufort Arms Coaching Inn & Restaurant ★★★ HL ⊛ ♀

**High St NP15 2DY ☎ 01291 690412 📄 01291 690935**
e-mail: enquiries@beaufortraglan.co.uk
dir: *0.5m from junct of A40 & A449 Abergavenny/Monmouth*

The Beaufort has been an inn since the time of the Civil War, when its proximity to Raglan Castle meant that Roundhead soldiers supped here during the siege of 1646. Later it became a coaching inn on the London to Fishguard route. The inn has been refurbished with many delightful design features, while holding strong to its traditional roots. A handsome display of fishing trophies dominates the country bar, where locals and visitors alike gather. Food is served in the lounge, with its carved bar, large stone fireplace and deep leather settees, as well as in the brasserie and private dining room. Bar meals range from light bites of classic Welsh rarebit, hot chorizo salad and paninis to local faggots served with chunky chips, crushed peas and red onion jus. The brasserie offers the likes of roasted pork belly with beetroot fondant and peppercorn sauce.

Open all day all wk Bar Meals Av main course £8.95 food served all day Restaurant L served all wk 12-3 booking required D served all wk 6-9.30 booking required Av 3 course à la carte fr £22 ⊕ FREE HOUSE ◀ London Pride, Reverend James, Warsteiner, Old Speckled Hen Ŏ Stowford Press. ♀ 12 Facilities Children's menu Garden Parking Rooms 15

# The Bell at Skenfrith ★★★★★ RR ⊛⊛ ♀

**NP7 8UH ☎ 01600 750235 📄 01600 750525**
e-mail: enquiries@skenfrith.co.uk
dir: *M4 junct 24 onto A449. Exit onto A40, through tunnel & lights. At rdbt take 1st exit, right at lights onto A466 towards Hereford Road. Left onto B4521 towards Abergavenny, 3m on left*

From its setting by the arched bridge over the River Monnow, this 17th-century coaching inn has views of Skenfrith Castle. An oak bar, flagstone floors, comfortable sofas and old settles ooze plenty of character. Locally sourced and mainly organic ingredients, many from the inn's very own kitchen garden, are used in regularly changing menus. One day's selection could include warm duck salad; slow braised shoulder of Talgarth lamb with pan-seared lambs' liver and mashed potato; and

continued

lemon meringue pie. A fixed priced carte proffers exquisite dishes which carefully combine finely judged flavours: an entrée of locally picked wild garlic served as a vichyssoise, with a warm fricassée of Hereford snails and spring rabbit ballotine bound with tarragon mustard is an excellent example.

**Open** Closed: last wk Jan & 1st wk Feb, Mon Nov-Mar **Bar Meals** L served all wk 12-2.30 booking required D served Mon-Sat 7-9.30, Sun 7-9 booking required Av main course £15 **Restaurant** L served all wk 12-2.30 booking required D served Mon-Sat 7-9.30, Sun 7-9 booking required Fixed menu price fr £19 Av 3 course à la carte fr £28 ⊞ FREE HOUSE ◀ Timothy Taylor Landlord, St Austell Tribute, Wye Valley Bitter ♂ Local cider. ♥ 13 **Facilities** Children's menu Dogs allowed Garden Parking **Rooms** 11

## TINTERN PARVA

## Fountain Inn ♥

**Trellech Grange NP16 6QW ☎ 01291 689303**
e-mail: fountaininntintern@btconnect.com
dir: *From M48 junct 2 follow Chepstow then Tintern signs. In Tintern turn by George Hotel for Raglan. Bear right, inn at top of hill*

A fire failed to destroy this fine old early 17th-century inn, and its character remains unspoilt. It enjoys views of the Wye Valley from the garden, and is close to Tintern Abbey. Home-cooked food includes grilled sardines with balsamic vinegar and cherry tomatoes; leek and Caerphilly sausages with onion gravy; and beef and Guinness pie. Also a good selection of steaks, omelettes, and seafood choices are available.

**Open** Closed: Mon (ex BH) **Bar Meals** L served Wed-Sun 12-2.30 D served all wk 6-9 **Restaurant** L served Wed-Sun 12-2.30 D served all wk 6-9 ⊞ FREE HOUSE ◀ Hook Norton, Spinning Dog, Ring of Bells, Interbrew Bass, Hobgoblin, Rev James, Kingstone Classic, Cats Whiskers. ♥ 10 **Facilities** Children's menu Family room Dogs allowed Garden Parking

## TRELLECH

## The Lion Inn

**NP25 4PA ☎ 01600 860322  📄 01600 860060**
e-mail: debs@globalnet.co.uk
dir: *From A40 S of Monmouth take B4293, follow signs for Trellech. From M8 junct 2, straight across rdbt, 2nd left at 2nd rdbt, B4293 to Trellech*

Summer drinkers enjoy supping in the garden of this well established free house, which features a stream, large aviary

and views over fields. The former brewhouse and coaching inn has a growing reputation soundly based on all that's best about a good British pub: a warm welcome, beams, wood fires in winter, as well as wholesome food, traditional ales, ciders and games. For hearty appetites, the menu embraces bar snacks and basket meals. Blackboard specials include fresh fish but, proving that homage to tradition is not total, ostrich or kangaroo may also be found. Also there are authentic Hungarian dishes, and hedgerow 'poacher's pocket' ingredients such as pigeon and wild boar harvested from the surrounding countryside. Children have plenty of favourites to choose from, while walkers' dogs are made most welcome.

**Open** 12-3 6-11 (Fri-Sat noon-mdnt Sun 12-4.30 Mon eve 7-11pm Thu eve 6-mdnt) Closed: Sun eve **Bar Meals** L served Mon-Fri 12-2, Sat-Sun 12-2.30 D served Mon 7-9.30, Tue-Sat 6-9.30 booking required Av main course £12 **Restaurant** L served Mon-Fri 12-2, Sat-Sun 12-2.30 D served Mon 7-9.30, Tue-Sat 6-9.30 booking required Av 3 course à la carte fr £23 ⊞ FREE HOUSE ◀ Bath Ales, Wye Valley Butty Bach, Sharp's Cornish Coaster, Rhymney Best, Butcombe Gold. **Facilities** Children's menu Dogs allowed Garden Parking

## USK

## The Nags Head Inn ♥

**Twyn Square NP15 1BH ☎ 01291 672820**
📄 **01291 672720**
dir: *On A472*

Owned by the Key family for 40 years, this 15th-century coaching inn overlooks the square just a short stroll from the River Usk, and boasts magnificent hanging flower baskets. The traditional bar is decorated with collections of horse brasses, farming tools and lanterns hanging from exposed oak beams. Game in season figures strongly among the speciality dishes, including whole stuffed partridge, pheasant in port, home-made rabbit pie and brace of quails. There is a good choice for vegetarians, too, such as Glamorgan sausage filled with cheese and leek and served with a chilli relish.

**Open** all wk Closed: 25 Dec **Bar Meals** L served all wk 11.45-1.45 D served all wk 5.30-9.30 **Restaurant** L served all wk 11.45-1.45 D served all wk 5.30-9.30 ⊞ FREE HOUSE ◀ Brains Bitter, Dark, Buckleys Best, Reverend James, Bread of Heaven ♂ Thatchers Gold. ♥ 8 **Facilities** Children's menu Dogs allowed Garden Parking

## Raglan Arms ◉ ♥

**Llandenny NP15 1DL ☎ 01291 690800  📄 01291 690155**
e-mail: raglanarms@aol.com
dir: *From Monmouth take A449 to Raglan, left in village*

This cosy, part-stone, part-wooden-floored, flint-built pub is tucked away in a small, attractive village. While the choice of dishes is limited, menus change daily and always includes a good selection of Welsh and English cheeses. Dine at rustic tables around the bar, or in the conservatory extension, on modern British dishes with a Gallic influence. Expect longhorn rib-eye of beef from a local breeder-cum-butcher; langoustines from Scotland, and scallops and turbot from Cornwall; slow-roasted pork with apples; and, compromising somewhat the modern British/Gallic theme, there's imam bayaldi, a Middle Eastern spiced aubergine and tomato-based dish, a long-standing favourite in the repertoire here. Try the deliciously creamy crème brûlée with red berry compote for dessert.

Open noon-3 6.30-9.30 Closed: Sun eve & Mon Bar Meals L served Tue-Sun 12-3 D served Tue-Sat 6.30-9.30 Av main course £11 Restaurant L served Tue-Sun 12-3 booking required D served Tue-Sat 6.30-9.30 booking required Av 3 course à la carte fr £25 ⊕ FREE HOUSE ◀ Wye Valley Bitter, Butty Bach, Guinness ☼ Thatchers Gold. ♀ 12 Facilities Children's menu Garden Parking

## PEMBROKESHIRE

### AMROTH

## The New Inn ♀

**SA67 8NW ☎ 01834 812368**
dir: *A48 to Carmarthen, A40 to St Clears, A477 to Llanteg then left*

A 400-year-old inn, originally a farmhouse, belonging to Amroth Castle Estate. It has old world charm with beamed ceilings, a Flemish chimney, a flagstone floor and an inglenook fireplace. Local lobster and crab are a feature, along with a popular choice of home-made dishes including steak and kidney pie, soup and curry. Enjoy food or drink outside on the large lawn complete with picnic benches.

Open all day all wk Mar-Oct 11am-11pm Closed: Oct-Mar Bar Meals food served all day Restaurant food served all day ⊕ FREE HOUSE ◀ Brains, Old Speckled Hen, Guinness, guest ales. ♀ 8 Facilities Children's menu Family room Dogs allowed Garden Parking ⏿

### LITTLE HAVEN

## The Swan Inn ♀

**Point Rd SA62 3UL ☎ 01437 781880 ▤ 04137 781880**
e-mail: enquiries@theswanlittlehaven.co.uk
dir: *From Haverfordwest take B4341 (Broad Haven road). In Broad Haven follow signs for seafront & Little Haven, 0.75m*

This unspoilt, 200-year-old seaside gem perches above a rocky cove overlooking St Bride's Bay. The views to Solva and Ramsay Island are spectacular, particularly from the terrace or the bay window in the beamed bar. Not long ago the Swan was boarded up, now it buzzes with chatter and contented diners, thanks to Paul Morris who has revitalised the pub. Expect a rustic and relaxed bar, with old settles, polished oak tables, and leather armchairs fronting a blazing log fire, an intimate dining room and, upstairs, an elegant, contemporary-style restaurant. Cooking is modern British with a commitment to seasonal and local produce, so bag a table and tuck into open soda bread sandwiches (Caerfai cheese and chutney) and St Bride's Bay dressed crab, at lunch, or venison casserole, brill with marsh samphire and sherry butter, or Welsh rib-eye steak

with red onion confit and béarnaise in the evening.

Open 11-3 5.30-mdnt (Sat-Sun 11am-mdnt) Closed: Mon (Jan) Bar Meals L served all wk 12-2 D served Mon-Sat 6-9 Av main course £10 Restaurant L served all wk 12-2 booking required D served Mon-Sat 6-9 booking required Av 3 course à la carte fr £28 ⊕ FREE HOUSE ◀ Worthington Best Bitter, Old Speckled Hen, Guinness, S A Brains. ♀ 8 Facilities Children's menu Dogs allowed Garden

### NEWPORT

## Salutation Inn ◮ ★★★ INN

**Felindre Farchog, Crymych SA41 3UY ☎ 01239 820564 ▤ 01239 820355**
e-mail: JohnDenley@aol.com
web: www.salutationcountryhotel.co.uk
dir: *On A487 between Cardigan & Fishguard*

Set right on the banks of the River Nevern, this 16th-century coaching inn stands in a quiet village in the heart of the Pembrokeshire Coast National Park. The oak-beamed bars are full of old world charm and country atmosphere. There is an emphasis on fresh local produce on the varied menu, including meat, poultry, fish, cheese and fruit and vegetables. Asparagus and smoked Cerwyn cheese, or rustic game pâté to start, with perhaps prime fillet of Welsh Black beef on rösti and roasted shallots to follow are fine examples of the fare.

Open all day all wk Bar Meals L served all wk 12.30-2.30 D served all wk 6.30-9 Restaurant L served Sun 12.30-2.30 booking required D served Sat-Sun 7-9 booking required ⊕ FREE HOUSE ◀ Felinfoel, Brains, Local guest ales ☼ Thatchers Gold. Facilities Children's menu Dogs allowed Garden Parking Rooms 8

### PORTHGAIN

## The Sloop Inn

**SA62 5BN ☎ 01348 831449 ▤ 01348 831388**
e-mail: matthew@sloop-inn.freeserve.co.uk
dir: *Take A487 NE from St David's for 6m. Left at Croesgooch for 2m to Porthgain*

Possibly the most famous pub on the North Pembrokeshire Coast, the Sloop Inn is located in beautiful quarrying village of Porthgain. The walls and ceilings are packed with pictures and memorabilia from nearby shipwrecks. The harbour is less than 100 metres from the door and there is a village green to the front and a large south-facing patio. A varied menu includes

continued

**Wales**

breakfasts, snacks, pub favourites, steaks from the grill and as much home-caught fish as possible.

Open all day all wk 9.30am-11pm Closed: 25 Dec Bar Meals L served all wk 12-2.30 D served all wk 6-9.30 booking required Restaurant L served all wk 12-2.30 D served all wk 6-9.30 booking required ⊕ FREE HOUSE ◀ Reverend James, Brains Draught, Felinfoel, IPA. Facilities Children's menu Garden Parking

## ROSEBUSH

### Tafarn Sinc

**Preseli SA66 7QT ☎ 01437 532214**
dir: *Please telephone for directions*

The looming presence of this large red corrugated-iron free house stands testament to its rapid construction in 1876. Now deserted by the railway it was built to serve, this idiosyncratic establishment boasts wood-burning stoves, a sawdusted floor, and a charming garden. Set high in the Preseli Hills, it is popular with walkers, who can stoke up on traditional favourites like home-cooked Glamorgan sausage with chutney, Welsh sirloin steak and chips, faggots and Preseli lamb burgers.

Open all day noon-11 Closed: Mon ex BH & summer Bar Meals L served Tue-Sat 12-2 D served Tue-Sat 6-9 Restaurant L served Tue-Sat 12-2 D served Tue-Sat 6-9 ⊕ FREE HOUSE ◀ Worthington, Tafarn Sinc, guest ale. Facilities Children's menu Dogs allowed Garden Parking

## POWYS

## BERRIEW

### The Lion Hotel

**SY21 8PQ ☎ 01686 640452 ▤ 01686 640604**
e-mail: trudi.jones@btconnect.com
dir: *5m from Welshpool on A483, right to Berriew. In village centre next to church*

Behind the black and white timbered grid of this 17th-century family-run coaching inn lie bars and dining areas. Menus, based on local produce, include loin of venison with wild mushrooms and redcurrant jus, and slow-roasted Welsh lamb shoulder with red wine mint gravy; and a fish board with sea bream, halibut, red snapper and salmon dishes. There is a separate bar area where you can enjoy a pint of real ale.

Open all wk noon-3 5-11 (Fri-Sat noon-11 Sun noon-3 6-10.30) Bar Meals L served all wk 12-2 D served all wk 6-9 Av main course £12.50 Restaurant L served all wk 12-2 D served all wk 6-9 booking required ⊕ MARSTONS ◀ Banks Bitter, Pedigree, Old Empire, guest ales. Facilities Children's menu Parking

## BRECON

### The Felin Fach Griffin ★★★★ INN ⚜⚜ ▾

**Felin Fach LD3 0UB ☎ 01874 620111**
e-mail: enquiries@eatdrinksleep.ltd.uk
dir: *4.5m N of Brecon on A470 (Brecon to Hay-on-Wye road)*

This much-feted country inn exemplifies owner Charles Inkin's passion for 'the simple things, done well'. In the bar are deep leather sofas and open fire. Food is served in rambling bare-floored rooms where original features are teamed with tasteful modern touches. The Griffin draws many of its ingredients from the surrounding area, while the garden provides the organic produce. The lunchtime menu includes Gorwydd Caephilly ploughman's with home-made soda bread and pickles, or Welsh pork and leek sausages. The freshest seafood could feature wild halibut fillet with young spring vegetables and fresh creamed morels. Other mains include rack of Herdwick lamb, shepherd's pie and carrot purée, and oak roast salmon on crushed Witchill potato and spinach.

Open all day 11-11 Closed: 24-25 Dec Bar Meals L served Mon-Sat 12.30-2.30, Sun 12-2.30 Av main course £11 Restaurant L served Mon-Sat 12.30-2.30, Sun 12-2.30 D served Mon-Sat 6.30-9.30, Sun 6.30-9 Fixed menu price fr £15 Av 3 course à la carte fr £35 ⊕ FREE HOUSE ◀ Breconshire Breweries, Wye Valley Butty Bach ♂ Thatchers. ▾ 20 Facilities Children's menu Dogs allowed Garden Parking Rooms 7

### The Usk Inn ★★★★ INN ⚜ ▾

**Talybont-on-Usk LD3 7JE ☎ 01874 676251**
**▤ 01874 676392**
e-mail: stay@uskinn.co.uk
dir: *6m E of Brecon, just off A40 towards Abergavenny & Crickhowell*

The inn was established in the 1840s, just as the Brecon to Merthyr Railway arrived. In 1878 the locomotive Hercules failed to stop at the former station opposite and crashed into the street, seriously disrupting conversations and beer consumption in the bar. The owner Andrew Felix is making sure you can still partake of interesting food like fried Celtic haggis and chilli dressing. Alternatively, opt for risotto of smoked garlic and porcini mushrooms, then half a honey-roast duck with apricot and tarragon, or a fish special, and home-made treacle tart to finish. The Brecon to Monmouth Canal runs through the village, in some places at rooftop level.

Open all day all wk 11am-11.30pm Closed: 25-26 Dec Bar Meals D served all wk 12-2.30 Restaurant D served all wk 6.30-9.30 ⊕ FREE HOUSE ◀ Hancocks HB, Brains, Guinness, Worthington, Rev James, Gold SA Ō Thatchers. ♥ 11 Facilities Children's menu Garden Parking **Rooms** 11

---

## The Old Hand and Diamond Inn

**SY5 9AR ☎ 01743 884379** 🖹 01743 884379
e-mail: moz123@aol.com
web: www.oldhandanddiamond.co.uk
dir: *9m from Shrewsbury*

Set in beautiful countryside close to the River Severn and the Welsh border, this 17th-century inn retains much of its original character. Open winter fires crackle in the beamed interior, whilst outside you'll find a children's play area and a beer garden with plenty of seating on the patio. Local produce underpins the extensive restaurant menu, offering dishes like braised haunch of venison with juniper berry and sloe gin, and whole sea bass filled with crab, soy and honey.

**Open** all day all wk 11am-1am **Bar Meals** L served Mon-Thu 12-2.30, Fri-Sun 12-9.30 D served Mon-Thu 6-9.30, Fri-Sun 12-9.30 Av main course £10.95 **Restaurant** L served Mon-Thu 12-2.30, Fri-Sun 12-9.30 D served Mon-Thu 6-9.30, Fri-Sun 12-9.30 Av 3 course à la carte fr £22 ⊕ FREE HOUSE ◀ Worthington, Shropshire Lad, guest ales.
**Facilities** Children's menu Play area Dogs allowed Garden Parking

---

## Nantyffin Cider Mill Inn ♥

**Brecon Rd NP8 1SG ☎ 01873 810775** 🖹 01873 810986
e-mail: info@cidermill.co.uk

dir: *At junct of A40 & A479, 1.5m W of Crickhowell*

Originally a drovers' inn, located at the foot of the Black Mountains, the Nantyffin dates from the 16th century. It became well known for the cider it produced in the 19th century and the original cider press has been incorporated into the Mill Room Restaurant. These days the Nantyffin is renowned for its pairing of traditional pub values with acclaimed French bistro-style food. Menus are based on locally sourced produce such as beef, pork, lamb and poultry from a farm only six miles away.

**Open** noon-3 6-11 Closed: Mon (ex BH), Sun eve Oct-Mar **Bar Meals** L served Tue-Sun 12-2.30 D served Tue-Sun 6.30-9.30 **Restaurant** L served Sun 12-2.30 booking required D served Fri-Sat 6.30-9.30 booking required ⊕ FREE HOUSE ◀ Reverend James, Rhymney Best Bitter, Felinfoel Stout Ō Stowford Press, Taffy Apples. ♥ 12 **Facilities** Children's menu Dogs allowed Garden Parking

---

## The Royal Oak Inn ♥

**HR5 3NR ☎ 01544 370669 & 370342**
e-mail: brianhall@btinternet.com
dir: *4m W of Kington, 10m from Hay-on-Wye on B4594*

The huge inglenook fireplace, heavily beamed ceilings and a flagstone floor set a scene befitting a 400-year-old inn that once welcomed drovers taking store cattle from Wales to England. Home-made fare is served in the lounge bar/dining area, including bar snacks, soups, jacket potatoes, sandwiches and salads. A roast is served every Sunday.

**Open** all wk Oct-Mar reduced hrs **Bar Meals** L served all wk 12-2.30 D served all wk 7-9.30 booking required **Restaurant** L served all wk 12-2.30 D served all wk 7-9.30 booking required ⊕ FREE HOUSE ◀ Brains Reverend James, Butty Bach, S A, Worthingtons Ō Stowford Press. ♥ 8 **Facilities** Children's menu Dogs allowed Garden Parking

---

## Kilverts Inn ♥

**The Bullring HR3 5AG ☎ 01497 821042** 🖹 01497 821580
e-mail: info@kilverts.co.uk
dir: *From A438 take B4351 to Hay. Turn right after bridge, left towards park and left again*

In the summer months, visit this inn's lovely garden, with its lawns, flower beds, pond and fountain. Indoors, there's a timber-framed, olde-worlde style bar offering a range of local beers. Expect robust, generous food – typical dishes include grilled goats' cheese with a pesto crust; Kilvert's famous home-made steak and pudding; home-made fisherman's pie and chilli con carne.

**Open** all wk **Bar Meals** L served all wk 12.30-2.30 D served all wk 6.30-9 Av main course £8.95 **Restaurant** D served Fri-Sat 6.30-9 ⊕ FREE HOUSE ◀ Wye Valley Butty Bach, The Reverend James, Pedigree, Guest Ales Ō Westons Old Rosie. ♥ 8 **Facilities** Children's menu Family room Dogs allowed Garden Parking

**Wales**

## LLANDRINDOD WELLS

# The Gold Bell Country Inn

**Llanyre LD1 6DX ☎ 01597 823959 📠 01597 825618**
e-mail: info@bellcountryinn.co.uk
dir: *1.5m NW of Llandrindod Wells on A4081*

Set in the hills above Llandrindod Wells, this former drovers' inn has a smart, modern interior. Two bars and a restaurant serve seasonally changing menus. A meal might include terrine of guinea fowl, organic chicken and woodland mushrooms on brioche followed by pork tenderloin stuffed with cider-soaked apricots, wrapped in ham and served with apple purée and cider sauce. Finish with sticky toffee pudding.

**Open** all wk noon-2 6-11.30 **Bar Meals** L served all wk 12-2 D served Mon-Sat 6-9 **Restaurant** D served Mon-Sat 6-9 booking required ⊕ FREE HOUSE ◀ Guinness, guest ales.
**Facilities** Children's menu Garden Parking

## LLANGYNIDR

# The Coach & Horses ♟

**Cwmcrawnon Rd NP8 1LS ☎ 01874 730245**
dir: *A40 from Brecon to Abergavenny, 12m from Brecon. Through Bwlch, pub after bend turn right*

This free house is just two minutes' walk from the canal. The talented chefs offer such dishes as smoked haddock, broccoli and mature cheese tart; roast peppered local venison haunch steak with juniper and redcurrant sauce; slow cooked Welsh lamb shoulder on minted mushy peas; and fillet of hake in crispy Welsh beer batter. There is a canal-side beer garden.

**Open** all day all wk noon-mdnt (closed Mon in Winter) **Bar Meals** L served all wk 12-2 booking required D served all wk 6-9 booking required Av main course £6.50 **Restaurant** L served Mon-Sat 12-2, Sun 12-4 booking required D served Sun 6-9 booking required Av 3 course à la carte fr £16 ⊕ FREE HOUSE ♟ 6
**Facilities** Children's menu Dogs allowed Garden Parking

## MONTGOMERY

# Dragon Hotel ★★ HL ◉

**SY15 6PA ☎ 01686 668359 📠 0870 011 8227**
e-mail: reception@dragonhotel.com
web: www.dragonhotel.com
dir: *A483 towards Welshpool, right onto B4386 then B4385. Behind town hall*

In a small quiet town amidst the stunning countryside of the Welsh Marches, this family-run black and white timber-framed coaching inn offers a friendly welcome. An enclosed patio has been created from the former coach entrance, while the bar and lounge contain beams and masonry allegedly removed from the ruins of Montgomery Castle after Oliver Cromwell destroyed it in 1649. The hotel prides itself on its use of fresh local produce in the kitchen too. In addition to daily blackboard specials and soups, the bar menu includes warm ciabattas; beef, chicken or vegetarian fajitas; and home-made fish pie. The carte may start perhaps with leek-laced Welsh cakes

topped with a Perl Las cheese sauce, and continue with breast of local pheasant wrapped in prosciutto, with blackcurrant jus and honey-roasted vegetables.

**Open** all wk noon-2 6-11 **Bar Meals** L served all wk 12-2 D served all wk 7-9 Av main course £8 **Restaurant** L served all wk 12-2 booking required D served all wk 7-9 booking required Fixed menu price fr £25 Av 3 course à la carte fr £29 ⊕ FREE HOUSE ◀ Wood Special, Interbrew Bass, guest.
**Facilities** Children's menu Dogs allowed Garden Parking Rooms 20

## NEW RADNOR

# Red Lion Inn

**Llanfihangel-nant-Melan LD8 2TN ☎ 01544 350220 📠 01544 350220**
e-mail: theredlioninn@yahoo.co.uk
dir: *A483 to Crossgates then right onto A44, 6m to pub. 3m W of New Radnor on A44*

Next door to this old drovers' inn is one of four churches named after St Michael that encircle the burial place of the last Welsh dragon. According to legend, if anything happens to them the dragon will rise again. The inn has a lounge and a locals' bar, two small restaurants and a garden. A broad menu draws extensively on local produce, including herbs from the garden. Mussels, served as a starter in white wine, garlic and cream, come from the River Conwy. Main courses might include game terrine with Cognac and grape preserve; Welsh Black beef fillet with béarnaise sauce; organic salmon fish cakes; and leek, wild mushroom and chestnut gâteau. Round off with Welsh cheeses and home-made walnut bread.

**Open** noon-11.30 (Sun noon-7.30) Closed: Tue **Bar Meals** L served Mon Sat 12-3, Sun 12-7.30 D served Mon-Sat 6-11.30, Sun 12-7.30 ⊕ FREE HOUSE ◀ Guest Ales Ŏ Thatchers.
**Facilities** Children's menu Family room Dogs allowed Garden Parking

## OLD RADNOR

# The Harp

**LD8 2RH ☎ 01544 350655 📠 01544 350655**
e-mail: info@harpinnradnor.co.uk
dir: *Old Radnor signed off A44 (Kington to New Radnor)*

Just yards from the church of St Stephen you'll find this village inn with spectacular views over the Radnor countryside. The building is a Welsh longhouse made from local stone and slate, dating back to the 15th century. Open the simple wooden door and step into a cosy lounge and bars with oak beams, open log fires, semi-circular wooden settles, flagstone floors, and lots of guide books. A lively menu, available in the two dining rooms, of modern pub food includes starters such as venison and juniper berry terrine or broccoli and celeriac soup, followed perhaps by spinach and ricotta cannelloni or Welsh Black rump steak with hand cut chips and roasted seasonal vegetables. Deserts range from apple and pear crumble to pannacotta with caramelised clementines.

Open 6-11 (Sat-Sun noon-3 6-11) Closed: Mon **Bar Meals** L served Sat-Sun 12-2.30 booking required D served Tue-Sun 6-9 booking required Av main course £11.95 **Restaurant** L served Sat-Sun 12-2.30 booking required D served Tue-Sun 6-9 booking required ⊕ FREE HOUSE ◀ Timothy Taylor, Three Tuns, Hopback, Wye Valley, Hobsons ♻ Kingston Rosie, Dunkertons, Stowford Press. **Facilities** Children's menu Dogs allowed Garden Parking

---

## TALGARTH

## Castle Inn

**Pengenffordd LD3 0EP ☎ 01874 711353**
📄 01874 711353
e-mail: castleinnwales@aol.com
dir: *4m S of Talgarth on A479*

Named after the Iron Age hill fort that tops the hill behind it – Castell Dinas, this welcoming inn enjoys a spectacular location in the heart of the Black Mountains, in the Brecon Beacons National Park. Numerous walks and mountain bike routes begin and end at its door, making it popular with outdoor enthusiasts. With a good selection of real local ales, substantial pub food includes sausage and mash and fisherman's pie.

Open noon-11.30 Closed: Mon (Nov-Etr) **Bar Meals** L served Sat-Sun 12-3 D served Wed-Sun 6.30-9 Av main course £7.95 **Restaurant** L served Sat-Sun 12-3 D served Wed-Sun 6.30-9 ⊕ FREE HOUSE ◀ Butty Bach, Rhymney Bitter, Rev James, Hobby Horse, guest ales ♻ Stowford Press. **Facilities** Children's menu Garden Parking

## TRECASTLE

## The Castle Coaching Inn

**LD3 8UH ☎ 01874 636354   📄 01874 636457**
e-mail: enquiries@castle-coaching-inn.co.uk
web: www.castle-coaching-inn.co.uk
dir: *On A40 W of Brecon*

A Georgian coaching inn on the old London to Carmarthen coaching route, in the Brecon Beacons National Park. Owned and run by John and Val Porter and their son Andrew, the hotel has been carefully restored, and has lovely old fireplaces and a remarkable bow-fronted bar window. The inn also offers a peaceful terrace and garden, and an open log fire burns in the bar throughout the winter. The bar menu is the same as in the restaurant, but also offers fresh sandwiches, ploughman's, hot filled baguettes and filled jackets. In both locations there will be minestrone or leek and potato soup; smoked haddock

topped with ham and tomato in Cheddar cheese sauce; and Japanese-style prawns with sweet chilli dip as starters. Main courses include fillet steak with melted Stilton and roasted red onions; supreme of chicken with mushroom, Gruyère and white wine sauce; Welsh lamb chops with rosemary and redcurrant sauce; steak and Guinness pie; pan-fried salmon with orange and tarragon; and Mediterranean vegetable bake. And finally, desserts of Dutch apple flan; cool mint fling; banana and amaretto cheesecake; and treacle sponge pudding and custard. Children may prefer a burger, breaded chicken goujons, cod fish fingers or a jumbo sausage.

Open all wk noon-3 6-11 (Sun 7-10.30) **Bar Meals** L served Sat-Sun 12-2 D served Mon-Sat 6.30-9, Sun 7-9 Av main course £10 **Restaurant** L served Sat-Sun 12-2 D served Mon-Sat 6.30-9, Sun 7-9 Av 3 course à la carte fr £18 ⊕ FREE HOUSE ◀ Fuller's London Pride, Timothy Taylor Landlord, Spitfire. **Facilities** Children's menu Garden Parking

---

# SWANSEA

### REYNOLDSTON

## King Arthur Hotel 🍷

**Higher Green SA3 1AD ☎ 01792 390775**
📄 01792 391075
e-mail: info@kingarthurhotel.co.uk
dir: *Just N of A4118 SW of Swansea*

A country inn, with real log fires, in a village at the heart of the Gower Peninsula. Eat in the restaurant, main bar or family room, choosing main menu or specials board dishes including seasonal game, Welsh Black beef, locally caught fish and vegetarian options. Try whole trout with cockle and laverbread sauce; crisp garlicky chicken Kiev; or tuna and bean salad.

Open all day all wk Closed: 25 Dec **Bar Meals** food served all day **Restaurant** L served all wk 12-2.30 D served Sun-Thu 6-9, Fri-Sat 6-9.30 ⊕ FREE HOUSE ◀ Felinfoel Double Dragon, Worthington Bitter & Bass, Tomas Watkins OSB, King Arthur Ale. 🍷 9 **Facilities** Children's menu Family room Garden Parking

---

# VALE OF GLAMORGAN

### COWBRIDGE

## Hare & Hounds 🍷

**Aberthin CF71 7LG ☎ 01446 774892**
e-mail: nicholasmassey@hotmail.com
dir: *1m from Cowbridge*

Transformed from a run-down boozer to a popular dining pub by the Masseys a few years ago, this 15th-century former mint stands in the village of Aberthin. The bar is traditional, while the dining room has a contemporary look, with warm decor and modern furnishings. At lunch, tuck into chicken liver parfait with plum chutney or quail's egg and bacon salad for starters or a light bite, or a main dish like cottage pie and gammon,

continued

egg and home-made chips. Evening dishes take in pan-fried venison with fondant potato and roasted pear jus; braised pork belly with cider apple jus; and wild mushroom risotto with basil dressing. On fine days dine by the stream in the garden.

Open all day all wk noon-mdnt (Mon 4-mdnt Fri-Sat noon-1am) Bar Meals L served Tue-Sat 12-3 Restaurant L served Tue-Sun 12-3 booking required D served Tue-Sat 6-9 booking required ⊞ MARSTONS ◀ Ringwood Best, Pedigree. 4 guests Ŏ Thatchers Gold. ♇ 11 Facilities Children's menu Family room Dogs allowed Garden Parking ⊛

---

## MONKNASH

### The Plough & Harrow
**CF71 7QQ ☎ 01656 890209**
e-mail: info@theploughmonknash.com
dir: *M4 junct 35 take dual carriageway to Bridgend. At rdbt follow St Brides sign, then brown tourist signs. Pub 3m NW of Llantwit Major*

In a peaceful country setting on the edge of a small village with views across the fields to the Bristol Channel, this low, slate-roofed, 14th-century building was originally built as the chapter house of a monastery, although it has been a pub for 500 of its 600-year existence. Expect an atmospheric interior, open fires, real ciders, up to eight guest ales on tap, and home-cooked food using fresh local ingredients.

Open all wk noon-11 Bar Meals L served all wk 12-2.30 D served all wk 6-9 Av main course £7.50 Restaurant L served all wk 12-2.30 D served all wk 6-9 Fixed menu price fr £9 Av 3 course à la carte fr £18 ⊞ FREE HOUSE ◀ Archers Goldon, Shepherd Neame Spitfire, Hereford Pale ale, Sharp's IPA, Bass, guest ales Ŏ Black Dragon, Fiery Fox, Barnstormer. Facilities Children's menu Garden Parking

## WREXHAM

## HANMER

### The Hanmer Arms ★★★★ INN ♇
**SY13 3DE ☎ 01948 830532  ▤ 01948 830740**
e-mail: hanmerarms@brconnect.com
web: www.hanmerarms.co.uk
dir: *Between Wrexham & Whitchurch on A539, off A525*

Standing beside the parish church in a peaceful, rural location on the borders of Shropshire, Wales and Cheshire, this traditional inn is the heart of the community. Head for the

---

beamed and wooden floored bars, warmed by log fires, for pints of local ale, and plates of pork terrine with home-made chutney, lamb rump with mustard mash and thyme gravy, and sticky toffee pudding.

Open all day all wk Bar Meals L served all wk 12-2.30 D served all wk 6-9.30 Av main course £11 Restaurant L served Mon-Sat 12-2.30, Sun 12-9 D served all wk 6-9.30 Fixed menu price fr £11.95 Av 3 course à la carte fr £20 ⊞ FREE HOUSE ◀ Timothy Taylor, Adnams, Stonehouse Ŏ Stowford Press. ♇ 12 Facilities Children's menu Dogs allowed Garden Parking Rooms 12

---

## LLANARMON DYFFRYN CEIRIOG

### The Hand at Llanarmon ★★★★ INN ⊛ ♇
**LL20 7LD ☎ 01691 600666  ▤ 01691 600262**
e-mail: reception@thehandhotel.co.uk
web: www.thehandhotel.co.uk
dir: *Exit A5 at Chirk follow B4500 for 11m. Through Ceiriog Valley to Llanarmon D C. Pub straight ahead*

Built beside the old drovers' road from London to Anglesey, this 16th-century farmhouse was a natural stopping place for drovers and their flocks. Yet The Hand only became a fully-fledged inn as recently as the late 1950s. Chef Grant Mulholland has built a strong reputation for superb cuisine, and the pub menu includes traditional favourites such as ploughman's with Welsh cheeses and home-made bread; as well as hot dishes like gammon, eggs and chips. Restaurant diners can expect starters like grilled red mullet with celeriac and ginger purée; followed, perhaps, by leg of Welsh lamb with cranberries and red wine. Desserts are just as inviting; try sticky date pudding, or honey and cranberry pannacotta.

Open all wk Bar Meals L served Mon-Sat 12-2.20, Sun 12.30-2.45 booking required D served all wk 6.30-8.45 booking required Restaurant L served Mon-Sat 12-2.20, Sun 12.30-2.45 booking required D served all wk 6.30-8.45 booking required ⊞ FREE HOUSE ◀ Worthington Cream Flow, Guinness, guest ale. ♇ 7 Facilities Children's menu Dogs allowed Garden Parking Rooms 13